# RESEARCHING SOCIETY AND CULTURE

## 3RD EDITION

Edited by

# CLIVE SEALE

Los Angeles | London | New Delhi
Singapore | Washington DC

First edition published 1998, reprinted 2002, 2004,
Second edition published 2004, reprinted 2005, 2006 twice, 2007,
2008 twice, 2009, 2010, 2011

SAGE Publications Ltd
1 Oliver's Yard
55 City Road
London EC1Y 1SP

SAGE Publications Inc.
2455 Teller Road
Thousand Oaks, California 91320

SAGE Publications India Pvt Ltd
B 1/I 1 Mohan Cooperative Industrial Area
Mathura Road
New Delhi 110 044

SAGE Publications Asia-Pacific Pte Ltd
3 Church Street
#10-04 Samsung Hub
Singapore 049483

**Library of Congress Control Number: 2011929421**

**British Library Cataloguing in Publication data**

A catalogue record for this book is available from the British Library

ISBN 978–1–84920–798–0
ISBN 978–1–84920–799–7 (pbk)

Typeset by C&M Digitals (P) Ltd, Chennai, India
Printed and bound in Great Britain by Ashford Colour Press Ltd

# CONTENTS

# ACKNOWLEDGEMENTS

Paul Acourt (Goldsmiths) gave helpful comments on Chapter 3. Figure 6.2 is reproduced by permission of the British Library. Caroline Ramazanoglu (Goldsmiths) supplied guidelines for Exercise 12.1. Workshop Exercise 14.1 was developed from original materials written by Nigel Fielding (University of Surrey). Daniel Miller (University College, London) supplied the material for Box 14.6. Michael Fiegel gave permission to reproduce Figure 16.1. John Grady and Katja Mruck gave permission for reproduction on Figure 16.4, taken from Grady (2008). Sara Arber (University of Surrey) gave permission for use of the material in Box 17.7 and Table 17.1. Workshop Exercise 19.3 was developed from original materials written by Lionel Sims (University of East London). Table 20.1 is adapted from an original developed for teaching purposes by George Brown (Royal Holloway). Lyn Richards (QSR, Australia) gave permission for use of the screen shots of NVivo and the reproduction of the interview in Box 12.12. The Open University gave permission for use of the interview material in Box 21.8, for which they are copyright holder. William Trochim gave permission for use of the picture in Figure 30.1. We would like to thank all these people for allowing their ideas to be used in this book.

# AUTHOR BIOGRAPHIES

Suki Ali is a Senior Lecturer in the Department of Sociology at the LSE. She previously taught at Goldsmiths College, the Institute of Education and University of Greenwich. Her main interests focus upon feminist postcolonial theory, research methodologies, visual culture, and theories of racialisation and embodiment. Her work centralises the interplay between gender, sexualities, 'race' and class. She is author of *Mixed-Race, Post-Race: Gender, New Ethnicities and Cultural Practices* (Berg, 2003).

Milind Arolker is a medical doctor specialising in palliative medicine, studying for a PhD at Barts and The London School of Medicine and Dentistry, Queen Mary University of London. His PhD work is a qualitative study of decision-making about the use of sedation in end-of-life care.

Chetan Bhatt is Professor of Sociology and Director of the Centre for the Study of Human Rights at the London School of Economics and Political Science. He has previously been Professor of Sociology at Goldsmiths, University of London and has taught at the universities of Essex and Southampton. He has undertaken research in a range of areas, including religious violence, nationalism, discrimination, health and human rights. He is the author of *Liberation and Purity* (Routledge, 1997) and *Hindu Nationalism: Origins, Ideologies and Modern Myths* (Berg, 2001).

Alice Bloch is Professor of Sociology at City University London. She has carried out a number of research projects relating to forced migration. Recent publications include *Race and Ethnicity in the 21st Century* (Palgrave Macmillan, 2010 co-edited with John Solomos) and *No Right to Dream: The Social and Economic Lives of Young Undocumented Migrants* (Paul Hamlyn Foundation, 2009 with Nando Sigona and Roger Zetter).

Duncan Branley is Training and Information Officer at Goldsmiths, University of London and a part-time relationship therapist and bereavement counsellor. He has been a research student in sociology at Goldsmiths looking at religious and sexual identities through a Foucauldian lens. He provides research training to students carrying out literature reviews or planning presentations of their research work as well as teaching a range of specialist software for academic research.

Bridget Byrne is Senior Lecturer in Sociology at the University of Manchester. She has previously worked at Goldsmiths College, LSE and the University of Sussex. *White Lives: The Interplay of Race, Class and Gender in Contemporary London* was published in 2006 (Routledge) and she has published several papers based on qualitative interviewing. In 2010 she had a Leverhulme Fellowship to investigate Citizenship Ceremonies in Britain and is also Principal Investigator on an ESRC study on School Choice.

**Miran Epstein** MD, PhD, MA, is a Senior Lecturer in Medical Ethics and Law at Queen Mary, University of London. He studied medicine and history and philosophy of science at Tel Aviv University. He has published widely on the ethics of organ transplantation, end-of-life, and human research, and is currently writing a book on the history of the bioethical transformation.

**Ben Gidley** is a Senior Researcher at the Centre on Migration, Policy and Society (COMPAS) at the University of Oxford. He has extensive experience of social research, using archival, ethnographic, visual and other methods, working on issues around ethnicity, urban culture and migration. His most recent book, co-authored with Keith Kahn-Harris, is *Turbulent Times: The British Jewish Community Today* (Continuum, 2010).

**Ann Griffin** has a portfolio role as a doctor and an educator. She is a Clinical Senior Lecturer at UCL School of Life and Medical Sciences and an Honorary Consultant at Enfield Primary Care Trust, where she works clinically as a general practitioner. She is involved in all aspects of medical education and training. Educational research, with a particular emphasis on methodology, is an area of personal interest. She is a student at Institute of Education in the final phase of her own educational doctorate investigating the training to work transitions of new GPs.

**Moira Kelly** is Senior Lecturer in Medical Sociology at Queen Mary, University of London, where she teaches medical students and undertakes research. She has worked as a researcher in palliative care, health promotion, mental health and primary health care and has a particular interest in social interaction in health care settings. Her publications cover a range of health research topics and methods. She is currently working on a study of communication between clinicians and patients in diabetes consultations.

**Vanessa May** is Lecturer in Sociology at the University of Manchester. She has conducted research on lone motherhood, post-divorce parenting and intergenerational relationships, using a variety of methods including biographical, narrative and mixed methods. Her most recent work focuses on belonging. She is currently editing a book called *Sociology of Personal Life* and writing a book entitled *Connecting Self to Society: Belonging in a Changing World*, both to be published by Palgrave.

**Mike Michael** is Professor of Sociology of Science and Technology at Goldsmiths, University of London. His interests include the relation of everyday life to technoscience, and biotechnological and biomedical innovation and culture. Current research projects include examination of the ethical aspects of HIV pre-exposure prophylaxis (with Marsha Rosengarten), and the interdisciplinary exploration of energy demand reduction through sociological and speculative design techniques. Two recent publications are *Technoscience and Everyday Life* (Open University Press, 2006) and (with Lynda Birke and Arnie Arluke) *The Sacrifice: How Scientific Experiments Transform Animals and People* (Purdue University Press, 2007).

**Constantinos N. Phellas** is Professor of Sociology and Dean of the School of Humanities, Social Science and Law at the University of Nicosia in Cyprus. His research interests include sociology of health and illness, ageing and sexualities. His publications focus upon the intersection of gender, culture, and issues of sexuality among ethnic minority communities, HIV/AIDS, social and psychological aspects of public health domain. He is the President of the Cyprus Sociological Association. He is currently editing two books: *Aging in European Societies* (Springer) and *Researching Alternative Sexualities* (Ashgate).

Tim Rapley is a Staff Scientist at the Institute of Health and Society, Newcastle University. He is a medical sociologist with particular expertise in qualitative studies of medical practice and research. He is interested in understanding the everyday, taken-for-granted, aspects of medical and research work. His publications include *Doing Conversation, Discourse and Document Analysis* (Sage, 2007) and his 2001 article on 'The art(fulness) of open-ended interviewing' (*Qualitative Research*, 1 (3): 303–323) has been reprinted in several edited collections.

Carol Rivas is a research fellow at Queen Mary, University of London, and was previously based at St Mary's Hospital, London. She has worked as a photographer, medical journalist and writer of health communications and clinician training materials. She currently lectures in medical sociology and teaches qualitative research methods to undergraduates and postgraduates. She has undertaken several studies of access to healthcare and its improvement involving various approaches to data collection, mostly using thematic content analysis and grounded theory. Her special interests are ethnicity, communication and mental health. Her current project is a video-based exploration of communication in medical consultations.

Clare Rutterford After completing an MSc in Statistics with Applications in Medicine (Southampton University, 2004), Clare has spent six years working as a medical statistician and joined Queen Mary, University of London in March 2009. Clare has been involved in a wide variety of trials including a large HIV prevention trial, a trial to improve the safety of women experiencing domestic violence, and several trials in mental health. Clare also leads one of the core modules for the distance learning MSc in Clinical Trials provided by the London School of Hygiene and Tropical Medicine.

Clive Seale is Professor of Medical Sociology at Queen Mary University of London. He has previously been Professor of Sociology at Goldsmiths and Brunel University. He has carried out many social research projects relating to health, involving a variety of methods. Most recently, he has been working on projects investigating communication in medical consultations, decision-making in end-of-life care, and mass-media reporting of health issues. His books include *Constructing Death* (Cambridge University Press, 1998) and *Media and Health* (Sage, 2002), as well as a number of methods texts, several of which are referred to in this book.

David Silverman is Emeritus Professor of Sociology at Goldsmiths College and Visiting Professor, Management Department, King's College (both University of London), as well as Visiting Professor, Business School, University of Technology, Sydney. His research interests focus on medical encounters, conversation and discourse analysis. He is the author of *Interpreting Qualitative Data* (4th edition, Sage, 2012), *Doing Qualitative Research* (3rd edition, Sage, 2010) and *A Very Short, Fairly Interesting, Reasonably Cheap Book about Qualitative Research* (Sage, 2007). He is the editor of *Qualitative Research* (3rd edition, Sage, 2011).

Neil Spicer is a lecturer in global health policy at the London School of Hygiene and Tropical Medicine. He has previously worked as a researcher at Goldsmiths College, London and the University of Birmingham and has a PhD in Geography from the University of Glasgow. His interests include global health policy, HIV/AIDS, maternal and child health, health services research, and qualitative and mixed methods research. Most recently his work has focused on global HIV/AIDS initiatives and civil society advocacy in Central Asia and Eastern Europe and community-based maternal and child health programmes in Nigeria, Ethiopia and India.

Fran Tonkiss is Reader in Sociology and Director of the Cities Programme at the London School of Economics and Political Science. She has previously taught at Goldsmiths and at the City University, London. Her research interests are in urban and economic sociology. Her work includes books on *Contemporary Economic Sociology: Globalization, Production, Inequality* (Routledge, 2006), *Space, the City and Social Theory* (Polity, 2005), *Market Society: Markets and Modern Social Theory* (co-authored with Don Slater, Polity, 2000), and *Trust and Civil Society* (edited with Andrew Passey, Macmillan, 2001).

David Walsh was a senior lecturer in sociology at Goldsmiths until his retirement in 2002. He died in 2008 and tributes and fond memories of him can be found here, some from people who have contributed to this book:

www.gold.ac.uk/sociology/dave-walsh

With others at Goldsmiths, he published the influential *New Directions in Sociological Theory* (MIT Press, 1972) which presented a critique of positivist sociology and outlined the basis for sociological work that embraced phenomenological and ethnomethodological approaches. More recently, his interests drew on his extensive knowledge of opera and musical theatre, resulting in *Musical Theater and American Culture* (Greenwood, 2003) written with Len Platt.

Be sure to visit the companion website at http://www.sagepub.co.uk/seale to find a range of teaching and learning materials for both lecturers and students, including the following:

FOR STUDENTS:

- Web links

The internet provides a bewildering range of material and resources. Here you can go straight to the most useful websites related to each chapter to help you with your studies.

- Workshop and discussion exercises

Here you will find a range of exercises that will help you understand and engage with the theories discussed in the book.

- Journal articles

Full access to selected SAGE journal articles related to each chapter, providing you with a deeper understanding of the topics presented.

- Glossary

Sociology can often present new concepts and ideas that can be a little daunting to grasp at first. This resource provides a useful and accessible collection of those key concepts and terms.

- Second edition chapters

You will also have full access to useful chapters from *Researching Society and Culture*, 2nd Edition.

FOR LECTURERS:

- PowerPoint slides

We provide PowerPoint slides for each chapter for use in class. The slides can be edited by instructors to suit teaching styles and needs.

# 1

# INTRODUCTION AND GUIDE TO USING THIS BOOK

## Clive Seale

This third edition of *Researching Society and Culture* provides, like its predecessor (Seale 2004a), theoretically informed guidance to practising the key social research methods for investigating society and culture. It is a text in both methods and methodology, reflecting the belief that social researchers do not just apply a set of neutral techniques to the issues they investigate. Research is part of a dynamic, reflexive engagement with social and cultural worlds, and the way in which we learn and apply 'methods' requires a continual awareness of this.

The first edition, published in 1998, arose from my involvement with members of the Department of Sociology at Goldsmiths, University of London, many of whom contributed chapters to the book. This department had been one of the leading centres for the practice of qualitative social research, with significant strengths in social theory, and the first edition reflected that history. Because of the success of that first book, which was adopted widely as a core text in methods courses in different universities, a much-expanded second edition was published in 2004.

The second edition included additional chapters on the history of qualitative methods to complement the existing one on the history of quantitative methods, and chapters on how to

review literature, use focus groups, make audio recordings, use visual materials, data archives and the Internet for research, and several other additional topics. This edition continued to draw on the significant strengths of authors associated with Goldsmiths sociology. As a result, quantitative social research was covered in the book, but somewhat less so that in other popular general methods texts. The second edition proved even more popular than the first, again being widely adopted as a core text.

This new edition is significantly revised to meet the needs of a wider range of students than either of the previous books. This partly reflects my own biography, as I now work outside sociology, in Barts and the London School of Medicine and Dentistry, part of Queen Mary, University of London. This has brought me into contact with people working in a wide range of other disciplines, and has enabled the inclusion of chapters from authors skilled in the use of quantitative methods to a much greater extent than in the first two editions. Thus, there are now three instead of two chapters on statistical analysis; the single chapter on carrying out social surveys has now been greatly expanded so that there are now separate chapters on research design – which itself covers experimental and quasi-experimental design as well as different kinds of social survey – sampling and structured data collection methods such as questionnaires, structured interviewing and structured observation, all of which mean that this book contains a more balanced coverage of both qualitative and quantitative methods than previous editions. In addition, there are new chapters on the qualitative methods of narrative analysis, and interpretative phenomenological analysis (IPA), whose importance has increased in the years since the earlier editions were produced, and on giving oral presentations – increasingly something that students and researchers need to know how to do.

Even in an expanded volume, the addition of so many new chapters has meant that some good chapters from previous editions have had to be left out. Because lecturers and students have indicated that they are valuable chapters, a selection of these chapters is freely available for downloading on the website associated with this book. These chapters include:

- Developments in social theory, by Paul Filmer, Chris Jenks, Clive Seale, Nicholas Thoburn and David Walsh
- History of social statistics and the social survey, by Fran Tonkiss
- History of qualitative methods, by Clive Seale
- Reading and writing research, by Les Back
- Representing otherness: collecting and analysing visual data, by Thomas Zacharias
- Embodiment, reflexivity and movement re-education: an ethnographic case study, by Jen Tarr
- My research practice, by Clive Seale

This book therefore outlines in a concise way the standard methods that a student beginning to learn how to do research will need to know, as well as some more advanced methods that enable a broader range of skills to be acquired than is often present in an introductory course. Although the origins of the book lie in sociology, the book is not solely addressed to sociologists. It will appeal to students and lecturers in a wide range of other disciplines, and the chapters are filled with examples of research studies from a diversity of disciplines making use of the methods described. These include, for example, geography, cultural and media studies, anthropology, psychology, health sciences, educational research and, of course, sociology. 'Social research' is the shorthand term used throughout this book to refer to work done in such disciplines, reflected too in the title of this book.

## Organisation of the book

At a more mundane level, this book addresses the practical constraint of student finances at a time when it is unrealistic to expect all students to buy three or four texts for each of the courses they may study during a typical year. Under one cover, *Researching Society and Culture* offers the opportunity to learn how to practise the main varieties of method used by social and cultural researchers today. To this end, the final part of each chapter contains practical exercises designed for use in workshops and discussion groups, all of which have been tried and tested with students by the contributors to this book. At the end of each chapter there is also guidance on further reading, which will allow a deeper understanding of the topic to develop.

Key terms are shown in blue type where a definition of the term is given in the text. Wherever possible, this occurs when the term is first used and sometimes such terms are defined more than once in the text, occurring in blue on each occasion. Every such occurrence of a key term is indexed at the end of the book, so that you can look up the definitions. Additionally, all of the key terms are explained in a separate glossary towards the end of the book. (The glossary also contains some terms that are not used in this book, but which you may find in other texts discussing methods).

However, it is inevitably the case that a book like this contains some variability in the level of language used in the chapters. Although both the contributors and the editor have tried to assume no previous familiarity with the topics discussed, learning this material is always going to feel a little like learning a new language. This variability is in part due to the fact that some of the ideas are more abstract and difficult than others, and this is especially so when the approach is explicitly seeking to generate a novel view of the social and cultural world, breaking with common-sense ideas. People sometimes express their feeling of strangeness about the language of social research by saying that it feels 'too technical' or that there is 'jargon' involved. We hope that you will find these feelings of strangeness reduce as you gain familiarity with the topics of the book.

The chapters are ordered so that the chapters in Part One: Starting Out cover the matters that require consideration before beginning data collection on a research project. These include chapters on the philosophical foundations of science and social research and the relationship between research and both theory and policy. Ethical issues in research are next discussed, before a chapter on how to proceed with a literature review. The next chapter discusses the formulation of research questions and proposals, and is followed by an associated chapter on the overall design of different kinds of research investigation. Sampling considerations run though all social research, whether quantitative or qualitative, so a chapter on this is next. This first part ends with a chapter on doing a dissertation, which pulls together much of what has preceded it and gives practical advice on how to go about carrying out a student research project in the social and cultural research disciplines.

Part Two: Doing Research outlines the main methods for the collection and analysis of both quantitative and qualitative data. To reflect the belief that firm divisions between quantitative and qualitative research are not helpful, these chapters are not separated into these two modes. Clearly, some do fit the 'quantitative' label very firmly (for example, the chapters on statistical analysis). Others are clearly 'qualitative' (for example, the chapters on ethnography, discourse analysis or qualitative interviewing). But several are not so easily classified – some of the approaches described in the chapter on content and linguistic analysis are not easily classified as either quantitative or qualitative, but are hybrid forms. In addition, 'crossover' is possible even with methods that seem firmly in one camp: structured interviews can be used to collect qualitative data under certain circumstances; counting things in 'qualitative' research is often very helpful. Reflecting this, this substantial part of the book ends with a chapter on combining qualitative and quantitative methods.

Part Three: Writing, Presenting, Reflecting is brief, containing just four chapters, but important. Chapters giving advice on both written and oral presentations are followed by reflection on validity, reliability and quality in research. And if things seem to 'go wrong' on your research project, Mike Michael's final chapter offers a variety of innovative suggestions for how to 'rescue' your work.

A number of features in the text aim to increase the clarity with which ideas are presented and give you pointers in how to explore particular topics further, using both conventional library sources and resources available on the Internet, which have improved and expanded enormously since the first edition. These include:

- Use of bullet points, figures and text boxes for the provision of key points, examples and illustrative material.
- A glossary of key terms at the end of the book.
- References to further reading.
- References at the end of each chapter to relevant readings from a student reader (Seale, 2004b), citing also the relevant chapter numbers, that contains a selection of edited classic readings on methods and methodology and to an advanced text on qualitative research practice (Seale et al., 2004) which contains accounts of methods written by leading practitioners.

- References to journal articles that report studies discussing methodological issues or which use the methods described in the chapter. These journal articles are all either published by Sage and available free to readers or are in journals which offer free access. If you visit the website for this book, you can click on these and jump straight to the article.
- Web links at the end of most chapters to indicate relevant Internet resources.
- A list of the key concepts in each chapter with instructions on how these can be used, with the glossary and the index, to test your knowledge of the chapter contents.

- Review questions that further test your knowledge of the chapter.
- Workshop and discussion exercise for use in teaching in learning, supported by data extracts where appropriate.
- An associated website[1] for the book in which you will find reproduced most of the things listed above, featuring links to websites, journal sites and extra data. The web site also contains:
  - Selected chapters that appeared in earlier editions, not included in this edition
  - PowerPoint slides with relevant figures, boxes and tables from the text.

## Web links

These are some websites worth exploring. Each covers many methods topics.

Social Research Update: http://sru.soc.surrey.ac.uk/

e-Source: Behavioral and Social Sciences Research: www.esourceresearch.org

Web Center for Social Research Methods: www.socialresearchmethods.net

Forum: Qualitative Social Research: www.qualitative-research.net

## Workshop and discussion exercises

Go to the end of any chapter that you have not yet read and pick a 'key concept' from the list at the end. Use the index of the book, and the glossary, to look up the meaning of this key concept. Do it again for three or four more.

Go to the website for this book at www.rscbook.co.uk. Pick a chapter you have read and explore the web links associated with that chapter. What extra information did you discover? Are there any other good websites on this subject that you can find? Check Wikipedia to see if the topics in this chapter are discussed and whether they seem accurate and reliable.

---

[1]The website for the book can be found at www.rscbook.co.uk or by visiting the Sage website www.sagepub.com or www.sagepub.co.uk and searching for 'Researching Society and Culture' where there is a link to the book's website. As web addresses sometimes change, links shown on the website are regularly updated.

# PART ONE
## STARTING OUT

# 2

# INTRODUCTION TO THE PHILOSOPHY OF SCIENCE

## Miran Epstein

| Chapter Contents | |
|---|---|

This chapter attempts to explain what science is by discussing competing answers from philosophers of science to six different questions.

- The first question deals with *the foundations of science*, namely, the nature of its underlying premises. We shall see that science rests on premises which are not scientific at all, in the sense that they are grounded in belief rather than experience. This conclusion raises the possibility that science and belief are somehow linked to each other and that the divide between them is, if not fictional, then at least bridgeable.

- The second question deals with *the nature of the things which science explores*. Here we shall encounter the possibility that science actually studies abstract objects, not concrete ones. If this is so, then its claims can actually be tested in theory only.

- The third question deals with *the objectives of science*. We shall see that science produces testable generalisations about its objects. However, it cannot establish their veracity with certainty.

- The fourth question is about *the evolution of scientific knowledge*. We shall notice that some philosophers take a normative position in relation to the question (how science ought to evolve) and others a descriptive one (how science actually evolves).

- The fifth question deals with *the distinction between science and other knowledge systems* as well as *between the natural sciences and the social ones*. Regardless of the answer, we might discover a tension between the philosophical and the political importance of the question itself.

- The sixth and last question deals with *the relationship between science and morality*. Here we shall examine two competing ways of ensuring that science remains moral.

By the end of the chapter, you will be able to:

- identify some of the philosophical premises upon which science rests

- outline the three main philosophical conceptions concerning the origin of objects, and describe the controversy about the nature of a scientific object

- distinguish between scientific and non-scientific explanations

- recognise the impossibility of verification or falsification of scientific claims

- describe and explicate the conflict between normative and descriptive positions regarding the evolution of science

- outline the major philosophical views about the distinction between science and non-science and between the natural and the social sciences

- explain the impossibility of drawing moral conclusions from scientific statements and describe two competing approaches to protecting science from abuse.

You may rightly wonder why a book that deals with social research should have a chapter on philosophy of science, when even books on physics or chemistry are not inclined to dedicate space to philosophical contemplations. If, as physicist Richard Feynman apparently said, 'philosophy of science is about as useful to scientists as ornithology is to birds' (unsourced), then it must be even less useful to those who study society. After all, some forms of social research do not associate themselves with science at all, others have been accused of pretending to be scientific, and even the incontrovertibly scientific ones have rarely received nearly as much respect as the 'hard' natural sciences.

Yet it is social research which teaches us that Feynman was wrong: humans are different from birds because they can reflect on themselves. Moreover, they can use such reflections to transform themselves and in doing so come to realise that they can become authors of the play in which they act.

But why does it have to be philosophy of science? Can't we just consult our experience and common sense? After all, they teach us quite a lot about science. For instance, they tell us that the term 'science' (from the Latin *scientia*, meaning 'knowledge') refers to a wide variety of knowledge-producing practices, to the community that engages in these practices, and the body of knowledge thereby produced. Experience and common sense tell us that scientific explanations differ somehow from explanations given by other knowledge systems such as everyday experience, intuition, religion, mysticism, philosophy, and perhaps even literature and poetry. Science may be fallible, but also has an unrivalled capacity to produce technology and transform our economies. Yet from time to time we may also question the morality of science.

Philosophy of science tries to go deeper than these considerations. It is the branch of epistemology that reflects on the particular nature of science (epistemology is the philosophy of knowledge in general; it explores the possibility of knowing, the generation and evolution of knowledge, and its validity). The classical questions it has been dealing with are:

1  What are the fundamental premises of science?

2  What is the kind of reality it could in principle explore?

3  What are the objectives of science?

4  How does it evolve?

5  What distinguishes it from other knowledge systems? What distinguishes its disciplines, particularly the natural and the social ones, from each other? In which sense, if any at all, can science claim to be superior to any other knowledge system?

6  Can it become immoral? And if so, how could we ensure that this does not happen?

This chapter has been written particularly for readers who are interested in the social sciences, although it deals with social science only as part of the wider discussion about science in general. The chapter offers a brief introductory overview of some of the most influential philosophical perspectives on each of these questions. By no means is it exhaustive; it should be seen rather as an invitation for further reading and discussion. Nor does it intend to take a position on any of the competing perspectives. On the contrary, it wishes to expand the debate, not to restrict it.

## The metaphysical basis of science

Science and philosophy are different. Science is in essence an explanatory enterprise, whose explanations are said to be 'testable' (the meaning of testability and its very possibility shall be discussed later on). Philosophy may produce explanations, but it is essentially justificatory. Whatever the case, its assertions are untestable: this is what is meant when we say that it is metaphysical. This does not mean that scientific assertions are necessarily true. Nor does it mean that philosophical assertions are necessarily false. One thing should be clear, however: the validity of science is grounded in *experience*, whereas the validity of philosophy is grounded in *belief*.

Philosophers and scientists commonly assert that science is or ought to be (which presupposes that it can be) completely non-metaphysical (logical positivism, a pro-science modern epistemology, goes farther, saying that *any* assertion that is not testable by contact with an external reality is meaningless).

Others, though, take the view that science actually rests on metaphysical premises and that it could not do without them. As philosopher Daniel Dennett (1942–) put it, 'there is no such thing as philosophy-free science; there is only science whose philosophical baggage is taken on board without examination' (Dennett, 1996: 21). Box 2.1 shows some examples of premises, fundamental to science, which are essentially metaphysical.

BOX 2.1

## SOME METAPHYSICAL PREMISES OF SCIENCE

- *Ontological realism* – the belief that reality and its components exist independently of any consciousness. (**Ontology** is the branch of philosophy that attempts to answer questions regarding the existence/non-existence of things and their nature).

- *Epistemological realism* – the belief in the 'knowability' of things, which presupposes that propositions about reality must be either true or false, regardless of which is which.

- Belief in the principles of *formal logic* (A = A; A = either A or non-A; A cannot be both B and non-B) including *deductive reasoning* (**deduction** involves working out that something will follow necessarily from given premises, i.e. if A then B).

The belief in some sort of *causality*, i.e. a generative rather than accidental link between successive states of affairs (A as a result of B).

The view that science rests on metaphysical foundations has significant implications. It means that science cannot claim to be superior to metaphysical arguments, such as those based on religion. Contrary to what both atheists and religious people often maintain, science and religion are not necessarily contradictory. The two could indeed be reconciled under certain conditions. For example, the religious belief that God created an evolving world with misleading apparent traces of an infinite past and the scientific belief that this world was not created at all and really has an infinite past are equally metaphysical. Moreover, both are perfectly compatible with evolutionary explanations.

## The object of scientific inquiry

Science explores reality, but not the whole of reality. It focuses on particular *objects*. Most generally speaking, the objects of science are the things it wants to explain. Philosophy of science raises some important questions about the nature of such objects and how scientists and social scientists define and study them.

The first question is about objects in general. It concerns what makes them intelligible and

open to any inquiry. Another way of putting this is to say that philosophers are interested in the *epistemic possibility of objects*.

## The epistemic possibility of objects

There are three main positions on this within epistemology: the empirical, the rationalist and the transcendental. Each in turn will be considered.

Philosophers who subscribe to empiricism regard any object as a distinct class of observable phenomena. Most (though not all) empiricists maintain that objects exist regardless of whether we have any sense or consciousness of them – they are 'out there' – quite apart from whether we know about them. Empiricism assigns cognition (i.e. our thought processes) a passive role similar to that of a camera film: our brain does not produce the object, but rather records its image. Since the object is concrete, the image is concrete too. Yet to be thought about, an object must be regarded as, at least potentially, one of many such similar things, and this requires us to use a *concept*. The idea of the general object, the corresponding *concept*, is therefore formed by a logical process known as *induction*, on the basis of repeated observations of concrete objects. Induction is a process of reasoning whereby a generalisation is inferred from a series of specific cases that either makes the whole group (strong induction) or is just part of it (weak induction).

Philosophers who subscribe to rationalist epistemology, in contrast, give no role whatsoever to the senses or to any external input. Rationalists regard reason as the active producer of concepts *ex nihilo* (out of nothing). They maintain that concrete objects are deduced from the general concepts that describe them, *deduction* being the logical process of drawing specific conclusions from generalisations.

Transcendental philosophy makes a synthesis between empiricism and rationalism. Invented by philosopher Immanuel Kant (1724–1804), it maintains, like rationalism, that a concrete intelligible object (also called 'the thing for us') is deduced from a general concept. However, it rejects the rationalist claim that the concept is a product *ex nihilo*. Transcendentalists argue that concepts are formed in our consciousness through a senses-mediated interaction between previously existing empty templates of reason (also called 'transcendental/a priori categories') and some unintelligible raw material of the external reality (also called 'the thing in itself'). The interaction is dialectically constructive, meaning that the templates of reason and the sense data transform and retransform each other reciprocally ad infinitum. In short, the transcendental mechanism of this interaction produces perpetually evolving concepts and objects. Contrary to what both empiricism and rationalism imply, concepts and objects are therefore not fixed. The history of science bears this out, showing that almost all the concepts and objects of science have changed over the years: how scientists think, and what they think about, has never been fixed for all time.

The role of reason in the construction of knowledge and the nature of its interaction with reality are subject to considerable dispute among transcendentalists. Logical positivists and neo-Kantians, for example, tend to assign reason a *passive* role in the construction of concepts: it simply lets itself be transformed by reality. From this follows the conclusion that the construction of knowledge is a fundamentally *individual* (non-social) process. Marxists, on the other hand, maintain that passive exposure to reality would not yield any conceptual knowledge whatsoever. They assign reason an essentially *active* role, meaning that to produce concepts it has to manipulate and transform reality. Marxists regard reality as social and natural at the same time. For this reason, they take the construction of knowledge to be a *social* process in essence.

Box 2.2 describes what empiricists, rationalists, neo-Kantian transcendentalists and Marxist transcendentalists think would happen to the cognitive development of baby A growing outside of society, but in front of a television screen that shows exactly the same content as what his social counterpart, baby B, is exposed to in real life. Note that baby A maintains a totally passive position vis-à-vis the reality to which he is exposed. Unlike baby B, he cannot transform it in any way. Does this difference matter?

BOX 2.2

## PHILOSOPHERS AND COGNITIVE DEVELOPMENT: AN EXAMPLE

**The question:** Baby A grows up outside of society, but in front of a television screen that shows exactly the same content as the reality that Baby B, born at the same time, experiences – what would happen to the cognitive development of each baby?

- **Empiricists, neo-Kantians:** if given sufficient time, both babies will acquire similar cognitive skills and knowledge.

*(Continued)*

*(Continued)*

- **Rationalists:** If given sufficient time, both babies will acquire similar cognitive skills and knowledge, and would do so even if they were not exposed to either television or particular experiences in real life.

- **Marxists:** Baby A will fail to develop any conceptual thinking whatsoever regardless of how long it is exposed to the television. Baby B will develop conceptual thinking, but the specific content will depend on the particular social circumstances experienced by the baby.

## The nature of a scientific object

The second set of questions that philosophers ask about scientific objects concerns their nature. Can any object be studied by science? Do the objects of science have to be 'natural' (e.g. chemical compounds, physical masses, cellular membranes etc.), or can they also be 'social' (e.g. religion, psychology, economy, identity etc.)? Do they have to be material (e.g. stars, waves, particles, forces etc.), or can they be theoretical as well (e.g. language, wars, nationalism etc.)? Do they have to be general and abstract (e.g. Canis lupus familiaris) or can they be concrete (e.g. Fido, Abraham Lincoln's dog, at the moment of the President's assassination)?

Empiricists regard an object as a potential candidate for scientific inquiry if it could give rise to a testable explanation, namely, one that makes predictions which could be verified or falsified by observation. This means that objects must have some observable regularity in order to be studied by science. At any rate, science will deal with *concrete* objects only. After all, for an empiricist only concrete objects expose themselves to observation.

But there is a different way of looking at this question, particularly so for transcendentalists. In this view, science cannot and does not explore concrete objects at all, since they are universally complex, contingent, erratic and hence essentially untestable. Instead, it studies their simplified theoretical models, which, as opposed to their concrete counterparts, are absolutely predictable. The objects of science are thus general, abstract, isolated and closed. In short, they are imaginary.

Box 2.3 contains two examples which illustrate this, one from the natural sciences and one from the social sciences.

---

**BOX 2.3**

### A SCIENTIST AND A SOCIAL SCIENTIST WHO STUDIED 'IMAGINARY' RATHER THAN CONCRETE OBJECTS

Johannes Kepler's (1571–1630) astronomical theory claimed to explain the orbital motion of planets, moons and other satellites around a 'sedentary' body. Did Kepler derive his laws from the *concrete* solar system, a system consisting of oddly shaped, three-dimensional, erratically behaving planets, placed in a particular point in space and time, each affected by an infinite number of vectors from all corners of the universe? Probably not. He had to clean it from its concrete observed properties before he could say anything general about it. Indeed, only a system containing dimensionless planets that revolve in perfect elliptical tracks around the only object with which they interact, a dimensionless sun, could give rise to the strict geometrical laws that make up his theory.

Karl Marx (1818–1883) invented the *labour theory of value*, which claims to explain the origin of profit. His theory pertains to a closed, abstract and isolated system in which buyers and sellers maintain perfectly symmetrical positions vis-à-vis each other. Such a system does not exist in reality.

If science tested its explanations on concrete objects, then the likelihood of *any* of its predictions to *ever* be perfectly successful would be virtually zero. Meaningful tests, so it seems, can only take place on abstract models. The controlled experiment (described in Chapter 8) – perhaps the quintessential tool of science, although social scientists do not use it very often – may thus turn out to be nothing but a physical attempt, and never a fully successful one, to abstract the concrete object from its concrete properties. Actually, the physical experiment becomes absolutely controlled only in the 'ideal laboratory' – the scientist's mind. Indeed, thought experiments universally complement physical experiments. Moreover, the former often replace the latter altogether, especially where these cannot or ought not to take place. Aren't thought experiments perhaps the only really scientific experiments there are? Isn't it in our thought where theories are ultimately tested? Again, these considerations question the extent to which scientific knowledge differs from metaphysical knowledge.

## The objectives of science

Historians of science have succeeded in showing that science has had more than one objective at a time and that its objectives have changed over the past three centuries or so. In our society, for example, scientists generally try to solve practical and theoretical problems, but science is also recruited by politicians and others in attempts to save money, attract funding, generate profit, and, occasionally, to promote certain political and other institutional ends. Things were somewhat different in the seventeenth century, prior to the Industrial Revolution, when science had not attained the prestige that it now occupies in the minds of the powerful. It is unfortunate that philosophers have appeared unaware of these historical changes. Instead, philosophers fluctuate between the *view* that science *has* an inherent and immutable objective and the view that it *ought to have* a certain objective. In general, however, both approaches agree that science aims, or ought to aim, to *produce 'scientific' explanations*. But what counts or ought to count as 'scientific' explanation is often disputed.

Philosophical debates on the nature of scientific explanation rest on two assumptions. The first one holds that all explanations, whether scientific or not, have something general in common that distinguishes them from other propositions about the world, such as explications (clarifications of vague propositions), descriptions (characterisations of things), predictions (telling what is or is not to happen under certain conditions), judgments (evaluations – e.g. moral or aesthetic), and justifications (arguments that support judgments). The second assumption holds that all scientific explanations have something general in common that distinguishes them from other explanations. It is this general essence that philosophers of science are seeking.

## Explanations in general

In terms of form, all explanations contain two elements: an explanans (the thing that explains) and an explanandum (the thing to be explained, i.e. the object of the scientific inquiry or, in other words, the scientific question). In terms of function, an explanation is supposed to expose the essence behind the appearance. This conclusion follows from philosopher Georg Hegel's (1770–1831) understanding of the relations between the essence of a thing and its appearance: they do not necessarily coincide, but they are not independent of each other either: the essence gives rise to appearance; hence it explains it (Hegel, 2010). This Hegelian conception is implicit in Marx's claim that '[all] science would be superfluous if the outward appearance and the essence of things directly coincided' (Marx, 1967: 817).

Box 2.4 demonstrates how this conception would view the difference between the Aristotelian geocentric model of the solar system (all planets and the Sun revolve around Earth) and the Copernican heliocentric model thereof (all planets including Earth revolve around the Sun)

BOX 2.4

## APPEARANCE AND ESSENCE IN THE GEOCENTRIC VERSUS THE HELIOCENTRIC MODEL

For both models the appearance of things is the same: the Sun rises in morning and sets in the evening.

According to the *geocentric* model, the essence behind this appearance is as follows: the Sun moves around the Earth. This is a convincing explanation. However, it is intuitive: it regards the essence to be coinciding with the appearance.

According to the *heliocentric* model, the essence behind this appearance is as follows: the Earth moves around the sun. This explanation is equally convincing. However, it is counterintuitive. Is this perhaps what makes it scientific?

Explanations can be classified according to general categories, each containing several subcategories:

- **Scope**: universal (pertaining to all cases in the category in question), particular (pertaining to some cases only); abstract (pertaining to objects that are abstracted from their contingent features); concrete (pertaining to real objects); overly general; general; specific.

- **Form**: causal; statistical; teleological (regarding purpose as cause).

- **Structure**: reductionist (seeking the explanans in another, more basic system); non-reductionist (seeking the explanans in the same system to which the explanandum belongs).

- **Testability**: metaphysical, non-metaphysical; idealist (ideas explain matter); materialist (matter explains ideas).

- **Validity**: true; false; meaningless.

For the moment, do not worry if some of the terms in the above list (e.g. 'truth) have not been defined as yet. Later in this chapter they will be discussed in more depth. Box 2.5 gives examples of several explanations together with some of their properties, and the text that follows will discuss these in a way which will help you understand what these terms mean.

BOX 2.5

## EXPLANATIONS WHICH VARY ON PARTICULAR DIMENSIONS

- God created man: metaphysical, idealist, universal, overly general, abstract.

- Man created God: metaphysical, materialist, universal, general, abstract.

- I hit him, because he annoyed me: non-metaphysical, non-scientific, particular, specific, concrete.

- $E=MC^2$ explains the interchangeability of matter and energy: non-metaphysical, scientific, universal, general, abstract.

- Nuclear fission of 1 kg of uranium releases huge amounts of energy, because $E=MC^2$ and 1 kg of uranium is a certain mass: non-metaphysical, scientific, universal, specific, abstract.

- Giraffes developed a long neck in order to be able to feed on leaves that grow on top of trees: metaphysical, teleological, universal, specific, abstract.

- Men are more intelligent then women, because their brain is bigger on average: statistical, non-metaphysical, scientific, biological, reductionist, universal, general, abstract.

## Scientific explanation

Philosophers of science believe that, to be scientific, an explanation must meet certain criteria. Some of the pertinent debates about these criteria are discussed below.

### Scope

A scientific explanation must be based on a universal law. Put differently, this law must apply to *all* particular cases in the category in question. An explanation that does not rest on a universal law (ad hoc explanation) may or may not be true, but it is not scientific. Here is a commonly cited example of an ad hoc explanation:

> *I was healed from cancer by God!*
>
> *Really? Does that mean that God will heal all others with cancer?*
>
> *Well … God works in mysterious ways.*

In this example, God is the explanans and the fact that 'I' was healed from cancer is the explanandum. God is said to explain *my* healing *only*. This is therefore an ad hoc explanation: God is not obliged by any law to heal *all* cancer patients. Ad hoc explanations may be true or false, but they are not scientific. Science is not interested in them.

A scientific explanation can be either general or specific. An explanation that pertains to a general explanandum is general, whereas one that pertains to a subspecies of that explanandum is specific. The difference between general and specific explanations is only relative, however. For example, an explanation for the rise of nationalism, say, in post-Tito Yugoslavia is *specific* relative to an explanation for the rise of nationalism is general. However, it is *general* relative to an explanation for Bosnian, Serbian or Croatian nationalism, for example.

Scientific explanations maintain a certain hierarchy in relation to their generality. The explanans in the most general explanations is referred to as a principle. Below this level is a scientific law and below this is a theorem. Different laws may obey the same principle, but they cannot be deduced from it. In contrast, theorems are deduced from laws. A set of laws that pertains to a composite explanandum, namely, one that gives rise to diverse phenomena – the universe, the atom, society, for example – is called a theory.

It should also be emphasised that not every generalisation is a law, and that a generalisation that is not law is not explanatory. For example, the generalisation 'all American presidents in the nineteenth century were bald' would not explain why any one of them was bald even if it were true. It is purely accidental.

Whereas scientific explanations must be general in some sense, they must retain some degree of specificity. Overly general explanations – the attribution of *everything* that happens to God's will, for example – cannot be scientific. Such explanations may or may not be true, but they are non-informative and hence useless.

### Form: models of scientific explanation

Following philosopher David Hume (1711–1776), empiricists have consistently rejected the idea of causality (i.e. a 'necessary' relation between events) as utterly metaphysical (untestable), hence unscientific. They maintained that the objective of science was merely to describe regularities in relation to successive or co-existing events.

Carl Hempel (1905–1997) and Paul Oppenheim (1885–1977) were the first to formalise this conception of scientific explanation. Their model is known as the deductive-nomological (D-N) model. 'Nomos' means 'law' in ancient Greek, so 'deductive-nomological' refers to the capacity of the law to generate deduction. (This model has also been called the *covering law model*.) According to this model, a scientific explanation contains two elements: (1) the specific explanandum (the sentence describing the phenomenon to be explained) and (2) the explanans (the sentence containing explanation), the latter being the logical conclusion of (a) a general law, plus (b) initial conditions pertaining to the specific explanandum.

Box 2.6 illustrates this, with explanations taken first from natural science and second from social science.

BOX 2.6

## THE DEDUCTIVE-NOMOLOGICAL MODEL OF SCIENTIFIC EXPLANATION IN GALILEO GALILEI'S (1564–1642) THEORY OF FALLING BODIES AND IN SOCIOLOGIST ÉMILE DURKHEIM'S (1858–1917) THEORY OF SUICIDE

| | | Galileo: falling objects | Durkheim: suicide rates |
|---|---|---|---|
| *Explanandum* | | Object x falls. | Suicide rates among Catholics are lower than among Protestants. |
| *Explanans* | Law | Objects with mass attract each other. | Suicide rates vary inversely with the degree of social cohesion. |
| | Initial conditions | Body x and Earth are objects with mass. | Catholicism is associated with greater social cohesion than is Protestantism. |

The D-N model purports to describe all scientific explanations. However, it has been criticised for being overly abstract. In particular, it does not tell us which generalisations could count as laws. As we saw earlier, generalisations that merely describe regularities are not explanatory. In the absence of a consensus on the criteria of lawhood the D-N model is unclear.

The model raises yet another difficulty. It describes an explanation as a deduction from deterministic laws. But what about the explanatory status of statistical laws, laws that speak of probabilities? Do they explain anything and if so, what do they explain? Hempel himself distinguished between two varieties of statistical explanation. The *deductive-statistical (D-S) explanation* involves the deduction of a statistical uniformity from a more general statistical law. For example, the law that describes the 1:4 chance of two parents each carrying one gene of cystic fibrosis to give birth to a baby with this condition can be deduced from the law pertaining to the heredity of heterozygote conditions in general. Clearly, this model conforms to the same general pattern of the D-N model. The *inductive-statistical (I-S) explanation*, on the other hand, involves the subsumption of individual events under a statistical law. This kind of explanation takes the following form, for example: 25 per cent of babies born to parents who carry the gene for cystic fibrosis will have the condition; X's parents carry the gene for cystic fibrosis.

Philosopher Wesley Salmon's (1925–2001) *statistical relevance (S-R) model* attempts to capture the 'causal' essence of a scientific explanation as a *conditional dependence relationship*. To illustrate this model, let us consider the following example. Women and men who are taking birth control pills are unlikely to conceive. If you are a male, taking the pill is statistically irrelevant to whether you become pregnant. However, if you are a female, it is relevant. In this way we can grasp the idea that taking birth control pills is explanatorily irrelevant to pregnancy among males but not among females.

Salmon eventually abandoned the attempt to characterise explanations or causal relationships in purely statistical terms. Instead, he developed another account, which he called the *causal-mechanical (C-M) model* of explanation. We may think of this model as an attempt to capture the 'something extra' involved in causal relationships over and above facts about statistical relevance. The C-M model employs the idea that a causal process is a mechanical process that is characterised by the ability to transmit a mark in a continuous way. A collision between snooker balls is a simple example. This model does not reflect many scientific laws, if any. One cannot argue, for example, that Isaac Newton's (1643–1727) classical mechanics contains laws that are the cause of the particular motion of bodies. Nor can one argue that Karl Marx's (1818–1883) historical materialism contains laws that cause the transition from one economic formation to another. At best one can say that bodies and economic transitions obey their respective laws.

A teleological explanation is an explanation that appeals to purpose/end. Some teleological explanations appeal to purpose only. They take the form of 'A in order to B' – the chair has four legs in order to be stable, for example. Such explanations may make sense. Other teleological explanations confuse the purpose for the cause. They take the form of 'A because of B', when in fact they should at best take the 'in order to' form cats have come to exist because they prey on mice. In any case, teleological explanations are not scientific. Science is not interested in purposes.

One of the more recent accounts of scientific explanation is the *unificationist model*. It holds that a scientific explanation aims to provide a unified account of a range of different phenomena previously thought to be unrelated. A typical example is physicist James Maxwell's (1831–1879) unification of electricity and magnetism.

The question whether there is or ought to be just one model of scientific explanation is still open. We shall later attempt to find out whether explanations in the natural sciences differ in principle from those in the social sciences.

## Structure: reductionism versus non-reductionism

It is commonly accepted that the foundations of some fields of study are rooted in another field: chemistry in physics and microbiology in chemistry, for example. There is also wide agreement that some 'basic' fields can affect and inform 'higher' ones: psychology in the case of economics and biology in the case of psychology, for example. Scientific reductionism takes a more radical approach, however. Taking a complex system to be no more than the sum of its parts, this literally mechanistic approach attempts to explain the former in terms of the latter. Reductionist conceptions and practices can be found in all areas of science, including medicine, social sciences and psychology among many others.

Scientific-reductionist explanations are often criticised merely because they happen to be reductionist. For example, sociobiologists, who seek to explain the social world as if it were entirely the product of biological forces, such as evolutionary competition, are often dismissed by critics as 'reductionist'. This is not justifiable. Scientists are under no obligation to produce reductionist explanations, but there is no reason why they should not try. Reductionist explanations should be judged on a case-by-case basis according to the same criteria that apply to non-reductionist explanations. For example, scientists who propose reductionist explanations have the onus of showing that the explanandum can be reconstructed from the explanans. Their success would be our gain, their failure our loss. In some cases they could possibly succeed. Perhaps eye colour could one day be reduced to proteins and genes, for example (so far we have only come up with regularities, not explanations). Yet it seems that some objects could never receive plausible reductionist explanations. For example, it seems highly unlikely that we will ever see a plausible explanation of the history of humankind that rested on quantum physics. Scientific reductionism can take a subtler but no less contentious form. In this version, the explanation is not reductionist in itself. It is reductionist only in relation to an alternative explanation that frames the explanandum and the explanans in terms of a more complex system. For example, the conception that a particular disease is a biological phenomenon that requires a biological explanation does not seem to be reductionist in itself. Of course, cancer is caused by a mutation of cells. However, it transpires to be reductionist in relation to the conception that regards the same disease as a social phenomenon that requires a social explanation. Cancer occurs with differing regularity in people occupying different social classes. The traditional (reductionist) tendency of modern medical science to focus on biological explanations to the relative neglect of social ones has had profound, often disturbing, social implications.

## Testability: verificationism versus falsificationism

To be scientific, an explanation has to be testable. An explanation that is untestable is unscientific regardless of any other considerations. Metaphysical explanations, such as theistic explanations for the creation of the world (as well as atheistic explanations for the invention of God), are unscientific, because they cannot be tested. In general, empiricism regards an explanation as testable, if it entails rigorous and specific (i.e. conditional) predictions that, if successful, can reveal its truth value. What these predictions are supposed to predict (events which are compatible with the explanation or events that are incompatible with it) and what exactly they should reveal about the truth value of the explanation (its veracity or its falsity) is debatable, however.

Verificationism, a traditional empiricist conception, maintains that a scientific explanation should entail predictions that are compatible with the explanation. Thus if successful, these will validate, which is to say confirm, its veracity. Relatively modest predictions required a relatively large number of confirmatory observations before the explanation is declared true, whereas for exceptionally bold ones even a single successful observation may suffice. For example, a single observation of light bending around the Sun made in 1918 as predicted by Albert Einstein's (1879–1955) general theory of relativity is said to have confirmed this theory. The justification for this position and its shortcomings warrant a brief discussion.

Verificationists regard generalisations as the basic units of any genuine knowledge, let alone scientific knowledge. However, they differ from others in their explanation of the origin of generalisations. They maintain that these are derived from consistent observations of cases or individual facts, a thought process called induction. For example, it is a fact that when a stone is dropped it falls to the ground, and we will find that it does so again and again if we keep on trying this. Verificationists would argue that the law of gravity is scientific because its prediction that things will fall under certain circumstances could in principle be found consistently successful. Verificationists would regard the law as scientific even if these predictions were eventually to be found unsuccessful; the verificationist would then simply conclude that this (scientific) law is false.

There is no doubt that the predictive capacity of scientific explanations, more than anything else, makes science socially useful: it instructs the engineer, the technologist, the astronaut, the doctor and a host of others. But do consistently successful predictions imply veracity? This is not clear. Induction may perhaps be a necessary thought process and no doubt it plays a role in the formation of some generalisations. But it is *not* a logical process. There is no necessity that the next observation will yield the same result as the previous ones, no matter how consistent and numerous they have been. The Sun may have risen since time immemorial, but this is no guarantee that it will rise tomorrow. Besides, the number of actual observations is always infinitesimally small compared to the infinite number of possible observations, so that it is always possible that an event has occurred that contradicts the law, but which has not been observed. Any generalisation that is based on induction is thus fallible: its veracity cannot be established with certainty. Known as the problem of induction, this had already been recognised by ancient philosophers. It was reintroduced by David Hume in the eighteenth century and then again by philosopher Karl Popper (1902–1994) two centuries later on.

An empiricist himself, Popper agreed that an explanation must be testable in order to be scientific. However, he rejected the verificationist assumption that explanations could be validated by successful predictions. He maintained, instead, that a scientific explanation should entail predictions, which, if successful, will falsify (i.e. refute) it. Popper's falsificationism regards an explanation as scientific if it is able to describe conditions in which it would be proved false by observation. Accordingly, the generalisation 'all swans are white' is scientific not because it can be confirmed – in fact, it cannot be confirmed – but rather because it can be refuted. Indeed, one observation of a non-white swan will falsify the generalisation.

Yet falsificationism itself is problematic no less than verificationism. (Interestingly, Popper was aware of that. He had other reasons for embracing the conception. These will be discussed later on.) Whatever their number, observations of an allegedly law-refuting prediction may be faulty in themselves. Moreover, there is no procedure or criterion that could guarantee their soundness. A swan may appear to be non-white just because it is dirty or because it has been painted black.

A student of Popper, philosopher Imre Lakatos (1922–1974) attempted to overcome the problems of both verificationism and falsificationism. He maintained that the nature of the predictions which an explanation entails has nothing to do with its truth value. It is merely a rational measure allowing us to compare competing explanations. Explanations that make many, new, and bold predictions are stronger than those that do not, regardless of whether they are 'confirmative' or 'refutative'. Lakatos seems to have saved the requirement of testability from emptiness by assigning it a functional, rather than epistemic role.

Yet the question could be tackled from a different direction. Let us note that the empiricist practice of observations presupposes that explanations are being confirmed and falsified on the basis of predictions about concrete reality. Think back, though, to the early part of this chapter where the nature of scientific objects was discussed and you will recall that it is debatable as to whether these objects can be considered concrete or abstract entities. If the object of scientific inquiry is abstract, then such predictions are purely theoretical. They succeed or fail in theory only, and it is theory and not observation that confirms or refutes them.

## Validity: truth and objectivity

Following philosopher Pierre Duhem (1861–1916), instrumentalists maintain that scientific theories are useful conceptual constructs that have no truth value. Realists, in contrast, regard them as explanatory constructs that do have a truth value. Excluding naïve realists, most realists are fallibilists, which is to say that they regard scientific theories as hypothetical and always corrigible in principle. They may happen to be true, but we cannot know this for certain in any particular case. But even when theories are false, they can be closer to the truth than their rivals. But what is truth? Can it be identified? Does it play any role in science? If so, should it?

One 'true' thing that can be said about *truth* is that it has received many definitions (see Box 2.7). Against this backdrop, it would be absurd to ask which one of them is true. Although the box shows many such definitions, just three will be discussed here. The first definition is known as the correspondence theory of truth, which goes back at least to some of the classical Greek philosophers including Socrates, Plato and Aristotle, and is still the most popular theory of truth. It posits a superposing (sometimes called 'matching' or 'corresponding') relationship between thoughts and objects. In other words, a judgment is said to be true when it conforms to the objective reality. According to this theory, the terms truth and objectivity seem to be interchangeable. However, the relation between them is not straightforward, and it would be sensible here to divert the discussion of truth definitions to consider this matter of objectivity.

Empiricism defines objectivity as the property of knowledge designating its independence of any consciousness. Accordingly, objective knowledge is true knowledge. If Newton's classical mechanics is false, then it is cannot be objective. If Einstein's special theory of relativity is true, then it is objective. But there are those who would argue against this. Transcendentalists, for example, regard objectivity as the property of knowledge designating its independence of any individual consciousness, but not of any consciousness. In fact, they regard it as an inter-subjective or social artefact. Newton's theory and Einstein's theory were thus both objective (referring to different objects, though), but only one of them, at most, can be true.

The second definition of truth is known as the coherence theory of truth, which maintains that truth is primarily a property of whole systems of propositions, and can be ascribed to individual propositions only according to their coherence with the whole. Coherence theories have been embraced by rationalists and logical positivists because they considered them as non-metaphysical in contrast to correspondence theories.

The third definition is that of social constructionism, which holds that truth is constructed by social processes, is historically and culturally specific, and is in part shaped through the power struggles within a community. Constructionism denies that our knowledge reflects any external realities. Rather, perceptions of truth are contingent on convention, human perception, and social experience. Constructionists maintain that representations of physical and biological reality, including race, sexuality and gender, are socially constructed.

---

**BOX 2.7**

## DIFFERENT CONCEPTIONS OF TRUTH

- *Correspondence theory:* A statement is true if it describes reality accurately.

- *Coherence theory:* A statement is true if it makes sense in the context in which it is made.

- *Social constructionism:* A statement is true if society constructs it as true.

- *Consensus theory:* A statement is true if it has been agreed upon.

- *Epistemological subjectivism/relativism:* A statement is true for those who take it to be true.

- *Epistemological nihilism:* Truth is a meaningless concept; nothing is knowable.

- *Pragmatic theory:* A statement is true if it works.

- *Performative theory:* Truth assertion is a speech act signalling one's agreement with the assertion.

- *Redundancy theory:* Asserting that a statement is true is equivalent to asserting the statement itself. Thus truth is a redundant concept; just a word that is used for emphasis, nothing else.

The plurality of definitions of truth reflects disagreements about the meaning of truth. Yet even if we embraced, say, the correspondence theory, we would still need some foundational criterion by which the veracity and the falsity of statements could be established. Unfortunately, philosophical inquiry has failed to uncover such a criterion. One view is that it is impossible to prove any truth even in the fields of logic and mathematics, since the very assertion from which the truth of the statement is deduced must be proved true by another assertion in a process requiring infinite regression. Another view holds that it is impossible to test a scientific hypothesis in isolation, because any empirical test of the hypothesis would require one or more background assumptions (auxiliary assumptions) whose own test requires other assumptions ad infinitum. According to these arguments, there is no point in looking for the truth in science or in any other knowledge even if it exists. Whatever it is, we shall never be able to identify it (ironically, even the truth of this assertion must be taken with a grain of salt).

This has therefore led many philosophers to argue that nonfoundationalism is the only way we can really think about science and social science. This position has several important implications. First, we could conclude that science is not superior to other forms of knowledge in any way. This possibility was discussed at the outset of this chapter when arguments for the metaphysical basis of both religion and science were discussed, and will be considered again in what follows. Alternatively, we could conclude that if science is indeed superior to other forms of knowledge, then this is not because of its veracity. To support this argument, then, we would need to come up with other points, such as the willingness of scientists to abandon scientific explanations that are in irremediable conflict with experience (a much trumpeted feature of science according to some who support it), or the systematic

attempt by scientists to construct stronger explanations or of course, the practical usefulness of science in instructing the production of various technologies. We might also compare the strength of competing scientific and non-scientific explanations based not on epistemic criteria, but rather on aesthetic ones, asking, for example, whether an explanation seems 'elegant'. Taken together, we might then argue that explanation P will be stronger than explanation Q, all other things being equal, if:

1  P accounts for more phenomena, or predicts a larger number of events.

2  P is simpler (more 'parsimonious').

3  P is more elegant.

4  P persists in the face of new knowledge, whereas Q does not.

5  P can explain why Q cannot explain the phenomena which it can.

The nonfoundationalist premise could take us to yet another place and help us realise that we must have chosen to embrace some scientific assertions and reject others under circumstances that had nothing to do with their 'real' truth value. These circumstances, for example, might include our psychological preferences or our social position, which predispose us to want to accept one scientific idea above some other idea. In other words, these are the conditions of our ideological choices, which under this view should concern us much more than the truth value of the knowledge which we accept. Philosophy cannot reveal this because it is unable to tell us why we find some of its assertions more attractive than others. This task belongs to social scientists who may study the way in which scientific (and social scientific) communities decide on what to count as true or false, and why some segments of the general population agree with them and others disagree. In fact, the sociological study of science, and of the public understanding of science, is a flourishing area.

## Methodology and progress

Philosophical accounts of the evolution of science are partly normative (how science *ought* to evolve) and partly descriptive (how it *actually* evolves). At any rate, philosophers regard its evolution to be the direct result of its particular methodology or the lack thereof. In this section five different accounts of the evolution of science will be considered.

The first is known as the hypothetico-deductive method, sometimes also known as the *cumulative model* of scientific progress. This was first proposed by the philosopher William Whewell (1794–1866) as a seemingly descriptive model, although it in fact contains normative elements. According to this clearly empiricist model, the scientific process starts with hypotheses. These are then tested: positive predictions corroborate them and negative ones refute them. Hypotheses that are corroborated thus add up to the existing aggregate of positive knowledge in an infinitely progressive process, which is why the model is also known as the cumulative model. In line with this model, some historians have argued that the acquisition and systematisation of scientific knowledge are the only human activities that are truly 'cumulative' and 'progressive'.

Second, associated with Karl Popper, is the falsificationist view of scientific progress. This is very much a normative view, which accepts the hypothetico-deductive method but holds that science ought only to try to falsify its hypotheses and, when successful, replace them with new hypotheses, which ought themselves to be falsifiable on other grounds. Popper regarded this process as a critical-rational condition for approximating to the truth, even without ever being able to know how close to it we are.

Third, are the ideas of philosopher Thomas Kuhn (1922–1996) who was influenced by historical study of how communities of scientists actually seemed to work, so might be considered to provide a descriptive rather than a normative view of scientific progress. He took a transcendentalist point of view in proposing that science progressed via a series of scientific revolutions. He maintained that scientific observations are always embedded in some broad context consisting of the theoretical premises, methods and practices used by a particular community, or generation, of scientists as a backdrop, or set of largely unquestioned assumptions, to their scientific work. This collection of background assumptions Kuhn called a scientific paradigm. Thus corroborations and refutations of hypotheses do not take place in the realm of observation, but rather in the reciprocal interface between observation and paradigm. According to this view, the evolution of science oscillates between periods of normal science – a routine, cumulative, 'puzzle-solving' work involving experimentation within a paradigm without actually challenging it – and a paradigm shift or a scientific revolution, namely, a critical situation where an irresolvable tension between normal science and paradigm results in a change of paradigm. Kuhn maintained that competing or consecutive paradigms are incommensurable, and that the choice between them is made on the basis of partly logical but also partly sociological reasons.

Fourth in the list of accounts of scientific progress is the idea that science proceeds by means of research programmes. Attempting to reconcile the differences between Popper and Kuhn, Lakatos suggested that research programmes are sets of theories which share a certain 'hard core'. Scientists involved in a programme will attempt to shield the theoretical core from attempts to falsify it behind a protective belt of auxiliary hypotheses. Whereas Popper regarded such ad hoc measures as unacceptable, Lakatos argued they rather reflected rationality (within limits).

Fifth and finally, philosopher Paul Feyerabend (1922–1994) argued that there is no single scientific methodology, pointing out that evidence about how scientists actually work shows that all 'scientific' methods have, in practice, been violated by individual scientists at some point in order to advance of scientific knowledge. He therefore embraced the view that science was – and perhaps needed to be – anarchic, so that he embraced scientific anarchism. At one level, Feyerabend appears cynical and dismissive of science. For example, he maintained that hypotheses came to be embraced or rejected not because of their accord or discord with any scientific method, but rather because their proponents and opponents used some tricks, including lies, in order to advance their cause, respectively. But Feyerabend also said that anarchism was, in practice, the source of scientific creativity and the secret of its achievements. Breaking methodological 'rules' has sometimes been necessary for scientific advances.

## Problem(s) of demarcation

Boundaries are often drawn between science and other knowledge systems. Moreover, they are drawn within science itself as well: between the natural and social sciences and among individual natural and social disciplines. But where exactly should the boundaries be drawn, what do they imply, and what purpose do they serve?

## Science versus pseudoscience

According to empiricists, the difference between science and other knowledge systems rests on the particular methodology which each employs. For logical positivists and verificationists, the scientific methodology, as they see it, reflects the meaningfulness of scientific assertions, if not also their unrivalled validity. For falsificationists, it reflects the difference between science and pseudoscience, practices that purport to be scientific, when in fact they only attempt to capitalise

on the reputation of science as the most rational system of knowledge. Indeed, Popper himself used the criterion of falsifiability primarily to reject certain theories to which he also happened to be politically opposed, notably, of deterministic interpretations of Marxist theory of history, which he regarded as unfalsifiable and therefore pseudoscientific. He applied the same critique to the ideas of Sigmund Freud, Alfred Adler and even Darwin.

For Kuhn and Lakatos, the boundary should be drawn between lively and degenerated scientific paradigms or research programmes, respectively. Thus it seems they would regard obsolete scientific theories as non-scientific, at least tentatively (although Lakatos did not preclude the possibility of resurrecting old research programmes). Feyerabend went one step further, maintaining that science does not occupy any special place in terms of its logic or methodology and is an integral part of the larger body of human thought and inquiry in which 'anything goes'. Such views are shared by postmodernists, who criticise any over-arching position, including positions that draw boundaries, as being ideological and at any rate oppressive.

## Natural versus social sciences

The relationship between natural science and social research is uneasy, with the suspicion that the application of the label 'science' to the study of social and cultural matters is unjustifiable always lurking behind debates. There are a variety of responses to this, ranging from attempts to make social science adhere to the methods and principles of natural science as closely as possible, to the opposite extreme, whereby social and cultural researchers actively reject the label 'scientific', claiming instead to be pursuing something quite different.

Naturalists hold that all phenomena are natural, thus society can be studied by science just like nature. Some of them, notably positivists like sociologists Auguste Comte (1798–1857), Émile Durkheim, Talcott Parsons (1902–1979) and Robert Merton (1910–2003), demand that social science embrace the empiricist conception of objectivity. Durkheim, for example, required the social scientist to 'embark upon the study of social facts by adopting the principle that he is in complete ignorance of what they are, and that the properties characteristic of them are totally unknown to him, as are the causes upon which these latter depend' (Durkheim, 1982: 245).

Interpretivists, on the other hand, contend that the study of society requires an interpretative approach. Some of them reject the positivist claim that empirical science is the only science. Others, like Alfred Schutz (1899–1959), Hans-Georg Gadamer (1900–2002), Paul Ricoeur (1913–2005), Clifford Geertz (1926–2006), Jürgen Habermas (1929–) and Charles Taylor (1931–), who accept the positivist claim, also accept the positivist conclusion that much of what social science is doing is not really science. As far as they are concerned, the study of society involves a search not for facts, but rather for meaning.

Reconcilers attempt to bridge the divide between naturalism and interpretivism. They typically embrace the transcendentalist perspective that all science, including the natural sciences, is anyway interpretive. Max Weber (1864–1920), for example, regarded detachment (complete conceptual neutrality of the observer) and objectivity that depends on 'pure' observation as utterly inconceivable, but he did not dismissed objectivity as a social construct. Karl Marx and Friedrich Engels (1820–1893) went even farther. They reduced all science, including the natural sciences, to one science that is essentially social: 'we know only a single science, the science of history. One can look at history from two sides and divide it into the history of nature and the history of men. The two sides are, however, inseparable; the history of nature and the

history of men are dependent on each other so long as men exist' (Marx and Engels, 2004: 39). It should be emphasised that most reconcilers distinguish between science in general and other knowledge systems. They are aware then that not every knowledge that is produced by science, natural or social, is necessarily scientific.

Determined to challenge any boundary in particular and in fact any positive knowledge in general, postmodernists often express attitudes toward science that differ radically from those we have discussed in this section. Their extreme relativism leads them to conclude that science is a 'myth' that does not differ in essence from any other 'narrative'. Moreover, they often claim that since all narratives make positive assertions which necessarily imply some negations, they must be essentially oppressive (ironically, this applies to this assertion as well). Indeed, postmodernists often attack science on this ground. In social science, they have typically targeted Marxism. However, they have attacked the natural sciences as well. For example, the feminist theorist Luce Irigaray (1932– ) criticised $E=MC^2$ for privileging the speed of light over other speeds that are vitally necessary for us. Other postmodernists seem to have ridiculed any boundary between natural and social science by importing concepts from natural science into the humanities without any justification. The alternative, allegedly 'subversive' knowledge, which they offer instead, is deliberately fragmentary and incomprehensible. This point was taken ad absurdum in 1996 by Alan Sokal, a physics professor at New York University and a harsh critic of postmodernism. He submitted a quasi-postmodernist article to *Social Text*, an academic journal dedicated to postmodern cultural studies, in attempt to learn whether it would publish an article liberally salted with nonsense. The article, 'Transgressing the boundaries: towards a transformative hermeneutics of quantum gravity' (Sokal, 1996: 217–252), which proposed that quantum gravity is a social and linguistic construct, was accepted for publication.

## The moral question

### Facts and values

Naturalists sometimes maintain that moral claims can be inferred from the natural properties of the object. The object would thus be inferred as 'good' from the fact that it is, say, 'desirable', 'pleasant', 'more evolved' etc. Think about it - we do it all the time: when someone says 'good boy' this involves inference from the boy's behaviour. Philosopher G.E. Moore (1873–1958) showed, however, that this position ('if it is natural, then it must be good'), called the *naturalistic fallacy*, is logically flawed: no natural property implies 'goodness'. And yet it often seems that people draw moral (ought to) conclusions from descriptive or explanatory (is) statements. David Hume regarded this cognitive leap as utterly illogical. For example, the statement 'Switzerland is a central European country' does not entail that Switzerland is good or bad. Max Weber held a similar view, noting that '[an] empirical science cannot tell anyone what he should do, but rather what he can do' (Weber, 1949: 54). For example, the statement 'E=MC$^2$' can tell us that we can build an atomic bomb, but it does not say we ought to do so.

Hume and Weber were right in arguing that science is morally neutral. But they were only partially right. Science is morally neutral only when it is considered in the abstract, that is to say, out of its social context. In social context, however, the conception that science is morally neutral becomes as absurd as the claim that music is emotionally neutral. Let us not forget that the social context contains general moral laws and concrete interests that are informed by 'is' statements. When this happens, the latter loose their moral neutrality. For example, a society that (a) embraced the general moral law that 'central European countries are bad' and (b) faced the factual statement that 'Switzerland is a central European country' would be bound to draw the conclusion that 'Switzerland is bad'. This deduction would not be illogical at all, as Hume thought.

### Good science: conservative versus radical ethics

Like any other social enterprise, science may also be subject to moral criticism. For example, the history of ethics in medical research involving humans in the past six decades can be described as a continuous reaction to moral outrage following revelations about crimes and wrongs committed in the name of science (Chapter 5 discusses research ethics in more detail).

In general, the morality of science can be judged with respect to three areas:

- its attitude to and impact on researchees, consumers and other populations (e.g. whether people participate in scientific studies on the basis of informed consent or not)

- the nature of its agenda, namely, the problems it chooses to deal with and those it chooses to ignore (e.g. scientists may study nuclear fission and contribute to weaponry, and they may ignore the science of global warming, or vice versa)

- the nature of the interests which it serves (e.g. the military-industrial complex or the pharmaceutical industry).

The moral action required in each of these areas has particular political implications. The action pertaining to the first area requires science to offer some protection to the pertinent groups. This is a most important sphere of action; however, without tackling the last two areas as well it is bound to become an ideological smokescreen. The moral actions regarding the last two areas are radical. They demand that we challenge the powers that determine the historical character of science.

## Conclusion

This chapter has tried to figure out what science actually is by presenting various answers to several specific questions. For each question, the discussion has raised issues which are pertinent to social researchers.

- First, we saw that science rests on several metaphysical premises, and that it probably cannot free itself from all metaphysics. Critical science, particularly social science, should be aware of its fundamental premises, scrutinise them, and be able to defend or reject them as necessary.

- Second, we saw that philosophers of science differ about the source of the intelligibility of objects in general and about the nature of the objects it can in principle investigate in particular. In view of these perspectives, social researchers should ask whether social objects are really different from 'natural' objects and what the conditions for making them amenable to scientific inquiry are.

- Third, discussing the objectives of science, we learned that science is fallible (interestingly, there is a wide consensus about this point among both scientists as well as philosophers of science). This means that its claims to any superiority cannot rest on its validity. Perhaps it is just *rational* and that is what makes it so special. Can social science be as rational as natural science? There is no reason why not.

- Fourth, we discussed theories that describe how science evolves or how it ought to evolve. This debate has given rise to the question of whether or not science is in fact rational. Whatever the case, we saw again that there is no reason why the proposed models of scientific progress should not apply to social science as well.

- Fifth, discussing problems of demarcation, we came across an extreme conflict between theories that push for a very narrow hence exclusive definition of science and theories that reject any positive assertions, including assertions about demarcation. Social researchers should be aware of the implications of both kinds of theories for their own enterprise.

- Finally, discussing the interface between science and morality, we saw that, in context, science tends to acquire a moral dimension and there are two complementary ways to strengthen its morality. A similar conclusion applies not just to science, natural and social, but also to any other knowledge system.

## FURTHER READING

Martin and McIntyre (1994) is a treasury of important articles in the philosophy of science. Hollis (1994) is an exceptionally good introductory text. Smith (1998) has excellent coverage of contemporary developments. Machamer and Silberstein (2002) provide a thorough, comprehensive guide.

### Student Reader (Seale, 2004b): relevant readings

3   Emile Durkheim: 'Laws and social facts'

4   Walter L. Wallace: 'The logic of science in sociology'

5   Thomas D. Cook and Donald T. Campbell: 'Popper and falsificationism'

26   Paul Feyerabend: 'Against method'

27   Thomas S. Kuhn: 'The structure of scientific revolutions'

59   Renato Rosaldo: 'Grief and a headhunter's rage'

62   Zygmunt Bauman: 'Intellectuals: from modern legislators to post-modern interpreters'

67   Max Weber: 'Science as a vocation'

71   Sandra Harding: 'Is there a feminist method?'

## Journal articles discussing issues raised in this chapter

Mulkay, M. and Gilbert, G.N. (1981) 'Putting philosophy to work: Karl Popper's influence on scientific practice', Philosophy of the Social Sciences, 11: 389–407.

Potter, J. (1984) 'Testability, flexibility: Kuhnian values in scientists' discourse concerning theory choice', Philosophy of the Social Sciences, 14: 303–330.

## Web links

Stanford Encyclopedia of Philosophy: http://plato.stanford.edu/contents.html

Routledge Encyclopedia of Philosophy. Social sciences, philosophy of: www.rep.routledge.com/article/R047

Philosophy since the Enlightenment, by Roger Jones: www.philosopher.org.uk

e-Source: Chapter 2 on '"Science" in the Social Sciences' by Jeffrey Coulter: www.esourceresearch.org

## KEY CONCEPTS FOR REVIEW

Advice: Use these, along with the review questions in the next section, to test your knowledge of the contents of this chapter. Try to define each of the key concepts listed here; if you have understood this chapter you should be able to do this. Check your definitions against the definition in the glossary at the end of the book.

Coherence theory of truth

Correspondence theory of truth

Deduction

Deductive-nomological (D-N) model

Empiricism

Epistemology

Explanans/explanandum

Explanations (scope, form, structure, testability and validity of)

Falsificationism

General and specific explanations

Hypothetico-deductive method

Idealism

Induction

Instrumentalism

Interpretivism

Law, theorem and theory

Logical positivism

Materialism

Metaphysical

Naturalism

Nonfoundationalism

Normative and descriptive accounts of science

Objectivity

Ontology

Postmodernism

Principle

Rationalist epistemology

Realism

Reductionism

Scientific paradigm

Scientific revolution

Social constructionism

Specificity of scientific explanations

Teleological

Testable explanation

Transcendentalism

Universal law

Verificationism

## ■ Review questions

1 Describe in which respects science resembles metaphysics and in which respects it differs from it.
2 Explain why science cannot claim to be superior to other knowledge systems based on the validity of its statements.
3 Describe the problem of induction and suggest an alternative way of producing generalisations.
4 What are the problems which falsificationism purports to address? Does it tackle them satisfactorily?
5 Describe the difference between normative and descriptive theories of scientific progress and give some examples of each.
6 Describe Feyerabend's view on the demarcation problem and compare it to a radical postmodernist view.
7 Give an argument why *all* science is necessarily interpretive and explain on which epistemology it draws.
8 Explain why Hume was right saying that a leap from 'is' statements to 'ought to' statements is illogical. Describe the conditions under which the transition from the former to the latter could nevertheless be done in a logical way.

## Workshop and discussion exercises

1 What, in your view, are the major features of a *science*?
2 Explain the arguments for:
    (a) treating social sciences as analogous to natural sciences
    (b) rejecting the notion of the methodological unity of natural and social sciences.
3 What do you understand by the terms *value freedom* and *objectivity*?
4 Are emotions best kept out of social science?

# 3

# RESEARCH AND THEORY

David Silverman

---

## Chapter Contents

Until recently, the different social sciences seemed to vary in the importance that they attached to theory. To take just two examples, psychologists and anthropologists, for all their differences, seemed to downplay theory. In psychology, the benchmark was the laboratory study. For psychologists, the motto seemed to be: 'demonstrate the facts through a controlled experiment and the theories will take care of themselves'. Anthropologists were just as interested in 'the facts'. However, their most important facts were revealed in observational case studies of groups or tribes usually found in faraway lands. Nonetheless, until recently, most English-speaking anthropologists followed psychologists in elevating facts above theories. This can be described as an *empiricist* approach in that facts are assumed to exist prior to the theories that explain them. In Chapter 2 there is a discussion of this empiricist vision which elucidates these points.

More recently, theory has become more important in both anthropology and psychology. Psychologists, for example, have become interested in discourse analysis (see Chapter 23). Anthropology has been particularly influenced by postmodern theories and theories of gender. By contrast, generations of British sociology students have long been made very aware of the primary importance attached to theory in their discipline. For instance, although undergraduate sociology courses tend to be split into three main areas (the 'holy trinity' of social theory, social structure and research methods), it is the course in social theory which is usually given the most prestige. Using the example of sociology, it is worth examining how far this elevation of theory is appropriate or fruitful.

Thus, when you have read this chapter, you should know what a theory is, be able to distinguish between a theory, a model and a concept, and to understand the ways in which models shape your research problem.

## Do we need theory?

The main complaint about courses in social theory heard from students relates to the complex and confusing philosophical issues which are raised and the use of impenetrable jargon. It may seem that students have to learn a new language before they can begin to ask properly accredited questions and, moreover, that this new language seems to be of doubtful relevance to the social or political issues which may have brought them to the subject in the first place.

Even if they can penetrate the jargon, students may be puzzled by discovering that, just as they have learned the ideas of one social theorist, the rug appears to be pulled out from under their feet by an apparently devastating critique of those ideas. So Durkheim, they learn, is a positivist (obviously disreputable) and mistakes society for a biological organism. And Marx's social theories are largely inappropriate to the age in which we live. As each succeeding theorist is built up, only to be torn down, people become understandably concerned about the point of the whole exercise.

The situation would not be so bad if theoretical ideas could be applied to research studies. But even brilliant contemporary syntheses of social theory – like those in the works of Anthony Giddens (e.g. Giddens, 1991a, 1991b) – seem to have an uncertain relationship to actual research. Moreover, when you open a typical research study, although you may see a passing reference to the kind of social theories you have learned about elsewhere, you will very likely find that theory is rarely used or developed in the study itself, except as some kind of ritual reference to add legitimacy to an otherwise 'factual' piece of research.

Does that mean that we do not need theory to understand social research? To answer that question let us take a concrete example from Eric Livingston (1987). Livingston asks us to imagine that we have been told to carry out some social research on city streets. Where should we begin? He sets out four 'data possibilities' for such a study: official statistics (traffic flow, accidents); interviews (how people cope with rush hours); observation from a tower (viewing geometrical shapes); observation or video at street level (how people queue or otherwise organise their movements). The different research projects that arise from these different data possibilities are outlined in Box 3.1.

As Livingston points out, each of these different ways of looking involves basic theoretical as well as methodological decisions. Very crudely, if we are attached to social theories which see the world in terms of correlations between social facts, we are most likely to consider gathering official statistics. Social facts are regularities of social life that appear to have an independent existence, such as 'social class' or religious values. Sociologists like Emile Durkheim were interested in how these things determined people's conduct – for example, whether they were likely to commit suicide.

By contrast, if we think, like Max Weber, that social meanings are important, we may be tempted by the interview study. Weber promoted the idea of verstehen, a German term referring to the study of intersubjectivity (the way in which our subjective experiences are involved in social life). Or if we have read about contemporary American theories like interactionism or ethnomethodology, we are likely to want to observe or record what people actually do in situ and elect the third or fourth options. Interactionists emphasise how social life is organised around events and symbols to which people orient themselves, and are often seen as providing the ideas that lie at the root of the ethnographic method (see Chapter 14). Ethnomethodologists examine the ways in which people produce orderly social interaction on a routine, everyday basis and their ideas provide the underpinning for conversation analysis (see Chapter 24). But note the very different views of people's behaviour we get from looking from on high (the third option), where people look like ants forming geometrical shapes like wedges, or from street level (the fourth option), where behaviour seems much more complex.

---

## BOX 3.1

### DOING RESEARCH ON CITY STREETS

| Data | Theory | Research question |
|---|---|---|
| Official statistics | Social facts | Are accidents more common when traffic flow is highest? |
| Interviews | Meanings | What attitudes to cyclists are expressed by car drivers in the rush hour? |
| Observation from above (videos, photographs) | Interactionism | How do cyclists negotiate their hybrid identity (neither pedestrian nor powered vehicle)? |
| Observation at street level (videos, photographs) | Ethnomethodology | How do people use body position and gaze to signal that a queue has formed? |

*Source*: Adapted from Livingston, 1987

---

The point is that none of these views of data is more real or more true than the others. For instance, people are not really more like ants or complex actors. It all depends on our research question. And research questions are inevitably theoretically informed. So we *do* need social theories to help us to address even quite basic issues in social research. Let me underline this point through an extended example.

## Theory in the field: who are the Lue?

In this section, I will look in greater detail at a study by Moerman (1974) of the Lue tribe living in Thailand. As an anthropologist, Michael Moerman was interested in learning how a people categorised their world. Like most anthropologists and Chicago School ethnographers (see Chapter 14), he used native informants who, when asked questions like 'How do you recognise a member of your tribe?', produced a list of traits which Moerman called *ethnic identification devices*. For example, an informant might say Lue people were characterised by their generosity, or were tall, or believed in several gods rather than one.

Moerman was troubled about what sense to read into the Lue's own accounts. His questions often related to issues that were either obvious or irrelevant to the respondents. As he puts it: 'To the extent that answering an ethnographer's question is an unusual situation for natives, one cannot reason from a native's answer to his *normal* categories or ascriptions' (1974: 66, emphasis added). So

Moerman started to see that ethnic identification devices were not used all the time by these people any more than we use them to refer to ourselves in a Western culture. This meant that, if you wanted to understand this people, it was not particularly useful to elicit from them what would necessarily be an abstract account of their tribe's characteristics. So instead, Moerman started to examine what went on in everyday situations through observation.

However, it was not so straightforward to switch to observational methods. Even when ethnographers are silent and merely observe, their presence indicates to people that matters relevant to 'identity' should be highlighted. Consequently, people may pay particular attention to what both the observer and they themselves take to be relevant categorisation schemes – like ethnic or kinship labels. In this way, the ethnographer may have 'altered the local priorities among the native category sets which it is his task to describe' (1974: 67). What, then, was to be done? A clue is given by the initially opaque subheadings of Moerman's article: 'Who are the Lue?', 'Why are the Lue?', 'When are the Lue?'.

Moerman argues that there are three reasons why we should *not* ask 'Who are the Lue?' These are shown in Box 3.2.

---

**BOX 3.2**

### THREE REASONS FOR NOT ASKING 'WHO ARE THE LUE?'

1   It would generate an inventory of traits. Like all such inventories, it could be endless because we could always be accused of having left something out.

2   Lists are retrospective. Once we have decided that the Lue are a tribe, then we have no difficulty in 'discovering' a list of traits to support our case.

3   The identification of the Lue as a tribe depends, in part, on their successful presentation of themselves as a tribe.

---

As Moerman puts it: 'The question is not "Who are the Lue?" but rather when, how and why the identification "Lue" is preferred' (1974: 62). He adds that this does *not* mean

that the Lue are not really a tribe or that they fooled him into thinking they were one. Rather their ethnic identity arises in the fact that people in the area use ethnic identification devices some of the time when they are talking about each other.

Of course, some of the time is not all the time. Hence the task of the ethnographer should be to observe when and *if* ethnic identification devices are used by the participants being studied. Moerman neatly summarises his argument as follows:

> Anthropology [has an] apparent inability to distinguish between warm ... human bodies and one kind of identification device which some of those bodies sometimes use. Ethnic identification devices – with their important potential of making each ethnic set of living persons a joint enterprise with countless generations of un-examined history – seem to be universal. Social scientists should therefore describe and analyse the ways in which they are used, and not merely – as natives do – use them as explanations. (1974: 67–8)

It is possible to conduct causal enquiries into social phenomena such as the use of ethnic identification devices. In Chapter 20, for example, a statistical approach to investigating causation is outlined. Moerman preferred a qualitative approach to explaining 'Why are the Lue?', drawing on his observations of when the devices were used and what his informants said about them. He suggests that they are used in order to provide the Lue with a sense of distinction and self-esteem in distinguishing themselves from 'hill' or 'jungle' people, whom they consider to be barely human, and 'officials' or 'townsfolk' who would otherwise be understood as insufferably superior. The Lue occupy a somewhat ambiguous position in a nation experiencing tensions between movement from a 'tribal' to a 'civilised' society and this gives added motivation for the display of characteristic labels of 'identity'.

Moerman's study can be understood as relating to broader theories of social constructionism now prevalent in contemporary social theory

(see Chapter 2). It reveals that any empiricist attempt to describe things 'as they are' is doomed to failure. Without *some* perspective or, at the very least, a set of animating questions, there is nothing to report. Contrary to crude empiricists, who would deny the relevance of theory to research, the facts *never* speak for themselves.

Moerman's research points to the way in which idealised conceptions of phenomena like 'tribes' can, on closer examination, become like a will-o'-the-wisp, dissolving into sets of practices embedded in particular settings. Nowhere is this clearer than in the field of studies of the 'family'. As Gubrium and Holstein (1987) note, researchers have unnecessarily worried about getting 'authentic' reports of family life given the privacy of the household. Thus researchers may be satisfied that they have got at the 'truth' of family life only when they have uncovered some hidden secret (e.g. marital disharmony, child abuse), regarding public presentations as a 'false front'. This, classically, is the perspective of Chicago School ethnography, which often involved a sense of triumph in revealing matters hidden from view by official smokescreens. But this implies an idealised reality – as if there were some authentic site of family life which could be isolated and put under the researcher's microscope. Instead, discourses of family life are to be found largely in people's talk, in a range of contexts. Many of these, like courts of law, clinics and radio call-in programmes where people often reveal what they mean by the term 'family', are public and readily available for research investigation.

If 'the family', like a 'tribe', is present wherever it is invoked, then the worry of some researchers about observing 'real' or 'authentic' family life looks to be misplaced. Their assumption that the family has an essential reality looks more like a highly specific way of approaching the phenomenon, most frequently used by welfare professionals and by politicians.

## The different languages of qualitative research

Thinking about the nature of institutions like 'tribes' and 'families' implies different theories about how the social world operates. Gubrium and Holstein's *The New Language of Qualitative Method* (1997) classifies qualitative research according to researchers' orientations towards data. In particular, Gubrium and Holstein focus on how each qualitative approach (e.g. discourse analysis, ethnography, conversation analysis) uses a particular analytical language to emphasise a particular facet of social reality. As the authors put it:

> Our strategy for understanding the diversity of qualitative research is to treat each variant as an enterprise that develops, and is conducted in, a language or idiom of its own. Accordingly, each idiom represents a distinctive reality, virtually constituting its empirical horizon. (1997: 5)

At the heart of this classification system is the division between substance and process, or between *what* is being studied and *how* it is constructed. Take the topic of nudity, for example. A qualitative researcher might, for example, ask *what* are the deviant traits that characterise nudists and *what* practices are associated with a nudist? Another researcher studying the same topic could examine *how* nudity could be made normal or routine. In 'The Nudist Management of Respectability,' Martin Weinberg (1994) explores how nudist colonies achieve the 'respectability' of the unclothed body through a set of locally defined and enforced norms like 'no body contact' and 'no accentuation of the body' (e.g. sitting with one's legs open). Weinberg's goal is to answer the question, 'How can they see their behavior as morally appropriate?' (1994: 392).

With this distinction between *how* (process of constructing reality) and *what* (reality as substantive truth), let us now look at two models of qualitative research discussed in Gubrium and Holstein's book: naturalism, and ethnomethodology and constructionism.

## Naturalism

As a model of qualitative social research, naturalism focuses on the factual characteristics of the object under study (this issue of the term 'naturalism' is distinct from the use of the term by philosophers, who mean something quite different when they use this word, for which see Chapter 2). Gubrium and Holstein cite William Whyte's *Street Corner Society* (1943) as a classic example of naturalism. In this urban ethnography from the 1940s, Whyte's goal is to describe what life is really like in an inner-city Italian neighbourhood located in Boston. To do this, he used the method of participant observation (see Chapter 14). The observations and analysis are intended to objectively reflect *what* Whyte saw and heard in this real world of poverty. Naturalism's strength is its representational simplicity. A naturalistic ethnography is almost formulaically built around the following tasks:

- entering the setting
- establishing rapport
- recording observations with an eye toward social scientific concepts (e.g. social status and group dynamics)
- presenting the findings.

The major shortcoming of naturalism, according to Gubrium and Holstein, is this:

> Because they view the border [between the topic of study and the way in which it is socially constructed] as a mere *technical* hurdle that can be overcome through methodological skill and rigor, they lose sight of the border as a region where reality is constituted within representation. (1997: 106).

This criticism suggests that naturalists overlook *how* people create meaning in their lives. Respondents are treated as mere sources of data without any interpretive capacity of their own. In a naturalistic framework, the participants' 'interpretive practice' (Gubrium and Holstein, 1997), or how they make sense of their own world, is irrelevant.

## Ethnomethodology and constructionism

A second qualitative approach reviewed by Gubrium and Holstein is ethnomethodology, which could roughly be translated into the study of people's methods of constructing reality in everyday life. Unlike the other two approaches, ethnomethodology is very much concerned with *how* social reality is constructed in everyday interaction. Ethnomethodologists' primary aim is to understand how people go about doing things in their everyday lives by creating meaningful categories for themselves and others. Thus, for example, an ethnomethodologist might ask seemingly curious questions like: 'What does it mean to be a "woman"?' The researcher would then *bracket* any prior knowledge about the topic (i.e. keep preconceived understandings from entering the analysis). In essence, bracketing means ontological detachment from the topic. Therefore, in representing the analysis, the word *woman*, for example, would be placed in quotation marks to indicate its bracketed usage for the purpose of the study. A study such as this would then aim to describe the signals, such as body movements, clothing, hair styling, that designate the sender of these signals as a 'woman'.

For Gubrium and Holstein, although analytically powerful, the problem with ethnomethodology is that it risks losing sight of the topic of analysis in the name of focusing on the process of its creation. As they put it:

As the substantively meaningful aspects of local culture are shunted aside in order to concentrate on constitutive interactional activity, the content of lived experience becomes almost incidental. (1997: 107)

For example, the study described above of how a person might constitute themselves as a 'woman' does not provide insights into the subjective experience of being a woman.

While ethnomethodology's analytical rigor can, on the one hand, free us of trite or stereotypic understandings of a research problem, by questioning the basic categories that make up research questions (e.g. 'family', 'Lue', 'woman') it does, on the other hand, impose restrictions on what a researcher can explore. For example, one cannot study poverty ethnomethodologically without bracketing its meaning, or placing it in quotation marks (i.e. 'poverty'). In this way, poverty loses its significance as a global social problem and becomes a particular achievement at a particular place and time. As a whole, a strict ethnomethodological analysis appears to neglect understanding the substance of everyday life in favour of a rigorous understanding of the activities that define it.

Nonetheless, it is possible to learn from the important insights of ethnomethodology without drowning in a whirlpool of intellectual nihilism. The most important of these insights is an emphasis on the rhetorical and constructive aspects of knowledge. That is, the realisation that facts or phenomena in the social world (like Moerman's tribe, or like 'the family' or a 'woman') are socially constructed in particular contexts. In some respects, this defines the constructionist model, concerned with questions of 'what?' and 'how?', which informs so much qualitative social research (see Holstein and Gubrium, 2008).

Of course, these are not the only kind of assumptions that may properly inform social research. Depending on our preferred theoretical framework, we might take a completely different position. For instance, researchers interested in the effects of social structure (as Durkheim was in his study of suicide) or feminists would argue that social structures (which Durkheim called social facts, as was shown earlier), such as social class, ethnic identity or family type, exist beyond face-to-face interaction. Many feminists would focus as much on what people were thinking (and feeling) as on what they were doing. The issue, for the moment, is not which theoretical framework is 'best' or even most useful. Instead, I have been suggesting that *some* theory of human or social action necessarily informs any piece of social research. Given this, we always need to try to specify our theoretical assumptions rather than to use them unconsciously or uncritically. In this way the practice of research becomes more fully reflexive.

## Theories, models and hypotheses

I have so far concentrated on showing how theories are used in social research through the use of concrete examples. But what precisely is a 'theory'? And how does it differ from a 'hypothesis'? Table 3.1 defines these and other basic terms in research.

As we see from the table, models provide an overall framework for how we look at reality. In short, they tell us what reality is like and the basic elements it contains. In social research, examples of such models are *functionalism* (which looks at the functions of social institutions), *behaviourism* (which defines all behaviour in terms of 'stimulus'

and 'response'), *symbolic interactionism* (which focuses on how we attach symbolic meanings to interpersonal relations) and *ethnomethodology* (which encourages us to look at people's everyday ways of producing orderly social interaction).

Concepts are clearly specified ideas deriving from a particular model. Examples of concepts are *social function* (deriving from functionalism), *stimulus/response* (behaviourism), *definition of the situation* (interactionism) and *the documentary method of interpretation* (ethnomethodology). Concepts offer ways of looking at the world which are essential in defining a research problem.

Theories arrange sets of concepts to define and explain some phenomenon, for example the nature of 'tribes' and 'families', or the conditions under which a phenomenon (such as a tribe) emerges. As we have already seen, and as was pointed out in Chapter 2 where the nature of scientific objects was discussed, many philosophers believe that without a theory the objects of science, or the phenomena which social researchers study, cannot be understood. In this sense, without a theory there is nothing to research. So theories provide the impetus for research. At the same time, as living entities, theories are also developed and modified by good research. You saw in Chapter 2 that the relationship between theory and research observations is a topic that has attracted philosophical debate (e.g. between verificationists and falsificationists). As used here, models, concepts and theories are

TABLE 3.1    Basic terms in research (adapted from Silverman, 2006: 13)

| Term | Meaning | Examples |
| --- | --- | --- |
| Model | An overall framework for looking at reality | Ethnomethodology, constructionism, feminism, naturalism |
| Concept | An idea deriving from a given model | Social practices, oppression |
| Theory | A set of concepts used to explain some phenomenon | Ethnic identification devices are used to construct tribal identities |
| Hypothesis | A testable proposition | 'Tribes invoke ethnic identification devices more frequently when threatened by external enemies' |
| Methodology | A general approach to studying research topics | Quantitative, qualitative |
| Method | A specific research technique | Social survey, conversation analysis |

self-confirming in the sense that they instruct us to look at phenomena in particular ways. This means that they can never be disproved but only found to be more or less useful.

This last feature distinguishes theories from hypotheses. Unlike theories, hypotheses are tested in research. Examples of hypotheses, discussed in Silverman (1993), are: 'how we receive advice is linked to how advice is given'; 'responses to an illegal drug depend upon what one learns from others'; 'voting in union elections is related to non-work links between union members'. As we shall see, a feature of many qualitative research studies is that there is no specific hypothesis at the outset but that hypotheses are produced (or induced) during the early stages of research. In any event, unlike theories, hypotheses can, and should, be tested. Therefore, we assess a hypothesis by its validity or truth.

A methodology is a general approach to studying a research topic. It establishes how one will go about studying any phenomenon. In social research, examples of methodologies are *quantitative* methodology, which uses numbers to test hypotheses and, of course, *qualitative* methodology, which tries to use first-hand familiarity with different settings to induce hypotheses. Like theories, methodologies cannot be true or false, only more or less useful.

Finally, methods are specific research techniques. These include quantitative techniques, like statistical correlations, as well as techniques such as observation, interviewing and audio recording. Once again, in themselves, techniques are not true or false. They are more or less useful, depending on their fit with the theories and methodologies being used and the hypothesis being tested or the research topic that is selected. So, for instance, behaviourists may favour quantitative methods and interactionists often prefer to gather their data by observation. But, depending upon the hypothesis being tested, behaviourists may sometimes use qualitative methods – for instance, in the exploratory stage of research. Equally, interactionists may sometimes use simple quantitative

methods, particularly when they want to find an overall pattern in their data.

The relation between models, concepts, theories, hypotheses, methodology and methods is set out schematically in Figure 3.1. Reading the figure anti-clockwise, each concept reflects a lower level of generality and abstraction. The arrow from 'findings' to 'hypotheses' indicates a feedback mechanism through which hypotheses are modified in the light of findings.

Let me now try to put flesh on the skeleton set out in Figure 3.1 through the use of some concrete examples. Imagine that we have a general interest in the gloomy topic of death in society. How are we to research this topic? Before we can even define a research problem, let alone develop a hypothesis, we need to think through some very basic issues. Assume that we are the kind of social scientist who prefers to see the world in terms of how social structures determine behaviour, following Durkheim's injunction to treat social facts as real things (see earlier). Such a model of social life will suggest concepts that we can use in our research on death. Using such a model, we will tend to see

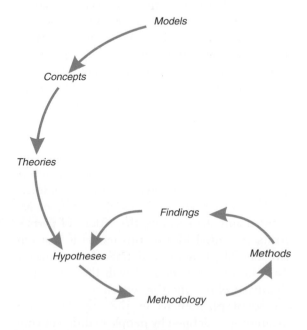

FIGURE 3.1 Levels of analysis

death in terms of statistics relating to rates of
death (or 'mortality'). And we will want to
explain such statistics in terms of other social
facts such as age or social class.

Armed with our concepts, we might then construct a theory about one or other aspect of our
topic. For instance, working with our assumption
that death is a social fact, determined by other
social facts, we might develop a theory that the
rate of early death among children, or 'infant
mortality', is related to some social fact about
their parents, say their social class. From this
theory, it is a quick step to the hypothesis that
the higher the social class of its parents, the lower
the likelihood of a child dying within the first
year of its life. This hypothesis is sometimes
expressed as saying that there is an inverse relationship between social class and infant mortality.

As already implied, a model concerned with
social facts will tend to favour a quantitative
methodology, using methods such as the analysis
of official statistics or the use of large-scale social
surveys based on apparently reliable fixed-choice
questionnaires. In interpreting the findings of such
research, one will need to ensure that due account
is taken of factors that may be concealed in simple
correlations. For instance, social class may be associated with quality of housing and the latter factor
(here called an intervening variable) may be the
real cause of variations in the rates of infant mortality. Research design for quantitative studies
aiming to answer questions like this is discussed in
Chapter 8. Multivariate analysis to investigate
causal propositions is discussed in Chapter 20.

This overall approach to death is set out schematically in Figure 3.2. Figure 3.3 sets out a very
different way of conceiving death. For interactionist social researchers, social institutions are
created and stabilised by the actions of participants. A central idea of this model is that our
labelling of phenomena defines their character.
This, in turn, is associated with the concept of
*definitions of the situation*, which tells us to look
for social phenomena in the ways in which
meaning gets defined by people in different contexts. The overall message of the interactionist

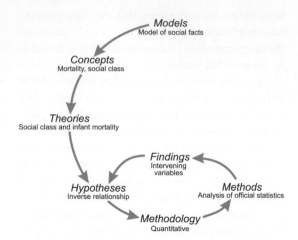

FIGURE 3.2    Death as a social fact

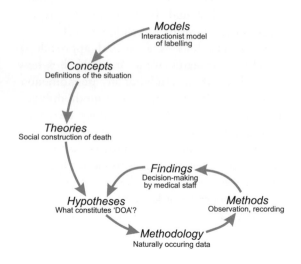

FIGURE 3.3    Death as a social construction

approach is that 'death' should be put in inverted
commas and hence leads to a theory in which
'death' is treated as a social construct.

Of course, this is very different from the
social fact model and, therefore, nicely illustrates the importance of theories in defining
research problems. Its immediate drawback,
however, may be that it appears to be counter-
intuitive. After all, you may feel, death is
surely an obvious fact. We are either dead or

not dead and, if so, where does this leave social constructionism?

Let me cite two cases which put the counter-argument. First, in 1963, after President Kennedy was shot, he was taken to a Dallas hospital with, according to contemporary accounts, half of his head shot away. My hunch is that if you or I were to arrive in a casualty department in this state, we would be given a cursory examination and then recorded as 'dead on arrival' (DOA). Precisely because they were dealing with a President, the staff had to do more than this. So they worked on Kennedy for almost an hour, demonstrating thereby that they had done their best for such an important patient.

Now think of contemporary debates about whether or when severely injured people should have life-support systems turned off. Once again, acts of definition constitute whether somebody is alive or dead. And note that such definitions have real effects. Of course, such a constructionist version of death is just one way of theorising this phenomenon, not intrinsically better or worse than the social fact approach. But, once we adopt one or another model, it starts to have a big influence upon how our research proceeds. For instance, as we have seen, if 'dead on arrival' can be a label applied in different ways to different people, we might develop a hypothesis about how the label 'dead on arrival' is applied to different hospital patients.

Because of our model, we would then probably try to collect research data that arose in such naturally occurring (or non-research-generated) settings as actual hospitals, using methods like observation or audio or video recording. Note, however, that this would not rule out the collection of quantitative data (say from hospital records). Rather, it would mean that our main body of data would probably be qualitative. Following earlier research (e.g. Jeffery, 1979; Dingwall and Murray, 1983), our findings might show how age and presumed moral status are relevant to such medical decision making as well as social class. In turn, as shown in Figure 3.3, these findings would help us to refine our initial hypothesis.

## Generalisations and theory building in qualitative research

Theorising about data does not stop with the refinement of hypotheses. In this section, I will show how we can develop generalisations out of successfully tested hypotheses and, thereby, contribute to theory building, an approach to social research that is discussed in depth in Chapter 22 on 'grounded theory.' First, we need to recognise that case studies, limited to a particular set of interactions, still allow one to examine how particular sayings and doings are embedded in particular patterns of social organisation. We first caught sight of this earlier in this chapter when I mentioned how Moerman (1974) used his research in Thailand to suggest generalisations which included English-speaking societies.

A classic case of an anthropologist using a case study to make broader generalisations is found in Mary Douglas's (1975) work on a central African tribe, the Lele. Douglas noticed that an ant-eater that Western zoologists call a 'pangolin' was very important to the Lele's ritual life. For the Lele, the pangolin was both a cult animal and an anomaly. It was perceived to have both animal and human characteristics. For instance, it tended to have only one offspring at a time, unlike most other animals. It also did not readily fit into the Lele's classification of land and water creatures, spending some of its time on land and some time in the water. Curiously, among animals that were hunted, the pangolin seemed to the Lele to be unique in not trying to escape but almost offering itself up to its hunter. Fortunately, Douglas resisted what might be called a 'tourist' response, moving beyond curiosity to systematic analysis. She noted that many groups who perceive anomalous entities in their environment reject them out of hand. To take an anomalous entity seriously might cast doubt on the naturalised status of your group's system of classification.

The classic example of the rejection of anomaly is found in the Old Testament. Douglas points out that the reason why the pig is unclean, according to the Old Testament, is that it is anomalous. It has a cloven hoof which, following the Old Testament, makes it clean, but it does not chew the cud – which makes it dirty. So it turns out that the pig is particularly unclean precisely because it is anomalous. Similarly, the Old Testament teachings on intermarriage work in relation to anomaly. Although you are not expected to marry somebody of another tribe, to marry the offspring of a marriage between a member of your tribe and an outsider is even more frowned upon. In both examples, anomaly is shunned.

However, the Lele are an exception: they celebrate the anomalous pangolin. What this suggests to Douglas is that there may be no universal propensity to frown upon anomaly. If there is variability from community to community, then this must say something about their social organisation. Sure enough, there is something special about the Lele's social life. Their experience of relations with other tribes has been very successful. They exchange goods with them and have little experience of war. What is involved in relating well with other tribes? It means successfully crossing a frontier or boundary. But what do anomalous entities do? They cut across boundaries. Here is the answer to the puzzle about why the Lele are different.

Douglas is suggesting that the Lele's response to anomaly derives from experiences grounded in their social organisation. They perceive the pangolin favourably because it cuts across boundaries just as they themselves do. Conversely, the ancient Israelites regarded anomalies unfavourably because their own experience of crossing boundaries was profoundly unfavourable. Indeed, the Old Testament reads as a series of disastrous exchanges between the Israelites and other tribes.

Douglas, applying an historical and comparative method, moves from a single-case explanation to a far more general theory of the relation between social exchange and response to anomaly (Box 3.3). Glaser and Strauss (1967), in their outline of grounded theorising (see Chapter 22), have described this movement towards greater generality as a move from substantive to formal theory. In their own research on hospital wards caring for terminally ill patients, they show how, by using the comparative method, we can develop accounts of people's own awareness of their impending death (a substantive theory) into accounts of a whole range of 'awareness contexts' (formal theory – see also Boxes 21.6 and 22.1).

---

BOX 3.3

## BUILDING THEORY FROM CASE STUDY OBSERVATIONS: MARY DOUGLAS AND THE LELE

- *Observation 1*: The Lele celebrate the pangolin, an anomalous animal. The Lele have good relationships with their neighbours.

- *Observation 2*: In the Old Testament an anomalous animal, the pig, is regarded as unclean. The ancient Israelites were frequently at war with their neighbours.

- *Theory*: The experience of crossing boundaries (as in relations with neighbours) can be generally good or bad and this influences whether anomalies are celebrated or shunned.

Douglas's account of the relation between responses to anomaly and experiences of boundary crossing can also be applied elsewhere. Perhaps bad experiences of exchanges with other groups explains why some Israeli Jews and Palestinian Muslims are so concerned to mark their own identity on the 'holy places' in Jerusalem and reject (as a hateful anomaly) multiple use of the same holy sites?

In any event, Douglas's study of the Lele exemplifies the need to locate how individual elements are embedded in forms of social organisation. In her case, this is done in an explicitly *Durkheimian* manner, which sees behaviour as the expression of a 'society' that works as a 'hidden hand' constraining and forming human action. Alternatively, Moerman's work indicates how, using a constructionist framework, one can look at the fine detail of people's activities without treating social organisation as a purely external force. In the latter case, people cease to be 'cultural dopes' (Garfinkel, 1967) and skilfully reproduce the moral order.

## How to theorise about data

Unlike Moerman or Douglas, most readers will not bring to their research any very well-defined set of theoretical ideas. If you are in this position, your problem will be how you can use data to think in theoretical terms. The list below is intended merely as a set of suggestions. Although it cannot be exhaustive, it should serve as an initial guide to theorising about data. It can also be read in conjunction with the discussion of grounded theorising in Chapter 22. In carrying out your research, I suggest that you think about the following six issues.

1 Consider *chronology*: Can you gather data over time in order to look at processes of change? If not, it is worth searching out historical evidence that may at least suggest how your research problem came into being (see also Chapter 15).

2 Consider *context*: How are your data contextualised in particular organisational settings, social processes or sets of experiences?

3 For instance, as Moerman shows, answering an interviewer's question may be different from engaging in the activity which is the topic of the interview. Therefore, think about how there may be many *versions* of your phenomenon.

4 Make use of *comparison*: Like Mary Douglas, who generated her theory by comparing how different groups treated anomalies, always try to compare your data with other relevant data. Even if you cannot find a comparative case, try to find ways of dividing your data into different sets and compare each. Remember that the comparative method is the basic scientific method.

5 Consider the *implications* of your research: When you are reporting your research, think about how your discoveries may relate to broader issues than your original research topic. In this way, a very narrow topic (e.g. how the Lele perceive the pangolin) may be related to much broader social processes (e.g. how societies respond to anomalous entities).

6 Be like the Lele and engage in *lateral thinking* if you can: Don't erect strong boundaries between concepts but explore the relations between apparently diverse models, theories and methodologies. Celebrate anomaly!

## Conclusion

The philosopher of science Thomas Kuhn (1970) has described social science as lacking a single, agreed set of concepts (see Chapter 2). In Kuhn's terms, this makes social research pre-paradigmatic, or at least in a state of competing paradigms. As I have already implied, the problem is that this has generated a whole series of social science courses which pose different approaches to research in terms of either/or questions. Classically, for example, qualitative methodology is thought to be opposed to quantitative.

Such courses are much appreciated by some students. They learn about the paradigmatic oppositions in question, choose A rather than B and report back, parrot fashion, all the advantages of A and the drawbacks of B. It is hardly surprising that such courses produce very little evidence of independent thought. This may, in part, explain why so many undergraduate social science courses actually provide a learned incapacity to go out and do research.

Learning about rival 'armed camps' in no way allows you to confront research data. In the field, material is much more messy than the different camps would suggest. Perhaps there is something to be learned from both sides, or,

more constructively, perhaps we start to ask interesting questions when we reject the polarities that such a course markets. Even when we decide to use qualitative or quantitative methods, we involve ourselves in theoretical as well as methodological decisions. These decisions relate not only to how we conceptualise the world but also to our theory of how research participants think about things. Theory, then, should be neither a status symbol nor an optional extra in a research study. Without theory, research is impossibly narrow. Without research, theory is mere armchair contemplation.

## FURTHER READING

A brief discussion of current theoretical ideas in qualitative research can be found in Silverman (2010: Ch. 7). An excellent book-length treatment is provided by Gubrium and Holstein (1997). Holstein and Gubrium (2008) provide an encyclopaedic handbook on constructionist research. Silverman (1998) offers an introduction to the work of Harvey Sacks, a key figure in constructionist theorising. The value of 'naturally occurring' data is discussed in Silverman (2007: Ch. 2).

### Student Reader (Seale, 2004b): relevant reading

29 Alfred Schütz: 'Concept and theory formation in the social sciences'

46 Udo Kelle: 'Theory building in qualitative research and computer programs for the management of textual data'

56 Alvin W. Gouldner: 'Toward a reflexive sociology'

64 Arthur W. Frank: 'Can we research suffering?'

See also Chapter 9 *The Foucaultian framework* and Chapter 10 *Ethnomethodology* by Paul ten Have in Seale et al. (2004).

### Web links

Social Theory Research Network (European Sociological Association): www.social-theory.eu

Social Theory Pages: www.socialtheory.info

e-Source: Chapter 3 on 'Theory development' by Stephen Turner: www.esourceresearch.org

Social theory and the study of popular culture: www.theory.org.uk

### Journal articles illustrating issues raised in this chapter

Hesmondhalgh, D. and Baker, S. (2008) 'Creative work and emotional labour in the television industry', Theory, Culture & Society, 25: 97–118.

Rhodes, T. (1997) 'Risk theory in epidemic times: sex, drugs and the social organisation of "risk behaviour"', Sociology of Health & Illness, 19 (2): 208–227.

Ryan, R.M. and Niemiec, C.P. (2009) 'Self-determination theory in schools of education: can an empirically supported framework also be critical and liberating?', Theory and Research in Education, 7: 263–272.

## KEY CONCEPTS FOR REVIEW

**Advice:** Use these, along with the review questions in the next section, to test your knowledge of the contents of this chapter. Try to define each of the key concepts listed here; if you have understood this chapter you should be able to do this. Check your definitions against the definition in the glossary at the end of the book.

| | |
|---|---|
| Concept | Model |
| Constructionism | Naturalism |
| Ethnomethodology | Reflexivity |
| Hypotheses | Social facts |
| Interactionism | Substantive and formal theory |
| Methodology | Theory |
| Methods | Verstehen |

## Review questions

1  What are models, theories, concepts and hypotheses?
2  What are Constructionism and Naturalism?
3  Why do we need theories in social research?

## Workshop and discussion exercises

1  This exercise asks you to think further about the different research strategies used by Moerman and Douglas:

(a) How far do (i) Moerman and (ii) Douglas make use of the five points listed towards the end of the chapter to help them theorise about data? (These were *chronology, context, comparison, implications* and *lateral thinking.*)

(b) Imagine that you were carrying out a study of a small group already known to you (e.g. a family, a friendship group or club). How could you use either Moerman's or Douglas's ideas to help you work out a research problem and to theorise about your data?

(c) In what respects is Moerman's or Douglas's work constructionist or naturalistic? How far would either's work be different if it used a different model?

2 This exercise encourages you to think further about the different ways of conceiving family life. Imagine that you wish to do an observational study of the family. Now consider the following questions:

(a) What are the advantages and disadvantages of obtaining access to the family household?

(b) In what ways may families be studied outside the household setting? What methodology might you use and what questions could you ask?

(c) What might observation tell you about the 'family' in each of the following settings: law courts, doctor–patient consultations, television soap operas?

(d) Either do a study of one of these settings or write hypothetically about all three.

3 What does it mean to say that you are studying the 'family' (i.e. within inverted commas)?

# 4

# RESEARCH AND POLICY

David Silverman

In my experience, researchers at the beginning of projects often make two basic errors. First, they fail to distinguish sufficiently between research problems and problems that are discussed in the world around us. The latter kind of problems, which I shall call social problems, are at the heart of political debates and fill the more serious newspapers. They are often the focus of social policies and researchers may find themselves commissioned by policy makers to address such problems in their research. However, I will be arguing that although social problems, like unemployment, homelessness and racism, are important, by themselves they cannot provide a researchable topic.

The second error to which I have referred is sometimes related to the first. It arises where researchers take on an impossibly large research problem. For instance, it is important to find the causes of a social problem like homelessness, but such a problem is beyond the scope of a single researcher with limited time and resources. Moreover, by defining the problem so widely, one is usually unable to say anything at great depth about it. It is often helpful instead to aim to say a lot about a little problem. This means avoiding the temptation to say a little about a lot. Indeed, the latter path can be something of a 'cop-out'. Precisely because the topic is so wide-ranging, one can flit from one aspect to another without being forced to refine and test each piece of analysis.

In the first section of this chapter I shall focus on the first of these errors – the tendency to choose social problems as research topics. However, in recommending solutions to this error, I shall imply how one can narrow down a research topic and thus deal with the second error. The second section of the chapter will illustrate some of these issues by describing my ethnographic research in health care settings. Finally, I discuss how such research can contribute to dealing with social problems and explain why it is sometimes resisted by policymakers.

By the end of this chapter, you should be able to distinguish between research problems and

social problems, work out researchable topics and understand how social researchers contribute to society (and why such research can be resisted).

## What is a problem?

One has only to open a newspaper or to watch television news to be confronted by a host of social problems. From time to time in the British news media there are references to a 'wave' of crimes committed by children – from the theft of cars to the murder of old people and other children. There have also been stories about how doctors infected by HIV, or who have not been vaccinated against infections like 'swine flu', continue to work and, by implication, endanger their patients or themselves. The stories have this in common: they assume some sort of moral decline in which families or schools fail to discipline children and in which physicians fail to take seriously their professional responsibilities. In turn, the way each story is told implies a solution: tightening up discipline in order to combat the presumed moral decline.

However, before we can consider such a cure, we need to consider carefully the diagnosis. Has juvenile crime increased or is the apparent increase a reflection of what counts as a good story? Alternatively, might the increase have been an artefact of what crimes get reported? Again, how many health care professionals actually infected their patients with HIV? I know of only one (disputed) case – a Florida dentist. Conversely, there is considerable evidence of patients infecting the medical staff who treat them. Moreover, why focus on HIV when other conditions like hepatitis B are far more infectious? Could it be that we hear so much about HIV because it is associated with stigmatised groups?

Apparent social problems are not the only topics that may clamour for the attention of the researcher. Administrators and managers point to 'problems' in their organisations and may turn to social scientists for solutions. It is tempting to allow such people to define a research problem – particularly as there is usually a fat research grant attached to it! However, we must first look at the terms that are being used to define the problem.

Let us imagine that a manager defines problems in their organisation as problems of 'communication'. The role of the researcher is then to work out how people can communicate 'better'. Unfortunately, talking about communication problems raises many difficulties. For instance, it may assume that the solution to any problem is more careful listening, while ignoring power relations present inside and outside patterns of communication. Such relations may also make the characterisation of 'organisational efficiency' very problematic. Thus administrative problems give no more secure basis for social research than do social problems. Of course, this is not to deny that there are real problems in society. However, even if we agree about what these problems are, it is not clear that they provide a researchable topic.

Take the case of the problems of people infected with HIV. Some of these problems are, quite rightly, brought to the attention of the public by the organised activities of groups of people who carry the infection. But social researchers should try to contribute the particular theoretical and methodological skills of their discipline, giving an initial research topic their own theoretical and methodological 'twist'. So:

- *Economists* can research how limited health care resources can be used most effectively in coping with the epidemic in countries with different overall levels of wealth.

- Sociologists using *social surveys* can investigate patterns of sexual behaviour in order to try to promote effective health education.

- Sociologists using *qualitative methods* may study what is involved in the 'negotiation' of safer sex or in counselling people about HIV and AIDS.

For instance, in my research on HIV counselling (Silverman, 1996), I used tape recordings and detailed transcripts, as well as many technical concepts derived from my interest in the qualitative method of conversation analysis (see Chapter 24). It is therefore usually necessary to refuse to allow our research topics to be totally defined in terms of the conceptions of social problems as recognised by either professional or community groups. Ironically, by beginning from a clearly defined social science perspective, we can later address such social problems with, I believe, considerable force and persuasiveness. I shall seek to show this later in the chapter.

## Sensitivity and researchable problems

I have been arguing that it is often unhelpful for researchers to begin their work on the basis of a social problem identified by either practitioners or managers. It is a commonplace that such definitions of problems often may serve vested interests. My point, however, is that if social science research has anything to offer, its theoretical imperatives drive it in a direction that can offer practitioners, managers and policy makers *new* perspectives on their problems. Paradoxically, by refusing to begin from a common conception of what is 'wrong' in a setting, we may be most able to contribute to the identification both of what is going on and, thereby, how it may be modified in the pursuit of desired ends. The various perspectives of social science provide a sensitivity to many issues neglected by those who define social or administrative problems. I will discuss three types of sensitivity in turn: historical, political and contextual.

## Historical sensitivity

Wherever possible, one should establish historical sensitivity by examining the relevant historical evidence when we are setting up a topic to research. This is a point dealt with at greater length in Chapter 15, which outlines the uses of historical and archival methods in social and cultural research. Box 4.1 gives two examples of the way historical sensitivity can offer us multiple research topics that evade the trap of thinking that present-day versions of social problems are unproblematic.

---

**BOX 4.1**

## TWO EXAMPLES OF HISTORICAL SENSITIVITY

- *Example 1*: In the 1950s and 1960s it was assumed that the nuclear family (parents and children) had replaced the extended family (many generations living together in the same household) of pre-industrial societies. Researchers simply seemed to have forgotten that lower life expectancy may have made the extended family pattern relatively rare in the past, and historical research has broadly confirmed that this was so (Laslett, 1966).

- *Example 2*: Historical sensitivity helps us to understand how we are governed. For instance, until the eighteenth century, the majority of the population were treated as a threatening mob to be controlled, where necessary, by the use of force. Today, we are seen as individuals with 'needs' and 'rights' which must be understood and protected by society (see Foucault, 1977). But, although oppressive force may be used only rarely, we may be controlled in more subtle ways. Think of the knowledge about each of us contained in computerised data banks and the pervasive CCTV cameras which record movements in many city streets (see Gobo's (2008) discussion of what he calls the Observation Society).

---

### Political sensitivity

Allowing the current media scares to determine our research topics is just as fallible as designing research in accordance with administrative or managerial interests. In neither case do we use political sensitivity to detect the vested interests behind this way of formulating a problem. The media, after all, need to attract an audience just as administrators need to be seen to be working efficiently.

So political sensitivity (see Box 4.2 for an example) seeks to grasp the politics behind defining topics in particular ways. In turn, it helps in suggesting that we research how social problems arise.

Political sensitivity does not mean that social scientists argue that there are no real problems in society. Instead, it suggests that social science can make an important contribution to society by querying how official definitions of problems arise. To be truthful, however, we should also recognise how social scientists often need to accept tacitly such definitions in order to attract research grants.

---

**BOX 4.2**

## AN EXAMPLE OF POLITICAL SENSITIVITY

Barbara Nelson (1984) looked at how 'child abuse' became defined as a recognisable problem in the late 1960s. She shows how the findings of a doctor about the 'battered baby syndrome' were adopted by the conservative Nixon administration through linking social problems to parental 'maladjustment' rather than to the failures of social programmes.

---

## Contextual sensitivity

This is the least self-explanatory and most contentious category in the present list. By contextual sensitivity, I mean the recognition that apparently uniform institutions like 'the family', 'a tribe' or 'science' take on a variety of meanings in different contexts. This is linked to ideas about identity and anti-essentialism, ideas through which social theorists and researchers have increasingly come to see personal identity as being socially constructed in interaction with others, rather than being fixed. This contrasts with 'essentialist' views of identity and human nature, which claim some basic, often universal feature of human beings, like their gender or their genetic makeup, determines the kind of person they are.

Contextual sensitivity is reflected most obviously in Moerman's (1974) study of the Lue tribe in Thailand (discussed more fully in Chapter 3). Moerman began with the anthropologist's conventional appetite to locate a people in a classificatory scheme. To satisfy this appetite, he started to ask tribespeople questions like 'How do you recognise a member of your tribe?'. He reports that his respondents quickly became adept at providing a whole list of *traits* which constituted their tribe and distinguished them from their neighbours, as well as others which they said they shared with their neighbours (see Box 4.3).

---

**BOX 4.3**

### LUE 'ETHNIC IDENTIFICATION DEVICES'

The Lue claimed that these made them *different* from their neighbours, the Yuan:

- the use of mattresses and blankets
- the possession of a village 'spirit house'
- the singing of particular types of folk song

These, though, they shared with the Yuan:

- the use of pillows and mosquito nets
- working in cooperative labour groups
- using a rice pounder to make rice flour

---

But Moerman began to feel that such a list was, in purely logical terms, endless. Perhaps if you wanted to understand this people, it was not particularly useful to elicit an abstract account of their characteristics, which Moerman called *ethnic identification devices*.

So Moerman stopped asking 'Who are the Lue?'. He came to believe that ethnic identification devices were not used all the time by these people any more than we use them to refer to ourselves in a Western culture. Instead, Moerman started to examine what went on in everyday situations. Looked at this way, the issue was no longer who the Lue essentially were but when, among people living in these Thai villages, ethnic identification labels were used and what were the consequences of invoking them. For example, a common cause for their display was the presence of strange, Western anthropologists asking the people to identify themselves! Curiously enough, Moerman concluded that, when you looked at the matter this way, the apparent differences between the Lue and ourselves were considerably reduced. Only an ethnocentric Westerner might have assumed otherwise, behaving like a tourist craving for out-of-the-way sights.

But it is not only such large-scale collectivities as tribes that are looked at afresh when we use what I have called 'contextual sensitivity'. Other apparently stable social institutions (like the family) and identities (gender, ethnicity and so on) may be insufficiently questioned from a social problem perspective. For instance, commentators say things like 'the family is under threat'. But where are we to find the unitary form of family assumed in such commentary? And doesn't 'the family' look different in contexts ranging from the household, to the law courts or even the supermarket? Rather than take such arguments at face value, the researcher must make use of contextual sensitivity to discover how things actually operate in a social world where, as Moerman shows us, people's practices are inevitably more complex than they might seem.

One final point: the three kinds of sensitivity we have been considering offer different, sometimes contradictory, ways of generating research topics. I am not suggesting that *all* should be used at the beginning of any research study. However, if we are not sensitive to *any* of these issues, then we run the danger of lapsing into a 'social problem'-based way of defining our research topics.

So far I have been talking rather abstractly about research. Let me concretise matters by showing how my own research sought to address particular social problems.

## The contribution of social science

Between 1979 and 2000, I conducted ethnographic research in a range of health care settings from outpatient clinics to AIDS counselling sessions (see Silverman, 1987, 1996). In this section, I will explain two practical contributions of my research in hospital clinics, namely: the revelation of surprising facts; and the possibilities for influencing practice.

Sometimes, in my own research, without any intellectual intent, I have revealed things opposed to what we might readily assume about how people behave. In work I was doing in a children's heart unit in the early 1980s, we interviewed parents of child patients. Parents told us that one of the things that made their first outpatient consultations so difficult was that there were so many people in the room. This was a very serious occasion; for many parents their child would be given a sentence of life or death. They said it was confusing and intimidating because of the many doctors, nurses and sociologists present.

We found this quite convincing, but used a problematic kind of measure to look at this further. We looked through our tape-recorded consultations where there were different numbers of people in the room and then we counted the number of questions asked by parents. Table 4.1 presents our findings.

As you can see, our findings went against the common-sense expectation that the more people in the room, the fewer questions would be asked since the parents would have been, as they claimed, more intimidated. The *p*-value of less than 0.05 means that a result like this would happen by chance less than 5 out of every 100 times, if the study were to be repeated that many times (see Chapter 19 for an explanation of *p*-values).

Based on its crude measures, Table 4.1 shows that, in our sample, parents asked more questions

TABLE 4.1   Questions asked by parents by number of medical staff present

| | Number of consultations | Total questions | Average questions |
|---|---|---|---|
| 1–4 medical staff | 17 | 48 | 2.8 |
| 5+ medical staff | 23 | 99 | 4.3 |

$p < 0.05$

when there were five or more people in the room. I will not go into detail about what we made of this. But let me reassure you that we did not say that this meant that parents were wrong. On the contrary, there was evidence that parents were trying to behave responsibly and were appealing to the number of people present at the consultation as one way of depicting the pressures they were under. The numbers present thus worked not as a *causal* factor in determining parents' behaviour but as something which could subsequently be used to rationalise their guilt at not asking as many questions as they would have liked.

We started to develop policy interventions in relationship to what the parents were telling us. For instance, how could a context be created where parents could display their responsibility to medical staff who, unlike researchers, could not visit them in their own homes? In due course, at our suggestion, the hospital created an additional clinic which was held some weeks after the first hospital interview. Here children were not examined and parents were free to interview doctors. The intervention was liked by both parents and doctors. Doctors liked it because it provided a good opportunity to get to know families before they were admitted to the ward. Parents said that they felt under less time pressure because their child did not need to be examined, and because several weeks had passed since their first hospital visit, they had had time to work out what they now needed to know. Moreover, many mothers commented that they felt that their children had benefited as well because, while their parents spoke to the doctor, they could spend time in the hospital children's play-room. Consequently, the hospital now seemed a less frightening place to elsewhere.

A further example of how new facts can be discovered appears in Box 4.4.

---

**BOX 4.4**

## ANOTHER EXAMPLE OF DISCOVERING NEW FACTS

This arose from my research on three cancer clinics (Silverman, 1984). In this research, I looked at the practice of a doctor in the British National Health Service (NHS) and compared it with his private practice. This study was relevant to a lively debate about the NHS and whether there should be more private medicine. I showed that the private clinic encouraged a more 'personalised' service and allowed patients to orchestrate their care, control the agenda, and obtain some 'territorial' control of the setting. However, despite these 'ceremonial' gains, in the 1980s the NHS provided cancer patients with quicker and more specialised treatment. So the cancer study serves as an example of how researchers can participate in debates about public policy.

---

## Debating public policy

There are two extreme positions about research and social change: what I have called the Scholar and the Partisan (see Silverman, 2006: Ch. 11). The scholar argues that research need never have any relation to public debates about social policy. By contrast, the partisan, while very interested in such debates, is likely to bring too many preconceptions to them. How have I tried to enter into such debates without limiting myself to the assumptions of either position? Box 4.5 shows an example of a finding from the same heart unit which we have already discussed.

BOX 4.5

## DIFFERENT APPROACHES TO PARENTS' RIGHT TO CHOOSE

At one point, we were looking at how doctors in the heart unit talked to parents about the decision to have a small diagnostic test on their children.

In *most cases*, the doctor would say something like: 'What we propose to do, if you agree, is a small test.' No parent disagreed with an offer that appeared to be purely formal, like the formal right (never exercised) of the Queen not to sign legislation passed by the British Parliament.

For a *subsample* of children, however, the parents' right to choose was far from formal. The doctor would say things to them like: 'I think what we would do now depends a little bit on parents' feelings', 'Now it depends a little bit on what you think', 'It depends very much on your own personal views as to whether we should proceed.'

In addition, the second type of consultations were longer and apparently more democratic than elsewhere. A view of the patient in a family context was encouraged and parents were given every opportunity to voice their concerns and to participate in decision making. In this subsample, unlike the larger sample, when given a real choice, parents almost always refused the test. It turns out that this smaller subsample was composed of parents of children with Down's syndrome, who had mental and physical disabilities in addition to their suspected heart disease. Moreover, the policy of the consultant at this unit was to discourage surgery, all things being equal, on such children. So the democratic form coexisted with (and was indeed sustained by) the maintenance of an autocratic policy.

The research thus discovered the mechanics whereby a particular medical policy was enacted. The availability of tape recordings of large numbers of consultations, together with a research method that sought to develop hypotheses *inductively* (see Chapter 2), meant that we were able to discover a phenomenon for which we had not originally been looking. More importantly, from the point of view of our present concerns, the research underlined how power can work just as much by encouraging people to speak as by silencing them (see Foucault, 1977, 1980).

'Democratic' decision making and 'whole patient medicine' are thus revealed as discourses with no intrinsic meaning. Instead, their consequences depend upon their deployment and articulation in particular contexts. So even democracy is not something that we must appeal to in all circumstances. In contexts like this, democratic forms can be part of a power play. As in the previous illustration, we had discovered a surprising fact. In this case, this fact was relevant to an important public debate about the care of disabled children.

Two practical consequences arose from the study of consultations with children with Down's syndrome. First, we asked the doctor concerned to rethink his policy or at least reveal his hidden agenda to parents. We did not dispute that there are many grounds to treat such children differently from others in relation to surgery. For instance, they have a poorer post-surgical survival rate and most parents are reluctant to contemplate surgery. However, there is a danger of stereotyping the needs of such children and their parents. By 'coming clean' about his policy, the doctor would enable parents to make a more informed choice.

The second practical point, revealed by this research, relates to my earlier remark about the limits of reducing social problems to issues of 'poor communication'. In some respects, this doctor's 'democratic' style seems to fit the requirements of 'good communication'. However, as good practitioners realise, no style of communication is intrinsically superior to another.

## Why policymakers prefer some methods over others

The studies I have just been discussing used ethnographic methods. Yet, in many societies, the only kind of qualitative research that policy-makers will commission are focus groups or 'exploratory' interview studies which, if successful, can form the basis of subsequent or revised quantitative surveys. Unlike more time-consuming ethnographic research, these kinds of qualitative studies can produce results within a few days or weeks and thus offer the kind of 'quick fix' that research commissioners desire.

Think, for instance, how focus groups have now become a major feature in how political parties orchestrate their election campaigns. The irony is that these relatively favoured techniques share with quantitative research an inability to access the (practically important) topic of how institutions are routinely enacted.

Part of the problem arises from two dangerous orthodoxies that lie behind the thinking of many social scientists and policy-makers who commission social research. The first orthodoxy is that people are puppets of social structures. According to this model, what people do is defined by 'society'. In practice, this reduces to explaining people's behaviour as the outcome of certain 'face-sheet' variables (like social class, gender or ethnicity). Let me call this the explanatory orthodoxy. According to it, social scientists do research to provide explanations of given problems (e.g. 'Why do individuals engage in unsafe sex?'). Inevitably, such research will find explanations based on one or more 'face-sheet' variables (e.g., 'Men do this more than women, so something about being a man must "explain" this').

The second orthodoxy is that people are 'dopes', in the sense that they do not know what is best for them, or what is true. Thus interview respondents' knowledge is assumed to be imperfect; indeed, they may even lie to us. In the same way, practitioners (such as doctors or counsellors) are assumed always to depart from normative standards of good practice. This is the divine orthodoxy. It makes the social scientist into the philosopher king (or queen) who can always see through people's claims and know better than they do.

What is wrong with these two orthodoxies? The explanatory orthodoxy is so concerned to rush to an explanation that it fails to ask serious questions about what it is explaining.

There is a parallel here with what we must now call a 'postmodern' phenomenon. I gather that visitors to the Grand Canyon in Arizona are now freed from the messy business of exploring the Canyon itself. Instead, they can now spend an enlightening hour or so in a multi-media 'experience' which gives them all the thrills in a pre-digested way. Then they can be on their way, secure in the knowledge that they have 'done' the Grand Canyon.

This example is part of something far larger. In contemporary culture, the environment around phenomena has become more important than the phenomenon itself. So people tend to be more interested in the lives of movie stars than in the movies themselves. Equally, on sporting occasions, the crowd's Mexican Wave and pre- and post-match interviews with competitors become as exciting (or even more exciting) than the actual game. In both cases, *the phenomenon escapes*.

This is precisely what the explanatory orthodoxy encourages. Because we rush to offer explanations of all kinds of social phenomena, we rarely spend enough time trying to understand how the phenomenon works. So, as I found when studying HIV-test counselling (Silverman, 1996), researchers may simply impose an 'operational definition' of 'unsafe sex' or a normative version of 'good counselling', failing totally to examine how such activities come to have meaning in what people are actually doing in everyday (naturally occurring) situations.

This directly leads to the folly of the divine orthodoxy. Its methods preclude seeing the good sense of what people are doing or understanding their skills in local contexts. It prefers interviews where people are forced to answer questions that rarely arise in their day to-day lives. Because it avoids looking at these lives, it condemns people to fail without understanding that we are all cleverer than we can say in so many words. Even when it examines what people are actually doing, the divine orthodoxy measures their activities by some idealised normative standard, like 'good communication'. So, once again, like ordinary people, practitioners are condemned to fail.

In such an environment, qualitative research has become the 'poor relation', its most problematic forms (interviews, focus groups) serving, at best, as a handmaiden to methods which can express findings in numbers – although there are some exceptions: market research has accommodated a number of reasonably sophisticated qualitative methods and proved very acceptable to business (Moisander and Valtonen, 2006). Even when good ethnographic research with clear practical implications is funded and published, vested interests can mount an effective attack based on its 'doubtful' scientific legitimacy. Animosity and resistance towards ethnographic research is demonstrated in the case study in Box 4.6.

---

## BOX 4.6

### THE 'MEDICAL ERRORS' CONTROVERSY

In 2005 a highly prestigious medical journal (the *Journal of The American Medical Association*) published a study by the ethnographer Ross Koppel and colleagues of a new software system which allowed computerised physician order entry (CPOE) of drug prescriptions in US hospitals (Koppel et al., 2005b). This study arose by accident when Ross Koppel was doing research on the stress experienced by junior house physicians. It turned out that the CPOE system produced not only stress among these doctors but a noteworthy number of errors (although, as Koppel points out, some of these errors may not be experienced as stressful at the time). Moreover, although studies had been completed of how CPOE worked, these were generally quantitative and none were based on interviews and observations of these younger physicians.

To establish the extent of the phenomenon, Koppel constructed a multi-method study which incorporated face-to-face interviews and focus groups with house physicians, shadowing doctors as they entered prescriptions into the system and observing nurses and pharmacists as they received prescriptions, interviews with senior medical and nursing staff and a 72-item questionnaire to a 90 per cent sample of house physicians. The prescribing errors discovered included doctors failing to stop one drug when they prescribed its replacement, confusion of which patient was receiving the drugs, and confusing an inventory list for clinical guidelines.

In the United States, it is estimated that medication errors within hospitals kill about 40,000 people a year and injure 770,000. According to Koppel's study, it turned out that CPOE systems can facilitate errors. Ironically, CPOE was most useful at stopping errors with few dangerous consequences. In particular, the way in which CPOE had been programmed had two unfortunate consequences: fragmented data displays meant that physicians had difficulty in identifying the specific patient for whom they were prescribing, and the system did not work in the way that doctors worked and this created confusion or extra work to address the ambiguities.

Given the amount of government and industry support for CPOE, it is not surprising that Koppel's findings were treated as highly newsworthy by the national media but also came under immediate attack. Many medical researchers suggested that such qualitative research could not produce 'real data'. The manufacturers of CPOE systems launched a campaign which said that Koppel had 'just talked to people' and reported 'anecdotes'. In particular, the public were told, Koppel's study was faulty because it offered no measure of adverse drug events and had identified no 'real' errors but only 'perceptions of errors'. Critics also complained that he had studied an older CPOE system; that new systems have fixed all of those problems.

In response, Koppel and his colleagues (2005a) made three arguments. First, they showed the limitations of previous research which had been used against them: 'Most of the research on CPOE was conducted to show its advantages over paper-based systems; almost all of the research was on reduction of potential rather than actual [adverse incidents]; many studies focused on physician satisfaction, barriers to acceptance, single outcomes, and very limited samples; several studies combine CPOE and clinical decision support systems, thus confounding the interpretation of CPOE's efficacy'. Second, Koppel and his colleagues argued that most of their critics had misunderstood the value of observing real time medical decision making. Third, further research by Koppel does not support the claims that new CPOE systems have fixed all the problems.

## Conclusion

In these examples, we see how social research can contribute to the community precisely by insisting on the relevance of its own social science perspectives and refusing to limit its vision to commonsensically defined 'social problems'. By pursuing rigorous, analytically-based research guided by its own sensitivities, we can contribute most to society.

Yet we should never forget that research reports are always written for an *audience*. Too easily, in later life, one takes from a college degree the assumption that writing is just about appealing to one person (your professor) and so getting a good grade. Even if you are lucky enough to go on to postgraduate study or get a university post, you continually need to remind yourself that fellow academics are only one of several potential audiences. At some stage, in some way, your audience should include policy-makers and practitioners and (barely dealt with in this chapter) lay audiences.

However, although recognising that there are such audiences out there is a necessary first step, by itself it is insufficient. Each group will only want to hear about your work if it relates to their needs. So you need to understand where such groups are 'coming from' and write in a manner, both in terms of form and content, which speaks to concerns which you share with them. This means implementing a skill which we use all the time in everyday life (for instance, relating current audience expectations to the way we issue an invitation or break bad news). Practitioners of conversation analysis call this skill 'recipient-design'.

In the final analysis, if you want to succeed in your research and beyond, you will have to be responsive to the various audiences who might be prepared to listen to what you have to say. As in so many other aspects of life, people who complain about the 'cruel world' are often the very people who disdain the occasionally difficult but generally rewarding business of listening to what others are saying.

## *FURTHER READING*

Silverman (2006: Ch. 11) presents a more detailed introduction to research and policy. A more advanced treatment of the topic is provided in Silverman (2007: Ch. 4). Silverman (2011) is a collection focused on qualitative methods which includes many chapters by distinguished scholars dealing with the relation between qualitative research and social problems.

*(Continued)*

## Journal articles illustrating or discussing policy-related research

Bradshaw, J., Ditch, J., Holmes, H. and Vilhiteford, P. (1993) 'A comparative study of child support in fifteen countries', Journal of European Social Policy, 3: 255–271.

Bonell, B. (2002) 'The politics of the research-policy interface: randomised trials and the commissioning of HIV prevention services', Sociology of Health & Illness, 24 (4): 385–408.

Lee, V.E. and Smith, J.B. (1997) 'High school size: which works best and for whom?', Educational Evaluation and Policy Analysis, 19: 205–227.

## Web links

The Policy Studies Institute (UK): www.psi.org.uk

The Brookings Institution (USA): www.brook.edu

Institute for Research on Public Policy (Canada): www.irpp.org

## KEY CONCEPTS FOR REVIEW

Advice: Use these, along with the review questions in the next section, to test your knowledge of the contents of this chapter. Try to define each of the key concepts listed here; if you have understood this chapter you should be able to do this. Check your definitions against the definition in the glossary at the end of the book.

Anti-essentialism

Explanatory vs. divine orthodoxy

Partisan vs. scholar

Social problems

 **Review questions**

1 In what ways are social problems different from research problems?

2 How can you transform a social problem into a research problem?

3  What are the advantages and disadvantages of quantitative research applied to social problems?

4  What are the advantages and disadvantages of qualitative methods applied to social problems (distinguish 'self-report' methods like interviews and focus groups from 'observational' methods like those used by ethnographers)?

## Workshop and discussion exercises

1  In the context of any social problem you choose (e.g. homelessness, racism, sexism), outline what you think to be a relevant research problem. Now discuss the following questions:

(a) How does your research topic differ from the common-sense version of your selected social problem?

(b) If your research topic sticks very closely to this common-sense version of the problem, how does it benefit from the insights of social science?

(c) If your research problem differs from how we usually see this social problem, how can your proposed research contribute to society?

2  Choose two research studies (one quantitative and one qualitative) on any social institution with which you are familiar (e.g. healthcare, organisations, law, politics, social work). Compare and contrast the contribution each makes either to (a) debates about public policy or (b) providing new opportunities for ordinary people to make their own choices.

# 5

# ETHICS AND SOCIAL RESEARCH

## Suki Ali and Moira Kelly

---

### Chapter Contents

Ethical issues are often difficult to define and harder still to work with, yet all social research involves ethical decision making. This may become relevant in the decision to undertake research in a particular area or population, in the formulation of a research question, when sampling, gaining access to data or research respondents, whilst collecting data, when analysing data or at the writing-up stage, when engaging with research audiences, and when publishing findings. In this chapter we will explain why ethical considerations are important to social research, provide an introduction to the development of ethical research practice, including inception of ethical guidelines and research committees, and go on to consider specific points in the research process at which ethics may play a significant role. We will also consider how the social and political contexts in which studies take place influence research decision making. Both conventional conceptions of research ethics and contemporary reflections on research ethics as they relate to power relations will be considered.

## Why do we need research ethics?

Many people consider ethics to be a minor part of the research process, one that may not even be relevant to their work at all. For example, in the past it has been usual to think about ethics predominantly in relation to social research with *people*, concentrating on the ways in which people are affected by their participation in research. Conventionally, and associated with the idea that research involves the pursuit of objective truths, it has been thought that the social researcher has certain obligations and responsibilities in considering the effects of such truths on both respondents and wider communities. In this kind of model, ethical practice is akin to a form of professional practice. Ethics here are centred on procedural issues and especially on the principle of informed consent. The emphasis on correct ethical procedures contains the danger

that somewhat prescriptive codes of practice are formulated which may allow researchers to think that as long as certain procedures are followed, research practice is automatically 'ethical'. The development of ethical practice is part of the craft of competent social research. It involves reflexivity, or the ability to reflect and learn from experience, and to use that learning during the research process. This may involve reflection on decision making at different levels. For example, given the history of research ethics, the underlying emphasis is often on protection of participants from unethical research procedures. However, if as social researchers we believe our work to be of value in improving the societies we live in, we may ask ourselves if it was ethical to decide *not* to undertake a study in an area which presents more complex ethical challenges.

In recent years, the way we think about ethics has changed and the topic has opened up, with its relevance becoming much wider. Increasingly there are challenges to the view that objective, knowable truths about the social world are uncovered by expert researchers. One of the most influential interventions into research ethics has come from feminist researchers who have challenged the idea that ethical practice per se can ensure non-harmful research practice. They have shifted emphasis onto the role of power relations at all levels of knowledge production, from epistemology, through research relationships, to the dissemination of findings. If we think about research in this way then the links between power, politics and research ethics become clearer.

The scientific tradition within social research has involved the view that the research should be judged according to whether it is a truthful description of social life, is value-free and that the product of neutral observation. This traditional view of social research was increasingly challenged by the anti-racist, feminist and gay liberation social movements in the 1960s and 1970s which focused on inequalities of gender, class, 'race', ethnicity, sexuality and ability. These concerns with issues of social difference not only informed changes in politics and policy, but also epistemology. Social researchers increasingly recognised the need for new models of research which were sensitive to diversity in social experience and aimed to challenge inequalities. With this came the view that researchers ought to consider not only *what* they know, but also *how* they come to know it.

Re-thinking research with this in mind we might see how research can never be fully 'objective', neutral or value-free because it is produced by 'knowers' who are situated in the social world and whose knowledge reflects its values. Within any given context under which social research is conducted there will be prior existing inequalities and differences which are often hierarchically ordered, and thus where power is often unevenly distributed. For feminists, for example, under these conditions, all knowledge is necessarily 'political' in that it not only reflects the positions of researchers and the contexts in which research is produced, but in a more direct way knowledge can have social consequences and impact upon politics and policies affecting individuals and groups. Donna Haraway argues that rather than thinking of knowledge as universally understood and applicable, we should understand it as situated. She does not suggest that we abandon rigorous research in favour of complacent solipsism but suggests that 'feminist objectivity means quite simply *situated knowledges*' (1991: 188). This 'opens the way to stronger standards of both objectivity and reflexivity. These standards require that research projects use their historical location as a resource for obtaining greater objectivity' (Harding, 1991: 163). This, then, is a radically different notion of objectivity to the one contained in traditional discussions. For Haraway our 'positionality' means that all research is only ever 'partial', but this does not make it less valid or useful.

By broadening the discussion of ethics to the entire research process, and connecting it to politics and power, we can see that even deciding on our research topic requires ethical awareness. For example, when a particular group have been 'over-researched' why would we also want to conduct research with them? What will our research add? Might it damage the group or persons we are working with, despite our best intentions? Will we contribute to the creation of a social problem rather than learn something about society?

We can see, then, that ethical considerations may be closely aligned to both moral and political considerations in research work. Whatever methodological approach a researcher might take, ethics will play a part. Even epistemological frameworks (see Chapter 2) can be informed by ethical considerations. In what follows we focus quite often on medical research ethics, as their historical development has been influential in the development of key ethical principles of practice for researching culture and society more generally.

## What are research ethics?

Ethics is the branch of philosophy, said to have been initiated by Aristotle, which takes human action as its subject matter (Finnis, 1983). This can mean opinions about human action, opinions about right human action, right opinions about human action, or all of these topics. Ethics in this classic sense is about practical knowledge and the application of theory to human activities. As Homan says, 'Ethics is the science of morality: those who engage in it determine values for the regulation of human behaviour' (1991: 1).

We are all aware of the moral debates that are discussed on a daily basis in the media on topics such as euthanasia, civil disobedience and genetic engineering. Much of this debate is related to the regulation and legality of these activities. Social and cultural researchers, too, are interested in the values that may regulate the conduct of research. The decisions we make at different stages in our research may have ethical implications even though we may not be aware of them. As we have suggested above, even when deciding on a topic for study we are making a choice about a population to investigate and this may have ethical implications.

## Influences on the ethics of social research

Contemporary research ethics has developed from the numerous philosophical debates that have gone on since the time of Aristotle. A central issue in ethics is the relationship between the individual and the social world. In research we need to consider how the imposition of the research on individuals (with their consent or otherwise) can be balanced with the benefit of making the world a better place to live in.

The complexity of human conduct means that there are no absolutes in practice: there is no single ethical theory that accounts for all possible contingencies. Differing philosophical perspectives may be presented as opposing perspectives. Utilitarian theory has been influential in thinking about the ethics of empirical research, with philosophers such as Bentham and Mill arguing that certain actions can be justified in terms of their contribution to the greater good. A research project may therefore be justified on the basis of its potential benefit to society, even if it may cause harm to an individual. Other philosophers, such

as Rawls, argue that the rights of the individual in terms of their freedom to choose (e.g. whether to take part in research) will always come first. Thus there is a tension between activities (such as research) that aim to improve the world in which we live and the rights of the individual.

The philosophical arguments of writers such as Mill and Rawls were not originally couched in terms of research practice, but were more general reflections on the nature of morality. However, they are still highly relevant to the conduct of a research project, potentially influencing decisions about what and how to study. In fact, achieving a balance between respecting the rights of the individual and making the world a better place often underlies contemporary discussions of research ethics. The role of such ethical debate, then, is to help decide on an appropriate course of action, but should never be reduced to a straightforward application of ethical principles regardless of context. As Hoffmaster has explained:

> The applied ethics model assumes that moral problems come neatly labelled and categorised and that their pre-assigned categories match those in the norms. But norms are not self-applying. Considerable moral work gets done in deciding how a situation is to be characterised, and that moral work can determine how issues are resolved. (1994: 1157)

---

BOX 5.1

## TWO PIVOTAL CASES IN MEDICAL ETHICS

### Nazi experiments

The importance of protecting human beings from invasive medical treatments was highlighted during the post-war Nuremberg trials. The trials of 23 doctors revealed that many people held in concentration camps had been made to participate in dangerous medical experiments, such as exposure to extreme temperatures, often with fatal results. This led to the Declaration of Helsinki, produced by the World Medical Association in 1964, which was to safeguard against future atrocities of this nature. This was revised for the fifth time in 2000 (Christie, 2000). It sets out international standards for conducting medical research with human subjects (Singer and Benatar, 2001).

*(Continued)*

---

## The Tuskegee experiment

In the Tuskegee experiment between 1932 and 1972, the US Public Health Service denied effective treatment to 399 African Americans who were in the late stages of syphilis, a disease which can involve tumours, heart disease, paralysis, insanity, blindness and death. The men were not told of the disease from which they were suffering and were, for the most part, illiterate and poor. The aim was to collect information at autopsy so that the effects of the disease in black sufferers could be compared with those in whites. In practice, the results of the study did not contribute to the control or cure of the disease. In 1997 President Clinton issued a public apology for these government-sponsored actions to the few remaining survivors (Jones, 1993).

## Medical research ethics

Emphasis on ethical aspects of social research has increased significantly in recent years. It has taken a lead from developments in medical research ethics that have taken place since the end of the Second World War, which have been fuelled by some ethical scandals (see Box 5.1). The practices of the Nazi doctors could be seen as an extreme case, but dangerous medical research practices did not end with the Nazis. In the Tuskegee experiment people were experimented upon without full knowledge of the procedures to be undertaken, causing them harm. The controversy surrounding Tuskegee led to a tightening-up of regulations concerning research ethics in the United States (Benatar and Singer, 2000).

Although there is considerable debate within medicine regarding ethical research practice, a number of principles are commonly regarded as fundamental. These have been set out by Beauchamp (1994: 3):

- **Beneficence** (the obligation to provide benefits and balance benefits against risks)

- **Non-maleficence** (the obligation to avoid the causation of harm)

- Respect for **autonomy** (the obligation to respect the decision-making capacities of autonomous persons)

- **Justice** (obligations of fairness in the distribution of benefits and risks)

These principles also underlie the development of social research ethics. They are not rules in themselves but are generally used as reference points for the development of ethical guidelines.

Whereas the ethics of medical research are often seen in terms of balancing risks against potential benefits, this is not always seen as useful in social research (Kelman, 1982). Concern with harms and benefits in medical research generally refer to physical responses to treatment. In social research such harms and benefits are harder to predict and therefore harder to 'balance' against risks. However, it can be taken that we have a moral obligation to avoid actions that reduce the wellbeing (broadly defined) of others or which may inhibit their freedom to express and develop themselves.

Our primary concern is with protecting and enhancing the wellbeing of research participants and of others who are, or may in the future be, affected by the research. We therefore have an obligation to minimise the risk of harm caused by the research and to forgo research that carries unacceptable risks (Kelman, 1982: 87).

## Ethical practice in social research

Despite the increasing regulation and monitoring of social research, ethical practice in effect comes down to the 'professional' integrity of the individual researcher. Reflexivity is relevant to professional integrity, as will become clear as this chapter progresses. The history of social research, like that of medical research, contains examples of questionable ethical practice (see Box 5.2) and regulation (in the form of codes of ethical practice, requirements for research ethics committees and the like) is partly a response to these incidents. In addition, feminist researchers have argued that, from a political standpoint, researchers need to pay attention to issues of power in knowledge production and that this is a matter of ethics. This has resulted in a particular (though not exclusive) focus on research relationships and issues of hierarchy.

## Relationships with research participants

### Contexts and power

Relationships with research participants are a key area in which issues of power differentials arise. It is common to think in terms of the researcher being all-powerful, as they are the ones who are actually conducting the research and in many cases are seen to 'control' it. Keeping an awareness of the political nature of research, it is easy to see that in some cases there are obvious power differentials that will impact upon the way in which data is gathered, and these might not only be between the researcher and their respondents. For example, in research about inequalities within a particular business organisation, conducting focus groups which contain workers and their managers in the same group will affect those taking part in a variety of ways, and this can last long after the researcher has left the site. In addition, having set up the study in this way, respondents may feel uncomfortable with the researcher and this may erode trust and confidence in the research process and affect participation.

Power differences between researchers and other participants in a study can also be exacerbated by social differences. Researchers may be working across social divides, with people who are a different class, 'race', ethnicity, gender and so on, so that the issue of power then becomes central to ethical practice. Although some people argue that it is a good thing if researchers are as similar to their respondents as possible in their gender, age or ethnicity, this is questionable. It may, for example, inhibit respondents from talking in a way that they might adopt with someone who is more distant from them, as they try to conform to what they think someone like them would expect. More generally, the consequences of differences in social identities and positions are not easy to predict, and perhaps the most that can be said is that it is important to recognise this complexity.

It is commonly argued (e.g. by the British Sociological Association, 2002) that research relationships wherever possible should be characterised by trust and integrity. If researchers work at gaining the trust and respect of the populations they study they are likely also to gain the trust of the wider community. Poor ethical practice causes potential harms to those studied and also muddies the waters for future efforts to undertake research in those populations.

---

**BOX 5.2**

## EXAMPLES OF ETHICALLY CONTROVERSIAL SOCIAL RESEARCH

### Example 1: Milgram (1974)

In an experiment done in 1963, Stanley Milgram was interested in why people were willing to harm other people if they thought they had been ordered to do so. The defence that 'we were only obeying orders' had been used by many who had perpetrated war crimes and other cruelties in the Nazi era. Pretending

*(Continued)*

that he was trying to see if punishment affected people's capacity to learn, unwitting research subjects were required to administer electric shocks to other 'subjects' if these people gave incorrect answers to questions, sometimes to the point at which people screamed and begged for mercy. The shocks, though, were not real and the people receiving the shocks were actors. Milgram was able to demonstrate that many people are willing to suspend moral doubts if authority over them is strong enough.

### Example 2: Humphrey (1970)

Laud Humphrey studied homosexual encounters in public toilets by acting as a lookout ('watchqueen'), not telling the people he studied of his true identity (although he did gain the trust of some after disclosing his purpose). As a covert researcher he could not interview men without revealing his identity, so he wrote down the car licence plate numbers of the men and found out where they lived. Changing his appearance he then interviewed them a year later in their homes on the pretext of carrying out a survey on a different subject. His study contributed to the de-stigmatisation of such men who at the time were harassed by police authorities, overcoming stereotypes that they were predatory in relation to non-homosexuals, for example.

These issues are often particularly acute when conducting ethnographic research (see Chapter 14). Indeed, some feminist researchers have argued that, although ethnography allows better knowledge of many research areas than other methods such as surveys, as well as involving less hierarchical relationships between researcher and researched, it also opens up greater potential for harm because of a deeper level of personal involvement and better access to otherwise hidden aspects of people's lives (see Stacey, 1988 and Skeggs, 1994). However, other methods (e.g. qualitative interviews) also involve these problems, if to a lesser degree, and these concern both the nature of developing relationships in the field and what happens to respondents after researchers have left. This is especially relevant when researching sensitive issues, such as sexual abuse.

Managing ethical involvement with participants involves two main areas of concern: issues of privacy and confidentiality and of gaining informed consent. We will take each in turn.

## Privacy, confidentiality and data protection

Most research studies involve an invasion of privacy at some level, even if this is as simple as being stopped in the street for a consumer survey. Invasion of privacy can be viewed both as a harm in its own right and also as a condition that subjects people to the possibility of harm by depriving them of the protection that privacy offers. The harms that may result from unwitting disclosure of personal information are both foreseeable and unforeseeable harms, and the researcher has a duty to protect people from both (Kelman, 1982).

In response to the increased potential for distributing personal information collected as part of a research study, policies and laws on data protection have developed. For example, the 1998 Data Protection Act in the UK sets out eight principles of good practice, saying that stored personal data (which includes both facts about and opinions expressed by people) must be:

- fairly and lawfully processed
- processed for limited purposes

- adequate, relevant and not excessive
- accurate
- not kept longer than necessary
- processed in accordance with the data subject's rights
- secure
- not transferred to countries without adequate protection.

Care regarding data protection needs to be taken at all stages of research, though particular sensitivity may be required at different stages. Note that unless the data sample is self-selected, such as through an advertisement, decisions about samples require the researcher to find out personal details even before people are recruited to the study.

Researchers usually explain to people, when approaching them about participation in a study, why they have been selected and how their name has been obtained. The potential participants may be assured at this point that the information they give will be confidential and that care will be taken to ensure that they will not be identified in a final report. Participants may also be assured that no information which could be used to identify them will be made available without their agreement to anyone outside the agency responsible for conducting the research. These promises, if made, mean that data must usually be anonymised, so all identifying names and places are taken out. This also protects other people and institutions to whom research participants may refer. The participant is likely to be told who will see the data in its original form (usually the research team). It is not always possible to ensure confidentiality or to do all of these things, and if so it should normally be made clear that this is the case so that consent to participate is given on this basis, and is therefore informed consent.

On a practical level, it is also usual that researchers store data in a way that is secure and promotes confidentiality. Each research participant may be given a code number, included on any transcripts or questionnaires. Data may be kept in a locked filing cabinet or secure computer file in a locked room. It may be destroyed when it is no longer needed or, if deposited in an archive (see Chapters 15 and 17), may be subject to varying levels of availability depending on the nature of the subject and the promises made to original participants.

Problems in maintaining confidentiality may arise when studying topics where the populations are small or easily distinguishable. For example, in a study of women chief executives in the motor industry the numbers are likely to be small, and it may therefore be difficult to maintain confidentiality and anonymity even if pseudonyms are used. This issue is not easily subsumed under a procedure or rule. However, if it looks likely that confidentiality or anonymity will not be assured and the participant refuses to waive this right, then the information they give you cannot be made public. Sometimes, in these cases, respondents are given the opportunity to delete particular segments in research reports, or there is restricted access to the final report. Another aspect to the relationship between confidentiality and anonymity arises in research involving group discussions where participants may choose to reveal to others the issues they have discussed. This may be more of a problem when working intensely within a specific site, for example a school. It may be impossible to control for this, so providing a *guarantee* of confidentiality to participants would be unrealistic, even if final dissemination of research returns to the principles of anonymity.

In some instances confidentiality may not be an issue. Some respondents may even be proud and pleased that their personal story is going to be shown to a wider public. Additionally, a researcher can go back to respondents and attempt to re-negotiate confidentiality agreements if they feel that circumstances have changed. Feminist researchers, as well as others, have argued that research participants have a moral right to see interview transcripts and other kinds of data in order for them to assess whether their words or actions have been fairly represented. This can make for a more equal research relationship between researcher and researched (see, for example, Maynard and Purvis, 1994).

The role of the Internet in providing for social networking through sites such as Facebook, Bebo and Twitter, and the sharing of information through blogs and other formats, has rapidly expanded over the last few years. These have also become sites for social research. However, although the general ethical principles behind internet research remain the same as for conventional research, there may be ambiguity in practice. For example, can data be treated as publicly available and therefore not requiring consent from authors for use as data? See Box 5.3 for further discussion on internet research ethics.

---

**BOX 5.3**

## ETHICAL PRACTICE IN INTERNET RESEARCH

Fox et al. (2005) highlight a number of ethical issues in their study of the 'pro-anorexia' online underground movement. They accessed a pro-anorexia site and collected data through posts from members and interviews. The research team discussed whether the research should be covert but decided that, given the provocative and sensitive nature of the issue, the research officer collecting data would disclose their identity as a researcher to the users of the website under study, including their name and place of work. Efforts were made to protect the anonymity of the research participants when reporting interview data. There is debate as to whether information publicly posted on websites requires permission from authors or whether it can be viewed as open to scrutiny without permission. Fox et al. decided to only use data from the website or discussion forum in papers and reports if permission was given by the authors.

---

## Informed consent

Following the Declaration of Helsinki (see Box 5.1), informed consent has been viewed as a focal point in any discussion of research ethics, in either natural or social science. Individuals are felt to have the right to know what is happening to them. Gaining informed consent is a procedure that aims to support the principle of individual autonomy and is widely agreed to be a safeguard for the rights of people participating knowingly and voluntarily in research. The aim is to ensure that research participants are able to decide for themselves what is in their best interest and what risks they are prepared to take. In order for consent to be 'informed', the reason for the study, the requirements of participants, and potential risks and harm need to be explained in appropriate detail and in terms meaningful to participants.

Potential research participants can be given information about the study both verbally and through an information sheet. Enough information needs to be given for the person to decide without overwhelming them with detail or specialist jargon. One way of presenting information in an accessible way is to include a number of questions and answers. Questions a potential participant may need to have answered could include:

- What is the study about?
- Why do you think I am suitable to take part in this research?
- How did you get my name/find out that I was suitable for the study?
- Why is this study important?
- How will the study be done?
- What does my participation in the study involve?

- Will this study benefit me?

- Are there any risks or hazards involved?

- Will people be able to find out my details because of this study?

- What if I change my mind or don't want to be involved?

- What will happen to the information I give you?

The research participant may be assured that they can stop participating at any time for any reason. Researchers, particularly if they are doing social surveys, are often under pressure to maximise response rates. However, it is important that this does not become coercion or lead to participants being misled. Ideally, written consent will be provided through a consent form signed by the participant and the researcher (although for self-completed questionnaires, such as those used in postal surveys, return of the completed questionnaire is normally regarded as an indicator of consent). A consent form may say that the participant has been informed about the study and what is required, that they understand the information collected will be confidential and that they can withdraw from the study at any time. Two copies may be signed, one kept by the researcher and one by the participant.

As with many ethical issues, this can also be a grey area. While researchers will for the most part follow the guidelines above, full disclosure about their research may not be desirable. For example, in order to encourage fresh and spontaneous answers, researchers might not want to disclose everything that they are interested in when they first explain their study, so as not to lead respondents to give answers that they feel are expected of them. Consideration of any ethical issues that this involves needs to be an ongoing concern for the researcher.

Although informed consent is considered the ideal in terms of respecting the autonomy of the potential research participant, it is also sometimes appropriate to study groups of people where this is not possible. For example, people with serious mental impairment may be unable to understand the purpose of a research study; people engaged in illegal or stigmatised activities may not want a researcher around them. If we believe in the value of social research it is important to learn about people who would be excluded if informed consent were always to be required in advance from individual participants. The issues this raises will be discussed further later in this chapter.

On the whole, practical arrangements for gaining informed consent are straightforward, particularly in interview studies, which may be one reason why they are so popular. However, there are some situations in which it is difficult to gain informed consent. For example, in studying a community or institution using methods such as observation it will usually be difficult to gain consent for each piece of data collected. Thus, if a public meeting is being observed it will be unwieldy to get written informed consent as described above beforehand from each person who may say something. One way around this is to provide information leaflets, posters or a verbal announcement about the research so that people can say if they do not want to be included. Another possibility is to gain consent from key figures and ensure that they know what the research entails. Many organisations that fund research require that representatives of those studied are included in planning and advising on the conduct of the research. This may be considered to be linked to the issue of consent in that researchers are then increasingly accountable to research participants.

## Covert research

There are situations where those researched are not informed about the study and consent is not sought prior to their participation in the research. Covert methods can range from misrepresenting the research to respondents at the outset, bugging or taping conversations, covert image collection (such as videoing and photo-graphing) and covert participant observation. Investigations of white supremacist organisa-tions, for example, have often involved covert methods (see Box 5.4). Researchers may inad-vertently use a form of covert method by using informal discussions which they later report in research, or by videotaping or photographing in public places. However, it is more likely that the issue of sustained covert participant obser-vation raises serious ethical considerations (as it did in Humphrey's study – see Box 5.2).

---

**BOX 5.4**

## EXAMPLES OF COVERT RESEARCH

- *Example 1*: In research on the far right political group, the National Front, Nigel Fielding (1981) used a combination of overt and covert methods. He gained consent for the study from the Front's 'head office', but in his participation in the activities of local groups he did not reveal his true status, display-ing instead an attitude that appeared sympathetic to the aims of these groups and participating in events such as marches.

- *Example 2*: In research on the use of the Internet by white supremacist groups, Les Back had to use a pseudonym to access much of the material. He reasoned that giving his real name and revealing his identity as a researcher would have resulted in danger to himself and lack of cooperation from research participants. (Ware and Back, 2001; see also Back's article at www.unesco.org/webworld/points_of_views/back.shtml)

---

There are many reasons for avoiding the use of covert methods if possible. Homan (1991) argues that covert methods:

- flout the principle of informed consent

- help erode personal liberty

- betray trust

- pollute the research environment for other researchers

- are bad for the reputation of social research

- discriminate against the defenceless and powerless

- may damage the behaviour or interests of participants

- are invisibly reactive, suggesting, for example, support for the aims of the group studied

- are seldom necessary

- have the effect of confining the scope of research.

Additionally, Homan says that if covert methods are used too readily the habit of deception may spread to other spheres of human interaction as they may become habitual in the everyday life of the person doing the research. They also place the covert researcher in conditions of excessive strain in maintaining the cover.

Given this litany of objections, is covert research ever justifiable? The answer to this is by no means unanimous, but seems to be a cautious 'yes' (see, for example, Spicker, 2011). Under certain circumstances secrecy may be the only way to collect data that is not 'contaminated' by the presence of the researcher, and if it does not harm respondents it may be justifiable. For example, in psychological experimentation it is often the case that small children may be observed in a controlled environment without their knowledge in order to assess their behav-iour. It is argued that if they knew there was an adult watching them play they would be likely to alter their actions and a 'true' representation of their behaviour would be impossible to obtain. In these circumstances, too, it may be considered that parental consent is adequate. For those studying people engaged in actions deemed illegal or anti-social, who may wish to conceal their actions from researchers, as in the case of the groups concerned in Box 5.4, concerns about harming the interests of the groups involved (if not the individuals concerned) may be less pressing than in other research situations.

As a rule of thumb, from an ethical perspective, covert research should be avoided unless it is absolutely essential. Where possible, too, where covert observation or deception has been involved in collecting information it is desirable to inform those involved that they have participated in the research, and sometimes to negotiate consent at that stage.

---

**BOX 5.5**

## MAKING ASSUMPTIONS ABOUT 'VULNERABILITY'

Valerie Hey's (1994) work with frail elderly people shows how the assumption of 'vulnerability' (implied also in the choice of the word 'frail') can have a *disempowering* effect on the autonomy of respondents. In her article about researching decision-making processes and community care, she argues that, in many cases, what might be considered by some as *incomprehension* of the purposes of research was in fact a form of *resistance* within the research process. Hey writes that we should not therefore conflate specific difficulties with gathering material from elderly people with mental and physical *incapacity*. Instead, we should respect people's accounts as thoughtful, perhaps strategic and certainly competent. This is part of Hey's commitment to ethical practice and awareness of political aspects to research processes in which power relations are held constantly under scrutiny.

---

## Vulnerable groups

If we take the question of power differentials seriously, we can see that almost *any* group or individual may be vulnerable in research. However, when we use this phrase we can usually point to groups who are at particular risk in society. These groups may include children, elderly people, people with learning disabilities, homeless or sick people and disenfranchised groups such as refugees. In all these cases, the vulnerability of the group is connected to issues of relative disempowerment within the social setting. However, we should be careful not to present an over-determined and constrained view of what constitutes disempowerment in the research setting, as Valerie Hey's (1994) research has demonstrated (Box 5.5).

In addition to the 'conventional' groups outlined above, it may be that the kind of research being conducted actually places people in a position of vulnerability. So if, say, you were interested in studying racism within a workplace, you might find that announcement of the research topic itself creates difficulties. It could suggest new racial or ethnic categorisations of co-workers to people in the organisation who had previously not thought of their colleagues in this way. This would be a clear example of where simply negotiating access and sampling respondents can have a negative effect even before any data collection, analysis or writing up has been done, and its effects may be lasting.

## Research with children

During the past 15 years there has been a shift in emphasis from research 'on' children to research 'with' them. This shift has implications for the ethical conduct of research since it emphasises that children are competent and knowledgeable respondents (see, for example, Alderson and Morrow, 2004). Research with children can give a particular focus to ethical issues that are common to all social research, though there are some age-specific issues too. Ethical guidelines for research with children have become increasingly important with the recognition of the high levels of abuse of children within families and institutional settings such as school and church. Researchers working with children must therefore be particularly aware of the potential abuse of power relationships between adult researchers and children. Anxieties about abuse have led to attempts to regulate researchers by means of police checks on criminal records. Although many researchers may be tempted to circumvent this requirement by using personal contacts, they ought to ask themselves whether this is right. Finally, legal considerations may come into play: adults in schools are considered to be *in loco parentis* (responsible in the place of parents if left 'in charge' of the child), and researchers left on their own with children may be held responsible if the child has an accident or is harmed in any way.

Informed consent has a particular resonance in work with children. In their discussion of ethics and informed consent with young women diagnosed with anorexia, Halse and Honey point out that 'A precondition of informed consent is that it is voluntarily and freely given. The concept of free will is premised on an autonomous liberal humanist subject who is able to make rational and independent judgments regardless of her context' (2005: 2149). The young women with whom these researchers worked did not fit neatly with this idea for many different reasons. Similarly, children are often not perceived to be as 'rational' and 'competent' as most adults. Do children really always understand the implications of taking part in research? Can they be said to fully consent to the process? Do they understand confidentiality? As we have seen, informed consent is one of the key areas of ethical research practice and yet one of the hardest to be sure about (see Box 5.6).

---

BOX 5.6

## WHAT DO CHILDREN MAKE OF GUARANTEES OF CONFIDENTIALITY AND PRIVACY?

The following excerpt is from research notes made in 1998 by Suki Ali in a study (Ali, 2003) of 'mixed-race' identities:

> I was talking to Marita today for the first time in a one-on-one interview. She is a very bright child in Year 4 in ******* School. I began with my 'blurb' about the research and what it was about and then asked her if she would like to take part in this next stage. I explained (I thought) that the interview would be confidential and explained what that meant. That it would be between us and not for other people to know what had been said and so on. She said 'sort of like a secret' and I said 'yes'. It was a key theme with the children that what they said should not be reported back to the teachers or to their parents.

Later in the interview she said: 'If the interview is confidential, why are you taping it?' It was an excellent question, because if confidential meant 'secret' it was indeed rather risky to be taping it! If it was only me who would use the information, and nobody else would hear what she had said, why tape it? I had to then re-think the way I explained 'confidential' and that it meant that she would not be identified but that what she said may be used in the research. I emphasised that it would be done in such a way that would be respectful of what she had said but would not get her into trouble.

---

One of the most obviously difficult and disturbing aspects of work with children is what to do if a child discloses abuse of some kind. Teachers are legally required to report this to the relevant specialists within the school. But the researcher who may have already promised confidentiality may find themselves with an ethical dilemma. Some schools will indeed be clear about the way that they will expect the researcher to respond, but in many cases decisions have to taken in the first instance by the researcher. This brings to the fore issues of trust, privacy and confidentiality that can also occur – if more rarely – in research studies done with adults.

## Ethical issues in data analysis

Some researchers may assume that once they have got through the difficulties of setting up a research project, working out a suitable question, accessing their sample and collecting data, they are now into an area that has no ethical implications: data analysis. In many cases that may be true, or at least be limited to some quite straightforward decision making. In other cases, it may be that urgent ethical issues arise at this stage (Box 5.7).

Both Mauthner and Song in Box 5.7 are clear that there are no easy answers to this kind of dilemma. They call for a rigorously reflexive approach to analysis and a recognition that whilst one respondent's account may be 'true' and the other 'false' they are both important contributions to the research. The processes of analysis and choice of examples to include in a report can also reflect the considerable power which the researcher has at this stage in a research project.

These issues relate to knowledge production and to questions of epistemology. Data analysis of all sorts involves decisions about which lines of analysis to pursue and which to put to one side. Choosing not to go down a particular route may have ethical implications: decisions made at this stage may 'silence' certain voices and give undue prominence to others. Thus the production of knowledge itself has to be understood as an ethical endeavour. Lorraine Code (1991) writes that objectivity and ethics in research are linked in a complex relationship which requires us to question who can know, and what they can know. Her work focuses on the exclusion of women from particular kinds of knowledge work, such as science, but is relevant to all kinds of marginal and 'vulnerable groups' who are not afforded status as competent knowers. She therefore argues for a form of knowledge production that is *responsible* and therefore ethical. Doucet and Mauthner (2002) have elaborated on this, arguing that in order to 'know well', to 'know responsibly' and to hold to what they call epistemic responsibility, researchers do not just need to have good research relationships but should also be clear that reflexivity and the ethical practice that it entails requires a strong engagement with social, institutional and political contexts as well as intellectual frameworks. These deeper-level ethical issues come into stark relief not only at the stage of data analysis, but also at the point at which research studies are published.

---

BOX 5.7

### EXAMPLES OF ETHICAL ISSUES WHEN ANALYSING CONTRADICTORY ACCOUNTS

- *Example 1*: Melanie Mauthner (1998) interviewed sisters about their relationships with each other, leading to some difficult questions about voicing and making public some very personal issues. In some cases one sister gave information that she did not want shared with the other. The interpretation of this material was potentially compromised by trying to hold back the confidential parts.

- *Example 2*: Miri Song (1998), also working with siblings, discusses the problems of being given competing accounts of the same relationships and events. She describes the difficulties with holding on to 'oppositional accounts' without 'stirring up trouble' or producing 'false' or one-sided accounts.

## Ethical issues in publishing and disseminating research

Considerable ethical issues arise when writing, publishing and disseminating research. There can be pressure from all sides to produce particular findings or present them in a certain way. This can be exerted by funders, other members of the research team or participants. An interesting example of this is described by Punch (1986), who details his experience of undertaking a PhD study on a progressive school in England in which the sponsors (the school's trustees, alumni and staff) were at best ambivalent throughout its course. The central problem was his difficulties in getting his sponsors to allow him to publish it at all.

Problems may arise in research teams where team members with less power may feel under pressure to go along with interpretations of the data they do not agree with. Regarding participants, in order to undertake research in the first place, a relationship usually needs to be built with those who are to be 'researched'. This can be either individuals or a community or organisation. This may place the researcher in the position of having to present negative findings or represent the population under study in an unflattering way. This means that it is especially important not to mislead participants at any stage. Box 5.8 looks at how confidentiality can suppress important findings.

---

### BOX 5.8

### THE DUTY OF CONFIDENTIALITY CAN SUPPRESS IMPORTANT FINDINGS

Baez (2002) describes a study where participants reported instances of discrimination on the basis of gender and race. However, despite Baez feeling that there was a strong need to highlight this in the analysis, the small numbers of ethnic minority members in the population studied would mean that they would be identifiable. The individuals refused to waive their right to confidentiality, leaving Baez frustrated that the discriminatory practice highlighted by his research could not be challenged.

---

Additionally, the need to maintain confidentiality at the dissemination stage can cause ethical tensions if important points are therefore suppressed (Box 5.8). Here the researcher can be caught between two ethical obligations: to publish the findings of research that may improve society, conflicting with an obligation to protect the rights of research participants.

In contemporary society, researchers are increasingly expected to involve members of the public with an interest in the research topic in the research process, and to feed back a summary of the findings to participants should they require it. This is particularly the case in applied research. Although this is less likely to be the case in a small-scale project, it is considered good practice to offer to feed back findings to those who have agreed to participate in research

or who have been involved in other ways, such as helping with access participants. As discussed earlier in this chapter, power relationships are inherent in research studies. In recent times there has been a move towards a more participative research model with researchers encouraged to disseminate their findings to participants and relevant practitioners as well as academic audiences. As the example in Box 5.8 illustrates, care may be needed in dissemination depending on the topic and sensitivity of the research.

## Ethical guidelines and review bodies

The expansion of social research and concern for the needs of participants and researchers, as well as cases of misconduct by researchers, have led to the development of guidelines and the setting up of research review bodies. Academic and other professional bodies involved in social research, as well as funders, publish guidelines on research ethics (see Web links for this chapter). Those undertaking social research will be expected to be aware of and attend to the ethical issues set out in the guidelines. In addition, some research studies may be required to be submitted to scrutiny by an ethical review body or committee based in an institution, such as a university or hospital. Obligations to get ethical approval for studies are sometimes seen as bureaucratic impositions. However, they can also be (and, we would argue, ought to be) treated as occasions for helpful advice. Most universities these days have ethical committees to review research proposals of staff and students, whereas even 20 years ago these were less common. Health services research is very commonly subject to the requirement that formal ethical approval be obtained before contacting potential participants and, sometimes, before seeking funding for research. This reflects the history of ethical debates, which as we have seen, have been highly influenced by events in medical research studies. The requirement to undergo ethical review also reflects legal requirements, such as those imposed by the conditions of insurance companies used by universities to insure their researchers against harm.

It may come as a surprise, too, to learn that good research design is often considered by formal research ethics committees to be a legitimate matter for comment and evaluation. Choice of research methodology and design would not appear to be intrinsically ethical, but it is generally viewed as ethically problematic to involve someone in a study that has been poorly designed. Participants often take part in research because they believe the results will be valuable for improving society, but if the study has been poorly designed it will not do so, meaning that participants have been misled and their time wasted.

## Conclusion

The central ethical issue for much social and cultural research is how the rights of participants (and researchers) are to be balanced against the potential benefits to society. The various facets of ethical practice we have discussed return, for the most part, to this issue. Ethical conduct requires attention to quite broad epistemological and political issues as well as matters pertaining to research relationships at the time a study is conducted. We have also argued that, at the end of the day, ethical practice depends upon the integrity of the researcher. Advice may be available from ethical committees. Guidelines exist to protect both the rights and safety of the research participants and the researcher (as well as the institution or subject discipline they represent). However, sticking rigidly to advice or guidelines cannot ensure that research is ethical: decisions still need to be made throughout the course of the research that demonstrate sensitivity to the local context of a project, for which the researcher takes ultimate responsibility. As Beauchamp comments, 'There is no such thing as a simple "application" of a principle so as to resolve a complicated moral problem' (1994: 11).

*(Continued)*

social research ethics. Renzetti and Lee (1993) provide a good review of the issues involved in researching sensitive topics. The Economic and Social Research Council Research Ethics Framework (ESRC, 2009) is a useful comprehensive review of ethics for social scientists. Ethical guidelines are produced by professional organisations, such as the British Educational Research Association (BERA) and the American Sociological Association (ASA). Use the Web links below to access these.

## Student Reader (Seale, 2004b): relevant reading

56 Alvin W. Gouldner: 'Toward a reflexive sociology'

69 British Sociological Association (BSA) and Council for American Survey Research Organizations (CASRO): 'Research ethics: two statements'

See also Chapter 16 'Ethical issues' by Anne Ryen in Seale et al. (2004).

## Journal articles illustrating the issues raised in this chapter

Corrigan, O. (2003) 'Empty ethics: the problem with informed consent', Sociology of Health & Illness, 25 (7): 768–792.

Dickson-Swift, V., James, E.L., Kippen, S. and Liamputtong, P. (2007) 'Doing sensitive research: what challenges do qualitative researchers face?', Qualitative Research, 7: 327–353.

Mellick, M. and Fleming, S. (2010) 'Personal narrative and the ethics of disclosure: a case study from elite sport', Qualitative Research, 10: 299–314.

Spicker, P. (2011) 'Ethical covert research', Sociology, 45 (1): 118–133.

## Web links

Information Commissioner's Office (UK) (Data protection Act): www.ico.gov.uk

Economic and Social Research Council Research Ethics Framework: www.esrcsocietytoday.ac.uk (type 'Research ethics' into search box)

Statement of Ethical Practice for the British Sociological Association: www.britsoc.co.uk/equality/Statement+Ethical+Practice.htm

American Sociological Association code of ethics: www.asanet.org/about/ethics.cfm

The Internet Encyclopedia of Philosophy (use it to look up entries on utilitarianism, Bentham, Mill, Rawls etc.): www.iep.utm.edu

Bioethics Resources on the Web (contains useful links to other sites on research ethics): http://bioethics.od.nih.gov

Social Research Association ethical guidelines: www.the-sra.org.uk/guidelines.htm

Ethical Guidance for Research with Human Participants: www.lancs.ac.uk/fass/resources/ethics

## KEY CONCEPTS FOR REVIEW

**Advice:** Use these, along with the review questions in the next section, to test your knowledge of the contents of this chapter. Try to define each of the key concepts listed here; if you have understood this chapter you should be able to do this. Check your definitions against the definition in the glossary at the end of the book.

| | |
|---|---|
| Confidentiality | Informed consent |
| Covert research | Privacy |
| Epistemic responsibility | Reflexivity |
| Ethical principles (beneficence, non-maleficence, autonomy and justice) | Situated knowledge |
| | Utilitarian ethics |
| *In loco parentis* | Vulnerable groups |

## Review questions

1 What is informed consent and how would you know whether consent is informed?
2 How does reflexivity contribute to ethical research practice?
3 What are the four principles underpinning research ethics outlined by Beauchamp?
4 What special considerations apply to doing ethical research work with children or vulnerable people?
5 What are the arguments for and against covert research?

## Workshop and discussion exercises

1 Select an issue from the following list (you may want to choose a subject that you are not familiar with, rather than one which you have studied before):

- the education of children aged 5–8 years at school
- self-harm in teenage children aged 12–16 years
- community responses to large sporting events taking place locally
- responses to being diagnosed with Alzheimer's disease in adults aged over 65 years
- attitudes towards graffiti.

Outline possible ethical issues that may arise in your study and describe the procedures you would use to address these.

2 You are undertaking a study in one of the areas outlined in question 1.

(a) You need to gain informed consent from participants (or guardians or carers) in order to do the study:
- Draw up an information sheet for participants.
- Draw up a consent form for participants.

(b) If working in a group or pairs, role play seeking and gaining consent for your hypothetical study. Swap roles (potential participant to researcher and vice-versa). After participation in the role play make a note of:
(i) As the research participant:
- how you felt receiving the information
- whether you felt the issues were fully explained to you
- did you feel that you had opportunities to ask questions?

**(ii) As the researcher:**

- how well you thought the potential participants understood the study purpose and process
- did you give opportunities to ask questions?

**Discuss your experiences. What have you learnt about ethical practice in social research?**

3  Download an ethics application form from your local research ethics committee/institutional review board. Using one of the topics in exercise 1, draft an ethics committee submission. If working in a group, critically appraise each other's draft submissions. Record what you have learnt.

# 6

# DOING A LITERATURE REVIEW

## Duncan Branley

What does it mean to 'do' a literature review? Feelings of apprehension when faced with an apparently overwhelming mass of information are understandable. Where do you begin? How do you make sense of it all? One approach is to treat it like eating an elephant (or a tree, if you are vegetarian): choose somewhere and take a bite. Chew it properly and, once you have swallowed, have another bite. Eventually the elephant (or tree) will be gone. This chapter will show you how to begin and help you to feel confident in taking your first bites. It will then take you through the stages of doing a literature review and will highlight the many useful research skills you will acquire as you do your own literature review. It is an academic exercise, but one that has many direct benefits for your research work both in terms of content and analytical skills. We will look at three broad areas in turn: research questions, finding references then managing them and your notes. We will then comment on writing before turning to other matters, such as 'systematic' reviewing.

When you have finished reading this chapter, you should have a better idea of where to look for relevant literature and know how to use keywords and search terms to interrogate a library database, including the use of reference management software. You will know what principles to apply when taking notes of your reading and writing a literature review. You will also understand the broad purpose and some of the procedures involved in carrying out systematic reviews.

## Getting started: research questions

Getting started with a literature review is also rather like walking through the door into a lively party. You probably have practical knowledge of how parties work, so you make your way to the kitchen where it is likely that you will be able to get a drink. Similarly, whether you are a student or an established researcher, you know that there are places where you can get information that is going to help you: libraries and the Internet. Importantly, there are also people you can ask too: librarians, academic staff and other students or researchers.

When you are choosing your drink at the party you might go for something you always have (staying in your 'comfort zone'); something familiar but with a slight twist (perhaps mixing an unusual combination); or you might decide to try something completely new. It might be that you limber up with something familiar and then experiment once you have relaxed a bit. To make these decisions you are drawing on your accumulated knowledge of drinks both from direct experience and from what others have told you. You are unlikely to be indulging in a substantial literature review until at least the last year of your undergraduate studies, more often in postgraduate research, so by this time you will have acquired a fair bit of knowledge about your subject and should be able to choose an area in which you are interested and about which you may well have some questions in mind. Chapters 3 and 4 contain some helpful guidance on how to incorporate theoretical and policy-related concerns in the formulation of research questions.

You must decide on your research questions (no matter how provisionally) before you begin. If you have no questions in mind, you will read with little focus and at the end will feel that you have achieved little. Not being clear and focused with a literature review will undermine your broad research aims.

---

BOX 6.1

### FIRST BRAINSTORM

Before you set off for the library write down:

- The general area that you want to research.
- What you know about it already:
  - who did or said what, when and how
  - what differences and similarities there are between these
  - some hunches about why.
- What you do not know and want to know — and why this is important or interesting.
- Where you might be able to find this information.
- A vocabulary of the specific words used in your area – include synonyms and antonyms.
- Possible theoretical models for constructing and arguing your case.
- The practical research skills you might need to use, if you are doing empirical research.

---

## Formulating your research questions

The formulation of research questions is discussed more fully in Chapter 7, but a few words about this are relevant here. It is important to realise that your initial definitions of your research questions will not constrain you completely – you are likely to refine your questions as you encounter new ideas, produce new data and have new thoughts. But you need to start somewhere so that you have got ideas that you can question and explore. One good way to get going is to do a 'first brainstorm' (see Box 6.1). The product of this is a working document that will form the basis of your research questions, will guide your reading and help you develop your argument. There may be gaps and you may not see how things can be made to relate at this stage – but if you know everything now, why do the research?

You now need to develop your brainstorming in the library in order to situate your ideas in a broader context. In the general reference section read up on the areas and questions you have noted in your initial plan. Look for discipline-specific and biographical dictionaries or encyclopaedias. Your aim at this stage is to fill out your initial knowledge and hunches, and to make your research questions better defined and therefore more researchable. You will find that you gradually revise your initial plans. If you note these changes, you can show how your thinking developed when you write up your research.

## Finding literature: where to search

When you start reading you will be referred to other sources, some of which will look like useful leads to follow. Each of those will, in turn, introduce you to other works. As you read you will make connections, guided by your research questions. Imagine meeting people at a party; it does not have to be a passive or random process, but something you partly direct. There may be many loud voices competing for your attention. Who do you go up to first? You'll probably recognise some people and so chat with them until you feel comfortable. Gradually you'll either be introduced to or introduce yourself to people you're not acquainted with. And those people in turn will introduce you to others. Sometimes someone will just catch your eye – serendipity.

## Library catalogues

Sometimes when browsing the library shelves you will come across other relevant books, but you should not rely on this informal approach when conducting a literature search. Academic knowledge is organised by librarians and 'information scientists' in the form of catalogues, usually searchable in computerised databases. A database is a structured way of holding related information. It can be a manual system in a book, on cards or an electronic system on a computer – what is important is that it is explicitly structured. The structure is there to help you find those specific bits of information quickly and accurately – and also to see gaps where you might want to complete the information later. So an address book is a manual database with specific places (known as fields) for different types of information: names, streets, cities, postcodes and telephone numbers.

The content of the fields which belong together (e.g. one person's contact details) is known as a record. All of the records together constitute the database (e.g. all the people in your address book). Figure 6.1 shows a simple database with three fields and two records. Notice the regular structure: if a telephone number were missing or in the wrong place it would be immediately apparent (compare this with the data matrix shown in Box 18.1).

A big advantage of computerised databases is that they enable you to enter information once and use it many times without having to re-enter it. For instance, you can produce mailing labels from a computerised address book instead of having to write out lots of addresses by hand.

Library catalogues are databases for holding bibliographic records (known as references), that is, the details of the books, journals etc., which the library owns. There are fields for the author's name, the title of the publication, the date of publication, the publisher etc. Libraries rarely catalogue individual (and separately authored) items in collections such as journals, conference proceedings or chapters in books like this one you are reading now. If you are looking for an article contained in a journal or an edited collection, the library will likely catalogue only the main title of the book or journal. See the next section 'Bibliographic indexes' for more information.

| | Field 1<br>*Name* | Field 2<br>*Address* | Field 3<br>*Telephone* |
|---|---|---|---|
| Record 1 | A Person | 1 London | 123 |
| Record 2 | A N Other | 2 London | 456 |

FIGURE 6.1  A database with three fields and two records

It is useful to have an understanding of how the library of your university is organised to help you both in searching and in retrieving resources. The two leading classificatory systems in the English-speaking world are the Dewey Decimal system and the Library of Congress system. They are hierarchical, working from general disciplinary headings to ever more precise headings. Dewey uses numbers; the Library of Congress uses letters. Thus resources about social groups can be found at 305 (a subsection of 300 Social Sciences) in the Dewey system and at HQ-HT (subsections of H Social Sciences) in the Library of Congress system (Hart, 2001: 13–14). Knowing this you can browse through a library catalogue at specific subdivisions to see what they hold of relevance to you before visiting the library itself (and also see what might be on loan).

## Bibliographic indexes

To find individual journal articles or book chapters, discipline-related bibliographic indexes or databases are published. Most are available over the Internet, are constantly updated, but they are often accessible only to subscribers. Ask your university library staff which indexes they have subscriptions for and what you need to do to get access to them.

Many of the indexes will have abstracts of the articles or chapters. These short summaries are a guide to the issues covered, how they are addressed and, if appropriate, some conclusions or results. The abstract should help you decide whether or not the article is going to be of any use to you. They may also suggest new terms or ways of thinking about your research questions before you have even read the article. Keep in mind your core research questions, though, so that you do not get distracted by each exciting new tangent or you will never get your project finished. Keep a separate note of exciting, but not quite relevant items to come back to once you have finished your current project.

## Other sources

Apart from library catalogues and bibliographic indexes there are other resources you may want to search, depending on your research project. Most major academic conferences and theses will be included in abstracts and indexes, although there are specific sites for theses and dissertations (see Web links for this chapter). The Internet is also a resource. You may want to consult official publications or government statistics – resources for accessing these do change and are often online, so it is best to talk to your university librarian or an academic adviser to point you at relevant resources in the first instance. Reports by non-official organisations (e.g. major charities) are known as grey literature and an online database for searching these exists (see Web links for this chapter). Newspapers and magazines often enable you to search some part of their archives online. Hart (2001) discusses this in detail over several chapters, but your first port of call should be your university librarians who will tell you which sources they have subscriptions to and may have suggestions for the best way of locating useful materials.

## Finding literature: how to search

### Keywords and search terms

Book or article titles are not always a good guide to their contents, and abstracts are not always available. Cataloguers and indexers use a system of keywords giving a more detailed guide to the contents of works. The keywords are used consistently whenever a work deals with a particular concept: listings of them are known as control lists. The actual keywords may not be used in the work at all, but a synonym will have been. For instance, works on sexual orientation might use any of the terms 'homosexual', 'gay' or 'queer', but all of the works might be found only under 'homosexual' and not under the other two terms. Control lists can function like a thesaurus, enabling you to broaden or focus your search terms.

Your preparatory work and initial library explorations will provide you with a good range of terms which map different facets of your research questions. Group related search terms together and think how groups of terms relate to other groups; this will enable you to stay focused in your searching.

With card catalogues the degree of cross-referencing between cards varies. You are often limited to searching for particular authors or for works catalogued at a particular point in the classification system. With printed indexes and abstracts look up each of the terms in your vocabulary list and note the references that appear to be relevant. It might be that you come across other concepts which you had not thought of at first; incorporate these into your search plan.

Most library catalogues can be searched using a web browser (see Figure 6.2). Computerised searching works on the principle of pattern matching, looking for a specified sequence of characters (letters, numbers, punctuation or other things you can enter through you keyboard). With a database you can tell the computer exactly in which field to look. To find all works in a library catalogue by Foucault, type 'Foucault' in the author field box. To find all works with 'power' in their title you use the title field, and you can even combine them (see Figure 6.2). Different library catalogues will have different fields which you can search, but most will have at least title, author, subject/keyword. When the results from your search appear on screen, you may often see a summary of all the search terms, known as a query (e.g. 'author = Foucault AND subject = power'). You can often search in every field at once too, if you want to find, for example, all books authored by *and* about Foucault, though this might produce too many results to be useful – remember your research questions.

## Wildcards, truncating and other variations

The term you are searching for is often a complete word and so by default most database searches will only look for complete words rather than just the sequence of characters (for instance, searching for 'ant' would not find 'fondant', 'mordant', 'antonym' etc.). If you find you get odd results, check the online help for 'complete words' or something similar.

If there are alternative spellings of a word, you may want to search for both of them at once. Perhaps you want to find a book by Alfred Smith, but cannot remember if that is the correct spelling of his surname or if it is Smyth. One solution is to use wildcards. These are characters which can stand in for any other character(s); when the computer does the search it substitutes all possible characters. Which wildcards work can vary with the database you are using, so you will need to check the online help.

For a single character you can often use a question mark to stand in: so you would enter 'Sm?th' as your search term. One word of warning: a wildcard can be replaced by any character, so you might also find Smath, Smeth, Smoth and Smuth and other, perhaps unexpected, combinations. Entering 'cent??' would return both 'center' and 'centre'; entering 'col*r', in many systems, would return 'color' and 'colour', since * used as a wildcard usually stands for any number of characters.

An associated search concept is truncation. This is where you limit the number of specific characters you search for rather than using a whole word to find a range of related terms. Often you will need to append a multiple character wildcard (*) at the end of the text pattern you have entered, and you need to ensure that you have enough of a text pattern to exclude words you do not want found. For example, searching for 'theol*', would find 'theology', 'theological', 'theologian', but not 'theodicy', 'theodolite', 'theogony' or 'theosophy'. Sometimes this is referred to as 'right-truncation'.

Often capitalisation will be ignored. If you are entering everything in lower case and not getting the results you might expect, check the

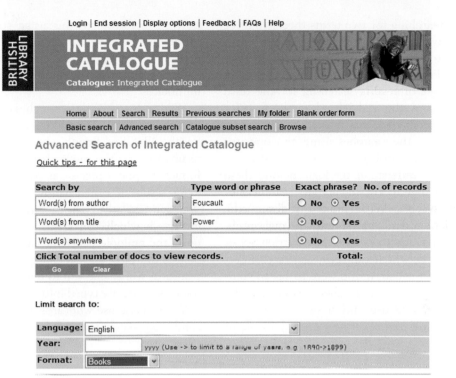

FIGURE 6.2   Searching a library catalogue

online help to see whether searching is 'case-specific'. If it is, then try searching for 'Foucault' instead of 'foucault'. Sometimes the database will include simple plurals automatically ('gloves' still contains the pattern 'glove' – though if you are limited to searching for a whole word then this will not work). If you are searching in a language other than English, say German, you might want to search for both Erlass and Erlaß and similarly ä (ae), ö (oe) or ü (ue). With other letters bearing diacritical marks, it might be best to search both with and without, for example, citta and città, manana and mañana or sante and santé. To do just one search you could use the single character wildcard (?) to substitute for the possibly accented character, or you could combine the search terms as discussed in the next section.

## Combining search terms: Boolean logic and proximity operators

Often if you search for just one term you will get too many references in your results, or if you have used a particularly specialist term you may get too few. There are standard techniques for combining search terms which enable you to narrow or widen your search; however, their implementation can differ between databases. Consult the online help to see how search terms are combined for the database you are searching. If you understand the principles involved, you should be able to understand the explanation in the online help, even if different terms are used. The name given to this system of logical relationships is derived from the work of a British mathematician called George Boole and so is known as Boolean.

When searching for two terms there are three common ways of combining them and a fourth which you may occasionally find. In the diagrams in Figure 6.3 the left hand circle represents the set of results searching for the term 'Foucault' and the right hand circle that for 'power'. The shaded area represents the results of combining the searches using the operator described (and in bold).

Once you understand the logic behind these you will be able to create complex searches not only on bibliographic databases but also on the Internet and in data analysis too. The main problem at first tends to be the rather strict use of OR and AND, which can seem contrary to everyday use in English. If you were to say to yourself 'I want everything about Foucault and power,' you might use 'and' to mean 'everything about Foucault *and* separately everything about

power'; to formulate this using strict Boolean terminology you would need to use OR. If you used AND, you would find only those items containing both terms – likely to be a far smaller number.

Wildcards and Boolean searches can sometimes be used to similar ends. You could use 'Alfred Smith OR Alfred Smyth' and should get similar results to using the single character wildcard (?). In fact it is more precise, as you will not get the extra results if other words meet the pattern 'Sm?th'. Similarly, using 'colour OR color' will not also find 'collar', 'colander' and 'collator' that using the multiple character wildcard (*) would. Sometimes there are data entry errors, and using wildcards will enable you to find things that have not been correctly typed into a database.

You can also use wildcards within elements of combined search terms. A search for 'foucaul*

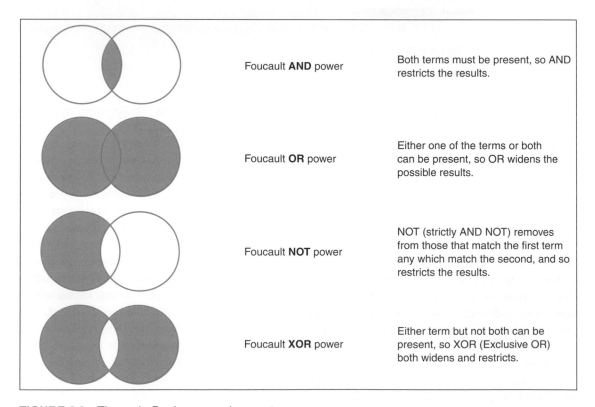

| | | |
|---|---|---|
| | Foucault **AND** power | Both terms must be present, so AND restricts the results. |
| | Foucault **OR** power | Either one of the terms or both can be present, so OR widens the possible results. |
| | Foucault **NOT** power | NOT (strictly AND NOT) removes from those that match the first term any which match the second, and so restricts the results. |
| | Foucault **XOR** power | Either term but not both can be present, so XOR (Exclusive OR) both widens and restricts. |

FIGURE 6.3   The main Boolean search operators

AND powe*' would find 'Foucauldian analyses of the powerful' as well as 'Foucault's concepts of power'.

If you are searching the abstracts in an index, there may be occasions when one term is at the beginning and another at the end and they are not related conceptually at all. To avoid finding such false positives you can control your searches by combining your search terms on the basis of their relative position using proximity operators.

Box 6.2 outlines the main relationships in increasing order of restrictiveness. The terms in capitals are common expressions for these relationships.

The methods of controlling searching using combination and proximity operators in catalogue and index database systems vary, so you should consult the online help for the exact syntax now that you understand the principles behind the relationships.

---

**BOX 6.2**

## PROXIMITY OPERATORS

| | |
|---|---|
| NEAR or WITHIN | Terms must be close to each other (WITHIN controls the maximum number of characters or words between the terms). |
| BEFORE or AFTER | Terms must be in a specified order (alternatives are PRECEDE or FOLLOWED BY). |
| NEXT, WITH or ADJACENT | Terms must be immediately next to each other with no intervening terms. You can also search for an exact phrase by putting it in inverted commas: 'Fine chocolate'. |

---

### Ordering of combined searches

Sometimes when combining search terms, the order in which the search is done is important. Rather than trying to learn or figure out each database's rules, it is easier to force the program to do the searches in the order you want. You can often do this using parentheses. The golden rule here is that the program will work out whatever is within parentheses first and then work with that result. You can enclose parentheses within other parentheses (known as nesting), but are unlikely to need to for a literature search, although you might when searching the Web. You are only likely to need to create complex queries for a literature search if you have used terms which are *homographs* because of a specialised usage in your area of research (e.g. 'fair' can mean 'a market' or 'beautiful' or 'just'; 'queer' can vary subtly in meaning according to whether it is used within philosophy or within studies of sexuality).

Examples of the effect of parentheses on the results generated are shown in Figure 6.4, with the shaded area showing the results returned when combining the search terms Foucault (left), power (right) and sexuality (bottom) in different ways. The first column shows the results of the combination within parentheses and the second combining these results with the term outside of parentheses. These are meant as examples to get you thinking about how your terms relate and are not exhaustive. An important thing to notice is that after the results for the search term in parentheses have been found, it is *these* results that are combined with the next level of search terms, *not* the search terms which produced them. For instance, in '(Foucault AND power) OR sexuality' there could be some results which were excluded in resolving the parentheses because they did not contain both 'Foucault' and 'power', but which when the results are combined with 'sexuality' using OR are then included again because they contain 'sexuality'.

---

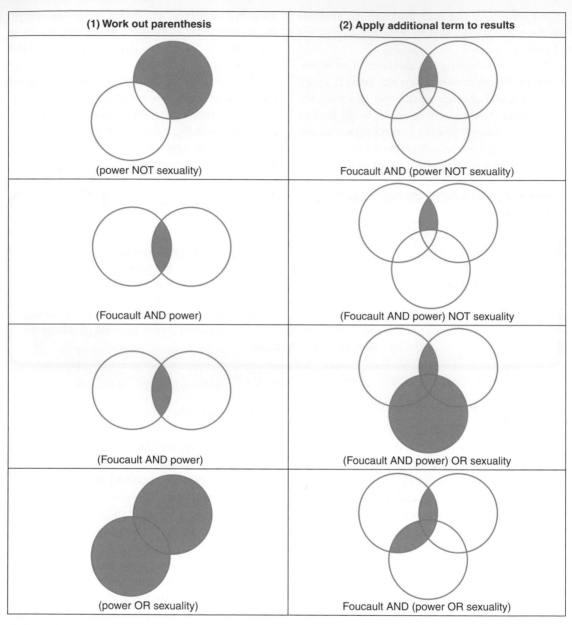

| (1) Work out parenthesis | (2) Apply additional term to results |
|:---:|:---:|
| (power NOT sexuality) | Foucault AND (power NOT sexuality) |
| (Foucault AND power) | (Foucault AND power) NOT sexuality |
| (Foucault AND power) | (Foucault AND power) OR sexuality |
| (power OR sexuality) | Foucault AND (power OR sexuality) |

**FIGURE 6.4**  Effect of nesting combined search terms using parentheses

Although this discussion of the mechanics of preparing search terms can be applied to any form of search, you need to be careful when you are not searching well-constructed databases, but the Internet generally.

## Organising your search

Keep track of what you have searched for so that you do not waste time repeating searches needlessly. It is a good idea to plan your searches and to have a number of alternative resources that you can search should one become unavailable to you temporarily. You should note:

- which resource you have searched
- which search terms you have used – any restrictions on dates
- when you did the search
- how many results or 'hits' you have got
- any initial thoughts or follow-up activities needed, including any problems encountered, which you need to resolve.

If you have downloaded or emailed results to yourself rather than printing them out (which often you cannot do directly), give the file or the email a title that summarises much of the above. For instance, 'soc-abs-identity-10–04–20–37.txt' would tell you that the files contained the results of your search of Sociological Abstracts for the term identity on 20 April 2010 which had 37 hits. The date portion is ordered year–month–day so that you can quickly sort files from subsequent searches of the same database by date.

Many databases will let you save a search so that you can run it again at a later date. They may also enable you to search only those records added since you last did the search (hence keeping that information). Other resources run an alert service, which stores your search and runs it against newly added records and then emails any hits to you. This enables you to keep on top of current developments. Journal publishers often run email alert systems to announce the contents of the latest issue of a journal or new books long before an article or book has been added to a bibliographic database. These can be useful if a particular journal or author is central for your research project.

You should be aware of the time delays in publishing too. It can take 3–4 years for a book to reach the shops from when it was written, and journal articles can take up to 2 years from first submission to appearing in print. Many journals now publish an online version of the article in advance of the hard copy being published. If you need to be aware of current developments, you will need to keep abreast of conferences and seminars where people often present drafts of articles or chapters on which they are working. You will need to network with others working in your field and monitor relevant websites and email lists.

## Managing the results of your literature searches

As you get results from your searches you need a system to organise them. You could use a notebook into which you write everything by hand, but there are distinct advantages to a more structured approach. Some researchers record their references on small note cards which are filed in boxes. More technically advanced and more flexible are easy-to-use bibliographic software programs (see Web links for this chapter). These enable you not only to keep your references organised, but also to import search results automatically. You can search your personal database, classifying references using keywords. You can then use your references with your word processor to insert formatted citations into your writing and to automatically produce a properly formatted bibliography.

## What information to keep

A major use of a bibliography is to enable a reader to locate and consult a copy of the work to which you refer, so keep as full a record of the bibliographic details as you can. You may also want to keep information for your own organisational purposes, which will not appear in the printed bibliography, such as:

- Where you found the reference.
- Where you obtained a copy. Library and class-mark is useful should you need to consult a work again. If it was by inter-library loan, note which library supplied

it and their reference. If you own a copy, perhaps note the ISBN in case you lose it and need to replace it.

- How useful each item was for your research. It is a good idea to devise a method of noting the usefulness of items so that you can prioritise study of the core ones.

## An overview of bibliographic software

Bibliographic programs are fairly similar, so you will not be locked into using a particular one for ever: the skills you will acquire are transferable. Further, you can easily exchange data between different bibliographic software programs. Some are web-based and enable varying degrees of sharing, creating a sense of academic community where people with similar interests can share the literature they're exploring.

## Different reference types

Bibliographic or reference management software programs are like a personal library catalogue. They are structured databases with separate fields for each part of a bibliographic reference. However, they differ in that you need to be able to store in one database information not only about books and journals as published, but also about the articles in journals and chapters in collections. This is significant because the *fields* required for books differ from those for articles, which in turn differ from those for chapters in books of collected chapters. These records have many fields in common, but some will only be relevant to one specific type of reference. For instance, the book record type has just one field for the publication title, whereas the article record type has a field for the article title and a separate field for the publication title.

To accommodate such differences, bibliographic databases contain different types of *record* within the same database. These may even include such things as newspapers, films, computer programs and works of art. For each different reference type the field names change appropriately. For instance, in the preceding list of reference types 'author' becomes 'journalist', 'director', 'programmer' or 'artist'. This flexibility improves accurate recording of references.

## Adding references

You can enter references by typing in each one yourself. However, because the data in library catalogues and indexes and abstracts are already held in a structured way, it is relatively simple to copy the data from them into your personal database. Sometimes you can search directly from within the software; otherwise you can download the references you find and import them.

Importing is done by matching each field in the source database with those in your database (often called *mapping*): the contents of the author field in the source should go into the author field in your database. Personal bibliographic software provides special import filters to facilitate this. There are numerous database producers who in turn license several large database vendors to market their databases to universities and other research institutions. Each producer and vendor has their own proprietary structure for organising the data they supply. For each producer and vendor combination there will be a different filter to ensure that the data go into the correct fields. You need to know which database you have been searching and which supplier has provided access to select the appropriate filter. They are often named explicitly, so this should not alarm you.

If you do not know the provider or the database, you will need to try to find as close a match as possible. See which filters use the same sort of tags as your downloaded references and try that. You may need to ask your library or IT support staff for assistance if you are using software supported by your institution. If that is not available, most programs have technical help available by email and also have email discussion forums which are frequented by experienced users who are willing to help.

If you can search a database from within your software, you could use it as a very quick way of entering all of the books on your shelf into your personal database. Connect to a large academic library (e.g. the British Library) and enter the ISBN for each book in turn. The full bibliographic record will be returned very quickly since you are searching for something very precise in a specific field. It is a lot faster than typing in the whole reference manually, though you will need to check that it has been downloaded correctly, especially with regard to capitalisation and author names.

## Writing and citing references in your personal bibliographic database

Using bibliographic software while you are writing in your word processor is one of the most productive benefits of this sort of technology. When you want to cite a work either in-text or in a footnote or endnote, switch to your bibliographic program and search for the reference. Copy and paste it into your word processor document and a temporary link to your bibliographic database is inserted. You can save your document and continue working on it for as long as you need to: those temporary links will remain in place.

Eventually, you will need to produce a copy of your work with the citations and bibliography formatted correctly. Tell the program to format them and select which bibliographic format to use. Look at the bibliographies in three books from different publishers and notice how varied their layouts are. For instance, it is fairly standard to have the first-named author first, but there is variety in how the name is shown: 'first name initials, surname', 'surname, first name initials' or simply 'surname, initials'. There will be variety with the other elements as well. Notice that the format of citations (in-text or within footnotes and endnotes) can vary between publishers. A common style in the social sciences and humanities is the 'name–date' system where reference is made in

brackets in the text to the author's surname and the year of publication (as in this book). Sometimes the specific pages are cited or superscript numbers in the text point to footnotes or endnotes, which give variously detailed bibliographic references.

There are several hundred formats with apparently minor differences between them. Some disciplines have preferred reference styles and some have become de facto standards, such as that recommended by the American Psychological Association, known as the APA style. Other common ones include Harvard, Chicago and the Modern Languages Association (MLA) style. It may be that your institution or department has regulations about which style you should use. When submitting a book or article for publication, you will need to follow the advice of the publisher. There are no hard and fast rules from the point of view of ensuring that your references enable people to consult the works you cite, other than ensuring that once you have selected a style to work with you should be consistent in its application throughout a single work. Since bibliographic databases are structured you can get formatted references out of your software very easily. You can also change the style just as easily. With the help of a manual you can also write your own styles.

It may be that you are planning to visit a reference library at some distance from your home. You have explored the library's online catalogue and have downloaded into your database all of the references you are interested in. You can produce a listing of all the books and journals, ordered by their class numbers together with volume and issue information for articles, rather than having to consult the library catalogue again.

## Making notes

### What sorts of notes will be most useful to me?

Whether you are attempting to write a separate section reviewing the literature or you are interweaving it with the whole of your writing, you need to show that you have understood what you have read and have thought about its relevance to exploring your research questions. You're not trying to regurgitate a mass of undigested literature to demonstrate how much work you have done in reading it. It needs to be a process of critical selection rather than encyclopaedic reproduction. You may have found an overwhelming mass of apparently relevant literature (perhaps you might want to sharpen the focus of your research questions to make them researchable within your time constraints). Your research questions are not just for finding the items which seem to address your concerns; they should also provide a focus for what you make notes on. Imagine your questions in conversation with the literature. Ask yourself how the literature addresses your questions: does it answer them, provide illumination, challenge them or refute the assumptions in your questions? By engaging with the literature like this, you will be able to both navigate through the literature and make a tight exploration of your concerns, which should result in a focused piece of writing.

## How can I make my notes?

You may find that the précis or abstract supplied by indexes is an adequate initial summary, but you should try to make it your own if possible. If you own a text (i.e. it is not a library's copy), you can converse with it by highlighting and making notes in the margin. But it is often better to make your own assessment of the arguments and evidence in a summary you create. You will make it more yours and so will be able to use many of your notes in initial drafts of writing. You may think that the real work is done in crafting the final text, but if you have skimped on this stage your writing will be a lot harder. More positively, if you seriously engage with the arguments of the literature you have found, you will find that your writing flows better and with more confidence.

Whether you are reading empirical or theoretical work, you need to assess if the evidence supports the conclusions. If not, why not? How does it seem that it does without actually doing so – what assumptions are made without support? What assumptions are suppressed – why are they not made explicit … is there a weakness in the argument? Identify any slippages in the logic – consult a book about arguments such as Warburton (1996) or Toulmin et al. (1979) or the chapter in Hart (1998) for more detailed guidance.

In short, note enough of the content to represent the points of engagement with your research questions and how this has been deployed rhetorically within the item of literature. Do so with humility and charity, but without being afraid to argue for your point of view. You will find it productive to subject your own engagement to a similar process of scrutinising argumentation.

## How should I manage my notes?

It can be useful to devise your own system of content keywords or tags to apply to notes for each item from the literature. These can flow from the vocabulary you created when you first brainstormed the dimensions of your research questions – and have probably amended. If you are using bibliographic software, you can often apply multiple keywords to each reference. Some allow you to have several notes attached to a reference (particularly useful for longer works where are number of themes will be explored) and then enable you to apply keywords to the separate notes. When you are writing a particular section, if you have used keywords judiciously you will be able to retrieve just the relevant notes. This pulling together of relevant notes will enable you to compare and contrast what the literature has to say about this particular aspect of your research questions and also where there are silences and absences – room for you to contribute something original. You can search your database and print out your notes along with the full bibliographic details. You can then think about and plan your work away from the computer screen, while still being able to reference accurately.

## Writing your literature review

Putting together an extended annotated bibliography is not the same as writing a literature review. Sometimes a formalistic concern with how to construct a literature review can deaden your work. Should you write a discrete section or should you use your limited words to engage with the literature throughout your work? Different disciplines have different conventions here (see also Chapter 28). For example, journal articles in more 'scientific' traditions will tend to separate the literature review from the rest of the text; 'results', too, may be strictly separated from commentary or discussion of their significance. In more 'literary' traditions, or theory-oriented writing, these things are much more interweaved (see Swales, 1990 for an account of these conventions and their history).

Although you are writing to demonstrate that you know the body of work which relates to your research questions, you want to do more than just provide a series of stark signposts. If you were a host at a party, you would not simply point people out to a new arrival with a bald, disinterested summary. Rather, you would pick those bits of someone's character and behaviour which you feel may interest the new arrival so that they will want to go and talk to that other person. So too with a literature review. You are demonstrating why you find various bodies of work interesting or productive for your research questions and you are trying to communicate your keenness to your readers.

You are also *situating* your research questions, teasing out a space for them by a close engagement with the detail of some core work and using a less central work to give a broader context. Frequently this will take the form of

demonstrating that no other study has approached the topic in the way that you propose, or show that certain questions remain unanswered. If you have written a research proposal, much of this writing will have been done at an earlier stage in order to justify the project, so much of the advice in Chapter 7 is also relevant to the writing of a literature review in a final report. Realising how your research is situated does not happen all at once after reading all of the literature. Rather, you read with your research questions in mind, testing them against existing work, reformulating and devising new questions when something novel strikes you or when you make new connections.

## How much is enough – or when to stop reading?

As you get further into your research you'll start finding fewer and fewer references to new sources. It is unlikely that you will ever be intimately acquainted with all of the works in any one field – there is too much published to achieve that and you have only a finite amount of time, and so must prioritise. You will also need to consider the relevance of older literature: it may have been subsumed or superseded by later works. You should be guided by both your evolving research questions and any advisers you may have for your project in determining which are the most important studies to be working with. At some point you have to focus on producing something rather than holding on, expecting to have absolutely the last word. One way to get to this point is to recall the metaphor of being engaged in a conversation with the works you have found. You are never going to meet *everyone* who might have something interesting to say, but if you have got a good coverage of the main people you can position yourself effectively to demonstrate the significance of your arguments. You may feel anxious at the premium placed on originality. Be assured, it is unlikely that something will be published completely unexpectedly which alights on just the same questions as yours. If you have done a systematic literature search and monitored developments in your area through academic networks, you will be aware who is working in broadly the same area as you. If someone is working in an area close to your interests, that may well be a strength, not a problem: it shows that others think it is an area of significance and it may give you someone with whom to explore some of the more arcane areas.

At some point you need to stop reading and to review all that you have covered. Frequently people engaged in an empirical research project will want to write a draft literature review before becoming too involved in data collection, returning to it later for revision. Although this can be a very helpful strategy, be aware that the experience of fieldwork can change ideas about the significance of particular research questions, so that the relevance of early literature reviews is placed in doubt. Some of your early writing will contain interesting ideas, but will undoubtedly require revision as your research questions evolve. Tying your final writing together into a coherent argument, although never easy, should be more straightforward if you have focused on your research questions for the duration of your project and put other interesting ideas to one side to pursue once you have completed the current project.

## Systematic review

Systematic review is a specific form of working with the literature which originated in health studies, but has also been used in more applied, social policy arenas. Its aims differ from the sorts of academic literature reviews we have been discussing in this chapter; but reflecting on the processes can bring both types of reviews into perspective. Its broad aim is to distil and summarise accumulated evidence gleaned from a wide range of sources to support clinical or policy decisions, rendering them evidence based. The synthesis aims to provide reliable evidence through explicit and transparent procedures of selection and evaluation of a range of relevant evidence (which is not limited to published and grey literature). The first step is to have a clearly defined and researchable question; this differs little from many research aims. The question then drives the selection of items to include in the summary: those which are found wanting in terms of content or methodology are excluded, based on explicit criteria – the aim being to avoid the risk of researcher bias, which is a possibility with expert 'narrative reviews' (Akobeng, 2005). Sometimes the data presented in included studies is agglomerated (again using explicit procedures) and a meta-analysis is performed. This approach aims to provide a robust and reliable summary of disparate research evidence to enable health or social policy practitioners to make more secure interventions.

**BOX 6.3**

## ABSTRACT OF AN ARTICLE REPORTING A SYSTEMATIC REVIEW OF LITERATURE

- **Purpose:** To review the effectiveness of cognitive behaviour therapy (CBT) as a treatment for anxiety disorders of childhood and adolescence.

- **Method:** Studies were included if they treated young people (under 19 years) with diagnosed anxiety disorder (excluding trials solely treating phobia, PTSD or OCD), had a no-treatment control group, and used diagnosis as an outcome variable. A search of the literature, incorporating electronic databases, hand search and expert consultation, yielded 10 randomised controlled trials that were appropriate for inclusion.

- **Results:** The outcome of interest was remission of anxiety disorder. Employing conservative criteria, the remission rate in the CBT groups (56.5 per cent) was higher than that in the control groups (34.8 per cent). The pooled odds ratio was 3:3 (CI = 1.9–5.6), suggesting that CBT has a significant effect.

- **Conclusions:** CBT is useful for the treatment of anxiety in children over the age of 6 years. However, we still know little about the treatment of younger children or about the comparative **efficacy** of alternative treatments. Most of the trials were efficacy trials, and have limited **generalisability**. Reporting of many aspects of the trials was weak.

*Source*: Cartwright-Hatton et al,, 2004

Box 6.3 shows the abstract of an article reporting a systematic review. Note that the purpose of review is clearly stated at the outset. Strict criteria were employed to decide which studies to include. The results reflect a pooling of the data from the 10 trials included in the review, so is the product of a meta-analysis. The relevance for health care practitioners who treat children with anxiety disorders is clearly spelled out, and limitations of the scope of the review, and the quality of the research evidence reviewed, is noted.

This process reduces complexity for good reason, but it is not the only way of approaching a research question. Returning to the metaphor of the conversations at a party I have deployed in this chapter helps give some perspective. To summarise what most people were saying at the party is not the only (or necessarily most) interesting thing that can be said about it: there are many stories which can be told about the conversations.

## Conclusion

The experienced sociologist Howard Becker advises a variety of methods for avoiding the trap of 'conventional ideas [becoming] the uninspected premises of their research' (1998: 7), including trying to develop research questions initially *before* a detailed examination of the literature. Of course, all of your previous study will contribute to formulating those initial questions, but they will still have a roughness and energy which you should not lose under the weight of the literature. Counterbalancing this, Becker stresses that it is not productive to reinvent the wheel: asking research questions that have already been answered is pointless. Rather, he describes producing research as akin to making a table: you do not have to make all the parts from scratch to make your very own table, but should use those prefabricated bits which have been tried and tested to enable your creative efforts to shine through on the other bits (Becker and Richards, 1986: 141–142). He concludes his chapter with advice that seems perfect for ending this one: 'Use the literature, don't let it use you' (1986: 149).

## FURTHER READING

Becker and Richards (1986) provides a helpful guide, written from the point of view of experienced researchers, to the writing of research reports in general, including literature reviews. Hart's books (1998, 2001) are more focused on the literature review per se, giving detailed guidance on finding materials and

*(Continued)*

*(Continued)*

writing creative literature reviews. Akobeng (2005), Greenhalgh (1997) and Kaczorowski (2009) give useful discussions of systematic reviews from a health studies perspective, while the websites of the EPPI-centre and the Campbell Collaboration give both brief overviews and links to studies in other areas of policy.

## Student Reader (Seale, 2004b): relevant readings

2    C. Wright Mills: 'On intellectual craftsmanship'

28   John M. Swales: 'Episodes in the history of the research article'

## Journal articles illustrating or discussing the approaches described in this chapter

A traditional, scholarly, critical literature review:

Scambler, G. (2009) 'Health-related stigma', Sociology of Health & Illness, 31 (3): 441–455.

A 'systematic' review of quantitative studies:

Horrocks, S., Anderson, E. and Salisbury, C. (2002) 'Systematic review of whether nurse practitioners working in primary care can provide equivalent care to doctors', British Medical Journal, 324: 819–823.

A 'systematic review' of qualitative studies:

Morton, R.L., Tong, A., Howard, K., Snelling, P. and Webster, A.C. (2010) 'The views of patients and carers in treatment decision making for chronic kidney disease: systematic review and thematic synthesis of qualitative studies', British Medical Journal, 340: c112.

An analysis and critique of the systematic reviewing movement:

Moreira, T. (2007) 'Entangled evidence: knowledge making in systematic reviews in healthcare', Sociology of Health & Illness, 29 (2): 180–197.

## Web links

Quoting and paraphrasing sources:

http://writing.wisc.edu/Handbook/QuotingSources.html

Writing a literature review:

www.canberra.edu.au/studyskills/writing/literature#fulltop

The literature review: a few tips:

www.writing.utoronto.ca/advice/specific-types-of-writing/literature-review

Systems for referencing citations:

www.lib.monash.edu.au/tutorials/citing/harvard.html

www.lib.monash.edu.au/tutorials/citing/vancouver.html

Sources of literature:

Library of Congress Gateway to Library Catalogs: www.loc.gov/z3950/

The British Library Public Catalogue: http://catalogue.bl.uk

Index to Theses (UK): www.theses.com

Online Dissertation Services (USA): www.umi.com/en-US/products/dissertations

The European Association for Grey Literature Exploitation: http://opensigle.inist.fr

ABYZ News Links – gateway to news media: www.abyznewslinks.com

Bibliographic software:

EndNote: www.endnote.com

RefWorks: www.refworks.com

CiteULike: www.citeulike.org

Systematic review:

Campbell Collaboration: www.campbellcollaboration.org

EPPI-centre http://eppi.ioe.ac.uk

The Cochrane Collaboration: www.cochrane.org

## KEY CONCEPTS FOR REVIEW

**Advice:** Use these, along with the review questions in the next section, to test your knowledge of the contents of this chapter. Try to define each of the key concepts listed here; if you have understood this chapter you should be able to do this. Check your definitions against the definition in the glossary at the end of the book.

| | |
|---|---|
| Abstracts | Library of Congress system |
| Alert service | Meta-analysis |
| Bibliographic indexes | Nesting |
| Boolean searches | Proximity operators |
| Control lists | Query |
| Database | Record |
| Dewey Decimal system | Reference management |
| Evidence-based | Reference styles |
| Fields | References |
| Grey literature | Search terms |
| Import filters | Systematic review |
| Importing references | Truncation |
| Keywords | Wildcards |

## Review questions

1 Where should you search for literature when planning a social research project?
2 Describe the use of keywords and search terms when interrogating a library database.
3 Explain what wildcards, Boolean operators and reference management software can be useful for.
4 What principles should you bear in mind when taking notes from reading?
5 How do you know when to stop reading for a literature review?
6 Describe the purpose and some of the procedures used in carrying out systematic reviews. How do these reviews differ from conventional (non-systematic) reviews?

## Workshop and discussion exercises

1 For a given research topic (take, for example, one of the topics listed in Box 27.10 on page 492 explore and compare the coverage of two or more of the following resources for finding academic literature on the subject:

(a) Your university library catalogue.
(b) A searchable journal database.
(c) An Internet search engine such as Google.

2 Examine a journal article reporting original social or cultural research on a topic that interests you. Consider answers to the following questions:

(a) To what extent is the literature review separated from the rest of the report?
(b) What connections are made between the analysis of data and the literature review?
(c) Many literature reviews have a funnel structure, with broad concerns being discussed at the outset, narrowing down to specific questions explored in the research study. Is this literature review like this? Identify sections where broad concerns are discussed and where specific research questions are identified.
(d) In the concluding section of the report, what references are made by the author to the concerns raised in the literature review?
(e) Try to find an important article or book on this subject that this researcher has failed to spot.

3 Find and consult a systematic review of randomised controlled trials:

(a) How explicit does it make its procedures?
(b) How do these differ from an article reporting a conventional (not 'systematic') review of literature?

# 7

# RESEARCH QUESTIONS AND PROPOSALS

Moira Kelly

| Chapter Contents | |
|---|---|

This chapter describes the process of developing a social research project and writing a research proposal. This process is closely linked to research design (see Chapter 8). A research proposal incorporates a research question, a plan for investigating it, and attends to the wider context in which a study conducted. The proposal is a key tool for developing a research project. It is a document that can be used to communicate your planned study to others, to manage your study as a project that produces data and analysis, and also serves as a template for writing up your study. The emphasis of this chapter is on the practicalities of developing research that works, or in other words, produces analysis that adds to what is already known, is rigorous, relevant and accessible to the audiences you wish to reach. After an initial discussion of the importance of developing skills in constructing viable research studies, this chapter will review approaches to devising good research questions and provide guidelines as to what a research proposal should contain, and why.

## From theory to practice

Becoming a social scientist as opposed to someone with a qualification in a social science is demonstrated by the ability to apply the knowledge gained during academic study to social research. As Weber (in Gerth and Mills, 1948) points out, unlike art 'scientific work is chained to the course of progress' (p. 137). As social scientists, we aim to build on what is already known. In the same way that medical practice is defined by

the application of medical knowledge in the treatment of illness, the craft of the social *scientist* is research (see, for example, Becker, 1998). To refer to Weber again, we need as social scientists to achieve a balance between creativity and passion for a topic with rigorous scientific endeavour:

> Ideas come when we do not expect them, and not when we are brooding and searching at our desks. Yet ideas would certainly not come to mind had we not brooded at our desks and searched for answers with passionate devotion. (Weber in Gerth and Mills, 1948: 136)

This can be taken here to apply to the relationship between creativity and practice in empirical social research. Practical skills in effective planning and application of the methodologies described in this text are valued by employers of social science graduates. These are sometimes referred to as skills in project management. For example, the main social research funding body in the UK, the Economic and Social Research Council (ESRC), states that its activities (as a research funding body) should 'advance knowledge and provide trained social scientists who meet the needs of users and beneficiaries' (ESRC, 2003). Contemporary research involves considerable attention to pragmatic concerns linked to good practice. Part of the training expected by institutions such as the ESRC is a hands-on understanding of research design and process. Social science students, whether undertaking undergraduate or postgraduate courses, are expected to carry out at least one research project. This is where the emphasis shifts from education to training in order to facilitate the development of transferable skills in developing, carrying out and writing up research projects, with researchers demonstrating the ability to apply skills rather than just to acquire them.

## Research questions

All research includes four basic ingredients: the initial research question; finding out what others have done; refining the initial question; and answering the question (Thomas, 2009: ix). The research question and its development is therefore the foundation stone for the whole research project (Thomas, 2009) and consequently it is necessary to take care in constructing it. This may seem counter-intuitive. We ask questions all the time, so how hard can it be? Developing good research questions, however, involves a level of craft. One way of thinking about the value of good questions is to consider how news interviewers ask questions. There are many news interviewers, but only a few are household names, known for their skill in framing questions in such a way as to find out what they want to know, from often resistant interviewees. Even seemingly straightforward research questions need to be considered critically. They need to be relevant, achievable and clear. New researchers often underestimate the importance of spending time working on research questions (and developing proposals around them), putting this work to one side in their enthusiasm to get going on the project.

Research questions provide direction for your study (O'Leary, 2010), so when asking a research question it is important to consider the possible ways in which it may be answered and refining it in relation to what you are interested in finding out about. This is the basis of devising a 'good' research question. Most questions have numerous possible answers and ways in which they can be answered. Take, for example, an apparently simple question such as a child might ask a parent: 'Why do people have wars?' They are likely to receive an answer such as 'Because people do not like each other'. A child may accept such an answer but an adult is unlikely to do so. As we get older and know more, we learn how to focus our questions and ask them in such a way that the response will add to what we know. When you ask a question it is framed, usually unconsciously, to elicit the answer you require in the form you would like it in. Research questions are also 'framed' in this way, but the process of developing them makes the framing more explicit, subjecting it to critique and justification, at a conscious level. Social research projects are not conducted in social isolation as a personal pursuit. They are meant to produce findings that contribute to current knowledge about topics, often for a range of audiences. This means that you need to be able to confidently describe how you came to make decisions regarding your choice of topic and question, such as 'Why this topic?', 'Why this research question?', 'Why now?' and 'Why not other questions?'.

Research questions take many different forms and may also be referred to as *research problems*, *research aims* or *hypotheses*. Some of the different types of research question can be seen in Box 7.1. There is often a lot of interest in asking questions that require explanations. However, it may be appropriate to undertake a descriptive study first. For instance, consider a study of political protests. Our question may be 'Why do people take part in political protests about climate change?' Before we ask this question we arguably need to know what political protests about climate change look like, whether there are different forms of protest, and what the different forms look like. In this sense we need a good description of political protests about climate change before we can ask why people take part in them. If we do not have this information, we make unexamined assumptions about the phenomenon we are studying. This information might already be available in the research literature, and if it is, we need to be clear about the context in which our question has been constructed.

BOX 7.1

## TYPES OF RESEARCH QUESTION

| | |
|---|---|
| Describing | What forms do political protests take? |
| Taking an aspect of the issue of interest and examining it in detail | What form does women's involvement in climate change protests take? |
| Explicitly drawing upon theory to examine an issue | Does social movement theory explain the emergence of climate change protest groups? |
| Comparing attributes | Does age group affect the likelihood of participating in a political protest? |
| Explaining | Why do some political protests involve violent conflict and not others? |
| Assessing whether an intervention works | Does specialist training for police officers who police large political protests reduce arrests? |

The way a research question is asked will be influenced by the social science discipline we come from. For example, a psychologist may frame the question 'Why do people take part in political protests?' in terms of the social psychology of group participation. A sociologist may frame it in terms of power relationships between the public and the state. An anthropologist may frame the question in terms of the culture of political protest. The way questions are framed also implies the methodological approach to be taken (see also Chapter 3 on theory and research). If it is framed as 'How many people take part in political protests?', a quantitative design will be appropriate. If it is framed as 'Why do people take part in political protests?', either a quantitative or qualitative design could be appropriate. If the question is 'What are the stories told by people who take part in political protests?', a qualitative design is most likely to be suitable. Decisions to use a quantitative or qualitative approach should be influenced by the nature of the research question, with the approach chosen being appropriate to the question asked. However, most researchers will have a preference for one methodological approach or

the other and this is likely to influence the way in which they formulate their research question.

## Quantitative research

Quantitative research involves deductive reasoning, meaning that all the relevant variables are identified before data collection begins. The two main quantitative research designs in social research are the *survey* and the *experiment* (see Chapter 8 for a full account of the design of these kinds of study). In survey research questions may be descriptive, such as 'Who takes part in political protests?' This would involve identifying a number of categories and possible characteristics of people such as age, gender, socio-economic status and ethnicity. If this information is already available, the relationship between different variables can be examined and comparisons made. These relationships are often presented in the form of a hypothesis. This is a statement specifying the relationship between two or more variables. The hypothesis is accepted or rejected depending upon there being a statistically significant difference between the variables.

For example, a hypothesis could be stated as: 'Men are more likely than women to take part in political protests.' This hypothesis would then be tested by seeing if gender and participation in political protests are associated, and often by using a statistical test to see if this association is likely to hold true in the population from which the sample of people included in the survey has been drawn at random (see Chapters 9 and 19).

The experimental method in social research is used to evaluate the effect of an intervention on behaviour. A hypothesis is set up at the start and then tested. A study may be set up with participants randomly allocated to an 'intervention' or 'control' group. For example, a hypothesis 'Exposure to negative information about climate change positively influences support for political protest against climate change' could be constructed. Under 'laboratory' conditions, volunteer participants in the intervention group could be shown a film about the negative effects of climate change and the control group shown a film about a neutral topic such as teaching languages to children. A questionnaire about political protests could then be given to assess whether support for protest against climate change differs between the control and intervention group.

## Qualitative research

Qualitative research is often based on *induction* (see Chapter 2). This means that efforts are made to avoid assumptions about what the research findings might look like before the data are collected and analysed. Given the inductive model, some qualitative researchers may be resistant to setting out a formal question and specifying details of how to answer it at the start of a project. However, even the most avowedly 'unstructured' qualitative research eventually involves the identification of a research question, even though this is developed and refined during data collection, having been no more than a 'foreshadowed problem' at the outset (see Chapter 14 on ethnography). At the very least, a general topic will need to be defined, and an initial research site chosen.

As with quantitative studies, qualitative studies may involve different types of research question depending on the methodology chosen. Some studies may set out to describe the content of a dataset in quite a general, relatively superficial way. A simple research question may be 'Describe people's views about climate change'. However, initial analysis of the data may highlight further subquestions to be explored in more depth, possibly drawing upon relevant theory. For example, the question may arise, 'How are political affiliations used by activists to explain their involvement in climate change protests?' inspired by 'new social movement' theory that indicates political affiliations to be of potential importance in influencing activism.

In most studies (qualitative and quantitative) a number of additional research questions arise following the first phase of data analysis. Depending upon time available, these questions can be either flagged up as questions for future research or set up as new questions (related to the core question set at the start) and examined in further, in-depth analysis (see Kelly, 2010). Decisions will need to be made about which questions to pursue in depth. Having described the issues involved in setting research questions, let us consider the practical issues involved in developing a research question.

## Developing a research question

What are you interested in investigating? You may have quite a clear question in your mind, or have a general topic you are interested in. Alternatively, you may have no ideas at all, or, as is more often the case, have too many ideas to choose from. Ideas for topics for social research projects may come from many different directions. Research projects often emerge from earlier research which has identified new research questions that need to be investigated. A researcher might want to see if findings from a study in one area can be replicated in another. For example, one could apply a research design used to investigate people in another country to the UK context. Alternatively, research questions may emerge in response to social problems or need, or a news story about an interesting issue.

Most people have a few ideas of things they would like to investigate at the start, though sometimes these may be quite general topics, such as 'climate change' or 'childhood obesity'. One way of developing research topics is to brainstorm ideas. Work with a whiteboard or take a sheet of paper and write down whatever comes into your head when you ask yourself: 'What research topics interest me?' If you have a general topic that you are interested in but no ideas for possible research questions, take a piece of paper, put your topic in a circle in the centre and start to consider different aspects of your idea. Think about what you know about your idea, and what you would like to know. Write these down and make links. You may want to go through this process for a few topics. Having done this, you will find that some ideas shift into the foreground and start to form up as prototype questions. You can then produce concept maps of your research questions (O'Leary, 2010), highlighting possible ways you could look at

them and the assumptions that underpin your ideas. This will expand the possible ways you can formulate questions. It will also help to identify which literature may be relevant to your research questions. It is good practice to think expansively at the start and then focus in. It is also useful to talk to others about your ideas and use their comments to facilitate your thinking. For example, in a study of political protests you might be interested in the views and experiences of protesters, but discussion with peers or a supervisor may highlight other possible questions such as the views and experiences of the police regarding political protests. It is good to consider a range of options at the start.

Once you have decided on a research question that interests you, you will need to review the literature to see what is already known about the topic. This may lead to further development of your question and focusing it to address a particular gap in knowledge about the topic. It is helpful to record the process through which decisions are made about research questions as you go along as you may be asked about this later in your research. Box 7.2 shows stages in developing a research question. At this point you will be ready to put together a research proposal.

---

**BOX 7.2**

## STAGES IN DEVELOPING RESEARCH QUESTIONS

- Identify possible research topics.
- Identify possible questions.
- Consider alternative questions.
- Break down your proposed question(s).
- Define your terms, identify assumptions that underpin the question(s).
- Choose a question.
- Check the literature to see whether the chosen question (in the form it is in) has already been answered.
- Refine your question if necessary.
- Develop a project proposal around your research question.
- If necessary, reframe question in the light of issues raised by constructing the proposal.
- Carry out your study.
- Go back to your question from time to time to check that you are still on the track you started on.

## Peer review and critical appraisal

The key tool in research design is the research proposal. The main reason for writing a proposal is to present your research design for critical appraisal. This may be informal, such as discussing your research with peers. This is the 'friendly' version of peer review. It can be valuable to receive comments from others at various stages when designing a study. These can be from a supervisor or tutor, fellow student, colleague, experts in the field, or increasingly a person representative of the group of people who are going to be studied. Presenting ideas to someone for comment at an early stage helps to develop them. Comments may reinforce some areas, and highlight areas not presented clearly or which need more work, or aspects which are untenable in some way. Feedback can be on academic or practical issues, both of which are important. For example, there is a need to know that the research question has been well constructed, but also that it is possible to gain access to the data needed to answer it.

Research proposals may also be formally reviewed or assessed as part of a course of study, as an application for funding or for ethics committee approval. Presentation of the research design for critical appraisal means that the audience for your research is a central consideration from the start. The proposal is also a link to the social scientific community and to a wider community who may have an interest in your research.

It cannot be assumed that the audience to which your proposed study is presented will be passive; they may well want to influence your study. A key issue in research design is the way in which the research problem is defined and, as is argued in Chapter 4, social and cultural researchers need to evaluate critically the definitions of social problems offered to them by policy makers. It is important that we, as social scientists, use our skills and knowledge to define the research problem. Although we can use common-sense concepts up to a point, we cannot expect such concepts to do the analytical work of theoretical concepts. The research proposal stage is often the point at which such issues are decided, and this will influence the conduct of the research. If you are clear about what you are doing and why, it is much easier to communicate this to others. Presenting the design in a proposal forces researchers to sort out their ideas and make them accessible to others at an early stage. This may seem like hard work but communicating our research to others is an essential part of the job. It also enables us to define the research on our terms, as social scientists.

## The research proposal as design tool

The need to produce a proposal in a particular format to satisfy the requirements of others may at times seem like a constraint. However, writing a proposal enables the researcher to set out the study from beginning to end so that the different elements that need to be included can be considered. It can be used to develop ideas and consider different methods, meaning that the initial draft of the proposal may look quite different from the final version. We often see things more clearly when we write them down. Drafting a research proposal allows you to design the study that you would like to do within the constraints you have, such as time, access to the population you are interested in and competence in particular methods.

Proposals for quantitative research could be said to be relatively straightforward, with information fitting into certain categories. Standards used in quantitative research have to some extent influenced expectations for qualitative research proposals. This can present a challenge for those proposing to carry out exploratory qualitative studies in which it may be counterproductive to pre-specify everything at the proposal stage. When using qualitative methods there is, therefore, the need to be creative and flexible in putting ideas across, especially if the audience is used to receiving proposals for quantitative work. The most important thing is to be clear about what you are doing and why.

## Writing a research proposal

The start of a research project is a time when you can think quite broadly about topics and methods. Later on you will need to focus in and be more specific about how you intend to turn your idea into a project. This is the stage at which it is useful to begin to identify and develop possible research questions. Let us consider developing a research proposal for a study about students' experience of paid employment.

Some possible questions related to this topic are given in Box 7.3. Writing down such questions is the first part of drafting a proposal. It can be seen how one topic can generate a wide range of possible research questions. To develop the project requires moving beyond the stage of jotting down questions, and structuring the project so that what you are planning to do, why you are planning it, and how you intend to do it are clear. Krathwohl (1988) suggests that signposts in the way a proposal is presented are helpful. These may be subheadings indicating main areas to be included. I will use one such sequence of subheadings now, to explain what can usefully be placed under each.

---

**BOX 7.3**

### POSSIBLE QUESTION FOR A STUDY OF STUDENTS' EXPERIENCE OF PAID EMPLOYMENT

- What is the proportion of students who work for pay and is this increasing?
- How many hours a week do students work on average in paid employment?
- What factors influence them working, for example class, age, sex, geographical region, ethnic group?
- What types of jobs do they do?
- How does having to work affect their studies?
- Does working while a student increase chances of getting future work?
- What sort of jobs do they do?
- How do they feel about having to work?
- How does working affect the social aspect of student life?

---

## Title

The title should describe briefly what the project is about. For example:

> Employment patterns in full-time undergraduates: proposal for a survey of students in London

In this title, information is provided on the subject area, target audience and where it will be carried out. Your name, and the names of any others involved if it is a collaboration, should also be stated with the title.

## Abstract

Research proposals often have a short summary of approximately 200–300 words after the title. This is usually written after the proposal has been developed. It should contain a short overview of your proposed study, including a brief introduction to your chosen topic, your research question, an overview of the methods to be used and how the findings are likely to be applied. It is good practice to develop the skill of writing abstracts as they can be used to tell people in a brief, clear way about your research. Abstracts for two proposed studies are shown in Box 7.4.

---

**BOX 7.4**

## ABSTRACTS FOR TWO STUDIES USING CONTRASTING METHODS

### Employment patterns in full-time undergraduates: survey of students in London

The reduction of state funding for undergraduate education in the UK means that an increasing number of students need to work part-time in order to support themselves during their degree courses. Little is currently known about the impact part-time paid employment has on students, both in terms of the effect on their academic performance and on their overall quality of life, including stress. This study aims to describe the patterns of part-time employment in a sample of second-year students studying at a large London university. A questionnaire will be sent to 500 students, randomly sampled from a list of all part-time and full-time students registered at the university, covering four main areas: demographic characteristics; type of job; academic performance; and quality of life. SPSS will be used to carry out the data analysis. Findings will be disseminated to students via relevant websites and to policy and research audiences with a focus on undergraduate education.

### Employment patterns in full-time undergraduates: qualitative interview study

The reduction of state funding for undergraduate education in the UK means that an increasing number of students need to work part-time in order to support themselves during their degree courses. Little is currently known about the impact part-time paid employment has on students, both in terms of the effect on their academic performance and on their overall quality of life, including stress. This study aims to describe the experiences of part-time paid employment in students at one London university. Qualitative interviews will be conducted with 20 second-year students (10 male and 10 female, in a variety of subject areas). The interview will cover four main areas: the nature of the paid work engaged in; reasons for working; effect on academic performance; and effect on their quality of life. Thematic analysis of the interview data will be conducted with the assistance of NVivo qualitative analysis software. Findings will be disseminated to students via relevant websites and to policy and research audiences with a focus on undergraduate education.

---

## Background or introduction

It is then important to introduce the subject and supply some background information. Social science covers all aspects of social life, and uses a wide range of theoretical perspectives and methodologies. Potential readers may need to be able to understand your proposal without necessarily having a thorough knowledge of the particular field. Similarly, they may not be an expert in the methodological approach chosen. The main aim of a reader may be to appreciate the nature and feasibility of the study, rather than to gain in-depth knowledge of the subject and methodology.

Continuing the example of a hypothetical study of students and paid employment, I would now write about the following things:

One reason for choosing this topic is the continuing debate about funding for higher education in the UK. State funding has been cut and there is a lot of media coverage on the hardship faced by students, suggesting that an increasing number of students have to work part time in order to support themselves. I would like to explore this phenomenon, to see if this is really the case, to what extent it is happening, and what effects it is having on students who have to work to help support themselves. For example, it may affect the time that students have to study, thus producing poorer examination results, or it may affect their social lives in adverse ways.

An introductory statement would point out all of this, but do so quite briefly, in order to give the reader a quick preview of the problems addressed by the research project.

## Literature review

Following the introductory statement, it would be important to undertake a brief review of the relevant literature (which would be expanded in the main research report). The literature review is important because one of the first things a reader will want to know is whether this research has been done before. Any major research in the field needs to be described. It can then be shown how the project will add to current knowledge. Librarians can advise on a range of resources which may be helpful. A major source of relatively up-to-date information can be accessed through the Internet and computer databases that contain abstracts of recently published research. Chapter 6 contains more detailed guidance on this aspect of doing research.

The literature review will reflect whether the study is aiming to influence social policy or social theory, as our continuing example shows:

One way of taking forward my proposed study of students is to include reference to current and previous higher education *policy* in the literature review. This emphasises the policy relevance of my research.

Alternatively, or in addition, I could discuss literature with a strong social *theory* perspective, such as interactionist studies (see Chapter 3) of the meanings students attach to paid employment while studying full time.

Thus, the type of literature explored here will have a bearing on the eventual use of the findings of your study. It is a good idea to highlight recent publications from both theory and policy. Most contemporary social research is expected to discuss policy implications on some level, and many policy makers now understand the value of social theory in providing novel ways of seeing social issues. The literature reviewed may therefore need to include reference to both of these.

The extent of the literature review at the proposal stage will depend on the nature of the study, the time available, and to whom it will be submitted. Funding bodies will send a proposal out for peer review, so you need to ensure that you have included research by any key people in the field. On the other hand, it is important to be selective in your reading, and stick to the things that are directly relevant to your research. This is a skill in itself. Finding and exploring the literature can be very time-consuming. If you have time, you may wish to contact people who are currently working in the field who can give you an idea of any work in progress.

A qualitative research proposal may involve a less comprehensive literature review at this stage, as data analysis may inform which literature is relevant. For example, if you are undertaking an exploratory study of students and paid work, you could assume that working is found to be stressful and undertake an extensive review of the literature on student stress. However, it may be that your data analysis indicates that students find working a positive experience which enables them to make friends outside college and gives them money to go out. In this case it would be better to review some of the relevant literature at the proposal stage, but allow the data analysis to inform a more extensive literature review. However, you will need to ensure that you build in time at the data analysis stage of the project to do this.

## Aims and objectives

Now that the relevance of the area to be investigated has been highlighted, the research question needs to be defined more precisely. In research proposals, research questions are often framed as *aims*, which describe what your research intends to achieve. How specific the research question is made at this stage will depend on what is to be discovered. You may wish to set up a hypothesis. For example, one could try to see whether the following statement is true or false:

> Full-time undergraduate students who are in paid employment are more likely to experience psychological stress than those who do not work.

On the other hand, a research question for a quantitative or qualitative study could be:

> To describe the effects of paid employment on the lives of undergraduate students.

A number of objectives may be drawn up which describe what you need to do to achieve your aim, and thus address your research problem. For example, in relation to a research problem similar to the first one shown in Box 7.4, an objective could be:

> To undertake a survey of full-time undergraduate students to describe the patterns of undergraduate employment in London.

This would include the number of students who work, their income, the number of hours worked per week, factors influencing the decision to take up or not take up work, their perceptions of the effects of the work upon their studies, and their examination results.

Objectives must be clear, and it should be easy to decide whether they have been achieved or not. Definitions of the research problem or hypothesis and objectives are, as previously stated, an important part of a proposal. It is therefore important to spend some time working these out. In exploratory research, the objectives may need to be quite broad. It is not uncommon for inexperienced researchers to get carried away with the methodology or idea and lose sight of whether the method will achieve the objectives. It is advisable to check them against each other regularly when developing your proposal. Pragmatic factors such as the time available may influence your research problem and objectives.

## Methods

The way in which aims and objectives will be achieved will be set out in this section. An explanation of the *methods* of data collection and analysis to be used (e.g. a survey based on random probability sampling, or discourse analysis of interview transcripts) and an explanation of why these methods are the most appropriate will be needed. For example, I could say:

> In order to ascertain patterns of part-time employment in students a survey of a random sample of 100 undergraduates in one university will be undertaken.

Alternatively, I could propose that:

> Unstructured interviews with five working and five non-working students will be carried out. A comparative analysis of interview transcripts will be carried out, using discourse analysis, to explore how the students construct the meaning of employment and studying in their lives.

The methods section should also include other information about how the research will be carried out, including the sampling, recruitment of respondents, establishing access to the field and, in quantitative studies, what variables you intend to include in the analysis. The emphasis here will be influenced by the method. For example, a survey of students could be through face-to-face interview, a postal questionnaire or telephone interview. Therefore I need to specify how I will carry out the survey. In a study using discourse analysis of interview transcripts, I need to set out what form the interviews with students will take, such as how I introduce the topic, and what areas will be covered.

## Data analysis

A short summary of how you intend to analyse the data should be included. This is relevant to both quantitative and qualitative research. For example, you need to include the key variables you will use for subgroup analysis such as age, sex, ethnic group. Any statistical data analysis packages you plan to use should be stated (e.g. SPSS). Methods of qualitative analysis should also be included where possible, and any qualitative data analysis computer programs specified (e.g. NVivo). How you will ensure the reliability and validity of your findings should be clarified here and in the methods section (see Chapter 30).

For example, in an online questionnaire survey of students, I might seek to establish trust in reliability and validity by saying:

> I will pilot the questionnaire with a small group of students before sending it out to the main sample. I will check to see whether any of the questions are ambiguous and interpreted differently by different people.

Statistical methods that will be used to ensure that findings from the survey are valid and reliable can also be stated. Statistical methods can be used to assess the likelihood of findings coming about through chance because a sample has been studied rather than the whole population.

In order to use such statistics you need to ensure that you have included enough people in your sample. Methods of sampling and making statistical inferences about the population from which the sample has been chosen are explored further in Chapters 9 and 19.

Reliability and validity are also important in qualitative research, though, as you will see in Chapter 30, it is sometimes felt necessary to modify quantitative criteria for establishing these things in qualitative studies. However, the broad principles are often the same, and frequently involve ensuring consistency and accuracy in the way the data are collected and analysed. In a study involving open-ended interviews with students I might say that:

> I plan to use a short topic guide with all the interviewees, but also to use open-ended questions which will allow any new topics I had not initially incorporated to be added to the topics included.

I would state that:

> In order to maximise the reliability of the findings all interviews will be transcribed and a number of categories produced based on an initial reading of the transcripts. Each interview will then be systematically analysed using these categories. Written analysis will be supported through extracts from the data.

## Ethical issues

As shown in Chapter 5, social researchers are expected to take ethical issues into account when doing research, and this needs to be discussed in the proposal. This largely involves attention to ethical principles regarding the treatment of research participants. The amount of attention to ethical issues required depends upon the sensitivity of the study proposed. For example, ethical issues surrounding interviews about sexual health are likely to be much more sensitive than interviews about work patterns. It is important that no harm, physical or psychological, will come to anyone taking part in your research.

Ethical issues in social research are not always clear-cut, but a key one is the preservation of confidentiality and the privacy of people involved. For example, in my proposed study I need to consider how I will ensure that individual students will not be identifiable when I present my findings. I also need to consider how I will gain consent from the students I want to interview. One possibility would be to state that:

> I will give all potential interviewees a letter with information about the study and its purpose, and ask them to sign a consent form. I will ensure that the interviews will be identifiable only by myself through a coding system.

Some organisations that sponsor or fund research require that under certain circumstances (e.g. research involving human or animal participants) formal approval from a research ethics committee is gained from the outset. This is particularly common in health-related research. If this is the case, a letter indicating approval by such a committee may need to be attached to the proposal.

## Dissemination and policy relevance

Dissemination of research findings is an issue that is receiving increasing emphasis, especially from bodies that fund research. Social and cultural research findings are used in two main ways: application to social policy, and building social theory. Social scientists have been criticised in the past for not sharing their research findings with those who may use them. Many funding bodies now require that applications for funding include plans for communication and details of how findings will be shared with users.

Continuing my hypothetical example, I might say that:

> The research will contribute to knowledge about the effects of employment on academic standards and student welfare.

I could argue that it has policy relevance in that:

> The research will provide direction for the development of support services for students and will contribute to policy debates about levels of government financial support for students.

The study could also contribute to the development of social theory. For example, I could argue that:

> Discourse analysis of interview transcripts will contribute to new understandings of how people construct narratives of self-identity in relation to work and studying.

Additionally, I might say that:

> A report will be written and submitted to the National Union of Students and the university Student Welfare Department, and it is planned to submit a paper to the next Psychology Association conference.

## References and appendices

Any references to other studies made in the text should be listed at the end of the proposal. Referencing should be done according to a standard system such as the Harvard referencing system (if you type this into Google, there are many links to websites with guides explaining this), which requires standard information about books and articles to be presented in a particular order (e.g. author, date, title, publisher). Place any appendices after the references, in the order in which they have been mentioned. Appendices will include any relevant papers you intend to use, such as questionnaires, topic guides and consent forms.

## Resources

Good project planning will consider what resources are needed in order for the proposed study to be successful. Resources include: money (funding); appropriate skills and training (e.g. in literature searching; computer-aided data analysis skills); access to sites and participants; time; and supervision and support. Possible resources needed for a survey and a qualitative interview study can be seen in Box 7.5.

study can be seen in Box 7.5.

---

BOX 7.5

## RESOURCES NEEDED FOR TWO DIFFERENT KINDS OF PROJECT

### Survey

- Training in questionnaire design.
- Printing costs of questionnaire.
- Postage of questionnaires.
- SPSS data analysis package.
- Training in statistical analysis.
- Conference registration fees and travel costs.
- Statistician's time.

### Qualitative study

- Training in qualitative interviewing.
- Training in qualitative data analysis.
- Digital recorder.
- Travel costs/interviewee expenses.
- Transcription of interviews.
- Qualitative data analysis program.
- Conference registration fees and travel costs.

---

Formal applications for funding will usually require detailed budget breakdowns. A proposal should show that plans have been tailored so that they are feasible within budgetary limits. Let us imagine that in my study I had planned to send a postal questionnaire to all the 2,000 full-time undergraduate students at my university. I have managed to gain a small grant from an interested organisation for postage and printing of questionnaires. However, taking into account all the postage and printing costs, I can survey only 500 students. Similarly, in the study involving unstructured interviews I need to visit interviewees in their homes, which means that I need a budget for travel. This, together with other factors such as the time involved in travelling, has prompted my decision to limit the number of interviews I will undertake.

## Schedule or timetable

It is valuable to have some form of structured timetable for a project. We often set ourselves unrealistic timescales for projects, such as underestimating how long it will take to gain access to

---

the people we need to interview, or by not fore-seeing that we may need to send out a second questionnaire to increase our response rate. For example, in considering my hypothetical project I realise that I need to allow time to negotiate access to student names and addresses through the university. The time available is 32 weeks from start to finish. I have been advised that it will probably be easiest to contact students during term time, so I need to take this into account in my plan. Box 7.6 shows a plan for the qualitative interview study.

---

## BOX 7.6

### TIMETABLE FOR A QUALITATIVE INTERVIEW STUDY

| | |
|---|---|
| Proposal to be submitted to university ethics committee | Week 2 |
| Contact university for names and addresses of students | Week 6 |
| Begin interviews | Week 8 |
| End interviews | Week 15 |
| Complete data analysis | Week 23 |
| First draft sent to others for comments | Week 26 |
| Submission of final report | Week 32 |

---

Box 7.7 shows the same thing for a survey proposal. It can be seen that a longer time has been allowed for data analysis in the qualitative study. This will include time to explore relevant literature. The plan for the survey study follows similar lines, but has more structure. Study timetables may also be presented as a chart, such as in a Gantt chart (see Figure 7.1).

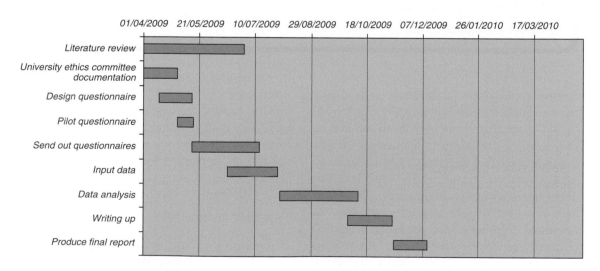

FIGURE 7.1   Gantt chart for a survey study

BOX 7.7

## TIMETABLE FOR A SURVEY

| | |
|---|---|
| Proposal to be submitted to university ethics committee | Week 2 |
| Contact university for names and addresses of students | Week 6 |
| First draft of literature review completed | Week 8 |
| Questionnaire ready for piloting | Week 10 |
| Complete pilot questionnaire | Week 12 |
| Send out questionnaire | Week 14 |
| Inputting of data completed | Week 22 |
| Data analysis completed | Week 25 |
| First draft sent to others for comments | Week 26 |
| Submission of final report | Week 32 |

## Revising the proposal

A proposal will start off as an outline and usually require several revisions. Each section mentioned here affects the others. For example, your time schedule will influence the method you have chosen, which has been influenced by your research problem. You need to make sure that all aspects of the proposal look as if they will work in relation to each other. It is useful to think in terms of how the human body functions. If we undertake strenuous physical exercise like running a marathon, we will need to drink a lot more fluid than usual in order not to become dehydrated and to last the course. We thus need to plan ahead and to make sure we have access to fluid along the way. The main thing to check is that the method will enable you to achieve your objectives. Researchers tend to be over-ambitious in the amount they set out to do. Feedback from others may be useful here. Alternatively, they may suggest new lines of inquiry, whose practical implications need to be thought through.

As discussed earlier, relevant audiences for your research need to be considered at an early stage. It is important to present work in a way that is accessible to other people. Strunk and White (2000) provide a useful guide, based on examples, on how to develop a good writing style. They suggest that 'the approach to style is by way of plainness, simplicity, orderliness, sincerity' (2000: 69). We all develop our own personal writing styles over time. It is valuable to ask others for their comments. For example, did they understand the reason for carrying out the research from the proposal? It is easy to get very wrapped up in the subject and think that, because we are convinced of the particular value of our research, others will be too. The way in which the proposal is presented can enable the reader to appreciate what you are planning to do. Box 7.8 shows an extract from Strunk's *The Elements of Style* (1918). Though originally written some 100 years ago, the advice in this book, which is available in full on the Internet, remains relevant today. Note that the examples totalling 38 words are reduced to just 12 words by the replacements suggested, indicating that brevity as well as clarity is enhanced by the application of Strunk's advice.

---

BOX 7.8

## THE ELEMENTS OF STYLE (STRUNK, 1918)

… the expression the fact that should be revised out of every sentence in which it occurs.

[For example:]

| | | |
|---|---|---|
| owing to the fact that [should be replaced with] | | since (because) |
| in spite of the fact that | " | though (although) |
| call your attention to the fact that | " | remind you (notify you) |
| I was unaware of the fact that | " | I was unaware that (did not know) |
| the fact that he had not succeeded | " | his failure |
| the fact that I had arrived | " | my arrival |

*Source*: www.bartleby.com/141/strunk5.html#13

---

Ideally, a research proposal should be concise. This may seem impossible considering the amount of detail given here about what to put into a proposal. This is where revision and writing style is important. The reader will want to see easily what you are proposing, whilst at the same time have their attention held by the content. Krathwohl (1988) suggests that the proposal should be easy for the reader to skim. Dividing the proposal up using some of the headings discussed here will help with this. Effective use of language is important. For example, where possible use short, simple sentences.

## Managing your research project

Producing a research proposal constitutes your study as a *project*, which implies that all the various aspects will be integrated. It provides the template for how you will manage your project. Researchers are accountable for the conduct of their research and need to demonstrate that they know what they are doing and that the project is likely to work as intended. This may seem daunting, but, as discussed earlier, you do not have to go it alone. It is often useful to access advice and

support from peers when planning and conducting research. Feedback from friendly peers can help to prepare you for later appraisal by less sympathetic audiences. Critical appraisal works as a form of quality control in the wider research community and is a feature of all research. However, whilst it is important to be open to the comments and advice of others, at the same time you need to make the research your own. You are the one who will have to describe and explain your rationale, and use the methods set out in the proposal. You therefore have to take responsibility for it.

Collaborating with others and submitting joint proposals for funding are common, which is another reason for getting used to sharing research ideas with peers. Collaboration might also include seeking advice from someone with particular expertise. For example, when undertaking quantitative research it is common to get advice from someone with statistical expertise at an early stage. Although it is not usual in research projects undertaken for a course of study, research is often undertaken by a team, sometimes including a range of different disciplines. Larger research projects usually have an advisory or steering group set up to discuss the study design and progress. If you are part of a research team it is important that all team members are clear about the research design and that agendas are made explicit. One way of doing this is to ensure that there is clear documentation of how all decisions are made and of how the research progresses.

As we all know, even the best laid plans can go off course. A common problem when collecting quantitative or qualitative data is unforeseen difficulty in recruiting the samples proposed. The likelihood of such problems will be minimised if time is taken to prepare the design at the start. If your study does not go according to plan, given accurate recording of the process of the research, it will be possible to learn from the experience and share that learning with others. Additionally, solutions may be available more easily than you expect if you are prepared to re-think your original aims so that failing to fulfil original plans is turned into a *strength* of a newly conceived project. Chapter 31 contains advice on how you can do this, together with some fully worked examples.

## Conclusion

A research idea is developed into a research project through the crafting of a good research question and research proposal. This involves developing and organising the study before data collection begins. The main features and benefits of research proposals are summarised in Box 7.9.

---

BOX 7.9

### FEATURES AND BENEFITS OF A RESEARCH PROPOSAL

- Sets up the research as an integrated 'project' with a start and end point.
- Research idea is conceptualised.
- Research question is defined.
- Theoretical framework is described.
- Methodological framework is described.
- Sets out standards for judging the quality of the study.
- Resources required are stated – for example, time, costs.
- Enables peer review and assessment.
- Provides a template for the conduct and writing up of the research.

---

Learning to design research and write proposals is part of the professional development of social scientists. Writing a proposal helps you to design your study and is a way of communicating to others what you are planning to do and why. Your research proposal is a way of setting out the way you will manage your project so that it is successful. Proposals can be simple or detailed, depending upon the scale of the study. A proposal for a small-scale study will usually be quite short, with maybe only a couple of sentences on some sections discussed here. All the areas covered should be at least given some thought. A proposal should be as short as possible, whilst at the same time containing all the necessary information the reader will need to appreciate what you plan to do and why.

## FURTHER READING

Bell (2005) and Thomas (2009) are good basic guides to carrying out a research project from start to finish. Kelly (2010) describes how to develop research questions in qualitative research studies. Punch (2006) is a helpful text on writing research proposals. Strunk and White (2000), first published in 1918, is an interesting and helpful little book on how to write well, containing lots of useful examples of good and not so good writing style.

### Student Reader (Seale, 2004b): relevant readings

2   C. Wright Mills: 'On intellectual craftsmanship'

8   Research design

See also Chapter 32, 'Preparing and evaluating qualitative research proposals' by Janice M. Morse in Seale et al. (2004).

### Journal articles discussing or illustrating the issues raised in this chapter

Sandelowski, M. and Barroso, J. (2003) 'Writing the proposal for a qualitative research methodology project', Qualitative Health Research, 13: 781–820.

Travers, M. (2009) 'New methods, old problems: a sceptical view of innovation in qualitative research', Qualitative Research, 9: 161–179.

A research proposal for a quantitative project:

Sayers, S.M., Mackerras, D., Singh, G., Bucens, I., Flynn K. and Reid, A. (2003) 'An Australian Aboriginal birth cohort: a unique resource for a life course study of an indigenous population. A study protocol', BMC International Health and Human Rights, 3: 1.

### Web links

Research Proposal Guide: http://researchproposalguide.com/

Developing a research question www.esc.edu/esconline/across_esc/writerscomplex.nsf/0/f87fd7182f0ff21c852569c2005a47b7

Examples of research proposals: https://webspace.utexas.edu/cherwitz/www/ie/sample_diss.html

Dissertation proposal workshop: http://iis.berkeley.edu/DissPropWorkshop

ESRC How to Write a Good Application – guidelines for writing a successful application for a social science research project: www.esrcsocietytoday.ac.uk/ESRCInfoCentre/Support/research_award_holders/FAQs2/Index1.aspx

The Elements of Style by Strunk (1918) – a guide to using good English: www.bartleby.com/141

## KEY CONCEPTS FOR REVIEW

**Advice:** Use these, along with the review questions in the next section, to test your knowledge of the contents of this chapter. Try to define each of the key concepts listed here; if you have understood this chapter you should be able to do this. Check your definitions against the definition in the at the end of the book.

| Dissemination | Research design |
|---|---|
| Harvard referencing system | Research questions |
| Hypothesis | Signposts |
| Objectives | Steering group |

 ## ■ Review questions

1  Name four types of research question.
2  Outline a question that can *only* be answered by quantitative methods, another that can *only* be answered by qualitative methods, and a third that could be answered by either.
3  What are the advantages and disadvantages of writing a research proposal at the start of a project?
4  What are the key components of most successful research proposals?
5  What is a Gantt chart and why is it useful in writing a proposal?

## Workshop and discussion exercises

1  Developing a research question:
   (a) Work in pairs or small groups.
   (b) Brainstorm topics that you're interested in studying and write them down on paper or a white board. Spend about 15 minutes doing this.
   (c) Organise the topics into groups if there are many.
   (d) Select a topic and start to consider different ways you could examine it using a concept map or spider diagram.
   (e) Consider alternative questions on the chosen topic.
   (f) Decide on a research question.

2  Developing a research proposal
   Take your research question and using the headings in this chapter begin to devise an outline research proposal. In particular set out the following headings and make notes as to what you would include under them.

   • Introduction
   • Research question or aim
   • Objectives
   • Methods
   • Data analysis
   • Dissemination

   This will not work as a linear process – go backwards and forwards between the areas and make adjustments.

   If you are working as a small group or pair as part of a larger group session, present your draft proposal to the larger group. Their questions and comments will help you to revise your research question and proposal.

   Ask a friend or fellow student to summarise back to you what you are planning to do.

# 8

# RESEARCH DESIGN

## Clare Rutterford

Have you ever wondered whether fish oils improve your intelligence, what the prevalence of violent crime is in the UK, how policy makers make and justify decisions, or whether drug use is associated with committing homicide? These are all examples of questions which can be answered through research. This chapter explores the different research designs you can use to answer these, and your own, research questions.

Producing high-quality research begins at the design stage, therefore it is important that adequate time and thought is dedicated to this process. Poorly designed studies often lack scientific credibility, are a waste of time and resources, and may not be able to adequately answer the research question of interest. Study designs can be classified broadly into two main categories, experimental or non-experimental (see Figure 8.1). In this chapter we consider some of the most frequently used study designs within these categories.

A non-experimental study is one in which the researcher does not directly influence the behaviour of the study participants, but observes and measures the study participants. By contrast, in an experimental study the researcher often imposes an intervention on some of the study participants and measures the effects. Randomised controlled trials (RCTs) are a particular type of experimental study and are regarded as the gold standard of research design where establishing a causal relationship is the chief aim, providing more valid results than non-experimental studies in proving cause and effect. However, they are not always feasible or appropriate for some research questions, particularly those that do not involve causal hypotheses. Non-experimental or quasi-experimental designs are sometimes used on these occasions.

The choice of the study design for your research will depend on many factors, such as the research question, practical constraints, ethical implications and cost. More than one study design may be appropriate and it is your job as the researcher to weigh up the advantages and disadvantages for the use of each

design within the context of your particular research setting.

This chapter discusses the design features of some of the most frequently used research designs, illustrated with examples taken from a range of social research situations. By the end of this chapter you should understand the key elements of each study design, be able to evaluate their appropriateness within the context of a research question, and be competent in applying to your own research.

## Non-experimental studies

In a non-experimental study a researcher does not directly influence the behaviour of the study participants, but rather observes and sometimes measures what occurs. This may sound straightforward, but if the researcher is to eliminate bias, these studies need to be rigorously designed and conducted. We will explore possible sources of bias as we consider these designs.

## Case studies

A case study is defined by (Berg, 2004) as 'a method involving systematically gathering enough information about a particular person, social setting, event, or group to permit the researcher to effectively understand how the subject operates or functions'.

Case studies tend to be associated more with qualitative data and analysis, but are not restricted to this. Materials and information for analysis can be gathered from a variety of sources and using different methods including, for example, documents, archival records, interviews, direct observation, participant observation and the identification of physical artifacts (Yin, 2003). These sources can provide data which are extremely rich and detailed. An example of a case study is given in Box 8.1.

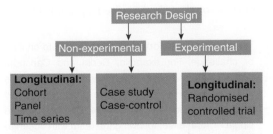

**FIGURE 8.1** Categorisation of common study designs

## THE CUBAN MISSILE CRISIS

The Cuban Missile Crisis during the cold war involved the Soviet Union, Cuba and the United States. In 1962 an American spy plane spotted nuclear missiles, built by the Soviet Union stored in Cuba. The Americans surrounded Cuba with navy ships in order to halt further production and demanded the missiles be destroyed. The confrontation could have led to a nuclear attack but came to a close when the Soviet Union dismantled and removed the offensive missiles.

Allison (1971) conducted a case study of this event using information in the public domain, declassified government files, and talking to those working in various positions and authority within the US government. He generated three alternative models for explaining government behaviour during the crisis:

- Model 1: The state acts rationally and in a unified manner to make *decisions*.

- Model 2: Different parts of the state (sub-units) follow standard operating procedures which, taken together, produce *outputs*.

- Model 3: Policy *outcomes* result from negotiations and bargains struck between key players, such as the Secretary of State, the Secretary of Defense etc.

For Allison, neither the 'decisions' not the 'outputs' nor the 'outcomes' model is 'best' in explaining government policies at this time, but each of them captures something of the realities that occurred in this particular case.

One of the first design issues in a case study is to select the case or cases for study. When we think of a 'case' we are thinking of an entity such as a single community, school, family, organisation, person or event which we wish to study. The choice of level at which to define a case will often follow logically from the research question. For example, if we ask, 'What obstacles to the implementation of anti-racist approaches in school curricula exist?', we would want to define our case as a school rather than an individual. If we ask, 'What psychological processes can lead to racially biased educational practices?', we would define our case as an individual rather than an institution.

The working definition of what to count as a case should be established from the start. When this is an event, as in Allison's study of the missile crisis, this may mean being precise about start and stop dates. When studying a community it may involve being specific about geographical boundaries. It may also be useful to

define cases similarly to other published case studies in order to be able to make comparisons between these and the findings of the planned study.

A case study may involve single or multiple cases. Yin (2003) suggests that, given the option, a multiple case design is preferred over a single case as the evidence from multiple cases is more compelling; however, this must be balanced against the time and resources required to gather very detailed information about each case. There are certain circumstances when a single case study is more appropriate. The following five rationales for this are described by Yin (2003):

1  We may have a theory that we may wish to confirm or challenge. For example, Berlin and Carlström (2008) wished to challenge idealised assumptions about how teams in health care are formed. They studied a trauma team at a university hospital as a single critical case, following the team with observations and interviews. They concluded that the

idealised model used at the time to explain team formation did not apply to the trauma team. (Allison used this rationale for his study of the Cuban Missile Crisis, described in Box 8.1).

2   The unique case is generally used for cases that are particularly rare. For example, a specific type of safety failure in industry may be so rare that an in-depth study of a single case will provide safety managers valuable information on how to avoid such safety failures in the future.

3   The authors of *Middletown: A Study in Contemporary American Culture* (Lynd and Lynd, 1929) wanted to create a portrait of American small-town life between 1890 and 1925. They chose a single case, Muncie in Indiana, to be what they considered to be a representative case, in that it had many features which were common across many American communities. They went on to generalise their results beyond this individual case.

4   In some situations the researcher may have a unique opportunity to undertake study, perhaps given access to a community or individual that has previously remained very private or inaccessible to researchers. These are known as revelatory cases. These studies can provide great insight. Liebow (1967) did just this when he was able to befriend a group of men living in a poor inner city and study their lifestyle and behaviour, which were previously poorly understood.

5   The longitudinal case occurs where you study the same single case at two or more time points, in order to examine changes over time. The Lynds did this when they returned to Muncie in 1935 to examine how the great depression had influenced the social structure of the town (Lynd and Lynd, 1937).

A summary of the aspects of case studies which can potentially be seen as advantages and disadvantages can be found in Box 8.2.

---

**BOX 8.2**

## ADVANTAGES AND DISADVANTAGES OF CASE STUDIES

### Advantages

- They can generate or test hypotheses.
- They allow us to gain detailed descriptions and understanding of a particular person, setting or event.

### Disadvantages

- Findings may not apply more widely (i.e. they are not generalisable).
- They cannot establish cause-and-effect relationships.
- They can be very time consuming to undertake and produce vast amounts of data.

---

## Cross-sectional studies

Cross-sectional studies can be thought of as taking a snap-shot in time. You select a group of people you are interested in and collect data on them at that one time point only. Your aim may be to find out how prevalent something is, such as unemployment, or whether it is more prevalent in some groups than others. In itself this can be very valuable, but there are disadvantages to this design too. For example, cross-sectional studies are not as good as experiments, case-control or cohort studies (all of which are described below) for establishing causality, due mainly to the fact that it is often hard to establish the temporal relationship required for this.

For example, in a study of unemployment you may see that those whom are unemployed tend to have poorer health. However, you may be unable to conclude whether being unemployed leads to worse health or whether having poor health leads to unemployment, because in a cross-sectional study you do not necessarily know which one of these things happened first. You will see later in this chapter that longitudinal studies offer better prospects for examining time order.

On the other hand, problems of time order do not always apply. If you want to discover whether gender influences adult occupational status, you can be fairly sure that (at least in most cases) a person's gender has been established long before adult occupational status was achieved. Here, though, we run into other problems: it could be that gender and occupational status are correlated, but some other variable is actually the true cause of this. Chapter 20 indicates methods of statistical analysis whereby causal analysis of cross-sectional data can be attempted.

Let us examine some of the considerations for cross-sectional design through use of an example from Teplin et al. (2005), shown in Box 8.3, in which a crime victimisation survey is described.

---

**BOX 8.3**

## CRIME VICTIMISATION IN ADULTS WITH SEVERE MENTAL ILLNESS

The objectives of this survey were to determine the prevalence of crime victimisation among persons with severe mental illness (SMI) in Chicago. At the time of the study 75 agencies in Chicago provided outpatient, day and residential treatment to people with SMI. Sixteen of these agencies were randomly selected for inclusion in the survey; participants were then randomly selected from within each agency stratified by gender, ethnicity and age to ensure equal numbers within each of these groups. Of 1,782 participants selected, 458 (25.7 per cent) refused to participate.

Participants were asked questions about their experiences of being victims of crime in the last 12 months. These results were compared to those collected through the National Crime Victimization Survey. The authors (Teplin et al., 2005) found that more than a quarter of people with SMI had been victims of violent crime, and this was 11 times higher than the general population.

As with many research designs it is important, given the topic that Teplin et al. were studying, that the sample be selected in order to be **representative** of the total population of interest (although see Chapter 9 for alternative rationales for sampling). Here the sample is of those with severe mental illness (SMI) who are connected to the mental health services. The authors point out that their findings may not be relevant for the almost 50 per cent of people with SMI who do not receive mental health services or are treated by private practitioners.

---

As with many designs, there is potential for inaccuracy and sources of bias in the data collection. One potential problem the authors report with their study is the potential for participants to sometimes relate incidents that occurred prior to the 12-month period the participants were asked about, thus possibly inflating the true prevalence of events.

Cross-sectional studies can also suffer from the problems associated with non-response.

There may be a systematic difference between those who respond and complete the survey and those who do not. For example, being a victim of crime may encourage a participant to respond, while all those who feel the research is not relevant to them may chose not to respond. This is likely to bias results by inflating the estimated prevalence. Non-response has been minimised in this study by using face-to-face interviews, whereas alternative data collection methods such as postal question- naires often have a larger non-response rate. See Box 8.4 for a list of advantages and disadvantages of cross-sectional study.

BOX 8.4

## ADVANTAGES AND DISADVANTAGES OF CROSS-SECTIONAL STUDIES

### Advantages

- Depending upon size, can be relatively cheap and easy to conduct.
- Depending upon size, results may be available quickly.
- There are no problems of loss to follow up (see longitudinal designs).

### Disadvantages

- Cannot easily establish time-order (e.g. whether a causal factor occurred before the event that is being explained).
- Potential for non-response.

## Longitudinal studies

The term longitudinal is a general term for study designs in which you survey or collect observations upon a sample of people from some population on at least two occasions. They can take place over a few weeks, months or many years. Under this longitudinal umbrella term a multitude of terminology is used to classify the study design. Cohort studies, panel studies, and randomised controlled trials are all examples of longitudinal designs.

Panel and cohort designs can be used to describe and explore changes over time; however, because of their longitudinal nature they can also be used to establish causal effects. For example, in the millennium cohort study (described in more detail in Box 8.6) it is of particular interest to see how the effect of parental education may impact upon a child's cognitive development during their lifetime.

This design could be displayed graphically, where we classify each child as to whether they have been 'exposed' to the factor of interest – in this case a high parental education. We then measure cognitive ability between the two groups

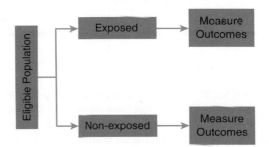

**FIGURE 8.2** Examining causal effects using the cohort or panel design

and make comparisons at the various time points. Figure 8.2 represents this graphically.

## Panel and Cohort studies

The distinction between a cohort and a panel study is at first hard to recognise and not always consistently used or stated in the literature. The distinction lies in the selection of the sample for the study. In a panel study a representative sample is taken across the whole population of interest. An example is the annual British Household Panel Survey, details of which are shown in Box 8.5.

## BRITISH HOUSEHOLD PANEL SURVEY

This is an annual survey which began in 1991. A nationally representative sample of 5,500 households are selected and all members of the household are interviewed. People are removed as they die or added once they reach the age of 16 within the household. The core questionnaire covers topics such as household composition, housing conditions, residential mobility, education and training, health and use of health services and income. The data is collected through various means such as face-to-face interview, telephone interviews and self-completion. The main objective of the survey is to understand social and economic change at the household and individual level in Britain.

For more details see www.iser.essex.ac.uk/survey/bhps.

One of the advantages of a panel study is to be able to generalise the results to the population of interest. In order to do this it is important that the panel be selected to be representative. In a cohort study, on the other hand, representing a particular population may not be so important. Here, the sample is a group of individuals who share a similar characteristic or experience, for example those who live within the same community, or British soldiers who fought in the Vietnam War, or children born within a particular time period. An example is the Millennium cohort study. This is a birth cohort of children born in the year 2000, details of which are shown in Box 8.6.

## THE MILLENNIUM COHORT STUDY

The Millennium cohort study is following the lives of a birth cohort of 19,000 children born in the UK in the year 2000. Surveys have so far been conducted at nine months, three, five and seven years. Over the course of the study data are collected on: parenting, childcare, school choice, child behaviour, cognitive development, and parental education and income. One of the primary aims of this study is to look closely at the first year of life and examine its long-term impact upon a child's development.

For more details see: www.cls.ioe.ac.uk

Sometimes a cohort is selected because it is a logistically convenient way to select or survey participants, but usually they are chosen because it is that specific group of participants you wish to make inferences about. One of the difficulties of cohort studies is that it is often hard to disentangle age effects (i.e. the effect of getting older) from cohort effects (i.e. the effect of a common experience such as being born in a particular year). This is mainly due to the fact that the members of cohorts generally tend to be of the same age, particularly in birth cohorts.

Both panel and cohort studies require repeat questioning of research participants, sometimes for many years. In such studies it is extremely important to ensure that you can maximise response rates year after year as the results become less reliable if people drop out – as some inevitably do – and the sample size diminishes. This decreasing participation in longitudinal studies is referred to as the loss to follow-up. This loss can be minimised by ensuring the data collection is not too burdensome for participants, having good methods for tracking and staying in touch with the participants, and trying to ensure that the participants remain engaged with the research. Many studies do this through sending birthday cards, newsletters about the research, or providing incentives for the participants.

One potential problem that can occur in longitudinal studies is that participants may modify their behaviour due to the fact that they are being studied. This is known as the Hawthorne effect, a term used to describe what was found during a study done at the Western Electrical Company's Hawthorne Works in Chicago in the 1930s. The investigators were looking into whether changes to the factory lighting improved productivity, and found that the mere process of studying the workers increased productivity rather than the changes to the lighting (Landsberger, 1958).

Due to the length of these longitudinal studies, there is also potential for the importance of the data being collected to change. A variable which was considered important at the start of the study may not be relevant by the end, and vice versa.

The advantages and disadvantages of longitudinal designs are listed in Box 8.7.

---

**BOX 8.7**

## ADVANTAGES AND DISADVANTAGES OF LONGITUDINAL DESIGNS

### Advantages

- Can establish a causal pathway.
- Can examine change over time.

### Disadvantages

- Cost.
- Loss to follow-up may make the sample less representative.
- Potential for Hawthorne effect.
- Potential for the importance of data to change.

---

## Case-control study

In a case-control study you select a group of people who have the event or characteristic of interest (cases) and a comparable group of people who do not (controls). A comparison of the past exposures between the cases and controls will indicate whether there is an association between exposure and the event or characteristic that you want to explain. Figure 8.3 shows this in a graphical way.

A case-control study designed to look for an association between methamphetamine use and homicide is shown in Box 8.8.

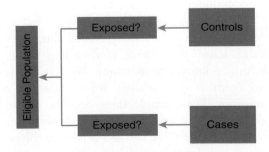

FIGURE 8.3 The case-control design

## HOMICIDE OFFENDING AND METHAMPHETAMINE USE

Methamphetamine is considered highly addictive and the relationship between this drug and violence is the topic of many debates. Cases were inmates who were at least 18 years old at the time of their crime and were incarcerated for murder or voluntary manslaughter. Controls consisted of a general sample of US adults aged 18 or older. Both cases and controls were asked about their past drug use, particularly whether they had ever used methamphetamine and whether they had used it in the month prior to being interviewed or arrested for homicide. Data was collected on other potential risk factors of homicide such as general drug use, alcohol intake, gender and social economic status. The author of this study (Stretesky, 2009) found that recent methamphetamine use was associated with an increased risk of homicide.

In such designs, we want the case and control groups to be similar in terms of their characteristics so that the only difference between them is their outcome status (in this case, whether or not they had committed homicide). This property gives our results credibility by allowing us to adequately examine the association between exposure (methamphetamine use) and outcome (homicide).

Imagine an extreme example where our cases were all male and controls all female. Gender may be an important factor in committing homicide; it may also be linked to drug use, with perhaps males more likely to participate in drug use. The gender of a participant is then said to be acting as a confounder. It is hard to say whether it is methamphetamine use or gender that is associated with increased risk of committing homicide. Confounders hide the true relationship between exposure and outcome.

Confounders can be dealt with to some extent at the analysis stage of these designs, but the ideal approach is to reduce confounding at the design stage. We reduce confounding using a technique known as matching. We match cases and controls on variables we consider to be important. For example, these could be age and gender. So for every case in the study we recruit a control of the same age and gender, so the two groups will be balanced in terms of these two characteristics of participants. It is therefore important not to match cases and control on the basis of the exposure of interest as this will mean you will be unable to assess the relationship between exposure and event as both groups will be similar in exposure status.

In the Stretesky study the cases were adults over 18 years old chosen from US prisons and controls were adults over 18 from the general population. But we can reasonably ask whether these two groups of people are comparable. Some might argue that those incarcerated are likely to be very different from the general population in other respects, apart from their use of methamphetamine, and that these factors (e.g. poverty, low levels of education, living in an inner-city environment) explain both higher homicide rates and drug use in the prison population. One way around this could be to consider selecting controls from within the prisons too – people who were imprisoned for crimes other than homicide, but who share the same social background as those who had committed homicide.

Case-control studies are retrospective studies, meaning the data is being collected about past exposure events. How this is done is an important issue. In the Stretesky study the data was collected by interview. It would be reasonable to question whether the data collected accurately reflected the truth, as often people cannot remember their exposure over many years. As well as a lack of accuracy there is also the potential for what is known as recall bias. This is when the ability to recall past exposures is different for the cases and controls. You can see how this could potentially happen in this study as perhaps those who have committed homicide will have spent more time looking back at their past and trying to determine what may have

caused them to do this. A time of drug use may stick out in their memory, whereas the same type of event may be completely forgotten by a control participant. At the end of the study we could see a difference in drug use between the two groups, but this could just be because the controls were not as good at remembering their use of drugs.

The advantages and disadvantages of case-control studies are listed in Box 8.9.

---

BOX 8.9

## ADVANTAGES AND DISADVANTAGES OF CASE-CONTROL STUDIES

### Advantages

- Several exposures can be studied at once.
- Useful in studying rare or uncommon events.
- Relatively cheap and easy to conduct.
- Do not suffer from loss to follow-up.
- Results available quickly.

### Disadvantages

- Potential for recall bias.
- Are not useful for studying rare exposures.
- Subjective assessment of exposure.
- Past data may be recorded in inconsistent format.
- Potential for selection bias.
- Choice of control group may be difficult.

---

## Experimental studies

In this section we consider randomised controlled trials (RCTs), a type of experimental design. In this design, the investigator imposes an intervention upon some of the participants and compares the results with those who did not receive the intervention. These designs were first used in the medical field, where the intervention was a drug and its effect upon disease was evaluated.

However, they are now used across many disciplines and the interventions to be assessed are varied, such as educational programmes to aid rehabilitation of prisoners, brain-training computer games to improve cognitive ability, or psychotherapy used to treat depression.

The results from well designed and conducted RCTs provide better evidence for causal claims than non-experimental studies. This is because they can eliminate many of the biasing issues that are inherent in the non-experimental designs we have seen. However, they are not as valuable as case studies if the aim of the research is to increase in-depth understanding of a phenomenon. RCTs require that initial hypotheses have been firmly established, and this is not appropriate in more exploratory research where the ideas of the investigator about what questions are important may change as the study progresses. Nor are RCTs of any use in establishing how prevalent something is in a population, or whether something has become more or less prevalent over time, for which a cross-sectional survey or a study comparing similarly selected samples at two or more different time points (called a time series study) is likely to be the most useful design.

## Trial design

There are several different design choices for the basic structure of RCTs. Probably the most common and simplest design is the parallel group design. In this design participants agree to take part in the study and are then randomly allocated to a particular group. The groups take place in parallel over the length of the trial, as illustrated in Figure 8.4. Most commonly we have two groups, a group who receive the intervention and a group who do not, although the design is not restricted to two groups. We refer to these groups as trial arms.

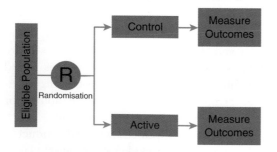

**FIGURE 8.4**  The parallel group design for a randomised controlled trial

## The control group

The control group is the name used for the trial arm which does not receive the study intervention. In order to understand why we need a control group let us think about what would happen without one.

Imagine we want to evaluate the effect of art classes on the mood of adults within a retirement home. We could measure the mood of all the participants at the beginning of the trial then give *all* the participants access to art classes. A few months later we measure their mood again and see an improvement. Now this improvement could have occurred for four reasons:

1  The art classes helped improve mood.

2  The mood of these participants would have improved in a few months regardless of attending the art classes.

3  The effect of being studied in a trial caused their mood to subsequently improve (Hawthorne effect).

4  The psychological effect of being part of an 'intervention', being looked after and listened to, made them feel better, even if it wasn't actually doing anything (placebo effect).

A placebo is a tablet or pill that contains an inert substance which has no effect on the body. The placebo effect as described by Beecher (1955) refers to a patient's subjective feeling that their condition has improved due to the fact that they have received a treatment even when that treatment does not contain any active ingredient.

In order to be able to rule out the last three options we must include a control group for comparison with the intervention group at the end of the study, and if we see a difference between the two groups we can be confident that this is due to the intervention rather than something else.

## Randomisation

In an RCT, after a participant has given consent to be involved in the study, the choice of which study arm he or she should receive should not be left for the investigator to decide. The participant should be randomly allocated to a study arm; this ensures that there is no selection bias occurring. Selection bias refers to where there is a systematic difference between the participants entered into each group. For example, given the choice, an investigator assessing the effectiveness of a new medical procedure may consciously or subconsciously put all the severe participants onto the new treatment in the hope they will benefit. The first clinical trial to implement randomisation was conducted by the Medical Research Council (1948) and looked at the use of Streptomycin as a treatment for pulmonary tuberculosis.

It is important to note here the difference between random sampling and random allocation. *Random sampling* is an unbiased method to select participants to study from a particular population (further details of which are in Chapter 9). *Random allocation* refers to the way participants in a study are allocated to a trial arm.

Randomisation is an attempt to ensure that the only difference between the two trial arms is the treatment they receive. All other factors (measured and unmeasured), such as age, gender, educational level or ethnicity, should be balanced across the groups when randomisation is successfully implemented. This helps us to establish that any effect seen is due to our intervention, protecting our conclusions from bias and confounding. This process of randomisation is the key difference and advantage of experimental compared to non-experimental studies.

In order to protect the randomisation process from bias you need to put procedures in place to ensure allocation concealment. Allocation concealment ensures that the investigator is unable to predict what the next participant will be allocated to. If you do not have allocation concealment then you risk introducing selection bias. For example, the investigator may change his or her mind about recruitment of a particular

participant if they know what treatment that participant would receive.

The randomisation sequence or list is a document created at the beginning of the trial which contains the sequence of treatment allocations for participants entering the trial. To ensure allocation concealment investigators may place each individual allocation into separate sealed envelopes stored in a central location. The next envelope is opened to reveal the allocation as each participant is recruited. This ensures that no one involved in recruiting participants would know what future allocations would be.

## Blinding

When we talk about blinding or masking in a trial we are concerned with restricting the knowledge about who has been allocated to each trial arm once this allocation has been performed. This may be knowledge by the participant themselves, by the person providing the intervention, the person collecting the data or anyone involved in the trial. Knowledge of the intervention may introduce bias into the trial. For example, if a participant knew they were receiving an experimental intervention they may report better outcomes because they believe the new intervention will help them. Similarly, if a person supplying the intervention – say, a teacher or a doctor – knew a study participant – say, a pupil or a patient – was receiving the new intervention they might communicate with the person in a different way from those in the control group.

If one of either the study participants or the people supplying the intervention know which treatment participants have been allocated to, then the trial is said to be single blinded. If neither the participant nor person supplying the intervention knows this, then the trial is said to be double blinded. A further elaboration of blinding is to ensure that the researcher who measures the outcome also does not know who is in which group, in case this influences how they apply the outcome measure.

The choice of control group also plays a part in aiding the blinding of treatment assignment. Blinding is improved if the intervention and control groups are indistinguishable. This is often easier to achieve in drug trials where a placebo can be made identical in taste and appearance to the trial drug. Of course, in some cases it is impossible to blind a trial. For example, if you wanted to find out whether brain-training computer games improved mathematical ability, it would be impossible to conceal from people whether or not they were allocated to use brain-training computer games. On the other hand, if you wanted to find out whether one brain-training game was better than another, then this could be easier, as people in both arms of the trial would be given a game to play.

## Sample size

One of the most important things to do at the planning stage of an RCT is to decide how many people you need to recruit into it order to make meaningful and precise conclusions. This is done by calculating a sample size using published sample size formulae (also referred to as power calculations). Try typing 'calculating sample size' into Google and you will find some sites explaining these somewhat complex calculations in more detail. Box 8.10 gives further reasons behind the importance of sample size calculations.

---

**BOX 8.10**

### REASONS FOR CALCULATING SAMPLE SIZE

A study that is too small may not show any significant differences between intervention and control groups, when in fact an important difference exists. The trial is too small to adequately answer the research question.

If the study is too large it will be a waste of resources as the cost of employing researchers and providing the intervention will increase as the size of the study increases. You could have answered your research question with fewer participants.

It can be considered unethical to enter people into a trial that is too large as the trial result could have been determined earlier, with fewer people, so that some participants in the control group may be denied the benefit of an intervention that is known to be successful.

Grant-awarding bodies will wish to see a sample size calculation to ensure that the study will provide valid results for the most economic price.

A sample size calculation can help in planning the study by allowing the researcher to work out costs and the timings for the study.

Peer reviewers will look at the sample size calculation to assess the credibility of your study when you submit for publication.

---

## Conclusion

Choosing the best study design to use to answer your research question will be one of many hurdles you will face as a researcher. The aim of this chapter was to show you that there is no 'one size fits all' when it comes to research designs. It is up to you to be able to evaluate all the potential difficulties that may be associated with different designs. Most importantly, every design should be evaluated in the context of your research problem. It is essential to remember that once the design has been chosen, the integrity of the design must be maintained throughout the study by careful monitoring and ensuring that the analysis you undertake is appropriate for the design you selected.

Understanding the design issues covered in this chapter will also allow you to evaluate published research. With a greater appreciation of the variety of research designs that can be used, you can decide whether the research has been conducted appropriately and whether it provides useful information for your own research area.

## FURTHER READING

This chapter covers the basic concepts involved in research design. The following literature builds upon these foundations. Berg (2004) is a good guide to research designs that involve qualitative methods, as is Creswell (2007), and Yin (2003) provides advice specifically geared to case-study research. Case-control studies are covered by Schlesselman and Stolley (1982) and randomised controlled trials by Pocock (1983). A good general text on research design is Hakim (2000).

### Student Reader (Seale, 2004b): relevant readings

7    Ray Pawson and Nick Tilley: 'Go forth and experiment'

78  Ann Oakley: 'Who's afraid of the randomised controlled trial? Some dilemmas of the scientific method and 'good' research practice'

See also Chapter 34 'Qualitative evaluation research' by Moira Kelly in Seale et al. (2004).

### Journal articles discussing the issues raised in this chapter

Foster, L.H. (2010) 'A best kept secret: single-subject research design in counseling', Counseling Outcome Research and Evaluation, 1: 30–39.

Holosko, M.J. (2010) 'What types of designs are we using in social work research and evaluation?', Research on Social Work Practice, 20: 665–673.

Ungar, M. (2006) '"Too ambitious": what happens when funders misunderstand the strengths of qualitative research design', Qualitative Social Work, 5: 261–277.

### Web links

www.esourceresearch.org for the following chapters:

e-Source: Chapter 1 on 'Determining appropriate methods' by John B. McKinlay

e-Source: Chapter 3 on 'Theory development' by Stephen Turner

e-Source: Chapter 7 on 'Observational studies' by Richard Berk

e-Source: Chapter 8 on 'Qualitative methods' by David Silverman

e-Source: Chapter 11 on 'Clinical trials' by Duolao Wang and Ameet Bakhai

Social research methods: www.socialresearchmethods.net/kb/design.php

Experiment-resources.com www.experiment-resources.com/research-designs.html

Methods@manchester, research methods in the social sciences: www.methods.manchester.ac.uk/methods/experiments/index.shtml

**Advice:** Use these, along with the review questions in the next section, to test your knowledge of the contents of this chapter. Try to define each of the key concepts listed here; if you have understood this chapter you should be able to do this. Check your definitions against the definition in the glossary at the end of the book.

| | |
|---|---|
| Allocation concealment | Non-response |
| Bias | Panel study |
| Blinding (or masking) | Parallel group design |
| Case study | Placebo effect |
| Case-control study | Power calculations |
| Cohort study | Randomisation |
| Confounder | Randomisation sequence/list |
| Control group | Randomised controlled trial |
| Critical case | Recall bias |
| Cross-sectional study | Representative case/sample |
| Double blind | Retrospective study |
| Experimental design | Revelatory case |
| Hawthorne effect | Selection bias |
| Intervention | Single blind |
| Longitudinal case | Time series |
| Loss to follow-up | Trial arms |
| Matching | Unique case |
| Non-experimental design | |

## Review questions

1 When is a case study the best research design and what are its disadvantages?
2 What is the best design for establishing a causal relationship and why?
3 What is the best design for establishing how commonly something occurs in a population and why?
4 How can you avoid threats to the validity of conclusions drawn from experimental research?
5 What are the characteristics, advantages and disadvantages of longitudinal studies?

## Workshop and discussion exercises

1 For each of the following study designs, formulate a research question that is best investigated using that design:

(a) **Case study**
(b) **Cross sectional survey**

(c) **Time series study**

(d) **Longitudinal study**

(e) **Case-control study**

(f) **Randomised controlled trial**

2 **You want to find out whether school examinations have got easier over time. Outline the design of a study that would do this.**

3 **You want to find out whether large retail organisations are better than small retail organisations at providing customer satisfaction. Outline the design of a study that would do this.**

4 **You want to understand how social workers interact with parents when they are assessing whether parental care is adequate. What kind of study would do this? How would you carry out such a study?**

5 **A government agency wants to find out whether a programme teaching people how to self-manage their chronic illness condition is effective in preventing hospital admissions. How would you design a study to determine this?**

# 9

# SAMPLING

## Clive Seale

Social researchers sample because it is very rare that they have either the time or the resources to carry out research on the whole population that could be potentially included in a study. In research involving social surveys the application of sampling theory enables researchers to take a random selection or sample of the population and from that to make generalisations – usually statistical ones – about the whole of the population. In such research sampling aims to provide good estimates about the nature of the whole population from a limited number of cases.

The way in which a sample is then designed will depend on the research goals. However, researchers need to consider whether or not they can generalise their findings to a wider group or population and the confidence with which they can do that. A sample which accurately reflects the *whole* population is called a representative sample. This chapter will, after saying something about how representative sampling techniques have developed historically, describe the procedures and considerations that are necessary in drawing up representative samples.

There are two broad types of sampling method: probability and non-probability sampling. A probability sample – which is generally regarded as more likely to provide representativeness – is one in which each person in the population has a known (usually equal) chance of being selected. A non-probability sample is one in which some people have an unknown, or no chance of being selected. Non-probability sampling and the various rationales that lie behind such approaches will be discussed in the second part of the chapter. By the time you have read the chapter, then, you should be equipped to assess what type of sampling is useful for particular types of study, and know how to actually proceed with a variety of different sampling techniques. A list of key types of sample is given in Box 9.1, divided into probability and non-probability methods.

---

**BOX 9.1**

## TYPES OF SAMPLE

### Probability

- Simple random
- Stratified random (proportionate and disproportionate)
- Cluster (single and multi-stage)

### Non-probability

- Quota
- Snowball
- Volunteer
- Maximum variation
- Theoretical
- Case study

It is important at the outset to dispel a common myth, namely that probability methods are only suited to 'quantitative' studies and non-probability methods are only suited to 'qualitative' studies. A moment's thought ought to be enough to realise that a representative, randomly chosen sample of people could be interviewed using depth interviews, and that a non-representative group of volunteers could be given a structured questionnaire asking fixed-choice questions that generated statistical information about the group thus studied. With some minor exceptions, sampling procedures are unconnected to the type of data collected.

## Probability sampling

### History of probability sampling

In the early days of the social survey this type of research required immense resources as it was felt that in order to discover the conditions of the population it was necessary to conduct a complete census of all its members. This is characteristic of the work of William Booth who, in the late nineteenth and early twentieth centuries, surveyed the entire population of London in order to discover the extent and causes of poverty (Box 9.2). This took him and a team of helpers 17 years, and he felt exhausted with his efforts by the end of it, as his own words show:

> I have at times doubted whether the prolongation of this work has had any other basis than an inability on my part to come to a conclusion. (Booth, 1902: 3)

> Never I should think has a book been the occasion of so much bad language on the part of its author – I cursed every minute I gave to it. (Booth, 1894)

---

**BOX 9.2**

## WILLIAM BOOTH'S APPROACH TO THE SOCIAL SURVEY, BEFORE SAMPLING WAS INVENTED

Booth's classic study of the *Life and Labour of the People in London* was based on the systematic collection of original and extensive data on the conditions of the urban population. Booth, a wealthy industrialist who was disturbed by the poor conditions of working-class life in late Victorian Britain, began his investigations in 1886 and published them in 17 volumes in 1902. His vast study into the working classes of London was framed by two chief concerns with the social and economic state (the 'life' and 'labour') of this population: focusing attention on the living conditions of working-class families, and the occupation and income of their 'breadwinners'. An in-depth study of this massive urban population was made possible not by surveying each household directly, but by interviewing the school board visitors who had access to each family with children in local schools. Their detailed knowledge of the households in their local district – including the details of their employment, rent and wages – was supplemented by further information obtained from local police, churchmen and district superintendents

*Source*: Tonkiss, 2004

---

The application of sampling theory to the social survey by Arthur Bowley made the sample survey possible, a cheaper method involving the random selection of a sample from a defined population. Generalising the results found in the sample to the population from which it was drawn became a matter of assessing the likelihood of results having occurred by chance. His survey of the wage-earning class in Reading (Bowley and Burnett-Hurst, 1915), instead of being a census of all of these households in that place, made use of sampling techniques, selecting every twentieth building on the borough residential register, and excluding non-working-class households. This left Bowley with a sample of 743 wage-earning households, each of which was visited and surveyed.

It was possible for Bowley to do this because of his use of a statistic called the standard error, though which researchers are able to measure the precision of the sample in relation to the population as a whole. The standard error decreases with increasing sample size, indicating a sample that is improving in precision. The importance of Bowley's contribution is explained here:

Bowley's paper itemises a set of ground rules that are still in use today: the construction of a sampling frame that defines exactly the population being surveyed, the selection of a method for sampling, the observation of all sampled units, and attention to possible biases and errors arising from violations in the sampling plan. ... Bowley stressed the fact that researchers engaged in sampling must have 'a complete absence of prejudice and a perfect willingness to accept the results, however unpalatable ... The universe from which the selection is made must be defined with the utmost rigour, [and] the rules of selection ... must be followed with perfect strictness' (Anderson and Fienberg, 1999).

Later statisticians refined Bowley's ideas to generate the idea of a confidence interval, which allows the researcher to be quite precise about the degree to which numerical results derived from a sample can be generalised to a population. Another term for this is the margin of error, and Figure 9.1 shows how this decreases as sample size increases. With a sample size of 96 the margin of error is 10

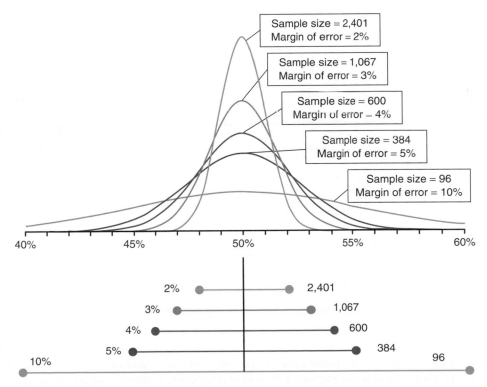

**FIGURE 9.1**  As sample size increases, the margin of error in generalising to the population decreases

per cent, but when it is 2,401 the error is just 2 per cent. This is shown in the upper figure by the contrast between the broad, almost flat curve relating to the sample of 96, and the peaked curve relating to the sample of 2,401. In the lower figure, the width of the lines represent the increasing margin of error as sample size decreases.

## Populations and sampling frames

The first step in drawing up a probability sample may seem a little bit counter-intuitive, but if you think hard about it, it is absolutely essential. Before starting on anything else, you need to define the population you wish to study. The population of a survey may not always be individuals. The relevant population could be made up of schools, hospitals, small businesses, local authorities, newspapers and so on. When the population to be studied consists of individuals it might be the population of a particular town, university students, refugees, people living in residential care homes, homeless people, people claiming disability benefits and so on. To draw up a probability sample the researcher then needs to find a list of all members of the relevant population. Such a list of the population is called a sampling frame.

Finding a suitable sampling frame is, in some cases, no easy task, and the absence of a suitable one is sometimes a reason to consider non-probability methods which do not have this requirement.

A number of sampling frames exist and are accessible to researchers (see Box 9.3). Samples of the whole UK population include the electoral register, telephone directories and the Postcode Address File (PAF), though they all have limitations in their coverage. The electoral register, for example, may under-represent people who frequently move house, while those who do not register to vote will not be included. Printed telephone directories are incomplete because they do not cover mobile phones, not everyone owns a land-line telephone and some people choose not to have their number listed anyway. The PAF is more up to date and has greater coverage of the population than the electoral register and has the advantage of being available electronically. However, because the file used for sampling is the 'small user file', which lists addresses receiving less than 25 items of post each day, included in the file are businesses that receive few items of post while private households that receive large amounts of post are excluded. The PAF is therefore not a full and accurate list of the population, though it is more accurate than many alternatives.

---

BOX 9.3

## EXAMPLES OF SAMPLING FRAMES

### Covering the general population

Register of electors; telephone directory; birth certificates; death certificates; postcode address file.

### Covering institutions

Directory of universities, schools or colleges; health services directory; directory of penal institutions.

### Covering professional groups

Medical directory; registers of psychologists, nurses, osteopaths; register of chartered surveyors.

### Some other groups

A university department's list of students attending a course; hospital admissions daily log book; a school register of pupils or students; an employer's records of employees; a solicitor's records of clients.

There are also sampling frames available for specific populations. For instance, there are lists available that cover institutions like the directories of universities, schools, colleges and penal institutions. There are directories that cover professional groups such as the medical directory, registers of nurses, psychologists and osteopaths. In addition, it is possible to gain access to lists other groups. For example, universities keep lists of students, schools keep registers of pupils, employers keep records of employees, a government department will keep records of social security or welfare benefit claimants. Some lists are more accessible to social researchers than others. Some lists are in the public domain while others are protected and remain confidential. But for some groups in the population sampling frames are not available and other methods must be found to study them, as we shall see later.

There are three types of probability sampling methods:

- simple random sampling
- stratified sampling
- cluster sampling.

All three approaches rely on the availability or the ability to compile a complete and accurate sampling frame. Once a sampling frame has been obtained, all the elements should be numbered and the size of the sample decided upon. The most basic type of probability sample is the simple random sample.

## Simple random sampling

To obtain a simple random sample, one can use a lottery method or a table of random numbers, or a systematic approach. The lottery method is akin to drawing numbers out of a hat. All elements of the population would be placed in a hat and the number required for the sample would then be drawn out. For example, if the population was 5,000 teachers and the sample size was 500, then the names of all 5,000 teachers would be placed in a hat and 500 would be drawn out. Here, each teacher in the population would have an equal, known chance of being selected: 1 in 10.

When the population is large the lottery method is unrealistic because it requires each member of the population to be listed separately, and random numbers or *systematic sampling* are used instead. Random numbers are generated by computers (see, for example, www.random.org) which, if each member of the population has been given a unique number, can then be matched with the same number in the sampling frame for inclusion in the study.

To obtain a systematic sample (which in this case is also a simple random sample) the researcher needs to calculate a sampling fraction by dividing the required size of the sample by the population. If a sample of 500 doctors were required from a population of 5,000, then the sampling fraction is 10. Starting with a randomly selected doctor with a number below 10, the researcher then selects every tenth person on the list. If you began with number 4, then you would select cases 4, 14, 24, 34, 44, 54 and so on to be included in the sample. With systematic samples you need to be sure that there is no inherent ordering to the lists as this would distort the sample. For example, if male and female teachers' names alternated so that every even number was a male and every odd number was a female, the sampling strategy just outlined would generate a sample consisting of men only.

The essential point about each of the above methods of sampling is that every member of the population has a chance of being selected. In fact, in simple random sampling, the chance is equal for each member of the population. The statistical procedures used to calculate the likelihood of sample results having occurred because an unrepresentative sample has been chosen (discussed in Chapter 19) can only be applied if this condition is met.

## Stratified sampling

A **stratified sample** is more accurate, and therefore more representative of the population than a simple random sample, but also more complex. Each member of the population is divided into groups or *strata* and then a simple random sample is selected from each stratum (perhaps using a systematic approach as described earlier). The strata are generally variables that the researcher wants to ensure are represented in the sample. Box 9.4 illustrates this.

---

**BOX 9.4**

### STRATIFIED SAMPLING: AN EXAMPLE

- *The study*: Of different levels and conditions of employment among university lecturers by ethnic group.

- *Stratifying factor*: Ethnic group.

- *Procedure*: List members of one ethnic group first, then list members of another ethnic group and so on until all of the members of the population are listed. Number each person in the list. Use a sampling fraction to select people for the sample.

- *Disproportionate stratification*: If the sampling frame describes the general UK university lecturer population it is likely that the majority of the sample would be 'white' because the majority of the population falls into the 'white' category. Using disproportionate stratified sampling techniques would ensure that different ethnic groups were included in the sample. Here, a smaller sampling fraction is used for smaller groups in the population, giving them a greater (but still known) chance of being selected.

*Source*: Bloch, 2004

---

Simple random sampling relies on chance to get a group of people (or elements) whose characteristics mirror those in the population concerned. Thus, we might hope in a simple random sample taken, say, from the population of people aged between 20–25 in a country, to see roughly equal numbers of men and women. The larger the sample, the more likely it is that this will occur (thus sample size influences representativeness, as we saw in Figure 9.1). However, in any such randomly selected sample it is always possible that, by some chance, we will select only one sex. Stratified sampling allows us to guard against this possibility. In the case of sex, for example, we might first list all of the women in the sampling frame, and then all of the men. If the sampling interval is still 100, every one hundredth woman is then selected, and then every one hundredth man, as in systematic sampling.

Here, sex is the **stratifying factor**, and in order to use this we need to know the sex of every member of the population listed on the sampling frame, so that it can be arranged accordingly. In fact, it is wise to use any information available on a sampling frame as a stratifying factor as this will almost always improve representativeness. One might, for example, stratify by age as well as sex, in which case one would arrange the sampling frame so that it listed 20-year-old women, then 20-year-old men, then 21-year-old women, then 21-year-old men and so on. All of this depends on this information being recorded against each person listed on the frame.

As an extra consideration, researchers sometimes select samples using **disproportionate** stratification. This can be useful if there is a minority group within a population of particular interest for the study. Thus, a sample of 100 from the general population of a country would be unlikely to contain many millionaires. If one were particularly interested in comparing the lives of such people with those of people less well off, and if one knew the incomes of every person listed in the sampling frame (quite a demanding requirement!), one could list the millionaires separately and choose every second one, as opposed to every hundredth person in the list of poorer people.

Seale's (2009a, 2009b) study of doctors' end-of-life decisions used disproportionate stratification. He wanted a study of a representative sample of doctors, but he was also particularly interested in doctors who specialised in looking after dying people, or very elderly people. If he had taken a simple random sample of doctors, he would only have selected a few such doctors, meaning that any generalisations about that particular group would have been based on low numbers.

He therefore chose (randomly) a disproportionately large number of palliative care and elderly care doctors, and a disproportionately small number of general practitioners and other specialties. When he wanted to produce statistics that applied to the whole population of doctors, he ensured that the results were weighted to adjust for this disproportionality, meaning that the replies from each palliative care doctor contributed less to the population statistic than did the replies of general practitioners. But when he wanted to compare the replies of general practitioners with palliative care doctors, he could do so without weighting the results in this way.

## Cluster sampling and multi-stage cluster sampling

Cluster sampling is particularly useful when the relevant population is widely dispersed because it economises on the time and costs incurred by travel. If, for example, a researcher wanted to interview university students, it would be more efficient first to sample (randomly) a group of universities from a list of all universities. Then students in the selected institutions could be selected. As well as travel savings this would have the added advantage of only requiring listings of students for selected universities. A random sampling procedure based on the whole population of university students would mean assembling a very large list of all students in the country.

Sometimes cluster sampling occurs in more stages than this, in which case it is called multi-stage cluster sampling. For example, the first stage might be to select several school districts or local education authorities (the first stage). Then, from lists of the schools in each selected area, a sample of schools would be chosen (the second stage). Next, from lists of the pupils in those schools, a random sample of pupils would be chosen (the third stage).

The accuracy of cluster sampling depends on how representative of the population the clusters chosen are. If a sample of 1,000 students was required, 200 students could be interviewed at five different universities, 100 students at 10 universities, 50 students at 20 universities, 10 students at 100 universities and so on. The researcher has to decide on the trade-off between a highly clustered sample and more variety. The smaller the number of clusters, the more likely that the sample will lack variation. The larger the number of clusters, the more representative of the population the sample will be.

## Response rates

It is important to maximise the response rate among those selected for inclusion in a study using probability methods because the higher this is, the more representative the sample is of the population. Generally, face-to-face interviews have higher response rates than postal surveys, though this will depend on the topic of the research. Self-completion surveys can achieve high response rates where the subject of the research is of interest to respondents. Table 9.1 shows the response to a survey using face-to-face interviews where sampling was done using the Postcode Address File. Table 9.2 shows response rates from a postal survey.

The reason stated most often for non-response among successful contacts eligible for the survey described in Table 9.1 was refusal to participate. Generally, government surveys achieve higher response rates than other surveys because of perceptions about their importance. However, skilled interviewers can encourage participation and increase response rates, though it is unethical to pressurise people into participating (see Chapter 5). The second reason was non-contact. Non-contact can be reduced by increasing the number of call-backs to each address and by varying the times of the day and days of the week that calls are made to increase the likelihood of finding the respondent at home. Some respondents cannot be interviewed because they are too ill, old and frail, or there might be a language barrier. Excluding some of these groups

from a survey might bias responses, and steps can be taken ensure their participation. For example, interviews can be carried out using community languages to ensure that those with less fluency in English can participate.

The responses to the postal survey shown in Table 9.2 were based on three contacts with each respondent: an initial letter and questionnaire, a follow-up letter and then an additional follow-up letter and questionnaire. A response rate of 67 per cent would generally be considered high for a postal survey.

In a probability sample survey the response rate should always be reported. Where known, information about the reasons for non-response and the characteristics of non-responders should be provided so that likely bias can be assessed.

Sometimes, survey researchers investigate the potential of non-response to have biased the results in more systematic ways. An example of this is shown in Box 9.5. In this survey, because the investigation measured the amount of bias introduced by variable response rates from different groups, it was possible to weight the results so that they more closely mirrored the profile of the population.

TABLE 9.1  Breakdown of a face-to-face interview sample

| Response category | Number | Percentage |
| --- | --- | --- |
| **Total addresses issued** | **1972** | |
| Non-eligible addresses | 223 | 11 |
| *Of which* | | |
| No trace of address | 50 | 22 |
| Business | 76 | 34 |
| Institution | 2 | 1 |
| Empty/boarded up | 86 | 39 |
| Other | 9 | 4 |
| Eligible addresses | **1749** | |
| *Of which* | | |
| Successful interviews | 1164 | 67 |
| Refusals | 310 | 18 |
| Non-contacts (after four calls) | 186 | 11 |
| Not interviewable (e.g. away, on holiday, language difficulty, ill) | 89 | 5 |

*Source*: adapted from Bloch and John, 1991

TABLE 9.2   Breakdown of a postal survey sample

| Response category | Number | Percentage |
|---|---|---|
| **Total number in sample** | **851** | |
| Not eligible (gone away, died, not known) | 75 | 9 |
| **Total eligible** | **776** | |
| *Of which* | | |
| Completed questionnaires | 519 | 67 |
| Returned but not filled out or incomplete (refusals, too ill etc.) | 44 | 6 |
| No reply | 213 | 27 |

*Source*: adapted from Bloch, 1992

---

**BOX 9.5**

## RESPONSE RATE AND RESPONSE BIAS IN A STUDY OF DOCTORS AND END-OF-LIFE DECISIONS

The overall response rate of doctors was 42.1 per cent. Specialists in palliative medicine produced the highest response rate (67.3 per cent), then specialists in care of the elderly (48.1 per cent), neurologists (42.9 per cent), other hospital specialties (40.1 per cent) and GPs (39.3 per cent). GP responders were more likely to be women (50 per cent of responding GPs compared with 44 per cent in the national medical workforce). Gender was proportionate for other specialties. Older doctors were more likely to reply. For GPs, this age bias applied to those over 45 and for other doctors to those aged over 35. Responders were more likely to report on a death from cancer (48 per cent of reported deaths) than occur in national mortality statistics (27.6 per cent) and less likely to report on a death from cardiovascular disease (18.9 per cent reported vs 34.7 per cent nationally).

In all, 66 doctors returned letters, notes or e-mails giving reasons for not responding. The most common reason was not having the time to complete the survey (28 doctors), and the second most common (19 doctors) was not being involved in care of dying patients or palliative care (even though the accompanying letter indicated that a response from doctors in this position would be welcomed).

Non-responders were sent a one-page form asking for their reasons for non-participation and some other questions, to which 348 replied. Table 3 [not shown here] shows the proportion agreeing with each of nine reasons for not responding. Non-responders were asked the first two questions that appear in Table 2 [not shown here]. No significant difference between responders and non-responders was found for question 1; non-responders were somewhat more likely to be opposed to allowing a doctor to assist in a death in the manner described in question 2 (72 per cent thought probably or definitely not, as opposed to 64 per cent of responders; P = 0.005).

In conclusion, it appears that non-responders tended to be younger and to have inadequate time to complete the questionnaire. The high response rate from palliative medicine specialists and, to a smaller extent, those involved in care of the elderly, coupled with the bias towards reporting on a cancer death and the perception of some respondents that it was unnecessary to complete the questionnaire if they did not normally attend dying patients, suggests that the survey tended to be perceived as being largely relevant to terminal care.

*Source*: Seale, 2009b

## Non-probability sampling

It is not always possible to carry out a random sample of the population and it is not always desirable. Non-probability techniques are often used to access groups whose activities are normally 'hidden' from public or official view, so that a sampling frame may not exist. In some circumstances a representative sample may not be desirable, because the study is aiming at something different. Typically, this is where not much is known about a subject, and the investigation therefore has an exploratory feel to it, or is devoted to the development of novel theories or other types of insight. Because exploration and theory development is often also a characteristic of qualitative research, it is sometimes assumed that non-probability sampling is only used in qualitative studies. As we saw at the outset of the chapter, though, there is no logical reason why a particular type of data (quantitative or qualitative) has to be inextricably linked to a particular method of sampling.

In some research studies the representativeness of the sample is less important than in others. For example, Geoffrey Baruch (1981) analysed the stories about medical consultations told by eight parents of children attending two medical clinics. If he had been trying to use these interviews to generalise about all parents' satisfaction with the quality of medical care in the country as a whole, we would feel this to be a hopelessly inadequate sample. However, his purpose was to analyse the language used during the interview to present parents' actions in a moral light, suggesting that 'atrocity stories' about poor behaviour by doctors were often told in order to achieve this effect, and that this tendency ought to be taken into account when assessing the results of 'patient satisfaction' exercises. Thus his purpose was not to estimate how commonly such atrocity stories were told in a population of parents, but to report what this phenomenon – which had not been noticed or described before – looked like.

Mary Douglas' work, discussed in Chapter 3, demonstrates a different rationale for generalising findings which has been called theoretical generalisation (Mitchell, 1983). You will recall that Douglas concluded from her case study of the Lele, when compared with the ancient Israelites, that groups faced with enemies and unused to crossing boundaries were less likely to celebrate anomaly in their classificatory thinking. This is a theoretical proposition arising from anthropological and historical case studies, chosen not because they represent some wider population, but because they exhibit features which help develop insights into social processes.

Let us first consider a type of non-probability sampling whose primary aim *is* to approach representativeness, known as quota sampling, before describing other non-probability methods.

## Quota sampling

Market researchers tend to use quota sampling techniques because they are relatively quick and cheap to carry out. Using this method, interviewers must find interviewees who fit specified criteria, such as age and sex, and often the quotas used in the sample mirror the population. For example, if it is known that 50 per cent of a population are male and 50 per cent of each gender are over 60, then a quota sample of, say, 100 people would ensure that equal numbers of men and women, both over 60 and below this age, are included. In this situation, people would be stopped in the street on the basis of the interviewer's estimation of their gender and asked their age. If they fit the requirements of the quota the interview proceeds if the potential respondent agrees to participate. Once 25 women aged over 60 had been interviewed, for example, the interviewer would no longer seek out such women for inclusion.

Quota samples have the advantage of being cheap as there are no costs associated with obtaining or compiling a sampling frame and there are no call-backs if a potential respondent is not at home first time. They are often also cheap because street sampling means that interview time is very short since you cannot keep people talking on the street for very long. The main problem with quota samples is that there are inherent biases. The quotas are usually obtained on busy shopping streets so frequent shoppers are over-represented and people who work outside the town centre are under-represented. Because there is no sampling frame that gives every member of a population a known chance of being selected, statistical tests that enable one to generalise from a sample to the population are not valid.

## Snowball and volunteer sampling

Snowball sampling (sometimes also called *network* sampling) involves obtained respondents through referrals among people who share the same characteristic and who know of each other. This technique relies on personal recommendations by people whom a respondent knows. This can be helpful if the researcher is trying to discover who are the important people to talk to about a particular issue, so can be useful in the study of elite groups where the connections between significant individuals are gradually being discovered as the study progresses. Conversely, this can be a useful technique when the study population is relatively hidden, as in the case of those engaging in illicit or stigmatised activities, such as drug users.

The main problem with snowballing is that there is a possibility of interviewing people within one network, which means that they might have similar experiences. More isolated members of a group, who may have had different experiences, are less likely to be included in the study. One way around this is to try to find multiple starting points for snowballing so that access to more than one network is obtained.

Another approach is to ask for a volunteer sample, as where a magazine prints a questionnaire for interested readers to return, or where an advertisement is posted on a notice board. This has an advantage in recruiting people who are particularly interested and willing to participate in the research study, and who may have particularly unusual or interesting insights to deliver. But the disadvantage of the volunteer approach is that such people may have different experiences and views compared to people who don't volunteer. For example, in a study asking for volunteers to take part on a study of the balance between work and leisure, volunteers may be those who have more leisure time to spare.

## Maximum variation sampling

This method is suited to small samples where there is no sampling frame, but the researcher still wants to feel that representativeness may have been achieved. Rather than seeking out people who seem 'average', the researcher uses his or her existing knowledge of the subject being studied to try to find people with widely varying experiences and characteristics. An example is given in Box 9.6. Through getting such a wide variety of views, the hope is that a complete range of possible experiences will be included. This would not be achieved were the researcher to seek out a sample of people who were mostly 'average'.

---

**BOX 9.6**

### AN EXAMPLE OF MAXIMUM VARIATION SAMPLING

With **maximum variation sampling**, you try to include all the extremes in the population. For example, in a small village, for a radio audience survey, you could ask to interview:

- the oldest person in the village who listens to radio
- the oldest who does not listen to radio

*(Continued)*

*(Continued)*

- the youngest who listens to radio
- a person who listens to radio all day
- a person who often talks about radio programmes he or she has heard
- a person who listens to radio in the middle of the night
- a person who has never listened to radio in his or her life
- the person with the most radios (a repairman, perhaps)
- the person with the biggest aerial
- a person who is thought to be completely average in all ways
- a person who spends a lot of time in the street and in public places
- a person who works nearly all the time

and so on – changing 'person' to 'man' or 'woman' alternately, to ensure equal representation of both sexes. Of course this only works when such information about other people is widely known. The above list of people could be produced in a village, where many people know many others, but would be much more difficult in a large city.

*Source*: List, 2004

## Theoretical sampling

Theoretical sampling is a method first developed by Glaser and Strauss (1967) as a component part of their method known as grounded theory. A whole chapter of this book (Chapter 22) is devoted to this and theoretical sampling is dealt with fairly fully in that chapter, so a brief account suffices here. Glaser and Strauss developed this approach in order to generate theories about the process of dying where their sampling elements were not people but different types of hospital ward. Applied to a study involving individuals as sampling elements, this method involves the selection of people for interview according to whether they have characteristics that are likely to help in developing an emerging theory.

An example taken from the PhD work of Marion Garnett (2000, 2003) concerns the topic of the use of alternative medical therapies by nurses. An initial three interviews showed that all of the nurses described therapies involving different types of massage as contributing to a new form of nursing expertise that involves the expression of care by touch. Note that Garnett had begun to analyse, or at least think about her interviews pretty soon after collecting them. This is a key characteristic of theoretical sampling and of grounded theory more generally: as the research proceeds with the study, they are constantly thinking about what they are discovering so that, in the case of sampling, decisions can be taken that maximise the possibility of developing an emerging theory. After her first three interviews Garnett then had to decide who to interview next. She decided that a fourth interview would be conducted with a nurse chosen explicitly on the grounds that she practiced an alternative therapy that did *not* involve massage or touch, to allow other, theoretically interesting meanings nurses claim for their use of these therapies to emerge.

## Sampling in case study research

If you are studying a single case, or only a few cases, as in ethnographic work where you may have decided to study in depth a particular setting, such as a village, an institution, a geographical area or even a single person, you will need to think about how cases are chosen. There are a number of possible rationales for choosing a particular case, shown in Box 9.7.

---

BOX 9.7

### ESTABLISHING THE 'TYPICALITY' OF A CASE

1  Take a case on the basis of it representing the future.

2  Provide full details of context to inform judgements of transferability to other cases.

3  Take a case typical of a cluster of characteristics.

4  Study more than one case.

5  Do team research to study different cases.

6  Choose cases on the basis of broader statistical picture.

---

As an example of the first rationale listed in Box 9.7, Cicourel and Kitsuse (1963) chose a particular school in the USA to study because it had a psychological counselling service. At that time this was unusual, but the researchers believed (rightly) that this represented the future for all American schools. Their results would therefore have relevance for the future of American schooling.

The second rationale for doing a case study is not really related to how a case is selected, but to how it is studied. This idea comes from Lincoln and Guba (1985), who argue that in case study research – especially if qualitative methods are used – 'transferability' of findings to other cases that have not been studied can be achieved. If the researcher immerses him or herself in the case that is being studied and provides a very full account of what that case is like, almost in the manner that a skilled novelist might paint a word picture of something so that the reader almost feels that he or she has 'been there', then transferability is enhanced. By providing such a thick description of a case, the reader of that description is empowered to make reasonable human judgements about whether things that are happening in the case that has been studied are likely to happen in some other case of which the reader

has experience. Thus a school teacher, reading Cicourel and Kitsuse's detailed account of how a school counselling service operates in a particular school, will be able to make a judgement about how a new counselling service would function if introduced into their own school.

The third and fourth rationales listed in Box 9.7 can be illustrated in a single example, again taken from educational research. Pratt et al. (1984) report a study of equal opportunities in secondary schools in the UK. Their task was to assess the degree to which such schools were conforming to the requirements of the 1975 Sex Discrimination Act. To start with, they carried out a postal survey of a representative sample of schools, chosen by a mixture of cluster sampling and simple random sampling. Using the results of this survey, and information about the characteristics of UK schools available in official statistics, they were able to choose 14 schools for further detailed study, involving visits for three day periods to each case study school by members of the team, in which teachers and pupils were interviewed about their experiences. Examples of five of the schools selected for case study are given in Box 9.8, showing that a variety of factors lay behind the selection of cases.

BOX 9.8

## SCHOOLS SELECTED FOR CASE STUDIES

- '*Midland Comprehensive*': 11–18 comprehensive; 720 pupils; Midlands; city centre catchment; Labour Local Education Authority (LEA); amalgamation of two single-sex schools; poor situation and catchment; 50 per cent of pupils non-European background; postal survey shows positive discrimination policy towards non-traditional choice, pioneered by headteacher.

- '*Inner City Comprehensive*': 11–18 comprehensive; 850 pupils; London city centre catchment; Labour LEA; postal survey shows it to have an active equal opportunities policy promoted by dynamic headteacher and widely supported by staff.

- '*Northern Modern*': 11–16 secondary modern; 760 pupils; mainly council estate catchment; northern region; Conservative LEA; postal survey shows low level of sympathy towards equal opportunities.

- '*Smallchange Secondary*': 12–18 secondary modern; 720 pupils; in southern rural catchment; Conservative LEA; postal survey indicates a passive view of equal opportunities.

- '*Oldboys Grammar*': 11–18 grammar school in prosperous London suburb; 700 pupils; Conservative LEA; highly traditional atmosphere and emphasis on academic excellence; postal survey shows little concern with equal opportunities.

## Sampling within a case

Of course, once one is carrying out a case study, there are further sampling considerations. In the study of equal opportunities in schools mentioned above, the researchers could not talk to all of the teachers and pupils in each school, so will have had to sample. Clearly, the principles of sampling that have been outlined so far in this chapter might be used to decide who to sample within a case. A random representative sample might be drawn up from a list of all of the people in the case, or a snowball or volunteer or some other non-probability method might be chosen.

But it is the experience of most people who carry out case-study research – perhaps particularly those using the ethnographic methods described in Chapter 14 – that who the researcher ends up speaking to will depend in part on the characteristics of the researcher. These can be the researchers fixed characteristics (e.g. their age or their gender) or their abilities or social skills. A man might have difficulty gaining access to a women's changing room, and vice versa. A researcher who knows nothing about football is likely to have trouble speaking with the fans if he or she is doing a study of a football club, so may end up communicating mostly with the management team. Box 9.9 contains an example of a researcher concerned about sampling within the cases he studied, and suggests a method for investigating whether biases have occurred as a result.

BOX 9.9

## IDENTIFYING SAMPLING BIASES WITHIN A CASE STUDY

In Sieber's (1979) study of schools he was concerned he had overestimated the job satisfaction of rank and file teachers, due to his having interacted disproportionately with their superiors in the hierarchy of the educational system. He writes:

[O]ur own fieldwork ... developed into a study of school boards, superintendents, and the leaders of the high school teachers. After conducting a survey, however, I was able to correct certain impressions that emerged from my elite bias. This can be shown quite simply. Prior to looking at the results of the survey, I predicted the proportion of teachers who would respond in particular ways to the survey questions. I then compared my predictions with the actual responses. It became obvious when observing these comparisons that I had unwittingly adopted the elite's version of reality. For example, I overestimated the extent to which teachers felt that the administration accepted criticism. Here are the relevant questions and the statistics: 'Do you think that teachers who are interested in administrative openings jeopardise their opportunities in this district by voicing criticism of present school policies and practices?' (per cent responding 'definitely' and 'possibly'):

|  | Predicted | Observed |
|---|---|---|
| System A............ | 40 | 60 |
| System B............ | 40 | 65 |

Similarly, I had assumed that the teachers were more satisfied with evaluative procedures than was in fact the case: 'All in all, how well do you think the evaluation of teachers is done in your school?' (per cent responding 'as well as possible' and 'fairly well'):

|  | Predicted | Observed |
|---|---|---|
| System A |  |  |
| Elementary............ | 80 | 65 |
| Secondary............ | 50 | 36 |
| System B |  |  |
| Elementary............ | 80 | 74 |
| Secondary............ | 75 | 56 |

Although to a lesser extent, I also overestimated the rank-and-file support for the leaders of the teachers association, with whom I had spent a good deal of time. In short, I had fallen prey to the elite bias, despite recent training in the dangers of giving greater weight to prestigious figures as informants.

*Source*: Sieber, 1979: 1353

## Conclusion

This chapter has divided sampling into probability and non-probability methods, emphasising that both approaches can be used to gather either qualitative or quantitative data. As the section on the history of survey sampling made clear, the idea of selecting a random sample from a population transformed the capacity to carry out social surveys. Further developments of simple random sampling were outlined, including stratified and cluster sampling and variations on these. A section on response rates and how to investigate and adjust for the biases introduced by skewed response rates then followed.

The chapter then turned to non-probability methods and different rationales for sampling than representativeness, including the aim of exploring a field and discovering new phenomena, and the aim of developing theories or special insights by sampling that maximises the possibility of this. First, quota sampling was introduced; this retains the idea of representativeness, providing a cheaper but less adequate alternative to random sampling. Snowball, volunteer, maximum variation and theoretical sampling were then outlined. The chapter ended with the considerations that apply when carrying our case studies, showing sampling considerations apply both in selecting cases and in the decisions taken about what or who to study within a case.

Sampling in large part determines what one can conclude from a research study. Using a non-representative sample to generalise results to a population is a mistake; similarly, who you take to, or observe, in an exploratory study is likely to determine what you discover. Good quality thinking about sampling, then, lies behind good social research and it is hoped that this chapter will have equipped you to think in this way.

## FURTHER READING

A good guide to survey sampling, emphasising representative random methods, can be found in Henry (1990). Another and more recent book in which this type of sampling is outlined in considerable detail is Barnett (2002). For non-probability methods, Flick (2006, Ch.11) has a good chapter on sampling. The same author has a further chapter on this in Flick (2003, Ch.3).

### Student Reader (Seale, 2004b): relevant readings

8   Barry Hedges: 'Sampling'

See also Chapter 29, 'Sampling, representativeness and generalisability' by Giampietro Gobo in Seale et al. (2004).

### Journal articles illustrating and discussing the approaches described in this chapter

Burton, M.L., Croce, M.D., Masri, S.A., Bartholomew, M. and Yefremian, A. (2005) 'Sampling from the United States Census Archives', Field Methods, 17: 102–118.

Mansergh, G., Naorat, S., Jommaroeng, R., Jenkins, R.A., Jeeyapant, S., Kanggarnrua, K., Phanuphak, P., Tappero, J.W. and Griensven, F. van (2006) 'Adaptation of venue-day-time sampling in Southeast Asia to access men who have sex with men for HIV assessment in Bangkok', Field Methods, 18: 135–152.

Thomas, M., Bloor, M. and Frankland, J. (2007) 'The process of sample recruitment: an ethnostatistical perspective', Qualitative Research, 7: 429–446.

## Web links

e-Source: Chapter 4 on 'Sample surveys' by Sarah M Nusser and Michael D Larsen: www.esourceresearch.org

Probability and non-probability sampling: www.tardis.ed.ac.uk/~kate/qmcweb/s2.htm

Sample size calculator: www.surveysystem.com/sscalc.htm

StatPac: www.statpac.com/surveys/sampling.htm

StatTrek: http://stattrek.com/Lesson6/SurveySampling.aspx

SlideShare: www.slideshare.net/sladner/sampling-methods-in-qualitative-and-quantitative-research-presentation

## KEY CONCEPTS FOR REVIEW

**Advice:** Use these, along with the review questions in the next section, to test your knowledge of the contents of this chapter. Try to define each of the key concepts listed here; if you have understood this chapter you should be able to do this. Check your definitions against the definition in the glossary at the end of the book.

| | |
|---|---|
| Census | Sample survey |
| Cluster sampling | Sampling fraction |
| Confidence interval | Sampling frame |
| Disproportionate stratification | Sampling theory |
| Grounded theory | Simple random sample |
| Margin of error | Snowball sampling |
| Maximum variation sampling | Standard error |
| Multistage cluster sampling | Stratified sample |
| Non-probability sampling | Stratifying factor |
| Population | Systematic sample |
| Probability sampling | Theoretical generalisation |
| Quota sampling | Theoretical sampling |
| Representative sample | Volunteer sample |
| Response rate | Weighting |

 **Review questions**

1 **Outline the steps involved in drawing up the following types of sample:**
   - **Simple random sample**
   - **Stratified sample**

- Cluster sample
- Multi-stage cluster sample
- Quota sample
- Snowball sample
- Volunteer sample
- Maximum variation sample
- Theoretical sample

2 What is the difference between probability and non-probability sampling? When is each approach useful?

## Workshop and discussion exercises

1 Pick one or more of the sampling frames listed in Box 9.2. Discuss the adequacy of these lists in covering the populations concerned. What omissions are there likely to be? What problems of access might there be in getting these lists, and in approaching people listed on them? What stratifying factors are likely to be present and useful for each sampling frame?

- *Covering the general population:* Register of electors; telephone directory; birth certificates; death certificates.
- *Covering institutions:* Directory of universities, schools or colleges; health services directory; directory of penal institutions.
- *Covering professional groups:* Medical directory; registers of psychologists, nurses, osteopaths; register of chartered surveyors.
- *Some other groups:* A university department's list of students attending a course; hospital admissions daily log book; a school register of pupils; an employer's records of employees; a solicitor's records of clients.

2 Imagine that you are engaged in a small-scale interviewing survey, designed to discover how people feel about balancing the demands of home life with those of their work life. You have the resources to interview about 20 people. How would you select people to interview?

3 Design a sampling strategy that would help answer the following research questions:

(a) What is the prevalence of euthanasia in the UK?
(b) How do school pupils approach their homework?
(c) What needle-sharing practices occur between injecting drug users?
(d) Does socio-economic status influence educational achievement?
(e) How has the public image of politicians changed over the past 20 years?

# 10

# DOING A DISSERTATION

Chetan Bhatt

---

| Chapter Contents |
|---|

Students in a variety of social and cultural disciplines are commonly required to write dissertations, often in the final year of an undergraduate degree. This is often seen as an opportunity to integrate and apply your previous learning while developing a personal project of your own. Employers can often look at CVs for evidence of having planned, undertaken and completed an independent project. Doing a dissertation will involve using some of the research methods described in other chapters of this book (or which you have learned about during your degree) and writing up your project as an extended document. Master's degrees also involve dissertations, though these are usually longer, more specialised and more demanding than at undergraduate level.

This chapter will guide you through the various stages of producing an undergraduate or Master's degree dissertation (also offering advice that may assist some PhD students or professional researchers). It necessarily overlaps with many of the other chapters in the book and references to these chapters are made at appropriate points. It is useful, though, to encapsulate in a single chapter the entire research process, from initial conception to final write-up, so that you can see more easily how the various elements of the research process can be combined into a single project.

## What is a dissertation?

A dissertation is not a long essay, but your own structured investigation or research into an interesting problem or topic. The topic might be chosen by you, or might be set by your tutor (you will need to find out the requirements that apply to you). Writing an extended piece of work on a subject of your own choosing is usually a pleasurable and interesting process; it is also challenging and requires careful thought and planning. In doing the dissertation, you are taking charge in setting your own topic (if allowed), developing your own ideas, undertaking the relevant reading, planning and doing your research, and writing up your research. On the other hand, you should also listen and respond to the advice and guidance of your supervisor and other advisers. *Both* your ideas and independence *and* listening carefully to advice from your supervisor are important to the successful completion of a strong dissertation.

A dissertation is normally expected to demonstrate:

* *Knowledge* and *understanding* relevant to a chosen or set dissertation topic or research problem.

* Your skills in *planning, organising, undertaking* and completing an independent project.

* Your ability to *apply* knowledge and understanding in investigating the topic.

* Your ability to *collect* or *produce, analyse* and *report on* information or data relevant to the topic.

* Your ability to *conclude* your analysis in relation to the initial topic or research problem.

You can view dissertations as being of four different kinds:

* *Empirical dissertations*: in which you discover, analyse and report on information you have collected yourself, usually by researching people or objects.

* *Dissertations based on secondary analysis*: in which you analyse existing information or data sets that have been created by other (usually professional) researchers.

* *Dissertations based on secondary sources*: in which you investigate a problem or topic by collecting other literature, analysing this, and proposing your own interpretation or argument.

* *Theoretical dissertations*: library-based dissertations in which you propose your own independent, critical approach or argument in relation to a body of *theoretical* literature from your subject.

However, the requirements for undertaking and submitting a dissertation vary across universities and courses. Universities have different regulations about matters such as dissertation length, referencing, style and whether you are required to undertake empirical research (such as interviewing people or doing a social survey). The length requirements can vary from 10,000 to 20,000 words. Because of these differing requirements, your first step in planning a dissertation that you have to submit for assessment must be to:

- gather information about the specific requirements of your institution or course
- be aware of the timescale during which you have to plan, produce and submit your dissertation.

Each discipline and course will have a particular view of the *academic contribution* a dissertation is expected to make. Your dissertation might also be assessed on the *transferable* or *employability skills* which are demonstrated within it. It may also be an essential part of the *learning outcomes* of your course or your overall degree that you are able to develop and apply specific research methods and data analysis skills relevant to your discipline. Therefore, familiarise yourself with the learning outcomes relevant to your dissertation and the purpose and the weighting of your dissertation within your degree. You will probably have been allocated a supervisor or tutor for your dissertation work. Meet them as soon as possible. Ensure that you discuss with them any aspects that are unclear in the dissertation guidelines specific to your course. It may also help to look at the dissertations of past students, if that is allowed by your institution. As for any assessed work, not following the expected requirements can affect your final mark, sometimes seriously. Be very clear about what is required from a dissertation in your course – and plan your dissertation early.

## Dissertation areas

Think about the full scope of your discipline and the range of areas it covers. You can use the latitude of your discipline to develop your approach. You should usually be able to consider any substantive topic or area that you can relate to your discipline as long as you can focus it down into a manageable research problem that can be completed in the time you have available and within the constraints of word length.

If you are doing a combined (joint) degree, you may be required to develop a dissertation that relates to both your disciplines. Many interesting issues emerge at the boundaries of two disciplines. You may need to seek the advice of your supervisor about how best to develop a research topic that addresses and integrates material from two different disciplines.

You should aim to formulate one or more research problems or questions that can be investigated within the constraints of a dissertation and which will provide you with an opportunity to develop and apply discipline-relevant arguments and interpretations. Your supervisor can tell you if you are straying too far from your discipline. You should think carefully how your research topic can be understood from the viewpoint of your discipline and how it can be related to existing knowledge. Chapters 3, 4 and 7 give guidance in the formulation of research questions that relate to broader concerns.

---

**BOX 10.1**

### WHAT IS THE DIFFERENCE BETWEEN AN EMPIRICAL DISSERTATION AND A THEORETICAL DISSERTATION?

Dissertations that involve your collecting information from people (using interviews, questionnaires, focus groups) or analysing items you have collected (such as images, text, film, video) are usually called **empirical dissertations**:

- For example, a dissertation considering the representation of Muslims in the UK and undertaken through an analysis of newspaper articles is an empirical dissertation because it involves empirical investigation on your part – in this case, of newspaper reports that you have collected.

*(Continued)*

Library-based dissertations undertaken by critically analysing and engaging with theoretical literature in your discipline are usually called theoretical dissertations:

- For example, a dissertation based on critically examining approaches to Orientalist scholarship about Islam during the colonial period would not be seen as comprising empirical research, but might be seen as dealing with a substantive theoretical area, such as Orientalism in colonial discourse, post-colonial theory or social theory. In this type of dissertation, you would be critically engaging with, and providing your own interpretations in relation to, the theoretical literature relevant to the topic.

Many dissertations do not *have to* involve *empirical* research (involving you in collecting original data), but nevertheless require engagement with a substantive topic or area (see Box 10.1). Check your local requirements or with your supervisor about this.

You should think carefully about your own creativity and independent critical approach in investigating a social or cultural issue. Examiners often mark dissertations based on, for example, interviews with young people about their attitudes to alcohol, drug use, sex, music, about their ethnic, cultural or religious identities or their consumer behaviour. No one will discourage you from doing a dissertation in these areas, but consider more creative approaches that pose a problem in a different and interesting way, or which investigate unexpected, challenging and uncommon questions (see Box 10.2). It can often be useful to think about projects that are concerned with the meanings of objects, identities or spaces that are unfamiliar to you or distant from how you might perceive your immediate 'identity', 'culture' or 'group'.

## BOX 10.2

### SOME DIFFERENT APPROACHES TO WELL-WORN PROBLEMS

- If you were to ask young people about their attitudes to water or paracetamol, might it give you more interesting and original results than asking them about their attitudes to alcohol or drugs?
- You could analyse the representation of men or women in popular magazine adverts for cosmetics; but would it make for a more interesting project to analyse the contents and state of a bathroom?
- Instead of investigating whether the identities of a minority ethnic or religious group are different from those of majority ethnic or religious groups, would it make for a more interesting project if the research were to investigate whether, and how, the everyday, lived cultures of both might be virtually the same?
- You could document the special features of the group you feel you belong to. In doing so, would you be discovering anything particularly new about the social world or would you simply be making

claims about your specialness (and that of your group) in the social world? Beware of the narcissistic fallacy: assuming that a demonstration of some (usually already well-known) beliefs or habits of a group one belongs to is the same as discovering new knowledge about the social world – including of that group itself.

- You could interview male and female students about their attitudes to sex and sexual relationships; would it make for a more interesting project if you investigated the same issue by analysing graffiti in male and female public conveniences?

- You could ask people about their food choices, shopping and cooking preferences, or you could record the contents of their kitchen.

- You could investigate attitudes towards the female hijab or niqab among your respondents. Alternatively, you could investigate their attitudes to modesty dress codes among men.

- You could investigate men's views of women by using interviews with men; but what about investigating men's views of men, or women's views of women using the same research technique?

- You could investigate associations between education and social class or education and ethnicity using a household survey data set; how about strengthening your dissertation by comparing your findings with published findings from UK labour force surveys, or analyses of ethnicity from the 2001 and 2011 UK censuses?

- You could investigate the experiences of racism faced by African Caribbean and South Asian people in the UK. But what about a more challenging project investigating the experiences of discrimination faced by Romani or other refugee populations from Eastern Europe living in France? Or experiences of civil/ethnic conflict abroad formerly faced by UK asylum seekers from Central African nations?

## The research process

Irrespective of what your dissertation is about, you will be following many of the stages, and going through several of the phases of a research process (see Figure 10.1). It is particularly suited to a dissertation involving empirical work, but many elements also apply to library-based dissertations. Many of these formal stages overlap considerably, and researchers often jump back to earlier stages. Hence, you should use Figure 10.1 as a general guide. You may not be expected to develop a formal hypothesis and test it. Nor might you be expected to create new concepts or theoretical terms (but see the next section on how to *combine concepts*). In an empirical dissertation, though, you will usually be expected to:

- Think about an area or interest.

- Focus this down to a manageable research problem.

- Undertake a literature review in the relevant area, typically using this to refine your research questions.

- Consider the strengths and weaknesses of, and apply appropriate research methods to, a defined group (or sample) of people or objects.

- Analyse your results.

- Report the analysis.

- Come to a conclusion about your original research problem, possibly also highlighting unresolved areas and debates, or other relevant theoretical or policy implications.

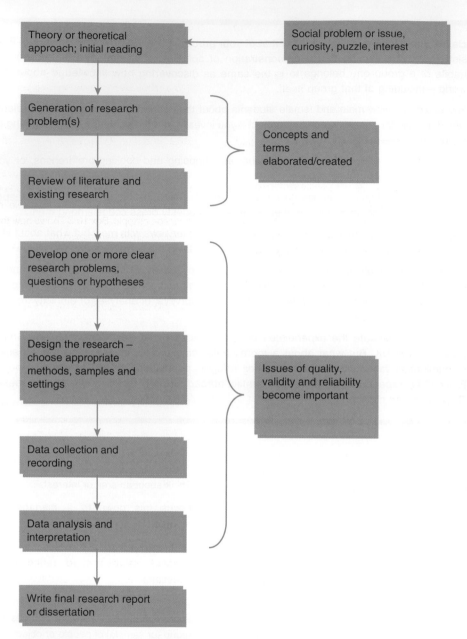

**FIGURE 10.1**  The research process (adapted from Giddens, 1993: 678)

## Defining your research problem

Students often start thinking about their dissertation by focusing on which research methods to use, together with a general idea of the research area. This is the *least* productive approach. The strength and quality of a dissertation is primarily determined by a fully thought-out, tightly focused research problem that directly relates to an interest of yours, which you can sustain interest in throughout the process of doing the dissertation, and which you can relate to existing debates, theories, or research in literature from your discipline. You should consider this stage to be the most important stage of the dissertation. Instead of starting off by, for example, thinking 'I am going to do some interviews to find out why people use social networking sites', push these ideas aside for the moment and instead *define and describe clearly a focused research problem*. Here is how you can proceed:

- Consider a strong interest or curiosity you have and which you think you might want to base your dissertation around. The initial curiosity may come from your reading, a lecture, a conversation with friends, the TV, a film, a blog, or just your own wandering thoughts. At this stage you can think on a grand scale, and you can think about grand statements. For example, consider the statement 'We are living in a surveillance society'.

- Convert your statement into a question: 'Are we really living in a surveillance society?' or 'In what ways are we living in a surveillance society?'. It is often useful to turn your statement into a 'how' or 'why' question.

- This next step is very important: process and focus your general question into a research problem or question which is in principle *researchable* and which

you can undertake to investigate within the time, financial and material constraints imposed on you as a student. Examiners will be looking for how your interests in a general area have been focused down into a manageable research project.

- There are various techniques that you can use to focus down your general interests, but one of the most useful is to spend a couple of undisturbed hours to 'brainstorm' your ideas and make use of visual representations, such as 'spider diagrams', flowcharts and lists. You may have to keep repeating this process until you get a sensible researchable question or topic. Box 10.3 shows how this can occur, using the surveillance example.

- You may end up with a research(able) problem that is some way from your original thinking or grand idea. You may decide to repeat the process until you are satisfied that you have a researchable problem which interests you enough to sustain this interest over a lengthy period. But the key point is that you will need to transform an original, perhaps grand-scale curiosity, interest or theoretical approach into a manageable, practical research project that you can complete over the allotted timescale. Notice also in the example in Box 10.3 that the methodology or research techniques have not, strictly speaking, been decided. This is as it should be.

---

**BOX 10.3**

## DEVELOPING A FOCUSED RESEARCH PROBLEM

### Are we living in a surveillance society?

Is the UK a 'surveillance society'? How does surveillance actually manifest in people's lives? – CCTV cameras? Internet footprints and personal data collection? Surveillance of consumer habits? Community policing? Audit and monitoring culture? Counter-terrorism legislation? Control orders? Restriction on civil liberties? Or is the idea of 'surveillance society' a reflection of other kinds of insecurity?

### What about social networking?

Social networking sites collect and monitor a great deal of information that people give voluntarily as well as inadvertently. They target advertising based on some of this information. Is this a kind of 'benign' surveillance? Is it like the government's collection of information? How much information are we giving up about ourselves with a click on an ad? What about personal information in radar type apps in smart phones?

… and so on …

*(Continued)*

*My draft topic:* I am interested in the broad idea of a surveillance society, but in thinking about this further I became interested in the kind of personal, consumption, marketing, retail and other information that is routinely collected by websites, especially social networking sites. The automatic and 'ordinary' way this information is collected results in very large social data stores about millions of people. My research problem is about how we are solicited to provide this information voluntarily to social network sites. My initial thoughts are that this is a kind of surveillance that works not by requesting information 'directly', as a government or social research agency might, but by flattering us and appearing to honour our choices and sensibilities. I am going to investigate this process using depth interviews with users of Facebook. I will also undertake a focus group by asking a small group of MySpace users to look at and discuss what parts of a dynamic social network site (pages, banners, targeted information) appeals to them and why. I will also undertake a brief analysis of a typical Facebook page to look at the processes of information solicitation. I will link this to theories of surveillance and governmentality. I also hope to examine the scale and scope of the kinds of personal, consumption and marketing data that such sites collect and link this to debates about the future of empirical social science.

In thinking about your research problem, it is useful to combine, and then explore, two or more, often radically different, key concepts – for example, 'power' and 'gender', or 'branding' and 'masculinity'. Combining concepts ('interrogative combination') is a useful study, learning and focusing strategy. The novelty and originality of your dissertation may be guided by exactly this process of combining and exploring the relations between two (or more) different conceptual areas. It can also be useful to combine one *theoretical* with one *empirical* area, and use this to develop your research questions. For example:

- 'visuality' with 'Christianity'
- 'underdevelopment' with 'Linux'
- 'symbolic interaction' with 'security guards'
- 'network society' with 'clothing'.

Such initial thinking processes are important in starting to help you focus your ideas into a practical, manageable project. It is as important to be convinced that this is the research problem you want to investigate. Try not to change your mind about your dissertation area halfway through the period you have in which to complete it; you may not have the time to start a new dissertation project afresh. Instead, seek the advice of your supervisor about how you can motivate yourself to make your existing project more suitable and relevant to your interests.

## Research design

A research problem can be investigated using a wide range of research methods and techniques. There is no one 'correct' method. For example, use of the social networking sites can be investigated using depth interviews, semi-structured questionnaires, large-scale social surveys, focus groups, ethnographic methods and observation research. You therefore should be able to make the case that the research methods (techniques) you have chosen are the most appropriate for your research questions, given time limitations and material constraints. Ideally, your research problem would have been formulated so that the research method chosen is clearly (one of the most) appropriate.

In thinking about your research design, it can be useful to distinguish between the methodology guiding your dissertation and the research methods (techniques) you are using. For example, a dissertation using broadly feminist approaches and partially based on statistical analysis of a data set on marriage and divorce might have a feminist *methodology* and be using quantitative research *methods*.

If you are doing a library-based, theoretical dissertation investigating a substantive area, there is likely to be some overlap between *theory* and *methodology* and you may need the advice of your supervisor. For example, a dissertation investigating the changing ways in which the female body has been represented in nineteenth and twentieth century art and literature might be undertaken using, say, Foucauldian social theory (see Chapter 4). In this case, you might want to also discuss Foucauldian *methodological* approaches (see also Kendall and Wickham (1999) for a guide to applying Foucault's approach).

Whichever research method(s) you select, you should think about the points described below.

## Strengths and weaknesses

You should be able to discuss and justify the research methods you have chosen based on their strengths and weaknesses *in relation to the research problem you are investigating*. You should also, even if briefly, be able to discuss why other methods were rejected, or were not considered appropriate.

## Sampling

Your sample refers to the *people* you have selected for interviewing or the *objects* (e.g. magazine advertisements) you have selected for analysis. How was your sample decided? What are the explicit criteria you have used to decide who or what is, and who or what is not, to be included in your sample? What other characteristics or attributes (age, gender, ethnicity, social class, employment, region, for example) do the members of your sample possess? Chapter 9 discusses sampling.

If you are doing small-scale qualitative research you will not be able to claim that your sample represents a larger population. This should be acknowledged when you write up your research, but you should also consider alternative rationales for sampling (e.g. theoretical sampling, discussed in Chapters 9 and 22) that may contribute significantly to the quality of your work.

Note, too, that use of large representative samples is quite feasible if you are doing secondary analysis of existing quantitative data sets (see Chapter 17). In such a case, you would usually be expected to include discussion about the nature of the sample – for example, the sample size, whether it is a random sample, if it is stratified in some way and the number of relevant missing cases or responses. These matters become especially important in quantitative analysis if you are generalising your results to (inferring something about) the population from which the sample came.

Box 10.4 looks at justifying qualitative sampling.

---

**BOX 10.4**

## JUSTIFYING QUALITATIVE SAMPLING: AN EXAMPLE

Your research may be based on an analysis of six selected issues of a magazine. You should ask:

- To what extent is this kind of magazine representative of 'the media' generally?
- To what extent can the magazine I have selected be considered representative of that subgenre of magazines?
- To what extent can the six issues be considered representative of the magazine?
- What social or historical period do those six issues seem to cover?

What (purposive) principles lay behind my selection of these six issues? Were these principles related to the research questions of the study, or informed by a search for variety?

## Validity, quality and reliability

Is your research 'instrument' – the questionnaire, the interview schedule, the focus group topic guide – and your overall research design, including your sample, capable of finding out what you want to discover (e.g. supporting your argument that one thing has caused another)? Would other people using the same research design get broadly the same research results? Would your research design generate broadly the same results among a different group of research participants sharing broadly the same characteristics? To what extent, if any, is it possible to generalise from your selected group (sample) to a wider 'population'? If you are doing a secondary analysis of a quantitative data set, you will usually need to address issues of statistical significance in your analysis: to what extent can you infer anything about the characteristics of the population from the sample which has been derived from it? These topics are discussed in Chapter 30 where their relevance for both quantitative and qualitative research designs is explored. Note that answering positively or affirmatively to all these questions may not (particularly in the eyes of some 'qualitative' researchers) guarantee quality of research and you may need to say more than that your results are 'limited because of the sample size' or your results 'are/are not replicable'.

## Reflexivity

What might be the consequences (actual or potential, intended or otherwise) of the research process on the research results? What might be the consequences of how your 'identity' was perceived and how you undertook the project, on the research process and research results? What are the various reflexive processes at play between you, the research process and your research participants (see Chapter 5)?

## Mixing methods

You should also consider more than one method (and in practice, you may well be implicitly using more than one method). For example, you may decide to use semiological methods to analyse some images (Chapter 16), but there is nothing to prevent you also considering a selected focus group's views of those same images (Chapter 13). You might interview individuals (see Chapters 11 and 12) and also analyse policy reports or documents (Chapters 15, 23 and 26) obtained from their organisation. Chapter 27 discusses the combination of qualitative and quantitative approaches. Using more than one method can strengthen your dissertation by allowing you to compare the results derived using one technique with those derived using another.

## Comparative research

You should think about the usefulness of comparative analysis in your research design. For example, you might interview a group of people about dance culture and methamphetamine use, and interview two representatives of a voluntary sector drugs agency. In this case, you are interviewing individuals from two different *groups* ('users' and 'key informants') and two different institutional *sites* ('club culture' and 'the voluntary sector'). It is very common for research questions to focus on documenting the experience of a particular group of people (e.g. women). The special nature of a group's experience, though, may be difficult to justify without a comparison with some other group (e.g. men). Comparative research therefore requires careful thought about sampling. You can also strengthen your dissertation if you compare your findings with those from relevant published research, or survey and census analysis.

## Research methods

You should find out whether your course learning outcomes mean that you are *required* to demonstrate your own skills of data collection in your dissertation. If your research problem requires empirical materials, you need to decide how you are going to gather and analyse these. You should also consider seriously whether you can use existing quantitative or qualitative data sets for your own secondary analysis (see Chapter 17). You are unlikely to have the resources to generate for yourself the quantity and standard of materials that teams of professional researchers may have deposited in data archives, particularly where large-scale government social surveys are concerned. If, however, you decide to undertake some small-scale empirical research, you need to decide on your method for generating as well as analysing data. A brief review of a range of methods is given here, most of which are described more fully in other chapters of this book.

## Depth interviews

These are popular with many students and can allow you to explore people's views, perceptions and understandings of an area, often providing you with rich and sensitive material (see Chapter 15). You should develop a topic guide (of usually about six to ten themes or questions) that you want to explore, together with a clear statement of the purpose of your research, a statement on ethical practice, and (if relevant) a guarantee of privacy, confidentiality or anonymity regarding the interview and your tapes or disc files. Pilot your interview schedule with a couple of volunteers, making any changes to the questions as necessary. Plan your interviews to last an hour or so. You can either take notes (which can be distracting for you and your interviewee) or tape and then transcribe the interview. Remember that transcription is very time-consuming, so be realistic about the number of interviews you can do. You should get permission to tape any interviews and do all that you can to make a good (hearable) recording. Interviews should ideally be conducted in a comfortable environment. Be prepared to elicit and probe in case of long or uncomfortable silences and monosyllabic answers. If you are researching sensitive areas (e.g. violence, sexuality, eating disorders, suicide, drug use, personal relationships), you may need advice

from your supervisor. Analysis can take the form of coding and qualitative thematic analysis (see Chapter 21) or content, discourse, keyword, narrative or interpretative phenomenological analysis (Chapters 23, 25 and 26).

## Focus groups

These are useful in quickly gathering rich and detailed material around a particular theme or issue, exploring new or 'experimental' areas or brainstorming ideas. Focus groups can also be used for practical, task-oriented work, such as viewing and discussing a poster or video. Typically, a focus group will have six to eight (but no more) participants. In the focus group, you are aiming to cultivate a strong group dynamic, while having a minimal and facilitating role in guiding the discussion towards your interests and making sure it stays on topic. A focus group session should not consist of you interviewing a group of people, but the group discussing among itself your themes and questions. Chapter 13 contains detailed advice on how to run focus groups, and many of the points made above about the conduct of depth interviews also apply to focus groups.

## Ethnographic methods and observational research

Ethnography, as is shown in Chapter 14, involves a multitude of methods, including observational research, documentary research, archival research, researching material culture, interviews and textual methods. It can be time- and labour-intensive, though brief episodes of observation can yield surprisingly rich data, particularly if these are electronically recorded and subjected to detailed scrutiny (as in conversation analysis – see Chapter 24). Participant observation is a valuable research method that can require considerable skill on the part of the researcher. It can be useful if you want to:

- 'step back' from the obvious and 'ordinary' and look at the social world and social interactions 'afresh'

- explore 'extraordinary' or 'unusual' beliefs, behaviours and practices
- learn about other groups or subcultures
- learn about how other people view *you*.

Observation research requires that you fully and systematically record and analyse your observations, either by keeping a diary or journal or by electronic recording. There are important issues regarding both ethics and access when undertaking covert and semi-covert ethnographic research, and your supervisor will be able to advise you further on this.

## Visual sociology, semiotics and content analysis

Semiotic analysis and visual research (Chapter 16) involve a range of powerful methods, based primarily (but not exclusively) on the structural linguistics of Ferdinand de Saussure, the semiology of Roland Barthes, the work of Stuart Hall and other approaches to the analysis of film, photography and new digital media. These approaches are used for the analysis of signs, images, symbols, texts and representations, as well as narrative structure in film and video. They are popular with students and are often combined with other methods (such as interviews, focus groups or documentary research). Realistically, using these method you will only be able to fully analyse a few (perhaps three or four) relevant or important images or short extracts of film or video from the ones you initially collect, although if a content analysis is planned (see Chapter 26) many more images will be involved. It is often helpful to include copies of still images that have been analysed as appendices to a dissertation.

## Textual and discourse analysis

Discourse analysis refers to a range of techniques, some highly formal, rigorous and systematic, others less so, that are used in the analysis of text, writing and talk (see Chapter 23). Raw materials might consist of small extracts of text, such as selected sections of newspaper reports or an extract from a political speech. Analysis typically focuses on the identification of 'discourses' – widespread systems of knowledge, beliefs or ideas – that speakers or writers draw upon in presenting their versions, particularly in so far as these make their text persuasive, or appeal to certain audiences while excluding others. Content analysis, both qualitative and quantitative, can be a useful adjunct here when looking for certain themes, phrases and recurring ideas.

## Documents

Documents are a very useful, somewhat neglected source of data and can be used in conjunction with several of the methods described in this section. You can collect documents that contain material appropriate to your research project, and then analyse them in a variety of ways. Documents can be of many different kinds: annual reports; pamphlets and leaflets; publicity materials; official statistics; policy documents and policy implementation strategies; personal diaries; personal letters; and a wide variety of other published and unpublished documents. You may have to visit a specialist archive (see Chapter 15) or access an electronic archive, or you may simply have to buy a newspaper in order to generate relevant documentary data. There are various techniques for the analysis of documents (including textual and semiological methods). In using them you should consider general questions of authenticity, credibility, authorship, intended audience, representativeness, interpretative context, genre, reliability and coherence (Scott, 1990). If your analysis is based mostly on unofficial documents accessed from the Internet, then issues of authenticity, credibility, representativeness and authorship become especially important.

## Material culture and artefacts

An imaginative analysis of the way that objects are situated in, and move through, space and time can provide an altogether different and enriching perspective on social life. There is a range of methods available for the analysis of material culture, mute objects and artefacts. If used creatively, these can help to provide rich and 'thick' descriptions of social settings (see Kingery, 1998; Miller, 1998). For example:

- Consider looking 'afresh' and objectively at a seminar room in which all the students have gone out for a short break but left their belongings. Think about the placement of the objects (bags, pens, pads, coats, desks, chairs), their styles and design, the colours of the objects, the arrangement of objects on a desk and the 'social symbols' they represent (such as 'barriers', 'enclosures', 'boundaries', 'gates', 'ownership').

- Look at the arrangement of mute objects in a nightclub just after closing time, but before it has been cleaned.

- Consider the assisted movement of people through the architecture and design of buildings or public and private spaces.

## Archival research

Archival research is altogether different from research in libraries (though most archives are deposited in libraries). As Chapter 15 indicates, there is an enormous variety of archives. Archival research needs to be systematic and will be time-consuming. If you are considering archival research, you will most probably (though not necessarily) be conducting historically based research. You can employ a variety of methods in archival research, but there are also important overall considerations regarding archives – access; the history of the objects in an archive; the process whereby the objects and documents have been catalogued by the archivist ('tertiary sedimentation') – and hence have forever lost their original associations with each other, incompleteness, issues of contextual interpretation and (usually historically informed) questions of intention and meaning (Hill, 1993).

## The social survey

Some students choose to undertake a small-scale social survey based on a highly structured questionnaire, and analysed using software such as SPSS (see Chapters 18–20). If you decide to do this (rather than statistical analysis of an existing data set) be realistic about the sample size you can manage. If you are thinking about generalising your results to a wider population, you will also need to think about and justify an appropriate random sample size in your research design. Structured interviews will take more of your time than a self-completion questionnaire and hence involve a reduction in the sample size. Survey research requires considerable care in matters of question construction and questionnaire design (see Chapter 11). You must also ensure that your questionnaire is directly related to the research problem you are investigating. You would usually be expected to discuss questions of *association* and *statistical significance* in your analysis. You will need to include your questionnaire in an appendix to the dissertation and describe how you undertook your data analysis.

## Using the Internet for social research

Some students often make strong use of the Internet their dissertations. This can be for scholarly and academic sources (such as electronic journals, databases of survey or other data, or research conference podcasts), other information (such as wikis and blogs), or as a social research site that provides primary social data – for example, through 'ethnographic' studies of social networking sites, YouTube videos, podcasts, blogs and blog comments, forum or email discussions or instant messenger communications. Other specialised approaches, such as data mining, social network analysis, Internet Protocol geography, can also be used in internet-based research (and for which you will need specialist advice). It is important to follow academic guidance from your supervisor about the use of the Internet for social research in your particular discipline. This advice this will depend greatly on your research problem, the research methods you have chosen and the type of data analysis you want to undertake. Generally, you should be careful not to confuse academic and scholarly sources (such as electronic academic journals and books) with opinion sources (such as blogs or forum discussions). While each of these may help you in your general research, you should also be aware of the Google–Wikipedia–YouTube–Facebook–Twitter 'funnel'. For example, you may enter a search term in a search engine. This will bring up results that have already limited and circumscribed what you can find out (because of the search engine's algorithms, page rankings and possibly paid rankings) – it is like a form of tertiary sedimentation, as in an archive. High up in the rankings will probably be a Wikipedia entry and possibly associated YouTube videos, Facebook pages and rolling tweets. You are unlikely to look past more than a few of the thousands of pages offered. This can result in a form of confirmation bias regarding what you read and what you can discover. It can work against you coming across new, unusual, interesting or controverting issues or reading. In a similar way, blogs and forums are often sites for the expression of strong or idiosyncratic – but not necessarily widely held – views. They might also shape your understanding or your research area in a way that would not be confirmed in, for example, face-to-face interviews.

## Ethical and practical issues

As a researcher, you have a range of ethical obligations towards the participants in your research project (see also Chapter 5). In some circumstances, you might be required to submit the proposal for your dissertation to an ethics committee, either within your university or outside it, before you can proceed with your data collection plans. It is wise to consult your supervisor and any ethical guidelines produced by the professional authorities in your subject discipline. This is particularly important when:

- conducting research in sensitive or potentially controversial areas
- a situation involves direct contact with the service users of hospitals, voluntary sector agencies, charities, schools, or local authority social and care services
- research involves children, young adults or any vulnerable people
- any kind of research is intended to be covert or semi-covert
- research is on terrorism, political violence or religious 'extremism', especially if it involves interviewing people, accessing related websites, downloading related material from the Internet or being in possession of such material, even if the material is available from public or official sources or appears innocuous. The legislation regarding this area varies in different countries and you should check with your supervisor and institution if you are doing any research on terrorism.
- research involves private information and records (such as personal diaries and documents).

Be clear about your role in emotionally charged or sensitive interview situations: you are not a counsellor or advisor, but a social researcher. Any attempt to provide counselling to an emotional or upset person might do more harm than good. It may be best to simply listen, using your human sensitivity, rather than intervene 'directively' or provide advice. Actions that might (though not always) make things worse are:

- Thanking a distressed person and then leaving.
- Trying to make a distressed person feel better by using platitudes, changing the subject, or minimising the nature of their difficulties – or conversely, by seeming to agree with them that their difficulties are overwhelming or insurmountable.
- 'Over-identifying' with them by telling them about a similar situation that occurred to you or attempting to

'create empathy' by describing similar or worse situations you know about.

- Using your interviewees to provide counselling or advice to you.

If relevant, it is good practice to prepare beforehand and give to interviewees a leaflet providing information on sources of local support or advice related to their difficulties.

When seeking interviews with service users of any voluntary or public sector service, you should write to the director, manager or co-ordinator of the service and get their written permission to approach service users for interview. In some cases, the organisation will even arrange the interviews for you. You must always seek the *informed consent* of each individual person you are interviewing, even if the organisation has already given you permission. Do not use improper authority (your university's name, the organisation's permission to approach people) to attempt to persuade people to give you interviews. Explain clearly that you are a student doing a dissertation, and explain fully the nature and purpose of your research. Similar criteria apply in interviewing employees of commercial organisations.

In conducting a focus group, some participants may disclose personal or sensitive information at that time which they had not originally intended. It is therefore always good practice to have a confidentiality statement and agree an appropriate *ground rule* at the start of each focus group (such as 'information disclosed by everyone stays in the room and should not be discussed outside the group'). Consider also providing research participants and interviewees with a clear statement that their interviews will remain confidential, that you will show them transcripts for their approval or veto, that you will destroy taped interviews after the research is over, or that they can be anonymised in your transcriptions and dissertation. It is also common practice in many universities to ask interviewees to sign consent forms before the interview.

You should also consider your *own* safety and security. It may not be appropriate to meet interviewees you do not know well or have never met in their private homes. It may be appropriate to be careful before accepting lifts from interviewees. Think of arranging interviews in public places and consider whether you should give people your home address details, telephone number, or Facebook or other social networking information.

## Other practical issues

### Interviewing friends and family members

Students often ask if they can interview friends or family members. This can have both positive and negative aspects. Your friends may respond by telling you what they think you want to hear about an issue. Conversely, you already have a relationship of empathy with your friends, and so you may be able to explore social issues in greater depth and find it easier to get them to participate in your research. However, you may also take less care and give greater flexibility to them in terms of your research questions than you might in a more formal interview situation. Some students find they get less useful practical data from friends and family, because those you know well may respond less fully to your questions since they assume you already know what they will say. It is important that you fully assess the consequences of your decision to interview friends and family and explain in your dissertation the methodological and reflexive issues involved. Unless your research question is directly related to researching family or friends, consider taking the decision *not* to interview them.

### Electronic interviews

Some students use email interviews, forum or blog posts, chatroom discussions or social network sites to collect data for their dissertations. This can have a range of positive and negative methodological consequences that vary considerably depending on the type of electronic forum being used to gather your information. For example, people may be very forthright about their opinions in, for example, chatrooms, blogs or forum posts – you may therefore believe you are getting information about their real views. But the same people may be more measured (or express very different opinions) in a face-to-face interview. They might also not respond 'honestly' in an electronic forum, or they might deliberately respond to you in a provocative way. With research participants found on the Internet, there is an important issue about authenticity and verification. Say, for example, in the blog you found on lesbian identity, how do you actually know that you are communicating with a married, bi-curious woman in her mid-40s from Medway, rather than a group of schoolboys from Enfield? Is the very informative reply, from a Hotmail address, to your request to a blog for information actually from a Savitri Gupta living in a Delhi suburb?

## Planning interviews

One of the key reasons why some students do not get to interview the number of people they would like to is poor planning. You cannot expect to telephone a busy voluntary sector organisation and ask them for an interview in the next day or so. You also cannot expect that your interviewees will have free time just when you do. Prepare and plan a timetable and give plenty of notice. Follow up with a letter explaining the purpose of your research, confirming the interview date and thanking the intended interviewee. If they cancel, ask them for another date or plan a telephone interview instead.

- Make sure you have background knowledge about the work and activities of the organisation and people you want to interview. If you do not know why the organisation was set up or what they do, they in turn may not take your project seriously.
- Start planning your interviews in the early stages of your dissertation.

- Be realistic about who you will be able to get to interview. The chief executive may be flying to a power lunch in Zurich, but her less senior staff might be more amenable. Conversely, you might not be satisfied with the information given by the organisation's press and publicity officer and you may want to be more tenacious in getting to speak to a frontline officer.
- Give plenty of notice to the interviewees.
- Provide alternative dates and times.
- Confirm interviews (in writing if necessary).
- Give the arrangement three chances to succeed, or place other realistic time limits on responses.
- Consider alternative or back-up organisations or interviewees.
- Try not to cancel the interview yourself, unless this is really unavoidable – you are unlikely to get the person's co-operation again.
- If you still have difficulty, seek the advice of your tutor and consider changing your research design.

Despite good planning, some students find it difficult to get interviews, or getting interview or focus group participants to turn up at pre-arranged times (obviously, important for all members of a focus group). They consequently feel they and their research are not being taken seriously. In the public and private sector, people often have busy schedules, and other contingencies may arise. Asking them to select appropriate service users and arrange the interview times for you may be the least of their priorities. If you cannot get to see any service users, consider:

- interviewing a representative of the organisation instead (a 'key informant' or 'stakeholder')
- approaching a different organisation
- asking the organisation for their annual reports, other publications, and advice and publicity material (this should be standard practice in any case)
- undertaking a documentary analysis instead
- interviewing fellow students or university staff about your topic.

## Payment to research participants

You should not enter into any financial relation or obligation to pay expenses to interviewees (unless your university makes provision, and has guidelines, for this). Make it clear that you are asking them to *volunteer* their time and expertise. Obviously, you may want to make interviewees comfortable, or thank them, by making sure they have tea and coffee. But do not make any other commitments regarding expenses and finance.

## Safeguarding your work

You must make sure that you save your work regularly, print out your dissertation in good time for the deadline, and anticipate any potential computer and memory stick problems. The latter may not be accepted as valid reasons for the late submission of your dissertation, and you therefore risk being penalised if your computer decides it wants to give up on you. Ideally, you should keep a copy of your dissertation and all related material – including all your raw materials or data – in two separate places, together with a third backup copy on floppy disk. You can send an ordinary or (if it is very large) a zipped attachment of your work and related material from your university email address to your home email address (or vice versa), or to a friend. In this case, you will still have another copy elsewhere if your computer develops problems.

## Using libraries and finding appropriate reading

In undertaking a dissertation, you are expected to carry out *independent* research in libraries. In addition to looking for books on your research topic in your university library, you should also search the indexes in relevant journals, carry out index and keyword searches on electronic bibliographies, and search the Internet and relevant newspapers, magazines, films and videos

(if applicable). Chapter 6 gives helpful guidance on this. You can also approach lecturers other than your supervisor and ask them for their advice or their course handouts. You should also be prepared to explore more libraries than just the one associated with your university if your search leads you to these. Your own university library will tell you about what access rights you have to other libraries and electronic resources, or may be able to negotiate access for you. Make sure that you record the full bibliographic details of the material you come across when you first see it. This will save you time later, when you construct your bibliography.

You may occasionally find that there is very little directly relevant literature in your area. If you face this situation, you should first ask whether this is because of the way you are thinking about the area, rather than deficiencies in the literature itself. First, you need to be realistic about the literature: there is no point looking for, and getting despondent when you cannot find *the* book on Émile Durkheim and Pop Idol. At the same time, your judgement about relevance may be too narrow. You may not find an article about the impact of network society on personal domestic habits, but you will find literature on changing forms of private and public behaviour and codes in history (e.g. by Norbert Elias) or behaviour in 'front stage' and 'back stage' regions (e.g. by Erving Goffman) that will contain many relevant insights.

Consider, too, the specialist libraries of relevant voluntary organisations and national charities; these often hold policy reports and other locally published information (*grey literature*) that may contain a wealth of information relating to your research area. Consider also searches in journals and magazines. If you still find there is very little relevant literature, you must state this in your dissertation, and describe what searches you did actually undertake. It is good practice to explain briefly in your dissertation how you went about finding relevant and appropriate reading.

## The structure of the dissertation

You should see the dissertation as your project and, unless your university specifies a particular chapter or section structure, its structure can normally be decided by you, with guidance from your supervisor.

## Empirical dissertations

The vast majority of students undertake empirical dissertations and their advantage is that they enable you to explore a particular topic and a body of literature of your choosing, and gain hands-on research and data analysis experience (useful for future careers and employment). *Empirical* dissertations should normally contain the equivalent of:

- An introduction that states clearly your research problem or topic
- A review of the relevant literature (reading) in your dissertation area
- A discussion of methods applied
- Analysis of data and reporting and discussion of results
- Conclusion
- References
- Appendices

### Introduction

Start with an introduction that establishes clearly and succinctly your research problem or questions, their relation to relevant debates and literature in your disciplines, how you intend to investigate your research problems, and very briefly, the methods used and how you analysed your data. You may also want to include a very brief description of what is covered in each chapter. This provides a signpost for the examiners about the structure of your dissertation.

### Literature review

Think of your literature review as having some of the following aims:

- Locating and situating clearly your research problem in the context of the relevant literature and existing debates.
- Presenting an *argument*, in the context of the relevant literature and debates, about why your research problem is an important one that requires investigation.
- Refining your research problems or questions.
- Demonstrating that you have read and understood the literature that is directly relevant to your research problem.
- Highlighting areas where there is insufficient literature or debate regarding the problem you want to investigate.
- Differentiating your own approach from that of the existing literature.
- Providing a theoretical 'grounding' for your dissertation.

If you are confused about what you should cover in a literature review, brainstorm your research problem and look at its key concepts (see Box 10.5). Think about the literature review as a 'conversation' between your research problem and the *relevant* material you have read, rather than an exposition of everything that you have read in the area.

### Methodology and methods

In your methodology chapter or section, you are expected to discuss and justify your overall research design, the methodological issues related to the research techniques you have used, their strengths and weaknesses, the way you specified and gained access to your sample, how you then generated data (including problems encountered) and how you analysed your data. You should also discuss any issues relating to validity, reliability, quality and reflexivity here.

It is often helpful to include a succinct *narrative description of the research process* itself. This can include information about any false starts or changes in plan or design. For example, if you organised a focus group and no one turned up, make sure you describe this and any subsequent changes in your research design, rather than ignore it as a 'failure' on your part. Similarly, if you were very nervous in conducting your first couple of interviews, describe this, as well as any potential reflexive consequences on the person being interviewed. Such occurrences are part and parcel of real world social research and the examiners are likely to be interested in your critical thinking about such problems. Examiners will also usually be interested in knowing how you might have done your research differently if you were starting again from scratch, or had more time or resources.

## Data analysis and reporting your results

These chapters or sections should report your main findings. Some of the main areas to consider if your analysis is of qualitative data are:

- The characteristics of your sample. It is good practice to report basic demographic information (age, gender, ethnicity, region, employment or social class) if your sample is one that involves people, and the equivalent if it involves other kinds of sampling (e.g. whether a newspaper article is from an American or British paper; whether it is front page news or from a lifestyle supplement).

- If you used a coding scheme, show this to the reader and describe how it relates to the research questions. Do not report your results according to the order of questions asked in an interview. Organise your reporting thematically and try to organise themes into *major* themes that could be subheadings in your data analysis chapters (see Chapter 22 on developing grounded theory).

- Consider which quotations from your interview data work best to illustrate themes, points and arguments. Consider opposite opinions and negative instances;

consider extreme viewpoints. Show short extracts that disrupt understandings as well as ones that illustrate your claims effectively.

- Do not reproduce long extracts of qualitative material. Be selective and economical, choosing carefully what you think are important extracts. If you have used a coding scheme, you can probably support your presentation of qualitative extracts with counts of the frequency with which particular themes occurred.

- Conclude your data analysis chapters with brief summaries. A certain amount of commentary or interpretation of the significance of your findings can be discussed in the 'results' section of your dissertation (and some disciplines strongly encourage this), but you might want to save your best and 'biggest' points for the concluding chapter.

## Conclusion

By the time you come to the conclusion, you might be tired of writing – or are rushing to meet a deadline – and so the conclusion can read like a quick summary, or an after-thought tagged on to the end. This is a serious mistake, as it is may be the concluding chapter that an examiner looks to first when seeking to assess the overall message of the work. In planning the writing of your dissertation, you *must* ensure adequate time for a strong, well-written *conclusion*. In this, you might want to:

- revisit your original research problem in the light of your key or strong findings

- discuss any implications for the theoretical areas you have explored

- discuss any implications for practical programmes of action or policy

- discuss how you might have improved upon the research or changed the research design

- highlight unresolved areas and debates

- point out areas for further research or debate

- *conclude* your dissertation.

## Appendices

Resist the temptation to use appendices as a way of inflating the length of your dissertation by including more results, analysis and so forth. Appropriate appendices would include:

- a blank questionnaire
- an interview schedule or topic guide
- a letter or email sent to research participants and (if relevant) the names of organisations approached
- any visual images analysed in the dissertation
- brief sections of transcripts to show the level of transcription used
- a coding scheme, perhaps accompanied by a short extract of interview material showing how the codes were applied (but not an entire interview transcript)
- a page of observation fieldnotes to illustrate the technique of data gathering used (but not an entire diary of fieldnotes).

---

**BOX 10.5**

## WHAT IS RELEVANT LITERATURE?

### Example 1

A dissertation focusing on the representation of women in young men's magazines would be concerned with issues of:

- Representation
- Gender
- Feminism
- Masculinity
- Youth culture

These keywords should then guide the searches you make for literature to read and discuss. In this example, you would not be expected to provide an assessment of, say, feminist theory, but you would be expected to provide a discussion of feminist theory in so far as it relates to the specific area you are researching: masculinity, representation and so forth.

### Example 2

A dissertation based on quantitative analysis of the association between population health and gross national product would be concerned with issues of:

- Development and underdevelopment
- Health and illness
- Political economy

These might be the keywords which can be combined to guide your initial literature search. Depending on what else you are investigating, you might also be concerned with some of the following concepts which can be used to refine your search:

- Infant mortality
- Gender
- Urbanisation
- Health policy
- Access to clean water

In this example, you would not be expected to provide an assessment of theories of development and underdevelopment, global political economy, the sociology of health and illness, or gender and development, but you would be expected to discuss these areas in *so far as* they relate to and help you refine the hypotheses you are testing.

## Dissertations based on secondary sources

A dissertation that is based on secondary sources should be distinguished from one based on secondary analysis. A secondary source consists of evidence which you have not collected yourself, but for which you want to propose a new or different interpretation from your own critical disciplinary position. Again, you must put forward a problem or issue you want to investigate in relation to the secondary literature. Starting with a bold statement (research problem) can often help (see Box 10.6). It is useful when exploring secondary sources to have a clear research problem that helps you stay focused, rather than getting overwhelmed with the amount of secondary material you may find.

---

**BOX 10.6**

## THINKING DIFFERENTLY ABOUT DISSERTATIONS BASED ON SECONDARY SOURCES

A dissertation based on a review of secondary sources relating to anti-depressants might make the bold claim that the technical development and marketing of new classes of antidepressant drugs by pharmaceutical companies precedes, and therefore may cause, the social phenomenon and social category of 'depression'. The relevant literature might be based on the sociology of health and illness, the sociology of mental health, academic literature on anti-depressants, publicity material from pharmaceutical companies, newspaper reports and epidemiological data. The theoretical approach might be based on 'social constructionist' perspectives on health and illness.

A dissertation on animal rights might argue that animal welfare organisations are key organisations responsible for the majority of unnatural deaths of animals in modern societies. The relevant literature might focus on the annual reports and material of the RSPCA, academic work on the sociology of environmentalism and animal welfare, and statistical data on the humane killing by animal welfare organisations of stray and unwanted dogs and cats in Britain. The theoretical approach might be influenced by Weberian ideas about the organisation and consequences of large-scale modern systems of bureaucracy.

A dissertation on 'counter-cultural' new age religious movements might make the claim that they are exemplary of rational, calculating, rigid and systematic methods of organisation in modern societies. Relevant literature might include the sociology of new age or new religious movements, and guides and instructions for personal change and transformation from a new age group. The claim might be backed up by Foucauldian theoretical approaches relating to 'technologies of the self'.

A dissertation based on a review of secondary sources relating to the events of September 11, 2001 might start by posing an unusual and controversial argument about the prominence of 'death'-related discourses in a variety of social movements and networks in late modern society, irrespective of religious or ethnic affiliation or identity. The relevant literature might focus on the sociology of death. Secondary sources might include newspaper and magazine articles, websites, political speeches, pamphlets and academic books and articles about the event.

## Theoretical dissertations

If you are thinking of writing a theoretical (or library-based) dissertation, you should first think carefully about whether you are comfortable with engaging with and providing your own independent or original interpretations in relation to the existing *theoretical* literature of your discipline. A theoretical dissertation should not simply be an extended essay, but should present and investigate a set of key problems which you have formulated in relation to a specific or substantive area. For example, a dissertation providing an exposition and evaluation of theories of globalisation would not in itself suffice. The theme of globalisation needs to be related to a key problem which you want to explore (e.g. 'existing theories of globalisation are inadequate because …'), or which you can relate to a substantive area (e.g. 'existing theories of globalisation do not address human rights …').

In a theoretical dissertation, examiners are typically looking for evidence of your independent critical judgements and original and creative approaches to the existing theoretical literature. You should not simply summarise, however cogently, existing theoretical debates and literature. You should also remember to discuss *methodological* issues, as relevant. For example, if you are undertaking a critical theoretical analysis of, say, post-structuralist feminism, what is the position from which you are undertaking your reading? What 'theoretical gaze' are you using in order to undertake your critical reading of feminism? Can this therefore be seen as a methodology of reading and analysis? Think broadly about methodological issues in relation to theoretical positions: can postmodern theory be used as a method, as well as a theory?

An ideal structure for a theoretical dissertation would be to have each chapter both dealing with a substantially different area and progressing your arguments and themes forward. You should conclude your dissertation strongly – do not just summarise what you have already covered, but conclude properly in relation to the problem you initially started with. You should also refer to unresolved areas and further debates.

Some students doing theoretical dissertations find that they 'get lost in the theory' and cannot bring their dissertation together or conclude it. Remember that you will not find 'an answer' by continuing to read more and more theoretical literature, and possibly getting overwhelmed by the number and range of theoretical issues you keep discovering. You should instead focus on what you initially started with, your own research or theoretical problem and your own critical independent viewpoint. The examiners are interested in this, rather than in the densities of the theoretical literature.

## Citations and references

Use a standard recognised format for acknowledging all the sources you have used, both in the body of your dissertation and in a separate reference list or bibliography. Chapter 6 gives guidance on bibliographic software that exports recorded references in various standard formats. In the body of your dissertation and following any quotation, you should typically state the (Author(s), Year: Page number). If citing more than two authors, use (First Author et al., Year: Page number). Your reference list should typically use a format such as that shown in Box 10.7. Box 10.8 shows how references in a dissertation might look.

---

**BOX 10.7**

### TYPICAL FORMAT FOR A LIST OF REFERENCES

- Author(s), (Year), Title. Place: Publisher. [Book]
- Author(s), (Year), 'Title', in Editor(s), Book Title. Place: Publisher. [Article in edited book]

- Author(s), (Year), 'Title', Journal Name, Journal Volume (Journal Number), Pages. [Journal article]
- Author(s), (Year), 'Title', Periodical Name, Date (where relevant), Page number. [Newspapers, magazines and other periodicals]
- Author(s), (Year or Date published), 'Title'. Full internet URL, Type of internet Document (e.g. 'web page'), Date the document was accessed by you. [Internet document]
- Author(s), (Year), 'Title'. Place: Publisher. Type of Electronic Medium (e.g. CD/DVD/Blu-Ray, PDF, Video), (Retrieved from: URL, date, if relevant). [Electronic sources]
- If you are referencing other material (films, videos, photographs, pamphlets, leaflets, posters, records, catalogues, CDs/DVDs, artefacts, personal records) or events (performances, speeches, installations, exhibitions) ask your tutor for detailed guidance.

---

**BOX 10.8**

## EXAMPLES OF DISSERTATION REFERENCING

In the body of the dissertation:

- … as argued by Smith (1998: 212) …
- … It has also been argued (Smith, 1998: 212) …
- … this view has also been countered by other writers (e.g.; Mooley,1996; Gosling, 1999) …
- As Madan has said:

'If globalization has allegedly advanced homogeneity, it has also differentiated peoples, ethnicities, cultures and nations in forms unimaginable in the nineteenth-century.' (Madan, 2003: 12)

- … was born in 1789, in Malden Grisp, Wokingham (Anonymous, 2002).
- … but it has recently been demonstrated that such interventions have clearly failed to 'socially include' groups from other communities (Tyler, not dated).
- … especially the new phenomenon of viral videos (HDCYT, 2007).

In the corresponding list of references:

- Smith, S. (1998) 'Revisiting "the cyborg": the dynamics of gender and technoculture', *Journal of Sociology & Culture*, 7(3), 198–223.
- Mooley, J. K. (1996) 'The economy of social time', in P. J. Holden & T. Matthews eds., *Social Theory Today*, London: Major Publishers.
- Gosling, J. (1999) *Social Spaces and Places*, Melbourne: Other Publishers.
- Madan, R. (April 2003) 'Globalization and its Discontents', *Students Journal of Social Theory*, volume 1, number 1, www.sjst.com/042003/~mad.html, web page, accessed 01.06.2003.
- Anonymous (2002) 'Josephine Bluntley – early life', *Microsoft Encarta 2002*. Redmond, VA: Microsoft Corp. DVD.
- Tyler, P. (not dated) 'Social inclusion?', www.anorg.co.uk/poppy/~scu/marginsuk.pdf, pdf document, accessed 24.08.2003.
- HDCYT (2007) *Charlie bit my finger – again!*, video, Retrieved from: http://www.youtube.com/watch?v=_OBlgSz8sSM, 1 January 2009.

## Plagiarism

Plagiarism is considered to be cheating and is a very serious academic offence. If you do not cite fully your sources, you may end up presenting other people's ideas and work as if they were your own. Copying or closely paraphrasing texts from whatever source without full referencing or acknowledgement of the source is called plagiarism. Copying from the work of other students is a form of plagiarism. Plagiarism also includes copying, closely paraphrasing or not referencing fully and properly:

- documents from the Internet, including web pages, Wikipedia or blogs, any other downloaded documents or files, and any materials obtained from Internet archives and Internet services
- other electronic sources, including DVD-ROMs and CD-ROMs, other electronically stored information, electronic magazines and newspapers, electronic journals and any electronic book libraries (e-libraries).

Avoid commercial sites offering ready-made dissertations and theses for sale, offering 'help' in writing your dissertation, or offering 'essay banks'. There are numerous sophisticated ways of identifying people who use these services, or identifying work that has been derived from such services, and the penalties in many universities for this type of cheating can be very severe. You need to be very clear about what is meant by plagiarism and consult your tutor if in any doubt.

## Conclusion

Doing a dissertation can be the most fulfilling part of a degree course, enabling you to put together the skills and knowledge you have learned, sometimes over a period of years, in a fully integrated research project that you plan and carry out independently. Using advice from your supervisor wisely (ideally regularly, and from an early stage in the process) is an important way of improving the quality of your eventual dissertation and, in some cases, rescuing you from situations that look as if they are going badly wrong. Using this chapter, in conjunction with the others in this book, can help you bring your dissertation to a successful conclusion.

## FURTHER READING

Perhaps the best book for advice on how to do an undergraduate dissertation is Walliman (2001). Bell (2005) is also very good, particularly if you are doing educational research. Aimed more at the doctoral student and focused on qualitative research, though still relevant at other levels, is Silverman (1999). Becker's (1998) book is aimed at anyone doing a research project, particularly in sociology, but will be rewarding reading if you are doing an empirically based dissertation.

### Journal articles illustrating and discussing the issues raised in this chapter

Li, S. and Seale, C. (2007) 'Learning to do qualitative data analysis: an observational study of doctoral work', Qualitative Health Research, 17: 1442–1452.

Li, S. and Seale, C. (2008) 'Acquiring a sociological identity: an observational study of a PhD project', Sociology, 42: 987–1002.

Smith, S.W., Brownell, M.T., Simpson, R.L. and Deshler, D.D. (1993) 'Successfully completing the dissertation: two reflections on the process', Remedial and Special Education, 14: 53–59.

## Web links

The Writing Center – thesis writing: www.rpi.edu/dept/llc/writecenter/web/thesis.html

Seven Steps to Effective Library Research: http://library.newpaltz.edu/assistance/tutorials/seven.html

Research Methods Knowledge Base: – the write-up: www.socialresearchmethods.net/kb/writeup.php

Drew University Writing Program – Web resources: www.users.drew.edu/~sjamieso/Webresources.html

## Websites to avoid!

Avoid commercial sites offering ready-made theses and dissertations for sale, or offering 'help' (at a price) in writing your dissertation. There are ways of catching people who use these services and penalties in many universities for such cheating can be severe.

## KEY CONCEPTS FOR REVIEW

**Advice:** Use these, along with the review questions in the next section, to test your knowledge of the contents of this chapter. Try to define each of the key concepts listed here; if you have understood this chapter you should be able to do this. Check your definitions against the definition in the glossary at the end of the book.

Combining concepts

Empirical dissertation

Methodology and method

Plagiarism

Research problem

Research process

Secondary sources

Theoretical dissertation

## ■ Review questions

1 What are the differences between empirical and theoretical dissertations?
2 What are the differences between dissertations based on secondary sources and secondary analysis?
3 Describe the steps involved in developing a research problem.
4 What ethical and practical issues are relevant in:

(a) a study of an internet discussion group?
(b) a study involving interviews with family and friends?
(c) a study involving direct observation of children?

5 How does citation and referencing guard against plagiarism?

## Workshop and discussion exercises

1 Outline the structure of:

(a) a theoretical dissertation investigating racism
(b) an empirical dissertation investigating the same topic.

What headings and subheadings might appear in each one?

2　Choose a social issue that is currently in the news (e.g. immigration, climate change, street protests, political corruption). Develop a researchable question about this that involves combining a theoretical and an empirical concept. What research design and methods would you use to answer it? What ethical and practical issues does the project raise?

3　Using a research question you have devised (perhaps in the previous exercise):

(a) investigate what secondary sources exist that might enable you to answer this question

(b) investigate what archived data exists that could be used for a secondary analysis answering the question.

# PART TWO
## DOING RESEARCH

# 11

# STRUCTURED METHODS: INTERVIEWS, QUESTIONNAIRES AND OBSERVATION

Constantinos N. Phellas, Alice Bloch and Clive Seale

## Chapter Contents

Learning how to design and use structured interviews, questionnaires and observation instruments is an important skill for researchers. Such survey instruments can be used in many types of research, from case study, to cross-sectional survey, to experiment. A study of this sort can involve anything from a short paper-and-pencil feedback form, to an intensive one-to-one interview asking a large number of questions, to direct observation of relevant behaviour. In general, these data collection instruments fall into three broad categories: self-completed questionnaires, interviews and observation schedules. This chapter concerns all of these, explaining how to design and administer structured interview schedules, design and distribute questionnaires intended for self-completion by respondents, and carry out structured observations.

## Interviews or self-completion questionnaires?

Choosing between an interview and a self-completed questionnaire on which the respondent writes their answers is an important decision. Within these there are also choices to be made, each with advantages or disadvantages. Thus, interviews can be done face to face or by telephone. A questionnaire can be sent and returned by post or email, completed on the Web, or handed directly to the respondent who completes it on the spot and hands it back. Additionally, some interviews contain pauses for respondents to complete questionnaire sections, so that the resulting instrument is a combination of things. This can be particularly advantageous if a topic is felt to be socially embarrassing to discuss face to face and has been used, for example, in surveys of sexual behaviour.

Interviews have certain advantages over self-completion questionnaires. The interviewer can explain questions that the respondent has not understood and can ask for further elaboration of replies (e.g. 'Why do you say that?'). In general, being asked questions by a sympathetic listener is experienced as more rewarding by respondents than the chore of filling in a form for some anonymous researcher, so it is generally found that fewer people refuse to take part and more questions can be asked of each person. However, interviews are more time consuming for the researcher and it may be the case that interviewer bias, where the interviewer influences the replies by revealing their own opinions, can be avoided by self-completion questionnaires.

Self-completion questionnaires have the advantage of being cheap, but are more suited to issues where there are only a few questions that are relatively clear and simple in their meaning, and the choice of replies can be limited to fixed categories. They are especially useful in surveying people who are dispersed over a wide geographical area, where the travelling demands on an interviewer would be excessive.

## Types of interview

The interview is a more flexible form than the questionnaire and, if intelligently used, can generally be used to gather information of greater depth and can be more sensitive to contextual variations in meaning. The classical survey research tradition, geared to producing quantitative data, is generally associated with interviews where the wording and order of questions are exactly the same for every respondent. Variation in responses can thus be attributed to respondents and not to variability in the interviewing technique. Wording the questions in the same way for each respondent is sometimes called standardising. Asking the questions in the same order is called scheduling.

Interviews, however, can be non-scheduled, though still partly standardised. This is sometimes called a semi-structured interview. Here, the interviewer works from a list of topics that need to be covered with each respondent, but the order and exact wording of questions is not important. Generally, such interviews gather qualitative data, although this can be coded into categories to be made amenable to statistical analysis.

## Face-to-face interviews

Using face-to-face interviews as a means of data collection has a number of advantages and disadvantages. The main benefits are:

- The presence of an interviewer allows for complex questions to be explained, if necessary, to the interviewee.

- Interviews can generally be longer than when self-completion techniques are used as interviewees are less likely to be put off by the length or to give up halfway through.

- There is more scope to ask open questions since respondents do not have to write in their answer and the interviewer can pick up on non-verbal clues that indicate what is relevant to the interviewees and how they are responding to different questions.

- Visual aids can also be used in the face-to-face situation.

- The interviewer can control the context and the environment in which the interview takes place. For instance, the interviewer can make sure that the questions are asked and therefore answered in the correct order and that the interview takes place in an appropriate setting which is conducive to accurate responses.

There are however, some problems with face-to-face approaches:

- The cost associated with face-to-face interviews can limit the size and geographical coverage of the survey.

- Interviewers can introduce bias, which will affect the reliability of responses. Such bias might emerge from the way in which questions are asked, or in the personal characteristics of the interviewer, or in respondents' wish to give socially desirable responses. For instance, there tends to be an over-reporting of voting activity and of participation in voluntary activities in data gathered through interviews.

## Telephone interviews

Telephone interviews using interview schedules are becoming increasingly efficient with developments in computer technology. Computer assisted telephone interviewing (CATI) systems are available and these provide clear instructions for the interviewer, display the interview schedule and allow electronic recording of responses as they are given. This cuts out the data entry part of survey research (i.e. transferring the responses from the interview schedule to the computer) because responses are recorded directly onto the computer. This makes CATI quick and cheap to use. There are other advantages associated with telephone interviews:

- Because the researcher does not have to travel, interviews can take place over a wider geographical area.

- There are fewer interviewer effects – that is, the personal characteristics of the researcher will be less obvious than in face-to face situations and is therefore less intrusive.

- The physical safety of the interviewer is not an issue.

- Telephone interviews are subject to greater levels of monitoring because supervisors can unobtrusively listen in to interviews to ensure that they are carried out correctly.

But telephone interviewing has disadvantages too:

- Questions have to be simple and interviews need to be kept short because they tend to have higher break-off rates (where people refuse to continue) than face-to-face interviews.

- It can be difficult to ask sensitive questions on the telephone.

- There is no opportunity to use visual aids or to pick up so easily on the non-verbal responses of interviewees.

- There are some groups that are underrepresented in telephone surveys. These include people without phones (often due to poverty), older people and people who are disabled or sick.

## Self-completed questionnaires

There are different types of self-completed questionnaire, and this chapter will help you decide whether to use postal, mailed, web-based or email questionnaires. First though, the good and bad points of such questionnaires can be summarised. With surveys delivered by these means, questions need to be simple and easy to understand and the questionnaire has to be clear and easy to complete because no interviewer is available to assist the respondent. Such surveys can be especially useful when respondents need time to gather information or consider their answers. For example, a survey of pay levels among university employees by gender would require complex information, so a self-completion survey would provide respondents with time to check their records before answering.

Surveys using self-completion questionnaires have some distinct advantages over face-to-face interviews:

- They are cheap to administer. The only costs are those associated with printing or designing the questionnaires, their postage or electronic distribution.

- They allow for a greater geographical coverage than face-to-face interviews without incurring the additional costs of time and travel. Thus they are particularly useful when carrying out research with geographically dispersed populations.

- Using self-completion questionnaires reduces biasing error caused by the characteristics of the interviewer and the variability in interviewers' skills.

- The absence of an interviewer provides greater anonymity for the respondent. When the topic of the research is sensitive or personal it can increase the reliability of responses.

The main disadvantages of self-completion surveys are:

- Questionnaires have to be short and the questions must be simple as there is no opportunity to probe or clarify misunderstandings.

- There is no control over who fills out the questionnaire, and the researcher can never be sure that the right person has completed the questionnaire.

- Those with low levels of literacy or poor access to email or the Internet are unlikely to complete a questionnaire, meaning that they are excluded from the study.
- Response rates tend to be low and it is difficult to know the characteristics of those who have not filled in the survey and how their non-response will affect the findings.

Response rates in self-completion surveys tend to be maximised when respondents have an interest in the subject of the research and are therefore motivated to complete the questionnaire. In addition, response rates can be increased by sending out reminder letters and emails and follow-up postings of the questionnaire, though this does mean that the fieldwork element of such surveys can be lengthy.

Ways of encouraging a good response rate are also discussed later in this chapter (and were mentioned in Chapter 9 too). In addition, the appearance and layout of questionnaires are important, and this chapter will cover this, as well as discussing different question types and the pre-testing of questionnaires.

## Designing studies using structured interviews and questionnaires

The most important goal of a study using such an instrument is to learn about the ideas, knowledge, feelings, opinions/attitudes and self-reported behaviours of a defined population. To carry out a survey the researcher must:

1 determine the information to be sought

2 define the population to be studied

3 construct the interview schedule or questionnaire and decide how it is to be administered

4 draw a representative sample

5 administer the instrument

6 analyse and interpret the data

7 communicate the results.

These procedures are overlapping and each demands careful work. We will focus in this chapter on steps 1 and 3 in particular. Other steps are more fully discussed in other parts of this book.

## Determining the information to be sought

Social research begins with an idea that sometimes might be quite vague and unclear. As a researcher you must systematically develop and refine your initial ideas, usually starting with a good understanding of the related literature (see Chapter 6). There will eventually be a need for concepts in the literature – if they are to be investigated in the study you are going to do – to be operationalised as questionnaire items, so that clear concept–indicator links are established. Therefore, you must make clear what you want to find out about. The research questions of the project determine who you will survey and what you will ask them. If your research questions are unclear, the results will probably be unclear. The more precise you can make these, the easier it will be to get usable answers.

Let us imagine that we are about to carry out a survey in order to answer the following research questions:

1 Does the possession of a university degree enhance the job prospects to a different extent in different ethnic groups?

2 Are people without degrees more likely to have jobs in which they experience alienation?

3 How do women and men graduates compare in balancing the demands of home and work?

If you examine these three questions you will see that they contain a number of concepts. These are possession of a degree qualification, ethnic group, having a job, alienation, gender and the demands of home and work. In designing questions, a researcher should ensure that the concepts contained within the aims of the study are *comprehensively* covered. If one forgot to ask a question about whether people had a degree qualification, for example, it would not be possible to fulfil the aims of the study.

The questions chosen for inclusion in an interview schedule or a self-completed questionnaire can be understood as indicating the concepts contained in the research questions. Ensuring good links between concepts and their indicators lies at the heart of good question design. Some concepts are easier to indicate than others. The concept of *sex* or *gender*, for example, is in most cases not controversial and might, in an interview, be indicated by the interviewer recording their impression rather than asking a question about it. The concept of having a degree qualification might also be indicated fairly easily, by asking a person to list their educational qualifications. Whether a person has a job, however, might pose more problems. What does one do about part-time workers, for example? Do we count housework as a 'job'? Decisions about how to categorise people into ethnic groups are often controversial.

Additionally, many of the more interesting concepts in social research are multidimensional concepts, which is to say that they are made up from several different things. Alienation is an example. Finding questions to indicate the extent of a person's alienation requires some further conceptual work, and perhaps some reading to see how different authors have used the term. A researcher interested in finding indicators for this concept would need to subdivide it into several components. Alienation involves, amongst other things, a sense of powerlessness, of normlessness (being outside normal society), isolation and self-estrangement (seeing a part of oneself as if it were a stranger). It is easy, for example, to see how one could be powerless without being isolated, so in order to count as 'truly' alienated a person would need to indicate that they experienced all of its components, requiring questions indicating each of the dimensions of alienation.

The chapter will return to how questions in survey instruments can be designed so that they reflect good concept–indicator links. First,

though, we will consider the decision as to how to administer a questionnaire or an interview.

## Deciding how to administer the questionnaire or interview

We saw earlier that there were several ways to administer a self-completed questionnaire, these being to send and return the questionnaire by post, and internet-based methods (web or emailed questionnaires). The advantages and disadvantages of each were summarised. Less often used, but nevertheless distinct from these approaches, are the group administered survey and the household drop-off survey. In addition, we saw that there were two main ways to carry out interviews: face to face or by telephone. Either of these might involve computer assistance at the data collection stage, with the interviewer entering responses and being prompted to ask questions as the interview proceeds, though this is more commonly used in telephone interviewing. The best approach will always be based upon a combination of factors such as time, the complexity of the data collection instrument, the sample profile and budget.

## Postal surveys

Postal surveys (sometimes called mail-out surveys) usually involve mailing self-completed questionnaires to a target group of people. The main advantages of postal surveys are that large numbers of questionnaires can be sent out at fairly low cost. Questions that are difficult to ask on the telephone or in face-to-face interviews can be asked in a postal questionnaire. For example, personally sensitive information (about income, sexual orientation, drinking behaviour) are best asked about in a way that saves the respondent the embarrassment of facing a stranger and reporting something they may feel awkward about. Box 11.1 gives an example of a study that asked about illegal behaviour in this way.

BOX 11.1

## EXAMPLE OF HOW TO ASK PERSONALLY SENSITIVE INFORMATION

A postal survey of UK doctors reported by Seale (2009a) asked them to report on whether they had taken various decisions about the end-of-life care of their last patient who had died. These decisions included things like withdrawing or withholding treatment, considered to unnecessarily extend life when a patient was already suffering a great deal. Doctors were also asked if they had prescribed or administered a drug with the sole intention of ending a patient's life (known as 'assisted dying', 'euthanasia' or 'physician-assisted suicide'). This last type of decision was not legal in the UK at the time of the survey. Doctors were sent a postcard when they were sent the questionnaire, and they were told that they could return the postcard separately to say that they had replied to the survey, so that they would not receive follow-up reminders to reply. The questionnaire itself contained no information that could link the particular questionnaire to the identity of any one of the 10,000 doctors who received it. This reassured respondents who reported illegal action that they could not be identified.

A serious problem with postal surveys is that response rates are usually lower than interview surveys. This is largely because people find talking to someone more pleasant than filling in a form on their own.

Factors that affect response rates are the questionnaire's length, the way it is laid out (e.g. is it easy to answer?), whether the issue it enquires about is important to the respondent, and whether incentives are offered. In addition, in populations of lower educational and literacy levels, response rates are lower. This makes it difficult, for example, to use postal surveys with groups that may be particularly important to understand, such as immigrant populations, or socially deprived people.

A low response rate is a problem because responders may not be representative of the entire population if they are systematically different on some dimension from non-responders. With self-completed questionnaires, as with any survey, you need to look at the characteristics of the people who responded and the people who did not respond. The respondents should have the same characteristics with the people who did not respond. Moreover, respondents should have the same characteristics as the overall population that you are sampling. If they do not,

then it may be possible to weight the results during the analysis so that the sample more closely reflects the population. Thus, if men were twice as likely to reply to a survey as women, the contribution of men's responses to an overall result could be reduced by dividing each response from a man by two, so that the sample result reflects the population. However, it is only possible to weight responses on variables that you know about; a low response rate may involve biases whose effect cannot be estimated.

If you design a sampling method that gives everyone in the population an equal chance of being selected as a potential respondent, your sample will be about the same as the overall population. But if there is poor level of response, most of the time it is almost certain that there will be some important differences between those who responded and those who did not. The assumption that your sample reflects the population as a whole fails, and with it, if weighting is not feasible, the possibility of doing any inferential statistics.

If you estimate that you will get a poor response rate no matter what you do, then you can extract some value from the data by reducing your survey to a few open questions. Read the comments that people give you and think about them. Although you may not be able to tell whether they are at all representative of your population, you will probably find that they do offer some interesting insights. There are several ways to improve response rates to postal surveys. These are listed in Box 11.2.

---

**BOX 11.2**

## WAYS TO IMPROVE RESPONSE RATES TO POSTAL SURVEYS

- Mail a postcard telling your participants to watch for a questionnaire in the next week or two.

- Mail non-respondents with reminders, including a further copy of the questionnaire in case they threw it away. The downside is that this method increases your mailing cost.

- Use incentives, such as vouchers, money, donations to a charity or a prize draw. An offer of a copy of the final research report can help in some cases.

- Ensure that the questionnaire can be returned with the minimum of trouble and expense (e.g. by including a reply paid envelope).

- Keep the questionnaire short and easy to answer.

- Ensure that you send it to people for whom it is relevant. It is no good sending a questionnaire designed for doctors to nurses too, as they will find some of the questions odd.

---

## Internet-based methods

The two main forms of internet-based methods are email surveys and web surveys. Online research is suited to most survey types, and for very personal and sensitive issues. Participants are also more often willing to give more honest answers to a computer or by email than to a person or on a paper questionnaire. The computer asks questions the same way every time, thus interviewer bias arising from the fact that different interviewers can ask questions in different ways is eliminated. Use the Internet for surveys mainly when your target population consists entirely or almost entirely of Internet users. Surveys of the general population usually will not be of this sort.

Email surveys involve sending questions in the text of an email, or in an attachment, which respondents fill in and send back. These surveys are both very economical and very fast. More people have email than have full Internet access. Email surveying can allow large numbers of respondents to be questioned. Geographical location is not a barrier, although this can sometimes mean having to produce questionnaires in non-English languages. Significant cost savings can sometime be made (e.g. postage and paper materials). This method of research has become increasingly popular for two main reasons: the rising penetration of computers and the increased ability to use computers by many people. This method may grow in importance as computer use increases.

There are problems, though. Some people will respond several times or pass questionnaires along to friends to answer. Many people dislike unsolicited email even more than unsolicited regular mail. You may want to send email questionnaires only to people who expect to get email from you. You cannot use email surveys to generalise findings to the general population. People who have email are different from those who do not, even when matched on demographic characteristics, such as age and gender. While email use is growing rapidly, it is not universal – three-quarters of the world's email traffic takes place within the USA. Many 'average' citizens still do not possess email facilities, especially older people and those in lower-income and education groups. So email surveys do not reflect the population as a whole. At this stage they are probably best used in a corporate environment where email is common or when most members of the target population are known to have email.

Email surveys cannot automatically skip questions or randomise the order of questions, or use other automatic techniques that can enhance surveys the way web surveys can. Many email programs are limited to plain text and cannot show pictures or other graphics. If the survey is sent by email attachment, the software used to create this must be of the sort that can be expected to be found on all of the potential respondents' computers. Box 11.3 shows the pros and cons of email surveys.

---

**BOX 11.3**

## ADVANTAGES AND DISADVANTAGES OF EMAIL SURVEYS

### Advantages

- Speed; an email questionnaire can gather several thousand responses within a day or two.
- There is practically no cost involved once the set-up has been completed.
- You can attach pictures and sound files.
- The novelty element of an email survey often stimulates higher response levels than ordinary 'snail' mail surveys.

### Disadvantages

- You must possess or purchase a list of email addresses.
- You may receive duplicate responses and instructions may be ignored.
- Many people dislike unsolicited email.
- You cannot use email surveys to generalise findings to the whole population.

---

Web surveys can be conducted by Internet or Intranet and are rapidly gaining popularity. They involve sending people a link to a web page containing a questionnaire that is filled in online. The questionnaire will have been designed with software that will ensure that skip instructions are accurately followed (i.e. an instruction to 'skip to Question 20 if you answer "yes" to Question 10'). These automatic skips are more accurate than relying on an interviewer or a respondent reading a paper questionnaire, and they have the positive benefit that respondents do not need to see a page filled with irrelevant questions.

Web surveys are extremely fast. A questionnaire posted on a popular website can gather several thousand responses within a few hours. Many of the people who will respond to an email invitation to take a web survey will do so the first day, and most will do so within a few days. There is practically no cost involved once the set-up has been completed. Large samples do not cost more than smaller ones (except for any cost involved in drawing up the sample). You can show respondents pictures, and some web survey software can also show video and play sound. Web page questionnaires, as well as supporting complex question-skipping logic, can involve randomisations of question order and other features not possible with paper questionnaires or most email surveys. These features assure better data. Colours, fonts and other formatting options that are not possible in most email surveys can be used. A significant number of people will give more honest answers to questions about sensitive topics, such as drug use or sex, when giving their answers to a computer instead of to a person or on paper. On average, people give longer answers to open-ended questions on web page questionnaires than they do to other kinds of self-administered surveys. Some web survey software can combine survey answers with the pre-existing information about individuals taking a survey, collected through other methods, such as at the sampling stage.

But the problems are also clear. Current use of the Internet is far from universal. Internet surveys do not reflect the population as a whole. This is true even if a sample of Internet users is selected to match the general population in terms of age, gender and other demographics. People can easily quit in the middle of a questionnaire. They are not as likely to complete a long questionnaire on the Web as they would be if talking with a good interviewer. If your survey pops up on a web page, you often have no control over who replies; anyone from New York to Tokyo cruising that web page may answer. Depending on your software, there is often no control over people responding several times to bias the results. You may also want to restrict access by requiring a password (good software allows this option) or by putting the survey on a page that can only be accessed directly (i.e. there are no links to it from other pages). Box 11.4 summarises these advantages and disadvantages of web-based surveys.

## BOX 11.4

### ADVANTAGES AND DISADVANTAGES OF WEB-BASED SURVEYS

#### Advantages

- Web page surveys are extremely fast.
- No cost is involved once the set-up has been completed.
- You can show pictures, video and play sound.
- Web page questionnaires can be set with skip instructions.
- Web page questionnaires can use colours, fonts and other formatting options not possible in most email surveys.
- A significant number of people will give more honest answers to questions.
- People give longer answers to open-ended questions.
- Survey answers can be combined with pre-existing information you have about individuals taking a survey.

#### Disadvantages

- Internet access is far from universal, so Internet surveys do not reflect the population as a whole.
- People can easily quit in the middle of a questionnaire.
- No control over who replies and how many times they reply, unless the software is set to accept only one reply and is password protected.

Self-completion surveys can also be group administered. For example, a researcher may ask a class of school pupils to fill in a questionnaire. If a pupil is uncertain about the meaning of a question, he or she can ask for help from the researcher, meaning that the quality of the data is improved. A school is an example of a setting where it is relatively easy to assemble groups of respondents; other places, such as places of work, may afford the same opportunities and therefore be particularly well-suited to this mode of administration. More rarely, the household drop-off survey may be used. The researcher using this method will go to a respondent's home and leave the questionnaire with a respondent to be returned later. This means personal contact with the respondent is made, which may involve the opportunity to explain the purpose of the survey and so increase motivation to respond. In addition, some questions from the respondent may be asked and answered, which can affect the quality of the resultant data.

Box 11.5, adapted from Trochim (2010), summarises the major features of group, postal and household drop-off surveys, comparing these with face-to-face and telephone interviews. You can see from this that interviews are particularly suited where a flexible method using open-ended questions is required, and that they possess the further advantage that the ability to read and write is not required of respondents, which can be important if interviewees are either not literate or are unfamiliar with the language of the inquiry. Questionnaires, on the other hand, have significant cost advantages, as well as the capacity to cover a geographically dispersed sample. Phone surveys retain some of the advantages that face-to-face interviews have over questionnaires, but not all. In some respects, the group (and drop-off) approach to administering questionnaires, while sacrificing the wide geographical coverage which questionnaires have, mitigates the impersonality of questionnaires, allowing for improved data quality due to the capacity to explain more about the study and the questionnaire to respondents.

## BOX 11.5

### GROUP, POSTAL AND HOUSEHOLD DROP-OFF SURVEYS, COMPARED WITH FACE-TO-FACE AND TELEPHONE INTERVIEWS

| Issue | Questionnaire | | | Interview | |
| --- | --- | --- | --- | --- | --- |
| | Group | Postal | Drop-Off | Personal | Phone |
| Visual presentations are possible | Yes | Yes | Yes | Yes | No |
| Long response categories are possible | Yes | Yes | Yes | Possible | No |
| Privacy is a feature | No | Yes | Yes | Yes | Yes |
| Flexible method | No | No | No | Yes | Yes |
| Open-ended questions feasible | No | No | No | Yes | Yes |
| Reading and writing is needed | Yes | Yes | Yes | No | No |
| You can judge quality of response | Yes | No | No | Yes | Possible |
| High response rates likely | Yes | No | Yes | Yes | No |
| Can explain study in person | Yes | No | Yes | Yes | Possible |
| Low cost | Yes | Yes | No | No | No |
| Low staff costs | Yes | Yes | No | No | No |
| Access to dispersed samples | No | Yes | No | No | No |
| Respondent has time to compose answers | No | Yes | Yes | No | No |
| Personal contact involved | Yes | No | Yes | Yes | No |
| Long survey is feasible | No | No | No | Yes | No |
| Quick turnaround | No | Yes | No | No | Yes |

*Source:* adapted from Trochim, 2010

## Constructing an interview schedule or questionnaire

### Keep it short

One principle that is consistent whether you are doing an interview or sending someone a questionnaire is that the instrument should be kept as short and simple as possible. If you send people a 25-page questionnaire, or tell them that an interview is likely to take an hour or more, most potential participants will give up before they begin, and particularly so when the instrument is a self-completion questionnaire, which is not as emotionally rewarding to fill in as it is to spend time talking about oneself with an apparently sympathetic, non-judgemental stranger. If you consider that a question is not essential, then do not include it. An effective way to avoid including pointless questions in a questionnaire is to ask yourself what you will do with the information gained from each question. If you cannot give yourself an acceptable answer, then leave it out. Stay away from the temptation to include just a few more questions. Try placing your questions into three groups:

1   Must know

2   Useful to know

3   Nice to know

Afterwards, discard questions in the last group unless the previous two groups are extremely short. Furthermore, it is vital the questions themselves are simple and unambiguous, particularly in self-completion surveys where participants, unlike interviewees, cannot ask the researcher 'What do you mean by that?' if they do not understand a question.

### Introduction or welcome message

Always start with an introduction or welcome message. In a postal questionnaire, this message can be in a cover page or on the questionnaire form itself; in an interview, this can be read or spoken by the interviewer. A good-quality introduction will encourage people to take part and increase the response rate. In contrast, having no welcome message will reduce the response rate. An example of an introductory message, for a survey in which the researcher remained present while the questionnaire was filled in, is given in Box 11.6.

---

**BOX 11.6**

### INTRODUCTION OR WELCOME MESSAGE: BELIEFS, ATTITUDES AND KNOWLEDGE ON HIV/AIDS

The University of Nicosia in association with the Ministry of Health, the Cyprus Family Planning Association and the Cyprus University of Technology are studying the attitudes, beliefs and knowledge of students and migrants from third countries (non-European) who live and work in Cyprus on the topic of HIV/AIDS.

The project aims to develop an HIV/AIDS Public Health Educational Programme for people who come to Cyprus to study and/or work in order to equip them with all the relevant information regarding HIV and AIDS.

Therefore, in order to carry out the above-mentioned research successfully, we need your own contribution by filling in this questionnaire and then inserting it in the envelope provided. Questionnaires are completely anonymous and the information collected will be used for the purposes only of this current survey. We urge you to complete the questionnaire alone. Should you have any queries or things you do not understand, please ask our researchers who stand nearby and they will be glad to assist you.

Thank you very much for participating in this survey.

Dr Constantinos N. Phellas
Dean of the School of Humanities, Social Sciences and Law
University of Nicosia

---

## Elements of an effective cover letter

Start with the title of the survey, for example 'Beliefs, attitudes and knowledge on HIV/AIDS'. If you are asking about opinions, personal belief or attitudes it is usually a good idea to give the name of the research organisation or university rather than the sponsor or the funding organisation. For example, it is better to tell respondents that a study is being done by the 'Research Unit on Social Issues' than it is being sponsored by a political party with which the respondent might have little sympathy. People prefer a neutral organisation.

In your covering letter you should introduce yourself, and say why you are doing the survey and how they have been chosen as a respondent. Do not go into depth about this, as respondents can try to influence the results with false answers if they know too much about your specific hypotheses. Mention the incentive, if any, and explain how to return the questionnaire. Include the name and telephone number of someone the participant can call if he or she has any questions. In addition, include instructions on how to complete the questionnaire itself. This may take the form of a sample question with one of its fixed-choice response options circled, ticked or crossed – however you want respondents to indicate their replies.

In addition, it is often a good idea to explain why taking part will improve some aspect of the respondent's life (e.g. make a health organisation/hospital better able to meet his or her needs), or provide him or her with the opportunity to express their viewpoint, or simply appeal to the respondent's sense of altruism, as in a plea to 'please help'.

## Deciding the order of questions

In general, it is desirable to start with the most important questions so that if a person gives up halfway through and still returns the questionnaire, or agrees that an interview can be used, at least you might get the most essential information.

But even if more personal or sensitive questions are important for the project, it is better to leave these until the end of the questionnaire or interview, since by then the participant should have built a 'rapport' with the project or with the interviewer that will encourage honest responses to such personal questions.

## Include all potential answer choices

You should include 'Don't know' or 'Not applicable' responses to all questions, except where they are clearly irrelevant, such as gender or age. This can be vital in dealing with participants who are frustrated because the response options do not fit them. On the one hand, sometimes options such as 'Don't know' or 'Not applicable' will really represent some participants' most sincere answers to some of your questions. On the other hand, participants who feel they are being forced into giving an answer they do not want to give commonly do not complete interviews or return questionnaires. For example, people will often abandon a questionnaire that asks them to specify their income, without offering a 'Decline to state' choice. For the same reason, include 'Other' or 'None' whenever either of these seems to be a reasonably possible answer. When the answer choices are a list of potential opinions, preferences or behaviours, you should usually offer these answers.

Leave a space at the end of a questionnaire for 'Other comments' and, in an interview, ask respondents if there is anything at all that they would like to add. This allows respondents whose feelings and thoughts are aroused by the questions to express themselves in their own way.

Occasionally, participants make casual remarks that are vital regarding some areas you have never thought of, but which they consider critical. You may decide to include the answers to sections like this, or to other open-ended questions, in the analysis. You can do this by 'post-coding' them. This involves inventing a category scheme into which each answer can be placed. If each category has a separate numerical value, these replies can be entered into a spreadsheet in the same way as fixed-response options.

Make sure you include all the appropriate alternatives as answer choices. Leaving out a choice can give misleading results. For example, if you ask participants if they eat after 6 p.m. and the choices are only 'Yes' or 'No' , then you will more likely find that the great majority of the respondents choose 'Yes'. Questionnaires that offer respondents more appropriate choices, such as 'Never', 'Some of the time', 'Most of the time' and 'Always' are likely to collect more realistic data.

## Questionnaire layout

An attractive layout in a self-completion questionnaire is important so that it appears easy to understand and relatively effortless to complete.

This can also be important in structured interviewing, as interviewers can be daunted, or confused, by poor layout. If you plan to enter data into a spreadsheet from responses marked on a paper questionnaire or interview schedule, you also want to make it uncomplicated for your data entry. Therefore, try to keep your answer spaces in a straight line either horizontally or vertically. A single answer choice on each line is best. The best place to use for answer spaces is the right-hand edge of the page. It is much easier for a participant or interviewer to follow a logical flow across or down a page. In addition, using the right edge is easier for data entry.

Squeezing questions into a small space (Figure 11.1) can make the questionnaire harder to complete, even though you can save a lot of paper.

Questions and answer choice grids (Figure 11.2) are popular with many researchers. They look

| 1 Circle the letters of the three courses in which your son or daughter has the best performance in class. 2 Circle the numbers of the three courses your son or daughter enjoys most. | | | | | |
|---|---|---|---|---|---|
| Mathematics | A | 1 | Religious Education | G | 7 |
| Modern Languages | B | 2 | Science | H | 8 |
| Art | C | 3 | Physical Education | I | 9 |
| Geography | D | 4 | Environmental Study | J | 10 |
| History | E | 5 | English Language | K | 11 |
| Music | F | 6 | Design & Technology | L | 12 |

FIGURE 11.1   Squeezing a lot into a small space

| | | Strongly disagree | Disagree | Uncertain or unsure | Agree | Strongly agree |
|---|---|---|---|---|---|---|
| Please respond to the following questions by circling the response that best describes you. | | | | | | |
| 1 | I am comfortable about people finding out that I am gay. | 1 | 2 | 3 | 4 | 5 |
| 2 | It is important to me to control who knows about my homosexuality. | 1 | 2 | 3 | 4 | 5 |
| 3 | Even if I could change my sexual orientation I wouldn't. | 1 | 2 | 3 | 4 | 5 |

FIGURE 11.2   A question and answer choice grid with responses in numbers

| Please respond to the following questions by circling the response that best describes you. | | | | | | |
|---|---|---|---|---|---|---|
| 1 | I am comfortable about people finding out that I am gay. | Strongly disagree | Disagree | Uncertain or unsure | Agree | Strongly agree |
| 2 | It is important to me to control who knows about my homosexuality. | Strongly disagree | Disagree | Uncertain or unsure | Agree | Strongly agree |
| 3 | Even if I could change my sexual orientation I wouldn't. | Strongly disagree | Disagree | Uncertain or unsure | Agree | Strongly agree |

FIGURE 11.3   A question and answer choice grid with responses in words

attractive and save paper. They also can avoid a long series of repetitive question and answer choice lists (Figure 11.3). But unfortunately, grids (Figure 11.2) are a bit harder than the repeated lists (Figure 11.3) for some participants to understand. Although both Figures 11.2 and 11.3 show the answer choices in neat columns and have space between the lines, Figure 11.2 is undoubtedly easier to read. The numbers in Figure 11.2 will also speed data entry. The creation of questionnaires is a mixture of science and art.

## Question types

A distinction is made between open questions, closed questions and fixed-choice questions. An open question asks the participant to formulate his own answer, whereas a closed question constrains the participant to a greater extent. A fixed-choice question requires the respondent to pick an answer from a given number of options. Examples of each are given in Box 11.7.

---

**BOX 11.7**

### EXAMPLES OF OPEN, CLOSED AND FIXED-CHOICE QUESTIONS

Open

• Why did you take up smoking?

   (Space for reply)

Closed question

• Do you want to quit smoking, or not?

Fixed choice question

• What type of assistance do you think would most help you quit smoking? (Please choose only one option)

   1   Medication

   2   Counselling

   3   Combination of medication and counselling

   4   More support from family and friends

   5   None of the above

   6   I do not want to answer

---

With an open question respondents are asked a question and can reply however they wish. In contrast, closed questions frame responses in a certain way, and fixed choice questions even more so. Closed and fixed-choice questions provide primarily quantitative data and are frequently used in confirmatory research.

## Levels of measurement

There are four levels of measurement: nominal, ordinal, interval and ratio. The four levels differ in how closely each matches the characteristics of the abstract number system.

Nominal variables (sometimes also called categorical) involve placing participants into separate categories such as diagnostic or political groups, so are said to have the property of identity. Use a nominal question when the potential answers are categories and the participant must fit into only one category. Examples are given in Box 11.8. Ordinal variables have both the property of identity and magnitude, which is to say that they involve some notion of order or rank between the categories (e.g. highest to lowest, largest to smallest), but no strong sense that the distance between two adjacent points on a scale is equal to the distance between two other adjacent points. Examples are shown in Box 11.9.

---

**BOX 11.8**

### EXAMPLES OF QUESTIONNAIRE ITEMS THAT PRODUCE NOMINAL OR CATEGORICAL VARIABLES

Gender: Male ..... Female .....
Marital status:

- Single
- Married
- Divorced
- Separated
- Widow/widower
- Remarried
- Cohabiting with sexual partner
- Other (please specify)

---

**BOX 11.9**

### EXAMPLES OF QUESTIONNAIRE ITEMS THAT PRODUCE ORDINAL VARIABLES

- Preference scores (e.g. ratings where 10=good, 1=poor, but the difference between a 10 ranking and an 8 ranking cannot be quantified)
- SES (low, middle or upper socioeconomic class)
- Grades in school (A, B, C, D, F; cannot determine how much higher the top ranked student is from the second)

---

Interval variables have the properties of identity, magnitude and equal intervals between points. A common example of an interval scale is the Fahrenheit scale of temperature. In the Fahrenheit temperature scale the distance between 10 degrees and 20 degrees is the same as the distance between 35 degrees and 45 degrees. However, since interval scales do not have an absolute zero point, the ratio of two scores will not be meaningful: it would not be appropriate to say that 40 degrees is twice as hot as 20 degrees. Other examples include IQ tests, neuroticism scores, attitude measures, personality measures, self-reported depression level, ability to solve problems. Such scales are normally constructed by adding together a number of separate questionnaire items that indicate a concept.

Ratio scales have all the properties of interval scales as well as a true zero point. Therefore, all mathematical operations are appropriate, including taking the ratio of two numbers. For example, someone who earns €3,000 earns twice as much as someone who earns €1,500. Data from ratio scales are also sometimes called *score data*. Examples include height, weight, age, annual income, number of responses, time duration, reaction time, heart rate, child's rate of hitting other children, number of acts of aggression, the number of stressful behaviours.

## Piloting the instrument

The last step in designing a questionnaire or interview schedule is to test (or 'pilot') it with a small number of participants prior to conducting your actual research. Preferably, you should test the questionnaire on the same type of people you will include in the real study. If that is not possible, at least ask a few other people to answer the questionnaire, such as friends or colleagues. The people used during the pilot study should be excluded from your final sample as their experience of seeing the earlier questionnaire may make them answer the real thing differently.

This kind of testing can reveal unanticipated problems with question wording, instructions to skip questions and so on. Crucially, it can help you see if both interviewers and participants understand the meaning of your questions in the way that you understand them. You can also see how long it takes to complete the questionnaire or interview and try to identify and eliminate items that will not generate usable data. Box 11.10 suggests the type of questions to ask when piloting a questionnaire or interview schedule.

BOX 11.10

## WHAT TO ASK WHEN YOU PILOT A QUESTIONNAIRE OR INTERVIEW SCHEDULE

- How long did it take to complete?
- Were the instructions clear?
- Were any questions ambiguous?

*(Continued)*

*(Continued)*

- Were any questions objectionable?
- Was the layout clear and easy to follow?
- Were any topics omitted?

## Structured observation

A comparison of structured observation with participant observation (for which see Chapter 14) is similar to the comparison between the structured interviewing or questionnaires described in this chapter and the qualitative interviewing techniques that are described in Chapter 12. Both participant observation and qualitative interviewing involve the researcher encountering the people and events studied with a relatively open mind as to what might become relevant to the research problem being addressed. They produce data amenable to qualitative analysis, and data gathered by such loosely structured methods is normally not subjected to statistical analysis, or if it is, usually of a simple sort. In contrast with these exploratory methods, the 'structured' approach means that the researcher figures out ahead of time what kind of event, or response, is going to be counted as relevant for the research problem.

The pay-off with these structured methods is to generate data that is reliable, generalisable and is often comparable with other studies if the same measurement instruments have been used. Although less structured methods can be valuable in discovering new things that could not have been anticipated at the start of a study, there are often problems in knowing whether they have been reliably described (would another researcher have seen it this way?) or there are doubts about whether newly discovered phenomena are particularly widespread – perhaps they only occur in the few cases that the qualitative researcher has been able to study in depth? What one qualitative researcher means when they describe a phenomenon may be different from what another researcher means, even if they use the same words to label it with. Structured methods try to avoid these problems.

Structured observation, like structured interviewing or the use of self-completion questionnaires, is suitable for projects where the researcher has quite specific questions or hypotheses to investigate. For example, a researcher might ask whether one group of doctors behaves differently from another group when interacting with patients, whether different types of patient are spoken to in different ways by the same doctor, or whether different school teachers vary in how much they allow pupils to ask questions in class. It could be that the researcher wants to know whether particular behaviours are related to other variables, such as coping better with an illness or passing school exams. If the researcher thinks they know what kind of behaviour is important (e.g. asking questions; giving information; eliciting feelings; maintaining eye contact), a standardised observation schedule can be used to categorise different bits of observed behaviour. The advantage of using an observation schedule that someone else has designed and which has been used on other studies is that the study about to be carried out using this same schedule will generate data that is directly comparable with the findings of other research work.

## The Roter Interaction Analysis System (RIAS)

The Roter Interaction Analysis System (Roter, 2000) is one of many structured observation tools, in this case a standardised schedule for coding talk in health care encounters. It is designed so that trained users can code interaction as it happens in real time, though ideally by viewing it on a videotape. RIAS and other structured observation tools are not normally used on typed transcripts of audio-recorded talk, because most researchers using such data collection tools wish to analyse a fairly large number of interactions in order to obtain sample sizes amenable to statistical analysis. To achieve reliability, inter-rater reliability tests involving comparisons of two raters who have independently rated several interactions are carried out (inter-rater reliability tests are discussed in detail in Chapter 26).

Box 11.11 shows the main categories used in this system. You can see that the RIAS divides speech into three broad categories:

- *process* statements, such as asking for clarifications or indicating that one is listening hard
- *affective* or emotional statements, such as providing reassurance or showing concern
- *content* statements, such as asking questions, giving answers or providing advice.

Box 11.12 describes a study in which the RIAS was used to examine communication in medical consultations. The researchers found that South Asian patients who were not fluent in English received significantly different consultations.

---

**┐BOX 11.11┌**

## MAIN CATEGORIES OF THE ROTER INTERACTION ANALYSIS SYSTEM (RIAS)

| Process | Affective | Content | None |
|---------|-----------|---------|------|
| 1. Social behaviour<br>3. Paraphrase<br>4. Verbal attention<br>8. Giving direction<br>9. Asking clarification | 2. Agreement<br>5. Showing concern<br>6. Reassurance<br>7. Disagreement<br>14. Counsels/directs – medical<br>15. Counsels/directs – social | 10. Asks questions – medical<br>11. Asks questions – social<br>12. Gives info – medical<br>13. Gives info – social | 16. Others |

*Source:* adapted from Neal et al., 2006

---

**┐BOX 11.12┌**

## COMMUNICATION BETWEEN SOUTH ASIAN PATIENTS AND GPS

Richard Neal and his colleagues (2006) wanted to compare the ways in which white and South Asian patients communicated with white general practitioners. They video-recorded 101 consultations with white patients and 82 with South Asians (mostly Pakistani and Bangladeshi) involving health centres in four different towns in West Yorkshire, including Bradford. Within the South Asian group, 51 classified themselves as 'fluent' in English and 29 regarded themselves as 'non-fluent', with two unable to be classified in this way.

The speech recorded in the videotapes was coded into categories by two researchers using the RIAS, who first independently coded 18 of the consultations and compared their results, to check whether each coder was coding in the same way. In addition, the researchers timed the length of the consultation, and the time each person spent talking within it.

*(Continued)*

*(Continued)*

South Asians fluent in English had the shortest consultations and those who were not fluent had the longest. The consultations with white patients contained significantly more affective statements, largely because of more statements that expressed agreement between doctor and patient. GPs asked most questions in consultations with non-fluent South Asian patients, but also spent the smallest amount of time giving information to this group.

The researchers note that the RIAS categories rigidly required statements which the researchers felt often had several functions under a single heading. They also wondered whether doctors' and patients' behaviour changed because they knew they were being recorded.

## Flanders Interaction Analysis Categories (FIAC)

Another, somewhat simpler structured observation tool which has been used widely in educational research is the Flanders Interaction Analysis Categories (FIAC) (Flanders, 1970), shown in Box 11.13. This is designed to be used so that an observer can sit in the corner of a classroom and code the interaction as it happens. Every three seconds, the observer records the predominant event that has happened during that period, so that 20 numbers are written on the recording sheet during each minute of observation. As you can imagine, this takes some practice, and inter-rater reliability is again an important issue to address, so as to ensure that any one observer is recording events correctly.

### BOX 11.13

#### FLANDERS INTERACTION ANALYSIS CATEGORIES (FIAC)

Teacher talk

- Response

  1 Accepts feeling

  2 Praises or encourages

  3 Accepts or uses ideas of pupils

- Initiation

  4 Asks questions

  5 Lecturing

Pupil talk

  8 Response

  9 Initiation

Silence

  10 Silence or confusion

*Source:* after Flanders, 1970

In broad terms, the FIAC can characterise teaching styles in terms of how teacher-centred they are. Clearly, if most of the time teachers occupy category 5 (lecturing), without asking questions (category 4) or allowing any pupil initiation (category 9) they are at the teacher-centred end of the spectrum. If, however, classroom interaction includes a lot of category 9 talk (pupil initiated talk), to which the teacher responds by accepting feelings, praising or encouraging, and accepting and using the ideas put forward by pupils (categories 1, 2 and 3), the teacher is more towards the pupil-centred end of the spectrum. It is possible that teacher-centred and pupil-centred styles have different impacts on pupil learning, so that the ready identification of such styles using the FIAC, if combined with measures of learning outcomes, can be revealing.

FIAC is a simple system which largely expects classroom interaction to occur as a dialogue between the teacher and one or more pupils. Clearly, if a group discussion took place between pupils, categories 8 and 9 would come into play a great deal, but to summarise the complexities of what might happen in such a discussion, these two categories are exceedingly simple. The teacher's behaviour, by contrast, is described by five different categories (1–5), so the FIAC contains the built-in assumption that it is this speaker whose behaviour is going to be of most interest to researchers, which may not be true of some research projects in which pupil behaviour is of greater concern.

Against this, the FIAC (and the RIAS) are both widely used instruments, so the researcher using one of these will be able to compare his or her results with those of many other studies – something which is hard to do when not using an instrument that has become as well established as these two have become.

## Deciding to use structured observation instruments

The researcher planning to use a structured observation instrument therefore faces choices similar to that of the person wanting to use structured interviews or questionnaires: whether to get a ready-made instrument (or items for a new instrument) 'off-the-shelf', or whether to make one up oneself. The latter choice means that something can be designed that relates precisely to the particular research questions being asked in a project. The former 'off-the-shelf' choice may involve some sacrifice on this front, but may gain the advantage of using something already well-validated and widely used.

If you do decide to construct your own observational instrument, a number of considerations then become relevant. For example, do you want to observe verbal or non-verbal behaviour, or both? In examining speech, do you want to look at 'extra-linguistic' features of speech (such as speaking speed, volume, interruptions), or the content of what is said? Sometimes you want to know how many times something happened, but sometimes you may want to know whether sequences of interaction occur; for example, is a question always followed by an answer? Are answers always followed by a response from the person who asked the question? And how long is devoted to each unit of behaviour that you have recorded? Do you observe a single individual for a period of time, or are you observing the whole group?

As well as deciding what to record and how to record it, you may need to decide whether (1) to devise an instrument that can be used by someone recording the scene who is on the spot, or (2) whether ratings should take place on viewing or hearing electronically recorded events, or (3) whether ratings should be done on the basis of typists' transcripts of talk. Option (3) is the most time-consuming, but perhaps the most reliable and valid approach, especially if combined with option (2). But there is a trade-off here with resources: it may be preferable to go for option (1) if large numbers of events are to be observed economically.

On the other hand, think of reactivity: is the presence of an 'on-the-spot' observer going to change behaviour more than the presence of a recording device? Observers doing on-the-spot observation have sometimes found that people in the setting try to interact with them, or behave in such a way that it is obvious they are reacting to the presence of an observer. In these situations, it is best to keep researcher interactions with research participants to minimal acknowledgments, and to get people habituated to being observed. If you observe a lot of sessions, you may find that interaction stabilises over time, people interact with you less and participants tell you afterwards that your presence has not affected them.

To develop your own observation schedule you should:

- relate the categories to your research question

- realise that you can't observe everything, so focus on the relevant

- be objective; require as little inference on the part of observers as possible

- define what is in or out of each category clearly

- always be able to assign behaviour to a code, even if an 'other' category

- ensure that categories are mutually exclusive (even if some behaviours attract multiple codes)

- make it easy to record behaviour

- carry out an inter rater-reliability test (see Chapter 26).

Additionally, in developing your categories, an exercise in blind coding (where two people attempt to use the instrument to observe the same event) can be helpful, as this can identify categories whose definitions are causing problems of interpretation and which therefore need further refinement. This is similar to piloting a questionnaire or an interview schedule.

## Conclusion

This chapter has elaborated a number of basic principles that should guide the design and administration of structured interview schedules, self-completed questionnaires and structured observation schedules. First, we discussed the importance of preliminary conceptual work and expressing the aims and objectives of your study so that good concept–indicator links could be established. The chapter also summarised the advantages and disadvantages of different kinds of self-completed questionnaires and interviews. The chapter then turned to the design of questions and questionnaires, emphasising the importance of good layout, design and question order, as well as other factors that influence response rates. Different levels of measurement and different response formats for questions were described and illustrated. The chapter then discussed the piloting, or testing, of questionnaires and interview schedules in order to develop them. Finally, the use of structured observation instruments was considered in more depth, with the examples of the RIAS and the FIAC to help. Familiarity with these topics should equip you to design and carry out a study involving one of these instruments with a high degree of competence.

## FURTHER READING

Textbooks often do not cover the topic of how to design an interview schedule or self-completed questionnaire at length, although Coolican (2004), Bryman (2001), Bernard (2000) and Robson (2002) all have useful chapters. Coolican discusses several different approaches and offers a good general guide as well as advanced information to new researchers. Bernard and Robson both present a refined discussion of different ways of approaching self-completed questionnaire design. Croll (1986) is a useful guide to structured classroom observation and Bryman (2001) has a chapter on this.

## Student Reader (Seale, 2004b): relevant readings

9  Sir Claus Moser and Graham Kalton: 'Questionnaires'

10  Herbert H. Hyman with William J. Cobb, Jacob J. Feldman, Clyde W. Hart and Charles Herbert Stember: 'Interviewing in social research'

11  A.N. Oppenheim: 'Attitude scaling methods'

12  Kim Sheehan and Mariea Hoy: 'On-line surveys'

21  Julius A. Roth: 'Hired hand research'

22  Aaron V. Cicourel: 'Fixed-choice questionnaires'

23  Cathie Marsh: 'The critics of surveys'

24  Hanneke Houtkoop-Steenstra: 'Quality of life assessment interviews'

25  R.C. Lewontin: 'Sex lies and social science'

## Journal articles illustrating the methods discussed in this chapter

Mills, M., Davies, H.T.O., Macrae, W.A. (1994) 'Care of dying patients in hospital', British Medical Journal, 309: 583–586.

Nichols, E. and Childs, J.H. (2009) 'Respondent debriefings conducted by experts: a technique for questionnaire evaluation', Field Methods, 21: 115–132.

Potter, J. (2003) 'Studying the standardized survey as interaction', Qualitative Research, 3: 269–278.

Smith, M.V. (2008) 'Pain experience and the imagined researcher', Sociology of Health & Illness, 30 (7): 992–1006.

## Web links

e-Source: Chapter 4 on 'Sample surveys' by Sarah M Nusser and Michael D Larsen: www.esourceresearch.org

e-Source: Chapter 5 on 'Social survey data collection' by Stephen Woodland: www.esourceresearch.org

Survey and questionnaire design: www.statpac.com/surveys

Questionnaire Design and Analysis: www.tardis.ed.ac.uk/~kate/qmcweb/qcont.htm

Observation – some examples: www.readingrecovery.org/reading_recovery/accountability/observation/index.asp and http://informationr.net/tdw/publ/INISS/Chap1.html

Super Survey Knowledge Base: http://knowledge-base.supersurvey.com/glossary.htm#survey_problem

Leeds University Guide to the Design of Questionnaires: http://iss.leeds.ac.uk/info/312/surveys/217/guide_to_the_design_of_questionnaires

StatPac survey and questionnaire design: www.statpac.com/surveys

Creative Research Systems: survey design: www.surveysystem.com/sdesign.htm

(Structured) observation: www.grahamtall.co.uk/Observation.htm

## Review questions

1. What are the advantages and disadvantages of interviews compared with self-completed questionnaires?
2. How do telephone interviews differ from face-to-face interviews?
3. Look at Box 11.5 and decide how the criteria listed would apply to email and web-based questionnaires.
4. Describe the main types of question used on structured interview schedules and self-completion questionnaires.
5. Explain the differences between nominal, ordinal, interval and ratio scales or variables.
6. What are the advantages and disadvantages of the use of structured observation instruments such as the RIAS of the FIAC?
7. What considerations should you bear in mind when designing your own structured observation instrument?

## Workshop and discussion exercises

1. Design 10 questions that could be used on a self-completion questionnaire investigating pupils' experiences of sporting activities in school, and type them onto a sheet of paper. Get some fellow students to fill in the questionnaire and ask them the questions in Box 11.9. What items of behaviour would you include if you decided to study the same topic using a structured observation instrument?
2. You want to study one of the following groups. In each case, outline the arguments for using either a structured interview, a self-completion questionnaire or structured observation, and describe how you would administer it.
   - Homeless people
   - Ex-offenders

- Politicians
- University students
- School pupils
- Social welfare claimants
- Small business owners
- Magazine readers

3   In a group of three or more, design a short interview schedule, containing some open, some closed and some pre-coded questions. The topic may be anything of which people in the group can reasonably be expected to have some experience (e.g. watching or participating in sports events, studying research methods).

One person should use the interview schedule to interview another person in the group while the others observe, considering the following issues:

- What difficulties were there in doing the inteview?
- Did the interviewer appear or feel at ease?
- Did the respondent appear or feel at ease?
- Did the respondent find the questions unambiguous and easy to answer?
- Did he or she find them relevant to his or her life experience?

Swap roles, until everyone has had a go at interviewing, replying and observing. How would you now redesign the interview schedule?

4   Use the FIAC (Box 11.13) to study interaction in a student seminar. What categories would need to be changed or added in order to more fully reflect what is going on?

# 12

# QUALITATIVE INTERVIEWING

## Bridget Byrne

---

This chapter will give an overview of what qualitative interviews are and what kinds of research they might be used for. It will consider the different ways in which qualitative interviews are used (as a resource or a topic) and will examine some of the ethical questions raised by qualitative research using interviews.

The chapter will also provide a practical guide to preparing for and conducting qualitative interviews, including questions of sampling and access. It will also consider what kinds of questions might be asked, how interviews should be recorded and questions of analysis of qualitative interviews.

The learning outcomes of this chapter will include:

- An understanding of what a qualitative interview is.
- An appreciation of what qualitative interviews can (and cannot) tell us (epistemological questions).

- An understanding of the ethical issues involved in qualitative interviewing.
- Practical understanding of how to design and conduct qualitative interviews.

For a commentary on successful interviewing, see Box 12.1.

---

**BOX 12.1**

## SUCCESSFUL INTERVIEWING

To interview successfully requires skill. But there are many different styles of interviewing, ranging from the friendly, informal, conversational approach to the more formal, controlled style of questioning, and good interviewers eventually develop a variation of their method which, for them, brings the best results and suits their personality. There are some essential qualities which the successful interviewer must possess: an interest and respect for people as individuals, and flexibility in response to them; an ability to show understanding and sympathy for their point of view; and, above all, a willingness to sit quietly and listen. People who cannot stop talking themselves, or resist the temptation to contradict or push an inform-ant with their own ideas, will take away information which is either useless or positively misleading. But most people can learn to interview well. (Thompson, 1988: 196)

---

## What are qualitative interviews?

Interviews are most importantly a form of communication, a means of producing different forms of information with individuals and groups. The interactive nature of their practice means that interviewing is a highly flexible but also somewhat unpredictable form of social research. In everyday life, there are many different forms of interviews, or conversations in which information is being elicited and/or shared with groups or individuals (see Box 12.2).

---

**BOX 12.2**

## INTERVIEWS IN EVERYDAY LIFE

- Market research surveys
- Doctors' consultations
- Job or university interviews
- Immigration interviews
- Interviews to receive welfare or social security
- Journalists' interviews
- Television interviews
- Therapeutic interviews

---

All of us will have experienced at least some of them, and we are also familiar with reading the results of journalistic interviews, and perhaps also published 'conversations' between academics, as well as watching televised interviews. We are also familiar with conversational forms, which would not be considered as formal interviews, where we share with greater or lesser depth our feelings and views with friends, relatives, lovers and also perhaps counsellors and therapists. This experience tells us that the kind of talk we do, or information and opinions we share, varies widely depending on the context, our mood and the nature of the encounter (see Chapter 24 for an account of how to analyse conversations). It also varies depending on how familiar the form of encounter is to us – this is likely to be affected by our gender, class and cultural backgrounds. We are also aware that sometimes we listen more carefully than others. As Les Back argues, 'Our culture is one that speaks rather than listens ... Listening to the world is not an automatic faculty but a skill that needs to be trained' (2007: 7).

Therefore, in thinking about interviewing as a tool of social research, we need to be aware of the many different variables which will affect the outcome. These will include who is doing the interviewing, who is being interviewed, the location in which the interview takes place and the form of questioning. These factors need to be thought about before and during research, but they are also worth bearing in mind when reading research based on interviews. Does the researcher give you a sense of the interview content and context, have they answered these questions for you and have they taken them into account in the analysis of their interview material?

Social research interviews range from the formal, structured interviews at one end of the spectrum (see Chapter 11) to totally open-ended interviews that might begin with a single prompt such as 'Tell me about your life'. The term qualitative interview generally refers to in-depth, loosely or semi-structured interviews,

and these have been referred to as 'conversations with a purpose' (Burgess, cited in Mason, 1996: 38). They are often used to encourage an interviewee to talk, perhaps at some length, about a particular issue or range of topics. This distinguishes them from the classical tradition of social survey work represented by the sort of interviews done by government social survey organisations, such as the UK Office for National Statistics, and the increasing number of telephone and street surveys conducted for marketing purposes. As you saw in Chapter 11, survey-based interviews tend to rely more on closed questions which follow a structured format in the form of an interview schedule and are designed to elicit specific information or 'facts' from the interviewees.

In a survey using structured interviews, the aim is to standardise the interviews in order to claim direct comparability between interviews with different people and to interview enough people so that the results could be held to be statistically representative of a particular population. The intention, therefore, is that the interview should be neutral (that is to say, not influenced by the words, actions or position of the interviewer) and generalisable (and therefore often quantifiable). The emphasis is on data collection and it is based on a particular epistemological position taken in the classical survey research tradition. Here, the social world is assumed to have an existence that is independent of the language used to describe it (see Chapter 2). In contrast to this realist approach, an idealist account would see interview data as presenting one of many possible representations of the world. This latter approach tends to view the interview as a process of data generation rather than collection. In qualitative interviews, the researcher is often regarded as a co-producer of the data, which are produced as a result of an interaction between researcher and interviewee(s) (Mason, 1996: 36).

There are many different forms which qualitative interviewing can take. These range from interviews following an interview schedule of topics or themes to be covered in a loosely planned order, to an invitation for the interviewee to talk on whatever they feel is relevant. Qualitative interviewing may not only be one-on-one interviewing. It can also include focus group discussions that bring together a group of interviewees to discuss a particular topic or range of issues. In these contexts, the interactions between participants can generate different data than would have emerged in a one-on-one interview. Chapter 13 gives a full account of focus group research.

Whilst qualitative interviews are often undertaken as a result of a particular epistemological position taken by the researcher (as will be explored below), they are also a flexible resource which may be used in conjunction with other research techniques. So, for example, in-depth interviews may be used to explore in more detail with specially selected interviewees questions that have also been covered in a wider questionnaire-based survey. Equally, focus groups or one-on-one interviews may be used as a part of an ethnographic approach (see Box 12.3). This raises the question of why one would choose to use qualitative interviews and what they offer the researcher.

BOX 12.3

## FOCUS GROUP INTERVIEWS

The method is particularly useful for allowing participants to generate their own questions, frames and concepts and to pursue their own priorities on their own terms, in their own vocabulary. Focus groups also enable researchers to examine people's different perspectives as they operate within a social network. Crucially, group work explores how accounts are articulated, censured, opposed and changed through social interaction and how this relates to peer communication and group norms. (Barbour and Kitzinger, 1999: 5)

## What the qualitative interview has to offer

Qualitative interviewing is particularly useful as a research method for accessing individuals' attitudes and values – things that cannot necessarily be observed or accommodated in a formal questionnaire. Open-ended and flexible questions are likely to get a more considered response than closed questions and therefore provide better access to interviewees' views, interpretations of events, understandings, experiences and opinions. They are also more open to hearing respondents' views 'in their own words', which allows for a more complex analysis. Therefore, this approach tends to be used by those who come from an ontological position which respects people's knowledge, values and experiences as meaningful and worthy of exploration. However, as we shall see below, few researchers believe that in the course of an interview, you are able to 'get inside someone's head'. What an interview produces is a particular representation or account of an individual's views and opinions.

One of the reasons why qualitative interviewing is a particularly suitable method for accessing complex issues such as values and understanding is that it is a flexible medium and, to a certain extent, allows interviewees to speak in their own voices and with their own language. Thus, qualitative interviewing has been particularly attractive to researchers who want to explore voices and experiences which they believe have been ignored, misrepresented or suppressed in the past. Feminists, for example, have used qualitative interviewing as a way of 'giving voice' to women's experiences, and much oral history is concerned with capturing voices and experiences 'from below'. As we shall see later, this raises important questions about the dynamics of power in the interview and research process.

A further advantage of using qualitative interviewing as a research method is its flexibility in allowing research topics to be approached in a variety of ways. Issues that might be of a sensitive nature, for example experiences of violence, or which interviewees may be reluctant to talk about (or unconscious of), such as racism or other forms of prejudice, can be approached with sensitivity to open up dialogue and produce fuller accounts. This again raises questions of power and ethics in the research process (see below and Chapter 5).

Perhaps the most compelling advantage of qualitative interviewing is that, when done well, it is able to achieve a level of depth and complexity that is not available to other, particularly survey-based, approaches. The non-standardised interview enables the researcher to become attuned to subtle differences in people's positions and to respond accordingly, both at the time of interviewing and in the subsequent analysis (see Box 12.4).

---

## BOX 12.4

### TALKING TO BEREAVED FAMILIES

A study by Chapple and Ziebland on the question of whether it was therapeutic for families to view the body of a loved one after a traumatic death which may have left the body damaged is a good example of the power of qualitative interviewing. As a demonstration of the *flexibility* of qualitative interviewing, the question of viewing the body was not an important issue for the researchers at the outset, but rather one which was raised by their interviewees. Nonetheless, the research can provide importance guidance for doctors and other nurses who deal with bereaved families. The authors found it was significant *how* the bereaved talked about their dead relative (as 'him' or 'her', by name; or as 'the body' or 'it'), and found that the most important factor was that families were given a choice in whether to view or not view their loved one, and that being forced to view a body for means of identification could potentially increase trauma. The qualitative nature of the study was essential for building trust and allowing interviewees to discuss difficult experiences in their own terms

*Source:* Chapple and Ziebland, 2010: 340:c2032

---

## The epistemological status of interviews

As we have seen, whilst qualitative interviewing offers particular advantages for researchers, it also raises epistemological, methodological and ethical issues for social researchers. However, it is also worth noting that many of these questions would also apply to other research methods.

Epistemological questions raised by qualitative interviewing centre around the status of the material produced:

- What can interviewees tell us and what do they not tell us?
- How do we assess and analyse the interview data?

Box 12.5 looks at what qualitative interviews can offer.

BOX 12.5

## WHAT QUALITATIVE INTERVIEWS OFFER

- Access to attitudes, values and feelings.
- Flexibility.
- Exploration of suppressed views.
- Sensitive issues can be broached.
- Achieve depth.
- Reflect complexity.
- Allow respondents to answer 'in their words'.

How we answer these questions depends largely on where we stand on the distinction between data collection and data generation mentioned earlier. In a realist approach, where the social world is assumed to have an existence independent of language, accounts given by interviewees are assessed according to how accurately they reflect this real social world. Thus, in this classical tradition, interviews are expected to act as a resource, providing real 'facts' about the social world. Thus interview data are scrutinised for bias – for the extent to which they present a distortion of the truth. In contrast, the idealist position takes the interviewee's account as one possible version of the social world. Here, the interview tends to be treated more as a social event in its own right, as a topic rather than a resource. In this approach, the researcher might be interested in analysing, for example, how the speaker uses various rhetorical strategies in order to achieve particular effects, or how the speaker is using particular discursive repertoires in their account (see Box 12.6 and Chapter 23).

BOX 12.6

## DISCURSIVE REPERTORIES OF WHITENESS

Ruth Frankenberg interviewed white women in the United States in order to explore their experiences of living in a racially hierarchical society. She identified different 'discursive repertoires', or ways in which race was spoken and written about in the United States. The dominant discourse was one of 'colour-blindness', or what Frankenberg named 'colour evasion': a way of thinking about race which 'asserts that we are all the same under the skin; that, culturally we are converging; that, materially, we have the same chances in US society; and that – the sting in the tail – any failure to achieve is therefore the fault of people of color themselves' (Frankenberg, 1993: 14).

Thus, Frankenberg was interested in identifying when her respondents were using this kind of discourse, as where interviewee Ginny Rodd said:

> To me, they are like me or anyone else – they're human – it's like I told my kids, they work for a living like we do. Just because they are Black is no saying their food is give to them [sic]. If you cut them, they bleed red blood, same as we do. (1993: 143)

*(Continued)*

*(Continued)*

Frankenberg contrasts these kinds of statements with those who she saw as drawing on a discourse of 'race cognizance', as in the words of interviewee Chris Patterson:

> When I look back, I think of myself as such a naïve white girl. Not even just naïve – naïve by isolation, by separation. Also coming from the white, privileged class … Means you don't have to look at anything else. You are never forced to until you choose to, because your life is so unaffected by things like racism. (1993: 161)

In practice, researchers are often using interview material both as resource and a topic. Interviews are often analysed both for *what* interviewees say about their lives and experiences (the interview as *resource*) and for *how* the information is communicated and the accounts are told (the interview as *topic*). Therefore it is not always possible to completely sidestep issues of 'truth' and reliability. Analysis of accounts is likely to need to consider some notion of how accurate the account is. If, for example, something is being misrepresented – a number or period of years being over-estimated – why does this happen? Why are certain things remembered more than others? Why is it more difficult to talk about certain subjects than others? As Luisa Passerini argues:

> There is no 'work of memory' without a corresponding 'work of forgetting' … So often forgetting indicates suffering, be it of the woman who 'does not remember' her housework because she has never been allowed to consider it important, or the silences of those who do not want to speak about the daily oppression of fascism and the massacres of Nazism. (1991: 194)

This 'work of forgetting' may be more interesting to the researcher than what is remembered, but interviews can only ever offer a partial view into the process. Of course qualitative interviews, by their nature, are reliant on people talking; however, some issues may be difficult to talk about.

As Kathy Charmaz writes, reflecting on her experience of research with people with chronic illnesses:

> [N]ot all experiences are storied, nor are all experiences stored for ready recall. Silences have meaning, too. … Certainly, silences derive from what people forget or do not know, understand, or take into account. Other silences occur when people grope for words to say something on the edge of awareness that had been unclear and unstated. And some silences result from people's awareness of and actions toward their situations. Such silences may either be intended or imposed: Some people are silenced. (2002: 305)

## Questions of power, difference and ethics

The interactive nature of the interview process can be the basis of many of its advantages as a research tool in that it allows for flexibility: the researcher can adapt in response to the reactions and responses of the interviewee. Whilst the nature of communication means that we can never be sure that two people's understandings of terms and concepts is exactly the same, the qualitative interview offers the possibility of exploring the interviewee's understanding in a more meaningful way than would be allowed by a less flexible survey questionnaire. However, the nature of interaction during interviews also raises some of the most critical questions that need to be dealt with by qualitative researchers.

Janet Holland and Caroline Ramazanoglu characterise interviews as 'stylized social events' and argue that 'differences such as age, class, gender, ethnicity and religion impinge on the possibilities of interaction and interpretation, and so on how the social world is known' (1994). This underlines the need to acknowledge and address difficult questions of reflexivity. Reflexivity involves critical self-scrutiny on the part of researchers, who need, at all stages of the research process, to ask themselves about their role in the research. Reflexivity involves a move away from the idea of the neutral, detached observer that is implied in much classical survey work. It involves acknowledging that the researcher approaches the research from a specific position and this affects the approach taken, the questions asked and the analysis produced. In the immediate context of the interview, reflexivity involves reflection on the impact of the researcher on the interaction with the interviewee.

Feminist researchers have been particularly alive to these questions. Ann Oakley wrote an influential critique of traditional standardised, structured interviews where these were based on the idea of a detached and neutral researcher who maintains control of the interview. Instead, Oakley argued that it

> becomes clear that, in most cases, the goal of finding out about people is best achieved when the relationship of the interviewer–interviewee is non-hierarchical and when the interviewer is prepared to invest his or her own personal identity in the relationship ... Personal involvement is more than just dangerous bias – it is the condition under which people come to know each other and to admit others into their lives. (1981: 41, 58)

Thus Oakley advocates the proffering of friendship and exchange within the interview process.

However, this may not always be possible or even desirable for either party involved. As Jane Ribbens points out, in some situations, the attempt of the researcher to place herself and give personal information may be seen as an imposition rather than as a welcome offer of friendship: 'After all, is not part of the research exchange that I have expressed an interest in hearing about the interviewees' lives?' (1989: 584). In addition, there is a risk that it is assumed that only women researchers should interview women respondents if they are to gain authentic accounts (see also Chapter 3). This overlooks other differences which may influence the interaction, such as age, social class and ethnicity. Thus in her article 'When gender is not enough: women interviewing women', Cathy Riessman contrasts her experience of interviewing middle-class Anglo women with that of interviewing working-class Puerto Rican women. Riessman found that in the interviews between an Anglo researcher and Puerto Rican interviewees, the interview 'was hindered by a lack of shared cultural and class assumptions' (1987: 190).

Some might therefore argue that there should always be 'race', gender and class matching between respondents and researchers. However, exactly matching all the characteristics of respondents and interviewers is likely to be very difficult and would restrict many research projects. Ann Phoenix, reflecting on her research experience on two studies – one on young mothers and the other on social identities in young people – argues that

> prescriptions for matching the 'race' and/or gender of interviewers and respondents are ... too simplistic ... If different types of accounts about 'race' and racism are produced with black and white interviewers this is in itself important data and may be good reason for using interviewers of both colours whenever possible since it illustrates the ways in which knowledges are 'situated'. (Phoenix, 1994: 49, 66)

Reflexivity in research requires that the impact of *both* similarities and differences on the research processes be examined. The impact of the social positioning of the researcher needs to be thought through and will be more significant to some research topics than others. For example, it might be more important to match gender when interviewing women about domestic violence. Questions about racism are likely to produce different responses depending on the racial identity of both interviewers and interviewees; being aware of when matching occurs or does not occur might be important in interpreting responses on such a research study.

The research relationship raises other ethical questions that need to be addressed (see also Chapter 5). Thus it is important to protect respondents from harm in the research process as well as to consider questions of disclosure, consent and anonymity. Informed consent should be obtained from interviewees wherever possible. This can be verbal, but should ideally be written, where interviewees are able to keep a copy of the agreement they have signed, including a statement about any questions of the copyright of the interview. It should also be clear to interviewees that they can stop the interview at any point if they want to. Depending on the research subject, it might be important to consider the extent to which interviewees are capable of giving informed consent. Do they understand the concept of research and what you are doing? Are they able to think through the implications? Should a third person be giving consent for them? This is particularly relevant to conducting research with children, but may also apply to others.

It is usual to offer anonymity to research respondents. But ensuring anonymity is not always a straightforward process. This is particularly true when dealing with in-depth biographical material which might be recognisable to friends and family unless some details are changed. Measures may also need to be taken in the recording and labelling of data to ensure that anonymity is preserved. Researchers need to think about where and how they will record and store their data during the research and writing-up process. It is important to separate the interview material from the real names of the interviewees at an early stage, for instance on the labelling of tapes and transcriptions.

British Sociological Association (BSA) guidelines on the ethical conduct of research studies state that:

> Sociologists have a responsibility to ensure that the physical, social and psychological well-being of research participants is not adversely affected by the research. (www.britsoc.co.uk/equality/Statement+Ethical+Practice.htm)

It should be clear that research should not inflict harm on interviewees, but in some cases the subject matter may be such that it is difficult to predict what is going to cause distress, and how much distress will be caused by taking part in an interview. Discussing violence, trauma, accidents, illegal activity and mistakes might all cause distress to interviewees. Researchers should ask themselves at all times if they are pushing too far in the questioning. In addition, they need to be aware that the interviewee might be saying too much – or things that they will regret disclosing. If you build up a good rapport with your interviewee it may start to feel like a counselling session, a role which the researcher is not necessarily trained to undertake. Where it is possible to predict that interviewees might become distressed by the interviews, it would be useful to have already researched the contact details of resources that might be available to them, such as support groups or sources of counselling which you can pass on.

Box 12.7 gives an example of ethical issues in interviews.

## ETHICAL ISSUES IN INTERVIEWS ABOUT SEXUAL ABUSE

In one study of the experience of sexual abuse, the researcher, Catherine Kirkwood, asked her respondents what they felt about the interview process. Of the 16 interviewed, three felt that the interviews pushed them too deeply into the emotional responses to abuse, leading to nightmares for two of them and the third being unable to finish the interviews (Kirkwood, 1993: 34–5).

Some people are clearly more vulnerable than others and some subjects more difficult to deal with, and careful consideration should be given to the likely impact of interviews on respondents.

## Doing qualitative interviews

This section will examine some basic questions that need to be addressed when undertaking research using qualitative interviewing. These include:

- Who do you interview (including how many people and how you contact them)?
- Where do you interview them?
- What do you ask them?
- How are you going to record the interviews?
- How will they be analysed?

Answering all of these questions requires forward planning and in particular will depend on establishing a clear sense of *why* you are conducting the interviews in the first place.

## Why interview?

Before you can plan your research, you need to have as clear a sense as possible about why you are proposing to undertake the research in a particular way and what you hope to achieve by it. This involves having at least a preliminary idea of how you will analyse your material (although in qualitative research this will often be a flexible process and subject to change). You can ask yourself:

- Is your aim to use the interview as an exercise in data *generation* or data *collection*? Related to this is the

issue of whether you will be treating the interview as *topic* or *resource* – or both.

- Are interviews the best way of conducting the research or are there other sources which would be more efficient ways of getting the information? Perhaps you should be pursuing the interviews in conjunction with other sources for your research.
- Is your aim to test or develop theoretical propositions?
- What kinds of comparisons are you likely to want to make?

The different answers that you have for these questions should help you frame both *who* you should interview and *how* you plan and conduct the interviews themselves.

## Who do you interview?

Qualitative interviewing is, by its very nature, relatively time-consuming compared to survey interviewing. Tom Wengraf argues that semi-structured interviews are 'high-preparation, high-risk, high-gain, and high-analysis operations' (2001: 5). The time involved limits the possibilities for covering large samples, and this is one reason why few attempts are made to achieve *random* or *probability* samples in qualitative interviews, although they may be conducted in conjunction with wider representative samples (see Chapter 9 for a discussion of this kind of sampling). So whilst the aim may not be statistical generalisation, there is still the need to consider who should be interviewed in order to achieve a good understanding of the issue under research.

As with more stringent versions of sampling, you need to begin by identifying the wider population from which you will select your interviewees. For instance, are you interested in researching the experiences of black women under 20? Of football supporters? Or of social workers who work in fostering and adoption? Or the whole population of people who live in a particular area of a large city? What is your particular interest in this population and how does it relate to your research? You will then need to make a selection of research participants or interviewees from this broader population. In order to do this, you need to establish a relationship between the selection and the wider population. There are several different types of relationship that can be established. These are outlined in Box 12.8.

---

**BOX 12.8**

## THREE POSSIBLE RELATIONSHIPS BETWEEN SAMPLE AND POPULATION

1  A *representative relationship* (as in *probability* sampling). This requires the selection of a sample which is representative of the total empirical population that the study refers to. It requires knowledge of the nature of the total population – so that proportions of social characteristics such as age, gender, ethnicity, class in the wider population can be mirrored in the sample. This requires the use of statistical conventions to enable you to argue that the general patterns discovered in the sample are representative of the wider population. As mentioned above, whilst this approach can be used in qualitative interviewing, it is not common.

2  A relationship designed to provide a close-up, detailed or *meticulous view* of a particular experience. This could be as narrow as selecting the life and narrative of a particular person for scrutiny, or a small set of people. This approach allows for the in-depth examination of a particular set of social processes in a particular context. However, you need to be able to argue how this narrow example relates to a wider population and how the interviewees do, or do not, compare with each other.

3  A relationship that covers a *relevant range* of people in relationship to a wider population, but is not designed to represent it directly. This does not mean an ad hoc sample, but involves a strategy of selection which ensures that a relevant range is covered.

*Source*: adapted from Mason, 1996: 91–92

---

Additionally, *theoretical sampling* is a common approach to selecting individuals for qualitative interviews. Here, people are selected according to how likely it is that their interview will contribute to the development of an emerging theory. The relationship of this to some population is generally not known. Theoretical sampling is discussed in Chapters 9 and 22. Roger Hewitt's experience in a study of processes of racism is helpful in showing how sampling decisions can be made in a qualitative interviewing study (Box 12.9).

The size and nature of your sample will depend partly on how it is designed to relate to the wider population (and the nature of that wider population). It will also be affected by the resources available to you. Identifying and gaining the cooperation of interviewees and conducting the interviews themselves are all time-consuming processes. But they are likely to be outweighed by the time spent listening to and annotating or transcribing the interviews and analysing the results. You should start out with a target number of interviewees which you think is suitable for your project. This may include target numbers of different people who have the required characteristics to supply the range of people who you want to interview. It might be helpful to set up a table of target interviewees who fulfil certain criteria (as in quota sampling – see Chapter 9). However (to introduce an element of theoretical sampling) this should be used flexibly by allowing for the development of new criteria and selection strategies as the research proceeds. For instance, you may realise after a while that there is a different group who provide a 'negative' comparison to those who form the bulk of your interviewees. It may be important to investigate this group. Or you may decide to follow up fewer interviewees but do so in more depth than originally planned, or conversely, increase your target number of interviews.

---

BOX 12.9

## SAMPLING IN A STUDY OF RACISM

We were concerned to build up a picture not simply of racial attitudes but of how young people who expressed racist opinions made the move into perpetrating racist acts. While we regarded understanding the experience of victims as central, it was the perpetrators of racist actions who were the major focus of our attention. At the same time, we were anxious to find out about those people who formed the social and family network of perpetrators. What did they think about racism and racist attacks? How did people in any neighbourhood allow harassment to go on? Who knew about it? What did they say to each other about it? This was part of what we called 'the social basis of racist action'. We believed that perpetrators of racist harassment probably did not behave in a social vacuum. It was somehow either allowed or even encouraged by others, and there was something in the local community that allowed it to happen.

In order to investigate the social basis of racist action, we interviewed as many young people as well as adult professionals including youth and community workers, teachers and the police. We attended community groups and other such meetings, talked to a wide range of adults in different neighbourhoods and interviewed both boys and girls – in groups in schools and youth clubs.

*Source:* Hewitt, 1996: 2

---

Once you have outlined your target selection, you then need to find the people and get them to talk to you. This can be a nerve-wracking process, but it is often surprising how willing people are to give you their time if approached in the right way. You need to think about how to contact potential interviewees. Are there organisations which will give you access to a certain population or specific ways of contacting them? For instance, if your target group is social workers working on adoption and fostering, are there professional bodies you can approach to help you find interviewees? Can you identify the agencies in which they work and approach them directly? Are there professional journals or magazines which also might help you locate interviewees? But you also need to think about how the route taken for your approach to interviewees may influence who you eventually interview. For instance, if you wanted to interview fathers who bring up single-headed families, you could contact the campaign groups that represent them. However, the men that are involved in these groups may have characteristics that are not shared by other men in similar situations. For instance, they might tend to have different class characteristics, or be more unhappy with their situations. In this case, if you were concerned to represent a full range of fathers in this position, you would need to develop alternative strategies for contacting single fathers who had different characteristics.

Sometimes getting access to interviewees requires going through intermediaries or gatekeepers (see also Chapter 14). For instance, if you want to interview elderly people, you might choose to approach a nursing home or social group for pensioners. You will need to get the permission of the head of the nursing home or group organiser. You will also want to ensure that the gatekeepers are not putting pressure on people to participate, and try to judge whether being introduced in a particular way by a person perhaps in authority may affect the interviewees and what they say.

As is shown in Chapter 9, another method of finding interviewees is to snowball, where you ask people you have interviewed to suggest friends or colleagues to interview. This can be a very successful method of making contacts, but it is likely only to introduce you to people who are similar to those you have already interviewed. It can be helpful to get a sense of networks or the ways in which people in similar situations use the same discursive repertoires. However, it is not likely to enable you to cover people across a range of differences (there is a tendency for people to know and introduce you to others who are broadly similar to themselves). In addition, it makes you dependent on your interviewees' choices of who you should talk to. They may have different selection criteria from you – for instance, suggesting people with unusual experiences where you want to interview more 'normal' cases.

However you contact your interviewees, you have to remain reflexive during this process, which is likely to happen over a period of time. You need to be aware of how your sample is developing and how it compares with your targets. Are there reasons for your changes to original plans? If certain people are particularly difficult to reach, can you find new approaches (see Chapter 31 on what to do 'When things go wrong')? If you are finding it difficult to find interviewees, this may *add* to your understanding of what you are trying to research. For example, it is often hard to find people for interviews about the experience of certain illnesses (e.g. HIV/AIDS), whereas others have conditions that they are more happy to discuss (e.g. heart disease). This may reflect the fact that some conditions attract more social stigma than others.

## Where do you interview?

In most qualitative interviewing, the interview takes place face to face. However, in some contexts, it may be impossible to meet with your interviewees. Telephone interviews are possible, although you will need to establish a way to record the interview (with appropriate consent). You also need to consider what is lost through the long-distance encounter. In particular, non-verbal cues and body language will be absent and you are less able to ensure that your respondent is not distracted. Finally, it is difficult to get people to settle down to a long conversation with someone that they do not know on the telephone. Some internet- and email-based research may involve interviewing (see Chapter 11). Even in face-to-face interviews, the setting in which you interview may also make a difference. For instance, you could get different responses from teenagers if you interview them in a classroom rather than a familiar café. You should therefore give some thought to *where* the interviews are conducted. Ideally, you need a space where you and the interviewee (or group) will be relaxed, able to talk and be undisturbed. This can sometimes be difficult to achieve. Often interviews are conducted in people's own homes as this is most convenient for them. However, this can have implications for privacy if other family members are around. You also need to have proper consideration of your own safety. Do you feel that this is a safe environment to go into? You should always have a responsible person who knows where you are going and when you expect to be finished. You should make an arrangement with that person that once you are out of an interview, you will call them to confirm your safety. Meeting in public places or at workplaces may influence the tone of the resulting interview in certain ways.

## What do you ask?

Qualitative interviews can be experienced by the interviewee as very similar to an informal conversation. However, this does not mean that they are totally unstructured or unplanned. Like sampling, the conduct of the interview needs to be planned, but it must also be responsive and, as the quotation from Paul Thompson in Box 12.1 suggests, it is a skill that needs to be learned. The key to a good interview is to adjust your approach so that the interviewee is encouraged to talk, but crucially to talk about subjects that you are interested in researching. You should also pilot (trial run) your approach or questions so that you know that they make sense to interviewees. Your questions need to be clear and in a style of language that your respondent understands. It is often best to keep questions simple (this can avoid the problem of asking more than one question in a single sentence).

---

**BOX 12.10**

### EXAMPLE OF INTERVIEW TOPIC GUIDE

1  First trying marijuana.

2  Circumstances surrounding first contact.

3  State of being following first contact.

4  Conditions for continual use.

5  Conditions for curtailment or stoppage.

6  Present situation.

7  Current attitudes towards usage.

Expansion of section 5 Conditions for curtailment or stoppage:

(a) Why did you decide to stop or cut down?

(b) What was happening to you at this time (e.g. were you still in school, working etc.)?

(c) Was the drug still relatively accessible to you?

(d) Did your decision to stop have anything to do with what was taking place in your life/career (i.e. was the usage of marijuana on a regular basis becoming too great a risk in moral, social or legal terms)?

(e) Did any particular person or persons influence your decision to stop or cut down? Who, and how did they influence you?

(f) [*To be asked of those who have stopped completely.*] Since having given up marijuana, have you felt any strong yearning to try it again or resume your use of it? Tell me about it (times, occasions, places and so on in which yearning is experienced). How do you handle these feelings when you get them – what do you tell yourself or do in order to resist the desire?

*Source*: quoted in Lofland, 1971: 78–9

---

Different researchers and research projects will adopt different approaches to qualitative interviewing. At one end of the spectrum would be conducting interviews with reference to a relatively structured topic guide, such as that in Box 12.10 which is taken from a study of people who had ceased using marijuana.

At the other extreme is the *single-question induced narrative* approach developed by Tom Wengraf (2001). Wengraf aims to elicit stories from the interviewee with a single question such as 'Tell me the whole story of your life' and no further questions except for clarification. Clearly, this is appropriate for some research projects, but not all.

Most qualitative interviewing falls somewhere between the single question and the relatively structured topic guide. They will involve the researcher having planned in advance the way in which he or she intends to introduce and open the interview and a range of topics which they hope to cover. Qualitative interviewing is a skilled process, as you need to develop the ability to listen carefully to what you are being told at the same time as you consider how to take the interview forward and what your next question will be. You also need to be aware of body language and other non-verbal signals that you are being given, as well as to attend to your means of recording the interview, either by taking notes or by making sure the recording equipment is still working. Juggling all these tasks takes practice.

As should be clear, conducting interviews is not the same as merely taking part in a conversation. It needs a different kind of listening and different responses. You need to take more care not to interrupt your interviewee's speech than you might in a normal conversation. Qualitative interviews generally concentrate on open-ended or 'non-directive' questions which require more response than a simple 'yes' or 'no'. There are various ways to encourage your interviewees to carry on talking or expand on what they are saying. Sometimes simply not rushing in with another question will give them time to reflect on what they have said and say some more, especially if you are giving encouraging semi-verbal cues such as 'uh-huh' and nodding encouragement. You can also repeat statements back to the interviewer in the form of a question. For example, if someone says 'When I was young, I didn't have much of a relationship with my sister,' you can ask them again as a question 'You say you didn't have much of a relationship with your sister?' as an encouragement to talk further about this topic.

In some cases, qualitative interviews may be covering quite sensitive material, or issues that the interviewees do not particularly want to talk about. It is important to raise sensitive issues in ways that make interviewees still feel comfortable about discussing them. This may involve using indirect questions. For example, rather than asking a white interviewee directly about their own attitudes – 'What do you think of Black people?' – it might be more productive to ask more general questions such as 'Do you think there is a problem of racism in this country?'. Interviews may also place researchers in a disturbing position where they have to respond to statements and opinions with which they disagree or even find offensive. There is no single appropriate response to these situations. You may need, for example, to weigh up your ethical and political desire to combat prejudice wherever you encounter it with a desire to maintain a good relationship with your interviewee. On the other hand, sometimes a more combative response may produce a discussion which is useful for your research (see Back, 1996; Wetherell and Potter, 1992: 99).

## How do you record interviews?

You need to think about how the interview material will be recorded and transcribed. This may depend in part on the form your analysis will take. For example, do you need exact transcription of the interviews (more important perhaps for discourse and conversation analysis)? Or will more summary notes be sufficient for your analysis? Will you be using a computer program to help you code your data? In this case, you will need to have all your material in electronic form, and this has important implications for the amount of time that the analysis will take.

The need to concentrate on what the interviewee is saying and how to respond and adapt to this is easier if you do not have to take notes of what is being said as you go along. This means that audio recording of interviews is often desirable, although it requires specific consent from the interviewee and may not be suitable in all cases. Recording also entails more post-interview work, as you will need to listen again to the interview and perhaps transcribe it.

Whether the actual interview is recorded electronically or not, it is wise, once the interview is over, to make field notes of the encounter. Often these will record aspects of the interaction and your sense of the interview, not otherwise included in your interview notes or transcript. This can be very helpful in reminding you of important things when you analyse the material (Box 12.11).

---

**▌BOX 12.11 ▌**

### WRITING FIELD NOTES AFTER THE INTERVIEW

Janet Holland and Caroline Ramazanoglu stressed the importance of field notes to accompany interview data in their work on young people's sexualities:

> Obviously the text of a transcript does not reveal all that went on in the interview: language was not the only thing exchanged. Body language, non-verbal exchanges, distress and laughter are all part of that interchange, and all need to be taken into account in understanding and interpreting what the young women and young men were trying to communicate about their sexualities. (1994: 141)

They feel that these field notes helped analysis by reminding them about each interview:

> Since no researcher can gain more than a glimpse of other people's lives through accounts given in an interview, much of the 'skill' of interview-based research lies in what sense we make of the interview after the subject has gone – how we interpret our interview texts. (1994: 126)

---

## How do you analyse interviews?

This section is short, but this does not reflect the importance of thinking about analysis: many chapters in the rest of this book guide you in doing this, since the considerations that apply to the analysis of qualitative interviews are really no different (and no less complex) than those that apply to other kinds of qualitative material. Thus, an interview might be analysed using qualitative thematic analysis (Chapter 21), as a part of a project in which grounded theory is being generated (Chapter 22), or using discourse analysis (Chapter 23), narrative analysis or interpretative phenomenological analysis (Chapter 25), content or linguistic analysis (Chapter 26) or (very occasionally) conversation analysis (Chapter 24). Combining qualitative with quantitative analysis (Chapter 27) may also be appropriate in some circumstances.

The distinction between analysis of interview material as a topic or a resource is key to understanding different approaches. Here, the basic decision is whether to 'read' interviews as a report of experience (the resource approach), or whether to treat them as events in their own right so that they become occasions that are observed (the topic approach). Qualitative thematic analysis often involves treating the interview as a resource; discourse analysis is one example of an approach which topicalises the interview, and occasional conversation analyses of interview data also do this. This distinction was also discussed in the section earlier on the epistemological status of interviews.

## Conclusion

This chapter has reviewed both practical considerations of qualitative interviewing and methodological issues that concern the underlying epistemological and political considerations that lie behind the use of this kind of material for research purposes. It should have equipped you both to do and to think about qualitative interviews. If you use this method, it is important to keep a note of all the decisions you make in planning and undertaking the interviews. This will help you when you come to writing up your research and providing a rationale for the way you have proceeded.

Finally, consider whether it is appropriate to have any follow-up with your interviewees. This might involve sending out a letter which tells them the results or progress of your research, or even giving a workshop or presentation where you explain the results of your research to a group of respondents and give them a chance to comment on what you have found.

## FURTHER READING

Denzin (1989) gives an overview of a variety of approaches to qualitative interviewing. Silverman (2001) presents a sophisticated discussion of different ways of approaching the analysis of qualitative interview data. Scott (1984) gives a feminist account of interviewing. Gubrium and Holstein's *Handbook of Interview Research* (2002) gives a comprehensive, up-to-date and authoritative account of a wide range of approaches to interviewing. Rubin and Rubin (2005) is a comprehensive guide to qualitative interviewing, as is Kvale and Brinkmann (2009). James and Busher (2009) and Salmons (2010) have a specific focus on online interviewing.

### Student Reader (Seale, 2004b): relevant readings

10  Herbert H. Hyman with William J. Cobb, Jacob J. Feldman, Clyde W. Hart and Charles Herbert Stember: 'Interviewing in social research'

36  Howard S. Becker and Blanche Geer: 'Participant observation and interviewing: a comparison'

37  Sue Jones: 'Depth interviewing'

38  Ann Oakley: 'Interviewing women: a contradiction in terms?' (and a subsequent exchange with Joanna Malseed)

79  Maureen Cain and Janet Finch: 'Towards a rehabilitation of data'

See also Chapter 2, 'Interviews' by Tim Rapley; Chapter 3' 'Oral history' by Joanna Bornat; and Chapter 4, 'Biographical research', by Gabriele Rosenthal in Seale et al. (2004).

## Journal articles discussing or illustrating the methods discussed in this chapter

Ogden, J. and Cornwell, D. (2010) 'The role of topic, interviewee and question in predicting rich interview data in the field of health research', Sociology of Health & Illness, 32 (7): 1059–1071.

Rapley, T.J. (2001) 'The art(fulness) of open-ended interviewing: some considerations on analysing interviews', Qualitative Research, 1: 303–323.

Seale, C., Charteris-Black, J., Dumelow, C., Locock, L. and Ziebland, S. (2008) 'The effect of joint interviewing on the performance of gender', Field Methods, 20: 107–128.

## Web links

Forum Qualitative Research – click on 'Search' then search for the term 'Interview': www.qualitative-research.net/fqs/fqs-eng.htm

Methods@manchester – creative interviewing: www.methods.manchester.ac.uk/methods/creativeinterviewing/index.shtml

Interview as a method for qualitative research: www.public.asu.edu/~kroel/www500/Interview%20Fri.pdf

Martin Ryder's qualitative research site – follow the links on interviewing: http://carbon.ucdenver.edu/~mryder/itc_data/pract_res.html

Oral History Society (UK): www.oralhistory.org.uk

Oral History Association (USA): www.oralhistory.org

Resources for Qualitative Research: www.qualitativeresearch.uga.edu/QualPage/welcome.html

## KEY CONCEPTS FOR REVIEW

Advice: Use these, along with the review questions in the next section, to test your knowledge of the contents of this chapter. Try to define each of the key concepts listed here; if you have understood this chapter you should be able to do this. Check your definitions against the definition in the glossary at the end of the book.

| | |
|---|---|
| Bias | Qualitative interview |
| Data collection vs. data generation | Reflexivity |
| Discursive repertoires | Snowball sampling |
| Informed consent | Topic vs. resource |

## ⌐■ Review questions

1 What is a qualitative interview, how does it differ from other kinds of interview, and what different approaches to carrying out qualitative interviews exist?

2 What kinds of research study are qualitative interviews best suited for?

3 What does it mean to say that an interview is treated as a topic rather than a resource at the analysis stage?

4 What kinds of ethical issues may arise in doing qualitative interviews?

5 What consideration arise when deciding who to interview, where to interview, what to ask and how to record qualitative interviews?

## Workshop and discussion exercises

1 The aim of this exercise is to produce interview data on students' experiences of studying and thus to experience some of the problems of asking questions and understanding answers in an unstructured interview.

(a) The workshop should be divided into groups of three or four.

(b) Each group should draw up a short *topic guide* for unstructured interviews with other students. Focus on a specific aspect of experience (e.g. reasons for coming to university, financial problems, reactions to lectures and classes) and work out some questions.

(c) Each group should choose an interviewer, an interviewee and one or two observers.

(d) The interviewer should interview the interviewee using the topic guide. The observer should write down as much as they can of what the interviewee says. Then change roles and do another interview.

(e) Compare the two interviews and discuss what you have found out. Consider the language of the questions. What do these take for granted? How far is the interviewer sharing understandings with the interviewee? How could the interview be improved?

2 Read the transcript of an interview with Joanna, an Australian woman interviewed for a research project concerning mothers' experiences of child day care centres (Box 12.12).

(a) How would you characterise the relationship between interviewer and respondent?

(b) What does this interview tell us about what has happened to Joanna and her child? Construct a list of key themes relating to this and say which segments of talk illustrate each theme.

(c) What does this interview tell us about the person Joanna wants to be, and about the child that she wants Jared to be? Construct a list of key themes relating to this and say which segments of talk illustrate each theme.

---

**◀ BOX 12.12 ▶**

### TRANSCRIPT OF A QUALITATIVE INTERVIEW

Interview with Joanna, separated, about Jared, aged 18 months, who has been going to a childcare day centre for three months:

| 1 | *Q:* | How did you feel during the first week or so that Jared was in |
| 2 | | day care? |
| 3 | *Joanna:* | Ah I worried. I worried a lot because he was very young then about |
| 4 | | three or four months old. Um but then I used to go and visit him say |
| 5 | | after two because I had a break and I'd go and visit him in between and |
| 6 | | he wasn't even interested in … I stopped doing it because I'd go in |
| 7 | | and after I'd been there an hour and a half two hours to play with him |
| 8 | | and he was busily involved in something else and um wasn't grizzly |

| 9 | | enough to want me. |
|---|---|---|
| 10 | *Q:* | You said you were rather worried. What were you worried |
| 11 | | about? |
| 12 | *Joanna:* | Um I was worried that it was going to affect him not |
| 13 | | being with me – that he wouldn't get the same love and attention – that |
| 14 | | he'd cry and miss me and but now I think it's ah I worry more about me |
| 15 | | missing him than him missing me. |
| 16 | *Q:* | How long has Jared been in day care now? |
| 17 | *Joanna:* | Since he was three months. So about a year and a bit. |
| 18 | | He virtually been going there really since he was about two months. I |
| 19 | | have found though that when we shifted from the country up here he didn't |
| 20 | | go for about eight weeks and he was … used to cry all the time for the |
| 21 | | first week or two um then I started to take him back to going into |
| 22 | | creche. |
| 23 | *Q:* | You found it difficult leaving him after? |
| 24 | *Joanna:* | Yes I found it difficult I don't know if it was a stage he was |
| 25 | | going through. That clingy stage or whether he just got so used to being |
| 26 | | with me he didn't want to … |
| 27 | *Q:* | Was that hard for you? |
| 28 | *Joanna:* | Yes terribly hard. I don't know if I could leave him if he was |
| 29 | | the type that cried all the time that I left him because I just … it |
| 30 | | makes me feel sick. I worry about him being away from me the whole |
| 31 | | time that he is away … so I'm really glad that he's happy and laughing |
| 32 | | when he walks in. |
| 33 | *Q:* | Have your emotions changed since the first weeks Jared was in day |
| 34 | | care? If so – how? |
| 35 | *Joanna:* | Well I think I've got a really positive outlook for it now I really |
| 36 | | feel that it's a really good thing for him to be going to day care as an |
| 37 | | only child – he doesn't have any brothers and sisters to mix with – it |
| 38 | | teaches him sharing and not being the centre of attention. Um and how |
| 39 | | to get on with other children and I think it's really important. And I |
| 40 | | think maybe an only child doesn't learn that early enough if they |
| 41 | | don't go to something where they are mixing with other children so I |
| 42 | | think really even if I didn't have to he would go at least a couple |
| 43 | | of times a week into a local childcare centre. |
| 44 | *Q:* | And if you were perfectly free to choose, how would you have arranged |
| 45 | | your life since the birth of Jared? |
| 46 | *Joanna:* | I'd have a nanny … If I was really going to choose anything I'd |
| 47 | | have a nanny/housekeeper. [*Jared appeared with something that he* |
| 48 | | *shouldn't have had – mother quickly removed it – Jared started to cry*]. |

*(Continued)*

(Continued)

| 49 | | I find he get very bored if he's at home with me I usually by ten o'clock |
| 50 | | have got to go down the street because he get so restless. |
| 51 | *Q:* | How about in the future if you were perfectly free to choose? |
| 52 | *Joanna:* | I'd still have him go into a creche maybe not quite as much as he |
| 53 | | does at the moment um and I think I would prefer to have more help at a |
| 54 | | night time. |
| 55 | *Q:* | So you'd still like a nanny? |
| 56 | *Joanna:* | A nanny/housekeeper. I mean I wouldn't like her to be bringing him |
| 57 | | up. But I suppose um somebody who could replace because my parents |
| 58 | | aren't up here. Somebody who would replace his grandmother I suppose. |
| 59 | | Somebody ah who I could just … more of a grandmother figure I suppose. |
| 60 | | Um just somebody who could help out occasionally a bit … It's very hard |
| 61 | | when you've got no … I've got girlfriends up here but none of them |
| 62 | | have got children so it's very hard to … yeah some are having children at |
| 63 | | the moment so it'll be different once they have them. But I wouldn't |
| 64 | | leave him with someone who didn't have children because it might put |
| 65 | | them off. |
| 66 | *Q:* | Is there anything else you would like to add? |
| 67 | *Joanna:* | Well I actually feel that it doesn't hurt any child going to |
| 68 | | child care I think it does depend on the child care centre um and I've |
| 69 | | been really lucky with both centres he's been to they've been really |
| 70 | | good. Really good in the way that they're brand new. So they have |
| 71 | | been very clean bright and new facilities bright windows a good |
| 72 | | playground which is really important. And the staff have all |
| 73 | | been new so they're all really enthusiastic um and they really like |
| 74 | | what they're doing and um I've found also that the children that go to |
| 75 | | them have been really nice types, and that makes a difference. And um |
| 76 | | I'm not being classist or anything but I'm not sure if I was living in |
| 77 | | a housing commission area and going to creche there in those areas I |
| 78 | | would find a difference. But both times he's been in really nice where |
| 79 | | the parents are nice types and ah it does affect even on really young |
| 80 | | children you can tell about the parents. In both the creches he's |
| 81 | | been in there have been no children swearing being naughty they've been |
| 82 | | taught discipline and I think that's good and actually the creche is good |
| 83 | | it teaches them a little more discipline than I do in a way. |
| 84 | | Sitting when he's eating and things like that where as a sole parent I |
| 85 | | can get a little bit soft on him so it's good that he does have a little |
| 86 | | stern-ness. |

*Source:* Reproduced with kind permission of Lyn Richards

# 13

# FOCUS GROUPS

## Fran Tonkiss

This chapter examines the use of focus groups within social and cultural research. It considers the different ways in which researchers use focus groups, their relationship to other methods of inquiry, issues involved in selecting and running focus groups, and their strengths and weaknesses as a research method. The aim of the chapter is both to outline some key methodological debates about the use and value of focus groups and to consider practical questions that arise in using the method.

## What is a focus group?

A focus group is, quite simply, a small group discussion focused on a particular topic and facilitated by a researcher. Focus groups originated in market research during the 1920s, and have been used within social science since at least the 1940s (see Kitzinger, 1994a; Merton, 1987). There has, however, been increasing interest since the 1980s in the use of focus groups across different fields of social, cultural and policy research. These include media and communications research (especially audience studies), sociology and social psychology, policy consultation and evaluation, organisational studies, environmental studies, health research and research into public attitudes. In the policy field, focus groups have featured not only in political campaign planning but also in strategies to promote user involvement in public services, or to create forms of deliberative democracy or citizens' juries that give people access to government debates and decision-making processes. In all of these contexts, focus groups offer a distinctive method for generating qualitative data on the basis of group interaction and discussion.

This interactive quality is the key feature of focus group research. The unit of analysis is the group, rather than the individuals taking part in the discussion. Focus groups in this sense are not simply a means of interviewing several people at the same time; rather, they are concerned to explore the formation and negotiation of accounts within a group context, how people define, discuss

and contest issues through social interaction. Underlying this approach is an assumption that opinions, attitudes and accounts are *socially* produced – shaped by interaction with others – rather than being discretely formed at the level of the individual (see Lunt and Livingstone, 1996: 90). Moreover, the group context makes visible *how* people articulate and justify their ideas in relation to others. Whereas a survey questionnaire can elicit what someone says they think about a specific topic and an interview can describe how an individual accounts for their views, group discussions show how such accounts emerge through a communicative process. Beyond their status as a practical strategy for generating data, then, focus groups involve a stronger methodological assertion that the group context is important (and not just handy) for exploring the way social and cultural knowledge, opinions and meanings are produced.

The 'focus' of the group discussion can take different forms, and be more or less structured. To focus, the interaction researchers might use:

- a fixed schedule of questions
- a *topic guide* of themes for discussion
- a group exercise
- visual cues (such as video clips, advertisements, press reports or photographs).

The size of focus groups varies from around 4 to 12 participants, with social researchers often preferring group sizes in the lower range, and market research typically using larger groups. There is no fixed rule; the 'right' group size will depend on the specific research problem you are exploring, the participants involved, issues of access – and simply on how many people actually turn up. The aim should be to work with groups small enough to allow all the members to participate, but large enough to capture a variety of perspectives and enable people to bounce ideas off each other. Most focus groups will last for one to two hours. While many research projects are based on a number of one-off groups, others involve a series of sessions with the same groups of people. Focus group research can be small- or large-scale. Researchers might, for example, use just one or two focus groups at the research design or pilot stage of their study. For small-scale research, three to five focus groups can be seen as sufficient in allowing access to a range of participants and for a variety of insights to emerge. However, focus groups can be used on a much larger scale – to take two studies discussed later in this chapter: Peek's work with second-generation Muslim Americans following the 9/11 attacks used 23 focus groups with 127 participants (see Peek and Fothergill, 2009), while Diane Reay's (2004) research (with co-researcher, Helen Lucey) on inner-city schools in London involved 77 focus groups with 454 children. Group discussions are usually audio- or video-taped, allowing researchers to concentrate on guiding the discussion and for the data to be transcribed for analysis. Before looking more closely at the practical conduct of focus groups, we can consider the range of contexts in which researchers use them.

## How are focus groups used?

Focus groups are used in a number of different research settings:

- In *media and communications studies* to explore issues of audience reception.
- In *consultation or evaluation research* to examine user demands and responses to services and agencies, especially in such fields as health, psychiatric, care and social services.
- In *organisational research* to look at staff or members' views and opinions.
- In *policy research* to analyse people's opinions about different political parties and policy issues.

- In *research on children and young people* to create an encouraging and comfortable environment for talk and interaction.
- More generally, in the *interpretive study* of social and cultural attitudes on a range of issues.

In these ways focus groups are relevant both to applied social research with a strong policy or practical orientation, and to theoretical research that seeks to explore social and cultural meanings, knowledge and discourses. Focus groups are effective both as an independent method for generating data and in conjunction with other techniques of data collection. Where focus groups are used together with other methods, we can think about this relationship on two levels:

- *Level 1:* focus groups provide a *tool* of research design, refining and clarifying the concepts and language used within a study, or helping to evaluate and interpret research findings.
- *Level 2:* focus groups can be used at the *core* of a research project, combining with other methods to produce different forms of data within a multi-method approach to social and cultural research.

Focus groups initially were used within social science as a supplement to quantitative research methods. The earliest example of a focus group in social research involved Paul Lazarsfeld and Robert Merton in 1941 (see Box 13.1). Merton (1987) describes the use of focused interviews to aid in the interpretation of experimental and survey data. Feeding results back to research participants in a group discussion allowed them to account for their responses in a qualitative manner.

---

**BOX 13.1**

### THE FIRST FOCUS GROUP IN SOCIAL RESEARCH

At Columbia University in 1941, Paul Lazarsfeld carried out experimental research on audience members' responses to radio broadcasts, having his participants press buttons to indicate positive or negative responses. Robert Merton extended this research by conducting group interviews after the broadcast to

*(Continued)*

discuss in more depth why people had responded positively or negatively at different times. Both such experimental and focus group methods remain common in media and communications research, especially in relation to political communication.

(See Lunt and Livingstone, 1996 and Merton, 1987 for an account.)

Whereas the experimental design could *indicate* people's responses, the group discussion was used to help *interpret* them. In recent years focus groups have been developed as a 'stand-alone' method, but they continue to have value as an element of research design, or when used with other approaches. At the start of the research process, for instance, focus groups can help researchers to *operationalise* their core concepts: that is, to define the main themes that the research aims to investigate, and how these might be studied in a practical way. Focus groups are valuable for exploring meaning in terms of participants' own understanding and terminology. For this reason, they can shed light on how respondents make sense of research problems or topics, helping to spell out key terms, issues and questions.

## Focus groups and survey research

It follows that this qualitative method for exploring social meanings works well in tandem with survey research (see also Chapter 27 for an overview of mixed methods research). Focus groups play a useful role in survey design, clarifying and defining the key research concepts, ensuring that the language used in the survey is likely to be understood by respondents, and even generating attitude statements for questionnaires.

---

**BOX 13.2**

## FOCUS GROUPS IN A STUDY OF MEDIA COVERAGE OF AIDS

Individual participants first completed a questionnaire, rating different categories of people on a scale of risk in relation to AIDS.

This exercise was then repeated in a group context: using a 'card game' format, the groups were asked collectively to allocate these same social categories to one of four levels of risk. Working in a group made it necessary for people to discuss and negotiate their risk assessments, and here researchers were able to observe the modes of reasoning, the assumptions and at times the misconceptions behind people's responses.

*Source*: Kitzinger, 1994b

---

Kitzinger describes an innovative combination of focus groups with surveys in her research on media coverage of AIDS (see Box 13.2). The focus group stage of the project was concerned with media 'effects' – how people consume and respond to media messages. Kitzinger and her colleagues were interested in using focus groups to explore the communicative processes through which knowledge is organised and opinions formed.

Knowledge about the topic, it was found, was shaped by values and personal experience as well as by information (and misinformation). A focus group of gay men, for example, placed 'male homosexuals' at lower risk than 'people who have sex with many different partners of the opposite sex', accounting for this assessment on the basis that gay men would be more likely to practise safer sex than would straight people with multiple sexual partners. Kitzinger comments that while other groups (including doctors, for instance) shared this knowledge about many gay men's awareness of safer sex, this did not necessarily inform those groups' collective assessment of risk. Moreover, these framing values and knowledge did not simply operate on an individual level; the group processes showed how attitudes were collectively shaped, both in confirming and hardening attitudes (around homophobia within certain groups of men or adolescents, for example), or in working out ideas and contesting assumptions (about the risk status of lesbians, for instance) (Kitzinger 1994b: 164–6).

The way in which group contexts shape individual accounts is also relevant to Hollander's study of violence in everyday life (see Hollander, 2004). In this study participants were asked to complete a lengthy postal survey prior to taking part in a focus group (see Box 13.3). The survey included questions about people's experience of fear and violence (as both victims and perpetrators). In comparing the results emerging from the two research methods, Hollander found several instances where the information reported in the survey was not disclosed in the group discussion. While a number of women in the sample reported experiences of sexual and physical violence in their survey returns, only a few discussed these in the focus group context – whether single- or mixed-sex. In contrast, in one of the all-male groups where the participants were members of the same college fraternity, the discussion elicited a number of accounts of individuals' own acts of violence, though none had reported such incidents in their survey. In making sense of these findings, Hollander refers to the problem of both 'problematic silences' and 'problematic speech' in the focus group setting, where participants can feel unable or unwilling to raise certain issues, but equally can be encouraged to 'strategically select' certain 'narratives that would boost the participants' apparent conformity' (2004: 625).

---

**▌ BOX 13.3 ▐**

## FOCUS GROUP RESEARCH ON VIOLENCE IN EVERYDAY LIFE

This study was based on 13 focus groups involving 76 participants recruited from a range of existing groups or organisations including churches, workplaces, apartment buildings, community centres, clubs and university classes.

Participants first completed a 14-page postal survey detailing their personal experience of fear and violence.

The researcher was conscious of potential gender differences both in people's experience of violence and victimisation and in their levels of fear. At the same time, she was alert to arguments that heterogeneous groups might produce richer discussion as individuals attempt to explain their experience or attitudes to others who do not share them. With both these issues in mind, the researcher conducted two-thirds of the discussions as single-sex focus groups, and one-third as mixed groups.

*Source:* Hollander, 2004

## Focus groups and interviews

Focus groups also have a critical relation to *interview* methods, particularly qualitative interviews (see Chapter 12), providing both a tool in research design and a complementary method of data collection. At the stage of developing or piloting research, one or more focus groups can help researchers to formulate qualitative topic guides: defining terms, raising themes for inclusion in a topic guide, clarifying the wording or order of questions, or assessing participants' understanding of key concepts and language. This is especially useful when researchers know what it is they want to study, but are less certain how their ideas can be turned into a relevant and meaningful set of questions. The two methods also can be used in conjunction with each other in the body of the research. Individual interviews can be valuable when different perspectives emerge from focus group discussions, or if potentially sensitive or contentious issues are at stake. In certain contexts, group discussions may encourage people to speak with greater openness than they would in a one-on-one interaction with a researcher; in others, the group context can be inhibiting. It will depend on the nature of the topic, the research design, and the make-up of the groups. Furthermore, where group discussions are used to open up topics in general ways – exploring a range of views using topic guides or visual cues, for example – individual interviews can be used to examine responses in greater depth or to draw out contrasting views and accounts.

One of the critical findings that emerged from Reay's (2004) study of children's transition to secondary school was the stigma attached to certain inner-city schools and their pupils, and how this reflected representations of social class and race (see also Box 13.4). In all of the 77 focus group discussions certain schools were 'demonised', but the researchers argue that children were positioned differently in these accounts in relation to the material and cultural resources associated with their social class, including the degree of effective choice they and their families had over where they would go to school (2004: 1008). Different voices in this way become audible within the group discourse of 'crap' schools, and are amplified through one-on-one interviews in which individual children negotiate their (lack of) choice, their attitudes towards their schooling, and their identity in relation to their peers.

In her research on religious and ethnic identity with young Muslim Americans following 9/11, Lori Peek began with a series of focus groups in the early period of the study followed by individual interviews (Peek and Fothergill 2009; see also Box 13.4). Initially Peek had intended to conduct only one-on-one interviews, but early in the study a person approached through a Muslim Students Association in New York suggested that he could bring a number of other members along to their meeting. This accidental twist in the research design was to prove valuable for the study in conceptual as well as practical ways. Most simply, Peek – who was travelling inter-state to conduct the research – was able to access a larger number of respondents during any one visit. Further to this, in the period following September 11, 2001 numerous Muslim Americans were subject to 'interview' by federal authorities – discussions in such group settings therefore seemed less likely to provoke anxiety in participants than either one-on-one interviews with a (non-Muslim) researcher or discussion in a group composed of strangers. While Peek conducted all-male, all-female and mixed focus groups, one respondent suggested that some Muslim men might be reluctant to take part in a one-on-one interview with an unknown female researcher in a semi-private space. The focus groups carried out in the first three months of the study not only allowed Peek to build up trust around the individual interviews; the discussions also generated issues and narratives that informed the interview stage of the study.

BOX 13.4

## FOCUS GROUPS AND INTERVIEW METHODS

### Study 1: Class, race and inner-city schools

This study was based on 77 focus groups with 454 children aged 10–11 in their final year of primary school in London. A sub-sample of 45 children took part in individual interviews, followed up with at least two further interviews in their first and second years of secondary school. Their parents and teachers were also interviewed. The focus group discussions generated strong views of 'sink' inner-city schools, often drawing on derogatory representations of race and social class. While these views were evident in all 77 focus groups, one aim of the interview study was to take seriously the voices of individual children in negotiating group discourses that pathologised certain schools and their pupils, particularly those working-class children who had limited choice over where they went to school.

*Source*: Reay, 2004

### Study 2: Religious and ethnic identity among young Muslim Americans

This study with second-generation Muslim Americans in New York and Colorado ran for two years between September 2001, just after the attacks of 9/11, and October 2003. In the first three months of the study, 23 focus groups were conducted, followed up by 83 semi-structured and unstructured interviews with individual participants. In total, 127 respondents took part in the study, which was supplemented by observation and fieldnotes. As well as producing data in their own right, the focus groups built up a sample of individual respondents for the latter stage of the study, promoted trust between researcher and respondents, and suggested more in-depth lines of inquiry for individual interviews.

*Source:* Peek and Fothergill, 2009

---

The difference between focus groups and individual interviews, however, is not simply a question of openness versus confidentiality or of generality versus detail. The two methods produce distinct forms of data, and it can be argued that they are premised on quite separate models of social action and meaning. A strong form of this argument holds that 'much individually based interview research is flawed by a focus on individuals as atoms divorced from their social context' (Morley, 1980: 33), when knowledge and opinions are in fact mediated by communication, and actors are irreducibly social. Focus group research, in this reading, does not seek to access individual opinions or even individual accounts, but is concerned with accounts that emerge through interaction. Its method of producing data is therefore more suggestive of 'real' social processes. As Lunt and Livingstone (1996: 94) point out, of course, interviews are no less 'social' than are focus groups, but one-on-one and group interactions are different contexts for the production of meaning and the shaping of accounts, and the data that result will reflect these differences in ways researchers should attend to in their analysis.

## Focus groups and ethnography

The interactive nature of focus group data is interesting in relation to a further approach to social and cultural research: *participant observation* or *ethnography* (see Chapter 14). The two methods share a number of practical and methodological features – including their use in the study of organisations and groups, their common emphasis on social meanings and communicative processes, and their concern with collective dynamics. The data produced by these two 'interactionist' methods are, though, rather different from each other. Focus groups can in a practical sense supplement observation methods, allowing researchers to elicit information or explore attitudes that are not easily accessible through observation alone. In this sense they add to the repertoire of methods that ethnographers draw on in field research (which also includes interviews or documentary analysis, for example), but in a way that appears especially well-suited to a broader ethnographic concern with social interaction and collective meanings.

In her study of rural social movements, Jennie Munday (2006) complemented the observation of public meetings, social events, protest marches and other political demonstrations with a series of focus groups and individual interviews (see Box 13.5). She argues that focus groups offer an especially valuable method for social movement research, allowing the researcher to explore how collective identities are formed and reproduced through communication and interaction. While the observation of rallies, events and protests could reveal how social movements are mobilised – that is, what they *do* – focus group research revealed how members articulated and reinforced group identities. The focus group dynamic in this sense mirrors the communicative context in which shared meanings and identifications are constructed.

---

### BOX 13.5

## FOCUS GROUPS AND COLLECTIVE IDENTITIES

This research used mixed methods in a study that challenged two conventions of social movement research:

- the focus on progressive or left-wing social movements
- the focus on urban social movements.

Bringing together observation and documentary analysis with focus groups and individual interviews, the research explored groups and individuals with particular relationships to a growing countryside or rural social movement in Britain. A key concern was how people articulated collective identity and politics in relation to the countryside, and in opposition to metropolitan political 'élites'. While the observation of protests and events provided insights into the public representation of a united countryside movement, the focus group discussions put into question the notion of a movement that was unified around class and regional differences, as well as around high-profile issues such as blood sports. Focus group research in this way allowed for a more in-depth engagement with how collective politics and identities are negotiated.

*Source:* Munday, 2006

---

In a stricter methodological sense, however, focus groups are an artificial intervention into a 'natural' observation setting, involving the researcher in a directive relation with their research participants and with the process of data production. Just as focus groups can be seen as more realistic than individual interviews, then, they can be seen as less naturalistic than observation. Approached in less purist mode, however, focus group techniques provide a valuable ethnographic tool, and can prove particularly useful for field research in organisations where the researchers' access to different actors and exchanges is subject to practical constraints. Focused group discussions can enable the researcher to examine issues that are not always or easily observable 'in the field', and moreover to define these issues in terms of members' own understandings and concerns.

## Focus groups and online research

Focus groups play an interesting role in the growing field of online social research. While critics might object that the online setting radically alters the interactive quality of the focus group, defenders point out that telephone surveys and interviews are generally accepted as legitimate versions of those research methods (Stewart and Williams 2005), and online survey research is now common. It might also be argued that online research captures *more* effectively the interactive and communicative contexts in which many people spend increasing parts of their live, for both work and leisure. Online focus groups are often 'asynchronous' – that is, individuals respond at different times via posts to newsgroups or discussion threads – but increasingly offer the potential for 'synchronous' interactions in real time via chatrooms and other virtual environments (see Box 13.6). Conducting focus groups online allows the researcher to bring together groups that are dispersed across space, including transnational 'communities' of users or interests. The downside is that it can be difficult for researchers to control who takes part in the study, to select participants in a purposive manner, or indeed to be certain of the basic demographic characteristics of their respondents – even at the level of sex or age.

The potential of online focus groups has been particularly apparent in health research, in which groups of practitioners or users can be accessed through online networks and support groups (see Murray, 1997). User groups might otherwise be hard to reach, and the anonymity of online interaction may encourage people to discuss problems or conditions they would be reluctant to talk about in face-to-face settings. These advantages equally can apply in other fields of research. Online focus groups follow similar 'rules' of method as conventional focus groups: above all, discussions are focused around a topic, are moderated by the researcher, and are based on the informed consent of participants who do not participate unwillingly or unknowingly (see Box 13.6). While it is possible simply to harvest existing discussions from newsgroups, blogs or social networking sites, the ethics of doing such research require careful thought (see also Stewart and Williams, 2005).

---

**▌ BOX 13.6 ▌**

## ONLINE FOCUS GROUP RESEARCH

Matthew Williams' study of 'deviance' in virtual graphical communities involved synchronous online focus groups of 45 and 15 participants over a period of 55 days. Williams developed a 3-D virtual environment for the focus group discussions, allowing participants to create avatars, to move around the 3-D space, and to interact with others visually as well as through posting comments using text. Setting up the study involved email negotiation via a gatekeeper and with research participants; while Williams had initial access to over 1,000 respondents, just five per cent of this sample agreed to take part over the two-month research period.

*Source:* Stewart and Williams, 2005

## Focus groups and data analysis

When used with other research methods in the ways described above, focus groups are often seen as particularly insightful at the data analysis stage of a project. In highlighting shared and contested meanings, focus groups can help researchers to explore the findings that emerge from surveys, interviews or observations. Their use here has the twin merits of adding interpretive weight to the researcher's own analysis, and seeking to integrate respondents' views and feedback in a participatory research process. Focus group work can be particularly valuable when results are puzzling (helping to dig deeper into inconsistencies or disagreements in responses) or surprising (helping to account in different ways for anomalies or blind spots). While this use of focus groups as an analytic tool echoes their earliest use in social science research, using focus groups to reflect on preceding stages of the research process is not only a convenient or consultative means of interpretation but can also add further layers to the research.

The following list summarises the diversity of uses of the method:

- On a *basic level*, focus group research is a practical means of generating data fairly quickly and reasonably conveniently – you can get six or ten people's views all at once rather than having to interview them separately. For this reason, focus groups can be a good option for student researchers or others who are working at a small-scale and with limited resources of time.

- On a *further level*, the focus group is a valuable tool of research design – helping you clarify your key concepts, refine your terminology, construct your questions – or of data analysis, aiding interpretation and seeking to reflect the understanding of research participants themselves.

- On a more *advanced level*, however, stronger methodological claims can be made for the focus group as a means of generating qualitative data. From this perspective, focus groups capture the inherently interactive and communicative nature of social action and social meanings, in ways that are inaccessible to research methods that take the individual as their basic unit of analysis.

Viewed in these terms, focus groups have moved some distance from their origins as a supplement to more orthodox social research techniques, to their current status as a distinctive method of social and cultural inquiry in their own right. In the following sections, I consider some of the more practical issues involved in using the focus group method, beginning with the question of how to go about selecting groups of participants.

## Sampling and selection

Focus groups are a means of generating qualitative data in order to explore different perspectives on a topic, rather than to access representative or generalisable views about it. Even so, issues of selection remain critical. Focus group researchers adopt a range of approaches to the selection of participants, and debates in this area reflect and add to more general questions about sampling in qualitative research (see Lunt and Livingstone, 1996; Krueger and Casey, 2008). In particular, there is the issue of selecting *individuals* for a method that is concerned with the analysis of *groups*. This has implications for the status of the data that emerge from focus group discussions, and how far these data can be taken to reflect either individual opinion or general social attitudes. In the discussion that follows, I review different approaches to sampling and selection that a focus group researcher might adopt, from those that follow a more standard *survey* logic, to the use of *theoretical sampling* as a strategy for generating data (see also Chapters 9 and 22).

## Random sampling

Random sampling is fairly uncommon in focus group research, given its association with larger-scale and quantitative studies (see Chapter 9). In some cases, however, researchers will be able to take a random sample of the population of interest. When researching a clearly defined organisation, for instance, one might use random sampling to select groups of employees in a workplace, students within a university, or people registered with a medical practice. The purpose of such research, however, is unlikely to be simply a broad measure of satisfaction within an organisation, or the highlighting of general problems or concerns. If that were the case, it would be easier and more reliable to use a survey instead. Focus groups offer evaluation and organisational research something different. The detailed nature of focus group data provides scope for greater insight into an issue. Why do different people say they are happy or unhappy with the service they get from their doctor? What do they say they want and what do they think might be done about it? Even where focus group research employs random sampling, it is not primarily for the purpose of generalising from individual responses to external populations. This is because focus group research does not provide access in any systematic way to individual responses, but rather to *interactive discussions*. For evaluation research, then, focus groups might be more time-consuming, more expensive and less clear-cut than surveys, but they can involve respondents in consultations that attempt to negotiate different views and work through issues collectively. Group discussions help to explore the reasons behind people's responses, suggest alternatives and solutions, and feed user, client or staff views into processes of evaluation, planning and change.

## Purposive sampling

While research within organisations offers potential for random sampling, focus group research more often is based on purposive sampling: where participants are selected on the basis of having a significant relation to the research topic. This works in different ways. In market research, for example, it might simply involve using a form of quota sampling – selecting a given number of men and women, of age groups, of income brackets or occupational types, to participate in focus groups that will be broadly *reflective* (if not strictly representative) of the population of interest, or that will provide an array of market views. The logic of selection is similar in the case of policy research into different groups' views about various issues or initiatives (middle-income voters, or rural voters, or young people, or women). The researcher here might be less interested in selecting groups that mirror the wider population, than in groups with a key relation to the topic.

The selection of focus groups, if rarely aiming to be representative, is often guided by these wider social debates. Social and political attitudes – as large-scale surveys, studies of electoral behaviour, patterns of newspaper readership and common sense all suggest – tend to be shaped by people's age or life-stage, their social class, their gender or ethnic background, their family status. Such knowledge can aid in the selection of focus groups:

- A researcher interested in attitudes towards the *legalisation of cannabis*, for example, might decide that *age* is a significant factor in selecting focus groups on the topic.
- Similarly, a focus group researcher looking at *public trust in the police service* might use *race or ethnicity* as a key selection criterion.

In these instances, the selection of focus groups is framed by broader public debates and social research knowledge about the topics under study. The aim of the research, however, will not be to 'prove' in either case that younger people are more likely to favour legalisation, or that black people are less likely to trust the police. Focus groups do not allow researchers to *measure* different responses and then generalise these to a larger population, but rather to explore how selected groups of individuals define, talk about and account for given issues. In these two examples, age and ethnicity respectively are being used as break characteristics: that is, categories that distinguish groups from each other. This is one of the central criteria researchers use in selecting members of focus groups.

As well as defining groups in terms of distinctive characteristics, researchers might apply control categories that remain stable across groups. For example, say a researcher is interested in using focus groups to investigate attitudes towards abortion. Box 13.7 shows two different approaches to selecting members of the focus groups for this study. In the first approach, gender is a 'control' category: all groups in the study have a common gender mix. In the second approach, gender is used as a 'break' characteristic: as a criterion which differentiates groups within the study.

Let us consider the other decisions the researchers have made in selecting these contrasting samples.

---

**BOX 13.7**

## TWO APPROACHES TO SELECTING FOCUS GROUP PARTICIPANTS IN A STUDY OF ATTITUDES TOWARDS ABORTION

*Approach 1*: Gender is a control category (all groups include the same gender mix: for example, women only or men only or the same number of men and women in each group).

| Groups | Age | Voting last election |
|---|---|---|
| Group 1 | 18–25 | Progressive |
| Group 2 | 18–25 | Conservative |
| Group 3 | 35–50 | Progressive |
| Group 4 | 35–50 | Conservative |
| Group 5 | 60+ | Progressive |
| Group 6 | 60+ | Conservative |

*Approach 2*: Gender is used as a break characteristic.

| Groups | Age | Gender |
|---|---|---|
| Group 1 | 18–25 | Female |
| Group 2 | 18–25 | Male |
| Group 3 | 35–50 | Female |
| Group 4 | 35–50 | Male |
| Group 5 | 60+ | Female |
| Group 6 | 60+ | Male |

- *Both researchers* agree that age is likely to be a relevant characteristic, and have divided their groups into broad generational ranges or life-stages. Notice that the age groups are quite clearly delineated by ten-year intervals, so as to mark out distinct age differences.

- The *first researcher* has decided that attitudes towards abortion potentially reflect general social and political attitudes, and so has chosen *voting behaviour* as a simple proxy for indicating 'progressive' or 'conservative' attitudes. (This criterion of selection reflects a general practice in social research of using voting behaviour as a fairly blunt instrument for indicating wider social and political attitudes – newspaper readership is another standard proxy.)

- The *second researcher* has decided that groups of men and women might talk differently about the topic of abortion, and so has used *gender* to divide groups.

In each case it is important to note that, while the researcher is interested in using focus groups to explore attitudes towards abortion, the design of the groups is already based on a number of assumptions about how those attitudes might be shaped. Gender in particular is a relevant issue for the selection of focus groups. This is partly due to the way that gender is understood to shape individuals' attitudes and experiences, but also reflects a recognition that mixed focus groups can reproduce wider dynamics of gender power. The studies mentioned earlier by Hollander and by Peek, for example, both involved female-only and male-only focus groups (see Boxes 13.3 and 13.4). While some of Peek's young Muslim American contacts saw it as convenient and comfortable to meet in a mixed group, other respondents requested single-sex groups – Peek reports that 'students in the sex-segregated groups seemed more comfortable and talked more openly about sensitive topics' (Peek and Fothergill 2009: 40). Gender was highly sensitive for Hollander's study of violence, given the gendered character of sexual and domestic violence. While the single-sex groups did not appear to increase either women's or men's disclosure of their *own* experience of sexual violence, Hollander suggests that the discussion in a mixed setting was dominated by 'men's concerns with property violence' (involving theft or vandalism, for instance), while discussion of sexual violence and fear was largely missing – leading her to argue for the importance of 'not only what is said in focus group discussions but also what is *not* said' (2004: 622).

## Homogeneity and knowing other members

A standard argument within focus group methodology is that group members should be *homogeneous* in respect of the relevant selection criteria, but unknown to each other (Krueger and Casey, 2008; Morgan, 1997). This is so as to avoid established relations of power, disagreement or consensus being brought into the research setting, where assertive voices are more likely to direct the group discussion and where it might be difficult for individuals to dissent from an apparently collective view. In practice, however, there are many research contexts where focus group members are likely to be known to each other. This is clearly the case where participants are recruited from within organisations or associations – employees in a workplace, members of a voluntary group, trade union or political association, residents on an estate, students on a course, users of a service and so on.

On another level, however, this is not simply a practical question about how researchers access their participants. The question of how groups are constituted opens up larger methodological debates about the distinctive nature of the research method. For some critics, the textbook view that participants should be homogeneous in terms of certain social characteristics, but unfamiliar to each other, is evidence of a survey logic that sees the focus group as somehow typical of wider social categories (see Lunt and Livingstone, 1996: 87). Alternative approaches select focus groups not as quasi-experimental subsets of larger social categories, but as actual groups or networks in their own right (see Box 13.8). This rationale for selection can be seen as a form of theoretical sampling, where participants are selected with the aim of developing conceptual insights in relation to the topic (see also Chapter 22).

## Running focus groups and analysing the interaction

Like other forms of research, the quality of the data generated by focus group research will depend on the quality of the research design, but execution – how effectively the researcher runs the focus group – is particularly important in this case. Focus group research is distinctive in allowing participants to work through and re-define key research concepts and questions in an interactive way; furthermore, they provide a 'mechanism for placing the control of this interaction in the hands of the participants rather than the researcher' (Morgan, 1993: 17–18). This also means that group discussions can be hard for researchers to manage. Running focus groups therefore requires the researcher to draw on certain skills, such as:

- facilitating *interaction* and discussion

- enabling space for different group members to make their views known

- keeping the group discussion focused around the core themes

- dealing with dominant or inappropriate voices

- sustaining a pace of discussion that ensures key topics are covered without constraining or rushing the talk.

The skills required in running focus groups, then, are rather different from the skills called upon in other kinds of social research, including individual interviews and surveys. In many respects they are closer to the range of skills needed to run a seminar, chair a meeting or convene a jury.

While it is important for the researcher to be able to observe interactions within the focus group so as to direct the flow of discussion, it can be difficult for the researcher to manually record the process. Focus groups are routinely audio- or video-taped – as in other research contexts, with the permission of the participants. Researchers can make basic notes during the group interaction, or use flipcharts or whiteboards as a way of facilitating the discussion which then provide a set of research notes. Researchers might consider having colleagues act as an observer and note-taker, although the advantage of this in terms of recording data needs to be balanced against the effect a non-participant might have on the flow of the group discussion. In any case, it is important to make the role of any researcher (including the facilitator) quite clear to the group members before the discussion starts.

One of the most basic practical issues involved in running focus groups is getting six to ten people together at the same time and in an appropriate space. Whereas interviewers often arrange times and locations for their meetings at the convenience of their participants, focus groups researchers need to bring participants together in a common place. It is good practice to pay the travel costs (and, if relevant, the childcare costs) of participants, and focus group researchers frequently offer refreshments, which also help to promote a relaxed and social atmosphere. Researchers will need to arrange a room that is private, quiet, comfortable and accessible. The duration of focus groups varies, but a rule of thumb would be to allow around two hours for the whole process, and participants should be informed in advance of how long the researcher expects the session to last. Researchers will also need to make judgements about including breaks, both for the benefit of the participants and to make sure different themes are covered.

Particular issues of confidentiality and anonymity arise in the group setting. In general, individuals should not be identifiable outside the discussion context, and taped records should only be heard or seen by people directly involved in the research. As well as outlining to participants the purpose and nature of the research in advance of the meeting, sessions usually begin with an opening statement to the group, outlining the research aims and who is doing (or funding) it. This is an opportunity to reiterate the researcher's position on confidentiality and anonymity, and to agree ground rules for the discussion, falling into two main areas:

- *Practical:* addressing the need to record the session in order to keep track of what people say; explaining the role of the researcher in guiding the process but allowing participants to take up the discussion in their own terms; stressing the importance of turn-taking and not talking over one another so as to make the discussion clear; encouraging people to voice their own opinions.

- *Ethical:* such as seeking agreement within the group over the use of offensive language, allowing for others' opinions and voicing disagreements in a reasonable way, and maintaining confidentiality outside the group.

In addition to setting up the terms clearly, researchers will need a strategy for closing the session, facilitating the discussion so as to allow the talk to 'wind down' in a fairly smooth way at the end.

There are no special techniques for analysing focus group material, which rather draws on the range of methods common to qualitative data analysis. However, analysis does need to attend to the distinctive nature of the data that emerge from focus group discussions. This, to re-state an argument made earlier, is interactive data, where the group discussion (rather than the individual discussants) is the unit of analysis. One cannot simply read off individual opinions from collective exchanges; neither can one easily translate from the specific group context to any wider social groupings represented by the participants. For many researchers, this is the particular strength of focus group methods, allowing the data to capture something of the situated communicative processes through which social meanings are made and reproduced. For this reason, focus group data often are well-suited to techniques of *discourse* or *conversation analysis* (see Chapters 23 and 24). These methods are concerned with how language is used to create and confirm meanings, how competing accounts are negotiated and how speakers draw on certain interpretive repertoires in making their arguments within a given discursive context.

## Conclusion

Focus groups have developed from a practical supplement to other research methods into a technique of social and cultural inquiry based on distinct methodological claims. Their relative strengths and weaknesses, too, range from the practical to the methodological. Focus groups:

- can be a convenient method of data collection, which can be undertaken on a small scale by researchers with limited resources

- are good at accessing respondents' own definitions and understandings, and at giving them a significant degree of involvement within the research process

- work well with other research methods – either in multi-method approaches to data collection or in terms of refining research problems and interpreting data produced by other methods

- generate data on the basis of social interaction and communication; in this sense, they reflect the social and cultural processes through which meaning, opinions and attitudes are shaped.

Problems in using focus groups also are practical and methodological in character, and tend to mirror the advantages of the method:

- Researchers have less control over the data that emerge than they have with individual interviews or surveys. The potential gain to the participants, in this sense, can be seen as a loss of power on the part of the researcher.

- Focus groups provide an insecure basis for generalisation. It follows that the claims a researcher makes in terms of developing insights into social attitudes cannot simply be matched by systematic claims about the representativeness of these attitudes. Focus group researchers explore a range of views,

and analyse how particular groups of respondents account for and negotiate these views. The qualified approach taken in most social research contexts to the wider validity of focus group findings often contrasts with the claims for representativeness implied in the use of focus groups for market research and political polling.

- While focus groups seek to reproduce the interactive nature of 'real' social processes, they are not in themselves naturally occurring interactions, and offer no guarantee about what people say or think, or how they interact, outside the research context.

These are valid problems. However, for many social researchers they are outweighed by the value of focus groups on a range of fronts: in clarifying and refining concepts; in accessing information that is not available through observation; in placing communication and interaction at the centre of the research process; and in exploring attitudes, opinions, meanings and definitions on participants' own terms.

## FURTHER READING

Krueger and Casey (2008) and Morgan (1997) are two well-known and very useful textbooks on the use of focus groups in social research; Barbour and Kitzinger (1999) bring together a range of interesting chapters on the politics, theory and practice of focus groups; Puchta and Potter (2004) focus on the practice of running focus groups, bridging market and social research. For article-length discussions, see Lunt and Livingstone (1996) for a valuable overview of the role of focus groups in media and communications research; Kitzinger (1994b) for an interesting account of how focus groups were used together with questionnaires and interviews in a project exploring perceptions of risk in relation to HIV/AIDS, and Hollander (2004) for a thoughtful reflection on the problems and potential of focus group research.

### Student Reader (Seale, 2004b): relevant readings

39 Jenny Kitzinger: 'The methodology of focus groups: the importance of interaction between research participants'

See also Chapter 5, 'Focus groups' by Phil Macnaghten and Greg Myers in Seale et al. (2004).

### Journal articles illustrating and discussing the methods raised in this chapter

Allen, L. (2005) 'Managing masculinity: young men's identity work in focus groups', Qualitative Research, 5: 35–57.

Griffin, C., Bengry-Howell, A., Hackly, C., Mistral, W. and Szmigin, I. (2009) '"Every time I do it I absolutely annihilate myself": loss of (self-)consciousness and loss of memory in young people's drinking narratives', Sociology, 43 (3): 457–476.

Kitzinger, J. (1994b) 'The methodology of focus groups: the importance of interaction between research participants', Sociology of Health & Illness, 16 (1): 103–121.

Wutich, A., Lant, Y., White, D.D., Larson, K.L. and Gartin, M. (2010) 'Comparing focus group and individual responses on sensitive topics: a study of water decision makers in a desert city', Field Methods, 22: 88–110.

## Web links

Anita Gibbs: 'Focus groups', in issue 19 of *Social Research Update:* http://sru.soc.surrey.ac.uk/SRU19.html

Carter McNamara, *Basics of Conducting Focus Groups:* www.mapnp.org/library/evaluatn/focusgrp.htm

Methods@manchester – focus groups: www.methods.manchester.ac.uk/methods/focusgroups/index.shtml

Focus groups and research on politics: www.pollingreport.com/focus.htm

## *KEY CONCEPTS FOR REVIEW*

Advice: Use these, along with the review questions in the next section, to test your knowledge of the contents of this chapter. Try to define each of the key concepts listed here; if you have understood this chapter you should be able to do this. Check your definitions against the definition in the glossary at the end of the book.

| | |
|---|---|
| Break characteristics | Purposive sampling |
| Control categories | Quota sampling |
| Interaction | Random sampling |
| Naturalism | Theoretical sampling |

## Review questions

1 Why would a researcher choose to use focus groups rather than other research methods?
2 What difference, if any, is there between data produced by focus group interviews and data produced from individual interviews?
3 What problems might arise from using focus groups where people know each other? What might be the potential benefits?

1 Working in small groups, choose a topic that you could explore through focus group research. Such topics might include questions about public attitudes (e.g. attitudes towards immigration), how audiences interpret media (e.g. responses to news content; the impact of violence in the media), or the study of meanings and beliefs (e.g. perceptions of national identity). Having agreed your topic of study, discuss and note down your responses to the following questions:

   (a) How would you select groups to participate in the study? How does the selection of these groups relate to your research problem?

   (b) Are there any methodological or ethical problems you might encounter in researching this topic via group discussions?

   (c) Could this study be extended by using other research methods?

2 This exercise involves running a focus group to discover students' experience of alcohol and drug use at university. One person should act as moderator and four to ten others should act as members of the focus group. You may wish to have two observers who can take notes on the interaction and provide an assessment of the effectiveness of the exercise in producing relevant data. The moderator should use the following questions to stimulate discussion and can also make other interventions in the discussion where appropriate:

   (a) Can we begin by talking about how people socialise at your university? What kinds of after-hours events and activities are on offer, and which do you take part in?

   (b) How much of a role does alcohol play in socialising at university?

   (c) Do you have some thoughts on how your university is doing regarding alcohol and drug problems with students? Can you describe to me what you know about this?

   (d) Do you think drugs or alcohol are easily available to students?

   (e) What kinds of personal rules do you have about alcohol and drugs?

   (f) If you ever had a problem with alcohol or drugs, who would you approach to talk about it? Can you explain your thoughts about your choice of this individual?

   (g) Can you talk about your thoughts on how alcohol and drugs affect a person? What about friendship groups or families?

# 14

# DOING ETHNOGRAPHY

David Walsh

---

**Chapter Contents**

The definition in Box 14.1 describes the essence of ethnography, showing it to be based in what is known as participant observation. This makes the researcher, as participant observer, the primary research instrument. Ethnography, then, contrasts with 'scientific' methods of social science research which, based upon a universalistic model of science, emphasises its neutrality and objectivity, attempting to generate data untouched by human hands. Ethnography belongs to the theoretical tradition which argues that the facts of society and culture belong to a different order from those of nature (see Chapter 2).

## Theoretical foundations

Anthropologists developed ethnography to become their primary and almost exclusive method. Faced with non-Western societies that largely possessed an oral culture, anthropologists were encouraged by a perception of their diversity to take an attitude of cultural relativism, whereby the values and institutions of any given society were seen to have an internal logic of their own.

Any attempt to judge other societies as inferior or superior, in this view, is condemned as ethnocentric. Eventually this attitude was to lead to the view, amongst some, that rationality itself was simply a value position promoted by Western societies. Anthropologists took the view that society and culture could only be studied from inside by the immersion of the researcher in the society under study.

Later, sociologists pursuing action theory and symbolic interactionism came to use the method (see Filmer et al., 2004 for a definition of these terms). It is, however, in phenomenology that we can see the most evocative conception of the ethnographer's role. Phenomenology focuses on the inter-subjective constitution of the social world and everyday social life. Schütz (1964), in a seminal essay on 'The Stranger', shows how a social group has its own cultural pattern of life – folkways, mores, laws, habits, customs, etiquette, fashions and so on – that, as far as its members are concerned, are taken for granted, are habitual and almost automatic (see Box 14.2).

Schütz's stranger provides a model for the ethnographer using participant observation. The ethnographer tries to treat the familiar world of 'members' as anthropologically strange, to expose its social and cultural construction. This is particularly demanding when a researcher is studying a group with which he or she is familiar, but represents an ideal attitude of mind for the researcher to pursue nevertheless.

problematic and questionable. Yet the stranger can become a member of the group through *participation*, becoming transformed into an insider, inhabiting it in the same taken-for-granted way as existing members. At the same time, being a stranger creates an attitude of objectivity because the stranger must carefully examine what seems self-explanatory to the members of the group. The stranger knows that other ways of life are possible.

*Source*: summary of Schütz, 1964

Constructionism is the view that society is to be seen as socially constructed on the basis of how its members make sense of it and not as an object-like reality. It is latent in symbolic interactionism, but more apparent in phenomenology. It has now become the primary theoretical foundation of contemporary ethnography. One can also see ethnomethodology as forming a part of this constructionist approach. Ethnomethodologists, though, are less interested in how people *see* things than more conventional ethnographers, and are more interested in how people *do* things, particularly in their uses of language. Chapter 24 shows how the method of conversation analysis has arisen from these concerns. Although such approaches share a view that the subject matter of social and cultural research is different from that of the natural sciences, they are nevertheless characteristically committed to a realist and scientific view of the world.

However, an altogether different version of ethnography has also emerged out of constructionism which urges a radical break with all ideas of objective scientific inquiry. This position involves not simply seeing ethnography as a revelation of social construction but seeing ethnographic research as *itself* participating in the construction of the social world. Bauman (1987) has summarised this by distinguishing a traditional form of social research which is legislative, in that the ethnographer rules some accounts of the world true and others false, and a newer form that is more genuinely interpretive. This view involves seeing social research as one possible interpretation amongst many. The American anthropologist Clifford Geertz has played an

important part in forming this different sense of ethnography. Geertz argues that

> man [*sic*] is an animal suspended in webs of significance he himself has spun and I take culture to be those webs, and the analysis to be therefore not an experimental science in search of law but an interpretive one in search of meaning. It is explication I am after, construing social expressions on their surface enigmatical. (1973: 5)

This leads Geertz to the view that the task of ethnography is to produce its own distinctive form of knowledge, which he calls thick description. Although the ethnographer continues to use the same techniques of data collection as conventional ethnographers, the focus of analysis turns much more to seeing culture as a system of *signs*. Here, the ethnographer comes close to doing a semiotic analysis (see Chapter 16). The easiest way to understand this is to imagine the ethnographer as being like a literary critic attempting to understand the organisation, construction and meaning of a literary text. The ethnographer then finds a whole web of cultural structures, knowledge and meanings which are knotted and superimposed on to one another and which constitute a densely layered cultural script.

Famously, Geertz analyses the many layers of meaning involved in Balinese cockfights in a demonstration of this approach. He sees the event of a cockfight as an example of a cultural script being written, or enacted. Through an intensive and dense description of a cockfight, Geertz makes broader cultural interpretations and generalisations. Yet Geertz understands his own analysis of the various meanings of the event as a reflexive interpretation of it, rather than an objective description. This, of course, raises the issue of validity. If ethnographers are simply in the business of introducing new texts into a society and culture that is little more than an interplay of 'texts', we must give up any notions of science or truthfulness.

There have been some very interesting deconstructions of ethnographic writing. These emphasise that ethnographers are story-tellers and, like all such, create narratives of tragedy, irony and humour which make their writing a literary activity. They use the same fundamental resources of literature and the same sorts of recipes and material in conveying arguments and persuading readers that their accounts are plausible reconstructions of social actors and social scenes.

But it seems wrong for social researchers wholly to accept this postmodern discourse, to abandon all forms of realism as the basis for doing ethnography, and to accept that all is textuality and construction. It could be argued that this takes reflexivity too far and shuns the empirical too much. The rhetorical strategies of ethnographic writing should be acknowledged, but this cannot be the end of the story. The social and cultural world must be the ground and reference for ethnographic writing, and reflexive ethnography should involve a keen awareness of the interpenetration of reality and representation.

## Doing ethnography

Quantitative research committed to a positivist vision of the unity of science (the philosophical term for this is naturalism – see Chapter 2) attempts to establish correlations between objectively defined variables as a basis for explanation. This proceeds through a research design that is organised as a logically sequential and separate series of stages, beginning from theory and going through hypothesis generation and data gathering to hypothesis testing. Frequently, one-off interviews or questionnaires are used. Ethnography departs from this. First, ethnographers study people in their natural settings (also said to be 'naturalistic', somewhat confusingly), seeking to document that world in terms of the meanings and behaviour of the people in it. It places in doubt the variables that quantitative research analyses, examining instead their socio-cultural construction. Second, it does not follow the sequence of deductive theory testing because it is in the process of research itself that research problems come to be formulated and studied. Often these prove to be different from the problems that the ethnographer had initially intended to study. Theory is often *generated* rather than solely tested. Indeed, the 'discovery of grounded theory' during fieldwork has been the subject of much debate in the literature on ethnography (Glaser and Strauss, 1967) and is discussed in Chapter 22.

Ethnography is distinctive in three ways:

- First, as stated above, there are *no distinct stages* of theorising, hypothesis construction, data gathering and hypothesis testing. Instead, the research process is one of a constant interaction between problem formulation, data collection and data analysis. The analysis of data feeds into research design; data collection and theory come to be developed out of data analysis and all subsequent data collection is guided strategically by the emergent theory.

- Second, ethnography brings a *variety of techniques* of inquiry into play, involving attempts to observe things that happen, listen to what people say and question people in the setting under investigation. So it involves, as McCall and Simmons put it:

  > genuinely social interaction in the field with the subject of study ... direct observation of relevant events, some formal and a great deal of informal interviewing, some counting, [the] collection of documents and artifacts, and open-endedness in the directions the study takes. (1969: 1)

- Third, *the observer is the primary research instrument*, accessing the field, establishing field relations, conducting and structuring observation and interviews, writing field notes, using audio and visual recordings, reading documents, recording and transcribing and finally writing up the research.

So ethnography has a large constructional and reflexive character. It is essentially the observer who stands at the heart of ethnography and of its open-ended nature.

## The observer position

Observation, inquiry and data collection depend upon the observer gaining access to the appropriate field and establishing good working relations with the people in it. They need to be relationships that are able to generate the data the research requires. The identity that the observer assumes determines the success of this.

A first issue is whether to take an overt or covert role in the setting. This, in turn, very much depends on the situation and on the gatekeepers who control access to it. Gatekeepers are the sponsors, officials and significant others who have the power to grant or block access to and within a setting. Sometimes, the ethnographer is faced with situations in which relevant gatekeepers are unlikely to permit access, so that covert or secret research is the only way of studying them. This has been done, for example, in studies of the police (Holdaway, 1982), religious sects (Shaffir, 1985), organised crime (Chambliss, 1975) and right-wing political movements (Fielding, 1981). Here, the observer seeks to present himself or herself as an ordinary, legitimate member of the group. This may solve the problem of access and observation as long as the covert role can be maintained, but successful maintenance produces major problems of an ethical and practical kind and a massive problem if the cover is 'blown'. Normally, then, totally covert research is rare in ethnography. More commonly the researcher lets some people know

about the research and keeps others in the dark or only partially informed about the purposes of the research. Some ethnographers argue on ethical grounds that the researcher should always adopt a completely overt role in which the purposes of the research and its procedures are explained to the people being studied. But Hammersley and Atkinson (2007) argue that, whereas deception should be avoided if possible, telling the whole truth about research may not be wise or feasible. Since research problems will change over the course of fieldwork, what the researcher can say about aims is often little more than speculation. Additionally, to produce too much information ahead of time may influence the behaviour of the people under study in such a way that it invalidates the findings.

Generally, then, a series of potential observer roles are open to the ethnographer. Junker (1960) identifies four (Box 14.3).

First, there is the *complete participant*. This entails complete covert research. Although it seems to carry the attraction of generating a complete knowledge of the situation, apart from the problems outlined above it produces others too. It can place a severe restriction on the character of the data collected because the observer, as a completely participating member of it, becomes hedged in by the expectations of the role he or she has adopted. So many lines of inquiry will be missed and optimal conditions for data collection may not be available. Finally, it carries the risk of 'going native', where the observer abandons the position of analyst for identification with the people under study.

Second, Junker describes the role of the *complete observer*. Here the researcher simply observes people in ways that avoid social interaction with the observed, as Corsaro (1981) did in a study of nursery school children in the classroom which involved observing them through a one-way mirror. This reduces the possibilities of people reacting to being observed (known as reactivity) or of 'going native', but introduces the potential problem of ethnocentrism instead, in which the observer, by not interacting with the people under study, cannot get at their meanings and so imposes an alien framework of understanding on the situation. Moreover, it places severe limits on what can be observed, although it can be a valuable supplement to other forms of ethnographic research.

The third role is that of the *participant as observer*. Here, the observer and the people being studied are aware that theirs is a field relationship, which minimises the problems of pretence. It involves an emphasis on participation and social interaction over observing in order to produce a relationship of rapport and trust. The problem is that it carries the danger of reactivity and of going native through identification with the people being studied, unless the intimacy created in social interaction is restrained by attempts to maintain the role of the stranger on the part of the observer.

---

**BOX 14.3**

## FOUR ROLES IN PARTICIPANT OBSERVATION

1  Complete participant

2  Complete observer

3  Participant as observer

4  Observer as participant

*Source*: Junker, 1960

---

The fourth role is that of the *observer as participant*. Here the balance is in favour of observation over participation. This prevents the researcher from going native but restricts understanding because limited participation in social activities heightens the possibilities of superficiality, so that important lines of inquiry may be missed or not pursued, things go unobserved and the activities of participants are not properly understood. Typically, most overt ethnography takes up a position somewhere between the third and fourth roles. Overt observer roles can never be entirely fixed and can and do change (the opposite is true if research is covert). Indeed, changes in the observer's role in the field over the course of fieldwork may be vital in producing new information, generating new data and creating new and fruitful problems and lines of inquiry that extend the scope of the research. In the end, however, the best observational position for the ethnographer is that of the marginal native, which will be described later in the chapter.

## Beginning an ethnographic study

Although ethnography does not work with a logically sequential research design that compartmentalises it into distinct stages, it does have phases and activities that give it a **funnel structure** in which the research is progressively focused over its course. At the start of this funnel the researcher will be involved in formulating ideas about the sort of problem to be investigated. In ethnography, however, what the researcher initially sets out to investigate may change over the course of fieldwork, as problems are transformed or emerge in the field. The process of observation itself establishes problems and the possibilities of inquiry into them. Yet all ethnography begins with some problem or set of issues, which some call fore-shadowed problems, that are not specifically formulated hypotheses and which can have many sources. As is shown in Chapter 7, the requirement to write a research proposal may be the opportunity to lay out the nature of such foreshadowed problems. At the same time it is important not to let such an exercise close down avenues of inquiry that deviate from the proposal. One of the strengths of ethnography is its open-ended nature.

To begin with, the ethnographer needs to consult relevant *secondary sources* on the problems and issues under consideration, which can range from allied research monographs and articles through to other sources like journalistic material, autobiographies and diaries and even novels (see Chapter 6). But the focusing of research problems cannot really be started until initial data have been collected. As Geer says, one begins with early working hypotheses but ultimately goes on to generate 'hypotheses … based on an accumulation of data … [that] … undergo a prolonged period of testing and retesting... over the period of [research]. There is no finality to them. They must be refined, expanded and developed' (1964: 152). Even at the early stage theory enters into the selection of research problems, as was shown in Chapter 5. Moreover, the initial consideration of foreshadowed problems has to begin a process that moves between the immediate empirical situation and an analytical framework.

However, the research problem is very much shaped by the nature of the setting chosen for study. Choice of setting may have arisen on an opportunistic basis. For example, a natural disaster may have occurred, or the researcher may come across the reconstruction of an organisation, or the replanning of a city, or may find an entry opened through personal contacts. In choosing a setting the researcher may then need to 'case' it, with a view to

assessing its suitability and feasibility for research purposes. This will involve assessing the possibilities for access to it, collecting preliminary data on it, interviewing relevant participants and finding potential gatekeepers. Finally, the practical issues of the time and money needed to do research will need to be considered.

It is important that the setting is a naturally occurring one, although it need not be geographically self-contained. It can be one that is constituted and maintained by cultural definitions and social strategies that establish it as a 'community'. For example, a study of green political movements would be like this. It may be necessary to go outside the setting to understand the significance of things that go on within it.

If the setting is a single case, this can pose problems of representativeness and therefore of the external validity of the study (see Chapter 30). This, though, can be circumvented by selecting on the basis of intrinsic interest and theoretical usefulness. Sampling *within* settings also occurs, so it is important to make decisions about what to observe and when, whom to talk to, and what to record and how. Here three dimensions of sampling are relevant:

- *Time:* attitudes and activities may vary over time so a study may have to represent this.
- *People:* people vary, so a range of types should be investigated.
- *Context:* people do different things in different contexts, so a variety of these will have to be studied. Such **contextual sensitivity** is vital to ethnographic study.

## Access

Initial access to the field is essential but is also an issue to be resolved throughout the whole of the data collecting process. There are numerous aspects to the problem. At a first level, gaining access to a situation is an entirely practical matter which entails using the ordinary interpersonal resources, skills and strategies that all of us develop in dealing with the conduct of everyday life. But access is also a theoretical matter in ethnography because, as Hammersley and Atkinson (2007) argue, the discovery of obstacles to access can help one to understand the social organisation of a setting, showing, for example, how people respond to strangers.

'Public' settings (e.g. the street, a beach), although seeming to offer no difficulties of access, are, in fact, difficult for research. This is because deliberate and protracted observation can place the observer in a potentially deviant position, perhaps appearing as someone loitering with the intent to commit a crime. More typically, access to 'private' settings is governed by gatekeepers who are not always easy to identify, though common sense and social knowledge can provide the vehicles for doing so. In formal organisations the gatekeepers will be key personnel in the organisation, but in other settings the gatekeepers may be different. Whyte's (1943) classic study of slum ghetto life and its gang structure depended on his finding and being befriended by 'Doc', a leading gang leader, who provided the sponsorship through which the ghetto was studied. But whoever the gatekeepers are, they will be concerned with the picture of their community, subculture, group or organisation and may want it and themselves painted in a favourable light. This, in turn, means they are likely to keep sensitive things hidden. They may also prevent the study of mundane matters because they take them for granted and see them as uninteresting.

Access affects the accuracy of ethnographic study because it determines how and where fieldwork can be organised. Relations with gatekeepers can either be facilitative, because friendly and cooperative, or the reverse and so obstructive. But even facilitative relations with gatekeepers will structure the research since the observer is likely to get directed to the gatekeeper's existing networks of friendship, enmity and territory. It may not be possible for the observer to become independent of the sponsor, so the observer can be caught in a variety of webs of client–patron relationships in which all kinds of unsuspected influences operate. The observer must find a way of using this to get relevant information. For example, Hansen's (1977) study of a Catalonian village in Spain became possible only when he accepted aristocratic sponsorship and worked with the aristocrat–peasant hierarchy since the assumptions and interactions of village life were based on this.

Gatekeepers will have expectations about the ethnographer's identity and intentions, as will other people in the field. Hammersley and Atkinson (2007) argue that it is particularly important as to whether the host community sees the researcher as an expert (and thus a person to be welcomed because he or she is helping to sort things out) or a critic and very unwelcome. On the other hand, if the researcher is defined as an expert this may conflict with the cultivated naivety involved in being a stranger. Moreover, even with a friendly gatekeeper, the researcher will be faced with the fact that not everything is equally available to observation. People will not, or cannot divulge everything, or may even be unwilling to talk at all. So access to data is a recurrent problem that only subtle negotiations with gatekeepers and careful manoeuvring of the researcher into a position to get data can resolve. This requires patience and diplomacy.

Internet ethnographies pose unusual access issues to consider, which centre not so much on the difficulties of gaining access, but more on the consequences of access that, initially at least, seems almost too easy. Christine Hine explains the thinking behind this in Box 14.4.

BOX 14.4

## ACCESS IN VIRTUAL ETHNOGRAPHIES

What makes using the Internet a sensible thing to do? … answers to this question can fruit-fully draw on a reflexive perspective on the experiences of the ethnographer both online and off-line … Recently, the Internet explosion has provided an apparently natural 'field' for ethnographers. … The accessibility of the Internet attracts ethnographers to a field site which lives on the desk top, and a community which can apparently be joined without complex rituals and access negotiations. This very accessibility, however, tends to focus attention on the on-line community, to the exclusion of links with off-line lives, identities and activities. It also tends to leave unquestioned the status of the Internet as a communication medium and as a technology. (Hine, 1998)

## Field relations and observation

Essentially, ethnography entails a learning role in which the observer is attempting to understand a world by encountering it first-hand. Once access to a setting has been achieved, the success of observational work depends on the quality of the relations with the people under study.

First, the researcher needs to consider the initial responses of people in the field and how to gain their trust. People will inevitably try to place the researcher within their own experience because they need to know how to deal with him or her. If they know nothing about research, they are likely to be suspicious and wonder if the researcher is acting as some kind of agent or spy for an outside body. For example, Kaplan (1991) reports that the New England fishermen she studied thought she was a government inspector at first. On the other hand, if people are familiar with research and so view the researcher in a favourable light, there may be a mismatch between their expectations of what a researcher should do and the eventual research product. This can lead to a challenge to the legitimacy of the research and the credentials of the researchers. For example,

Keddie (1971), although originally welcomed by teachers to do research within classrooms, was denounced later by them when her findings conflicted with their claims not to have streamed pupils in their mixed-ability curriculum. In the face of this, the researcher needs to create a professional front.

But this raises a second issue in field relations, concerning impression management by the researcher. What is needed is an impression that facilitates observation and avoids producing obstacles. This, in turn, will require dress that is familiar to the people in the setting and the cultivation of demeanour, speech and habits that fit. The researcher must be able to create different self-presentations for different settings. Above all, the researcher must establish a large degree of ordinary sociability and normal social intercourse. Without this, pumping people for information can become threatening. Most anthropological field studies show that the researcher must meet local customs and decorum before research can be done at all. Yet the researcher must prevent sociability, rapport and trust from deteriorating into exploitation or 'going native'. This means some degree of frankness and self-disclosure on the part of the researcher is needed. This is not easy. The researcher will have to suppress some things as he or she will have to interact with people whose views he or she disagrees with but cannot challenge.

Rapport, then, is a delicate matter to be decided by progressive initiation into the field.

Box 14.5 lists issued that arise when conducting relations in the field.

---

**BOX 14.5**

## ISSUES IN CONDUCTING RELATIONS IN THE FIELD

- Gaining trust and managing initial responses.
- Impression management.
- Awareness of the consequences of non-negotiable characteristics.
- Dealing with marginality.
- Deciding when to leave.

---

Third, the researcher will not be able to negotiate all aspects of his or her personal front, and these non-negotiable characteristics of identity will have to be monitored for their effects on the research. Such characteristics are largely the *ascribed* ones of gender, age, ethnicity and race, which tend to be institutionalised in society in terms of style and expected forms of social interaction. In the early stages of research, the researcher will simply be like any other stranger in the setting who watches and asks questions to make sense of it. But gradually the researcher will establish a version of himself of herself as a naive participant. In doing this, he or she must retain a self-conscious position in which incompetence is progressively substituted by an awareness of what has been learned, how it has been learned and the social transactions that inform the production of knowledge. Complete participation in the situation is impossible; such immersion would risk going native, and so a degree of marginality in the situation is needed to do research. Marginality is a poise between a strangeness that avoids over-rapport and a familiarity that grasps the perspectives of people in the situation. Thus the researcher can be understood to be a *marginal native*. This position creates considerable strain on the researcher as it engenders insecurity, produced by living in two worlds simultaneously: that of participation and that of research. The researcher will be physically and emotionally affected by this.

Finally, the researcher has to take a decision as to when to leave the field. This can be decided on the basis of the necessary data having been collected. Glaser and Strauss (1967) offer the concept of theoretical saturation to indicate the state of affairs that suggests that it is time to leave the field (see also Chapter 22). As a part of their scheme for generating theory, they say that saturation occurs when no new ideas are generated by empirical inquiry, after the researcher has made strenuous efforts to find instances in the field which might contradict, or help develop further, the emergent theory. Leaving the field will have to be negotiated, as it entails closing relations with participants that may have been firmly established and which they may not wish to relinquish.

## Interviewing

Interviewing has a particular character in ethnography. Some ethnographers, following the dictates of naturalism, argue that people's accounts should always be unsolicited, so as to avoid the reactivity of formal interviews. But interviewing may be the only way of collecting certain data, in which case the researcher needs to decide whom to interview. People in the field may select themselves and others as interviewees because the researcher has used them to update himself or herself on events. Or again gatekeepers may try to select interviewees, either in good faith or to manipulate the research. The researcher may have to accept both because access to data is not available otherwise. The researcher may consider that conventional notions of representativeness should dictate the selection of interviewees. Alternatively, informants may be selected on the basis of their particular value to the investigation: people who are outsiders, naturally reflective, or who have strong motives to reveal inside stories for a variety of personal reasons. Another principle may be that based on theoretical sampling (see Chapter 22): the selection of informants whose information is more likely to develop and test emerging analytical ideas.

Largely speaking, depth interviews are done (Chapter 12), requiring active listening on the part of the researcher to understand what is being said and to assess its relation to the research. The ethnographic analysis of interviews should focus on the context in which the interview occurred. All of the considerations about the analytic status of interview data raised in Chapter 12 apply.

## Documents

Most settings in contemporary society are literate and much of everyday life in them is organised around the production and use of documents. These are a valuable resource for ethnographic study. Official statistics, for example, are documents. But from an ethnographic point of view they are often understood in terms of their social production rather than their truth. Another kind of key document is the official record. Records

are central to work in large organisations and are made and used in accordance with organisational routines. Such records construct a 'privileged' reality in modern society because they are sometimes treated as the objective documentation of it. But like official statistics, such records should be interpreted by the ethnographer in terms of how they are written, how they are read, who writes them, who reads them, for what purposes, with what outcomes and so on.

Yet other documents, too, of a literate society are relevant for the ethnographer. Fiction, diaries, autobiographies, letters, photographs and media products can all be useful. These can be a source of sensitising concepts and suggest foreshadowed problems largely because they recount the myths, images and stereotypes of a culture. But as accounts biased by social interests and personal prejudices, such documents can be used only to sensitise the ethnographer and open up potential worlds for scrutiny. (Approaches to the analysis of texts are described in Chapter 26.)

## Recording data

The typical means for recording observational data in ethnography is by making field notes, which consist of fairly concrete descriptions of social processes and their contexts and which set out to capture their various properties and features. The initial principle of selection in this will be the foreshadowed problems of the research, and in the beginning of inquiry this requires a wide focus in selection and recording. The systematic *coding* of observations into analytical categories comes later (see also Chapter 21). The central issues for making good field notes concern:

- *What* to write down.
- *How* to write it down.
- *When* to write it down.

In terms of *when*, field notes should be written as soon as possible after the events observed. Leaving this to a later point produces the problem of memory recall, and the quality of the field notes deteriorates. But note-taking has to fit in with the requirements of the setting under study, so the researcher must develop strategies for doing this. Buckingham, for instance, who adopted a secret observational role in a hospital by posing as a terminally ill patient, told anyone who inquired that he was 'writing a book' to explain his note-taking activities (Buckingham et al., 1976).

As to *how* to write down observations, field notes must be meticulous. This raises simultaneously the issue of *what* to write down. As social scenes are inexhaustible, some selection has to be made. At the beginning this must be wide, but as research progresses the field notes need to be relevant to emerging concerns. This requires focusing on the concrete, the detailed and the contextual. So the researcher should try to record speech verbatim and to record non-verbal behaviour in precise terms. Notes can then later be inspected in the secure knowledge that they give an accurate description of things. Field notes should also, wherever possible, record speech and action in relation to who was present, where the events occurred and at what time. Final analysis of data will draw on this knowledge of context. With interviewing, audio recording and with observation, visual recording can be used as an additional and valuable aid. But audio and visual recording are still selective, and so is the transcription of tapes. This is partially resolvable by following the now well-established rules of transcription that conversation analysis has produced (see Chapter 24). But to transcribe at this level of detail is really only practicable for very short extracts. Documents can be collected and photocopied but they too will involve note-taking in terms of indexing, copying by hand and summarising. In all, the primary problem of recording is always the same: as literal data are reduced, more information is lost and the degree of interpretation is increased.

Additionally, the researcher should write down any analytical ideas that arise in the process of data collection. Such analytic memos identify emergent ideas and sketch out research strategy. They provide a reflexive monitoring of the research and how ideas were generated. Ultimately, analytic memos may be best assembled in a fieldwork journal which gives a running account of the research.

All data recording has to be directed towards the issue of storage and retrieval. This usually begins with a chronological record, but then moves to the conceptualisation of data in terms of themes and categories to create a coding system that actively fosters discovery (see Chapter 21). This provides an infrastructure for searching and retrieving data, providing a basis for both generating and testing theory. Here, computers often prove useful.

## Data analysis and theorising

In ethnography the analysis of data can be said to begin in the pre-fieldwork phase with the formulation and clarification of research problems. It continues through fieldwork into the process of writing up reports. Formally, it starts to take place in analytic memos and fieldwork journals but, informally, it is always present in the ideas and hunches of the researcher as he or she engages in the field setting and seeks to understand the data being collected.

The fragmentary nature of ethnographic data introduces problems. Checking the reliability of a particular interpretation may be difficult because of missing data. Representativeness, the typicality of crucial items of data, may be hard to establish. It may not be possible to investigate comparative cases in order to demonstrate validity. The generation of theories may not be the main aim of the researcher. The procedures of coding, whereby devices like typologies or careers may be developed, is the start of generating theory from data. Thus, ideally, theories are grounded in the data. Highly abstract theorising, where concepts are not exemplified with data extracts, goes against the spirit of most ethnography.

In the funnel structure of this type of research, the initial task in the analysis of fieldwork data is to establish some preliminary concepts that make analytic sense of what is going on in the social setting. These can arise in a variety of ways. One is a careful reviewing of the corpus of the data in which the researcher seeks patterns to see if anything stands out as puzzling or surprising, to see how data relate to social theory, organisational accounts or common-sense expectations, and to see whether inconsistencies appear between different people's beliefs in the setting or between people's beliefs and their actions. Concepts can be generated in terms of *observer categories* derived from social theory, or from *folk categories*, terms used by participants in the field. But this initial conceptualisation cannot be anything but sensitising, a loose collection of orienting categories which gives a general sense of reference and guidelines in approaching the field.

The second stage is to turn such *sensitising* concepts into *definitive* concepts, a stable set of categories for the systematic coding of data. These will refer precisely to what is common to a class of data and will permit an analysis of the relations between them. Glaser and Strauss (1967), describing the 'discovery of grounded theory', argue that the method for this in fieldwork should be that of constant comparison, in which an item of data that is coded as a particular category is examined and its similarities with and differences from other items in the category are noted. In this way categories can be differentiated into new and more clearly defined ones and subcategories established. So this method, through its systematic sifting and comparison, comes to reveal and establish the mutual relationships and internal structure of categories. An example of the use of the constant comparative method is given in Chapter 22.

The discovery of grounded theory supplies a logic for ethnographic research, helping it gain scientific status. But whether this process of systematisation is an entirely inductive and exclusively data-based method of theory generation, as Glaser and Strauss argue, is debatable. If the role of theory in structuring observation is recognised (see Chapter 2), then theory, common sense and other various assumptions precede theory generation, so grounded theory has a constructive character and not simply a data-based one. Whatever level of systematisation takes place in the direction of theory construction, it is of value only if it offers a revealing purchase on the data.

## Validation and verification

Ethnographic research has produced two suggested forms of validation: respondent or 'member' validation and triangulation. These are both discussed in Chapter 30 so will not be discussed at length here, except to point out some limitations of these techniques. Member validation consists of the ethnographer showing findings to the people studied and seeking verification in which the actors recognise a correspondence between the findings and what they, the actors, say and do. Thus verification is largely reduced to a matter of authenticity. But there are problems with this. Actors may not know things; they may not be privileged observers of their own actions or consciously aware of what they do and why. They may have an interest in rationalising their beliefs and behaviour and so reject the ethnographic account of these, or indeed they may have no interest at all in the ethnographic account. So respondent validation cannot be a simple test of ethnographic findings, but it can be, as Bloor (1983) argues, a stimulus to generate further data and pursue new paths of analysis.

On triangulation, it is worth noting the experience of West (1990), who used triangulation in a study of what mothers said to him in interviews about medical consultations. West wanted to know whether the accounts given in interviews were true or not. He therefore observed actual consultations and compared these with the interview accounts. Broadly speaking, he found the mothers' criticisms of the doctors to be supported. But this method of triangulation has its problems, too. West's validation exercise is potentially limitless, as the next question to ask is whether his observations were true. At most, if different data tally, the observer can feel a bit more confident in his or her inferences, but can hardly conclude that a final truth has been reached.

Indeed, if we apply the perspective of constructionism to ethnographic writing itself (as was suggested earlier in the discussion of theoretical foundations for ethnography), the whole issue of the 'validity' of the method becomes more complex. Ethnographers in recent years have become very interested in this perspective on their own work and have experimented with a variety of reporting forms that attempt a more self-aware approach towards ethnographic authority.

## Conclusion

Ethnography presents both problems and opportunities for social and cultural research because of its largely qualitative character and its essential basis in the participant observer as the research instrument itself. The problems are not entirely analytical but are ethical too. The fact that ethnographic research depends on building up relations of rapport and trust with people in the field, whilst using this to generate and collect data from them, raises issues of manipulation, exploitation and secrecy. These are maximised in covert research, but exist even in overt research because of the degree to which the researcher must withhold disclosure about his or her activities in order to maintain sociability in the situation and to gain access. These ethical considerations also affect the publication of research. There may be political implications that damage the people whose lives have been investigated. Yet ethnography, through participant observation of the social and cultural worlds, opens out the possibility of an understanding of reality which no other method can realise.

## FURTHER READING

Hammersley and Atkinson (2007) is the best textbook-length introduction to doing ethnography. Atkinson et al. (2001) is an edited collection that outlines a broad range of approaches to doing, writing and reading ethnography. Coffey (1999) discusses the researcher's position in relationship to both ethnographic fieldwork and writing.

## Student Reader (Seale, 2004b): relevant readings

29  Alfred Schütz: 'Concept and theory formation in the social sciences'

30  William Foote Whyte: 'First efforts'

31  Buford H. Junker: 'The field work situation: social roles for observation'

32  Barney G. Glaser and Anselm L. Strauss: 'Theoretical sampling'

33  John Lofland: 'Field notes'

34  Clifford Geertz: 'Being there'

35  Martyn Hammersley: 'Some reflections on ethnography and validity'

36  Howard S. Becker and Blanche Geer: 'Participant observation and interviewing: a comparison'

43  Robin Hamman: 'The application of ethnographic methodology in the study of cybersex'

57 James Clifford: 'Partial truths'

58 Paul Atkinson: 'Transcriptions'

59 Renato Rosaldo: 'Grief and a headhunter's rage'

61 John D. Brewer: 'The ethnographic critique of ethnography'

See also Chapter 15, 'Ethnography and participant observation' by Sara Delamont and Chapter 17, 'Working in hostile environments' by Nigel Fielding in Seale et al. (2004).

## Journal articles illustrating and discussing the methods described in this chapter

Andrews, H. (2005) 'Feeling at home: embodying Britishness in a Spanish charter tourist resort', Tourist Studies, 5: 247–266.

Bourgois, P. (1998) 'Just another night in a shooting gallery', Theory, Culture & Society, 15: 37–66.

Forsey, M.G. (2010) 'Ethnography as participant listening', Ethnography, 11: 558–572.

## Web links

Laura Zimmer-Tamakoshi's 'Anthropologist in the Field': www.theanthropologistinthefield.com

How to do ethnographic research – a simplified guide: www.stumbleupon.com/www.sas.upenn.edu/anthro/anthro/cpiamethods

Forum Qualitative Social Research – use the search facility with the words 'ethnography' and 'participant observation': www.qualitative-research.net/fqs/fqs-eng.htm

Methods@manchester – ethnographic methods: www.methods.manchester.ac.uk/methods/ethnographic-methods.shtml

Royal Anthropological Institute: www.therai.org.uk

American Anthropological Association: www.aaanet.org

## KEY CONCEPTS FOR REVIEW

**Advice:** Use these, along with the review questions in the next section, to test your knowledge of the contents of this chapter. Try to define each of the key concepts listed here; if you have understood this chapter you should be able to do this. Check your definitions against the definition in the glossary at the end of the book.

| | |
|---|---|
| Analytic memos | Cultural script |
| Anthropological strangeness | Ethnocentricism |
| Constant comparison | Ethnomethodology |
| Constructionism | Field notes |
| Contextual sensitivity | Foreshadowed problem |
| Cultural relativism | Funnel structure |

*(Continued)*

*(Continued)*

| | |
|---|---|
| Gatekeepers | Participant observation |
| Impression management | Phenomenology |
| Marginality | Reactivity |
| Member validation | Sponsorship |
| Naturalism | Theoretical saturation |
| Naturalistic | Thick description |
| Overt vs covert role | Triangulation |

## ■ Review questions

1 What does making the social world appear 'anthropologically strange' involve and why would an ethnographer want to do this?
2 What aspects of ethnography make it naturalistic?
3 Describe the different roles available to the participant observer and summarise their advantages and disadvantages.
4 At what point in an ethnographic study do research questions become finalised?
5 What sources of data do ethnographers use and how do they record these?

## Workshop and discussion exercises

1 This is a field-based exercise in ethnographic methods using observation techniques:

(a) Choose a social setting where you can act as an observer more than a participant. Examples of suitable settings are: council meetings; student union meetings; libraries; interaction between people providing a service (shop workers, doctors' receptionists and so on) and clients; pubs; launderettes; public transport; waiting rooms.

(b) Record what you see and hear as fully and as neutrally as possible, that is, without making inferences about why people are doing whatever they are doing. Note the sequence of events, the frequency, any patterns you can discern as well as groupings and non-verbal behaviour. Briefly describe the physical setting of the room. You may find it necessary to concentrate on a particular group or person.

(c) Write on-the-spot observations on the left page of a notebook; on the right (opposite) page, write down your own thoughts about what is going on, so that you separate your observation from your interpretation. Write down any difficulties you experience and note any instances of when your observing seems to be affecting the scene you are observing. If you are doing this with a partner, you may find it interesting to compare notes, looking for any similarities and differences in what you recorded.

(d) Then try to interpret what you have seen. You should be concerned with trying to explain what you have been observing and hearing, and to a degree participating in. Your interpretation should try to understand what has been going on from the perspective of those you have been observing.

(e) Consider whether there are any aspects or themes that seem worth exploring further. Discuss what you have learned about the problems and possibilities of participant observation as a method of data collection.

*Some advice:* People beginning this sort of research often have difficulty in seeing the unusual in situations that initially seem pretty routine. To avoid producing a purely descriptive account of 'what happened', try observing two contrasting examples of the setting (e.g. compare an academic library with a public one; compare queuing at a bus stop with queuing in a takeaway restaurant). This can often help you see the underlying rules of interaction that are being used by participants. If you are observing a social situation that is strange to you, see if you can find a person to 'guide' you through it; such an informal sponsor can help by explaining the underlying rules of the situation, as well as showing you how to pass successfully as a member.

2 In Box 14.6 is an extract from the field notes of a practising ethnographer, Daniel Miller, who did field-work in Trinidad in 1988 (Miller, 1994, 1995). These sections of the notes contain records of conversations, observations and other techniques relevant to how Trinidadians liked to view and talk about a US-made soap opera, *The Young and the Restless*, which in Miller's words concentrated 'on the domestic life and turmoil of wealthy families in a generalized American city' (1994: 247–8). In his final research report Miller argues that Trinidadians use their viewing of this programme to express a spirit which they call 'bacchanal', which 'can refer to

[a] general level of excitement and disorder, [but also involves] the emergence into light of things which normally inhabit the dark ... directed against the pretensions of various establishment forms, revealing their hollow or false nature. (1994: 246–247)

Examine these field notes and answer the following questions:

1 Which of them describe people's actions, and which their words?
2 What details of the context of actions and words are given? Are there any notes that suggest what Miller was doing? For example, is there any evidence of his having questioned people?
3 Is any counting involved? Where do the numbers appear to come from, and what do they tell us?
4 Are there any analytic memos, in which Miller reflects on what the observations mean to him?
5 How objective and representative do these observations appear to be?
6 How could notes like this be improved?

---

**❙ BOX 14.6 ❙**

## FIELD NOTES EXTRACT

507:     Longdenville women, both addicts of Y&R [*The Young and the Restless*], since view it daily, say – it's about young people, about relations between rich and poor, tend always to go back to the first person you loved, e.g. in own family elder sister went with moslem boy, married off by parents to hindu man but she left husband, gone back to first man and had child by him.

614:     result of my survey of all media: note 70% watched Y&R, news just less but then nothing else over 30%, asking who watched (I guess regularly 50% women, 30% men).

622:     even panmen watch Y&R.

*(Continued)*

---

*(Continued)*

641:  *Rene*:  I discuss TV with sister, neighbours or with people in the health centre – have to get back by 12 to see it, when my neighbour gets back from her friends where she watches – we discuss, very exciting right now. Where Brad's first wife taken him away but he doesn't know why he's doing it; people who come from America saw it already.

(*Me*: most Trinidadians asked to describe the character of their islands in one word would say 'bacchanal' with a smile that suggests affectionate pride triumphing over shame.)

EY18:  Women talk about Y&R: 'I prefer that, you see it is safer to talk about the celebrities business than to talk about people business, you won't get into trouble, nobody won't cuss you if you say Chancellor was with this one's husband you just won't get into trouble. Although it is gossip won't be anybody's personal life ... but it is just bacchanal, all them soaps is just bacchanal ... even if you don't like what is happening on the show you could even admire their earrings or their pearl necklaces; their hairdressing is exotic ... I would copy Brad's wife although I won't like to have a husband like Brad. I like Cricket, I like Tracy and I like Lauren.' Talking about marriage in Trinidad: 'I find it should be 50–50 not 30–70. The woman have to be strong, she have to believe in her vows no matter what ... that make me remember Y&R – Vickie want her marriage to work but Victor is in love with somebody else, but she is still holding on.'

ET21:  Everybody does watch Y&R, 'when they tell me Mamy they like so and so's clothes in the picture, so I would sit down on Friday evenings and watch it to see the style. I don't have ties during the day. If watch it from TV I can copy the style. The last style copied was a style Ashley had – low cut across with a frill and a mini.' It is a black and white TV so she buy a black skirt, don't know what colour it really was. Copied Cassandra's jacket with the gathers on top; got the T-shirt from Young and Restless.

*Source*: Miller, 1994

# 15

# DOING HISTORICAL AND DOCUMENTARY RESEARCH

Ben Gidley

---

## Chapter Contents

Doing documentary or historical research is not a 'method' in the way that, say, doing ethnography is. Instead, we are talking about using a particular type of data – data generated in the past, stored in archives – which can be researched using a variety of methods. This chapter will show you what kinds of data are available in archives, tell you how to gain access to archives and introduce you to methodological issues relevant to their use. The chapter is intended to give practical guidance around some of the difficulties which those starting out in documentary research might encounter, but also to help you think through some of the conceptual issues around what to do with historical data once you have found it.

## Sources

The first matter to consider in approaching historical and documentary research is the different types of available source material. Each of these can be used in different ways, depending on what our research question is. The types of historical source we can use include primary and secondary sources, and oral and documentary sources. In the first section of this chapter we will see what these different types of sources are, which will also allow us to get to grips with the basic terminology used in this field of research.

## Primary and secondary sources

The most common distinction made between types of historical source is that between primary and secondary sources (Box 15.1).

Primary and secondary sources have different strengths and weaknesses. Just because someone witnessed something, we should not see it as a completely accurate account; the witness might have some particular motive for highlighting certain aspects of their experience rather than others. This might make the primary source 'unreliable', but it remains interesting to social researchers because of what it reveals about the way that the account was produced.

---

■ BOX 15.1 ■

### PRIMARY AND SECONDARY SOURCES

Primary sources are actual records that have survived from the past, which may include texts, such as letters or diaries, or material artefacts such as articles of clothing or shards of bone, visual artefacts such as photographs, audio-visual sources such as film or tape recordings. These were produced in conditions of proximity (in time and space) to the events described.

Secondary sources are accounts created by people writing at some distance in space or time from the events described. For example, a historical textbook, written by someone one who did not experience or witness the events being described, is a secondary source. But it will draw on primary sources, on the recollections or reports of those who actually did experience or witness the events.

---

## Oral and documentary sources

Another key distinction is between oral and documentary sources (Box 15.2).

Oral sources can be used in a huge variety of ways. To give a couple of examples, anthropologists Richard and Sally Price have worked intensively with the oral history of the Saramaka Maroons – descendents of runaway slaves in Suriname, South America – culminating in their book *Two Evenings in Saramaka* (1991), which records verbatim two long sessions of Maroon story-telling, while historian Jerry White, in his books *Rothschild Buildings* (1980) and *The Worst Street in North London* (1986) present a complex picture of the recent history of two tiny neighbourhoods in London. Many of the methodological issues that concern oral history are similar to those concerning qualitative interviews in general (see Chapter 12).

---

**BOX 15.2**

### ORAL AND DOCUMENTARY SOURCES

- *Oral sources* are the memories of people who lived through a historical moment, as related out loud, usually to an Interviewer some time after the event. These are generally recorded and transcribed.

- *Documentary sources* are written sources – personal letters, diaries, scrapbooks, memoirs, legislation, newspaper clippings, business accounts, marriage contracts. These might have been produced at the time of the events described, or some time later.

---

Documentary sources will often have survived because they were kept in someone's personal collection, in a file somewhere, or an archive. There is a vast range of documentary sources, some personal, such as diaries or letters, some official, such as police reports or council memos, some corporate, such as a company's accounts. Some documentary and primary sources have been digitised or put on microfilm or microfiche, or collected and printed in anthologies and sourcebooks. When using these, you should be aware that you are looking at something different from the original documentary sources.

## Public and private, internal and external

Sometimes a distinction is drawn between documents for internal consumption, such as a memo between two civil servants, and documents for external consumption, such as a report those two civil servants wrote for publication. Related to this distinction is whether the document is publicly accessible today, regardless of whether it was intended for public consumption. In this sense, documents can be categorised into four further types (Scott, 1990):

- *Closed*: such as top secret espionage reports.

- *Restricted*: documents which a researcher must get special permission to access.

- *Open-archival*: something held in an archive such as the UK National Archives (NA), which can be consulted by anyone who goes there.

- *Open-published*: something fully in the public domain because it has been published, which today includes documents published on the Web.

In making these sorts of distinctions, it is important to remember that the category into which a document falls might change over time. For example, the British government keeps secret documents 'closed' for a set period of time before making them accessible in the NA. The way the NA works is bound by the Official Secrets Act, and if you are researching politically sensitive topics, such as the IRA or the Communist Party, you may come up against the restricted or closed data.

## Why might I use archival sources?

Social research is often thought of in terms of researchers engaging directly with members of society, with methods such as interviews and participant observation. Archival research, on the other hand, is often seen as dry and dusty work, associated with other disciplines such as history. However, as John Scott (1990) points out, some

of the classic texts in social science have been based on documentary or archive research:

- *Durkheim's* seminal work on *Suicide* (1970) was based on an analysis of official records.
- *Weber's* research on religion that led to studies such as *The Protestant Ethic* (2002; first published 1905) was based on historical material.
- *Marx's* great texts, such as *Capital*, (1967) were based on an analysis of government records archived in the British Museum (see Box 15.10).
- *Florian Znaniecki* used what he called 'concrete materials' in his study *The Polish Peasant in Europe and America* (Thomas and Znaniecki, 2007, first published 1918), including letters home, newspaper articles and institutional records.

There are a number of reasons why you might want to use archival and documentary sources to research society or culture. These are outlined in Box 15.3 and examples of each are given below.

---

**BOX 15.3**

### REASONS FOR USING ARCHIVAL SOURCES

Archives may:

- be the only means of access
- allow a glimpse 'behind the scenes'
- allow for triangulation
- allow us to trace the genealogy of ideas
- provide another dimension to our data
- provide access to marginalised voices and allow communities to connect to their histories.

---

### The only means of access

Most obviously, the archive might be the best or only way of *accessing* the data that exist on your research question: 'Data on the phenomenon you are interested in may simply *not be available*

*in other forms*' (Mason, 1996: 73). There may be no witnesses left alive or willing to talk or available to you.

For example, in my own research, I set out to examine East London Jewish radicals in early twentieth-century London, to find out how they understood their sense of identity and belonging. I originally contemplated oral history interviews, but as I began to focus on a historical period over 80 years earlier, I realised that I would not be able to interview many people involved in this milieu and so turned to archival sources.

## A glimpse behind the scenes

Archives can give you a glimpse behind the scenes. We can think of the insights archives offer in terms of Erving Goffman's analogy of 'frontstage' and 'backstage' identities, which he developed in his classic book *The Presentation of Self in Everyday Life* (1959). Goffman contrasted the 'official stance' of an organisation or team or its members, visible in their 'frontstage' presentation, to their 'backstage' or 'off-the-record' performances. 'Backstage', Goffman suggested, conflicts, contradictions and ambiguities are more often expressed.

An example of this can be found in Clive Harris's work, which draws meticulously on official documents from the Public Record Office, now part of the National Archives. He examined the racialisation of black people in twentieth-century Britain, working closely on the text to trace the emergence of black identities within official discourses. He writes that:

The documentation ... clearly demonstrates the extent to which racism permeated the culture of the British establishment long before the introduction of formal immigration control ... [It] is drawn extensively from government archives only recently made available to scrutiny. (1991: 2)

He shows that even when the official 'frontstage' pronouncements of senior civil servants seemed not to use racist language, in their minutes and memos to each other, when they presented their 'backstage' identities, they frequently used a language that racialised black people.

Another reason why the glimpse behind the scenes that the archive allows provides a useful research tool is that we can see the workings that led to particular policies or practices emerging. For instance, using official archives we can see the discussions that went on behind the scenes before decisions were made, or we can see how particular languages or phrases came into use. An example of this is given in Box 15.4.

Another sense in which documentary research gives us a glimpse behind the scenes is that it can allow us to understand the web of social relations in which social actors are enmeshed. For example, Brett St Louis's (2007) work on the Caribbean intellectual C.L.R. James drew heavily on unpublished documents scattered across archives in North America, Europe and the Caribbean, including letters and drafts of political leaflets, which enabled St Louis to develop an understanding of the correspondence between James's everyday life, his social thought and his political interventions, in ways which are not visible in James's extensive published output.

---

**BOX 15.4**

## BEHIND THE SCENES OF MI5

This example comes from the government files of Vernon Kell, the first head of what was to become MI5, who took the codename 'K', a name said to have led James Bond's creator Ian Fleming to call 007's boss 'M'.

During the First World War, Kell was involved in deciding which foreigners should and should not be interned in camps to protect public safety. He wrote a circular to the police that certain enemy aliens should be exempted from the internment 'because, although subjects of an alien power, they are assumed on racial or political grounds to be friendly' (NA HO 45/19881/338498/2).

*(Continued)*

---

In the Home Office files, we can see a civil servant, Troup, amending this to read: 'because, although technically subjects of an alien power, they have been ascertained to be on racial grounds friendly to the allies and hostile to the enemy' (NA HO 45/19881/ 338498/2).

In these changes, we can see the emergence of a way of thinking that contrasted the 'technical' subjecthood of empires with a 'racial' belonging to nation-states. This way of thinking is interesting because it was to inform the British government's support of the creation of a mosaic of 'racial' nation-states in Europe at the end of the war, and because it is the first time that 'racial' criteria were used in Britain as part of immigration control.

## Triangulation

Many archives provide great opportunities for triangulating data (see also Chapter 30). A government archive on conscientious objectors during a war – such as can be found in the Home Office files of the NA – includes not just the government's view of the issue, but also a wealth of materials that provide other perspectives. There might be, for example, pacifist leaflets, police transcriptions of speeches given at anti-war meetings, clippings from newspapers of different persuasions, notes of delegations made to ministers by anti-conscription groups. Sources such as these can be compared with the official views to provide a more reliable account of the moment. Similarly, when looking at recent history, documentary sources can be triangulated against oral sources.

This sort of approach has been used in sport studies, for example by Symons (2009), whose work on gay sportspeople over the last three decades combines detailed archival research with oral history and participant observation. In health research, historical materials have been used extensively. Examples can be found on the website of the Centre for History in Public Health (http://history.lshtm.ac.uk).

## The genealogy of ideas

Historical research allows us to trace the genealogy of ideas or institutions that are important today. Geoff Pearson (1983), for example, traced the way in which discussions of criminality and violence had been conducted over the years. He was able to question the idea that we are living in a time of exceptional criminality and violence compared with 'the good old days' by examining texts from the past that revealed identical 'respectable fears' being expressed in every generation.

## Adding another dimension

Historical and documentary research can enable you to add a further dimension, that of change over time, to the real-time data provided by other methods. For example, it can add explanatory depth to ethnographic description. This has become increasingly important in anthropology, which, in an earlier period, had sometimes placed the communities it troubled outside time and history, a tendency that was criticised by many anthropologists from the 1980s onwards (Wolf, 1982; Fabian, 2002). For instance, Karen Fog Olwig (1987), an anthropologist who studies the Caribbean, has drawn on archival material from the Danish West Indies to show how forms of social life that were developed during the period of slavery – sometimes even on the passage across the Atlantic from Africa – have left their traces in contemporary social practices, such as funerals, in the region. More recently, the anthropologist Laura Bear (2007) has worked on the family and institutional archives of Indian railway workers, alongside ethnography, to give a fuller picture of the complex histories that shape their lives today.

## Marginalised voices and forgotten histories

Archives are useful because they provide access to voices that have been marginalised in previous historical literatures. Clive Harris, whose work was mentioned earlier, concludes his article on his archival research by saying:

> No apologies are offered for not trying to document … the lives of the victims of racism. That I leave to others. What I have aimed to do is shift attention to those structures of power which have proved so resistant to change, and thereby examine the micropolitics of the different institutions within the state in order to disclose the way in which techniques and practices were codified to secure the exercise of social control and domination. Only in this way can the silences of history be made to speak and fractured narratives restored. (1991: 28–29)

In other words, there is an ethical or political reason to work with archival material. This ethical imperative can be seen, for example, in sociologist Nirmal Puwar's (2007) work on South Asian cinema scenes in Britain where she combined oral history work with her own and her parents' generation of British South Asian people with the collection of an archive of ephemeral materials, such as photographs, to retrieve a history that has largely been forgotten or repressed in official histories of multicultural Britain.

## How to access an archive: practical issues

How you go about using an archive will depend on your research question. In general, though, it is advisable to begin with a *preliminary investigation*. This means finding out about the archives that may be useful in answering your research questions. You can go about this in several ways:

- *Secondary sources* on topics similar to yours will often have drawn on primary sources which you might also find useful. Check their references to find what these were.

- There are a number of *guides to primary sources* available. These range from the very general to the very specific (see 'Further reading' at the end of this chapter).

- Once you have located the archives you want to use, they will have **indexes**, sometimes in printed form, sometimes electronic. As more and more indexes are being digitised, they are becoming easier to search, for instance using keywords or dates (see Box 15.14).

- Major archives such as the UK National Archives publish *leaflets and guides* to the sorts of materials they have.

Once you have conducted a preliminary investigation, you can begin to gather your data. A few practical issues arise at this point, some of which might be obvious, others less so:

- *Find out when the archive is open!* Specialised archives are notorious for having peculiar opening hours.

- *Consider how you want to take notes.* Many archives charge a lot for photocopying or are very particular about what you can copy – this is because of their duty to preserve documents. Many do not allow you to use a pen when taking notes; this is the case in the NA and the Rare Manuscripts room of the British Library, both of which require you to use a pencil. Some provide power sources for laptop computers; others do not let you carry a bag. You might want to consider taking digital photos of key documents, if the archive permits you to. Some researchers use hand-held scanners, although many archives forbid this. If you are using a private room in the archive, you could consider dictating your notes into an audio recorder.

- *Plan timings for your visits.* There is only so much time you can spend doing archival research in one go. If you are looking at handwritten documents, this can strain your eyes, as can working with microfiche or microfilm.

- *Make sure you take a note of the source.* As with other kinds of research, make sure, when you are taking notes or making copies, that you take a note of the source. Where possible, you should use the standard referencing systems archives themselves use, such as the codes used in their catalogues or indexes. This is partly so you remember where you found things, in case you want to go back and to cite when you write it up (you'll regret it later if you don't!), but also as part of good practice in responsible scholarship so future researchers can know how you found things and check how you used them.

Many researchers, when starting archival research for the first time, are overwhelmed by the sheer amount of material available. A short sentence in the index might turn out to refer to a box file bulging with documents; references in the documents to other documents open up rich new veins of inquiry that take time to exhaust. Poring over this paperwork can be enormously time-consuming, and sometimes researchers are seduced by the material, sucked in and pulled in directions they did not anticipate. When conducting a time-limited project, this can be problematic. For example, you may have made a trip to a different town where the archive is located, and cannot spend unlimited time there. And the quantity of data that you generate can then be difficult to analyse and write about. All of this points to the vital importance of two related tasks: preparation and prioritisation. Box 15.5 contains tips on how to prepare and prioritise.

---

**BOX 15.5**

## PREPARATION AND PRIORITISATION

### Preparation

- *Familiarise yourself in advance* as much as possible with what you might find. For example, search an on-line catalogue beforehand, if one is available.
- *Be prepared to join or register.* This may require supporting documentation.
- *Order documents in advance.* Check in advance what the procedure is, and find out if it this is possible, otherwise you could waste a lot of time.
- *Come with the right equipment*, for example, a pencil, change for the lockers or the photocopiers.
- *Come intellectually prepared:* the more you know your field, the better.

### Prioritisation

- *What can you see another way?* For example, exclude stuff you can see online anyway.
- *What can you copy?* Different archives have different set-ups for copying and different rules for what can be copied.
- *Did someone else get there first?* Focus on the undiscovered: it is one of the great satisfactions of archival work to realise you are the first person to unearth a document which makes us think differently about our social world.
- *How does it relate to your research question?* Don't get distracted by things that lead you away from your purpose.

## Methodological debates

In approaching historical documents, we can identify two broad ways of working. These relate to the broad distinction between realism and constructionism that was introduced in Chapter 2.

The realist approach to archival work involves gathering as great a volume of texts as possible and scouring them for details of 'who', 'when', 'where' and 'what' – to use texts as evidence, as a representation of reality. This approach has often taken the documents themselves at face value – seeing them as a research resource. This approach reflects a decision made at the epistemological level (i.e. in terms of the theory of knowledge and truth involved). The problem with it, from an idealist or social constructionist point of view, is as follows: just as ethnographic interviews are never completely transparent windows into present social reality, archived documentary sources are never perfect windows into the past. Rather, they are socially produced:

> People who generate and use such documents are concerned with how accurately they represent reality. Conversely, ethnographers are concerned with the social organisation of documents, irrespective of whether they are accurate or inaccurate, true or biased. (Silverman, 1993: 61)

Atkinson and Coffey make a similar point when they describe documents as 'social facts': produced, shared and used in socially organised ways, not transparent representations of realities (1997: 47).

The social constructionist approach sees archived texts as *topic* rather than *resource* – as realities in themselves rather than a way of accessing some other reality. This approach is not concerned with the accuracy of the descriptions given in the documents, but in their social organisation. That is, how are different discourses (and the different identities which emerge from them) produced?

These different approaches imply different ways of attending to *how* documents are produced. Those who see documents in a realist manner – as a window onto social reality – might be concerned about issues of authenticity, for example. Those who see documents from a constructionist perspective would be concerned, in contrast, to analyse the various ways in which social reality is constructed in documents. We will look at some of these issues here.

## Issues of validity and reliability

If archived texts are to be used as evidence, as they are from a realist viewpoint which takes them to be a means of accessing past social realities, a number of issues of validity and reliability arise. Archives are partial: certain documents are archived whilst others are not. For example, the views of a managing director are more likely to survive in a company's archive than the views of a receptionist, while a managing director's views that come to be considered embarrassing might be shredded. Because of this, it is possible to argue that archival data is insufficiently reliable and valid.

Scott (1990: 6) suggests that we should judge an archived document by four criteria:

- *Authenticity:* is it genuine?
- *Credibility:* is it undistorted?
- *Representativeness:* is it typical of its kind?
- *Meaning:* is the evidence clear and comprehensible?

On one level, authenticity is a key issue for archival research. Documentary sources can, for example, turn out to be fakes (see Box 15.6).

Among the historians who showed that the 'Hitler diaries' were fake was David Irving. Irving came to greater prominence in 2000, when he sued historian Deborah Lipstadt and her publisher Penguin Books for libelling him. In her book *Denying the Holocaust: The Growing Assault on Truth and Memory* (1993), Lipstadt had alleged that Irving had persistently and deliberately misinterpreted and twisted historical evidence to minimise Hitler's culpability for the Holocaust, which Irving claimed was defamatory. The judge eventually ruled against Irving. Box 15.7 shows some comments made after the case was decided. This example points to how seriously we must take issues of reliability and validity if we want to use documents as evidence of some reality that exists outside the documents.

## Producing documentary realities

You can see from the last comment from the historian David Cesarani that he had a slightly different view of the trial than the other commentators. He argued that it was important for historians to take part in public debates, but expressed doubts about translating historical argument to a court of law. He argues that context and circumstance are central to the way that social scientists must use historical data. In support of this more constructionist view of documents, Atkinson and Coffey write:

> Texts are constructed according to conventions that are themselves part of a documentary reality. Hence, rather than ask whether an account is true, or whether it can be used as 'valid' evidence about a research setting, it is more fruitful to ask ourselves questions about the form and function of texts themselves. (1997: 61)

Silverman writes similarly about official files:

> Like all documents, files are produced in particular circumstances for particular audiences. Files never speak for themselves. The ethnographer seeks to understand both the format of a file (e.g. the categories used on blank sheets) and the processes associated with its completion. (1993: 61)

There are three main aspects of archived documents to which we should attend in thinking about how they construct social and cultural meanings:

- The relationships between documents (their intertextuality).
- The genre conventions according to which they are written.
- Their actual material production.

## Relations between documents: intertextuality and genre

Documents are related to each other intertextually in two key ways: there are relationships of sequence and relationships of hierarchy. These are shown in Box 15.8.

---

### BOX 15.8

### INTERTEXTUALITY: RELATIONSHIPS OF SEQUENCE AND HIERARCHY

A relationship of sequence might be the order in which documents were intended to be read or the order in which they were produced. For example:

- a memo replying to another memo
- the 'Matters Arising' section of a set of minutes which refers back to the minutes of the previous meeting
- the sequence in which two documents are filed or archived.

Relationships of hierarchy between documents are not so straightforward, but here are some examples:

- Who in an organisation *writes* a document; to whom it is *sent*; who has *the right* to *correct* it; who *reads the summary* of a document and who *summarises* it; who has to *act* on it.

These things depend on the formal and informal division of labour in an organisation, a hierarchy which is inscribed in the documents.

---

Atkinson and Coffey (1997: 55) use the term intertextuality to talk about the relationships between documents. This term comes from literary theory and refers to the hidden connections between texts, the way texts echo within other texts, whether explicitly or implicitly. The examples of 'Matters Arising' in minutes or a memo responding to another memo are examples of an *explicit* relationship between documents, as would be a citation of a newspaper report in a government file. *Implicit* relationships between documents might include shared conventions or style.

As Atkinson and Coffey note, documents are also often marked by the use of characteristic *registers* or genres, by which we can recognise what type of document we are looking at. We can easily recognise a set of corporate minutes, for example, by the way they are set out – and the same goes for a menu, a trial transcript, a set of medical notes, a diary and so on. To say that documents share a genre is to say that they may follow prescribed formats, or have particular conventions and assumptions built into them. For example, in the minutes of a meeting, 'Matters Arising' always comes near the beginning and 'Any Other Business' near the end – just as the soups and starters section of a menu comes before the list of desserts and coffees. The conventions of documentary genres include not just the order they are set out in but also the language they use. Official documents, for example, often use the passive voice and the third person ('it is felt that' rather than 'we feel') and often avoid expressing explicit opinions, emotions or beliefs. These characteristics of the linguistic register of documents may give them facticity, the sense of neutral, objective truth that we associate with bureaucracy. Another term for this is to say that official documents often naturalise the categories with which they deal, making these seem 'natural' and therefore unquestionable. This is a very different usage of the term 'natural' from *naturalistic* (used to describe the advantages of studying people in their natural settings – see Chapter 14) and *naturalism* (used to indicate the view that the natural and social sciences are unified at the level of methodology – see Chapter 2).

As well as the linguistic register, non-textual elements such as layout also follow genre conventions. To follow the same example, official documents often use bullet points, lists and tables, and rarely use extravagant typefaces – again reinforcing the sense of facticity and authority.

Genre also helps determine what is *excluded* from the text. Thus Casement (Box 15.9) put in his diary facts about his sex life and his daily expenses, as well as his emotional reactions to the atrocities he was witnessing; he did not put these in his official reports. Diaries rarely record the number of times the diarist visits the bathroom in a given day. Menus rarely record the amount of fat or vitamins in a dish, while frozen food packaging is required to. Minutes do not record every comment made at a meeting, but they will record the decisions reached – thus preserving the dominant or prevailing opinions for future archival researchers, but not necessarily the marginalised or minority ones.

---

**BOX 15.9**

## ACHIEVING FACTICITY IN DOCUMENTS

Anthropologist Michael Taussig has worked from various archival sources on atrocities which occurred in the rubber trade in the Putumayo in Colombia in the early twentieth century. He discusses the reports of Roger Casement, the British Consul-General in the Putumayo, who investigating these events, as well as the edited versions of those reports produced by Casement's superior, the Foreign Secretary, Sir Edward Grey. Taussig describes the way in which the publication of stories in print and their repetition in legal spaces 'facilitated shifts in reality involved in the metamorphosis of gossip into fact and of story into truth' (1987: 33). He describes the shift in the mode of description between Casement's informants in the Putamayo, Casement's write-up of their stories and finally the editing of Casement's report by bureaucrats back in Whitehall. Taussig suggests that Casement's report (in contrast to his diary) and Grey's editing exemplify 'what we could call the "objectivist fiction", namely, the contrived manner by which objectivity is created, and its profound dependence on the magic of style to make this trick of truth work' (1987: 37).

Another example of archival research which treats the texts as research topics in themselves and works to unpack the official document's naturalising 'trick of truth' is Karl Marx's work. Marx's use of documents as evidence is in many ways characteristic of how archives can be read critically to research society and culture. Box 15.10 shows how he approached official documents relating to laws regulating factory work.

---

**BOX 15.10**

## OFFICIAL DOCUMENTS IN MARX'S *CAPITAL*

### The documentary material

The chapter in *Capital* (1967) called 'The Working Day' largely consists of a close reading of the body of official documentation relating to the Factory Acts. The Factory Acts were a series of laws passed in nineteenth-century England regulating the length of the working day and the conditions of labour within factories. A key provision of the first Factory Act, which was passed in 1850, was the creation of a small army of Factory Inspectors, who enforced the terms of the Act, collating reports on conditions which were passed to the government. 'Let us listen for a moment to the factory inspectors,' Marx writes.

### Children depicted as units of time

The Inspectors write about workers as 'full-timers' and 'half-timers'. Under the provisions of the Factory Acts, children under 13 were only allowed to work six hours a day, and it is these children who are being described when the Inspectors speak of 'half-timers'. Marx comments: 'The worker is here nothing more than personified labour-time. All individual distinctions are obliterated in that between 'full-timers' and 'half-timers.'

### Constructing the 'working day'

The category of the working day itself, which seems to have a common-sense meaning, is far from natural and obvious, but is likewise produced socially. As Marx puts it: 'The working day is not a fixed but a fluid quantity.' He argues that it was the struggle of the workers to reduce the length of the working day, and the struggle of capital to keep it long, that produced the definitions of the working day that are then inscribed in the law through legislation such as the Factory Acts.

---

When Marx speaks of 'listening' to the Inspectors, he is suggesting that the official texts produced by the Inspectors – supposedly neutral and objective – had a *voice*, a particular register, to which we can listen, in order to produce a critical understanding of the social reality the reports described and sought to naturalise. Marx's method involves taking the official categories, the analytical boxes into which the government inspectors place the phenomena they observe, and shows how these categories are *produced*, shows the human stories of suffering and struggle which shape these categories. The apparently common-sense official categories of 'full-time,' 'half-time' and 'the working day', he reveals, were produced socially, and carried particular cultural and historical baggage which can be traced through the *genealogies* of these terms.

## The production of documents

What Taussig and Marx alert us to is that we cannot take the formats of official texts for granted: they are not *natural* but are *culturally constructed*.

---

**▐ BOX 15.11 ▐**

### AUTHORS WHO HAVE INVESTIGATED THE WAYS DOCUMENTS ARE MADE

- *Garfinkel* (1967) examined the way in which death certificates are written.

- *Sudnow* (1965) looked at how crime records are generated through plea bargaining.

- *Cicourel* (1963) studied the way records were assembled on 'juvenile delinquents' in the American criminal justice system.

- *Silverman* has looked at how a UK local government organisation's selection interviews constituted a file (Silverman, 1975, Silverman and Jones, 1976).

- *Dingwall* (1977) looked at how health visitors produce their notes and how these are filed.

- *Latour and Woolgar* (1979) examined the way scientific facts are produced.

---

We must *learn* to produce documents like these – and *learn* to read them. A number of studies since the 1960s have highlighted the social processes at work in the production of particular types of document (see Box 15.11). These sorts of studies, rather than being concerned with whether the files were 'true' or 'false', have used files to reveal the social conditions of their own production. This sort of work makes us go beyond the actual documents and files themselves to the social context in which documents are produced, filed and archived.

## The production of archives

To understand the growth of archives themselves, it is appropriate to delve into their history.

First, the archive is intimately connected to the law, to the state and its power. Derrida (1996) excavates the etymology of the word 'archive', tracing its Greek roots in the *arkheion*, the home of the 'archons', the magistrates. Official documents were stored in the home of the archons, who had the right to make law, to act as the guardians of the law, to keep and interpret the archive.

Second, the archive is intimately connected with the modern nation-state and its monopoly on law and the violence of law: 'archives, libraries and museums help to store and create modern "imagined communities" … archives construct the narratives of nationality' (Brown and Davis-Brown, 1998: 20). See Box 15.12 for a further elaboration of this idea.

## NATION-STATES AND APPROACHES TO ARCHIVING

[The shared features of archives can be traced to the] enlarged systems of surveillance, first established in the Europe of the eighteenth and nineteenth centuries as states adopted more bureaucratic forms of administration. Central to such systems were practices of 'moral accounting', whereby a state initiated a system for monitoring the activities of its members through the policing of the population ... Administrative records therefore are not, and never were, merely neutral reports of events. They are shaped by the political context in which they are produced and by the cultural and ideological assumptions that lie behind it ....
(Scott, 1990: 60–2)

Third, the archive is intimately connected with the development of capitalist forms of power. Thus, in *Capital*, Marx used government archives to find a wealth of detail on the life and work of the proletariat – but he recognised that the production of these documents, this detail, was tied to administrative practices such as the Factory Acts, which were passed between 1831 and 1853 – that is, contemporary with the Public Record Office, which was inaugurated in 1838. In other words, the production of the documents Marx read was intimately tied to the political will and class interests of the British capitalist state. At the level of the specific workplace, production of knowledge was tied to workplace discipline, to the practice of supervision.

The supervisor thus embodied the authority of capital, and documents representing factory rules and regulations, such as attendance registers and time sheets, became both symbols and instruments of his authority. Supervision, so crucial to the working of capitalist authority, was thus based on documents and produced documents in turn (Chakrabarty, 1989: 68).

Once we think of archives as socially produced within particular historical and cultural contexts, we can start to pay attention to different features of the archive. These include:

- the technologies that are used to produce files
- the way in which documents are filed (their serialisation)
- the way in which bits of files go missing (fragmentation)

## Technologies

Working with archives, it is important to pay attention to the changing technologies involved. Changing technologies of printing, typing and reproduction affect the way in which files are produced – but so did the invention of the ballpoint pen. The invention of carbon paper, and later the mimeograph and more recently the photocopier, mean that multiple versions of the same document can be preserved. Paperclips are a relatively recent invention, and the staple even more so; these affect how files are kept together or not. The shredder has a profound impact on what is archived.

In recent decades, the production of documents has shifted from paper to the computer screen. With the spread of the electronic memo, the e-mail and the electronic diary, increasingly documents may never exist in a paper form; environmental and financial concerns have made the 'paperless office' an aspiration for many organisations, and on-line tools for the sharing and shared production of texts make this a possibility. All of this creates a challenge for those responsible for creating archives and will increasingly create challenges for researchers using them.

## Serialisation

When documents are archived, they are filed in particular orders; we can call this process serialisation. The post-colonial theorist and historian Ranajit Guha describes serialisation as one of the ways in which the archive brings off its appearance of coherence: 'Historians know all too well how the contents of a series in an official archive or a company's record room derive much of their meaning from the intentions and interests of the government or firm concerned' (1997: 37). Richard Harvey Brown and Beth Davis-Brown also highlight the political structures underlying the way that archives are serialised or classified:

> [C]lassifications never emerge solely from the material to be classified since our ways of defining the material itself are shaped by the dominant intellectual or political paradigms through which we view it … Insofar as categorical systems appear to organize their relevant material 'correctly', all their ideological functions are thereby more disguised and, hence, all the more powerful. (1998: 25)

I came across a good example of this in my own research, when reading a Home Office file on a woman named May Peters, the wife of a Bolshevik named Jacob Peters. The changing meanings in a sequence of case notes are shown in Box 15.13. In this file, we can see what Taussig calls the archive's 'trick of truth' at work: hearsay and rumours acquiring the status of fact through sounding like truth, through the use of specific modes of writing and filing.

---

**■ BOX 15.13 ■**

## THE FILE OF MAY PETERS

The file is ordered chronologically in reverse, so that the civil servant consulting it only needs to read the top document in the file, the most recent, and summarise that. With each successive summary, the stories deposited in the earlier layers – allegations, rumours and hearsay – gain the status of facts.

1   In the bottom, earliest, file, from 1918, a right-wing MP, Sir Henry Page-Croft, passes on an anonymous note about May Peters to the Home Office, accusing her of receiving money from the Soviet government, of fomenting strikes and practising free love.

2   The MP's letter, passing on 'confidential' information that was already second-hand (from an 'informant'), was then passed to the Criminal Investigation Department (CID), who found absolutely no evidence for the allegations whatsoever.

3   Nonetheless, the Home Office kept the file, and added press cuttings about the husband, Jacob Peters, which support the myth that he (who was an active Bolshevik in London who returned to lead the Cheka) was 'Peter the Painter', a Lithuanian terrorist involved in a 1911 gun battle known as 'the Siege of Sidney Street'.

4   When, a couple of years later, Mrs Peters found herself in Russia, divorced by her husband under Bolshevik marriage law, she applied to return to Britain, and the file was again consulted. A typed minute from a civil servant this time adds some more allegations, that she was a member of a 'notorious' socialist group 'from which she was threatened for expulsion for immorality' – and adds that she sends her daughter to modern dance classes, which 'can scarcely be taken as proof she has renounced her ways'.

## Fragmentation

At the same time as clerks and archivists arrange files in particular orders, documents go missing, are accidentally or deliberately destroyed and so on: a process Guha (1997) calls fragmentation. In the file on May Peters, for example, some of the police reports which discredited the allegations against her have disappeared, so that we will never know the 'truth' of her story. Fragmentation can come about quite innocently, from the effects of damp weather or war-time bombing, through fires or floods, or through clerical error.

## Digitisation and the Internet

Digitisation, combined with the Internet, has completely transformed the nature or archives and the ways researchers can relate to them. Box 15.1 lists features of the archive that have changed as a result of this.

## BOX 15.14

## THE ARCHIVE IN THE AGE OF DIGITAL REPRODUCTION

- *On-line indexes:* Most archives now have indexes or catalogues which can be searched on-line.

- *Metadata:* or data about data, has proliferated. This can involve the keywords used in indexing something, indicating something about its content or things like the date a document was produced or who produced it.

- *Digitised documents:* Many archives are in the process of digitising their holdings, partly to preserve them (at least virtually) and partly to open up access and make them more usable.

- *Towards the archive of everything:* The almost unlimited storage and sharing capacities apparently opened up by the Internet have led to the drive to digitally archive pretty much everything.

- *Citizen scholarship:* Archival scholarship has been greatly democratised by the Internet, the most famous example being Wikipedia.

- *Copyright, copyleft:* Digital reproduction and on-line ways of sharing material open up legal, ethical and practical questions about copyright. Copyleft initiatives have arisen (e.g. Creative Commons licences which allow people to share materials in different ways – see: http://creativecommons.org).

- *Fakes, forgeries and hoaxes:* Mark Twain once remarked that a lie gets half-way around the world before the truth has put its boots on. Digitisation and the Internet have vastly increased the velocity at which untruths can travel.

## Conclusion

Serialisation and fragmentation, as May Peters' story shows, mean that what we find in the archive are the *traces* of various past events. The Marxist historian E.P. Thompson, when describing his work, spoke of his task as rescuing working-class rebels of the late eighteenth and early nineteenth century 'from the enormous condescension of posterity' (1966: 12). Foucault, whose key works are based on archival research, collected together fragments from prison archives. He wrote of giving a chance to

these absolutely undistinguished people to emerge from their place amid the dead multitudes, to gesticulate again, to manifest

their rage, their affliction ... [I wanted to present] lives that survive only from the clash with a power that wished only to annihilate them or at least obliterate them, that come back to us only through the effect of multiple accidents. (2000: 163).

We can assemble some of the fragments of the lives of people such as May Peters, both tracing the way they were constructed in the archive – through processes such as serialisation, genre and so on – but also by hearing something of their voices across time. Hearing voices across time in this way adds explanatory depth to real-time forms of social research, and it can have a social impact by enabling the users of research to engage with different histories.

---

### FURTHER READING

Scott (1990) is a good general guide and gives a quick history of the UK Public Records Office and of the Official Secrets Act. His four-volume *Documentary Research* (2006) is the most comprehensive textbook on this type of research. Foster and Sheppard (1994) provide a guide to UK Archives. Another useful textbook is Prior (2003).

#### Student Reader (Seale, 2004b): relevant readings

41 Ken Plummer: 'On the diversity of life documents'

42 Martyn Hammersley: 'Qualitative data archiving: some reflections on its prospects and problems'

See also Chapter 3, 'Oral history' by Joanna Bornat and Chapter 25, 'Documents' by Lindsay Prior in Seale et al. (2004).

#### Journal articles illustrating and discussing the methods described in this chapter

Daley, B., Griggs, P. and Marsh, H. (2008) 'Reconstructing reefs: qualitative research and the environmental history of the Great Barrier Reef, Australia', Qualitative Research, 8: 584–615.

Knepper, P. and Scicluna, S. (2010) 'Historical criminology and the imprisonment of women in 19th-century Malta', Theoretical Criminology, 14: 407–424.

Prior, L. (2008) 'Repositioning documents in social research', Sociology, 42: 821–836.

## KEY CONCEPTS FOR REVIEW

**Advice:** Use these, along with the review questions in the next section, to test your knowledge of the contents of this chapter. Try to define each of the key concepts listed here; if you have understood this chapter you should be able to do this. Check your definitions against the definition in the glossary at the end of the book.

| | |
|---|---|
| Copyleft | Metadata |
| Documents for internal/external consumption | Naturalise (as in making something seem natural) |
| Facticity | Oral vs. documentary sources |
| Fragmentation | Primary vs. secondary sources |
| Genealogy of ideas | Realism |
| Genre conventions | Relationships of sequence vs. relationships of hierarchy |
| Indexes to archives | |
| Intertextuality | Serialisation |

 **Review questions**

1   What different types of source material are available to the historical or documentary researcher?
2   What are the reasons for using archival sources?
3   How should you prepare and prioritise when using an archive?
4   What methodological issues need to be considered when using documentary and archival sources?
5   How have digitisation and the Internet affected archives and archival research?

**Workshop and discussion exercises**

1   Consider the research topics listed in Box 27.10. Which ones could be investigated (either wholly or in part) by means of archival research? Pick one of them (or do this exercise for a project on which you are working) and consider:

(a) What kinds of *primary* and *secondary* sources might you hope to find?

(b) What kinds of *oral* and *documentary* sources might you hope to find?

(c) How would you gain access to these sources and what problems might you need to overcome in doing so?

2   Find a local or national archive that will allow you to do one of the following:

(a) Reconstruct the history of your house or home, focusing on its occupants or owners.

(b) Study the socio-economic composition of your street at one point in time more than 75 years ago.

(c) Study a major local event, occasion or institution from more than 75 years ago.

# 16

# VISUAL ANALYSIS

Suki Ali

In social and cultural research, visual and spoken means of communicating have generally been regarded as secondary to written methods. Yet we live in a society where visual images have proliferated and our ways of seeing and our experiences of and responses to visual spectacles are central to our understanding of who we are and where we belong. Vision should be, as Gillian Rose (2007) has argued, distinguished from visuality if we are to appreciate the socially constructed nature of what and how we see. Ways of seeing are not neutral matters of biology, but are structured in various ways that create social differences. Our visual experience plays a central role in identity formation, although this is of course dependent on us being able to see and is an 'ablist' understanding of the role of the visual. We can think of the field of vision as a transparent or neutral space with the job of 'visual culture' being to fill this space. Our analysis of visual culture in all its forms should attempt to reveal this illusion, and to make clear how this space is socially differentiated. In order to do this we need to recognise visuality as open to change over time. For example, technological advances that allow us to manipulate images make the relationship between what we see and what we know increasingly uncertain.

Studying the visual aspects of culture and society have been important to the fields of sociology, anthropology, cultural studies and media and communication studies. While vision and visuality have always been at the heart of other disciplinary traditions such as fine art, art history, drama or film studies, the growing interest from social and cultural researchers more generally reflects shifts in social theory, whereby it has become commonplace to think of all forms of representation as 'textual' in the broadest sense. This has meant that visual images in the form of photographs, films, bodies, sculptures, buildings and so on have all come to be regarded as 'texts' and worth analysing as cultural artefacts that can be 'read'. The expansion of work on and with the visual means that it is not possible to cover all aspects of visual methodologies in this chapter. The chapter will, however, guide you through some of the key methods that use visual materials in research.

The range of visual materials that can be used for research purposes is very broad. Before deciding which to use, it is wise to consider the range of things that might be done with visual images. This is linked to the important question of *why* one would wish to use such materials for research purposes rather than using other kinds of data. For example, one type of image that has proven very popular for research purposes is the advertisement, particularly print-media advertisements. Consider the ways in which such material might contribute to a research investigation. You could:

- investigate the production of the advertisement itself – the author or artist, the industry.

- analyse the site and advertisement itself – its position on the page, composition, hidden messages and so on, so that the research study becomes an investigation of representation.

- assess consumption by the 'audience' for the advertisement. This might involve conducting a focus group to discuss the image (see Chapter 13).

- look at other people's use of visual materials as research and assess what role it plays in the research process, what 'job it does' (Rose, 2007).

Taking these four areas alongside a consideration of *modalities* in relation to the image provides a comprehensive research agenda. Modalities include visual technologies, compositional aspects and the whole spectrum of the social context.

In this chapter we will be mostly concerned with using representations but in addition we will draw on methods (such as focus groups, surveys, ethnography) that are covered in other chapters in this book. Before considering the way images can be used in research, let us consider the kinds of visual materials that are available to you as a researcher, and some of their potential uses.

## Visual materials for research

A convenient way of classifying images is to separate moving from still images. Of course, it is possible to analyse stills from film, video and television, and indeed many people do so. With computer software and animation techniques it is also possible that photographs and drawings can be turned into moving images. In addition, it is important to be aware of possible variations in production between 'human-made' and 'natural' images, and between simple chemical and analogue technologies (video and photography) and digital data. Visual research now deals with increasingly astonishing amalgamations of the two: for example, 'real' images being digitally enhanced and films interspersing images of 'real' people with 'computer-generated' material to name but two. The range of digital data that is produced through digital cameras and videos and through the use of computer technologies is evident in much web-based material. It is commonplace for people to use multi-media such as sound, image, text and so on in one site. This means that we must increasingly attend to intertextuality in work with images (see, for example, Prosser and Loxley's 2008 discussion of these issues). Despite this blurring of boundaries, associated with the growing complexity of technology for producing images, there are nevertheless some methods of analysis that are associated with particular materials and thus make traditional distinctions useful.

## Moving images

Film and television have long been resources for social scientists. The development of film technologies was linked to other scientific advances, and in the early years of film there was an overlap between scientific uses of film and film as entertainment. Visual technologies and the magic of moving images of science were fed into entertainment and popular culture. Increasingly, though, the scientific 'truth' of film has been questioned, particularly in an age where digital technology allows for the enhancement and manipulation of initial footage.

In early anthropological work, *documentary* film was seen as a crucial way of recording the lives of 'others'. As with critiques of written ethnographies (see Clifford and Marcus, 1986), critiques of visual anthropological ethnographies (e.g. Harper, 1998) suggest that these films inevitably recorded a partial version of the truth. The power relations of production and dissemination favoured the anthropologist who could choose what to record and where and how to present it. Although there is debate about the extent to which such films in fact furthered imperial and colonial stereotyping (see Hallam and Street, 2000), it remains the case that these films helped to create and maintain ideas of 'primitive' versus 'civilized' people and making the notion of 'otherness' seem 'natural'.

*Entertainment* films, from Hollywood and Bollywood blockbusters to those produced by small 'art-house' independents, have been of interest to researchers for a number of reasons. There is considerable debate about whether films simply reflect or create problems in society. Films themselves have been scrutinised, addressing such key social issues as gender stereotyping, violence, sexual explicitness and racism. Psychoanalytic theory (see below), as well as other methods, have been used to investigate viewers' subjectivities and spectatorship. Other research may look at audiences.

*Television* is a medium that can be distinguished from cinema chiefly by the relatively private nature of the viewing experience. Many of the interests in film are relevant to discussions of television. Content analysis (see Chapter 26) has been extensively used to understand this medium and distinctions between different media genres has been important. Thus soap operas, television documentaries, serial dramas, news and current affairs all possess their own conventions of visual presentation. In addition to such studies of representation, studies of production and consumption have been important too. Ethnographies of newsroom activities, for example, can focus on how producers select certain images rather than others; investigation of audience response to television, viewing patterns and the like allow assessment of forms of identification and interpretation by viewers. Work has been done with children as audiences in relation to violence, with cross-cultural readings of soap operas, and with gendered patterns of family viewing. *Videos* can also be used by researchers, and interesting work has been done on short promotional films in music that allow an assessment of the interpretive work done by spectators.

## Still images

As with moving images, still images fall into many subcategories which often overlap. An important source of images for researchers has been the photograph. As a visual technology that emerged in the nineteenth century at a time of increased interest in the classification and study of humanity, its early history is associated (like that of anthropological film) with the documentation of 'otherness' so that photography has played a role in producing and maintaining social divisions. Much of this work involved scientists using photography to classify humanity into 'groups' or 'types' and the camera was used in this way by biologists, psychiatrists, anthropologists, philanthropists and historians. In addition to its scientific role, it became the preferred way for the middle classes to document the family. The camera was seen as an artistic tool as well. In fact, many painters bemoaned the 'death of the artist' that photography appeared to herald. There is still some debate today about the status of photography as art, and as a result of technological developments that allow for the digital enhancement of images, we are now entering the age of post-photography (Lister, 1995).

Documentary photography and photojournalism are important areas for research investigation.

In such cases images are often used in place of text, not simply as illustrations to written pieces. Certain visual images have made an enormous impact on public consciousness, recording and helping shape perceptions of key historical moments. It is often key still images from newspapers (rather than moving images) that are said to capture the most devastating events and eras and come to represent them forever. This power of the image means that the way they were produced, how and where they are reproduced, and how they may affect people involved are all areas that concern us as researchers. They reflect concerns with the burden of representation (Tagg, 1988).

Advertising images, as mentioned earlier, are some of the most popular for analysis. Many studies explore the links between consumption and identification with advertising images. By analysing examples such as car advertisements we can consider the issues of identity and social class, gender and 'race'. Advertisements for ordinary domestic products such as soap powders and daily foods are fertile territory for considering representations of families and gender relations. Perfumes and alcohol adverts often highlight issues about sexuality and gender. Adverts in magazines and newspapers are easily accessed and cheap to use. Like television and film, they are a major part of daily life in Western countries and are exported around the world. This makes them a rich source of socially relevant data.

Domestic photography has been described by Bourdieu (summarised by Krauss, 1991) as 'an agent in the collective fantasy of family cohesion, and in that sense the camera is a projective tool, part of the theatre that the family constructs to convince itself it is together and whole' (1991: 19). It is only in the past decade or so that ordinary family snaps have been treated to systematic analysis by researchers. In part this reflects an increasing interest in autobiographical and biographical work (frequently also investigated by means of qualitative, life history interviews – see Chapter 12). Family photographs, portraits, often follow quite strict conventions and even 'family snaps', although apparently informal, also show recognisable or generic features. Additionally, as Holland has pointed out, 'the personal histories they record belong to narratives on a wider scale, those public narratives of community, religion, ethnicity and nation which make private identity possible' (1991: 3). It is this combination of the distinct personal narrative and its intersection with wider social history that makes them useful tools for research. As historical documents, they may also be useful in facilitating memory work (see below).

Other sources of still visual images include painting, drawings and graphics. These kinds of images may range from the 'high culture' of traditional forms of fine art, to cartoons or children's finger paintings. Of course, the lines between these are increasingly blurred in contemporary visual culture, so that 'high' and 'low' distinctions may make little sense (see Figure 16.1).

Archives (see also Chapter 15) can be a useful source of visual materials, sometimes accumulated from family records but also from other sources. Eric Margolis (2000) has looked at archival materials in the United States to explore the ways in which gender and 'racial' difference has been constructed through school photographs (see also discourse analysis below). Margolis looked at two 'virtual' archives that have been used as resources for teachers and students searching for primary source documents for history and social studies projects. What is important about this work is that it shows that the production of the archive itself – the choice of images, location, cataloguing, absences and inclusions – produces biased views of the history of education in the United States. He also analyses the images themselves for the work they do in this process. In his article, Margolis uses only one or two sources, several images as samples, and multiple methods of analysis to provide an extremely rich research project (described in further detail later in this chapter).

**FIGURE 16.1** Mona with burger: high or low culture?

(www.ninjaburger.com/fun/creativity/art/mona-lisa-with-ninja.jpg; reproduced with permission)

## Methods for analysing visual materials

There are several different methods for analysing visual images. These need not be used exclusively, and indeed it is becoming more popular to use a combination or 'mixed-methods'. In fact, many debates at the moment focus on the need to embrace the multiple methods and approaches available to visual researchers. In this section I outline some of the main approaches to this before briefly considering ways of investigating consumption.

## Psychoanalytic theory

This method is often used with work in film studies and focuses as much on audiences as upon representations, though this is approached through the study of representations themselves rather than by questioning members of audiences. There is an emphasis on desire, sexuality and subjectivity, which means that psychoanalytic approaches are interested in emotional states and the role of the unconscious. Particular scenes may be looked at in great detail and the scene's spatial organisation (the mis-en-scène) is subject to considerable analysis. Screen ratios, frames and planes, multiple images, focus, angles, point of view, camera movements and so on are all investigated for the work they do in creating the 'gaze' of both protagonists and spectators.

Laura Mulvey (1975) wrote an influential text on 'the male gaze', arguing that both male and female spectators must identify with male protagonists in order to gain pleasure from viewing. Although there are critiques of her work, Mulvey and other feminist film analysts have shown how films can be 'phallocentric' and fetishise women. Lola Young (1996) used psychoanalytic theory in her work on 'race' and sexuality in the cinema to great effect. She uses these techniques of visual analysis with a selection of British films made from the 1950s through to 1987. She scrutinises how black women are portrayed in the earlier films and looks at continuities and discontinuities in later films (see Box 16.1). Young's work shows the need to make a gendered and racialised use of psychoanalytic ideas and she criticises other theorists for their failure to do this.

Other work in cultural studies has drawn on psychoanalytic theory to analyse still images. Kobena Mercer's (1994) work on Robert Mapplethorpe's series of photographs of black male (nude) bodies is exemplary of the genre. (See www.ocaiw.com or www.masters-of-photography.com for collections of Mapplethorpe's photographs.) Mercer uses the images to explore issues of racialisation and sexuality (see Box 16.2).

---

**▌ BOX 16.1 ▐**

## A PSYCHOANALYTICALLY INFORMED STUDY OF THE FILM *MONA LISA*

Lola Young's (1996) reading of the film *Mona Lisa* shows how it is that even without a significant number of black protagonists, racial differences are maintained. The two central characters are a white, male middle-aged newly released ex-convict, and a young, black, female prostitute. Young argues that the man, George, shows a 'phobogenic' response to black men: that is, he fears them. But he develops a relationship with the woman, Simone. Black people in the film are connected to low moral standards, and despite George's 'romanticisation' of Simone, the relationship fails. Young discusses the commodification of black female sexuality, and the need to control the body of the Other demonstrated in the film. She suggests that Simone's body is in fact only there to service white men, and she is the object of the white male gaze. Simone's sexuality is pathologised in a number of ways, including her relationship with another young woman. Even though George is a working-class man, he holds a position of relative power over Simone, despite both of them occupying a sordid and dangerous underworld. Young concludes that the film should also be understood as arising at the time of Thatcherism, in which a rampant form of individualism and neo-colonial conquering of 'foreign markets' harked back to older forms of colonial and imperial acquisition.

BOX 16.2

## KOBENA MERCER'S (1994) READING OF MAPPLETHORPE'S PHOTOGRAPHS

Mercer's analysis considers a range of photographs Mapplethorpe made during the 1980s. His choice of images include some nudes, some portraiture and a famous image, 'Man in a Polyester Suit', which is a cropped image starting mid-chest and stopping at mid-thigh level. The trouser zipper is open to allow the man's penis to be outside the fabric.

All of these images are problematic for Mercer. He argues that Mapplethorpe facilitates the imaginary projection of certain racial and sexual fantasies about the black male body. The black nude is presented as an aesthetic object to be looked at and this is achieved through 'specific visual codes brought to bear on the construction of visual space' (1994: 174). The conventional nude is the white female body, and Mapplethorpe substitutes the black man. Mercer suggests Mapplethorpe is constructing a white, gay male gaze which embraces a colonial fantasy of black male sexuality and otherness. Sexual mastery is conveyed by the fact that only one male appears at a time, disallowing a collective identity.

Mercer describes how Mapplethorpe uses several camera codes to achieve these effects: sculptural, feminised objet d'art portraiture, cropping and lighting. The latter facilitates a view of black skin as a sexual fetish. In all he suggests, then, that there is a form of racial fetishism involved in looking at these images. He draws on the Freudian concept of splitting used by feminist analyses of gender fetishism and adapts it to discuss the 'Man in a Polyester Suit'. Despite Mapplethorpe's intentions, Mercer argues, the images are problematic and ambivalent.

In Mercer's reconsideration of this article he argues that he may have overlooked the 'polyvocal' quality of Mapplethorpe's work: that is, that it can be read in many ways. In addition, Mercer later stresses the homoerotic nature of the imagery which undermines traditional forms of masculinity. Mapplethorpe did succeed in challenging the status quo of white, heterosexist masculinist cultural space with these images. Mercer concludes that they had significant political impact on 'readers'.

## Content analysis

Content analysis is described more fully in Chapter 26 where its application to the analysis of written and spoken texts is emphasised. I will not repeat the detail of that discussion here. As you will have gathered by now, though, a text in the broadest sense includes more than just words: it incorporates images as well as material artefacts such as clothes, hairstyle, buildings, architectural plans, maps and so on. All of these things both reflect social processes and help construct perceptions of the social and cultural world. Content analysis, then, can be applied to the kinds of visual material discussed in this chapter. For example, a content analyst interested in gender in soap operas might ask questions like these:

- How prevalent in soap opera are sexist images of women?

- How often are women depicted in soap operas as mothers, as opposed to sex objects, workers or mainstays of the community?

- To what extent do women characters become less important in soap operas as they get older?

Cantor and Pingree (1983) studied soap operas with these and other questions in mind. The content analyst might aim to identify instances of 'sexist images' or roles in which women might be portrayed, and count the number of cases in a well-defined sample. The controlled and replicable counting of elements within a range of images should allow comparison and generalisation across a field, so that one could speak about the role of women within a clearly defined population of images (e.g. all soap opera, or American versus Mexican soap opera).

Trends over time can also be identified. For example, an analysis of samples drawn from a particular soap opera once a month from 1960 to 1997 might reveal much about changing representations of women not only in that soap opera, or soap operas in general, but by extension across much popular televisual culture. The point of such exercises is descriptive, but often takes the form of statements either about the accuracy with which the media represent aspects of the world, or about the kind of world to which viewers are exposed.

Box 16.3 describes a study using content analysis to understand trends in advertising. There are many advertisements (indeed, they may have become increasingly important) in which the very small amount of text is memorable and crucial.

---

**BOX 16.3**

## CONTENT ANALYSIS OF ADVERTISEMENTS

Leiss et al. (1990), in *Social Communication in Advertising*, aimed to investigate how certain features of advertising changed over the twentieth century. Specifically, they were interested in looking at how new communicative strategies had altered the ways in which representations of people, products and their relationship had changed over time.

To this end, they took a sample of advertisements for several product types (smoking products, cars, clothing, food, personal care items, alcohol products and corporate advertisements) that appeared in two Canadian magazines, one primarily directed at men, the other at women, over the period 1910 to 1975.

Amongst other things they wanted to see whether advertising had come to rely more on visual than verbal techniques. This is obviously a complex interpretive issue involving questions about the structure and meaning of a vast range of images. The authors get round this by measuring the proportion of space, in square inches, taken up by text versus image in every advertisement in their sample. Of course, the measurement of image space gives a very crude sense of the 'importance' of image versus text, paying no attention, for example, to the structural position (as opposed to size) of each, or of the importance that the text might have in actual readers' understandings of these advertisements.

*Source*: adapted from Slater, 1998

---

One can also think of advertisements in which the text *is* an image: for example, logos like Coca-Cola are both words and images. This illustrates a key tension in content analysis, where objectivity and the avoidance of interpretive ambiguity or unreliability may have to be traded off against in-depth contextual understandings of individual images.

## Semiotic analysis

Semiotic analysis involves a greater reliance on personal interpretations of the researcher and is less concerned with objectivity and generalisability. It is based on the view that the meaning of an image (or indeed of a word, since semiotic theory can also be applied to these) is derived from its *interrelation* with other images. As Slater has pointed out:

> Where content analysis is all method and no theory, hoping that theory will emerge from observation, semiotics is all theory and very little method, providing a powerful framework for analysis and very few practical guidelines for rigorously employing it. Above all, semiotics is essentially preoccupied with precisely that cultural feature which content analysis treats as a barrier to objectivity and seeks to avoid: the process of interpretation. (1998: 238)

Saussure's (1974) structural linguistics forms the theoretical background to semiotic analysis. He argued that a system of signs generated the meanings of linguistic units. Thus, the meaning of a word such as 'flower' does not come from the things that this word describes, but from the relationship which this word has with other words, such as 'tree' or 'vegetable'. Different cultures and languages have different ways of representing the world, so that the English may have many different words for 'rain' (drizzle, fine mist, sheets, buckets), whereas people in a drier country or more stable weather conditions may make fewer distinctions. These then become the mode of thought in which people in that linguistic culture operate, so that it may be hard to appreciate the distinctions made in other cultures and languages. Box 16.4 gives further details of Saussurian concepts and distinctions.

---

**| BOX 16.4 |**

## SAUSSURE'S METHOD: CONCEPTS AND DISTINCTIONS UNDERLYING SEMIOTICS

1 **Diachronic analysis** looks at the arrangement of elements in a system at a single point in time (e.g. the items on a restaurant menu). This is the focus of semiotic analysis and is distinct from **Synchronic analysis**, which examines the historical development of languages, as in the discipline of etymology, and looks at how the meanings of words change over time. This is not of great interest to semioticians.

2 Language (**langue**), the system of signs, *is distinct from* speech (**parole**), individual instances of the use of language resources to make particular utterances or speech acts.

3 Reality is **bracketed** so that the relations between words or signs and the things that these refer to (their **referents**) are treated as arbitrary.

4 A **sign** comprises two components: a **signifier**, which is the sound or the image of a word like 'cat', and a **signified**, which is a concept that we attach to the signifier ('four-legged furry beast that meows'). There is nothing immutable about this relationship, which is purely a convention that members of the same linguistic culture 'agree' to use. This can be seen in the fact that 'tom' can also signify cat, and that 'cat' can also be used to signify 'catamaran'.

*Source*: adapted from Slater, 1998: 238

---

The meaning of a sign arises from the relationship between signifier and signified, *not* from the relationship between sign and referent (which is 'bracketed out' for analytic purposes). Understanding that a conversation about cats is about four-legged animals is based on 'linguistic context' our conversation sets up a relationship for the linguistic elements. Recognition of the conventional basis of sign systems has profound consequences for our knowledge of the world. As Slater puts it:

Not only is the sign I use not determined by its referent, but my sense of what is out there in the world – my sense of the referent – is clearly structured by words and images through which I come to represent the world. Language as a system of difference *constructs* or *produces* our idea of the objective world, of referents. Languages do not neutrally reflect or mirror or correspond to the objective world, but rather different languages produce a different sense of the world. (1998: 239; emphasis added)

Our view of the world depends less on the actual way things in the world are arranged, more on the means that we use to perceive and represent the world. Thus semiotic theory is a social constructionist approach to theories of knowledge (see also Chapter 2).

Although Saussure was a linguist and he intended his system, first and foremost, to be relevant to the analysis of words, it was clear to him that semiotic theory could be applied more widely. Indeed, a variety of objects can be thought of as 'signs'. Roland Barthes (1977a, 1986) is one of the best-known semioticians to extend the ideas of Saussure to a wide variety of objects serving as signs. Barthes went on to consider what he regarded as higher orders of meaning, which he called codes or ideologies. The concept of code involves a further distinction, between denotation and connotation. Denotation refers to the basic factuality of an image for example. Does it appear to be a flower? Connotation, on the other hand, is more interesting: a rose may have connotations of beauty or romantic love. Thus flowers may form a part of more general codes or ideologies. Box 16.5 shows how Barthes applied these distinctions to the analysis of the photograph in Figure 16.2.

**FIGURE 16.2** Salute (*Paris Match*, 1955)

---

**BOX 16.5**

## SEMIOTIC ANALYSIS OF THE *PARIS MATCH* COVER

- *Denotation*: the figure is male rather than female, black not white, young not old. The cap is a uniform, not a matter of personal choice. The young man is saluting someone or something. The caption and text shows us that the magazine is French. This is what the picture is of, at a basic descriptive level.

- *Connotation*: ideological meanings are 'coded' in the image. The picture does not actually show the French flag, but it is connoted by the way the young boy has his eyes raised and focused on the middle distance. At the time, Algerians were fighting to be freed from French colonial rule. The image 'argues' that nevertheless colonial troops are loyal to France, which may be a racially diverse 'nation' but is nevertheless unified in its Frenchness. Thus, the photograph is a sign that acts as a signifier in ideological systems of meaning about colonialism, nationalism and patriotism.

Barthes argued that images like this were a part of 'mythologization', by which he meant something similar to naturalisation: they help create an assumption that it is natural for colonial subjects to feel loyalty to France. Something that is in fact a convention, an ideologically informed, partial version of the world, is made to look neutral and acceptable.

*Source*: adapted from Slater, 1998, describing analysis in Barthes, 1986

Barthes's understanding of the connotations of this image may reflect as much his personal biography and preferences as anything else. One of the strengths of semiotic analysis lies in the detailed analysis of elements of visual images in context; however, one person's analysis may differ from another's. The polysemous nature of interpretive analysis of this sort reflects the fact that different people will have different 'readings' and is a central part of discourse analysis.

## Discourse analysis

Chapter 23 focuses exclusively on discourse analysis, so this section provides only an overview of how it relates to the analysis of images. Many researchers have become interested in investigating the intentions of image *producers* as well as the multiple readings made by different audience members – the *consumers* of images. Hall (1980), for example, argues that consumers sometimes accept but also sometimes resist the dominant messages intended by image producers. Thus producers may encode certain meanings, but consumers will decode them in a variety of sometimes unexpected ways. However, for the most part, it is possible to look for both preferred readings (what the producer intended) and other individual and collective readings made by spectators by using a discursive approach. Although individuals can read texts/images in multiple ways, they often do so by drawing on a range of discourses that are 'out there', so in order to find an image 'racist' or 'sexist' you will probably have an understanding of that term. You may also have different opinions about the same image depending on where it is located and so on. This forms the basis for much feminist media analysis (see, for example, van Zoonen, 1994).

We can see how Margolis (2000) used a broadly discursive framework in his study of history of education archives containing the pictures shown in Figure 16.3. He analysed the historical context in which the images were shot, the way the archive was put together, the organisation of the index, the choice of images, the images themselves and so on. Margolis not only provides the marginal groups but makes visible the invisible category of whiteness. The archive is as revealing in its absences as it is in what it includes.

Margolis points to the framing of the first two photographs in Figure 16.3: in the imposing doorway (a gateway to learning), the white children being carefully posed to create an image of obedience and order. The swords at the boys' sides and white dresses of the girls emphasise the production of gender. Children at Indian schools (the third photograph) were dressed in European clothes and their hair was cut. The photograph shows how overtly these children were disciplined into conforming to white American values. Margolis tells us that these children were not allowed to speak their own language, and were forced to assimilate. By drawing on the wider discourses of ethnic and 'ablist' segregation he can demonstrate how the archive itself, as well as the images contained within it, function to further segregate marginal groups.

## Photo elicitation

Photo elicitation is a straightforward way of using images in conjunction with other methods. It is most commonly used in the context of interviews or focus groups (Chapters 12 and 13). Most often researchers use photographs that they already own or chose specifically for the purpose of eliciting comments on a subject. In this case the choice of images is an important part of the research process. Some authors offer clear guidelines for how to proceed and what kind of questions should be asked.

For example, you may want to use images like the ones in Figure 16.3 in relation to discussions of gender, ethnicity and education. Here are

'School Girls' created between 1900 and 1905 (Detroit Publishing Co., American Memory, Library of Congress)

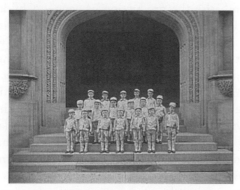

'School Boys' created between 1900 and 1905. Note says 'Students holding swords at their sides' (Detroit Publishing Co., American Memory, Library of Congress)

Very early class of young boys with flags at the Albuquerque Indian School, c.1895 (National Archives and Record Center, Still Picture Branch (NWDNS), National Archives)

**FIGURE 16.3** 'Race', gender and ability in school photographs

some choices and questions you would need to make and ask in setting up the process:

- You could structure your work around individuals or focus groups of same or mixed sex; how would this choice make a difference to the project?
- Would you conduct only one session or follow up with further work?
- What kind of questions could you ask? Would you ask directly about the image or the text or the participants' responses to it?
- What difference would age, sex or ethnicity make to the reading of the image? How could you ascribe different responses to these differences?

This is an interpretive approach, and although you can ask supplementary questions about how someone responds to an image, you cannot know for sure why this is different from someone else. However, using discourse analysis (as above and Chapter 23) you could reveal some of the discursive formations that participants draw on to make sense of the image. Or you could apply a psychoanalytic analysis to the participants' fantasies or desires in relation to the image.

## Memory work

Memory work is often used seen as a form of photo-elicitation but has its roots in a quite different process. Feminists have developed methods that have been used very successfully to encourage autobiographical recollection. Here, photographs taken by interviewees themselves, or held in their own collections, can help facilitate memory work. This process involves not only recollection but also the production of new memories. The kinds of question that can be useful with family photographs are:

- What does the photo represent to you? How do you feel when you look at it?
- Who is in it? Who is not in it?
- Who took the picture?
- What do you remember about the picture being taken?

- What do you remember about the time it was taken, the event?
- Can you describe anything in the picture that is important to you, and explain why? (Adapted from Kuhn, 1995)

Again, these are not exhaustive. They do show that the kind of questions you ask are more likely to engage the respondents with the emotional responses to the image, and are more flexible and open-ended than a more formal photo-elicitation method. The questions are deliberately vague so that the respondents can lead the research processes themselves into the areas that are important to them. This spontaneity can help to reduce the rigidity of the interviewer/interviewee positions in keeping with feminist research principles. Consideration for the respondents helps to minimise power relations between researcher and researched.

## Making images

For students in many areas of the social sciences, the possibilities for submitting images for assessment may be somewhat limited. Practical courses in art and media, of course, require the production of images. But in most cases, although images can be submitted as illustrations, or as part of appendices to show the role they played in the research process, they require further textual explanation. Nonetheless, the process of making images can provide a creative way into researching topics as well as presenting the results of research. On the one hand, the researcher can make images; on the other, research participants can make images.

Creating a documentary is one of the most obvious ways a researcher can produce images for research purposes. It can be that the researcher sets out to make a visual record of an event, situation or process. With colleges and universities providing technologies, it is possible to make a film or video as well as photographs. However, you could ask research participants to do the same, and in this way would get a different perspective of the same thing. British television is now saturated with the 'video diary', which purports to give participants a 'say' in programmes. Ironically of course, as with 'reality television', what we as viewers get to see is a highly edited version of the whole film and so meaning can still be controlled by the producers. This is something to be aware of when working with participants in your research. Another factor to consider is time and cost. Making films and videos and processing photographs can take a lot of time in the post-production phase, time that needs to be generously factored into the overall project. Nonetheless, this can be a very rewarding way of working.

Rather than using existing images for photo elicitation, you can ask people to create their own images, perhaps by drawing, painting, photographing or choosing to create images from a series of other images (collage). This is a fairly simple and cheap way of encouraging research participants to become creatively involved in the research. Getting participants to make photographs is sometimes called photo-voice, and is often used in conjunction with photo-elicitation. There are numerous examples of this kind of work with children, and examples are given in Box 16.6.

---

**BOX 16.6**

### GETTING CHILDREN INVOLVED IN PRODUCING VISUAL IMAGES FOR RESEARCH

My own research with children (Ali, 2003) involved a number of visual methods. One of them required the children, aged 8–11 years old, to take pictures with throw-away cameras. The children used the cameras to show what 'family' and 'home' meant to them. In many cases, the results were not as expected.

*(Continued)*

I accumulated numerous pictures of objects rather than people. These included some of doors, cars, gardens, pets and so on. By using a form of memory work with the children I still accumulated a fascinating wealth of data. The children reported enjoying using the cameras and that they felt they had some role in the research process.

The Artlab site is a multimedia site hosted by a group working at the University of Westminster using creative research methods. One of these involved children making videos about the environment. You can find a lot of information on this at their website: www.artlab.org.uk/videocritical/.

The three maps shown in Figure 16.4 come from a project (Grady, 2008) which asked college students to map their room layouts. The students provided an inventory of the possessions displayed in the map, photographs of three 'favourite things', how these things were obtained and why

Student Map 1

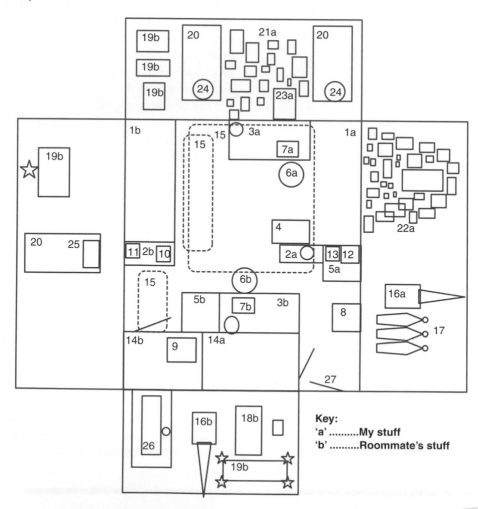

Key:
'a' ..........My stuff
'b' ..........Roommate's stuff

Student Map 2

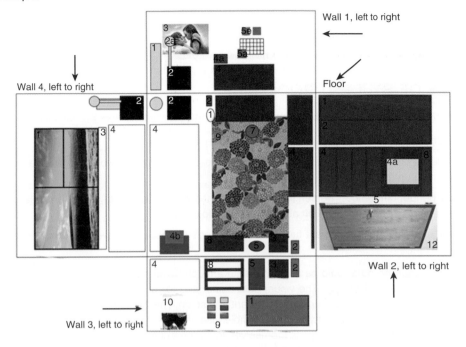

Student Map 3

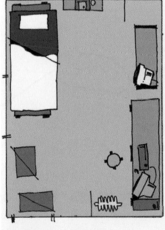

FIGURE 16.4   Student maps of their rooms at Wheaton College, MA (Grady, 2008)

they matter. We can see that the participants went to some trouble with these maps and produced some fascinating images. In Box 16.7, John Grady discusses some of the ways of analysing this data.

---

BOX 16.7

## ANALYSIS OF STUDENT ROOM MAPS

John Grady (2008) suggests that you can draw some general conclusions from this visual data:

1   An easy shared aesthetic value with roommates (if they have one).

2   Most students produced a 'shrine' for their valuable possessions which evolves over time to include their current situation.

3   There are gender differences: women valuing things that are associated with people and relationships, while men display possessions such as technological toys.

4   Generally, students' most important functional furnishings are beds! However, laptops are becoming more important.

Grady also says that the data could be used to create a much richer picture of people's relationships to private space and material objects. The visual data could also tell us much more about their personal relationships, views on issues they think are important and so on. The method could be used with a range of age groups in different settings. In fact, this example also shows us the multiple layers to relevance of the visual – from the artefacts and objects themselves to the production of image, the discussion of both and the further representation of these in the research.

---

Grady's maps contrast strongly with the map shown in Figure 16.5. This image comes from research conducted by Jon Prosser and Andrew Loxley (2007). The map of friendships was produced by a young girl who is on the autistic spectrum, has learning disabilities and speech limitations. They argue that this simple image says a great deal, not least about the trust established within the research process. They say that the graphical-elicitation method along with other sensory methods has a particular power for work with those who do not readily access experience through words. This image is no less a rich source of data than the complex and sophisticated ones produced by the students. This kind of method has a long history in other social and life sciences, such as psychology, but can be useful to sociological and cultural researchers as well.

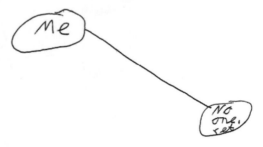

**FIGURE 16.5** 'Me and No-one Yet'

## Visual ethics

Finally, it is important to note that using visual methods can throw up some particular ethical issues. Obviously if you use images that show people, places and things, questions of confidentiality, anonymity and consent are particularly acute. For example, you may gain consent to work with a person who brings in family photographs, but when it comes to showing the image as part of a project, or in a publication or exhibition, you would need permission of the other people in the image to use it. The issue of copyright is also important when using found images, and legal questions about filming and photographing in public places are important. It is crucial that you consider these aspects of visual ethics very carefully when beginning your research (see also Chapter 5 on ethics).

## Conclusion

Many of the methodological considerations that concern the use of visual images in social and cultural research are the same as they are for other kinds of research material. This chapter has sought to give you a guide to some of the main ways in which researchers have found it helpful to incorporate such materials in their work. Visual research has, historically, played a secondary role to research involving talk, text and numbers, but is growing in importance. As you can see, there are many different approaches to researching visual culture and using visual methodologies, and the complexity can be daunting. If you combine this introductory account with some of the recommended further reading, you may find yourself re-orienting your own research plans towards exploiting more fully the potential of visual methods.

## FURTHER READING

Rose (2007) and Pink (2007) both provide good general outlines of visual methodologies. The journals *Visual Studies* and the *Journal of Visual Culture* both engage with the whole range of visual methods. Chandler (2007) gives a good introduction to semiotic analysis. Knowles and Sweetman (2004) is a collection of writing on the possibilities of visual sociology emphasising a reflexive approach. Jon Prosser's (1998) collection presents a good range of essays on image-based research. Leiss et al. (1990) provide an excellent comparison and outline of both semiotic and content analysis, showing the application of this to the study of advertisements. Wiles et al. (2008) is a good overview of visual ethics with practical suggestions of managing ethical issues and further resources.

### Student Reader (Seale, 2004b): relevant readings

40 John Collier Jr and Malcolm Collier: 'Principles of visual research'

50 William Leiss, Stephen Kline, Sut Jhally: 'Semiology and the study of advertising'

See also Chapter 26, 'Visual methods' by Sarah Pink in Seale et al. (2004)

### Journal articles illustrating and discussing the methods described in this chapter

Harrison, B. (2002) 'Seeing health and illness worlds – using visual methodologies in a sociology of health and illness: a methodological review', Sociology of Health & Illness, 24 (6): 856–872.

Keller, C., Fleury, J. and Rivera, A. (2007) 'Visual methods in the assessment of diet intake in Mexican American women', Western Journal of Nursing Research, 29: 758–773.

Woodward, S. (2008) 'Digital photography and research relationships: capturing the fashion moment', Sociology, 42: 857–872.

*(Continued)*

*(Continued)*

## Web links

Methods@manchester – visual/sound methods: www.methods.manchester.ac.uk/methods/VisualSound.shtml

'Introducing Visual Methods' by Jon Prosser and Andrew Loxley: http://eprints.ncrm.ac.uk/420/

'Semiotics for beginners' by Daniel Chandler (article): www.aber.ac.uk/media/Documents/S4B/semiotic.html

International Visual Sociology Association: www.visualsociology.org

British Sociological Association Visual Sociology Study Group: www.visualsociology.org.uk

Software for anonymising visual images: www.yowussup.com/pixelating-images.php and www.virtualdub.org and http://compression.ru/video/cartoonizer/index_en.html

Visual Anthropology resources: www.visualanthropology.net

Manchester eResearch Centre: www.merc.ac.uk

## KEY CONCEPTS FOR REVIEW

Advice: Use these, along with the review questions in the next section, to test your knowledge of the contents of this chapter. Try to define each of the key concepts listed here; if you have understood this chapter you should be able to do this. Check your definitions against the definition in the glossary at the end of the book.

| | |
|---|---|
| Bracketing | Polysemy |
| Codes | Post-photography |
| Consumption, production and representation | Preferred readings |
| Denotation and connotation | Referents |
| Diachronic vs. synchronic analysis | Signifier and signified |
| Encoding and decoding | Signs |
| Langue and parole | Social constructionism |
| Media genres | Text |
| Mis-en-scène | Intertextuality |
| Photo elicitation | Visual ethics |
| Photo-voice | Visuality |

## Review questions

1 Describe different types of moving and still images and explain how they can be used for research purposes.

2 What are the key characteristics of (a) psychoanalytic theory, (b) content analysis and (c) semiotics when used to analyse visual images?

3　How can visual images be analysed using discourse analysis?

4　How would you collect material relevant to a research study using photo-elicitation?

5　What are the different ways in which (a) a researcher and (b) other participants in a research project can make visual images for a research investigation?

6　What ethical issues are specific to visual research?

## Workshop and discussion exercises

1　In this exercise you will do a semiotic analysis for which you will need to have collected a number of advertisements featuring women. For instance, select from a women's magazine all the advertisements for perfume. The overall concern is to gain knowledge of how meanings about gender are used, organised and produced within visual texts. For example, questions you might ask are: How are women portrayed? How is sexual difference represented? How are relationships between men and women depicted? Use semiotic concepts (*sign, signifier, signified, connotation, denotation*) to consider the following questions for each image (these are suggestions):

(a) What are the elements of the sign (the advertisement)? Look at images of people, settings, products, written text. Consider what they *signify*: what kinds of meanings and associations do they bring into the image? What kinds of codes of meaning do they draw on? How are these elements organised and related to each other (do they support or contradict each other, do they comment on each other)?

(b) How are the different meanings in the text related to the product advertised, and what meaning is thereby given to the product?

(c) Is there an overall ideological structure of meaning which emerges from the advertisement (e.g. what conclusions about gender do you think the advert leads the reader to)? How are other kinds of social difference such as 'race', class and sexualities intersecting with gender?

(d) In comparing the different advertisements, what can you infer about the range of possible constructions of gender available within advertising?

You can apply this approach to other types of image too – such as images of children in clothes catalogues.

2　Consider each of the following research projects:

(a) An investigation of communication in medical consultations.

(b) A social history project about experiences of wartime.

(c) A study of children's experiences of play.

(d) A study of far right ideology.

For each, consider what sources of visual images would be relevant for such a project, how they would be collected, how you would analyse them, and consider the ethical issues that may arise and how these might be addressed.

# 17

# SECONDARY ANALYSIS AND OFFICIAL STATISTICS

## Clive Seale

Collecting data for social research can take a lot of time and money. Frequently data sets, both qualitative and quantitative, are analysed by their original investigators for certain purposes, but the researchers then move on to other projects. In the past a lot of these original materials were simply thrown away. Fortunately, though, data archives now exist in a number of countries to preserve materials so that other researchers can use them – often for purposes unimagined by the original researchers. The main advantage of this, of course, is that the effort that went into assembling the materials does not have to be repeated: research can begin at the analysis stage. As well as such secondary analysis by other researchers, data archives have other uses too. This chapter gives a guide to using such resources and will assess the advantages and disadvantages of different approaches to the use of archived data.

## Data archives

Such archives exist in a number of countries and most are now easily accessible via the Web. In many cases data can be downloaded from websites in forms readable by standard software packages such as SPSS or NVivo (see Chapters 18–20). In some other cases, though, immediate open access would violate promises made to research participants about confidentiality, so certain paperwork procedures are necessary. Sometimes, too, the supply of data may incur small charges to cover expenses of, say, copying to a CD and posting to the researcher. The web links listed at the end of this chapter are to popular data archives and sites offering information on how to find out about others.

## Official statistics and survey data

A huge range of statistical data sources are available through data archives. These are often derived from surveys done by central government agencies, though researchers from other organisations – such as opinion polling agencies, or academic researchers based in universities – also deposit their data in archives. Box 17.1 lists some of the major surveys available through the UK Data Archive.

---

**BOX 17.1**

### MAJOR SURVEYS IN THE UK DATA ARCHIVE AT WWW.ESDS.AC.UK

- Annual Population Survey
- British Crime Survey
- British Social Attitudes
- British Election Studies
- British Household Panel Survey
- Census of Great Britain
- Families and Children Study
- Family Resources Survey
- General Household Survey/General Lifestyle Survey
- Great Britain Historical Database, 1841–1939
- Health Survey for England
- IEA (International Energy Agency) World Energy Statistics and Balances
- Labour Force Survey
- Millennium Cohort Study
- National Child Development Study
- National Food Survey
- National Travel Survey
- OECD Education Statistics
- Young People's Social Attitudes
- Workplace Employee Relations Survey
- World Bank World Development Indicators

---

A survey that is particularly heavily used is the General Household Survey (GHS), now known as the General Lifestyle Survey, and an exploration of this will show you how you can find out more about survey data available in archives.

If you are planning a study on a particular subject and are looking for available data sets, it is important to know whether a particular survey contains relevant information. Information about the coverage of archived surveys is normally available on the archive's website. In the case of the GHS, the following summary information is available on the UK Data Archive website:

> The General Household Survey (GHS) is a continuous national survey of people living in private households, conducted on an annual basis by the Office for National Statistics (ONS). The main aim of the survey is to collect data on a range of core topics, covering household, family and individual information. This information is used by government departments and other organisations for planning, policy and monitoring purposes and to present a picture of households, family and people in Great Britain ... The GHS started in 1971 and has been carried out continuously since then, except for breaks in 1997–1998 when the survey was reviewed and 1999–2000 when the survey was redeveloped. (www.esds.ac.uk/government/ghs)

Clearly, then, it is going to be possible to compare trends over time, going back to 1971, if we examine several years of this survey. It is a very large survey, beyond the resources of most researchers to carry out on their own, which makes it an attractive prospect. But the questions asked, and the way they are asked, may not suit our way of seeing our research problem. Clearly, we need to find out more about the actual questions used. It is possible to download full documentation for the GHS questionnaires, including information about how answers were coded and entered onto the computer, from the archive's website. Alternatively, another website exists that is an invaluable guide to UK government surveys: the *Survey Question Bank* (http://surveynet.ac.uk/sqb) is a resource designed for a variety of purposes (including the provision of ready-made items for questionnaires), but also containing the information we need. The full questionnaire for each year of the GHS is reproduced on their website in a downloadable form.

It can also help to see what other researchers have done with the GHS data sets, and information about this is also available. Over 100 publications by secondary analysts of the GHS are listed on the Archive's website. Box 17.2 shows just four of these, covering issues concerning sport, binge drinking and sexually transmitted infections, caring for elderly parents, and women in the labour market. Further exploration of these articles, books and reports is of great value in evaluating the potential of the data sets. (Further examples of journal articles reporting studies that used archived data are given at the end of the chapter.)

---

**BOX 17.2**

## FOUR PUBLICATIONS USING THE GHS DATA SETS

Downward, P. and Riordan, J. (2007) 'Social interactions and the demand for sport: an economic analysis', Contemporary Economic Policy, 25 (4): 518–537.

Harkness, S., Machin, S. and Waldfogel, J. (1997) 'Evaluating the pin money hypothesis: the relationship between women's labour market activity, family income and poverty in Britain', Journal of Population Economics, 10 (2): 137–158.

Henz, U. (2009) 'Couples' provision of informal care for parents and parents-in-law: far from sharing equally?' Ageing & Society, 29 (3): 369–395.

Standerwick, K., Davies, C., Tucker, L. and Sheron, N. (2007) 'Binge drinking, sexual behaviour and sexually transmitted infection in the UK', International Journal of STD and AIDS, 18: 810–813.

While this example has concentrated on a single data set in a particular archive, you will find that quite similar procedures for discovering more about data sets are available through other archives. At the University of Michigan archive (www.icpsr. umich.edu), which I visited for about five minutes between writing this sentence and the last one, I found a data set on the grim topic of 'Capital punishment in the United States, 1973–2008', for example. The description said this:

> This data collection provides annual data on prisoners under a sentence of death and prisoners whose offense sentences were commuted or vacated during the period 1973–2008. Information is supplied for basic sociodemographic characteristics such as age, sex, education, and state of incarceration. Criminal history data include prior felony convictions for criminal homicide and legal status at the time of the capital offense. Additional information is available for inmates removed from death row by year-end 2008 and for inmates who were executed. (www.icpsr.umich.edu/icpsrweb/ICPSR/studies/27982/detail)

I discovered that I could download both the data set and the 'codebook' that describes the original questions and their variables if I filled in a form that had to be approved by the archive managers.

On the other hand, if I wanted some data right now, I could download an earlier version of the data set without needing to fill in a form (for cases between 1973 and 1999, for example). If I wanted, I could begin my analysis now, using SPSS, by simply clicking on the downloaded data file.

## Qualitative data archives

Archives of statistical data are well established, but there is also a growing trend towards the creation of qualitative data archives in a number of countries. The Qualitative Data Archival Resource Centre (Qualidata) was established at the University of Essex in 1994, later becoming a part of the Economic and Social Data Service (ESDS) which also archives quantitative data sets. At last count (December 2010), Qualidata displayed details of 330 data sets on its website. Other archives containing qualitative social research data include the Finnish Social Science Data Archive and the Life-Course Archive in Germany. There are links on the Qualidata website to qualitative data archives in Finland, Northern Ireland, Germany, France and Switzerland. In the USA a leading archive of this sort is the Henry A. Murray Research Archive; Box 17.3 shows descriptions from the archive of just two of the many qualitative studies deposited there.

---

**❙ BOX 17.3 ❚**

## TWO QUALITATIVE STUDIES ARCHIVED AT THE HENRY A. MURRAY RESEARCH ARCHIVE

### Antecedents of Artistic Success: A Study of the Early Lives of Women Visual Artists (1978: Nancy Wilton)

This study examined the early development and family backgrounds of ... female visual artists, [differentiating] the more successful from the less successful artists. ... Data were collected in a personal interview session with each participant ... [including] ... a personal data questionnaire, which included typical background and demographic items [and] ... an in-depth interview, which included sections concerning recollections of childhood activities and interests, parents' child-rearing techniques, and the participant's present life situation.

*(Continued)*

---

**Abortion and the Politics of Motherhood (1980: Kristen Luker)**

The purpose of this study was to explore factors influencing the attitudes of pro-choice and anti-abortion activists and to weigh individual commitments to the abortion debate. The study examines the values and moral beliefs of activists on both sides of the abortion issue. Both pro-choice and anti-abortion activists were interviewed, including men and women between the ages of 19 and 73.

Although qualitative data archives often contain data in electronic form, many studies are only available through other means – particularly older studies. Thus a secondary analyst may need to travel to consult original paper documentation, or view and listen to videotapes or audiotapes. This is in part because qualitative data can take many forms (such as videotapes) that may not be easily translated into another medium, but also because electronic analysis of qualitative data only became feasible and popular from the mid-1980s onwards, whereas the analysis of statistical data with computers started much earlier than this. Early generations of qualitative researchers therefore had no need to store data in electronic form.

An example of this is a study by Professor Hilary Wainwright, deposited in the UK Qualidata archive. This concerned events surrounding the 1984–1985 miners' strike in the UK. The research material is described as arising

> from the depositor's personal involvement with organisations supporting striking miners and their families, including 'Women Against Pit Closures' and 'Miners and Families

Christmas Appeal'. The deposit provides information on the development of grassroots organisations and the level of public support for miners and includes news-paper cuttings, reports about pit closures, correspondence and organisations' own literature (pamphlets and newspapers). (www.esds.ac.uk/qualidata/news/virtualdata.asp)

To study this, a researcher must consult the original files, housed at the National Museum of Labour History in Manchester.

On the other hand, another data set in this archive contains some transcripts of qualitative interviews in electronic form. These were done in the 1970s by Paul Thompson, a founder of the archive, for a study of everyday life in Edwardian Britain (1901–1918). They are retrievable either as whole transcripts of each interview or as thematic sections taken from each of several interviews. Themes include topics such as 'School', 'Marriage' or 'Politics'. Box 17.4 shows extracts from two interviews in which different respondents describe the role that meat had played in their diets as children.

**BOX 17.4**

## EXTRACTS FROM 'EDWARDIANS ONLINE' AT QUALIDATA: TALKING ABOUT FAMILY MEALS

**Respondent 1**

Well – never really did have a lot of meat you know, 'cos she'd make what I – we called a great – a big meat pud – pudding, well there was more pudding than there was meat.

Oh we were very lucky with meat. Of course she was a woman who would get stewing beef, rather than steaks, I've known her to get stewing beef for us and make – and rabbit we've had hundreds of rabbits. Of course you can make such good meals, and she was a good cook. She'd either stew a rabbit and make broth and then mince the rabbit up and make sandwiches for your tea, out of it, and perhaps have broth and vegetables for dinner. ... But she did used to have a piece of beef, you know, something like that, occasionally. But we didn't have it very often but I know when she wanted to get me father a bit of something nice she – I've gone across to the butcher, he used to live opposite, almost opposite to us, for a quarter of beefsteak, very tender please. A quarter of beefsteak! That would be me father's. Ours, we've done with these beef soups and stews, but I suppose she'd think he'd get sick of that all the time. She'd done him plenty of vegetables with it. We've lived very well considering we had a big family and not much money.

## Using archived data

Corti and Thompson (2004), in an account of the uses of archived qualitative data that could equally be applied to statistical data, list six main uses for such materials (Box 17.5).

---

**BOX 17.5**

### SIX USES FOR ARCHIVED QUALITATIVE DATA

1 *Description*: For example, a study of the City of London business district (Kynaston, 2001) drew on interviews done by other researchers (Courtney and Thompson, 1996) for accounts of working lives. This is rather similar to the use made by historians of data archives (see Chapter 15).

2 *Comparative research, re-study or follow-up*: For example, Franz et al. (1991) used data in the Henry A. Murray Research Archive to follow up the children of mothers interviewed in 1951 about their child-rearing practices, comparing this later sample with the earlier one.

3 *Re-analysis or secondary analysis*: For example, Fielding and Fielding (2000) reanalysed data collected by Cohen and Taylor (1972) on men in long-term imprisonment, identifying new themes in the material.

4 *Research design and methodological advancement*: For example, the interview guides of other researchers investigating similar topics can assist a researcher's own development of an interview; the Survey Question Bank (see http://surveynet.ac.uk/sqb/) can be used to find questions that have worked well in indicating particularly difficult concepts.

5 *Verification:* If a study makes important claims, other researchers can examine its original data to assess the evidence in support of those claims (see the discussion of auditing in Chapter 30).

6 *Teaching and learning:* Examining original research materials can be an important resource in learning how to do research. The 'Edwardians Online' (Box 17.4) project has been designed with this purpose in mind. In the field of statistical analysis, special 'teaching data sets' have been prepared from subsets of GHS data, together with suggested lines of inquiry, available from the UK Data Archive.

The focus of the present chapter is on secondary analysis, but it is worth saying a little about the use of data sets for 'verification', since some of the problems with this raise important issues for secondary analysts as well. Hammersley (1997) has identified these in relation to archived qualitative data, though once again his discussion has some relevance to statistical analysis too. Replication is difficult in qualitative research – probably more so than in research using experimental designs and quantitative data – since time often elapses between study and re-study of a setting in which social change takes place. Another reason for such difficulty is the differing perspective, interests and characteristics of the researcher on each occasion which, in qualitative research, often leads to researchers 'seeing' different things in a social setting. For example, a man studying childbirth in some cultures would simply not get access to certain events that a woman might be allowed to witness.

As a result, auditing or 'peer review' (see Chapter 30) has been proposed as a way of generating trust in a study's findings. Here, the original researcher records as much as possible about the methods, decisions and data collected in a study. This body of material is then inspected by other researchers not involved in the project to see whether the links made between claims and evidence seem good. Clearly data and other materials deposited in archives could constitute such an 'audit trail'.

Hammersley, though, points out problems with this use of archived qualitative data. In qualitative research in particular, he argues that there is a great deal of room for argument about what counts as adequate evidence for a claim. Additionally, a lot of decisions made by researchers go unrecorded. One researcher, writing about anthropological field notes, has argued that

[field notes are] … the anthropologist's most sacred possession. They are personal property, part of a world of private memories and experiences, failures and successes, insecurities

and indecisions … To allow a colleague to examine them would be to open a Pandora's box. (Bond, 1990: 275)

Hammersley feels that if researchers are aware that their personal diaries and log books, as well as records of data, are likely to be scrutinised by outsiders, they will be 'tidied up' as they are written, in much the same manner as politicians often write their diaries in the certain knowledge that they will one day be published. Thus auditing of this sort will encourage researchers to hide their secrets.

Clearly, Hammersley is identifying something very important about the research process: a lot of what goes on in a research project is quite messy and illogical; the final report tends to reconstruct the whole process as more rational than perhaps it really is. He goes on to discuss secondary analysis, drawing on this depiction of the research process, saying that although secondary analysis has many advantages it also has some inherent problems resulting from this informal, messy nature of the research process. This is because research contains a considerable intuitive component. Perhaps qualitative researchers are particularly sensitive to the idea that 'data' are not simply 'given' but are at least in part 'constructed', thus they rely on their knowledge of context in presenting their analyses. Hammersley says about this:

There is a difference between how ethnographers read the fieldnotes they have produced themselves and how someone else will read them. The fieldworker interprets them against the background of all that he or she tacitly knows about the setting as a result of first-hand experience, a background that may not be available to those without that experience … The data collected by different researchers will be structured by varying purposes and conceptions of what is relevant. As a result, users of archives are likely to find that some of the data or information required for their purpose is not available. (1997: 139)

Clearly, this is a useful warning against using other researchers' data in an uncritical fashion. However, it is not a problem that is new to people who have thought hard about the issues involved in secondary analysis. But secondary analysis developed first in relation to statistical data, and an unfortunate divide has existed between quantitative and qualitative research workers (see Chapter 27 for an assessment of this). Let us see how analysts of statistical material have approached these problems.

## Secondary analysis of quantitative data

One of the best texts on this is by Dale et al. (1988), researchers who were at the time based at Surrey University (UK) and had considerable experience of analysing the GHS and teaching the methods involved. They advocate careful inspection of the methods of studies that produced data sets before beginning analysis. Six questions need to be asked (Box 17.6).

It will be seen that, if taken seriously, such questions represent a rigorous assessment of the adequacy of data for analysing issues for which they were not originally intended, taking into account much of the context in which the data were produced. On the other hand, it can be argued that methods for collecting qualitative materials are more dependent on the personal quirks of individual investigators than are quantitative methods. In my view, though, the production of both qualitative and quantitative data ought to be subject to similar levels of critical scrutiny and assessment.

---

**BOX 17.6**

### SIX QUESTIONS TO ASK ABOUT A DATA SET DOING SECONDARY ANALYSIS

1   What was the purpose of the original study and what conceptual framework informed it?

2   What information has been collected and is it on subjects relevant to the concerns of the secondary analyst and in the form needed?

3   How was the sample drawn up and what biases in responders and non-responders were evident?

4   What sort of agency collected the data and how adequate were their procedures for ensuring its quality?

5   Which population does the survey represent?

6   When was the data collected and is it still relevant to the circumstances the secondary analyst wishes to investigate?

*Source*: Dale et al., 1988

---

In fact, the broad principles of secondary analysis are similar to those of any researcher engaged in statistical reasoning (Chapters 18–20): be aware of the conditions under which data have been produced, and ensure that any generalisations (particularly those that involve causal statements) have been fully exposed to possible counter-arguments.

But unlike the researcher who has designed a tailor-made survey, the researcher using officially produced data has little control over the variables measured. Sometimes little can be done about this, but at times creative solutions can be found in the transformation of existing variables into derived variables. An example of this is found in the work of Arber and Ginn (1991), who draw upon secondary analysis of the 1985 British General Household Survey (GHS) to present a series of compelling arguments about the disadvantages faced by elderly women.

The derived variable generated by Arber and Ginn is shown in Box 17.7. The 'disability index' was created by combining answers from six questions (each of which had three possible answers) to form a scale ranging from 0 to 12, where people with no disability scored 0 and people with very severe disability scored 9 or more. The percentages are the proportion of people aged 65+ in the survey who fell within each broad category of disability. The production of this variable was not the original intention of the people who designed the GHS, but Arber and Ginn found it to have considerable construct validity (see Chapter 30). That is to say, as one might expect, scores on the index increased with age and it correlated well with high use of health and welfare services.

---

**BOX 17.7**

## CONSTRUCTION OF A DISABILITY INDEX

Coded from answers to six questions: 'Do you usually manage to …?'

- Get up and down stairs and steps
- Get around the house
- Get in and out of bed
- Cut your toenails yourself
- Bath, shower or wash all over
- Go out and walk down the road

The answers are scored:

0   On your own without difficulty

1   On your own, but with difficulty

2   Only with help from someone else, or not at all

| Degree of disability | Scale values | Scale items |
|---|---|---|
| None | 0 | None |
| (49%) | | |
| Slight | 1 | Has difficulty cutting toenails |
| (25%) | 2 | Needs help/cannot manage to cut toenails |
| Moderate | 3 | Has difficulty in going up and down stairs |
| (14%) | 4 | Has difficulty managing to go out and walk down the road |
| | 5 | Has difficulty having a bath/shower or wash all over |
| Severe | 6 | Needs help/cannot manage to go out and walk down the road |

| (7%) | 7 | Needs help/cannot manage to go up and down stairs |
| | 8 | Needs help/cannot manage to have a bath/shower or wash all over |
| Very | 9 | Has difficulty in getting around the house |
| severe | 10 | Has difficulty in getting in and out of bed |
| (4%) | 11 | Needs help/cannot manage to get in and out of bed |
| | 12 | Needs help/cannot manage to get around the house |

100%

(3,691)

*Source*: Arber and Ginn, 1991: 202

Table 17.1 illustrates how this index of disability was then used to show differences between elderly men and women. It shows, for example, that half (51.9%) of severely disabled elderly women lived alone compared with only a quarter (26.1%) of the men. This meant that more women needed to rely on people from outside their homes for help. Men, on the other hand, were much more likely to be able to rely on their spouse. As well as gender-specific cultural expectations about who should give care, demographic factors lay behind this: on average women live longer than men, and tend to have married men older than them, so are more likely to be widowed. Clearly, qualitative research could be done to show how the broad statistical pictures relate to the finer details of family life.

**TABLE 17.1**   Caring contexts for elderly men and women, by level of disability (column percentages)

| | Elderly person has: | | | | | |
| | All elderly people | | Severe disability (score 6–8) | | Very severe disability (score 9–12) | |
| | Men | Women | Men | Women | Men | Women |
|---|---|---|---|---|---|---|
| All care is extra-resident | | | | | | |
| Elderly person lives alone | 19.8 | 47.5 | 26.1 | 51.9 | 14.3 | 29.2 |
| Co-resident care in elderly person's own household | | | | | | |
| Lives with spouse | 70.1 | 36.4 | 58.5 | 31.2 | 69.0 | 27.4 |
| Lives with others | 5.9 | 8.4 | 9.2 | 9.0 | 7.1 | 17.7 |
| Co-resident care: elderly person is NOT householder | | | | | | |
| Lives with adult children | 2.1 | 4.6 | 6.1 | 6.3 | 4.8 | 21.2 |
| Lives with others | 2.2 | 3.1 | — | 1.6 | 4.8 | 4.4 |
| Total | 100% | 100% | 100% | 100% | 100% | 100% |
| N = | (1,477) | (2,155) | (65) | (189) | (42) | (113) |

*Source*: Arber and Ginn, 1991: 145, Table 8.4

## Secondary analysis of qualitative data

The best way to show how this can proceed is to provide an extended example, taken from the work of Mike Savage (2007), who used material from the UK Mass Observation archive (www.massobs.org.uk) to investigate changes in the way social class was narrated in 1948 compared with 1990. Hosted at the University of Sussex, this archive contains the writings of those participating in this long-standing project to document everyday life in Britain since 1937. Because of the large amount of material available, he studied only 10% of the replies written at each time point.

In the 1948 sample, it was common for observers to contest the value of talking about class, although most would identify as belonging to one if pushed. Examples include:

> I hate class distinctions and do not think any definite lines can be drawn between social classes, but if there has to be a division, I consider myself to belong to the upper middle class.
>
> I try to eliminate all class distinctions from my social life … however I suppose I have been brought up with a middle class outlook as …. For the most part of ten years my father has been a regular army officer.

Observers wrote brief statements which identified themselves as belonging to a class (usually the middle class) because of 'ties of birth, through having appropriate manners, and other social ties' (Savage, 2007: 4.13). For example:

> From a materialistic point of view, I would place [myself] in the middle class. Whereas we do not live in a large mansion with a staff of servants, have a 'Rolls Royce' and mix socially with 'country folk', we possess a house plus one acre of garden, two cars, and enough money to give us a good annual holiday at a first class hotel. This type of living could hardly, I think, be called that of a working class family. (2007: 4.13)

In 1990, replies on this subject were much more extensive, prompting observers in several cases to tell detailed stories about their lives and their continuing negotiation of class identity. A number of respondents narrated hybrid family histories in which different members of a family were regarded as belonging to different classes. Others remarked that their class identity was related to whether they lived in a working-class or middle-class location, suggesting that this had been a choice they had exercised. Observers in 1948 did not regard their class identity as fluid in this way, portraying it as something which was fixed by virtue of birth or occupation.

Several observers demonstrated knowledge of sociological discussions of class, suggesting to Savage that the double hermeneutic (Giddens 1991b), whereby social scientific ideas about a subject themselves become incorporated into lay thinking about that subject, is at play. For example, Savage (2007) reports that one mass observer wrote:

> Mary Daly, in her book Gyn-ecology, suggests that the setting up of divisions or barriers is typical of patriarchy, so I am always reluctant to fit my thinking into what, tangibly and socially exists, circumscribing, nay defining my life.

Savage comments: 'respondents use class talk reflexively to show their sophistication – very different to the Mass-Observers of 1948 who saw talking about class as a sign of vulgarity' (2007: 5.6). Savage ends by commenting that such qualitative sources enable a better appreciation of the complexities and ambiguities through which class is lived at certain points in time than is provided by survey research which simply asks people whether they believe they belong to a particular class.

It is clear that this work shows the value of an archive in enabling comparison over time. Significantly for Hammersley's arguments described earlier, where he said that a secondary analyst would inevitably be at a disadvantage compared with a primary researcher who had been present at original data collection, Savage's knowledge of the context in which Mass Observation data is collected was similar to that which anyone may have – the original data collectors do not have privileged knowledge here, since contributors of data ('observers') respond in writing to written requests for information. The wording of these written requests is reported in Savage's paper so that readers can also share in knowledge of context. Savage reflects on the way in which question wording may have influenced responses at the different time points, and notes the consequences of relying on a sample consisting largely of middle-class respondents.

Clearly, Savage's investigation benefitted from the foresight of the archivists who established the Mass Observation archive without knowing all of the uses to which it might be put in the future. Worries about the secondary analyst not having 'been there' when the data was collected are not relevant, as the primary researchers were also not 'there' in a situation where the material was gathered in response to a written request (although it might be argued that, as they were themselves part of the generation of people who wrote comments in 1948, whereas Savage was not, their general understanding of the background to the comments is bound to have been different from that of Savage). The awareness demonstrated by the analyst of the ways in which the social environment may have influenced the nature of the data is very much in the foreground of the analysis nevertheless.

Finally, it is worth noting that the fact that data is 'qualitative' does not mean that analysis also needs to be qualitative. In Chapter 26, quantitative approaches to the analysis of text are described, and one of the projects described in particular detail involves analysis of archived qualitative interviews.

## Conclusion

Secondary analysis of archived qualitative and quantitative data, then, places a method of great potential in the hands of researchers who have appropriate skills. It is always necessary to take account of the conditions of their production, and unwise to assume that the meaning of data is precisely as the original researchers intended. A careful assessment of the conditions under which the original data were produced needs to be made. In statistical secondary analysis, new variables may have to be created from old, and there will be times when the ingenuity of researchers in doing this will face the limits of the original data forms. In the analysis of archived qualitative data it is possible that the secondary analysts' lack of first-hand knowledge of the circumstances in which data was collected will influence the type of conclusions drawn. Nevertheless, this chapter should have given you a lead in identifying the ever-growing range of data sources available for research purposes and may encourage you to search through these when you plan a research project, so that you can benefit from the time and effort other researchers have put into the collection of research materials relevant to your research problem.

## FURTHER READING

Dale et al. (1988) supply an excellent account of the procedures involved in secondary analysis of statistical data, together with a guide to sources of data. On qualitative data, a chapter by Corti and Thompson (2004) provides an overview. Heaton (1998, 2004) provides similar advice. Seale (2010) addresses objections some qualitative researchers have put forward to secondary analysis.

*(Continued)*

*(Continued)*

## Student Reader (Seale, 2004b): relevant readings

15 Ian Hacking: 'The taming of chance'

16 K. Jill Kiecolt and Laura E. Nathan: 'Secondary analysis of survey data'

17 Angela Dale, Sara Arber and Michael Procter: 'A sociological perspective on secondary analysis'

42 Martyn Hammersley: 'Qualitative data archiving: some reflections on its prospects and problems'

See also Chapter 22, 'Secondary analysis of archived data' by Louise Corti and Paul Thompson and Chapter 23, 'Reanalysis of previously collected material' by Malin Åkerström, Katarina Jacobsson and David Wästerfors in Seale et al. (2004).

## Journal articles illustrating the use of the methods described in this chapter

Arber, S., Gilbert, N.G. and Dale, A. (1985) 'Paid employment and women's health: a benefit or a source of role strain?', *Sociology of Health & Illness*, 7 (3): 375–400.

Fielding, N.G. and Fielding, J.L. (2000) 'Resistance and adaptation to criminal identity: using secondary analysis to evaluate classic studies of crime and deviance', *Sociology*, 34: 671–689.

Payne, J. (1987) 'Does unemployment run in families? Some findings from the General Household Survey', *Sociology*, 21: 199–214.

## Web links

e-Source – Chapter 6 on 'Administrative data systems' by Vincent Mor: www.esourceresearch.org

### Some popular data archives

Australia Social Science Data Archive: http://assda.anu.edu.au

Life-Course Archive in Germany: www.lebenslaufarchiv.uni-bremen.de

The National Archives of Canada – Ottawa, Ontario: www.archives.ca

UK Mass Observation archive: www.massobs.org.uk

The UK Data Archive: www.data-archive.ac.uk

Economic and Social Data Service (UK): www.esds.ac.uk

New Zealand Social Research Data Archives: www.nzssds.org.nz

Social Sciences Data Services, University of California, San Diego: http://ssdc.ucsd.edu/

The Roper Center for Public Opinion Research (USA): www.ropercenter.uconn.edu

Inter-University Consortium for Social and Political Research: www.icpsr.umich.edu

Henry A. Murray Research Archive: www.murray.harvard.edu

### Guides to data archives

This page on the University of Toronto Data Library Service website lists links to data archives throughout the world: www.chass.utoronto.ca/datalib/other/datalibs.htm

See also: The International Federation of Data Archives (IFDO): www.ifdo.org

Council of European Social Science Data Archives (CESSDA): www.nsd.uib.no/Cessda

Advice: Use these, along with the review questions in the next section, to test your knowledge of the contents of this chapter. Try to define each of the key concepts listed here; if you have understood this chapter you should be able to do this. Check your definitions against the definition in the glossary at the end of the book.

Data archives                                          Knowledge of context

Derived variables                                      Secondary analysis

## ■ Review questions

1   What is secondary analysis?
2   In what ways is the secondary analysis of qualitative and quantitative data similar? How do they differ?
3   What is a derived variable?
4   Why might knowledge of context be important in analysing qualitative data? In what circumstances is it not important?
5   What are the key considerations to be addressed when analysing (a) archived quantitative data and (b) archived qualitative data?
6   What are the arguments in favour of the secondary analysis of data?

## Workshop and discussion exercises

1   If you are planning a research project involving data collection, see if you can find a data set in a data archive on the Web that will help you answer your research questions. Investigate its adequacy for this purpose. If you are not currently working on a research project, try doing this for one of the following research problems, or for a research problem that you invent:

    (a) In what ways does ethnic origin affect life chances?

    (b) How do American (US) attitudes towards world affairs compare with the attitudes of people in other countries?

    (c) How do people use home entertainment technology (e.g. VCRs, home computers, hi-fi, television)?

2   Go to the 'Edwardians Online' website: www.qualidata.essex.ac.uk/edwardians. Use the various ways of searching these interviews ('Browse themes' or 'search') to investigate specified topics, comparing what each interviewee has to say about the topic.

    Alternatively, you can copy and paste the full transcripts into a word processor such as Word. Either print it out and analyse it 'manually', or save each transcript as a 'rich text format' file and import it into NVivo (see Chapter 21) or a similar qualitative analysis package. You can then code and search the transcripts for themes.

3   Go to the ICPSR (Inter-University Consortium for Social and Political Research) website: www.icpsr. umich.edu/icpsrweb/ICPSR/access/index.jsp; click on 'Analyze Data Online'.

    There are over 90 different studies there, containing statistical data on a wide range of topics. You can analyse them 'online' without having any statistical software on your computer. Find out about how you can do this for a particular survey data set that interests you by clicking on relevant links on the website (e.g. you will need to look at the study's 'codebook' for information about the variable names). Produce some frequency counts, tables or other data displays and comment on what they tell you about the social and cultural processes involved.

4 Choose a topic of interest to you, for example, ethnicity, gender differences, class inequalities, educational inequalities, family structure, health differences. Find some tables of official statistics on your chosen topic in the reference section of your library. Do not choose data that are already presented in graph form. Some examples of UK statistical series that you are likely to find are: Social Trends; General Household Survey; Annual Abstract of Statistics; Population Trends; Mortality Statistics; Decennial Census; Marriage and Divorce Statistics.

Present an analysis of up to four tables of data from such publications relevant to your chosen topic. Consider questions like: What do the tables tell you about the topic? What might explain the patterns you see? How might the way in which the statistics were collected affect the conclusions that can be reached? How would the tables need to be modified (in other words, broken down by other variables) in order to take your inquiry further? What further data would need to be collected in order to take your inquiry further?

You may find it relevant to recalculate and represent data in simpler or graph form to clarify the main messages of the tables analysed. Speculate on the links between the tables chosen: conduct an *inquiry* into the topic by analysing the data from the various tables. Make sure you consider critically the measurement validity of the variables involved.

# 18

# PREPARING DATA FOR STATISTICAL ANALYSIS

*Clive Seale*

---

## Chapter Contents

Social and cultural research involves taking a particular view of the world, choosing a way of seeing a topic that is different from other possible ways. The selection of certain things rather than others to be called 'data' is an important part of this, but once a researcher is faced with a pile of questionnaires, interview transcripts, field notes or tape transcripts, a further selection occurs. Certain parts of the data will be considered more relevant than others. Additionally, the researcher will usually be interested in detecting *patterns* in the data. A pattern demands that things that are similar are identified. Coding involves placing like with like, so that patterns can be found.

Coding is therefore the first step towards data analysis. Decisions taken at this stage in a research project have important consequences. The quality of a coding scheme influences the eventual quality of data analysis, for it is in coding schemes that a researcher becomes committed to particular ways of categorising the world. Coding schemes can be narrow, artificial devices that hinder thought, or they can contain the seeds of creative new insights. In this chapter I describe the coding of data gathered by structured interviews or questionnaires (see Chapter 11) to prepare it for the statistical procedures described in Chapters 19 and 20. With this kind of material, data is often pre-coded to a large extent by the format of the fixed-choice questions asked. Therefore, the focus of this chapter is how to transfer such material into spreadsheets of the sort used by statistical software (such as SPSS).

## The data matrix

At the heart of the statistical analysis of structured data from, for example, a social survey lies the data matrix, as is suggested by Catherine Marsh in her definition of the social survey:

[A] survey refers to an investigation where … systematic measurements are made over a series of cases yielding a rectangle of data … [and] the variables in the matrix are analysed to see if they show any patterns … [and] the subject matter is social. (1982: 8)

Box 18.1 shows a small data matrix, derived from a hypothetical social survey in which five people were asked four questions: their sex, their age, whether they were working full-time, part-time or not at all, and the extent of their satisfaction with their work. This last question gave people five options, ranging from 'very satisfied' (1) to 'very dissatisfied' (5). These questions become the variables in the matrix. In other words, they are qualities on which the cases (in this instance cases are people) vary. If you read the section in Chapter 6 in which library catalogue databases are described, you will detect similarities.

---

**BOX 18.1**

### A DATA MATRIX

| | Variables or questions | | | |
|---|---|---|---|---|
| People | Sex | Age | Working | Jobsat |
| Case 1 | Male | 66 | No | Missing |
| Case 2 | Female | 34 | Full-time | 1 |
| Case 3 | Female | 25 | Part-time | 2 |
| Case 4 | Female | 44 | Full-time | 5 |
| Case 5 | Male | 78 | No | Missing |

---

It will be seen that there is a simple pattern in the matrix, with people beyond conventional retirement age (cases 1 and 5) being out of work. Additionally, the people in work are all females; the people out of work are all male. People out of work were not asked an irrelevant question about job satisfaction, so the *Jobsat* variable for these cases shows data to be missing.

The variable called *Sex* is a nominal variable (sometimes also called *categorical*). This means that it applies a name to the quality, but that

there is no sense of magnitude between the different categories of that quality. In this respect it is different from the *Jobsat* variable, where there is a sense in which the categories of the variable have magnitude. Someone who says they are 'very satisfied' can be understood as having 'more' satisfaction than someone who says they are 'very dissatisfied'. Variables like this, with a sense of rank order or magnitude, are known as ordinal variables. *Age* clearly has a sense of magnitude as well, but this is known as an interval variable. This is because there is a fixed and equal distance between the points on the scale. Thus the 'distance' between a person who is 25 and another who is 20 years old is the same as that between a 15-year-old and a 20-year-old. The mathematical operations of addition and subtraction 'make sense' with an interval level variable, whereas they do not with an ordinal variable (where the 'distances' between the points of a scale are unknown quantities). The distinction between nominal, ordinal and interval variables becomes important when data analysis begins.

Another feature of the variables in Box 18.1 is that they are expressed in either string or numeric form. String variables use letters to indicate values; numeric variables use numbers. *Age* and *Jobsat* are numeric; the rest are string. When entering data like these into a computer it is generally advisable to give string variables numeric values. Although most computer packages accept string variables, some place restrictions on the analyses that can be performed with them. The variable *Sex* could be transformed into a numeric variable by giving 'male' the value of 0, and 'female' the value of 1. The variable *Working* could be transformed by the following: 'none' = 0; 'part-time' = 1; 'full-time' = 2. Finally, some variables are dichotomous (consisting of only two values). *Sex* is an example of a dichotomous variable. It is not difficult to imagine how the information in Box 18.1 might have been recorded originally on a form or questionnaire for each of the cases, and then transferred from such forms into the data matrix.

Looking carefully at Figure 18.1 (the SPSS Data Editor window) is also revealing, since this too

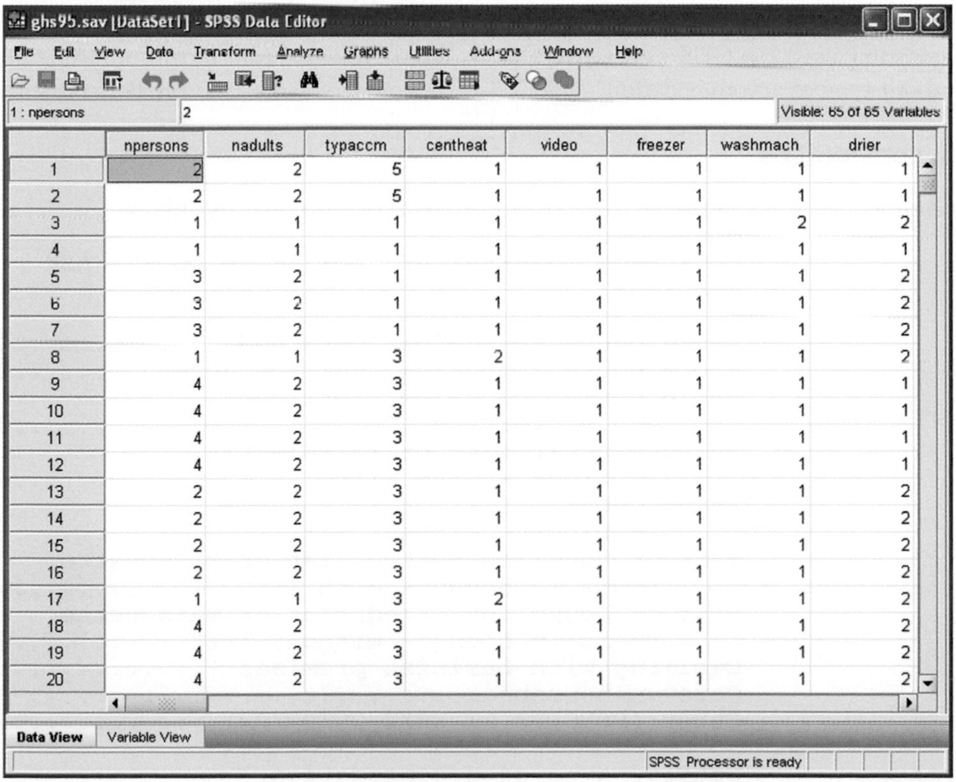


| | npersons | nadults | typaccm | centheat | video | freezer | washmach | drier |
|---|---|---|---|---|---|---|---|---|
| 1 | 2 | 2 | 5 | 1 | 1 | 1 | 1 | 1 |
| 2 | 2 | 2 | 5 | 1 | 1 | 1 | 1 | 1 |
| 3 | 1 | 1 | 1 | 1 | 1 | 1 | 2 | 2 |
| 4 | 1 | 1 | 1 | 1 | 1 | 1 | 1 | 1 |
| 5 | 3 | 2 | 1 | 1 | 1 | 1 | 1 | 2 |
| 6 | 3 | 2 | 1 | 1 | 1 | 1 | 1 | 2 |
| 7 | 3 | 2 | 1 | 1 | 1 | 1 | 1 | 2 |
| 8 | 1 | 1 | 3 | 2 | 1 | 1 | 1 | 2 |
| 9 | 4 | 2 | 3 | 1 | 1 | 1 | 1 | 1 |
| 10 | 4 | 2 | 3 | 1 | 1 | 1 | 1 | 1 |
| 11 | 4 | 2 | 3 | 1 | 1 | 1 | 1 | 1 |
| 12 | 4 | 2 | 3 | 1 | 1 | 1 | 1 | 1 |
| 13 | 2 | 2 | 3 | 1 | 1 | 1 | 1 | 2 |
| 14 | 2 | 2 | 3 | 1 | 1 | 1 | 1 | 2 |
| 15 | 2 | 2 | 3 | 1 | 1 | 1 | 1 | 2 |
| 16 | 2 | 2 | 3 | 1 | 1 | 1 | 1 | 2 |
| 17 | 1 | 1 | 3 | 2 | 1 | 1 | 1 | 2 |
| 18 | 4 | 2 | 3 | 1 | 1 | 1 | 1 | 2 |
| 19 | 4 | 2 | 3 | 1 | 1 | 1 | 1 | 2 |
| 20 | 4 | 2 | 3 | 1 | 1 | 1 | 1 | 2 |

FIGURE 18.1 SPSS (www.spss.com) software for statistical analysis, the Data Editor showing data from the 1995 General Household Survey (GHS)

shows a data matrix. You may find the appearance of this screen familiar if you have worked with spreadsheet software. Like the data matrix in Box 18.1, the cases (also, in this instance, people) are listed down the side and the variables across the top. For the person listed first (Case 1), we can learn that two people lived in that household (the variable *npersons*) and that both of these were adults (*nadults*). The accommodation was type '5' (*typaccm*), and a '1' is given for the variables *centheat*, *video*, *freezer*, *washmach* and *drier*.

We can discover what these numbers mean by seeing how each question was coded when it was entered into SPSS. For example, a '1' for the variables concerning central heating, video ownership and so on means 'yes', the household has this; a '2' would have meant 'no'. The value labels for the variable *typaccm* are shown in Figure 18.2. These indicate that the number '5' has been assigned to people who live in a purpose-built (PB) flat with no lift. Figure 18.3 shows the original question used by GHS interviewers to find out about type of accommodation.

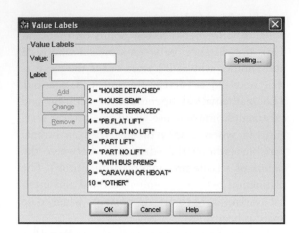

FIGURE 18.2    Value labels for the variable *typaccm*

## Different question formats

Box 18.2 shows some examples of questions in different formats. For each format there are different ways of transferring information into a data matrix. Note that the first three questions

**ALL HOUSEHOLDS**

TypAccm          Type of accommodation occupied by this
                 household.
                 CODE FROM OBSERVATION, BUT IF IN DOUBT, ASK
                 INFORMANT

                 Whole house, bungalow, detached .............1
                 Whole house, bungalow, semi-detached .......2
                 Whole house, bungalow, terraced/
                     end of terrace...........................3
                 Purpose-built flat or maisonette
                     in block - with lift....................4
                 Purpose-built flat or maisonette
                     in block - without lift.................5
                 Part of house/converted flat or maisonette/
                     rooms in house - with lift..............6
                 Part of house/converted flat or maisonette/
                     rooms in house - without lift...........7
                 Dwelling with business premises ............8
                 Caravan/houseboat ........................... 9
                 Other (SPECIFY AT NEXT QUESTION)............10

XTypAccm         Specify type of accommodation

FIGURE 18.3    Extract from the 1995 General Household Survey questionnaire

in Box 18.2 are closed and largely pre-coded (see Chapter 11), which is to say that they allow answers from a range of pre-specified choices. The fourth question is an open one. Question 1 can easily be transferred to a data matrix as a numeric variable. What would one do, though, if someone did not know their age in years, or refused to answer, or forgot to answer that question? A missing value would then be entered at that point in the matrix. If 0 or 99 were chosen to represent a missing value, we would have to be sure that there were no newborn babies or 99-year-olds in the sample, otherwise we would have used up a value needed for these people. One solution is to incorporate negative numbers as missing values (e.g. 'missing' = −1). Another would be to treat *Age* as a variable with three digits, so that a 99-year-old would be recorded as 099, and the missing value could then safely be allocated a number such as 999.

---

**BOX 18.2**

## DIFFERENT QUESTION FORMATS

1   What is your age in years?

2   Would you say that your health, for your age, is?

| | |
|---|---|
| Excellent | 1 |
| Good | 2 |
| Fair | 3 |
| Poor | 4 |

Other (please specify)

3   Please indicate which of the following you have experienced in the past year by underlining the conditions that apply:

(a) Persistent cough

(b) Cold or flu

(c) Measles

(d) Mumps

(e) Rubella

4   At times people are healthier than at other times. What is it like when you are healthy?

---

Question 2 is a bit like the 'job satisfaction' question represented in the data matrix shown in Box 18.1, or the question about the type of accommodation in the GHS (Figure 18.3). People, or cases, can be given a value between 1 and 4 in the matrix to indicate the judgement they made about their state of health. However, as is common on this sort of item, a space was allowed for respondents who wanted to describe their health in terms different from those offered by the question. Managing this at the data entry stage depends on how many people chose this option, and whether the detail of their replies is important in achieving the aims of the research study. If replies are rare and the issue is of low importance, one could simply categorise these people as a 5. Alternatively, one could go through all of the questionnaires where people had chosen this option and devise a category system to place replies into categories with common elements, each of which would be given a separate number: 5, 6, 7, 8 and so on. This procedure is in fact the same as that which will be described for question 4, the open question, below.

Question 3 is an example of a multiple response item. Here, respondents can underline (or tick or 'check') as many or as few items as they wish. It is best to treat this as a question containing five *dichotomous* variables. If an item is ticked/checked, for example, one could record the person as saying 'yes' to that question; if an item is not ticked/checked, the person has said 'no'. These could be given *numeric* values ('yes' = 1; 'no' = 2, for example), so that the answer of a person indicating they had a cough and a cold but none of the other conditions might be a row of the following numbers: 1 1 2 2 2. The first number is the person's answer to question 3(a), the second to question 3(b) and so on.

The fourth question is an open one, asked on an actual interview survey of 9,000 people's health and lifestyles (Blaxter, 1990). Such a question gathers qualitative rather than quantitative data, but it is possible to categorise replies so that quantitative analysis can proceed. In one sense, this is done in *all* quantitative data analysis. The world is essentially a qualitative experience; the quantitative researcher imposes categories upon the world and counts them. In pre-coded items, such as question 2, the categorising occurs as the respondent answers the question. In question 4, the information can be post-coded, that is, coded after the answer has been recorded. This means that respondents are less constrained by the question wording to respond in the researcher's fixed terms, and the researcher has more knowledge about the variety of meanings that have contributed to answers and to the development of coding categories. This is likely to improve the measurement validity (Chapter 30) of a question. though, as with most of the good things in life, better-quality work demands more time and effort. There is always a temptation to opt for a badly designed pre-coded question in order to save the effort required to analyse qualitative data.

Mildred Blaxter devised a coding scheme for replies to the question about health based on a close reading of 200 of the 9,000 interviews in the survey. The categories devised, together with illustrative examples, are shown in Box 18.3, which shows that a five-category variable was derived.

---

## BOX 18.3

### CATEGORISING QUALITATIVE ANSWERS TO AN OPEN QUESTION: 'AT TIMES PEOPLE ARE HEALTHIER THAN AT OTHER TIMES. WHAT IS IT LIKE WHEN YOU ARE HEALTHY?'

1   Unable to answer:

'I don't know when I'm healthy, I only know if I'm ill'; 'I'm never healthy so I don't know'

2   Never ill, no disease:

'You don't have to think about pain – to be free of aches and pains'; 'Health is when you don't have a cold'

3   Physical fitness, energy:

'There's a tone to my body, I feel fit'; 'I can do something strenuous and don't feel that tired after I've done it'

4 Functionally able to do a lot:

'Being healthy is when I walk to my work on a night, and I walk to school to collect the grandchildren'; 'Health is being able to walk around better, and doing more work in the house when my knees let me'

5 Psychologically fit:

'Emotionally you are stable, energetic, happier, more contented and things don't bother you so. Generally it's being carefree, you look better, you get on better with other people'; 'Well I think health is when you feel happy. Because I know when I'm happy I feel quite well'

*Source*: Blaxter, 1990: 20–30

## Cleaning data

Once entered into a spreadsheet or into SPSS, the data may need to be cleaned. This is because data entry often involves errors. This may, for example, be due to pressing the wrong key. There are ways of setting up SPSS so that this is more difficult; for example, one can 'tell' SPSS only to accept certain values for a particular variable, but mistakes creep in nevertheless. With modern spreadsheets it is often quite a simple matter to run one's eye down a column of figures to check that no 'out of range' values occur. Alternatively, a variety of data cleaning procedures can be helpful in the early stages of analysis. (Chapter 19 contains explanations and examples of the following procedures.) A frequency count for a variable will detect out of range values. A cross-tabulation can be used to see if people have answered a question which, according to the values of another variable, they should not have done. Additionally, cross-tabulations can show illogical combinations: if someone is aged 25 it is likely to be an error if they are recorded as having a child aged 20.

## Coding meaning

Categorising the qualitative replies to open-ended questions in a structured interview is one way of turning quality into quantity so that patterns can be detected in data analysis. It is, however, possible to go a step further than this and code material derived from almost any kind of qualitative material, making it available for statistical analysis.

Unstructured interviews (such as those discussed in Chapter 12), where different respondents are asked different questions, or simply encouraged to tell the story of their lives, can be coded in this way. This was done by George Brown and Tirril Harris (1978) in their study of the role of life events in causing depression. Brown and Harris rejected what they called the 'dictionary approach to meaning' evident in other researchers' methods for measuring the importance of life events in disrupting people's lives. In such an approach, which relies on people simply reporting whether particular things happened to them in a certain period, different events are given different 'weightings' according to how disruptive the researchers feel the event would be. Thus in one such device (Holmes and Rahe, 1967), researchers gave a weighting of 100 to 'death of a spouse', 73 to 'divorce', 47 to 'dismissal from work' and 11 to 'minor violations of the law' to indicate the severity of each event. The problem with this approach is that an event like 'dismissal from a job' will not have the same meaning in everyone's life. An actor, well accustomed to moving in and out of different jobs, will find this less distressing than a 50-year-old miner, made redundant after a lifetime of work in an area with no alternative sources of employment. Another way of putting this is that

Holmes and Rahe's approach demonstrates a low level of contextual sensitivity to the variable way in which people constitute the meaning of life events.

Brown and Harris therefore proposed that in order to measure the impact of life events on people it was necessary to gather a great deal of qualitative information about the person's life. This was done in lengthy qualitative interviews in which women were encouraged to talk freely about their circumstances. A group of researchers then read the transcripts of these interviews and rated different aspects of the impact of the various life events reported. Examples of how events were rated according to the long-term threat they posed for people's lives are given in Box 18.4.

Brown and Harris were then able to incorporate the measures into a sophisticated analysis of the social causes of depression. Coding at this level involves more than just transferring information from a form into a computer, and is linked with complex issues of measurement validity (see Chapter 30). This example also shows how to overcome simplistic notions of a quantitative–qualitative divide (see Chapter 27).

---

**BOX 18.4**

## SEVERITY OF LIFE EVENTS IN TERMS OF LONG-TERM THREAT

1  Severe

   (a) Woman's father died aged 81. She was married and he had lived with her for 7 years.

   (b) Woman's husband was sent to prison for two years; woman was pregnant.

2  Non-severe

   (a) Woman had to tell her husband that his sister had died.

   (b) Woman was in a car accident. In a rainstorm a woman 'walked into the car'; her husband was driving. The woman left hospital the same evening as the accident. There were no police charges.

*Source*: Adapted from Brown and Harris, 1978

---

## Recoding variables

Variables often contain a lot of categories, some of which may only apply to a few cases. For example, in the 1995 GHS only 11 people (0.2 per cent of the 5939 people surveyed) lived in a caravan or a houseboat. Most people (86.6 per cent) lived in one of the first three types of accommodation listed in the question shown in Figure 18.3. We may decide that we would like to compare this majority with the rest (in other words, people living in whole houses with who

do not), thus transforming the ten-category variable *typaccm* into a new two-category one (i.e. a dichotomous variable). Recoding the original variable is therefore required. The variable can be given a new name (e.g. *typaccm2*) and the values may be just '1' and '2', to indicate 1 = 'whole house' and 2 = 'other'.

In SPSS this is a straightforward procedure which involves the logical operation shown in Box 18.5. SPSS will save the new variable as well as keeping the old one, so both can be used during analysis where appropriate.

BOX 18.5

## RECODING TYPACCM INTO TYPACCM2

| Old values for | | New values for |
|---|---|---|
| *typaccm* | | *typaccm2* |
| 1, 2, 3 | = | 1 (people who live in whole houses) |
| 4,5,6,7,8,9,10 | = | 2 (people who do not) |

## Weighting cases

Sometimes disproportionate sampling (see Chapter 9) is used so that certain groups that are rare in the population from which the sample is drawn are included in sufficient numbers in the sample. For example, I once surveyed doctors in the UK (Seale, 2009b), asking them their attitudes towards the legalisation of assisted dying (by which is meant euthanasia and assisted suicide). I wanted to know about the opinions of doctors as a whole, but was also particularly interested in doctors specialising in palliative care because they specialise in looking after people with terminal illnesses. However, there are not many doctors in this specialty and if I had chosen a simple random sample of, say, 1,000 doctors then by chance I might have selected just 10 or so palliative care doctors.

Keeping to these numbers (the actual numbers were different, but explaining weighting is easier if we keep this aspect of things simple), let us say that I proceeded to sample 500 doctors in palliative care and 500 in other specialties. With a sample like this I can easily compare palliative care doctors with other doctors and not worry about having too few palliative care doctors. But what do I do when I want to make a statement about doctors as a whole, regardless of specialty?

One solution would be to randomly exclude most of the palliative care doctors, so that the few who were left in the sample paralleled the proportion of palliative care doctors in the population. It seems a shame, though, to lose all that information. A better solution is to weight the cases, so that the replies of palliative care doctors contribute less to the eventual result than do the replies of other doctors. A weight factor is applied to each case, this being different according to whether the doctor is a palliative care specialist or not. The logic of this is shown in Box 18.6. Here, if the sample proportions are to be restored to the population proportions, the responses of palliative care doctors need to be multiplied by 0.02; if the doctor is in some other specialty, the replies need to be multiplied by 1.98. Again, SPSS allows for the temporary application of weight factors to data sets while particular analyses which require this are carried out.

Weighting is not only used where disproportionate sampling has occurred. Sometimes, different subgroups in a population may respond or participate in a social survey at different rates, meaning that the eventual data set under represents some groups and over represents others. Weighting can also adjust for such variability on response rates, so making a sample more representative of the population from which it has been drawn.

## ILLUSTRATION OF WEIGHTING

| Specialty | UK population of doctors | Sample of doctors | Weight factor | Weighted proportions |
|---|---|---|---|---|
| Palliative care | 1,000 (1%) | 500 (50%) | 0.02 | 10 (1%) |
| Other | 99,000 (99%) | 500 (50%) | 1.98 | 990 (99%) |
| Total (100%) | 100,000 | 1,000 | – | 1,000 |

## Conclusion

This chapter has reviewed methods for coding data in order to prepare them for statistical analysis. Such coding involves transferring data from collection instruments like questionnaires or structured interview schedules to spreadsheets. Different questions formats mean that careful thought needs to be given to the different ways in which this can be done. Errors in data entry or in data collection can be guarded against to some extent by the various techniques of cleaning data that have been described. Although pre-coded and fixed-choice items are the data collection methods that usually contribute numbers for statistical analysis, the postcoding of qualitative data is also feasible, making it amenable to statistical analysis. Finally, the chapter described two important procedures that are often needed before data analysis proper can proceed: recoding variables and weighting cases.

## FURTHER READING

De Vaus (2002a) contains a helpful discussion of coding for statistical quantitative analysis.

### Student Reader (Seale, 2004b): relevant readings

18 A.N. Oppenheim: 'The quantification of questionnaire data'

### Web links

SPSS basic skills tutorial – data entry: http://my.ilstu.edu/~mshesso/SPSS/data_entry.html

Harvard/MIT Guide to SPSS: www.hmdc.harvard.edu/projects/SPSS_Tutorial/spsstut.shtml

e-Source – Chapter 4 on 'Sample surveys' by Sarah M. Nusser and Michael D. Larsen: www.esourceresearch.org

**Advice:** Use these, along with the review questions in the next section, to test your knowledge of the contents of this chapter. Try to define each of the key concepts listed here; if you have understood this chapter you should be able to do this. Check your definitions against the definition in the glossary at the end of the book.

Cleaning data

Coding

Cross-tabulation

Data matrix

Frequency count

Multiple response item

Nominal, ordinal, interval variables

Pre-coding and post-coding

Recoding

String, numeric variables

Value labels

Varlables

Weight, weight factor

## Review questions

1   What different types of variable can be entered into a data matrix?
2   How would you enter data from a multiple response item?
3   What is the difference between pre-coding and post-coding?
4   Why might you need to (a) clean data, (b) recode variables and (c) weight cases?

## Workshop and discussion exercises

1   For this exercise you will need some questionnaire items, some of which are *pre-coded*, others *closed* and others *open*. Look for examples of these in Boxes in Chapter 11 and in Box 18.2 in this chapter. Otherwise, find some structured interview schedules containing such things by searching the Economic and Social Data Service (UK) www.esds.ac.uk.

   (a) Having chosen a number of items you will need to generate answers to the questions, either by asking them of at least five people or by using your imagination. Now you have some data that you can prepare for quantitative analysis.

   (b) Draw up a coding scheme which indicates the variable names and the value labels. Using a square grid of boxes, fill in the values of the data matrix. If you are learning SPSS or some other statistical software package, you can try entering these data and producing some frequency counts.

# 19

# STATISTICAL REASONING: FROM ONE TO TWO VARIABLES

Alice Bloch

---

The use of statistics in social research has a long history, with the production of social statistics being closely tied to programmes of legislation and social reform (Tonkiss, 2004). Research reports in the quantitative tradition often present statistical tables with the author's interpretation of them in the surrounding text. It may be tempting to concentrate on the text rather than 'read' the table and draw one's own conclusions. The purpose of this and the following chapter is to help you to read research reports that include statistical analysis, so that you can understand and then assess whether a researcher's conclusions are supported by the numerical data they present. The chapters will also help you to construct statistical arguments of your own.

This first chapter on statistical reasoning will begin by outlining some key ideas about univariate statistics, before going on to bivariate statistics. That is to say, it will discuss the presentation of single variable analysis before discussing ways in which two variables can interact. This will lead, in the chapter that follows, into a discussion of how statistical reasoning can be used to construct arguments about causality, the idea that one variable has caused another variable to vary.

## Univariate statistics

As you saw in the previous chapter, the product of a social survey is a data matrix that can be analysed, most efficiently, by entering data into statistical software such as SPSS. Figure 18.1 in that chapter showed you an example of some data that had been entered. Figure 19.1 is another image of the SPSS data editor, but this time showing 'variable view', a screen which allows you to enter information about variables. Here, the researcher can specify information about each variable and assign numerical labels to each category for the purpose of analysis. Figure 19.1 shows this with value labels for the variable *jobsat* showing.

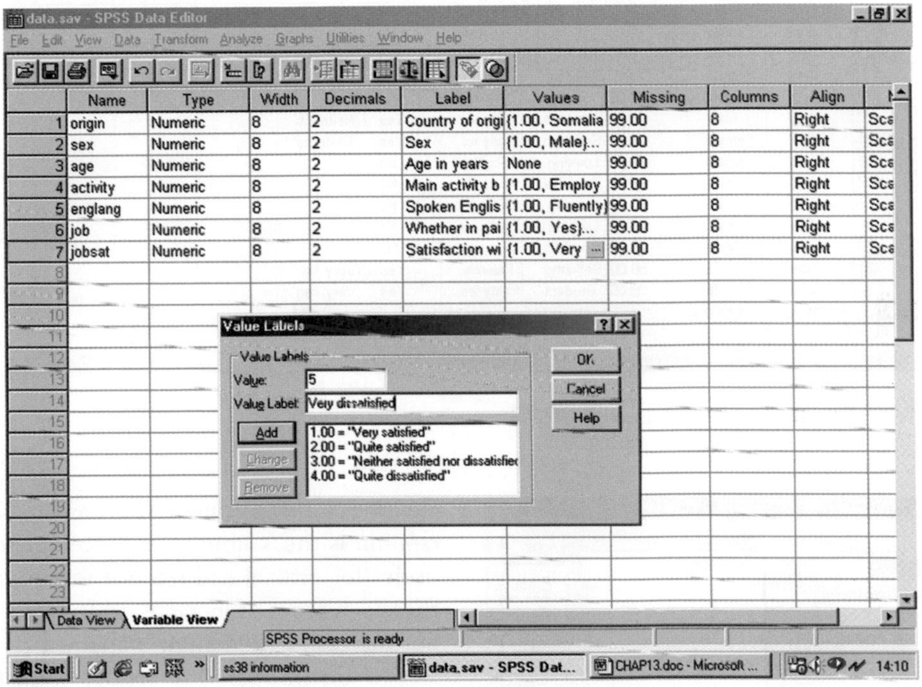

FIGURE 19.1   Variable view and value labels dialogue box (SPSS)

If a raw data matrix such as that in Figure 18.1 were presented in a research report it would be difficult to see the main patterns that exist in the data. Using SPSS makes the analysis of data simple and quick and also provides options for the numerical or graphical presentation of the data.

Univariate statistics are those that present the analysis of a single variable. Such analysis might involve the production of frequency distributions – the distribution of data from a single variable showing the number of times each score or value occurs. Using SPSS, the data from a frequency distribution can be presented as both absolute numbers and percentages. Figure 19.2 shows the SPSS commands to open the frequencies dialogue box.

Clicking on 'frequencies' in the right hand menu brings up a frequencies dialogue box (Figure 19.3). In order to specify which variables are required for analysis the variables are transferred from the source list (left-hand side) to the target variable list (right-hand side) by using the arrow in the middle of the dialogue box. In Figure 19.3 the variable *sex* has been transferred to the target variable list while *age* is highlighted in order to be transferred.

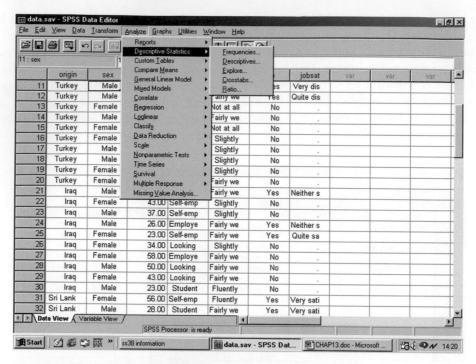

FIGURE 19.2    Descriptive statistics with SPSS

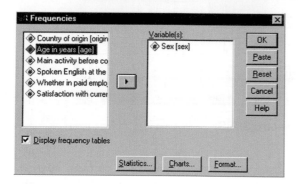

FIGURE 19.3    Frequencies dialogue box (SPSS)

Clicking on 'OK' generates an analysis and SPSS output (see Figure 19.4). The information for the variable *sex* shows that there were 25 men and 25 women in the survey (see 'Frequency' column). Another way of putting this is that 50 per cent were males and 50 per cent were females, and this is indicated in the column marked 'Percent'. The column 'Valid percent'

excludes missing values if there are any. The final column is the 'Cumulative percent' and is most useful for ordinal and interval variables because there is a sense of increase or decrease, which is not the case with nominal variables.

The distribution for *spoken English at the moment* shows a more complex picture than that of *sex*. It shows that eight people spoke English fluently, which was 16 per cent of respondents or 16.7 per cent of valid respondents. The per cent and valid percent differ because two respondents did not answer the question and were therefore not included in the valid percent and instead were coded as missing (99). The final column, cumulative percent, shows that if we add the 16.7 per cent who spoke English fluently to the 33.3 per cent who spoke English fairly well, a total of 50 per cent of valid cases spoke English either fluently or fairly well.

As well as presenting frequency distributions numerically, it is also possible to present them

**Sex**

| | | Frequency | Percent | Valid Percent | Cumulative Percent |
|---|---|---|---|---|---|
| Valid | Male | 25 | 50.0 | 50.0 | 50.0 |
| | Female | 25 | 50.0 | 50.0 | 100.0 |
| | Total | 50 | 100.0 | 100.0 | |

**Spoken English at the moment**

| | | Frequency | Percent | Valid Percent | Cumulative Percent |
|---|---|---|---|---|---|
| Valid | Fluently | 8 | 16.0 | 16.7 | 16.7 |
| | Fairly well | 16 | 32.0 | 33.3 | 50.0 |
| | Slightly | 17 | 34.0 | 35.4 | 85.4 |
| | Not at all | 7 | 14.0 | 14.6 | 100.0 |
| | Total | 48 | 96.0 | 100.0 | |
| Missing | 99.00 | 2 | 4.0 | | |
| Total | | 50 | 100.0 | | |

FIGURE 19.4   Frequency tables for the variables 'sex' and 'spoken English' (SPSS)

graphically using SPSS. Bar charts and pie charts are used most often. Within the frequency dialogue box (see Figure 19.3), SPSS provides output options including charts. Figure 19.5 shows the chart options with 'bar charts' selected and the output that results when, first, bar charts and, secondly, pie charts are selected for the variable *spoken English at the moment*.

While numerical frequency distributions and graphical representations for ordinal level variables such as English language can be very useful, for interval or ratio level variables there are generally too many categories. Using the example of *age*, which is an interval level variable, one strategy would be to *recode* the variable into age band categories that make it into an ordinal level variable and then use bar charts or pie charts to display the results. This is easily done in SPSS (use the 'recode' button on the drop-down menu at 'transform') and can be useful. However, collapsing categories involves losing

information about fine differences between cases. If we wish to keep the details of the raw data then we can summarise the distribution of an interval level variable using descriptive statistics: the mean, mode, or median. These are all measures of central tendency, which means that they are statistics that help to indicate the central point of a particular distribution. Another statistic, the range, measures the distance between the highest and lowest scores. In the frequencies dialogue box there is a sub-menu that will produce these statistics, shown in Figure 19.6.

The mean is the average of the distribution of the variable. The mean is calculated by adding together all the ages (the sum) and dividing by the number of cases. From the output shown in Figure 19.7 we can see that the mean age of respondents in this data is 36.54. The median is the number positioned in the middle of a distribution, below which half the values

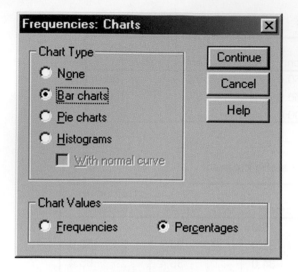

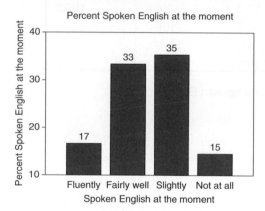

Percent Spoken English at the moment

Spoken English at the moment

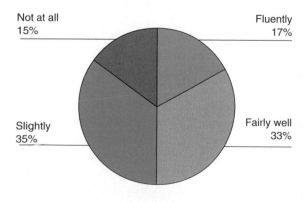

**FIGURE 19.5** Charts in SPSS

fall: it is 34. The median is more suited to variables measured at ordinal level than interval level. The third measure of central tendency is the mode and this statistic is normally used for nominal variables, being the most frequently occurring value in a distribution, which in this case is 19.

In addition to these measures of central tendency, you will sometimes find social researchers referring to the standard deviation in research reports. This is a statistic which indicates how widely cases are dispersed around the mean. If many of the values of cases are far away from the mean, the standard deviation will be high. If most of the values are close to the mean, it will be low. In the case of age the standard deviation (sometimes written as SD) is 14.05, indicating quite a narrow dispersion for age. If a researcher reports the mean and standard deviation of interval variables this tells us a great deal about the variable, even without seeing the raw data that led to them. Another measure of dispersion is the range. Figure 19.7 shows that in this example the range is 46. The range is the difference between the highest score or maximum (64) and the lowest score or minimum (18).

One way of visualising the distribution of interval level variables is to obtain a histogram in SPSS. Figure 19.8 shows a histogram produced by SPSS for the variable *age*. Note that SPSS has grouped the data so that patterns can be easily seen. Statistics have been requested, appearing to the right of the histogram, and a normal curve has been superimposed onto the data. The normal curve is a theoretical distribution based on an infinite number of cases. If the distribution of this variable was truly 'normal' the curve would be perfectly symmetrical, whereas in fact it is skewed in this case. Superimposing the normal curve onto the histogram allows the researcher to see whether the distribution of a variable is skewed. Figure 19.8 shows that the variable *age* is skewed towards the younger age groups.

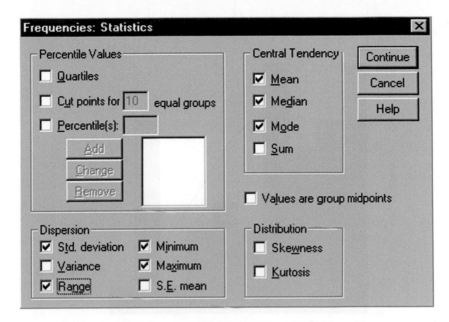

**FIGURE 19.6** Dialogue box for specifying univariate statistics in SPSS

**Statistics**

Age in years

| N | Valid | 50 |
|---|---|---|
| | Missing | 0 |
| Mean | | 36.5400 |
| Median | | 34.0000 |
| Mode | | 19.00 |
| Std. Deviation | | 14.0541 |
| Range | | 46.00 |
| Minimum | | 18.00 |
| Maximum | | 64.00 |

**FIGURE 19.7** Output of descriptive statistics for the variable 'age in years'

## Bivariate analysis

Univariate analysis can show us how a single group of people varies on some characteristic, such as sex, age or job satisfaction. However, to really understand data and to think about it theoretically or in terms of policy development or evaluation it is necessary to explore the relationship between two or more variables. Bivariate analysis involves exploration of relationships between two variables. For instance, a researcher might seek to discover the relationship between sex and economic activity, or between country of origin and levels of spoken English. (Where the researcher is concerned with the relationship between three or more variables, multivariate statistics are used, covered in the next chapter.)

## Contingency tables

The best way to approach bivariate analysis is through the analysis of contingency tables, though such analysis can also be presented in graph form. Contingency tables are devices that show the relationships between two variables, each of which has only a few categories. Interval

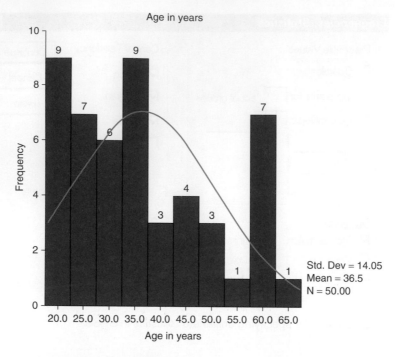

FIGURE 19.8   A histogram of the variable 'age'

level variables (such as *age in years*), if not recoded, generally have too many values for inclusion in tables, so if they are to be used in tables they are often re-coded into categories.

In SPSS, the production of contingency tables is done using the 'crosstabs' option in the 'descriptive statistics' submenu of the main 'analyse' menu. Figure 19.9 shows the resultant menu, with two variables selected from the left hand list and pasted into two of the right hand boxes.

The researcher must decide which variable should be the row variable (going across the table) and which the column variable (going down the table). The third box allows for the selection of a third 'layer' variable, which is used for multivariate analysis (see Chapter 20). You can see, too, that there are options for 'statistics' and 'cells'. Under the 'statistics' menu the researcher can select a number of statistics including measures of association and chi-square tests. These will be explained in a later section

below. Under the 'cells' menu the researcher can choose how the data is displayed in each box or cell of the resultant table. This idea is best explained by looking at the output from this procedure in Figure 19.10.

Both these variables are dichotomous, which means that within each variable there are two categories. The resultant output is a 2 × 2 contingency table. The 14 in the top left-hand group of numbers, or cell as it can be called, represents in this case the number of male respondents in paid employment. Adding the 4 women who were also in paid employment means that a total of 18 people were working (the row marginal). By adding 14 to 4 in this way, we are going across the top row of the table to calculate the row marginal of 18. Marginal numbers are the ones around the 'margins' or edges of the table. Going down the columns of the table, we can see that in each case the column marginal is 25, since there were equal numbers of men and women

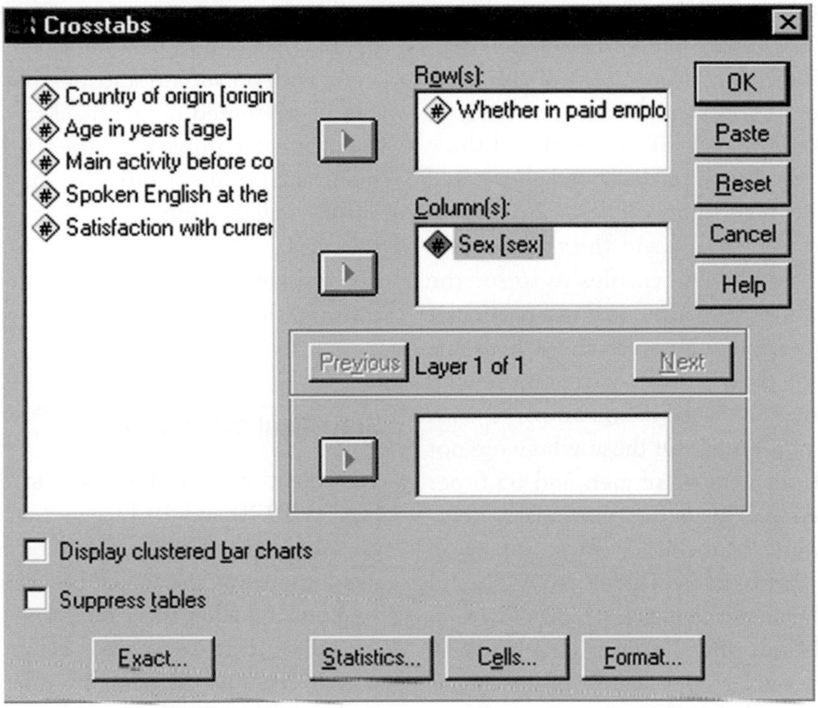

FIGURE 19.9   Cross-tabulations in SPSS

**Whether in paid employment * Sex Crosstabulation**

| | | | Sex | | Total |
|---|---|---|---|---|---|
| | | | Male | Female | |
| Whether in paid employment | Yes | Count | 14 | 4 | 18 |
| | | % within Whether in paid employment | 77.8% | 22.2% | 100.0% |
| | | % within Sex | 56.0% | 16.0% | 36.0% |
| | No | Count | 11 | 21 | 32 |
| | | % within Whether in paid employment | 34.4% | 65.6% | 100.0% |
| | | % within Sex | 44.0% | 84.0% | 64.0% |
| Total | | Count | 25 | 25 | 50 |
| | | % within Whether in paid employment | 50.0% | 50.0% | 100.0% |
| | | % within Sex | 100.0% | 100.0% | 100.0% |

FIGURE 19.10   Sex by Whether in paid employment

interviewed. Conveniently, SPSS prints out the percentage of the total represented by each marginal figure. Thus 18 is 36 per cent of the total, which is 50 (or 100 per cent).

Inside each of the cells SPSS has placed three numbers: first the count, as described above, and then two percentage figures. These are, respectively, the row percentage and the column percentage. The first of these enables us to see the proportion of those who answered in a particular way to the question who were in each group. Thus, we can say that 77.8 per cent of those who were in employment were men, compared with 22.2 per cent of women. Of those who were not working, 34.4 per cent were men and 65.6 per cent were women. This is not particularly helpful, as we want a more direct comparison between men and women. Therefore, we should look at the column percentages, which show that 56 per cent (14 out of 25) of men were working compared with only 16 per cent (4 out of 25) of women. If we were using this output to write up results in this case we would use column percentages. Deciding whether row or column percentages are appropriate is sometimes difficult, though generally the independent variable (see Chapter 20) is placed across the top of the table

and the percentage used when describing the data is the column percentage.

As with univariate statistics, bivariate statistics can be presented in graphical form, often giving them greater impact. Figure 19.11 shows how men and women differed in terms of paid employment by means of a bar chart. The vertical axis (y axis) shows the percentage working or not working while the horizontal axis (x axis) distinguishes between men and women.

## Statistical significance

We might stop at this point in our analysis of Figures 19.10 and 19.11 and conclude that men are more likely than women to be in paid employment. However, this would be a mistake. How can we know whether this result is not simply caused by chance? Perhaps we have, at random, picked an unrepresentative sample. In other words, how likely is it that we can generalise from the sample of 50 to the population from which it is drawn, which in this case are all refugees eligible to work in Britain? Estimation of the likelihood that a sample result is true of the population involves statistical inference. A variety of statistics that

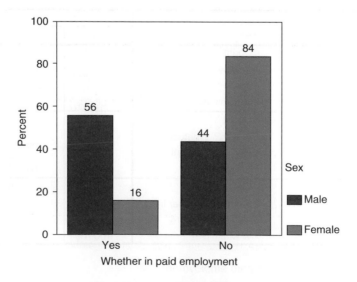

**FIGURE 19.11**   Graphical representation of a contingency table

help to do this are available, but the one most commonly used for contingency tables is known as the chi-square test. Using SPSS it is possible to obtain statistics for contingency tables (see dialogue box in Figure 19.9). Figure 19.12 shows SPSS output when a chi-square test is specified.

The information given in the SPSS output is much more detailed than is necessary for basic data analysis and interpretation. The top line of output is all that is needed here. Pearson's chi-square test produces an estimate of the statistical significance of the result in the associated table (in this case, the table in Figure 19.10). If the significance value is small (conventionally less than 0.05), then we reject what is known as the null hypothesis of no association between the two variables and say that they *are* related. That is to say, as one variable changes, so the other one changes too. A condition of using the chi-square statistic is that the sample has been collected using a probability sample (see Chapter 9). In the above example, the significance of the Pearson chi-square is 0.003, which is less than 0.05, so we can say that the result is probably not due to chance and if we had been able to study the entire population of refugees eligible for employment, then we would find the same sort of difference between men and women.

The significance of the chi-square value is sometimes known as the *p*-value with *p* standing for probability. The value of chi-square is affected by sample size. Intuitively it makes sense because a random sample of 1,000 is going to be more representative of the population than a random sample of 10 where we are more likely, by chance, to have selected atypical individuals that skew the distribution. A statistically significant result (in other words, a low *p*-value) is more likely with large samples. Additionally, the principles underlying chi-square require that the expected values in at least 20 per cent of the cells in a contingency table are more than 5. Thus, SPSS (in note b to the output shown in Figure 19.12) has produced a 'minimum expected count' of 9, indicating that it is valid to use the results of chi-square. Expected values for particular cells are those that we would expect by chance given the distribution of the marginal figures in a table. The expected value for the top left-hand cell is calculated by multiplying the left-hand column marginal (25) by the top row marginal (18) and dividing by the total sample size (50) to get 9. You will see that the actual value (usually called the observed value) in that cell is 14. The calculation of chi-square involves comparing the observed values with the expected values in cells.

The mathematical calculations that underlie the chi-square statistic are not particularly complex. It is unnecessary to learn them in

**Chi-Square Tests**

| | Value | df | Asymp. Sig. (2-sided) | Exact Sig. (2-sided) | Exact Sig. (1-sided) |
|---|---|---|---|---|---|
| Pearson Chi-Square | 8.681[b] | 1 | .003 | | |
| Continuity Correction [a] | 7.031 | 1 | .008 | | |
| Likelihood Ratio | 9.062 | 1 | .003 | | |
| Fisher's Exact Test | | | | .007 | .004 |
| Linear-by-Linear Association | 8.507 | 1 | .004 | | |
| N of Valid Cases | 50 | | | | |

a. Computed only for a 2x2 table

b. 0 cells (.0%) have expected count less than 5. The minimum expected count is 9.00.

FIGURE 19.12  Statistical output for chi-square in SPSS

order to analyse data. The suggestions for further reading at the end of this chapter contain books where these calculations are shown if you wish to take this further. The important thing to grasp is the meaning of statistics such as the chi-square rather than the underlying mathematics.

Finally, the chi-square is not the only test of significance. Others exist for data that are not arranged in contingency tables. However, all have the same underlying purpose of allowing estimates to be made about the likelihood of a sample having produced a chance result. Whatever the underlying statistic, this likelihood is usually expressed as a *p*-value.

## Measures of association

In contingency tables statistics can also be used to indicate the strength and direction of association between variables. Such statistics are known as measures of association and they are produced in SPSS using the same dialogue box as the one used for producing chi-square statistics. Output relevant to Figure 19.10 is given in Figure 19.13, showing two of the many tests of association available: *phi* and *Cramer's V*.

Each measure of association has slightly different characteristics, and the choice of which to use is governed by the level of measurement of the variables in the table (e.g. whether nominal or ordinal), and by how many cells there are in the table. SPSS gives on-screen help in selecting the test most appropriate for each type of table. For a 2 × 2 contingency table (in other words, a table with two variables each with two categories), the most appropriate statistic to use is *phi*. For larger tables *Cramer's V* is a more appropri-

ate statistic and will give a slightly different result where such tables are involved. Association can vary between 0 and +1 or −1. An association can therefore be positive or negative. A perfect positive association is indicated by +1, a perfect negative association by −1 and the absence of association by zero. An association of 0.417, as shown in Figure 19.13, suggests a moderate positive association between the variables.

You should note that the concept of association is not quite the same as the concept of correlation. As you will see in the next section, variables can sometimes be associated but not correlated. It is very important to distinguish between these two concepts and the very different concept of significance. For example, a relationship can show an association or a correlation, but may nevertheless fail to be significant if the sample size is too small.

Although it is good practice to report both a test of significance and one of association when writing up the results of a research project, measures of association are often omitted when considering data in tables. This is because a judgement of strength and direction can be made simply by examining the percentages in the table. Additionally, the various tests of association for tables do not always 'behave themselves'. For a variety of reasons, some do not indicate the direction of associations, or may indicate stronger or weaker associations than really exist. For these reasons they are rather rough-and-ready tools, compared with the more consistent chi-square test.

## Using interval variables

When variables have many values, as is often the case with interval variables such as *income*, or as mentioned earlier *age*, they can be recoded into a few categories so that they can be presented in bar charts or tables. However, this represents a loss of information and the raw data can be used graphically and statistically to explore the relationship between variables. Using an example of the *number of hours worked* and *income*, Figure 19.14 shows four graphical representations of possible

|  |  | Value | Approx Sig. |
|---|---|---|---|
| Nominal by Nominal | Phi | 0.417 | 0.003 |
|  | Cramer's V | 0.417 | 0.003 |
| N of Valid Cases |  | 50 |  |

**FIGURE 19.13**  Tests of association for a crosstabulation produced by SPSS

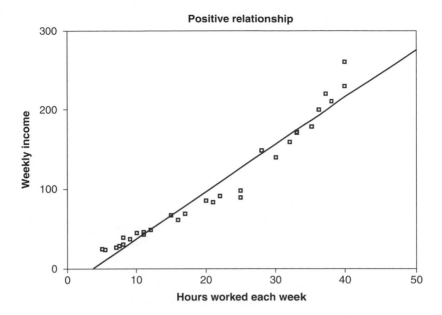

**Positive relationship**

$r = 0.976$
$p < 0.000$ (significant at 0.01)

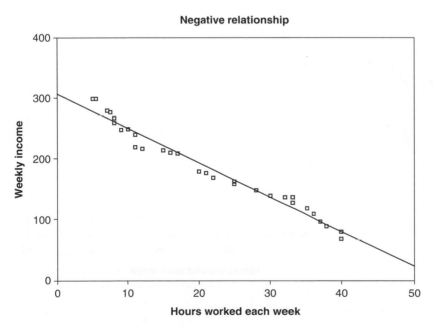

**Negative relationship**

$r = -.985$
$p < 0.000$ (significant at 0.01)

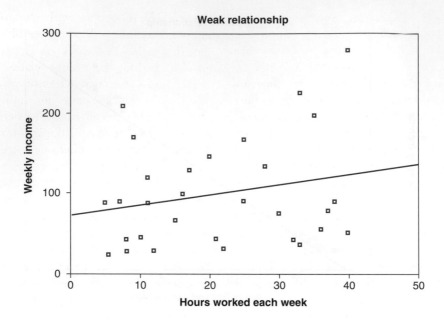

r = .220
p = .243

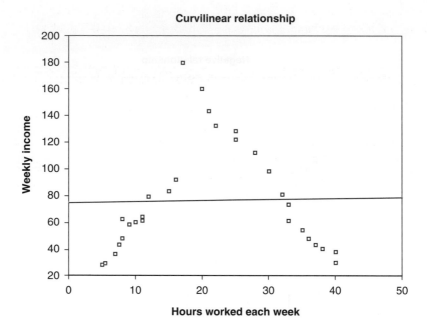

r = .023
p = .902

**FIGURE 19.14** Scattergrams showing different relationships between the number of hours worked and income

relationships between the number of hours worked and income.

Scattergrams (or scatterplots as they are sometimes known) are produced in SPSS by pulling down the 'graph' menu and choosing 'scatter'. The statistics are produced by pulling down the 'analyse' menu, choosing 'correlate' and then 'bivariate', as Figure 19.15 shows. From the bivariate correlations dialogue box the *Pearson coefficient* and the *two-tailed test of significance* were selected to produce the output in Figure 19.14. By selecting a two-tailed test the researcher is making no assumptions about the direction of the correlation – in other words, whether it will be positive or negative.

The first scattergram in Figure 19.14 shows a positive relationship between the variables *number of hours worked* and *income*. That means it shows a scatter of points rising from the bottom left corner to the top right. Each of the points represents a person about whom two facts are recorded: the number of hours worked and their weekly income. The first scattergram shows that the more hours people work, the greater their income. In other words, as one variable increases, the other variable increases too. This is the defining characteristic of a positive relationship.

The next scattergram demonstrates a negative relationship, which means that the more hours worked the less people earn. The defining characteristic of a negative relationship is that as one variable increases, the other one decreases.

The third scattergram demonstrates a relationship that is so weak it is almost absent, while the fourth one shows a curvilinear relationship. Here, there is an initial increase in income in line with the increase in the number of hours worked. However, after a peak in income at 17 hours a week, the amount of income starts to decrease with an increase in hours.

The line that runs through the points in each of these scattergrams is the line of best fit or regression line. It is the single straight line that can be drawn through the cluster of points that involves the least distance between it and all the points. It is useful in making predictions.

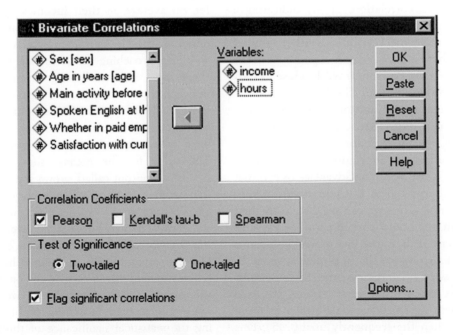

**FIGURE 19.15** Getting correlations in SPSS

With a scattergram that shows a strong relationship between variables it is possible to predict the values of one variable from the values of another, in this case income and hours worked, by using the points on the regression line. Thus, in the first scattergram, we might reasonably predict that someone working 20 hours a week would earn roughly 100 income units. Predicting income by hours worked where there is no relationship or where there is a curvilinear relationship would be misleading as, in practice, the points are very far away from the regression line. Making predictions only makes sense if there is a positive or negative linear relationship where most of the points are reasonably close to the line.

Below the scattergrams there is also a value for $r$ (which is Pearson's $r$) and a $p$-value, both generated by SPSS. The value of Pearson's $r$ is a measure of *correlation* (sometimes called a correlation coefficient) and it indicates how close the points are to the line, measuring how *strong* the relationship is. If most of the points are close to the line, this statistic will be close to +1, indicating a strong positive correlation, or −1, indicating a strong negative correlation. In fact, if all the points fall on the line, Pearson's $r$ is either +1 or −1 exactly. If there is broad scatter of points, as in the third scattergram, Pearson's $r$ will be close to zero, indicating no correlation. The Pearson's correlation coefficient is an indicator of association suitable for use with two interval variables. Sometimes, $r$ is squared; for example, the $r^2$ for the first scattergram in Figure 19.14 would be $0.976 \times 0.976 = 0.953$. The advantage of $r^2$ is that it can be interpreted as the percentage of variance explained. Thus we can say that, in the first scattergram, the hours worked per week explains 95.3 per cent of the variability in weekly income.

You will also notice that a $p$-value is given. In the first two scattergrams the SPSS output shows that the relationship between the two variables was significant at 0.01 (which is more significant than the frequently used 0.05). This indicates that the relationship is very likely to hold true in the population, if this is a random

sample drawn from that population. In both of the first two cases we would say that the relationship is strong and statistically significant. In the last two we could not say this as $p > 0.05$. You should notice that Pearson's $r$ is not suited to indicate curvilinear relationships. Unless we saw the fourth scattergram, we would not be aware that this relationship actually existed. This why, earlier in this chapter, we noted that association and correlation are not exactly the same thing. A curvilinear relationship is an association between variables, but because it is not linear (that is to say, the points are not close to a straight line) it is not a correlation.

## Comparing the means of two groups

So far, we have considered relationships between two variables measured at the same level. Quite frequently, however, the social researcher is concerned with comparing the average values between two or more groups of people. Thus, we might be interested in how men and women differ, on average, in their incomes. This type of relationship can be understood as one between a nominal variable and an interval variable. One way of approaching this is to establish whether there is a statistically significant difference between the means of the two groups.

Figure 19.16 shows SPSS output from a data set containing 10 men and 10 women who have been asked to indicate their annual income. The value for the means (shown under the first bit of output called 'group statistics') shows that women earn more, on average, than men: £14,780 compared with £9,255 for men. The standard deviations for each are given, indicating a greater spread of incomes for men. The question that then arises, though, is whether this difference is likely to hold true in the population from which this sample of 20 has been drawn (we assume) at random. This, then, becomes a problem concerning the statistical significance of the result, the same problem for which (as you saw earlier) the chi-square is used when tables are involved.

**Group Statistics**

| | SEX | N | Mean | Std. Deviation | Std. Error Mean |
|---|---|---|---|---|---|
| INCURV | Male | 10 | 9255.0000 | 6202.6182 | 1961.4401 |
| | Female | 10 | 14780.00 | 3489.9220 | 1103.6102 |

**Independent Samples Test**

| | | Levene's Test for Equality of Variances | | t-test for Equality of Means | | | | | 95% Confidence Interval of the Difference | |
|---|---|---|---|---|---|---|---|---|---|---|
| | | F | Sig. | t | df | Sig. (2-tailed) | Mean Difference | Std. Error Difference | Lower | Upper |
| INCURV | Equal variances assumed | 6.914 | .017 | -2.455 | 18 | .024 | -5525.0000 | 2250.6005 | -10253.3 | -796.6637 |
| | Equal variances not assumed | | | -2.455 | 14.179 | .028 | -5525.0000 | 2250.6005 | -10346.3 | -703.6631 |

FIGURE 19.16   SPSS output comparing levels of income of men and women

The estimation of statistical significance here, though, is based instead on the significance of the *t*-value (this procedure is known as a *t*-test) and two of these are shown under the heading 'Sig (2-tailed)'. These are .024 and .028, so $p<0.05$ and we can conclude that this difference between men and women's income holds true in the population from which this sample was drawn.

The statistics shown in Figure 19.16 are obtained in SPSS from a submenu of the 'analyse' menu. Once the 'analyse' box is pulled down, the next step is to click on 'compare means' and then 'independent samples t-test'. The dependent variable is placed in the test variable box and the 'grouping' variable – which is the independent variable – is placed in the grouping variable box. The 'define groups' box then becomes active and the variable values have to be specified as shown in Figure 19.17. In this case women are coded 1 and men are coded 2.

Sometimes in social research it is important to compare the means of more than two groups. Thus, for example, social class might be measured as upper, middle and lower. If we wished to compare the mean income of groups defined in this way, the *t*-test would be inappropriate, and a

related procedure known as the analysis of variance would be used. Details of this are beyond the scope of this chapter, but can be explored in further reading.

## Conclusion

In this chapter we have moved from the analysis of single variables to a consideration of two-variable analysis. You should by now be familiar with the idea of a frequency distribution and of statistics such as the mean that measure the central tendency of such distributions. You were introduced to the use of the standard deviation to indicate the dispersal of cases around the mean. Further on in the chapter, contingency tables were discussed, followed by a discussion of statistical significance and the way this is indicated for tables by the *p*-value derived from chi-square. It is important to distinguish the idea of statistical significance from the idea of association. The former enables us to judge whether we can infer from a sample to the population from which it is drawn. The latter describes the strength and direction of relationships between variables,

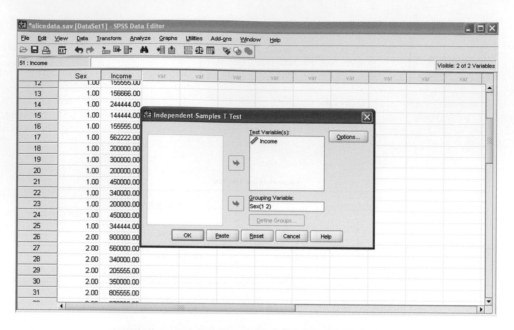

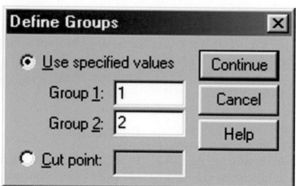

**FIGURE 19.17** Comparing means and carrying out *t*-tests in SPSS

regardless of sample size. With large samples even quite weak associations will be significant; with small samples it will be hard to attain significance whatever the strength of association.

The discussion of association moved us away from tabular analysis to consideration of scattergrams and relationships between interval variables. Different strengths and directions of association were illustrated. The use of regression to predict values of one variable from another was briefly touched upon, before the application of tests of association to data in tables was explored. Finally, we considered the use of the *t*-test to indicate the significance of differences between the means of two groups. Throughout the chapter there have been screen shots from SPSS to show the commands needed to analyse data as well as the output that is generated both numerically and graphically. Combine your reading of this chapter with some hands-on experience of SPSS (which has superb 'help' facilities if you get stuck) and you will find that you too can generate and interpret the kind of statistical analyses shown here.

A good way to begin analysing quantitative data is to start using SPSS for Windows, which has a helpful tutorial, a demonstration data set and good on-line help. There are a plethora of books available. Fielding and Gilbert (2000) offers a clear introduction both to statistics and to SPSS. De Vaus (2002a) gives a brief but clearly explained guide to the main principles of quantitative data analysis. De Vaus (2002b) presents clear and simple solutions to the problems researchers face when carrying out data analysis. Bryman and Cramer (2008) relate their explanations of statistical methods to output from SPSS.

## Student Reader (Seale, 2004b): relevant readings

18  A.N. Oppenheim: 'The quantification of questionnaire data'

19  Paul F. Lazarsfeld: 'Interpretation of statistical relations as a research operation'

20  Morris Rosenberg: 'The strategy of survey analysis'

## Journal articles illustrating use of the methods described in this chapter

Im, E-O. and Chee, W. (2005) 'A descriptive internet survey on menopausal symptoms: five ethnic groups of Asian American University faculty and staff', Journal of Transcultural Nursing, 16: 126–135.

Seale, C. (2009) 'Legalisation of euthanasia or physician-assisted suicide: survey of doctors' attitudes', Palliative Medicine, 205–212.

Smith, H.P. and Kaminski, R.J. (2011) 'Self-injurious behaviors in state prisons: findings from a national survey', Criminal Justice and Behavior, 38: 26–41.

## Web links

Tabulating and graphing data: http://glass.ed.asu.edu/stats/lesson1

Online analysis of data (you don't need SPSS to do statistical analysis!): http://glass.ed.asu.edu/stats/online.htm

Free statistics: www.freestatistics.info

SPSS tutorial: http://it.chass.ncsu.edu/training/SPSS/

Hyperstat Online statistics textbook: http://davidmlane.com/hyperstat/index.html

Selecting statistical tests: a decision aid tool: www.socialresearchmethods.net/selstat/ssstart.htm

**Advice:** Use these, along with the review questions in the next section, to test your knowledge of the contents of this chapter. Try to define each of the key concepts listed here; if you have understood this chapter you should be able to do this. Check your definitions against the definition in the glossary at the end of the book.

*(Continued)*

*(Continued)*

Analysis of variance

Association

Bar charts

Bivariate, univariate and multivariate analysis

Bivariate statistics

Causality

Cell

Charts

Chi-square test

Column marginal

Column percentage

Column variable

Contingency tables

Correlation

Correlation coefficient

Count

Curvilinear relationship

Descriptive statistics

Expected and observed values

Frequency distribution

Histogram

Mean

Measures of association

Measures of central tendency

Median

Mode

Negative association or relationship

Normal curve

Null hypothesis

Pearson's $r$

Percentage of variance explained

Pie charts

Positive association or relationship

$p$-value

$r^2$

Range

Recoding variables

Regression line or line of best fit

Row marginal

Row percentage

Row variable

Scattergram or scatterplot

Skewed distribution

Standard deviation

Statistical inference

$t$-test

Two-tailed test

Uniivariate statistics

Value labels

x axis

y axis

## ◖ ▪ Review questions

1  Describe the difference between univariate and bivariate statistics.
2  What information does a frequency distribution provide?
3  What information does a contingency table provide?
4  Describe three measures of central tendency.
5  What is statistical inference?
6  What is a chi-square test used for?
7  What is the difference between correlation and association?

8  What kind of variable are *t*-tests suited to and what does a *t*-test tell you?

9  What is the difference between a test of association and a test of significance?

10  Describe the purpose of (a) a pie chart, (b) a histogram and (c) a scattergram.

# Workshop and discussion exercises

1

  (a) Using the data matrix in Table 19.1, draw a frequency distribution for the variable *Working.* Do the same for *Age,* recoding it into three broad categories. Draw a bar chart of these distributions. Calculate the mean, median and mode for each variable.

  (b) Construct contingency tables that show the relationship between: *Sex* and *Working; Sex* and *Jobsat; Working* and *Jobsat.* Ensure that each cell contains a count and column and row percentages. Describe the character of the relationships which you find.

  (c) Draw a scattergram, plotting *Age* against *Jobsat.* Describe the character of this relationship.

  (d) Using the recoded version of *Age* construct contingency tables showing the relationship between this variable and each of the other three variables. Describe the character of the relationships you find.

  (e) If you are learning SPSS or another statistical package, try inputting these data. You will find it easier to get the computer to do the analyses specified above. You can also generate tests of association and significance and consider the meaning of these. Try using the software to produce output in the form of graphs (e.g. pie charts, histograms).

TABLE 19.1  A data matrix

| | Variables or questions | | | |
| --- | --- | --- | --- | --- |
| | Sex | Age | Working | Jobsat |
| Case 1 | Male | 66 | No | Missing |
| Case 2 | Female | 34 | Full time | 1 |
| Case 3 | Female | 25 | Part time | 2 |
| Case 4 | Female | 44 | Full time | 5 |
| Case 5 | Male | 78 | No | Missing |
| Case 6 | Male | 40 | Full time | 2 |
| Case 7 | Male | 33 | Full time | 1 |
| Case 8 | Male | 16 | No | Missing |
| Case 9 | Female | 35 | Full time | 1 |
| Case 10 | Female | 45 | Full time | 2 |
| Case 11 | Male | 30 | No | Missing |
| Case 12 | Female | 56 | Part time | 4 |
| Case 13 | Male | 79 | No | Missing |
| Case 14 | Male | 60 | Part time | 4 |
| Case 15 | Female | 55 | Part time | 4 |
| Case 16 | Female | 54 | Part time | 5 |
| Case 17 | Male | 55 | Full time | 1 |
| Case 18 | Male | 17 | No | Missing |
| Case 19 | Female | 23 | Full time | 3 |
| Case 20 | Female | 20 | No | Missing |

2  Table 19.2 consists of four contingency tables (a–d) demonstrating different types of relationship between the two variables of social class and home ownership. Below each is a *p*-value and the result of a test of association (Q). For each table, describe the character of the relationship and explain why the *p*-values and tests of association vary.

**TABLE 19.2** Tables showing different relationships between social class and home ownership (column %)

| Home ownership | (a) Social class | | | Home ownership | (b) Social class | | |
|---|---|---|---|---|---|---|---|
| | Lower | Middle | Upper | | Lower | Middle | Upper |
| Owner | 20 | 30 | 50 | Owner | 60 | 40 | 3 |
| Private, rented | 30 | 40 | 30 | Private, rented | 35 | 35 | 45 |
| Council, rented | 50 | 30 | 20 | Council, rented | 5 | 25 | 52 |

$p < 0.01$, Q = 0.6                                   $p < 0.01$, Q = −0.8

| Home ownership | (c) Social class | | | Home ownership | (d) Social class | | |
|---|---|---|---|---|---|---|---|
| | Lower | Middle | Upper | | Lower | Middle | Upper |
| Owner | 33 | 32 | 36 | Owner | 56 | 10 | 59 |
| Private, rented | 30 | 28 | 33 | Private, rented | 23 | 20 | 22 |
| Council, rented | 37 | 40 | 31 | Council, rented | 21 | 70 | 19 |

$p < 0.05$, Q = 0.04                                   $p < 0.01$, Q = −0.02

3 This is a structured exercise in reading a statistical table that aims to give you a general strategy for perceiving the main messages of such tables. You could apply this approach to Table 17.1 in this book, or find tables as suggested in the fourth workshop and discussion exercise associated with Chapter 17. You will find that not all of the questions are relevant to every table, but experience has shown that these steps, if followed carefully, enable a deeper understanding of any statistical table.

(a) Read the title before you look at any numbers. What does this reveal about the content of the table?

(b) Look at the source: who produced the data, with what purpose? Was it a census or a sample?

(c) Look at any notes above or below the table. How will they influence its scope and your interpretation?

(d) Read the column and row titles. They indicate which variables are applied to the data.

(e) How many variables are there and what are they? Can any be considered independent or dependent?

(f) How are the variables measured? Are there any omissions or peculiarities in the measurement scale? How else might such a measure have been constructed?

(g) What units are used – percentages, thousands, millions? If you are dealing with percentages, then which way adds up to 100 per cent?

(h) Look at the 'All' or 'Total' column. These are usually found on the right-hand column and/or the bottom row (the 'margins' of a table). What do variations in the row or column tell you about the variables concerned?

(i) Now look at some rows and/or columns *inside* the table. What do these tell you about the relationships between variables? What social processes might have generated the trends you find?

(j) Is it possible to make causal statements about the relationship between variables? If so, do any of these involve the interaction of more than two variables?

(k) What are the shortcomings of the data in drawing conclusions about social processes?

(l) What other enquiries could be conducted to take this analysis further?

(m) Finally, consider the issue of whether the table reveals something about social reality, or creates a particular way of thinking about reality.

## 20

# STATISTICAL REASONING: CAUSAL ARGUMENTS AND MULTIVARIATE ANALYSIS

## Clive Seale

| Chapter Contents |
|---|

It was argued in Chapter 2 that the search for causal explanations has often been a part of a positivist enterprise, reflecting a desire to generate law-like statements about the workings of society, so that social life is thought of as analogous to a physical structure, or at best a biological organism. Additionally, in Chapter 3, concerning the uses of theory in social research, it was argued, using the example of Moerman's (1974) study of the Lue, that qualitative research is particularly suited to showing *how* people generate meaningful social life. For example, the Lue achieve their ethnic identity by using 'ethnic identification devices' strategically in interactions with, say, visiting anthropologists. (Thus, they claim to like certain foods above others, or to possess certain beliefs, which they say are 'characteristic' of their particular ethnic identity.)

The sociologist Max Weber, who is often associated with the interpretive approach to social research aspired to by many qualitative researchers, was interested in causal reasoning too. Weber's criteria for adequate explanations of social life involved explanations adequate at the levels of both cause and meaning (Marsh, 1982). Put in another way, we could argue that as well as asking *how* people achieve various effects (or meanings) in their social lives, we should also be concerned with *why* certain effects are achieved rather than others. Examples of such 'why' questions might be:

- Following Mary Douglas's theory about anomalies (Box 3.3), we could hypothesise that more threatened social groups are less likely to tolerate anomalies, this being reflected in the frequencies with which certain foods were eaten.

- We know that male asylum seekers are more likely to be in paid employment than female asylum seekers (see Chapter 19). Could this be because they are better qualified, or is there some other explanation?

- Does getting a good degree result in better pay in the long run?

These are examples of causal hypotheses. Quantitative methods can help to establish whether such hypotheses can be supported. Crude beliefs in the unity of science (e.g. that people and molecules are similar classes of being), or a lack of interest in how people actively construct meaningful worlds, are not necessarily involved when pursuing an interest in causal explanations. This chapter will show you how to construct causal arguments with statistics. It depends on a thorough understanding of the concepts introduced in Chapter 19. You should also review Chapter 8 on research design before proceeding, because this also introduces ideas that are essential in understanding how to construct causal arguments. In fact, I'll remind you now about some essential ideas about research design, drawing on the more extended discussion you will find in Chapter 8

## Research design

### Experiments and quasi-experiments

In social research, it is very hard to conduct experiments like the randomised controlled trial described in Chapter 8. For the most part, it is difficult to manipulate people's social worlds to the extent required in a full experiment. To test the hypothesis that social groups under threat tend to have different views about the consumption of 'anomalous' foods, one would have to randomly allocate people to groups that were either threatened or not threatened. To test the hypothesis that higher education causes income levels to vary, one would have to randomly allocate people to different types of lifetime educational experience. Clearly this is going to be difficult, if not impossible. While it is sometimes possible in social research to use such experimental designs, the intervention often changes people's social realities so much that the setting involved becomes artificial (e.g. the psychology laboratory), so that generalising results from the experimental setting to the real world becomes difficult (an issue of the external validity of the experiment, for which see Chapter 30).

In dealing with data derived from social surveys, therefore, one is usually faced with the necessity to adopt a quasi-experimental approach. This involves the manipulation of data so that a causal *argument* is gradually built up from the data, in which associations between variables are demonstrated, arguments for and against the view that these are causal associations are considered, and then further data analysis is done to test out these arguments. There are a variety of ways in which this can be done, but the most accessible of these is to conduct analysis via contingency tables. The elaboration paradigm is a term used to describe this type of analysis of tables, which was developed by quantitative social researchers in America in the 1940s and 1950s. Rosenberg's *The Logic of Survey Analysis* (1968) provides a classic account of the approach. The present

chapter will first explain the techniques of the elaboration paradigm before going on to discuss other techniques of multivariate analysis.

## Cross-sectional and longitudinal designs

Because time order is important in establishing causality (see Chapter 8), it is also important to know whether data arise from a cross-sectional study, in which people (or other units of analysis) are studied at a single point in time, or from a longitudinal study, in which they are followed over a period of time.

In the example in Box 20.1, a longitudinal design would enable time order to be established. If the same people were followed over a long period of time, the researcher would know when things happened and would treat differently cases where respiratory illness occurred before the move into damp housing.

---

**BOX 20.1**

### PROBLEM WITH TIME ORDER

- *Research question*: Do damp housing conditions cause respiratory illness?
- *Variables*: Does the person live in damp housing or not? Does the person have a respiratory illness or not?
- *Time order problem*: Did the illness start before moving into the damp housing conditions, or after?

---

A cross-sectional study could also deal with the time order problem, but with greater difficulty. Questions would have to go into *when* things happened. People's capacity to remember things like the onset of illness is not always very reliable.

Although longitudinal studies have an advantage in controlling time order problems, they also have some disadvantages. They can be expensive, since following people at time intervals involves more visits for data collection and keeping in touch with a large sample can be difficult. People taking part in longitudinal studies

may drop out, leading to poor response rates (see Chapter 9) at the later follow-up points, or they may start to feel special in some way because they are taking part in a research project and therefore act differently (the problem of reactivity, also described in Chapter 14).

A compromise between cross-sectional and longitudinal designs is the time series design, in which a cross-sectional survey is repeated at intervals. At each point the same method for sampling from the population and the same questions are asked, but the people studied are (or may be) different. This enables comparisons and trends over time to be established, but does not necessarily deal with time order problems in causal analysis. The General Household Survey (see Chapter 17) is an example of a time series study.

A brief description of the three research designs is given in Box 20.2.

---

**BOX 20.2**

### THREE RESEARCH DESIGNS

- *Cross-sectional*: a sample is studied at a single point in time.

- *Longitudinal*: a sample is studied at intervals over a period of time.

- *Time series*: samples chosen in the same way each time are studied using the same questions at different points in time.

(See Chapter 8 for a fuller discussion of these and other research designs)

---

## The elaboration paradigm

### Dependent and independent variables

Before beginning this section, it is worth pausing for a moment to define what is meant by the division of variables into those called independent and those called dependent. Crudely, one can understand an independent variable as being a *cause*, and a dependent one as being an *effect*. The effect variables 'depend upon' variation in the cause variables. In the examples discussed earlier in this chapter, independent variables were:

- The degree to which social groups are under threat.

- Being a male or female asylum seeker.

- Getting or not getting a good degree.

Dependent variables were:

- The frequency with which certain foods are eaten.

- Being in paid employment or not.

- Level of pay.

Establishing whether a variable can be considered dependent or independent is sometimes not straightforward; it may, for example, depend on issues of time order. Take the example of education and income. Clearly, it is reasonable to assume that in a sample of middle-aged adults, their income might be determined to some extent by whether they were university graduates or not. But let us imagine that by 'income' we mean the overall wealth of people's family of origin. In this case, many people's 'income' will have been established long before they entered the education system. Indeed, it may have been established before they were born! Here, 'income' precedes education and, one could argue, could be considered to be the independent variable (the cause), with education being the dependent variable (the effect). Establishing the point in time at which variables are measured is important in constructing an argument about which can be considered dependent on the other. For this, one needs an understanding of the way in which the data being analysed were originally produced – in other words, the research design that lies behind the data.

### Relationships between three variables

For the moment, though, we will deal with situations that commonly arise when cross-sectional data, perhaps derived from a social survey, is being analysed with a view to constructing causal arguments. Here, the elaboration paradigm, in which contingency tables are broken down into subtables, often becomes relevant.

Table 20.1 shows a series of tables in which different sorts of relationships between three variables are displayed, below an initial or zero-order contingency table. Look first at this top table ((a) (i)) which shows the relationship between educational achievement and income. For simplicity, all the variables in the table are dichotomous; that is, they have two values. Thus educational achievement and income are divided into 'high' and 'low'. This is a rather crude measurement of these variables; the ideas of the elaboration paradigm can be applied to more sophisticated measures too.

Within each cell is a count and a column percentage. In the zero-order table, this indicates that 60 per cent of the 200 people with 'high' levels of educational achievement have achieved a 'high' income, compared with 40 per cent of the 200 people with a 'low' level of education. This is a moderate association, but is a statistically significant result. Phi, a measure of association, has a value of 0.20; gamma, another measure of association, and perhaps the one best suited to this type of table as it is designed for ordinal variables, gives a value of 0.38. You will recall from the previous chapter that tests of association generally conform to the rule that a value of 0 indicates the absence of association, and a value of +1 or −1 indicates either perfect positive or perfect negative association. The $p$-value, based on chi-square, is 0.00006, way below the level of 0.05 where one normally accepts that two variables are likely to be related in the population from which a sample is drawn.

One can imagine that a researcher might have generated this first table in order to present an argument that gaining educational qualifications tends to cause people to get more highly paid jobs. Initially, it seems, the zero-order table supports this view. But a counter-argument might be that in fact this is a spurious result. In other words, the argument would be that although there is a statistical association between these variables, it is in fact caused by some other factor. Gender, for example, may explain the association. Perhaps it is the case that, in the population from which this sample is drawn, boys are encouraged by their parents to do well at school and to think of themselves as high achievers in the job market. This factor of gender-biased parental encouragement may have produced the initial association, suggesting that it is caused by gender (or rather the things associated with gender) rather than representing any real causal relationship between what one learns in the education system and the jobs one can do as a consequence.

In order to *test* this counter-argument the research can break down the initial zero-order table into two tables, first examining the relationship for men, and then that for women. This generates conditional or first-order tables, showing how the relationship between the variables in the zero-order table looks when considered separately for different values (in other words, male and female) of the third or test variable. Replication is said to occur if the original relationship remains, as is the case in the first pair of conditional tables ((a) (ii)). Here, the researcher can conclude that gender does *not* affect the relationship between educational achievement and income. This is reflected both in the percentages and in the two tests of association, which show little change when compared with the zero-order statistics (although note that the $p$-values are no longer so low, as the sample size has reduced in each of the two tables compared with the size of sample in the zero-order table).

In the next pair of conditional tables ((a) (iii)) you will see that the tests of association are both close to zero in both tables. Additionally, the $p$-value indicates that neither table shows a statistically significant result. If you examine the percentages, you can confirm that there is no association between the variables.

**TABLE 20.1** Demonstration of the elaboration paradigm: the relationship between education and income, as affected by gender

*(a) (i) Zero-order table showing an association*

| | Educational achievement | |
|---|---|---|
| Income | High | Low |
| High | 120 (60%) | 80 (40%) |
| Low | 80 (40%) | 120 (60%) |
| Total | 200 (100%) | 200 (100%) |

$p = 0.00006$; phi = 0.20; gamma = 0.38

*(a) (ii) Replication*

| | Men | | | | Women | | |
|---|---|---|---|---|---|---|---|
| | Educational achievement | | | | Educational achievement | | |
| Income | High | Low | | Income | High | Low | |
| High | 40 (61%) | 26 (39%) | | High | 80 (60%) | 54 (40%) | |
| Low | 26 (39%) | 40 (61%) | | Low | 54 (40%) | 80 (60%) | |
| Total | 66 (100%) | 66 (100%) | | Total | 134 (100%) | 134 (100%) | |

$p = 0.01481$; phi = 0.21; gamma = 0.41         $p = 0.00149$; phi = 0.19; gamma = 0.37

*(a) (iii) Spurious or intervening*

| | Men | | | | Women | | |
|---|---|---|---|---|---|---|---|
| | Educational achievement | | | | Educational achievement | | |
| Income | High | Low | | Income | High | Low | |
| High | 112 (78%) | 64 (76%) | | High | 8 (14%) | 16 (14%) | |
| Low | 32 (22%) | 20 (24%) | | Low | 48 (86%) | 100 (86%) | |
| Total | 144 (100%) | 84 (100%) | | Total | 56 (100%) | 116 (100%) | |

$p = 0.78290$; phi = 0.02; gamma = 0.04         $p = 0.93038$; phi = 0.01; gamma = 0.02

*(a) (iv) Specification*

| | Men | | | | Women | | |
|---|---|---|---|---|---|---|---|
| | Educational achievement | | | | Educational achievement | | |
| Income | High | Low | | Income | High | Low | |
| High | 90 (60%) | 50 (33%) | | High | 30 (60%) | 30 (60%) | |
| Low | 60 (40%) | 100 (67%) | | Low | 20 (40%) | 20 (40%) | |
| Total | 150 (100%) | 150 (100%) | | Total | 50 (100%) | 50 (100%) | |

$p <0.00000$; phi = 0.27; gamma = 0.50         $p = 1.00000$; phi = 0.00; gamma = 0.00

*(b) (i) Zero-order table showing no association*

| | Educational achievement | |
|---|---|---|
| Income | High | Low |
| High | 120 (60%) | 120 (60%) |
| Low | 80 (40%) | 200 (100%) |
| Total | 80 (40%) | 200 (100%) |

$p = 1.00000$; phi = 0.00; gamma = 0.00

*(b) (ii) Suppressor*

| Men | | | Women | | |
|---|---|---|---|---|---|
| Educational achievement | | | Educational achievement | | |
| Income | High | Low | Income | High | Low |
| High | 20 (67%) | 20 (20%) | High | 100 (59%) | 100 (100%) |
| Low | 10 (33%) | 80 (80%) | Low | 70 (41%) | 0 (0%) |
| Total | 30 (100%) | 100 (100%) | Total | 170 (100%) | 100 (100%) |

$p < 0.00000$; phi = 0.43; gamma = 0.78          $p < 0.00000$; phi = −0.45; gamma = −1.00

Educational achievement appears to make no difference to income, once gender is taken into account (or 'controlled for'). If the original relationship disappears once a test variable is entered, as it does here, we may conclude either that the relationship was spurious, which is to say that gender has caused the association between educational achievement and income, or that the test variable is an intervening one. For a variable to be considered intervening, it must be caused to vary by the independent variable in the zero-order relationship, and in turn must cause variation in the dependent variable (see Box 20.3).

---

**BOX 20.3**

## AN EXAMPLE OF AN INTERVENING VARIABLE

Educational achievement could be seen as intervening in the relationship between people's social class of origin and their eventual social class in adult life. Here, the argument goes, people who are well off provide the type of education that allows their offspring to enter occupations of similarly high status to their parents.

---

In Table 20.1, though, it is not reasonable to argue that gender intervenes between educational achievement and income. This is because one's level of educational achievement does not cause one's gender to vary! Clearly, gender is largely established by the time one enters the educational system. In fact, the zero-order association is caused by the fact that boys tend to be both high achievers and high-income earners, while girls are the opposite. That is to say, gender is independently associated with both educational achievement and income. An argument about time order, then, must be generated in order to distinguish between spurious and intervening variables. The tables alone will not solve this problem for you.

A further possible outcome when a test variable is entered is that one of the conditional tables will demonstrate an association, whereas another will not. This is known as specification because the test variable has specified the conditions under which the original relationship holds true (this is also sometimes called interaction). Thus, in the third pair of conditional tables ((a) (iv)) the relationship between education and income is present for men but not for women. Try reading the percentages in the table, and the tests of significance and association, to see how this can be supported. Such a finding may lead the researcher into further theorising and data analysis. Could it be that men take more vocationally oriented courses than women, for example? Clearly, further data collection and analysis would be needed to explore such a relationship.

Finally, we can consider the idea that a test variable may hide or suppress the existence of a relationship in a zero-order table. It is often the case that social researchers faced with a table that suggests the absence of association between two variables give up on their hypotheses at that point, concluding that further reasoning along these lines is inappropriate. It is sometimes said that the presence of association is not enough, on its own, to demonstrate causation. However, it is not often appreciated that *absence* of association is not enough to prove *absence* of causation. Table 20.1 shows how this can occur. The second zero-order table ((b) (i)) suggests that 60 per cent of people have a high income, regardless of their educational achievement. The conditional tables ((b) (ii)), though, suggest that for men there is a strong positive relationship between educational achievement and income, while for women educational achievement appears to

militate against achieving a high income (a negative relationship). Clearly, if such a finding occurred it would be of particular interest, and would justify further argument and data analysis to establish what had led to this pattern.

Notice, too, what has happened to the tests of association (phi and gamma) in tables (b) (ii). In the left-hand table, these are positive values, reflecting the positive nature of the relationship. In the right-hand table, they are negative values. Note too that in the right-hand table gamma gives a value of −1.00, which in theory is supposed to indicate a perfect pure relationship. A glance at the table reveals this to be misleading; it is in fact an artefact of the way in which gamma is calculated that has distorted the value in a table where one of the cells has no cases in it. It is for this sort of reason that it was stated in the previous chapter that tests of association are somewhat crude devices, and that examination of percentages is recommended as well when interpreting tabulated results.

To summarise, the elaboration paradigm is a way in which tabular analysis can be used to assess the adequacy of causal arguments in social research. Through elaborating the relationships found in bivariate analysis by entering third variables as tests of causal propositions, one can gradually build up plausible arguments about what might be going on in an area of social life. One can never, eventually, prove beyond reasonable doubt that one event has caused another. In fact, this method of analysis follows closely the ideas of Popper, who proposed that science proceeded by sustained attempts at falsifying theories (see Chapter 2), as well as Campbell (see Chapter 30), who stressed the evaluation of threats to internal validity in a similar spirit. When all plausible counter-arguments to a proposition have been tested, progress has been made. On the way, deeper understanding will have been achieved through the fruitful interaction between data and argument that is the characteristic of good data analysis.

Box 20.4 give an explanation of the elaboration paradigm.

BOX 20.4

## THE ELABORATION PARADIGM

An initial zero-order relationship between two variables, when examined under separate values of a test variable, may result in:

- *Replication*: the relationship is maintained.

- *Spuriousness*: the relationship disappears and is due to the test variable preceding both of the others in time.

- *Intervening:* the relationship disappears and is due to the test variable occurring after the independent variable and before the dependent variable.

- *Specification*: the relationship only holds true under some values of the test variable.

- *Suppression*: a relationship appears that was previously hidden.

## Other methods for multivariate analysis

It is a good idea to begin to learn about multivariate analysis by using tables and the elaboration paradigm, since one can see in the cells in the tables, and in the percentages, exactly what happens to each case in the data matrix as variables are entered into the analysis. This helps in retaining a firm grounding in the data; one does not then become detached from it in a self-sustaining technical world of statistical procedures whose meaning and interpretation may be somewhat unclear. However, multivariate analysis with tables has some disadvantages. First, in order to use interval variables one must recode them into manageable categories (see Chapter 18), thus losing information. Second, as more variables are entered (and one can go on elaborating first-order conditional tables by entering fourth or fifth variables to produce second-order and third-order tables and so on), retaining a sense of the question one is testing becomes increasingly difficult. Problems also arise with low numbers in each cell, as subtables require the sample to be split up into ever smaller groups. This makes significance testing difficult.

## Multiple regression

A popular method of multivariate analysis that preserves interval variables as they are, and which enables the researcher to understand the interactions between quite large numbers of variables simultaneously, is multiple regression. This technique preserves the idea that in social statistics one must often recognise that events have *multiple* causes, rather than *single* ones. If one wishes, for example, to understand what causes people's income to vary, one must recognise that this is down to a number of factors, perhaps including parental income and social class, educational achievement and gender. Discovering the relative *strength* of different variables thought to be causal factors then becomes the task of data analysis. Multiple regression provides the researcher with statistics that enable an estimate of this.

In SPSS multiple regression is fairly easy to do, though interpreting the output can pose some challenges. A sketch of the main points is presented here, but you are recommended to read more detailed treatments if you wish to use this technique. Figure 20.1 shows the SPSS dialogue box that appears once 'linear regression' has been selected using the drop-down menus under 'analyse'. This concerns a data set in which the infant mortality rate (IMR), gross national product (GNP), female illiteracy rate (FIR) and the prevalence of contraceptive usage (PCU) across many different countries are measured. The research question that multiple regression allows us to answer concerns the relative influences of the last three of these on the infant mortality rate. Thus IMR is the dependent variable and the others are all independent variables.

Some of the output from this procedure is shown in Figure 20.2. As is usual in SPSS output, there is a great deal of information, some parts of which are more important than others. The first part of the output tells us that $R$ square is 0.837 (amongst other things). $R^2$ in multiple regression can be interpreted in the same way as $r^2$ in simple correlation and regression (see Chapter 24). It describes the percentage of variance explained by the three independent variables. Thus we can

say that 83.7 per cent of the variability in IMR can be explained by the three independent variables, leaving very little unexplained variance (only 16.3 per cent in fact).

The second part of the output in Figure 20.2 allows us to look at the impact of each independent variable separately, controlling for each of the others. The first column to examine is the first of the two unstandardised coefficients columns. B allows us to see the impact of a one-unit change in each independent variable on the dependent variable (IMR) while controlling for (holding constant) the influence of the other two independent variables. Thus we can say that an increase of 1 per cent in the female illiteracy rate leads to an increase of 0.701 infant deaths per thousand. An increase of 1 per cent in contraceptive prevalence leads to a *decrease* of 0.777 in IMR.

The standardised coefficients (Beta coefficient) allow different kinds of conclusions to be

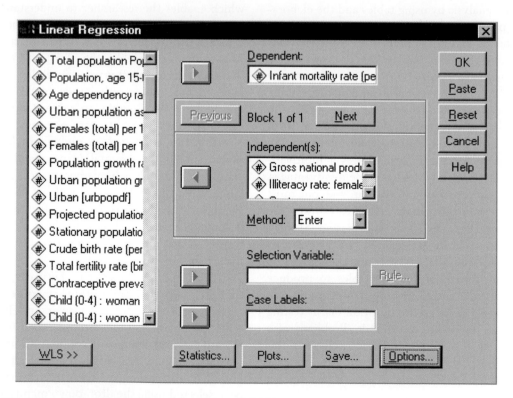

**FIGURE 20.1** Multiple regression dialogue box (SPSS)

**Model Summary**

| Model | R | R Square | Adjusted R Square | Std. Error of the Estimate |
|---|---|---|---|---|
| 1 | .915[a] | .837 | .830 | 17.7270 |

a. Predictors: (Constant), Contraceptive prevalence (% of females 15-49), Gross national product per capita ($US), Illiteracy rate: female (% of females age 15+)

**Coefficients[a]**

| Model | | Unstandardized Coefficients | | Standardized Coefficients | t | Sig. |
|---|---|---|---|---|---|---|
| | | B | Std. Error | Beta | | |
| 1 | (Constant) | 67.567 | 8.780 | | 7.695 | .000 |
| | Gross national product per capita ($US) | -1.13E-03 | .001 | -.074 | -1.311 | .194 |
| | Illiteracy rate: female (% of females age 15+) | .701 | .117 | .454 | 6.006 | .000 |
| | Contraceptive prevalence (% of females 15-49) | -.777 | .135 | -.469 | -5.739 | .000 |

a. Dependent Variable: Infant mortality rate (per thous. live births)

FIGURE 20.2   Multiple regression output

drawn, relating to the relative importance of each independent variable. The largest impact appears to be the negative one of contraceptive prevalence (–0.469), with the positive impact of illiteracy in raising the rate of IMR close behind (0.454). GNP, rather puzzlingly, appears to have a negligible impact on IMR. To understand this rather counter-intuitive result (after all, surely rich countries are less likely to have high infant mortality rates) we must turn to path analysis, a procedure that allows us to place the results of multiple regression into a model, closer to real life.

## Path analysis

The implicit 'model' of the world in our multiple regression so far is shown in Figure 20.3. This suggests that each of the three independent variables has a direct, independent influence on the dependent variable IMR. You will see that the standardised regression coefficients

and the estimate of unexplained variance (sometimes also called the error term) have been written in next to the path arrows, indicating the relative influence of the independent variables.

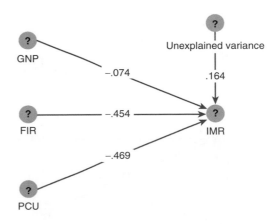

FIGURE 20.3   Implied model of influences on Infant Mortality Rate

A little thought about how things actually work in the real world suggests that this is not a very adequate depiction. When a country has a high GNP it is likely to be quite rich. This wealth tends to produce a better education system and is also associated with a degree of female emancipation. GNP, then, is likely to cause variation in both FIR (the female illiteracy rate) and PCU (the prevalence of contraceptive use). Figure 20.4 shows a more realistic path diagram, reflecting this reasoning.

The standardised regression coefficient for the influence of GNP on FIR was produced using the same SPSS dialogue as before (Figure 20.1), but with FIR as the dependent variable and GNP as the only independent variable. The influence of GNP on PCU was assessed similarly.

The path analysis and accompanying standardised Beta values suggest that GNP does indeed have quite a big impact on both FIR and PCU. In fact, we can say that FIR and PCU are both *intervening variables* in mediating the influence of GNP on IMR. Because GNP affects them, and both of them affect IMR, GNP really does influence IMR, but it does so *indirectly* rather than *directly*.

The *direct*, *indirect* and *total* influence of a variable can be calculated from a path analysis

diagram like that in Figure 20.4. Table 20.2 demonstrates this. The indirect effects are calculated by multiplying the standardised Betas in the relevant path. The total effects are calculated by adding all of the effects together. Reassuringly (perhaps!) for our view of the world they indicate that GNP does indeed have a major impact on infant mortality.

## Logistic regression

A technique related to multiple regression is that of *logistic regression*. While multiple regression is suited to estimating the impact of variables upon an interval level dependent variable (e.g. income measured in units of currency), logistic regression is suitable for assessing the influence of independent variables on a dichotomous dependent variable. It has the advantage of producing a statistic whose meaning is intuitively easy to grasp: the *odds ratio*. Here, I will demonstrate the use of this technique in a particular piece of data analysis in order to show the potential of the method. To learn how to use the technique yourself, you will need to consult more advanced texts (see further reading suggestions and web links). You should note, however, that

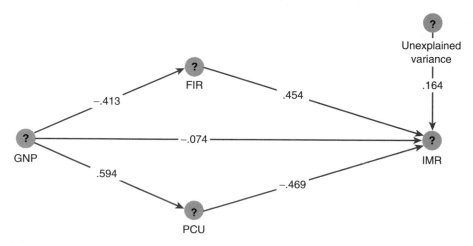

FIGURE 20.4   New model of influences on Infant Mortality Rate

**TABLE 20.2** Direct, indirect and total effects of GNP on IMR

| | | |
|---|---|---|
| Direct effect: | | −0.074 |
| Indirect effects | | |
| via FIR: | −0.413 × 0.454 = | −0.188 |
| via PCU: | 0.594 × −0.469 = | −0.279 |
| Total effects (direct plus indirect): = | | −0.541 |

the concepts learned in the elaboration paradigm underlie both multiple and logistic regression.

Table 20.3 presents results from an interview survey of the bereaved relatives, friends and others who knew a sample of people who had died (Seale and Addington-Hall, 1994, 1995a, 1995b). The respondents were asked whether, in their opinion, the person had died at the best time, or whether it would have been better if the person had died earlier than they did. They were also asked whether the person who died had ever expressed a wish to die earlier, or asked for euthanasia. It is commonly said by those who oppose the legalisation of voluntary euthanasia that if people are looked after well enough, particularly if they are looked after in hospices devoted to the care of dying people, this will remove people's desire for euthanasia, as they will learn to accept the benefits of a natural death. The data analysis set out to test this proposition.

Table 20.3(a) shows the proportion of people who said an earlier death would have been better, or who asked for euthanasia, according to whether they had received hospice care. It shows, for example, that of people who received no hospice care, 3.6 per cent were said to have wanted euthanasia. By comparison, 7.9 per cent of the 356 people who received domiciliary hospice care (e.g. visits at home by a specialist nurse), and 8.8 per cent of the 329 people who had inpatient hospice care (in other words, who were admitted to a bed in a hospice), were said to have asked for euthanasia. If you look at the percentages given for the 'better earlier' and 'wanted sooner' questions, a somewhat similar pattern is evident. In two cases, the difference

between the groups is statistically significant (shown by the $p$-value). Note that we are analysing three separate dependent variables here, represented by the three questions.

One might conclude from this that people who argue that hospice care reduces the desire for euthanasia have got it wrong. It appears to be the case that the opposite is true: hospice care actually seems to *increase* the incidence of requests. This, however, would be a superficial conclusion. First, there is a potential time order problem. The interview did not establish whether requests for euthanasia, or the expression of wishes to die sooner, occurred before, during or after episodes of hospice care. It is possible that some people became so distressed that they made this request, and subsequently entered a hospice where they changed their minds owing to the good care they received. However, this time order problem does not apply to respondents' own views about the desirability of an earlier death, since hospice care had occurred many months before the interviews were done.

Another objection is that a variety of other things are likely to cause people to want to die sooner, or relatives to feel that an earlier death would have been better. People who receive hospice care might be different from people who do not. We cannot conduct a randomised controlled trial here (McWhinney et al., 1994). Perhaps people who enter hospices have more distressing symptoms, or greater levels of dependency. Other analyses of the data (Seale and Addington-Hall, 1994, 1995b) had shown that older people were more likely to want to die sooner, and that respondents who were spouses rather than other types of relative or friend of the person who died were less likely to feel that an earlier death would have been better. Maybe these factors differed systematically between people who received hospice care and people who did not. In other words, a series of plausible reasons as to why the three zero-order associations reported in the top half of the table might be spurious were considered.

**TABLE 20.3**  Hospice care, euthanasia and the wish to die earlier: bivariate and multivariate analysis

*(a) Bivariate analysis*

| | Hospice care | | | |
| --- | --- | --- | --- | --- |
| | Domiciliary only | Inpatient | No hospice care | Significance (*p* value) |
| Proportion of respondents saying better earlier | 28% (of 327) | 36% (of 312) | 26% (of 1179) | *p*<0.01 |
| Deceased said wanted sooner | 26% (of 362) | 22% (of 338) | 22% (of 1277) | *p* > 0.01 (not sig.) |
| Deceased wanted euthanasia | 7.9% (of 356) | 8.8% (of 329) | 3.6% (of 1264) | *p* < 0.01 |

*(b) Multivariate analysis (logistic regression)*

| | Hospice care | | |
| --- | --- | --- | --- |
| | Domiciliary only | Inpatient | Number of people |
| Respondent: better earlier | 1.4 | 1.7* | 856 |
| Deceased: wanted earlier | 1.4 | 1.0 | 921 |
| Deceased: wanted euthanasia | 2.0 | 2.1 | 912 |

*Source:* adapted from Seale and Addington-Hall, 1995a

Notes:
* *p* < 0.05
Odds ratios have 'no hospice care' as reference category.

Logistic regression allows the data analyst artificially to hold certain variables 'constant' in order to assess the independent impact of key variables of interest. This impact is represented in terms of odds ratios. The odds ratios shown in Table 20.3(b) can be understood by giving a verbal interpretation of one of them: respondents for people receiving inpatient hospice care were 1.7 times more likely than respondents for people not receiving such care (the 'reference category') to say that it would have been better if the person had died earlier. The asterisk indicates that this is a statistically significant result. The odds ratios ensure that like is being compared with like; symptom distress, dependency, age and whether the respondent was a spouse or not, were all held constant in order to make this comparison.

Of course, other potential spurious variables could have caused the association. By thinking through plausible objections to a causal proposition (e.g. the rather surprising idea that something about hospice care caused respondents to feel that an earlier death would have been better), measuring the variables involved in these objections, and then including them in multivariate data analysis, a variety of arguments can be investigated.

## Conclusion

The ideas of the elaboration paradigm are a useful start in multivariate analysis. A really detailed explanation of more advanced techniques such as multiple or logistic regression are beyond the scope of this book, but the main features of these techniques have been outlined. I hope that this chapter, and the previous one, will have given you an introduction to quantitative data analysis that is sufficient to demystify the procedures involved. Good data analysis proceeds by being constantly aware of the main issues that are being investigated.

Statistics are a tool for taking forward an argument. It is unfortunate that technical complexity has sometimes been elevated to an end in itself, so that the researcher loses sight of the basic issues at stake in a piece of data analysis. It has been the aim of these two chapters to show you that these methods are within your grasp.

## FURTHER READING

De Vaus (2002a) gives a brief but clearly explained guide to the main principles of quantitative data analysis, including multiple regression. Bryman and Cramer (2008) relate their explanations of statistical methods to output from SPSS. Logistic regression is not often covered in introductory books on statistical analysis. One book that does introduce it in a reasonably accessible way is Field (2009). A good way to begin analysing quantitative data is to start using SPSS for Windows, which has a helpful tutorial, demonstration data sets and plentiful on-line help.

### Student Reader (Seale, 2004b): relevant readings

19  Paul F. Lazarsfeld: 'Interpretation of statistical relations as a research operation'

20  Morris Rosenberg: 'The strategy of survey analysis'

### Journal articles illustrating use of the methods described in this chapter

Dahl, E. and Malmberg-Heimonen, I. (2010) 'Social inequality and health: the role of social capital', Sociology of Health & Illness, 32 (7): 1102–1119.

Johnson, R.R. (2011) 'Suspect mental disorder and police use of force', Criminal Justice and Behavior, 38: 127–145.

Narcisse, M-R., Dedobbeleer, N., Contandriopoulos, A-P. and Ciampi, A. (2009) 'Understanding the social patterning of smoking practices: a dynamic typology', Sociology of Health & Illness, 31 (4): 583–601.

### Web links

SPSS tutorials, including regression techniques: http://pages.infinit.net/rlevesqu/spss.htm

Social Sciences Research and Instructional Council – SPSS guide: www.csub.edu/ssricrem/spss/spsfirst.htm

Andy Field's website for his book (Field, 2009) on statistics and SPSS: www.uk.sagepub.com/field3e

*Statnotes:* an online textbook by G. David Garson (includes multiple and logistic regression, path analysis and a host of other topics): www2.chass.ncsu.edu/garson/pa765/statnote.htm

*(Continued)*

Web pages that perform statistical calculations: http://statpages.org/

Methods@manchester – survey-related methods: www.methods.manchester.ac.uk/methods/survey-related.shtml

Correlation or causation?: http://jonathan.mueller.faculty.noctrl.edu/100/correlation_or_causation.htm

Introduction to statistical analysis: www.le.ac.uk/bl/gat/virtualfc/Stats/introst.html

Hyperstat Online statistics textbook: http://davidmlane.com/hyperstat/index.html

## KEY CONCEPTS FOR REVIEW

**Advice:** Use these, along with the review questions in the next section, to test your knowledge of the contents of this chapter. Try to define each of the key concepts listed here; if you have understood this chapter you should be able to do this. Check your definitions against the definition in the glossary at the end of the book.

| | |
|---|---|
| (Beta) standardised coefficient | Path analysis |
| Conditional or first-order tables | $R^2$ |
| Direct effect | Replication |
| Elaboration paradigm | Specification or interaction |
| Independent and dependent variables | Spurious variable |
| Indirect effect | Suppression |
| Intervening variable | Test variable |
| Logistic regression | Total effect |
| Model | Unexplained variance (or the) error term |
| Multiple regression | Unstandardised coefficient (B) |
| Odds ratio | Zero-order table |

 ■ **Review questions**

1  Describe the difference between a dependent and independent variable.
2  What is the purpose of the elaboration paradigm?
3  What is a zero-order table and how would you elaborate it?
4  Define: replication, a spurious relationship, an intervening variable, specification and a suppressor relationship.
5  What type of independent variable is suited for (a) multiple regression and (b) logistic regression?
6  What do standardised Beta coefficients contribute to path analysis?

1  Choose any article or book that reports the results of a *qualitative* research study. What sort of causal propositions does the author assume to be true? What sort of causal arguments are contained in the text? How could these be tested in quantitative data analysis? What would the independent and dependent variables be?

2  Table 20.3 and the discussion that accompanies it suggests that hospice care may cause people to want euthanasia. What plausible objections might there be to this causal argument? How could they be tested in further research? How could qualitative research be used to investigate this proposition?

3  Take Table 20.4 to be a zero-order table. Draw hypothetical conditional or first-order tables that you might expect to find by entering the test variable of *income,* measured as low or high. The pairs of tables should, in turn, illustrate:

(a) the existence of a *spurious* or *intervening* relationship between social class and home ownership
(b) *replication* of the original relationship
(c) *specification* of the original relationship
(d) *suppression* of a stronger relationship.

TABLE 20.4   Table showing relationships between social class and home ownership (column %)

| Home ownership | Social class | | |
| --- | --- | --- | --- |
| | Lower | Middle | Upper |
| Owner | 20 | 30 | 50 |
| Private, rented | 30 | 40 | 30 |
| Council, rented | 50 | 30 | 20 |

$p < 0.01$, $Q = 0.6$

4  Use SPSS to analyse a statistical data set. Chapter 17 has web links to data archives, from which such data sets can be downloaded. The website for this book (www.rscbook.co.uk) contains links to data archives and data sets. Use data transformations (e.g. Compute or Recode) as well as univariate, bivariate and multivariate statistical procedures to investigate the data. Try to pursue an argument, hypothesis or research question in your analysis, considering counter-arguments to yours and dealing with these, where possible, with further data analysis.

# 21
# CODING AND ANALYSING QUALITATIVE DATA

## Carol Rivas

---

### Chapter Contents

This chapter considers thematic coding as one way of looking at data of the sort often produced in ethnographic work or other qualitative methods. It is easier to make sense of the data when they are divided up into themes, or patterns in the data. Thematic coding can be used for transcripts, field notes, documents, images, internet pages and audio or video recordings. It reduces the volume of the original data and turns it into something meaningful and easy to digest. Sometimes themes may be used as a way of summarising and sharing the data, with selected themes described in reports and papers, illustrated with data extracts. But it is often instructive to move beyond simple reporting of themes, to consider underlying concepts.

In my own work on women who are being abused by their partners, I have produced a simple description of the theme 'hiding the abuse from others', showing for example how some abused women liken their experiences to the normal arguments that 'every relationship' has. This descriptive work should help domestic violence support services to be more effective; for example, it suggests the need to differentiate normal arguments from abuse when talking to abused women. In a separate report, I have subsequently considered something that the women do not say directly, but which I have deduced from carefully analysing a number of linked themes – the way that, by hiding the abuse, they maintain their standing with their families and in their community as women who have successful relationships. This provides a deeper layer of understanding that support services can use.

I based both levels of analysis on a systematic formalised coding process, called thematic content analysis, which I describe in this chapter. One impetus for the original development of this was to help qualitative researchers legitimise their methods, responding to critics who claimed that qualitative research is a softer option than quantitative research. By following the process and then describing it in their reports, researchers can enhance and demonstrate the quality, or validity and reliability, of their findings (see Chapter 30 for more on quality, validity and reliability). It is also helpful in providing novice researchers with a relatively simple approach to analysis.

Thematic content analysis involves looking across the data set rather than within one case. The approach is similar to that used in interpretative phenomenological analysis (IPA; see Chapter 25), and in the early stages of grounded theory development (see Chapter 22), but there are important differences. Simply put, thematic content analysis will often focus on what a phenomenon, event or social interaction 'looks like' to the individuals of interest (their lived experience). With IPA, on the other hand, which is a method used predominantly by psychologists, interviewers are interested in what things feel like. The difference in perspective is taken forward into the coding process, which is otherwise similar. A grounded theorist undertakes thematic analysis, and develops abstract concepts from the themes, but then builds up theory from the concepts.

Other analytical approaches have been developed that involve looking for themes and patterns in the data in very different ways to thematic content analysis, IPA and grounded theory. Semiotic analysis, discourse analysis, conversation analysis, and narrative analysis are considered in Chapters 16, 23, 24, and 25 respectively. These require detailed technical and theoretical knowledge and are not as accessible to the inexperienced researcher as is thematic content analysis. 'Content analysis' without the thematic prefix (i.e. analysis that focuses on counting the frequency of words or other small bits of data and then looking at the context in which they appear) is different to any of the other techniques mentioned in this section and is considered in Chapter 26.

## Preparation for thematic coding

Before coding, it is a good idea to think about theoretical sensitivity. This may be defined as the researcher's sensitivity to concepts, meanings and relationships within the data, and it comes largely from professional and personal experience. Theoretical sensitivity is also shaped by reading.

There is considerable debate as to how much literature an analyst should read before coding. Practically speaking, it is impossible to do research in a literature vacuum, and indeed a literature review will often inform the design of a qualitative study. However, you may need to do less reading if your approach is inductive rather than deductive. Box 21.1 illustrates the difference between these approaches.

---

**BOX 21.1**

### INDUCTIVE AND DEDUCTIVE CODING

Qualitative studies are often inductive, which is to say that they begin with a very broad research question, and the final research question and precise themes are suggested empirically from the data.

For example, you may wish to learn more about doctors' working lives but are not sure which particular issues might be important to them. It would be sensible to read broadly beforehand so that you know the sorts of questions to ask when collecting your data, and then focus on more specific topics once these are suggested by the data itself as analysis proceeds.

However, sometimes a more deductive approach might be required, with at least some themes developed before you begin analysis, from previous research or theory or researcher intuition and experience.

For example, you may already know that doctors are limited by the amount of time they can spend with patients and wish to explore this further. This might require fuller engagement with the literature before analysis begins to ascertain what is already known and what gaps in knowledge need to be filled. If your research is being undertaken to test, update or expand on an existing finding, for example the way that female doctors in primary care are more likely than their male counterparts to refer patients on for further tests, and how this relates to gendered health beliefs, your codes may be primarily derived from the literature.

---

By reading and re-reading your data several times before formally coding it – sometimes called immersion in data – your sensitivity to its meanings is likely to be enhanced. Keep memos (notes to yourself) of phrases and broad impressions that seem significant. During coding you will fragment your data into a number of different parts which then may seem disconnected from the whole. Being able to remember the context from which fragments are drawn, because you have immersed yourself thoroughly in the material, will help you make sense of them later.

### Memos

Memos are informal notes to yourself so you may use words and styles you would not draw on when writing for an audience. You can use memos to:

- write down impressions and ideas as a way of 'holding that thought' as you carry on working through the data

- record personal comments about your progress, decisions, difficulties and annoyances (this can be useful later when writing up)

- keep a note of problem codes that need later revision, and ideas that need to be checked with more data gathering

- help you when drafting your report.

Because of their multiple uses, it is a good idea to give memos titles for easy later identification, such as 'Why I changed the topic guide' or 'issues with method'.

To see how memo-writing might work, consider the following extract, which is part of a memo reproduced by Anselm Strauss and Juliet Corbin, about pain in childbirth (the asterisks and italics are in the original and mean something to their author):

> Pain is* part of a labor process, labor of course serving an end – the end of pregnancy, the delivery of the awaited child. Hmm. How do I describe this property? The pain itself is not purposeful, but associated with a *purposeful activity – labor*. (**** I'll note this though I'm not yet sure what to do with this. It doesn't necessarily mean acceptance (though it might to some people), or tolerance, but perhaps it gives the pain a certain degree of predictability? This still doesn't quite capture this phenomenon.) (1990)

## The zigzag approach

Thematic coding is often begun before all the data are collected, in a process of iterative data gathering and analysis, which has been aptly labelled the zigzag approach (see Figure 21.1). The idea is for early analysis to inform further data gathering so that gaps in the data are filled or new and unexpected themes unpacked. Ideally, the process ends when no new themes emerge from the data (which is called saturation of themes). Here is an example of how this works, taken from a study that involved interviews with men about their experience of having testicular cancer:

> An early respondent talked powerfully of his distress at people making 'bad jokes', or referring to cautious people as having no 'balls'. Alerted to this theme, the researcher asked other men if they had ever been subjected to 'bad jokes'. Humour was found to play an important role for men with testicular cancer, and was used by them to demonstrate that they were OK with the diagnosis (which has a very successful cure rate), were confident of recovery, and that they were still 'one of the lads'. (Ziebland and McPherson, 2006: 407)

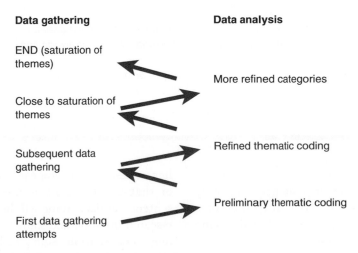

**Data gathering**

END (saturation of themes)

Close to saturation of themes

Subsequent data gathering

First data gathering attempts

**Data analysis**

More refined categories

Refined thematic coding

Preliminary thematic coding

FIGURE 21.1 'Zigzag' data gathering and analysis

With more deductive approaches to thematic coding, the zigzag approach may be redundant, with all data gathered before analysis begins.

## Open coding

Whether you use the zigzag approach or not, it is a good idea to begin by coding only a small amount of your final data and then building your codes up with progressively more data. This enhances your theoretical sensitivity. Immerse yourself in the first few bits of data and get a feel for what they say. Then the more formal coding can begin. The first stage of thematic coding is often called open coding, a term used by Barney Glaser and Anselm Strauss (1967) in their book *The Discovery of Grounded Theory*. Open codes are labels for chunks of data that capture something of the literal essence of the data. An example of open coding from my study of abused women is provided in Box 21.2.

---

**BOX 21.2**

### OPEN CODING: AN EXAMPLE

| Data extract | Open codes |
|---|---|
| [Y]ou know, there's a couple of girlfriends and we're always saying, what the hell are we doing? But we've been saying that for twenty years now! (*laughs*) For ten years, we've been saying … we spend our lives saying, 'Why am I with this man?' and they go, 'I don't know, why are you with him!' 'I don't know!' (*laughs*) … and you kind of look around and think, well, what relationship is actually worth staying together … you know, you think, I know very few … I maybe know two good … really good, strong relationships and the rest are kind of just … muddling through! (*laughs*) Because I guess that is just being with someone as well, you just … it isn't going to be plain sailing. But it is where you draw that line and I don't … I think maybe if [partner] had been more abusive, I would have left. You know, it's a more subtle … isn't it? If it was a more obvious type of … you know … I'd just go. | *Talking to friends* <br><br> *Jokes about exasperation with men* <br> *Reflecting on relationship for many years* <br><br> *Querying being with the man* <br><br> *When relationships are not worth it* <br><br> *Good relationships rare* <br><br> *Muddling through* <br><br> *Relationships not plain sailing (normalising)* <br> *Choosing where to draw the line* <br><br> *Abuse too subtle to leave* <br> *Abuse not obvious type* |

---

Coding line by line, or sentence by sentence (i.e. reading each line or sentence separately and seeing if it suggests a code to you) ensures that each part of the data is treated the same way, and thus that representative and also new and unexpected themes may be captured. This does not mean you will identify a code for each line or sentence, as you can see from Box 21.2, or that a data chunk is the same as a line/sentence of data. Some will be irrelevant to the research question and some will suggest two or more codes, while some codes may develop over two lines, several sentences or even a whole paragraph. Correspondingly, data chunks may be any size, from words and phrases to whole paragraphs and more.

Unless you are using an entirely deductive approach and have decided on all your themes before you begin analysis, your code names will often be very rough at this stage. You should simply aim to get down a word or phrase that describes the data well and does not involve any interpretation by you. You may find that your open codes are quite repetitive. This is to be expected. For example, in Box 21.2 I have the codes *Abuse too subtle to leave* and *Abuse not obvious type*. I did not try to group these into a code – called *types of abuse* perhaps – during open coding because had I done this too early, I might have missed something in the data. As it transpired, by keeping them separate I was able to see as I added more data that women downplayed the abuse (and so justified their behaviour in staying in the relationship) until it became obvious to others.

Had I combined the codes I would have simply concluded that women left abusive relationships when the abuse became more obvious.

## Inductive and deductive coding combined

Sometimes it is useful to combine deductive and inductive coding. You may have a general idea of what you are looking for and use broad, deductively determined codes to home in on the data, and then inductive coding to explore this in more detail. Or you may wish to add to existing knowledge, as in the example in Box 21.3, which comes from a study of antibiotic prescribing in children (Rollnick et al, 2001). Both deductive and inductive codes were applied to transcripts of talk between doctors and their patients (or patient's parent in this example); Box 21.3 shows some of the different codes used and their origins.

---

**BOX 21.3**

## SOME CODES FOR ANALYSING TRANSCRIPTS OF DOCTOR–PATIENT INTERACTION

| Code name | Definition |
| --- | --- |
| Elicitprobs* | Moves by doctor to elicit problems parent or child is having, or worries that they have. |
| Elicitexpect** | Moves by doctor to elicit expectations parent (or child) has of consultation. (This does not include offering parents the choice of whether to have antibiotics or not; this is covered by a separate code.) |
| Elicitaction* | Moves by doctor to discover what parents are doing to alleviate/solve the child's problems with the illness. |
| Pre-empt* | Pre-emptive strike – where doctor says things that are likely to preclude objections to a 'no' decision. This 'strike' may be renewed after the no decision is announced in order to make the decision secure. |
| Choice** | Offering parents the choice of whether to have antibiotics or not. |
| Delayed*** | Delayed prescription strategy. |
| Easy*** | Offering patients/parents easy access for a review of situation; e.g. 'I'll see you straight away if you find it gets worse tomorrow'. |

*Source*: Used in a study reported by Rollnick et al., 2001
* Arose from inspecting transcripts and discussing them.
** Arose from communication skills training philosophy/literature.
*** Arose from interviews with doctors on an earlier project.

---

## Inductive approaches: in vivo coding

Inductive codes are often, though not always, in vivo codes. This means that the codes are terms taken directly from the data, representing living language and they may include slang and metaphors. Language is rich and evolving, and words may be used in unconventional ways, for example: 'shooting up', a term for injecting drugs used by drug addicts as explored in a study by Howard Becker (1963); 'Bull and Cow', London Cockney rhyming slang for 'row' or argument; 'wicked', meaning either bad or good depending on your age; 'peng', as current youth talk for attractive. You might realise from these examples that using these term as codes could alert you to new understandings and new themes that you might miss if you glossed over the precise words used or wrongly assumed that you understood them.

---

**BOX 21.4**

### IN VIVO CODING: AN EXAMPLE

Naomi Quinn (1996), in her study of American marriages, realised that her interviews were peppered with metaphors, and used them as her initial open codes. She found people expressed their surprise at the breakup of a marriage by saying they had thought the couple's marriage was 'like the Rock of Gibraltar' or had been 'nailed in cement'. They assumed a common understanding that cement and the Rock of Gibraltar signify 'lastingness'. Quinn grouped the hundreds of metaphors in her data into eight linked themes that reflected her respondents' attitudes to marriage and which she labelled: lastingness, sharedness, compatibility, mutual benefit, difficulty, effort, success (or failure), and risk of failure.

---

By considering Naomi Quinn's approach in Box 21.4, you can see how open codes such as 'nailed in cement' are not interpretive (i.e. the product of the researcher's own interpretation) but feed into later interpretation by the researcher in forming a theme such as lastingness.

In vivo coding helps the analyst to avoid too early interpretation which could result in misinterpretation. Kathy Charmaz (2006) recommends using the *gerund* (words such as 'moving', 'finding', 'doing') for open codes, as this also helps to avoid misinterpretation, focusing attention onto the *actions* that are being done, rather than the *people* doing them. This is important because if you say someone is 'baking a cake' it has a very different meaning to saying they are 'a cake baker'. The gerund helps analysts to see how people have different behaviours in different situations. If instead you label the individual, you might miss nuances in the data. For example, the fact that the individual was baking a cake might have been extraordinary – perhaps they were stuck at home bored, or they were preparing for a celebration – whereas a cake baker would be expected to bake a cake. As a further example of this, consider the following: in my own research on abused women, I discovered that sometimes the women called themselves 'hard bitches'. I coded this as 'saying they were hard bitches', explored this further and discovered that it did not mean they were hard bitches, but rather that they were uncomfortable with standing up to their partner.

Do not worry if you find it difficult to use the gerund or in vivo codes. Many people prefer to use the type of coding shown in Box 21.3. This chapter provides tips not prescriptions, and you should experiment and choose what approach to coding works for you. But do remember to avoid too much interpretation at an early stage if you are committed to an inductive approach, as you need to allow the data to 'speak for itself'.

## Asking questions of your data

The 'open' of open coding might be taken to reflect both the freedom the researcher has in choosing the coding style they are most comfortable with, and the way they need to be open to whatever the data says. You should constantly ask questions of your data as you code, for example, 'What is happening?' and 'From whose point of view?' The literature is replete with checklists of suggested questions. An example of one such checklist, designed for interviews and focus groups, is provided in Box 21.5. Lists may be constraining if rigidly applied, so only use them as springboards to further thought. Periodically refer back to the research question to make sure you are maintaining your focus.

---

**BOX 21.5**

### LIST OF QUESTIONS TO ASK OF THE DATA DURING ANALYSIS

- *Words*: How are specific words used, and what do they mean to the participant?
- *Context*: When does the participant raise a topic? Does it relate to anything else?
- *Internal consistency*: Are topics talked about differently at different times? Can this be related to anything?
- *Frequency*: Why are some things repeated more frequently than others? Does this reflect their significance to the participant, and is this because they have problems coming to terms with something, or because they wish to be seen in a certain light? Is it significant that a particular topic is rarely mentioned, avoided or missing?
- *Extensiveness*: How much coverage is given to particular topics (remember that a topic may be mentioned only once but take up half an interview, for example)?
- *Intensity of comments*: What positive and negative words and emphases are used and what is their significance?
- *Specificity of responses*: Do the data describe an actual event or a hypothetical situation? Is the first or third person used?
- *Big picture*: What major trends or topics are there that cut across cases?

*Source*: Adapted from Rabiee, 2004

---

Look for patterns in what is missing as well as what is not. Unspoken topics may be attempts at 'impression management' by your research participants (trying to make sure you get a particular impression of them rather than an alternative and probably less desirable one) or may represent taboos. When investigating birth planning in China, Susan Greenhalgh reported that she could not ask direct questions about resistance to government policy but was able to sense this indirectly:

I believe that in their conversations with us, both peasants and cadres [formal birth planning officials] made strategic use of silence to protest aspects of the policy they did not like. (1994: 9)

Alternatively, things may remain unsaid or unexplained because your participant believes they do not need to articulate what they assume everyone knows.

## Getting it down

Researchers have various ways of getting their initial codes down on paper or on their computer. Some people highlight words or parts of images on hard copy with highlighter pens. Others type or write codes in the margin alongside the relevant data in the transcript, document, picture or other data form. Similarly, software for supporting qualitative research allows the researcher to highlight a section of text and then apply a code to it (Figure 21.10, later in this chapter).

Whichever technique you use, it is good practice to number each line of any text at this initial stage, as this will help you when referring to your data later, in quotes, memos and discussions. Software packages may number paragraphs rather than lines.

If your approach is deductive and you knew what your themes were before you began analysis, this may be all the coding you need to do. In this case, you may choose to do open coding using software, and then to move on to the part of the analysis described later where themes are checked for completeness (perhaps using the concept maps described) and then written up. If you are using an inductive zigzag approach, it may be best not to code into software at this stage. Your codes are likely to change a great deal in the early stages of your analysis, and it can be quite tricky to make radical changes to your coding scheme within software packages.

Your open coding should have resulted in a long list of codes – too many for them to be used as they are. They now need to be grouped together into preliminary categories, then themes. Spider diagrams (Figure 21.2) are often useful in organising thoughts about this. By grouping related codes in this way, I can see that several of the codes in the diagram codes suggest

**FIGURE 21.2**   Spider diagram: experiences of abuse

a category of *playing down the abuse*, several relate to the *expectations of others*, and several relate to *changes in responses to abuse*. This suggests three potential categories that subsume the categories in the spider diagram.

## Developing categories and then themes

### Category formation and the process of constant comparison

Category formation is the second of three stages used in inductive or combined inductive-deductive thematic analysis. It is needed if the analysis is eventually aimed at more than just description, so that it provides themes which contain an explanation or indeed are part of a theory that will bring a new perspective to bear on the problem at hand. The second stage follows some form of coding, such as in vivo or open coding as just described. It involves grouping similar open codes together to form analytic categories. Develop them as your research proceeds using the zigzag approach if you can. This keeps the analysis manageable, and it also makes it more likely that you will spot the unusual and the unexpected, and develop richer interpretations of the data.

In the past, many researchers would physically cut their data into parts representing the different open codes, then group these into categories on a large table, on the floor, or pinned to the wall. Each piece of data might be accompanied by information about its source and its location in the original or transcript. With the advent of Microsoft Word and other word processing tools, and bespoke software such as *NVivo*, *Atlas.ti* or *MaxQDA* that supports qualitative data analysis, this is increasingly done on a computer. However, many researchers still prefer the physical approach.

Once you are happy with your categories, you should operationalise them by defining them so

that subsequently you or others can understand what you have done. Operationalisation means that you turn an abstract idea into something more concrete. This is particularly useful for write-ups and when you share analysis with others, have someone else undertake parallel coding of some data as a quality control measure, or return to your analysis after a long absence. The following is an operationalised category called *ending relationship* from my study of abused women:

> *Ending relationship:* includes both temporary and permanent endings. Considers reasons, feelings and agency, coming back, and also continued contact that is no longer an intimate relationship. Excludes continued contact within an intimate relationship but the couple can live in the same accommodation if they have separated.

In the above example, the last phrase about the couple continuing to live together without being in an intimate relationship was added after I discovered two cases of this happening in the data. It is usual for your categories, and therefore operationalisations, to change as you gather more data and continue to analyse. You need to check that categories fit new as well as already analysed data rather than checking that the data fit the categories – avoid trying to force data into the categories! The aim is for each category to be distinct, although it is almost certain to be related to other categories. A later section of this chapter describing typologies and careers will demonstrate how relationships between categories can be used.

The process of category formation requires constant comparison of all the bits of data within a category with each other, and constant comparison of the data across categories. In other words, each time you code and then categorise a bit of data, you need to check it against all the other pieces of data in its designated category. This may lead you to add a category, subsume one with another or rename it, or to change your understanding, as I did in the example above. Constant comparison of a gradual trickle of data ensures that your interpretations remain grounded in the data and that you are not so overwhelmed with data that you cannot see the finer detail.

In another example from my study of abused women, I decided that the code *saying they were hard bitches* belonged to the category *fighting the abuse*. Originally, the definition said this category contained examples of rebellion and anger and empowerment, and so it had to be amended to encompass the discomfort some women felt in fighting back and the negative terms they therefore used for themselves to describe this. Reflecting on this subsequently led me to change the category name to *stepping outside of expected behaviours*, which began to be more interpretive and revealing.

The function of category development is to systematically group multiple fragments of unconnected literal codes into something meaningful and more analytical and digestible; some interpretation may occur at this stage, but most of your interpretive work should be reserved for theme development. The process of constant comparison should mean that the themes developed from categories describe all the features and characteristics of each topic in the data as fully as possible and are conceptually as complete as the data allow.

In summary, constant comparison:

- stops you from being overwhelmed by your data

- provides a systematic way of working through the data

- keeps analysis grounded in the data

- helps you to develop categories that are as complete as possible

- shapes distinct categories that can be clearly operationalised.

## Getting themes from categories

Once you are happy with your categories, it is time to develop them into themes, the third step in moving from open or in vivo coding, through category development, to thematic coding. A dominant category may be used as a theme, in which case it is likely to remain quite literal. But often, themes are abstract concepts shaped from two or several more literal categories.

Tetyana Shippee (2009) described how she moved from literal/descriptive coding to a more abstract/interpretive understanding, and from open codes through categories to themes, when she analysed interview data from residents of a retirement village in America. Residents entered the village being able to live independently (IL) in accommodation on the complex. When they required moderate supervision and care, they were moved to assisted living (AL) spaces or, if they required more specialised care, into nursing living spaces (NL). According to Shippee, residents perceived transitions between types of living space as disempowering and final. One of the themes that helped her to arrive at this conclusion was *autonomy* (or lack thereof). Her development of this theme is shown in Figure 21.3. As you can see, she took initial open codes such as *lack of privacy* (an in vivo code taken from one interview) and *not allowed to go to the toilet by myself* (which was paraphrased from similar talk occurring across several interviews), and grouped these under the broader category of *threats to privacy and personal space* which keeps much of the sense of the open codes and so remains largely literal. She then grouped this category with others, such as *being told to move* and *rules regarding transitions*, to develop her final more conceptual theme of *autonomy*.

Shippee used her findings to suggest that retirement facilities should increase residents' privacy, challenge social boundaries that restricted social mixing between care levels, and educate residents to prepare them for transitions in care.

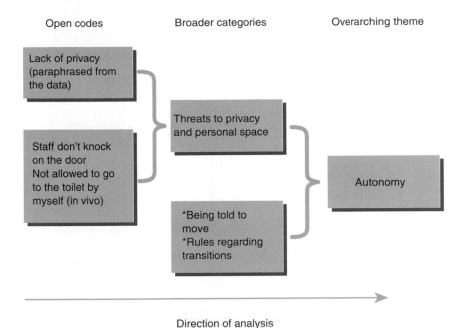

Open codes      Broader categories      Overarching theme

Lack of privacy (paraphrased from the data)

Staff don't knock on the door
Not allowed to go to the toilet by myself (in vivo)

Threats to privacy and personal space

*Being told to move
*Rules regarding transitions

Autonomy

Direction of analysis

**FIGURE 21.3** Code, category and theme development using data from the residents of a retirement village (adapted from Shippee, 2009)

*Shippee does not show how she developed these categories from open codes

## Concept maps

To see whether your themes provide good explanations of the data and also to check whether there are any gaps in the data, you may find it helpful to put together a concept map (concepts are abstract ideas – themes may be abstract or literal but they can still be developed using a concept map). Although these may look similar to spider diagrams, their development proceeds in a somewhat different manner.

The way I use concept maps is to choose a theme that seems significant in some way (e.g. it accounts for a great deal of the data) and that I therefore wish to focus on. I put the label for this theme at the centre of my concept map. Then I consider its qualities and features according to the questions shown in Figure 21.4, using the data I have analysed. These are written up as brief notes within the concept map. Figure 21.5

shows the application of this system to my own data on abused women, involving a concept map for the theme of *hiding the abuse from others*.

When I ask students to develop a concept map of what it is like to be a student, as a classroom exercise, some interpret the 'who' to mean themselves and some to mean the whole population of students. Each interpretation might be valid; the questions in the template should be interpreted in ways that suit your data, your approach and your research question. Keep your concept map simple. This is not brainstorming, but a way of creating meaning from the pieces of your data puzzle. It is always important to consider the negative instances (data that seems to be contradictory but that need to be accounted for in the analysis). These are represented by blue dashed arrows in Figure 21.4.

Concept maps may be used singly or integrated with other concept maps to help you to

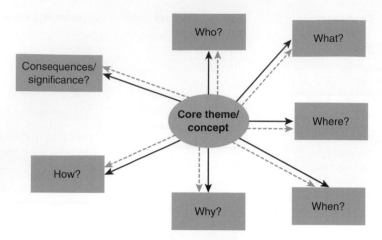

**FIGURE 21.4** A concept map template (blue dashed arrows indicate negative instances – Why not? etc.)

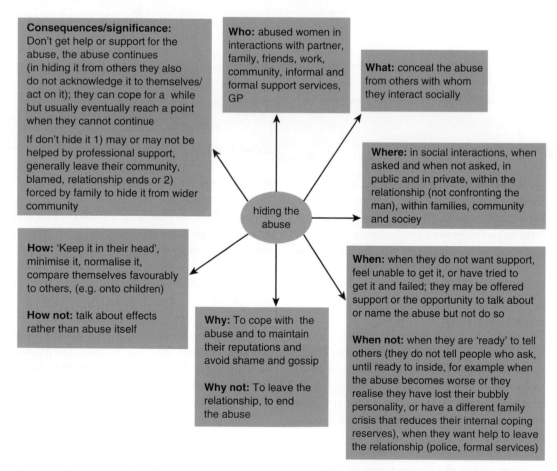

**FIGURE 21.5** Concept map to consider the theme of abused women hiding the abuse from others

write up your data as well as in developing your ideas and checking whether more data need to be gathered. They are useful for thematic content analysis, but not essential. However, if the anticipated final product is a 'grounded theory' (see Chapter 22), you may find them indispensable. Figure 21.5 was used for a descriptive report using thematic content analysis. Figure 21.6 shows a concept map based on the same data but using it to develop theory, in this case a theory involving the concept of *boundary setting* to explain responses to abusive relationships

Commercial concept mapping software has been developed and also physical toolkits. For example, Ketso (www.ketso.com) comprises felt mats and Velcroed leaf shapes to represent ideas or codes, as well as other comment, prioritisation and linking symbols, all of which may be placed and moved around on the mats as your ideas take shape and reform. Generalist qualitative data analysis software also includes modelling tools that serve a similar function.

## Presenting your findings – lists, careers and typologies

In thematic content analysis, themes (whether inductively or deductively formed) are typically written up either as descriptive lists, or as careers or as typologies. Examples of each will be given in this section.

### Lists

Rachel Millsted and Hannah Frith's (2003) report of their in-depth interviews with eight large-breasted women provides an example of a list format. Their interest was in exploring the ways in which the women make sense of and

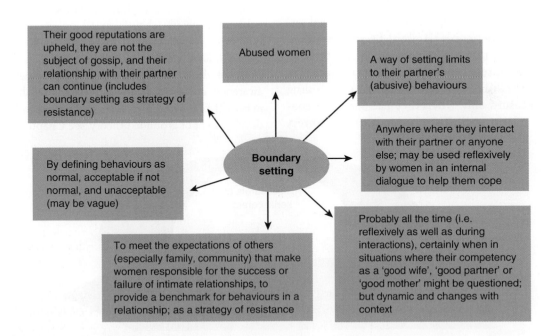

**FIGURE 21.6** Concept map to explore the way abused women set boundaries to their abusive partner's behaviours

experience their embodied selves. They focused on two themes which they described in turn. The theme of breasts as *objectified and visible* was supported by data extracts such as the following:

> Yeah, I do tend not to wear low-cut tops because even though they are still there when you wear a normal – not even high-necked – top, if things are on show then people do look more. (Nicola)

The theme of breasts as a *pleasurable marker of femininity and attractiveness* was supported by such data extracts as:

> I think it's important 'cos it [having large breasts] does make you feel more feminine and I think with me being on the skinny side it does give me a little extra shape. (Joanne)

## Careers

Careers (or 'trajectories') are sequential, showing the progress people make through social settings or experiences. Howard Becker identified three stages that individuals had to pass through in their 'career' to becoming a drug user. He argued that individuals were able to use a drug for pleasure only when they had learnt to conceive of it as such. They had to learn the correct technique for using the drug, learn to perceive the drug's effects and learn to enjoy these (Becker, 1963: 30, 51).

In another use of the career device, Mary Larkin (2009) considered the experience of people who had looked after dependent older adults until death of the dependant. She reported a post-caring trajectory with three experientially distinct phases:

- the post-caring void
- closing down the caring time
- constructing life post-caring.

Seventy per cent of her sample had cared more than once; she called these *serial carers*. Her analysis is summarised in Figure 21.7. Each stage in Larkin's and Becker's models accounts for a single theme of their analysis.

## Typologies

Typologies highlight differences between events, behaviours or people (but remember that the behaviours people show depend on context, so typologies of people need to be used with care). Barney Glaser and Anselm Strauss (1964), in their study of dying people, developed a typology of awareness contexts and their determinants, shown in Box 21.6. For more on Glaser and Strauss and the development of grounded theory, see Chapter 22.

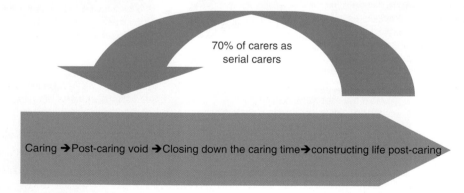

70% of carers as serial carers

Caring ➔ Post-caring void ➔ Closing down the caring time ➔ constructing life post-caring

**FIGURE 21.7** A model of the post-caring trajectory for carers of dependent older adults (adapted from Larkin, 2009)

BOX 21.6

## AWARENESS CONTEXTS: A TYPOLOGY AND ITS DETERMINANTS

### Typology

| | | |
|---|---|---|
| 1 | Open awareness | Everyone knows the person is dying |
| 2 | Closed awareness | The dying person does not know, but other people do |
| 3 | Suspicion awareness | The dying person suspects |
| 4 | Pretence awareness | Everyone, including the dying person, pretends that they do not know |

### Determinants of closed awareness

- Patients are inexperienced at recognising signs of impending death.
- Medical staff are skilled at hiding the truth.
- Staff have a professional rationale that says that it is best to withhold the truth.
- The patient has no family allies.

The examples in this section show how qualitative analyses make sense of the data in ways that can be shared with others. When analysts write up the data in this way, they may discover holes in their argument so that it may need to be reworked. This is such common practice that writing up can also be considered to be part of the analytical process (see also Chapter 28).

## Member validation and inter-rater reliability

Even deductive codes are shaped by what we bring to the data as individuals. As Ian Dey notes, 'there is no single set of [themes] waiting to be discovered. There are as many ways of "seeing" the data as one can invent' (1993: 110–111). This is one argument for *not* undertaking member validation, which means giving your research participants the opportunity to examine and comment on themes before your final write-up. It is appropriate to do this when a goal of your research is to identify and apply themes that are recognised or used by your participants and their peers. This can be very useful as a check that one has picked up everything that is important to participants and described it in a way that they can relate to. But in the light of Dey's observation, it may be wise to be careful in interpreting the results of any member validation exercise if the analysis presented to participants is framed by complex theory, as research participants are not always the best people to judge the 'accuracy' of this.

Because there are many ways of seeing the same data, many qualitative researchers also argue against using inter-rater reliability tests to see if more than one coder agrees on how to apply a coding scheme. Nonetheless, if a number of researchers independently code a piece of qualitative data, there is often remarkable concordance in what they find (Frost et al., 2010), and discussion of differences can be revealing and fruitful in devising better coding schemes. Inter-rater reliability exercises may be particularly helpful when researchers' own biases and preferences need to be discounted.

## The framework approach

The framework approach is increasingly used to manage qualitative data for thematic content analysis (it is not a method of analysis, as often stated). Applied research projects and projects that have been set up to inform policy often have short timescales, and framework may speed up analysis. It is a mainly deductive approach and often all the data are collected before analysis begins, so that the zigzag approach (see Figure 21.1) cannot be used. This may be seen as a disadvantage or as preventing the researcher from being biased by earlier interviews, depending on your viewpoint. One advantage is that the analysis can be more clearly matched to themes in quantitative analyses. Typically, analysts still look for unexpected themes grounded in the data, but only once the data have been grouped more deductively.

Figure 21.8 shows the stages involved in this approach. This follows the same basic steps as in more conventional thematic content analysis except that data are summarised in charts or matrices developed from a thematic framework, rather than being more simply grouped together under code and then category headings as more linear text. The charts then become the primary resource for analysis.

The charts are conventionally constructed using Microsoft Word tables or Excel spreadsheets (or can be handwritten), but bespoke software was released in 2009 (see www.framework-natcen.co.uk). Unlike other approaches to thematic content analysis, the data are summarised early on in the process.

In Figure 21.9 themes related to social support in my partner abuse interview-based study is shown. The themes form columns in the matrix, and cases (the people interviewed) are

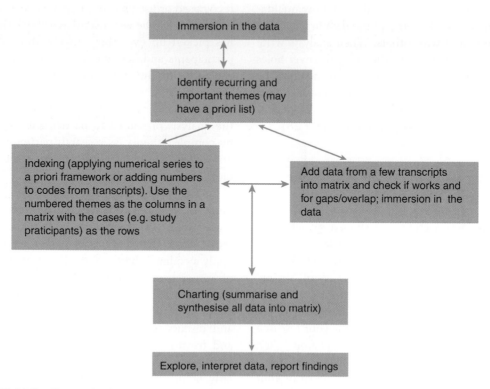

**FIGURE 21.8**  Stages in developing a framework

rows. Only two cases and three of the themes are shown in the figure here. Data are added to the cells as analysis proceeds. These can contain the researcher's own summaries of what each person said about the theme (in square brackets in Naomi's row) or edited quotes from respondents which are usually shortened by removing repetitious parts and extraneous words – in the figure the bits to be deleted are shaded in grey.

Comparisons are facilitated by this approach. A different chart is developed for each group of related themes, with the data summaries displayed as cases (the rows) and themes (the columns) such that comparisons can be made across cases or across themes on the same chart. This makes it easy to develop typologies as well as careers. It also makes analysis more transparent and means the data can be easily accessed and even re-assessed by others. The same data may be used in different charts, but using cross-referencing rather than repetition.

## Computers as a way of managing qualitative data

Computer software may be used to build concept maps and framework charts, but the main uses

| Theme 1: Social support | | | |
|---|---|---|---|
| Interview | 1.1 Family | 1.2 Friends | 1.3 Community |
| #1 (Naomi) | … my mum and dad, I didn't really get to know them properly because … I born here and they send me home when I was nine months, and then I grew up in Barbados with my grandparents. Naomi: 14 | *[Known close friends from childhood]* … my close friends they're like, since I was six, seven years old, my good girl friends, that girl that walked past, she's one of my close friends, I've known her for like 17 years …, they wouldn't they wouldn't, put it this way, 'they wouldn't stop coming to visit me because they didn't like him [*her abusive partner*]. Tracy: 358 | … you walk up the road and you meet someone you know. Everywhere you go, there's somebody that you know and If you haven't seen them for a long time, you'll stand and you'll have a chat and stuff like that, you know?  It's really nice. I wouldn't … I wouldn't like to move, from this town anyway, I wouldn't, because most of the people that I build up a relationship, they live around this town.  And it's really good. You walk up the road, and you meet someone and you have a chat.  Naomi: 172 |
| #2 (Zoe) | My brother's just bought a house near around here, they're just round the corner from me, and my sister, who's my best friend, anyway and then she, when I go to work she sleeps in my house with the kids, so that they don't have to be in her house. Zoe: 75 | A lot of my husband's friends,  they're married to my friends.  It's a common group. Zoë: 90 | If I had none of my friends and family, I might not be able to work. I would like um, you know, to have a good nursery that could take them. Zoe: 76 |

FIGURE 21.9  A framework chart for an analysis of social support and abused women

made by qualitative researchers of software for qualitative data analysis (QDA software) are to support thematic coding and analysis, as well as to organise, summarise and integrate different types and forms of data, such as interviews, focus groups, documents and pictures. It is important to know that computer programs help researchers manage their data; they cannot do the analysis for them, although the most recent versions automate some coding processes. The latest versions allow users to import, sort and analyse audio files, videos, digital photos, Microsoft Word, PDF, rich text and plain text documents (previous versions did not allow all these formats). In addition, the programs have various tools that enable you to annotate your data, search for specific content within it, model your ideas, and compare different groupings of data using matrices. Figure 21.10 is a screenshot from *NVivo*; other popular programs include *MaxQDA* and *Atlas.ti*.

All of these programs use variations of what in *NVivo* are called coding stripes – these are codes the researcher has applied to the data and are represented vertically so that the stripes match the corresponding parts of the transcript (in Figure 21.10, a video is shown on the left, with a transcript immediately to the right of the picture. To the right of the text are some vertical lines with words written above them; these are the coding stripes and the words are the code labels. Images, sound files and transcripts can be linked so that clicking on one takes you to the corresponding part of the other.

Metadata may be attached to the data files. These might be a feature of a participant (their gender or age, for example) or of a data transcript (e.g. whether a medical consultation led to a prescription). These metadata can be used to filter searches; for example, where an analyst who has interviewed men and women about their health experiences asks for the text coded as 'pain talk' to be provided separately for men and for women. Here, the gender of a respondent is metadata attached to each interview

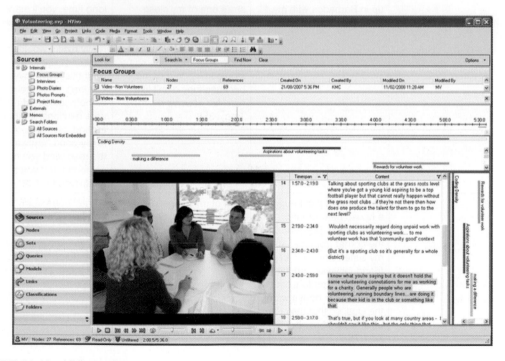

**FIGURE 21.10** NVivo software

transcript. The metadata can be treated like variables and in most programs they can be exported to spreadsheets or SPSS for numerical analysis in support of qualitative analysis.

Counts of code or theme frequencies and other numerical analyses may reassure the reader that the researcher has not simply cherry picked examples to support his or her particular bias. If phrases such as 'most people felt', 'usually people said' or 'it was rarely observed' can be backed up by actual numbers, the reader should have more confidence in the report's validity. Additionally, counts can be helpful in making comparisons between settings. David Silverman (1984), for example, found this in an observational study comparing medical consultations in private clinics with those in public health service clinics (Box 21.7).

---

BOX 21.7

## PRIVATE AND PUBLIC HEALTH CARE

Out of 42 private consultations, subsequent appointments with the doctor were fixed at the patient's convenience in 36 per cent of cases; in 60 per cent of cases the consultation involved polite small-talk about either the doctor's or the patient's personal or professional lives. The corresponding percentages in the 104 public health service clinics observed were significantly smaller (10 per cent and 30 per cent). This supported Silverman's impression that a more personal service was given in private clinics.

*Source*: Silverman, 1984

---

The programs also include search tools. A search of Rollnick et al.'s study described in Box 21.3, for example, might be used to retrieve all instances of the word antibiotics, embedded in surrounding text so that the context in which the word was used is not lost. Search functions might also be used to restrict analysis to particular transcripts, for example only those that resulted in a prescription, if this has been entered as metadata. In this way, analysis is not restricted to thematic codes but can be enriched by additional ways of mining the data, or the data may be used in multiple ways for different analyses. Word searches may also be used to double-check that you have not missed data and to clarify emergent ideas. Rollnick and colleagues (2001), using the search features of *NVivo* in their investigation of antibiotic prescribing, found that doctors were more likely to give advice on symptoms in consultations where antibiotics were not prescribed, suggesting that they might have a 'consolation prize' function. Similarly, an attribute like gender might be used to compare whether male or female doctors talk about symptoms in different ways. Boolean searches enable different kinds of search to be combined as a single operation. For example, a search might be made for all paragraphs containing the word 'antibiotics' that occur in consultations before training happened, comparing these with such paragraphs in consultations after training. Chapter 6 contains detailed advice on how to do Boolean searches, in the context of literature reviewing, but similar principles apply in relation to their use in qualitative data analysis

The programs also include matrices that compare coding frequencies, modelling tools, charts and other ways of representing the data that may aid analysis. Figure 21.11 shows a flowchart drawn with the modelling tool in *NVivo* during a project examining the representation of cancer experience in newspapers.

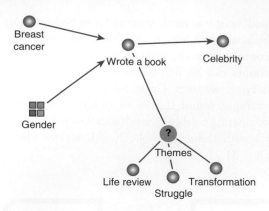

**FIGURE 21.11** Writing a book about cancer experiences: use of an early version of the NVivo modeller

Using this tool it became clear that women who had breast cancer wrote books about their experience more often than men with cancer or women with other kinds of cancer. These books frequently involved themes of life review, struggle and personal transformation. Many of the authors achieved celebrity status as a result. The software links models to the text used in their development so that clicking on the model takes you to the relevant data. The model can be used in this way as a thinking tool.

The programs also have memo tools. Some programs allow different team members to work on the same project, then merge their results, with each researcher's work still separately identifiable.

Searches (with or without the associated text), data aggregated in themes, screenshots, models, diagrams and charts can be printed out or exported to other programs. Reading these printouts is part of the analytical process. It helps you develop theoretical sensitivity to particular codes and categories and themes and refine and develop them.

As technology and demands change, bespoke software programs have become increasingly sophisticated and increasingly similar. However, each one has particular strengths:

- *Atlas.ti* specialises in hyperlinking, coding for grounded theory, and linking data flexibly so that it

can be rearranged until you are happy with what you have done, for example with uncoded text or spider diagrams.

- *NVivo* specialises in flexible coding and in bar and pie chart outputs.

- *MaxQDA* specialises in matrices, georeferencing (with direct links to Google Earth), text-based and mixed method approaches and keyword analysis (see Chapters 26 and 27).

Some programs have been developed for more specialist work; for example, popular dedicated video analysis programs are *Transana* and *Elan*. No single program does everything, and the program that is most suitable for you will depend partly on the purpose of your project and the type of analysis (e.g. grounded theory, framework), the type of data you are using, the unit of analysis (e.g. interview, image, video, participant) and the output you desire (e.g. linear text, models, matrices).

## Conclusion

This chapter has described how to code and analyse data for themes. It has shown that the basic process comprises three stages: open coding, category development, theme formation. With highly deductive coding, themes may be known in advance and therefore initial coding is used simply to apply the chosen theme and not as a preliminary stage in theme development. More inductive coding needs to pass through all three stages to provide credible, reliable, high-quality results. Analysis continues during write-up, whether the themes are developed inductively or deductively. This chapter has also shown that there is some flexibility in the way that thematic coding is undertaken – in terms of the types of words used to name codes and themes, the interplay of analysis and data gathering, the use of the literature and the bias towards induction or deduction. The data may be presented in a variety of ways, for example as descriptive lists, careers or typologies, and they may be augmented by counts of the data. Various data management approaches, some of which involve computer software, may be used to facilitate analysis by managing and displaying the data in useful ways.

## FURTHER READING

Coffey and Atkinson (1996) explain and illustrate a variety of approaches to qualitative data analysis, including those based on the sort of coding explained in the chapter, as well as some others. Gibbs (2002) is an excellent text which, although linked to the use of a particular computer package (*NVivo*), gives a good general guide to qualitative data analysis.

### Student Reader (Seale, 2004b): relevant readings

44 Anselm L. Strauss and Juliet Corbin: 'Open coding'

45 Graham R. Gibbs: 'Searching for text'

46 Udo Kelle: 'Theory building in qualitative research and computer programs for the management of textual data'

See also Chapter 31, 'Computer assisted qualitative data analysis' by Udo Kelle in Seale et al. (2004).

### Journal articles illustrating or discussing the methods described in this chapter

Bringer, J.D., Johnston, L.H. and Brackenridge, C.H. (2006) 'Using computer-assisted qualitative data analysis software to develop a grounded theory project', Field Methods, 18: 245–266.

DeCuir-Gunby, J.T., Marshall, P.L. and McCulloch, A.W. (2010) 'Developing and using a codebook for the analysis of interview data: an example from a professional development research project', Field Methods. Published online before print 27 December, doi: 10.1177/1525822X10388468.

Hsieh, H-F. and Shannon, S.E. (2005) 'Three approaches to qualitative content analysis', Qualitative Health Research, 15: 1277–1288.

Seale, C. (2001) 'Sporting cancer: struggle language in news reports of people with cancer', Sociology of Health & Illness, 23 (3): 308–329.

### Web links

e-Source – Chapter 10 on 'Software and qualitative analysis' by Eben Weitzman: www.esourceresearch. org

What is Qualitative Data Analysis?: http://onlineqda.hud.ac.uk/Intro_QDA/what_is_qda.php

The CAQDAS (Computer-assisted qualitative data analysis) project: http://caqdas.soc.surrey.ac.uk/

Qualis Research home page (makers of *The Ethnograph*, a tool for qualitative data analysis) – click on 'QDA paper' to download an excellent overview of qualitative thematic analysis: www.qualisresearch. com

*Atlasti* website: www.atlasti.com

QSR home page – more information about *NVivo* can be found here: www.qsrinternational.com

**Advice:** Use these, along with the review questions in the next section, to test your knowledge of the contents of this chapter. Try to define each of the key concepts listed here; if you have understood this chapter you should be able to do this. Check your definitions against the definition in the glossary at the end of the book.

| | |
|---|---|
| Boolean searches | Memos |
| Careers | Metadata |
| Coding stripes | Open coding |
| Concept map | Operationalising |
| Constant comparison | QDA software |
| Deductive coding | Saturation of themes |
| Framework approach to analysis | Search tools |
| Immersion | Spider diagrams |
| In vivo codes | Thematic content analysis |
| Inductive coding | Theoretical sensitivity |
| Inter-rater reliability | Typologies |
| List format | Zigzag approach |
| Member validation | |

## Review questions

1 Describe the difference between inductive and deductive coding.
2 What is the zigzag approach and how does it differ from framework analysis?
3 Define open coding and in vivo coding.
4 How can (a) spider diagrams and (b) concept maps help in analysing qualitative data?
5 What relationship do categories have to codes and to themes?
6 Describe the characteristics of a list format, a career and a typology.
7 What are the arguments for and against member validation and inter-rater reliability exercises?
8 What are coding stripes, metadata and Boolean searches?

## Workshop and discussion exercises

1 Examine either the transcript of a taped interview in Box 12.12 or the transcript in Box 21.8, taken from a study by Jocelyn Cornwell (1984), then do the following:

(a) Consider what themes you can find in this extract and use these to make a list of codes for the passage. Mark your transcript with code words that describe the themes on the margin.

(b) Consider what assumptions you have made. What have you found difficult?

(c) **Are your codes objective? What decisions have you taken in choosing particular codes to characterise particular words or phrases in particular ways? How do you account for similarities and differences in coding between other people in your group who have coded the extract? What has been left out? Can the use of such codes give us agreed interpretations of these data? If codes are not agreed, does this matter?**

(d) **Report back to the rest of the workshop. Can interviews of this sort be used as a basis for generalising about the beliefs, practices and feelings of women?**

(e) **If you are using a computer package for analysing qualitative data, such as *NVivo*, you may find it helpful to enter the data and your codes and use the computer to search for coded segments, or segments where codes overlap.**

---

**BOX 21.8**

## INTERVIEW TRANSCRIPT: JOCELYN AND WENDY

| | | |
|---|---|---|
| 1 | Jocelyn: | Last time we met, you told me that between the times |
| 2 | | that we'd seen each other, you'd been in hospital, and |
| 3 | | had had an operation. |
| 4 | Wendy: | That's right, I had er the hysterectomy done last year. |
| 5 | Jocelyn: | Can you tell me about that, about, take me back to the |
| 6 | | beginning with what happened. Were you unwell, what |
| 7 | | happened? |
| 8 | Wendy: | It was mainly cos I'd been on the pill for twelve years, |
| 9 | | and because of my age and the fact I smoked. I was |
| 10 | | reaching what they classed as erm a risk barrier, at risk |
| 11 | | age, and they wanted me to come off the pill. I'd been |
| 12 | | using the pill mainly to regulate my periods all that time. |
| 13 | | So I knew that if I come off, I'd be having a lot of |
| 14 | | problems, and basically the doctor suggested other forms |
| 15 | | of contraceptive, but it wouldn't have helped me as far as |
| 16 | | the bleeding was concerned. |
| 17 | Jocelyn: | What was the bleeding about? |
| 18 | Wendy: | My periods had never regulated from the time I'd started, |
| 19 | | so I used to bleed heavily, and maybe lose for ten, fifteen |
| 20 | | days at a time. The only thing that really regulated it was, |
| 21 | | was the pill. But it was getting to a stage that that wasn't |
| 22 | | easing it off any more. |
| 23 | Jocelyn: | Right. |
| 24 | Wendy: | It was unusual. I used to bleed for just five days while I |
| 25 | | was on the pill. I used to know exactly when my periods |
| 26 | | would start. It used to be sort of like 3.30 on a Wednesday |
| 27 | | afternoon, and then it started to change. I was starting to |

*(Continued)*

---

(Continued)

| | | |
|---|---|---|
| 28 | | lose maybe on the Tuesday, heavier and for longer. And |
| 29 | | I found that strange considering all them years it had |
| 30 | | stayed the same. |
| 31 | Jocelyn: | Did you talk to anyone about it before you went to see |
| 32 | | the doctor? |
| 33 | Wendy: | No, no. |
| 34 | Jocelyn: | No one at all? |
| 35 | Wendy: | No, I was just worried myself that there might be |
| 36 | | something wrong. |
| 37 | Jocelyn: | Did you ever talk about anything of that kind with either |
| 38 | | Sandra or with your mother? |
| 39 | Wendy: | No. |
| 40 | Jocelyn: | No, or with friends? |
| 41 | Wendy: | No, no. I would, I would tell them after I'd already sorted |
| 42 | | it out myself. But I would just automatically follow through |
| 43 | | on something myself. Go to my own doctor, or the family |
| 44 | | planning clinic. |
| 45 | Jocelyn: | And did they talk to you about that sort of thing or not? |
| 46 | Wendy: | No, no, it was never discussed. When I was younger nothing |
| 47 | | like that was ever discussed. Something that you just |
| 48 | | well I've always dealt with it on my own, I suppose I could |
| 49 | | talk to my mum about it, I just never did. Something I never |
| 50 | | spoke to her about. |
| 51 | Jocelyn: | So you went to see the doctor, and she said, she sent you |
| 52 | | to the hospital. |
| 53 | Wendy: | She suggested, well she said it was my body, and it was my |
| 54 | | choice. Cos, they said I could go on for quite a few years like |
| 55 | | it. But they did want me off the pill, and that I wasn't willing |
| 56 | | to do, just come off the pill and take a chance on what |
| 57 | | would happen. |
| 58 | Jocelyn: | Who was it who first mentioned having a hysterectomy then, |
| 59 | | you or them? |
| 60 | Wendy: | Me. |
| 61 | Jocelyn: | You? |
| 62 | Wendy: | Yes, on the, erm the second occasion when I went to the |
| 63 | | hospital, that was my suggestion. He asked me what I |
| 64 | | wanted done and I said I wanted the lot taken away, and |
| 65 | | he said fine. The first doctor didn't want to know, he |
| 66 | | said I wasn't old enough. There was nothing they could do. |

| 67 | *Jocelyn:* | How old, how old were you? |
|----|-----------|------|
| 68 | *Wendy:* | About 33, 32 or 33. And then they wasn't willing to do it. |
| 69 | *Jocelyn:* | What made you think of that as an option? Were you, you |
| 70 | | were given other options, were you given the option of |
| 71 | | being sterilized, or anything like that? |
| 72 | *Wendy:* | No, sterilization wouldn't have made any difference to the |
| 73 | | bleeding. |
| 74 | *Jocelyn:* | Right. |
| 75 | *Wendy:* | That's just a form of contraception. As far as the bleeding's |
| 76 | | concerned, it's a matter of trial and testing different drugs. |
| 77 | | And I know other women that have maybe done that for |
| 78 | | four years. Tried drugs, don't work. Tried a different one, |
| 79 | | it doesn't work, try another one, it doesn't work. And they |
| 80 | | still end up having the hysterectomy done anyway. I don't |
| 81 | | see why I should go through all that hassle for two, three, |
| 82 | | four years, just for the same end result anyway. Makes you |
| 83 | | feel rather like a guinea pig, just testing out the drugs for |
| 84 | | them to see if they work. It's annoying, most of the |
| 85 | | gynaecologists are men anyway, so they don't know what |
| 86 | | you're going through. It's fine for a doctor to sit there and |
| 87 | | say you can go on for another ten years. He doesn't have |
| 88 | | that problem every month. |
| 89 | *Jocelyn:* | You see I think that um a great many people would find it |
| 90 | | shocking that you chose that as an option. |
| 91 | *Wendy:* | Well. No not really. I've got my children. If you want to |
| 92 | | look at it that way, that's what the womb is for. The |
| 93 | | womb is for reproduction, I've done my bit. I've got my |
| 94 | | two, I didn't want any more, so it was fine for me to have |
| 95 | | it taken away. |
| 96 | *Jocelyn:* | Did you have any idea, have you ever had any idea |
| 97 | | about why you have always bled so much, why, why your |
| 98 | | periods haven't ever been regulated? |
| 99 | *Wendy:* | No, I'd never, from the time mine started when I was at |
| 100 | | school, I never knew when I would start, I never knew |
| 101 | | how heavy I would lose. I used to be at home maybe for |
| 102 | | three or four days in bed. I was that ill. And the only time I |
| 103 | | wasn't was when I was on the pill. The doctor at the family |
| 104 | | planning said like they will regulate. I said I'm thirty, if they |
| 105 | | haven't regulated in fifteen years I said I don't think they're |

*(Continued)*

*(Continued)*

| 106 | | going to now. But she just didn't want me to have it no |
| 107 | | more 'cos I smoked. That was it. She wanted me to stop |
| 108 | | smoking and I wouldn't. So I got my pills from my doctor |
| 109 | | instead! Just changed. |
| 110 | *Jocelyn:* | Did she give you any explanation for why you needed to |
| 111 | | stop smoking that was connected to whether or not she |
| 112 | | would prescribe the pill? |
| 113 | *Wendy:* | Because as you get older your blood thickens, you're more |
| 114 | | thickens the blood. And taking the pill also does the same, |
| 115 | | so for me I had three factors. |
| 116 | *Jocelyn:* | Getting older, taking the pill, smoking. |
| 117 | *Wendy:* | Getting older taking the pill, smoking. I can't stop getting |
| 118 | | older. I wanted to stay on the pill, but I could give up |
| 119 | | smoking, you know what I mean, so that was it, you cut |
| 120 | | out the smoking and you can keep the pill. |
| 121 | *Jocelyn:* | And what's the consequence of this been? You had the |
| 122 | | operation a year ago? |
| 123 | *Wendy:* | Yes, I had it done last year. And I felt fine, never had no |
| 124 | | problems. Obviously same problems as anyone has after |
| 125 | | an operation, but nothing drastic. |
| 126 | *Jocelyn:* | Um, has it made any difference to your sense of yourself? |
| 127 | *Wendy:* | Err, no. I mean some, some women sort of say they feel |
| 128 | | less of a woman for it, I don't. Not at all. I'm same as I |
| 129 | | was before. Just can't have children. That's it. I feel better |
| 130 | | in myself healthwise, because I don't have them problems |
| 131 | | every month that I had before. |

*Source*: Cornwell, 1984; © The Open University (reproduced with permission)

# 22

# GENERATING GROUNDED THEORY

Clive Seale

---

## Chapter Contents

---

Establishing good links between concepts, ideas or theories and the things that they refer to is an important aspect of the quality of research reports. In Chapter 30, it is pointed out that this concern to ensure good concept–indicator links is one that is shared by both qualitative and quantitative researchers. Grounded theorising is a set of techniques which emphasise the creation of theoretical statements from the inspection of data, largely gathered in qualitative observational studies of the sort described in the chapter on ethnography (Chapter 14). The participant observer using a grounded theory approach cycles between episodes of data collection and data analysis, the one informing the other, so that the eventual research report is very likely to exhibit good concept–indicator links.

Box 22.1 gives an example of a theory that is well-grounded in data. Wiener's research project involved interviews with people with rheumatoid arthritis as well as observation of their care. From close inspection of their accounts and the observational data, she found that the concept of 'normalisation' summarised a broad range of experiences. Normalisation was itself related to another concept, 'justifying inaction'. At every point in describing these concepts Wiener was able to show the reader what they meant by giving examples drawn from the interviews or observations.

In this chapter I will give an account of the main procedures involved in research using grounded theory as well as say something about the historical context in which this approach arose, explaining why it has gained such popularity. I will also assess some of the criticisms that can be made of the method.

---

**BOX 22.1**

## GROUNDED THEORY IN A STUDY OF PEOPLE WITH RHEUMATOID ARTHRITIS

How the analysis was done:

Analysis of field data was conducted in the following manner: indicators in the data (descriptions by the arthritic, or observations by the researcher, of an action, episode or event) were coded into categories and their properties. For example, all descriptions of behavioral attempts to continue a normal life were initially coded as normalization and then broken down into categories of normalization, such as covering-up, keeping up and pacing. Concepts which have been dictated by the data, and thus coded, can then be inter-related … and can be carried forward in the writing … one can carry forward a concept such as covering-up to demonstrate its relationship to another concept such as justifying inaction, but one cannot constantly carry forward a description such as 'When I walk, I walk as normally as possible' and demonstrate its relationship to another description such as 'My husband doesn't really understand' … It is intended that conceptually specifying behavior will strengthen its applicability as a guideline for health professionals. (Wiener, 1975: 97)

An extract from the report:

A successful repertoire for covering-up and keeping-up may at times turn out to be a mixed blessing. Relationships generally remain normal, but when the arthritic cannot get by, it is harder to justify inaction to others … This problem is increased when others have stakes in the arthritic's remaining active, as was the case with a young mother whose condition worsened when she tried to keep athletic pace with her husband and son: 'My husband really doesn't understand. He is very healthy and he thinks there is some magic formula that I'm not following – if I would just exercise, or have people over.' (Wiener, 1975: 100)

## The discovery of grounded theory

The original ideas of grounded theory were outlined by Glaser and Strauss (1967), arising from their work together on a research project that involved analysing the treatment of people dying in American hospitals. Grounded theory needs to be understood in its historical context, since it was fundamentally a reaction to a positivist, verificationist approach (see Chapter 2) which was then very dominant in American social research, threatening to overshadow the work of qualitative researchers with an approach that was almost exclusively quantitative and statistical. In this dominant approach, data was collected in order to test the truth value of theoretical propositions. Instead, grounded theorists favoured an approach that emphasised the inductive generation of theory from data. The scheme had an almost revolutionary appeal for a sociological 'proletariat' of qualitative research workers, keen to overthrow the twin domination of their field by 'theoretical capitalists' and big-time, government-funded quantitative survey research work, represented for Glaser and Strauss in the 1960s by the work of theoreticians such as Talcott Parsons or the quantitative methodologist Paul Lazarsfeld, who, with others, developed the elaboration paradigm (for which, see Chapter 19). In fact, Glaser had previously worked with Lazarsfeld and echoes of the elaboration paradigm can be found in the original book on grounded theory.

## Theoretical sampling and theoretical saturation

A commitment to continual re-examination of data in the light of developing arguments is the principle feature of grounded theorising. It is important to note that this extends to the collection of data as well. Too often, researchers go and do some qualitative interviews and then say that they have 'analysed them using grounded theory'. This is incorrect, since grounded theorising involves collecting data in episodes punctuated by periods of data analysis; it cannot occur if data collection takes place at a single point in the research process. In Chapter 21, you will have seen that the zigzag approach to data analysis, whereby it is punctuated with episodes of data collection, incorporates the same idea (see in particular, Figure 21.1)

The concept of theoretical sampling was designed by Glaser and Strauss to describe the approach grounded theorists ought to take. It modifies the principle (which at the time was well established by Becker (1970) and others) of searching for negative instances (see Chapter 30). Glaser and Strauss showed that this could be used in theory construction rather than (as in Becker) purely as a test of theory. Here, a difference becomes apparent with the elaboration paradigm whose authors, for practical reasons, could not envisage frequent returns to data collection so that a relatively rapid cycling between fieldwork and data analysis might occur. Large-scale social survey work does not permit very much repetition of expensive data-gathering exercises if a researcher discovers a key question has not been included in an interview schedule, thus limiting the exploratory potential of such work. The qualitative researcher, though, is more fortunate in this regard and Glaser and Strauss were able to exploit this very fully. They advocated that through theoretical sampling a researcher might extend and broaden the scope of an emerging theory. Such sampling involves choosing cases to study, people to interview, settings to observe, with a view to finding things that might challenge the limitations of the existing theory, forcing the researcher to change it in order to incorporate the new phenomena. Box 22.2 shows Glaser and Strauss outlining this aspect of their method.

BOX 22.2

# THEORETICAL SAMPLING AND THEORETICAL SATURATION

**Theoretical sampling:**

Theoretical sampling is the process of data collection for generating theory whereby the analyst jointly collects, codes, and analyzes his data and decides what data to collect next and where to find them, in order to develop his theory as it emerges. This process of data collection is controlled by the emerging theory ... The basic question in theoretical sampling (in either substantive or formal theory) is: what groups or subgroups does one turn to next in data collection? And for what theoretical purpose? In short, how does the sociologist select multiple comparison groups? The possibility of multiple comparisons are infinite, and so groups must be chosen according to theoretical criteria. (Glaser and Strauss, 1967: 45, 47)

**Theoretical saturation:**

The criterion for judging when to stop sampling the different groups pertinent to a category is the category's theoretical saturation. Saturation means that no additional data are being found whereby the sociologist can develop properties of the category. As he sees similar instances over and over again, the researcher becomes empirically confident that a category is saturated. He goes out of his way to look for groups that stretch diversity of data as far as possible, just to make certain that saturation is based on the widest possible range of data on the category ... The adequate theoretical sampling is judged on the basis of how widely and diversely the analyst chose his groups for saturating categories according to the type of theory he wished to develop. The adequate statistical sample, on the other hand, is judged on the basis of techniques of random and stratified sampling used in relation to the social structure of a group for groups sampled. The inadequate theoretical sample is easily spotted, since the theory associated with it is usually thin and not well integrated, and has too many obvious unexplained exceptions. (Glaser and Strauss, 1967: 61, 63)

Box 21.6 in the previous chapter described the grounded theory of awareness contexts and their determinants which Glaser and Strauss developed in their study of the conditions under which people die in modern health care settings. Here is their description of how they carried out the theoretical sampling that led to this theory:

Visits to the various medical services were scheduled as follows: I wished first to look at services that minimized patient awareness (and so first looked at a premature baby service and then a neurosurgical service where patients were frequently comatose). I wished next to look at dying in a situation where expectancy of staff and often of patients was great and where dying tended to be slow. So I looked next at a cancer service. I wished then to look at conditions where death was unexpected and rapid, and so looked at an emergency service ... So our scheduling of types of service was directed by a general conceptual scheme – which included hypotheses about awareness, expectedness and rate of dying – as well as by a developing conceptual structure including matters not at first envisaged. (1967: 59)

The process of theoretical sampling is, of course, potentially limitless, since it comes up against the general problem of induction, which concerns the ever-present possibility that a further case will exhibit properties that force some further changes in a theory. Undaunted, Glaser and Strauss propose a typically pragmatic solution by describing a state of theoretical saturation, also shown in Box 22.2.

## Constant comparison

In addition to the strategy of theoretical sampling and the recognition of theoretical saturation, the third core idea of grounded theorising is that of the method of constant comparison, which is used as a systematic tool for developing and refining theoretical categories and their properties. If applied rigorously, it can aid in taking researchers beyond common-sense reporting of participants' categories so that a study becomes genuinely relevant at a theoretical level. The method is not a loosely structured free-for-all, in which researchers glance impressionistically through their field notes looking for anecdotes that support their preconceived ideas. Instead, it is a rigorous strategy for producing thoroughly saturated theoretical accounts.

The method of constant comparison proceeds in four stages, shown in Box 22.3

---

### BOX 22.3

### FOUR STAGES OF THE CONSTANT COMPARATIVE METHOD

1  Code data into **categories** so that items with shared characteristics are placed together. (Example of a category: the 'social loss story'.)

2  Integrate categories and their **properties**. (Example of properties: age and education, which interact to influence the kind of social loss story told.)

3  Reach theoretical saturation.

4  Write the theory.

---

First, incidents in data are coded into categories so that the different incidents that have been grouped together by the coding process can be compared. Very quickly, this begins to generate ideas about the properties of the category. An example taken (and somewhat modified) from the work of Glaser and Strauss (1964) can be given.

As they observed nurses in hospital wards they noticed that when a patient died, nurses commonly would reflect on the death, expressing sentiments such as: 'He was so young', 'He was to be a doctor', 'She had a full life' or 'What will the children do without her?'. These moments were coded as *social loss stories* by Glaser and Strauss, indicating that some calculation was being made of the degree to which the death represented a loss. As they looked at these different incidents, they gathered that this category had certain properties. For example, age, social class and parental status appeared to influence the calculation of social loss.

The second stage of the constant comparative method involves the integration of categories and their properties, noting, for example, how properties interact. From detailed inspection and comparison of instances, it became clear that age and education interacted, so that educational level was very important in calculating social loss if the person who died was a middle-aged adult; for a very elderly person, though, educational level was of little importance. Additionally, at this second stage, the interaction of different categories is noted. Glaser and Strauss found that nurses sometimes lost their composure and wept when certain patients died, but did not do so in other cases. This, established through constantly comparing different instances, related to whether a social loss story constituted a successful rationale for the death. Death could be understood as a welcome relief in some cases, but a dreadful tragedy with which nurses identified in others.

The third stage is represented by theoretical saturation, discussed earlier, in which no new properties of categories appear, and no new interactions occur. Theoretical sampling will appear to have exhausted all such possibilities. The fourth stage, writing the theory, is then relatively straightforward, since categories and their interactions provide chapter headings or titles of papers, properties provide section headings and the coded data provide plentiful illustrative examples, which may even be counted so that the reader may assess the generality of the phenomena described. Theories developed in this way will, in the first instance, be substantive, in that they explain the immediate phenomena of interest to the researcher. However, they may be thought generalisable to other related settings, in which case their potential scope is considerably broadened. Thus, as a substantive theory, the idea of the social loss rationale may only be applied in the sort of health care settings in which the theory was developed. But in a formal extrapolation, it might be applied more generally to the relationships between professionals and their clients. Thus, it can be hypothesised that all professionals involved in the provision of human services (social workers, teachers etc.) may calculate the social value of their clients according to their age, social class, educational background and so on, and vary the quality of their service to suit this perceived social value. Glaser and Strauss therefore distinguish between substantive and formal theories.

## Later developments and disagreements

Both Glaser and Strauss have produced further book-length statements about the grounded theory approach (Glaser, 1978, 1992; Strauss, 1987; Strauss and Corbin, 1990). Of these, Strauss and Corbin (1990) is perhaps the best known, being a distillation of years of experience in supervising students and other researchers applying the original grounded theory approach, which in the 1967 book was expressed in language at times difficult to apply. The Strauss and Corbin volume has more the feel of a textbook to it, focusing on showing researchers how to apply a well-established method by applying some well-tried procedures.

Strauss and Corbin are also significant in introducing three distinctive ways of coding data (see Box 22.4).

---

BOX 22.4

### CODING IN GROUNDED THEORY

- *Open coding:* Marking instances of data according to emerging analytic themes.
- *Axial coding:* Exploring the interconnections of coding categories.
- *Selective coding:* Core categories are identified.

---

In open coding, the researcher is involved in naming and categorising phenomena through close examination of data. Without this first basic analytical step, the rest of the analysis and communication that follows could not take place. During open coding the data are broken down into discrete parts, closely examined, compared for similarities and differences, and questions are asked about the phenomena as reflected in the data. Through this process, one's own and others' assumptions about phenomena are questioned or explored, leading to new discoveries (Strauss and Corbin, 1990: 62).

Subsequently, axial coding becomes relevant, according to Strauss and Corbin. This involves intensive work with a single category, examining how it connects with other categories and seeking to explore its 'conditions, contexts, action/interactional strategies and consequences' (1990: 96). The third type of coding activity Strauss and Corbin called selective coding, and this they associate with the point at which a fully fledged theory emerges. Taking a single 'core category' – such as 'awareness contexts' (Glaser and Strauss, 1965) or 'dying trajectory' (Glaser and Strauss, 1968) – all other categories and their properties are regarded as subsidiary to the core. Strauss and Corbin give an example from Corbin's (1987) work (see Box 22.5).

---

BOX 22.5

## AN EXAMPLE OF SELECTIVE CODING

In Corbin's (1987) study of the approach of women with chronic illness towards their pregnancies, she found that the women played an active part in managing pregnancy risks. The core category which eventually emerged was that of protective governing, in which women were understood to be continually monitoring the risk status of their pregnancies, taking cues from a variety of sources including signs and the reactions of others. A variety of categories of action emanated from protective governing, including at times a trusting and cooperative relationship with health care staff, but at others a withdrawal from this relationship in order to 'save their babies'.

---

To call these three things 'coding' is something of a sleight of hand, as it is clear that only the first constitutes 'coding' as it was conceptualised in the 1967 book. Axial and selective 'coding' are in fact further elaborations of open codes, through a method of constant comparison. The book has a rather programmatic, formulaic feel to it and tends, according to Glaser (1992) in a critical response, to encourage an unwelcome degree of preconception. Glaser argues, too, that there is too much stress on verification in Strauss and Corbin, thus returning to one of the central issues of the original work on grounded theory. Indeed, a number of critics of grounded theorising (Hammersley, 1995b; Hammersley and Atkinson, 1995; Rose, 1982) have noted both that theory verification should be regarded as important to qualitative researchers, and that Glaser and Strauss failed to recognise in their own work strong elements of theory testing. Glaser's main point of disagreement, though, concerns the over-technical, rule-following behaviour which is expected of researchers following the Strauss and Corbin text. He prefers to stress the centrality of the idea of constant comparison as containing the simple central idea of grounded theorising:

> Strauss' method of labelling and then grouping is totally unnecessary, laborious and is a waste of time. Using constant comparison method gets the analyst to the desired conceptual

power, quickly, with ease and joy. Categories emerge upon comparison and properties emerge upon more comparison. And that is all there is to it. (Glaser, 1992: 43)

## Limitations and criticisms of grounded theory

A number of criticisms of grounded theorising have emerged, some of which simply point out limitations in its applicability to all kinds of research problems, others of which suggest radically different conceptions of the research process and are not so easily addressed.

### Limited applicability?

In the latter category is the point made by Brown (1973), who observes that grounded theorising is an inappropriate methodology for certain types of research problem. Brown, for example, was interested in unconscious processes at work in the connection between social factors and mental disorder, inferring the existence of these by demonstrating causal links that could be explained by no other means. Clearly, such things cannot be observed directly. Brown also notes that the study of certain types of long-term historical process would not be feasible with a grounded theory approach. For example, grounded theory could not be used to investigate the influence of economic recession on workers' willingness to strike, or the impact of warfare on the suicide rate. Thus he argues:

> [Grounded theory] may only be profitable in a fairly limited range of circumstances. The type of material best given to the development of grounded theory ... tends to involve relatively short-term processes, sequences of behaviour that are directly observed or can be easily reported upon, and behaviour which

has a repetitive character. Something missed can often be observed again. (1973 :8)

In defence of grounded theory, though, we can say that Brown's points relate not so much to the analytic methods described by Glaser and Strauss – the method of constant comparison, theoretical sampling and so on – but more to the common dependence of grounded theory on observational and interview data. In fact, there is no logical reason why other types of data cannot be included in the approach. Comparative analysis, using historical records that relate to large-scale societal developments, for example, has a distinguished history in social research (Llobera, 1998), though its practitioners will rarely have conceptualised their methods in terms of grounded theory.

### Modernist assumptions?

A more radical critic is Denzin who, in reviewing a book by Strauss (1987) in which grounded theorising was once again outlined, wrote the words contained in Box 22.6. This review does not so much criticise the approach as claim that it is now old-fashioned, with a variety of postmodernist approaches now being 'in'.

Denzin roots his criticism in the view that the modernist assumption of an empirical world that can be studied objectively by qualitative methods is no longer sustainable. He makes the apparently democratic point that the scientific emphasis on theories generated by researchers gets in the way of paying close attention to the theories people use in everyday life. Denzin also claims that Strauss's modernist demand to make generalisations across cases gets in the way of a detailed focus on the individual characteristics of particular cases, observing that 'By making qualitative research "scientifically" respectable, researchers may be imposing schemes of interpretation on the social world that simply do not fit that world as it is constructed and lived by interacting individuals' (1988: 432).

BOX 22.6

## DENZIN'S REVIEW OF STRAUSS'S (1987) BOOK *QUALITATIVE ANALYSIS FOR SOCIAL SCIENTISTS*

[T]his book marks the end of an era. It signals a turning point in the history of qualitative research in American sociology. At the very moment that this work finds its place in the libraries of scholars and students, it is being challenged by a new body of work coming from the neighboring fields of anthropology and cultural studies. Post-Geertzian anthropologists (Marcus, Tyler, Clifford, Bruner, Turner, Pratt, Asad, Rosaldo, Crapanzano, Fischer, Rabinow) are now writing on the politics and poetics of ethnography. They are taking seriously the question 'How do we write culture?' They are proposing that postmodern ethnography can no longer follow the guidelines of positivist social science. Gone are words like theory, hypothesis, concept, indicator, coding scheme, sampling, validity, and reliability. In their place comes a new language: readerly texts, modes of discourse, cultural poetics, deconstruction, interpretation, domination, feminism, genre, grammatology, hermeneutics, inscription, master narrative, narrative structures, otherness, postmodernism, redemptive ethnography, semiotics, subversion, textuality, tropes. (1988: 432)

## Over-reliance on coding?

Somewhat linked to the postmodernist critique of grounded theory are the points made by Coffey et al. (1996), who object to the narrow analytic strategy imposed by a heavy reliance on coding as a first step. This, they feel, is particularly encouraged by computer software for the analysis of qualitative data, based on a code-and-retrieve logic (see Chapter 21). Some approaches to qualitative analysis, say these authors, do not involve the coding and retrieval approach of grounded theorising. Thus, they argue that discourse analysis (Potter and Wetherell, 1987), or the analysis of formal narrative structure (e.g. Riessman, 1993), depend more on the thoughtful teasing-out of the subtle and various meanings of particular words, or on a global perception of whole structures within data, that are otherwise fragmented and decontextualised if discrete segments are coded and grouped with others under invented categories (see Chapters 23 and 25 for an account of these methods).

Coffey et al. (1996) propose instead an approach to data analysis and representation that is consistent with postmodern sensibilities. This depends on the use of 'hypertext' links, which preserve data in their original form, allowing the 'reader' or user to leap from one link to another in an exploration of data that is open-ended, akin to the experience of the original producers of the data themselves. They equate grounded theorising with an attempt to impose a single, exclusive interpretation of data, and advocate their hypertext alternative as allowing a much more open-ended presentation, recognising multiple meanings which both actors and readers may bring to instances of text.

Against this, Kelle (1997) has pointed out that the equation of coding with grounded theorising, and indeed with the imposition of singular interpretations, is somewhat forced. He argues instead that two broad possibilities exist for data analysts who wish to identify similarities and differences between particular text passages, and that these had been in existence in various branches of scholarship (including biblical hermeneutics) for hundreds of years before becoming an issue for social scientists. On the one hand are *indexes*, such as an author or subject index in a book. 'Coding' of the sort described by Glaser and Strauss might equally well be termed 'indexing', in this sense. On the other hand, *cross references* can be constructed, of the sort Coffey et al. describe in their advocacy of hyperlinks, whereby textual passages are linked together. A King James Bible contains such devices, so that a teaching of Jesus in one of the Gospels is linked with the Old Testament passage to which Jesus refers.

Kelle then observes that in biblical scholarship 'techniques for indexing or cross references are used similarly by all interpreters … whether they take into account or not the polyvocality and diversity of biblical authors' (1997: 2.4). The distinction between the two, made by Coffey et al., which equates indexing with univocality and cross-references with polyvocality is, Kelle argues, therefore unsustainable. This diversion into the deeper reaches of the scholarly tradition is helpful in addressing some issues raised by postmodern critics of grounded theorising.

## Conclusion

Many qualitative researchers are attached to the ideas of grounded theorising and do not wish to dismiss these as inconsistent with contemporary sensibilities or to opt, wholesale, for the postmodern alternative à la Denzin. Grounded theory emerged at a time when scientific conceptions of qualitative research were rather dominant and literary, postmodern conceptions had not yet taken off. More technical explanations of the procedures involved are sometimes unwelcome reminders of this, but the spirit that lies behind the approach can be simply explained, and does not have to be attached to a naively realist epistemology, or indeed to an oppressive urge to force readers to regard its products as true for all time. It demands a rigorous spirit of self-awareness and self-criticism, as well as an openness to new ideas that is often a hallmark of research studies of good quality.

## FURTHER READING

The best place to start in finding out more is the original book on grounded theory by Glaser and Strauss (1967). I have written a more extended outline of the method as Chapter 7 in Seale (1999). In addition, you can see how researchers have actually used the approach by reading a book edited by Strauss and Corbin (1997) called *Grounded Theory in Practice*, which contains reports of studies written by leading researchers using grounded theory.

### Student Reader (Seale, 2004b): relevant readings

32  Barney G. Glaser and Anselm L. Strauss: 'Theoretical sampling'

44  Anselm L. Strauss and Juliet Corbin: 'Open coding'

46  Udo Kelle: 'Theory building in qualitative research and computer programs for the management of textual data'

See also Chapter 6, 'Grounded theory' by Ian Dey in Seale et al. (2004).

## Journal articles illustrating use of the methods described in this chapter

Charmaz, K. (1983) 'Loss of self: a fundamental form of suffering in the chronically ill', Sociology of Health and Illness, 5 (2): 168–195.

Kennedy, B.L. (2011) 'The importance of student and teacher interactions for disaffected middle school students: a grounded theory study of community day schools', Urban Education, 46: 4–33.

Neill, S.J. (2010) 'Containing acute childhood illness within family life: a substantive grounded theory', Journal of Child Health Care, 14: 327–344.

## Web links

The Grounded Theory Institute: www.groundedtheory.com

The Grounded Theory Review: www.groundedtheoryreview.com

Grounded theory: – doing it as part of public discourse: www.habermas.org/grndthry.htm

Grounded Theory Online: www.groundedtheoryonline.com

Grounded theory – a thumbnail sketch: www.scu.edu.au/schools/gcm/ar/arp/grounded.html

Introduction to grounded theory: www.analytictech.com/mb870/introtoGT.htm

## KEY CONCEPTS FOR REVIEW

**Advice:** Use these, along with the review questions in the next section, to test your knowledge of the contents of this chapter. Try to define each of the key concepts listed here; if you have understood this chapter you should be able to do this. Check your definitions against the definition in the glossary at the end of the book.

Axial coding

Categories and properties

Concept–indicator links

Constant comparison

Open coding

Selective coding

Substantive and formal theories

Theoretical sampling

Theoretical saturation

 ■ **Review questions**

1   What is theoretical sampling and how might it be used in a research study?
2   How should grounded theory researchers decide when to stop collecting and analysing data?
3   Give an example from the chapter that involves constant comparison. What are the stages of constant comparison and how does the example illustrate these?
4   What types of coding are proposed by Glaser and Strauss?
5   What criticisms of grounded theory as a method have been made?

1  Choose a specific research study and ask of it:

   (a) How well are the concepts grounded in data; how adequately are central claims supported by evidence?

   (b) Can you identify core categories and subsidiary categories? What are the properties of these categories and what are the relationships between them?

   (c) What strategies from grounded theorising might the researcher have pursued in order to generate a more 'saturated' or 'thick' theoretical account? Consider, here, theoretical sampling decisions that might have been taken, or comparisons that might have been made.

2  Grounded theorising involves an attempt to construct an account that is well defended against threats to its truth status. To what extent does this allow for alternative voices? Is this a desirable feature of qualitative research?

# 23

# DISCOURSE ANALYSIS

## Fran Tonkiss

---

## Chapter Contents

---

This chapter considers the use of written and spoken texts as the basis for social and cultural research. It focuses on discourse analysis as a method for studying the use of language in social contexts. This method provides insights into the way speech and texts help to shape and reproduce social meanings and forms of knowledge. I define the term 'discourse', outline approaches to the social and cultural analysis of discourse, and explore discourse analysis in relation to four key stages of the research process:

1   Defining the research problem

2   Collecting data

3   Coding and analysing data

4   Presenting the analysis

This qualitative approach to textual analysis can sometimes seem a difficult method to pin down because it is used in different ways within different fields (see Hammersley, 2002; Wetherell et al., 2001a). While its origins lie most firmly in the disciplines of linguistics and social psychology (see Billig, 1987; Fairclough, 2003; Van Dijk, 1997), the method has been widely taken up within sociology, media and communications, politics and social policy, health studies, socio-legal studies, education, management and organisation studies. In this discussion I am concerned with these broadly *social* approaches to textual analysis, focusing on how social categories, knowledges and relations are shaped by discourse.

Discourse analysis takes its place within a larger body of social and cultural research that is concerned with the production of meaning through talk and texts. As such, it has affinities with semiotics, which is primarily concerned with visual texts (see Chapter 16) and with conversation analysis (see Chapter 24). While approaches to discourse analysis vary, they share a common understanding of language as an object of inquiry. To the discourse analyst, language is not simply a neutral medium for communicating information or reporting on events, but a domain in which people's knowledge of the social world is actively shaped. Anyone who has been in an argument with a skilled or slippery debater will be aware of the way that language can be used to compel certain conclusions, to establish certain claims and to deny others. Discourse analysis involves a perspective on language that sees this not simply as reflecting reality in a transparent or straightforward way, but as constructing and organising the terms in which we understand that social reality. Discourse analysts are interested in language and texts as sites in which social meanings are formed and reproduced, social identities are shaped, and social facts are established.

## What is discourse?

Discourse can refer to a single utterance or speech act (from a fragment of talk, to a private conversation, to a political speech) or to a systematic ordering of language involving certain rules, terminology and conventions (such as legal or medical discourse). This second definition allows researchers to analyse how discourses shape specific ways of speaking and understanding. Viewed in this way, 'a discourse is a group of statements which provide a language for talking about – i.e. a way of representing – a particular kind of knowledge about a topic' (Hall, 1992: 290). Such an approach is often associated with the work of the French thinker Michel Foucault, and his interest in how forms of discourse help to produce the very categories, facts and objects that they claim to describe (Foucault, 1972: 49). Discourse, in Foucault's sense, does not refer simply to language or speech acts, but to the way language works to organise fields of knowledge and practice. Thus, following the work of Foucault, one might ask:

- How is our understanding of sexuality shaped by various moral, medical, legal and psychological discourses?

- How is the concept of deviance (e.g. 'mad' or 'delinquent' behaviour) defined and talked about within discourses of psychiatry or criminology?

- How are these discursive constructions linked to social practices, to social institutions, and to the operation of social power?

A good example of this kind of approach is Bell's (1993) use of discourse analysis to examine how the crime of incest is constituted under English and Scots law (Box 23.1).

---

**BOX 23.1**

## BELL'S (1993) ANALYSIS OF POLITICAL DISCOURSES ON INCEST

Incest was criminalised in English law in 1908; while it has been criminal in Scotland since 1567, the law was modernised in 1986. Bell bases her analysis on the parliamentary debates surrounding both pieces of legislation (Bell, 1993: 126–127). Her interest is in how incest is defined as a criminal act in ways that draw on particular forms of expertise and evidence at these different historical moments.

---

Bell identifies three key 'knowledges' that shape the political and legal discourse about incest:

1 The first of these concerns issues of health – articulated in terms of the dangers of 'inbreeding' in the 1908 debates and 'genetic' risks in the 1980s (Bell, 1993: 130–1). While medical or scientific arguments appear in both debates, Bell points out that they are in themselves insufficient to define the offence of incest. For example, they do not explain why incest would be wrong if there was no chance of conception; they focus on the possible consequence of the act rather than the act itself. At the same time they define incest as a problem in rather limited ways, as referring only to sexual relations between men and fertile women, and to blood relatives rather than adoptive or step-family. The victim of incest, furthermore, is understood to be the potential offspring, rather than either of the parties directly concerned. In these terms Bell examines how medical knowledges shape the discourse on incest to produce particular definitions of the problem itself and the subjects it involves.

2 The scientific discourse of genetic harm is supplemented by a second body of knowledge that constructs the offence of incest in terms of sexual, psychological or child abuse. Here the speakers in the parliamentary debates are seen to draw on discourses of child protection, social welfare and psychology. Incest is constructed as wrong on the basis of mental harm, coercion and violence, defined in terms of power relations within the family. The victims of incest are represented within these discourses as children or young women who are vulnerable to (especially male) adults. While such a conception of incest might be seen as more in keeping with current understandings, Bell does not claim to assess the 'relative truth' of these competing accounts (1993: 129). Rather, she is concerned with the differing ways in which they produce incest as a legal fact, defining the problem and the victim in various terms.

3 The third key frame within which incest is constructed in these debates is as a threat to the family as a social institution. This is particularly important for the inclusion of adoptive and step-relations in the definition of incest under the more recent Scots law, in contrast to the scientific arguments seen earlier. Here, the offence of incest is construed in terms of a breach of trust within the family, and as violating the family as a social bond rather than simply a genetic one. Such an understanding involves an extended notion of the family unit, as well as its importance to a wider social and moral order.

Bell's analysis is interesting in showing how the category of incest, while often naturalised as a primary human taboo, can be understood as a legal artefact moulded by various political, medical and moral discourses. English and Scots law define incest differently; moreover, the parliamentary debates that inform these laws draw on contrasting and sometimes conflicting knowledges which go beyond the legal sphere. Incest is constructed as a legal fact via discourses of medical science, psychology, child protection, social welfare, the family and moral order. It follows that legal discourse – and the legal facts that it inscribes – is shaped by wider networks of language, knowledge and power. This point goes beyond semantics: discourse – ways of speaking about and understanding an issue – is important here because it helps to determine the practical ways that people and institutions define and respond to given problems.

## Critical discourse analysis

This social and historical approach to the study of discourse is often associated with critical discourse analysis (CDA) (Fairclough, 1995; Van Dijk, 1993, 2001; Wodak, 2004; Wodak and Meyer, 2001). Critical discourse analysis is concerned with the social and political context of discourse, based on the view that language is not only conditioned by these contexts, but itself helps to constitute them (Fairclough and Wodak, 1997: 258). Leading approaches in CDA examine how ideologies are reproduced through language and texts (Fairclough, 1995), and how discourse can be understood in relation to historical processes and events (Wodak, 2001). Critical discourse analysts go beyond the rhetorical or technical analysis of language to explore its social and political setting, uses and effects. They see language as crucial to the ways that power is reproduced, legitimated and exercised within social relations and institutions.

## Discourse in a social context

Perhaps the easiest way to think about discourses as linking language, knowledge and power is to take the model of 'expert' languages. Doctors, for example, do not simply draw on their practical training when doing their job; they also draw on a medical language that allows them to identify symptoms, make diagnoses and prescribe remedies. This language is not readily available to people who are not medically trained.

Such an expert language has a number of important social effects: it marks out a field of knowledge or expertise, it confers membership, and it bestows authority:

1   Medical discourse establishes a distinct sphere of *expertise*, setting out the domain of medical knowledge and the issues with which it is concerned. Consider, for example, ongoing debates as to whether chronic fatigue syndrome or ME should be considered as primarily a physical or a psychological problem, and, to an extent, whether such a condition can be said to exist at all (see Guise, et al., 2010). One way in which such debates play out is in the language used to describe the condition. The term 'myalgic encephalomyelitis' clearly *medicalises* the condition, while a term such as 'yuppie flu' does not. The use of language plays a notable part in arguments for recognising a condition as a 'proper' illness: as a valid object of medical expertise and a suitable case for medical treatment. Medical discourse in this sense helps to delimit a distinct field of knowledge, and to exclude certain facts or claims from this field.

2   Medical discourse confers *membership* in allowing health professionals to communicate with each other in coherent and consistent ways. Language in this sense represents a form of expert knowledge that professionals draw on in their everyday working practice and reproduce in their interactions. The internal conventions and rules of medical discourse act as a way of *socialising* individuals into the medical professions, and enabling them to operate competently within them. In this respect, discourse has a role to play in the institutional organisation of medical knowledge and its professional culture.

3   Medical discourse *authorises* certain speakers and statements. Doctors' authority is perhaps most routinely expressed by their access to an expert language from which most of their patients are excluded. On an everyday level, while we may at times be frustrated by the use of medical language to describe our symptoms, we may also be reassured that our doctor is an authority on these matters. More generally, medical authority is asserted in the use of expert discourses to dismiss competing accounts, such as those associated with homeopathic and alternative remedies.

Expert languages provide an obvious and a very fruitful area for research; discourse analysis, however, is by no means confined to this domain. Discourse analysts might study formal policy or parliamentary discourse, but also the popular discourses used in politicians' speeches and manifestos, the news and other forms of media, interviews and conversations. In all cases, the analyst is concerned with examining the way that specific forms of text and speech produce their versions of a social issue, problem, event or context.

## Doing discourse analysis

It is difficult to formalise any standard approach to discourse analysis. This is partly because of the variety of frameworks adopted by different researchers, partly because the process tends to be 'data-driven'. However, while there are no strict rules of method for analysing discourse, it is possible to isolate certain core themes and useful techniques which may be adapted to different research contexts. In the discussion that follows I consider some of these in terms of four key stages of the research process: defining the research problem; selecting and approaching data; sorting, coding and analysing data; and presenting the analysis.

## Defining the research problem

I have stressed the 'special' character of discourse analysis as a method of research – its distinctive approach to language and its resistance to formulaic rules of method. However, the discourse analyst is faced with a common set of questions that arise within any research process. What is the research about? What are my data? How will I select and gather the data? How will I handle and analyse the data? How will I present my findings?

Formulating a research problem can be one of the most difficult moments in social research. Sometimes it can seem like a very artificial exercise – qualitative research frequently is data-led, and the researcher cannot be certain precisely how the research problem will be defined until they have begun data collection and preliminary analysis (see also Chapter 7). This is underlined by the fact that this form of research is not so much *looking for* conclusive answers to specific problems ('What are the causes of juvenile crime?'), as *looking at* the way both the problem, and possible solutions, are constructed ('How is juvenile crime explained and understood within current political discourse?'). Explanations of juvenile crime might draw on accounts of moral decline, poor parenting, the absence of positive role models, inadequate schooling, poverty, lack of prospects, adolescent rebelliousness and so on. This is not to say that the issue – juvenile crime – does not exist or has no meaning, but to assert that social actors make sense of this reality in various, often conflicting ways. If a dominant understanding of juvenile crime within political and media discourse rests on the notion of poor parenting, for example, it is likely that the problem will be tackled in a different way than if it was commonly understood in terms of a language of material deprivation.

As with other forms of social and cultural research, discourse analysis often begins with a broad – even vague – interest in a certain area of social life. The way this broad interest becomes a feasible research topic is strongly linked to the choice of research methods (see Box 23.2).

---

**BOX 23.2**

### FORMULATING A DISCOURSE ANALYTIC PROJECT ON IMMIGRATION

A researcher has a broad interest in undertaking research on immigration – a topic of ongoing political, media and public interest. There are different ways of approaching research on immigration, and these will influence how the research problem is defined. You might, if you were not planning to do discourse analysis,

- explore statistical data relating to the number of people entering a country in each year, their countries of origin, and patterns of change over time, or
- select a sample of people who have settled in a place, and use interviews to research aspects of their experiences of immigration, for example: their experience of immigration bureaucracy, of the process of integration, questions of cultural difference, the notion of 'home'.

*(Continued)*

---

*(Continued)*

Using discourse analysis, you might:

- choose to examine political debates surrounding immigration legislation
- analyse press reports on immigration issues
- investigate anti-immigration literature published by right-wing organisations.

A discourse analyst might be concerned with how immigration is constructed as a political issue, the ways in which immigrants are represented within public discourses, the manner in which certain conceptions of immigration are warranted in opposition to alternative ways of thinking – for example, representations of immigration in terms of illegality or 'threat' (see Van der Valk, 2003; see also Philo and Beattie, 1999; KhosraviNik, 2009). A starting point for such a study could be as simple as 'How is immigration constructed as a "problem" within political discourse?' The analytic process will tend to feed back into this guiding question, helping to refine the research problem as you go along.

## Selecting and approaching data

Having set up a problem like the one in Box 23.2, the next step is to collect data for analysis. This will in part be determined by how you are defining the issue. Do you want to look at:

- Immigration policy?
- Immigrant identity?
- Media representations of immigration issues?
- Attitudes towards immigration within sections of the public?

Depending on how you are conceptualising the research problem, you could collect data from a number of sources. These include parliamentary debates, political speeches, party manifestos, policy documents, personal accounts (including interviews), press or television reports, and campaigning literature. As with textual analysis more generally, a discourse analyst potentially can draw on a very wide range of data. As a general rule of thumb, discourse analysis tends to be based on more textual data than conversation analysis and less than content analysis, where computer-assisted coding can allow the researcher to process a large amount of material. However, the primary consideration in selecting textual material is its relevance to the research problem, rather than simply the number of texts analysed. It is therefore especially important to make clear the rationale for your selection, and how it might provide insights into a topic. Box 23.3 shows how two discourse analysts selected texts for their studies.

---

## BOX 23.3

### SELECTING DATA FOR DISCOURSE ANALYSIS

#### Study 1: The historical construction of incest

Bell's study of the construction and criminalisation of incest considered the changing ways in which this problem is defined and understood over time and in different legal systems. Rather than undertaking a very large-scale historical study, however, Bell was able to identify two contrasting bodies of discourse at two different historical moments: the 1908 legislation in England, and 1986 legislation in Scotland. While both nations are governed by the British parliament, they maintain their separate historical legal systems.

In addition to the Acts of Parliament that constitute the letter of the law, Bell analysed the debates in both the upper and lower houses of the British parliament which framed these pieces of legislation, as well as reports of relevant parliamentary committees. In this way, she was able to examine the political discourses and arguments that shaped the law.

*Source*: Bell, 1993

## Study 2: Refugees, asylum seekers and immigrants in the British press

This study by Majid KhosraviNik examined the ways in which these groups were represented in a sample of British newspapers against the backdrop of two major events: the 1999 conflict in Kosovo, and the 2005 British General Election. In each case, the researcher chose a specific time-frame: March 1999, covering the NATO bombing of Serbian positions in Kosovo and the displacement of Kosovar refugees; and May 2005, covering the British election campaign. Note that in the first sample the 'problem' of refugees is constituted at a relative distance from the British public addressed by these newspapers, while in the second sample it becomes a more immediate, domestic issue in a context of heightened political debate. He also identified a specific sample of media texts:

> [T]hree representative newspapers (along with their Sunday editions) were selected in terms of their formats and socio-political ideologies as follows:
>
> *The Guardian* and *The Observer:* liberal quality newspapers
>
> *The Times* and *The Sunday Times:* conservative quality newspapers
>
> The *Daily Mail* and *Mail on Sunday:* "tabloid" newspapers.'
>
> (KhosraviNik, 2009: 482)

In selecting this sample, the researcher aimed to explore a range of press discourse on refugees, asylum seekers and immigrants, using a common social research strategy that distinguishes 'quality', 'serious' or 'broadsheet' press from more 'tabloid' or 'populist' media, and associates particular newspapers with more liberal or left (*New York Times*, *Le Monde*, *El País*) or more conservative (*Washington Times*, *Le Figaro*, *El Mundo*) political orientations.

*Source*: KhosraviNik, 2009: 482

As Bell (1993) found, political and policy discourse – whether parliamentary debates, formal legislation, committee enquiries, political speeches and manifestoes, or policy texts – are valuable resources for discourse analysts. In many countries such texts are freely available on the public record and increasingly are archived on-line, making them an accessible source of data for student researchers. Political or policy discourse is also an excellent example of the way that language helps to reproduce and reinforce social power, and has an impact on how institutions and individuals are governed. In selecting such data for analysis, however, the researcher needs to be sensitive to the different kinds of discourse that are at stake: a political speech on the campaign trail is not the same as a piece of legislation or a policy paper. As in all social and cultural research, the analyst should be clear about their rationale for choosing certain kinds of data, their strategy for collecting it (What range of textual data? Over what time period?), and how they understand the relevance and role of these data in their social context.

Like political and policy discourse, media texts of the type studied by KhosraviNik (2009) – whether press, radio, television or other media – are important resources for discourse analysts. They represent the powerful way in which discourse can shape attitudes and help to establish dominant meanings, as well as demonstrating the contested nature of many of these accounts. They are also easily accessible, increasingly on-line. The very abundance and availability of media texts, however, poses a real challenge for the researcher in selecting a manageable amount of relevant data. KhosraviNik could not have gathered, let alone analysed, everything that appeared in the British (print, radio, television, Internet) media on Kosovo or the 2005 election – he therefore had to be very selective in constructing his sample and accounting for those choices in writing up his research.

## Sorting, coding and analysing data

Discourse analysis has been called a 'craft skill' (see Potter and Wetherell, 1994: 55), and has been compared to riding a bike – a process that one picks up by doing, perfects by practising, and which is difficult to describe in a formal way. Doing effective discourse analysis has much to do with getting a real feel for one's data, working closely with them, trying out alternatives, and being ready to reject analytic schemes that do not work. While it has been argued that discourse analysis is not centrally concerned with 'some general idea that seems to be intended' by a text (Potter and Wetherell, 1987: 168), the overall rhetorical effect of a text provides a framework in which to consider its inconsistencies, internal workings and small strategies of meaning. Potter and Wetherell refer to these as the interpretive repertoires at work within a discourse, the ways of speaking about and understanding a topic that organise the meanings of a text.

When doing discourse analysis it is not necessary to provide an account of every line of the text under study, as can be the case in conversation analysis. It is usually more appropriate and more informative to be selective in relation to the data, extracting those sections that provide the richest source of analytic material. This does not mean that one simply 'selects out' the data extracts that support the argument, while ignoring more troubling or ill-fitting sections of the text. Contradictions within a text (including and perhaps especially those parts that contradict the researcher's own assumptions) can often be productive for the analysis.

If there is one rule of method that we might apply to discourse analysis, it would be Durkheim's first principle: abandon all preconceptions! At times it can be tempting to impose an interpretation on a sample of discourse, but if this is not supported by the data then it will not yield a convincing analysis. We cannot *make* the data 'say' what is simply not there. Most discourse analysts would reject the idea that texts are open to any number of different, and equally plausible, readings. Rather, analytical assertions are to be grounded in textual evidence and detailed argument. In this respect discourse analysis entails a commitment to challenging common-sense knowledge and disrupting easy assumptions about the organisation of social meanings.

Discourse analysis is an interpretive process that relies on close study of specific texts, and therefore does not lend itself to hard-and-fast 'rules' of method. Even so, we might take a cue from Foucault (1984: 103), who suggested that one might analyse a text in terms of 'its structure, its architecture, its intrinsic form and the play of its internal relationships'. Put simply, this directs our attention to the organisation and the interpretive detail of given texts. Here we can identify some useful pointers for analysis:

1  Identifying key themes and arguments.

2  Looking for association and variation.

3   Examining characterisation and agency.

4   Paying attention to emphasis and silences.

Note that these are devices or tools for opening up a text, rather than a fixed set of analytic strategies. The tactics that you adopt as an analyst come from engagement with the data themselves, rather than from any textbook approach.

## Identifying key themes and arguments

A common starting point for analysis is to locate key categories, themes and terms. Identifying recurrent or significant themes can help you to manage the data and bring a more systematic order to the analytic process. In this way, discourse analysis draws on more general approaches to handling and coding qualitative data (see Chapter 21). The analytic process involves sifting, comparing and contrasting the different ways in which these themes emerge. On a simple level, the repetition or emphasis of keywords, phrases and images reveals most clearly what the speaker or writer is trying to put across in the text. This can provide the basis for a critical analysis of the data:

- What ideas and representations cluster around key themes?
- Are particular meanings and images being mobilised?
- What other discourses or arguments are drawn on to define or justify the approach taken in the text?

KhosraviNik's (2009) study of the representation of refugees, asylum seekers and immigrants in the British press notes a basic contrast in the use of key terms in his sample (see also Boxes 23.3 and 23.6). In the coverage of the Kosovo conflict and NATO air-strikes in 1999, the common term used to describe displaced Kosovar people is 'refugee'. In the same newspapers' coverage of the 2005 British General Election, the language is that of 'asylum seeker' and 'immigrant'. KhosraviNik suggests that this linguistic shift marks a political shift to a more negative view of these groups. In the first case, the British newspapers are reporting on a distant humanitarian crisis in which the claims of the refugees are not in question: Kosovars are represented as victims of forced and unwilling displacement. In the second case the newspapers are reporting on people who have arrived in Britain. Whereas the use of the term 'refugee' assumes the legitimate status of this claim, the use of the term 'asylum seeker' implies that such a status is unclear, uncertain or even illegitimate.

Bell's analysis (Box 23.1), to take another example, was organised around the three core arguments she identified as shaping the political debates on incest: potential genetic risks; the abuse of children and other vulnerable individuals; and the threat to the family structure – or as Bell sums it up, discourses of 'health, harm and happy families'. Her analysis also highlights the wider fields of discourse and knowledge that inform legal argument in this setting. The criminalisation of incest rests not only on legal definitions and knowledge, but on medical and psychiatric knowledge, child psychology and welfare discourses, moral and socio-cultural understandings of the family. These shape the interpretive repertoires – the ways of speaking and modes of understanding – at work in the texts she studied.

## Looking for association and variation

Another useful tactic for opening up a piece of discourse is to look for patterns of association and patterns of variation within the text. What associations are established between different actors, groups or problems? Van der Valk's (2003) study of right-wing French discourses on immigration (Box 23.4) points to the way that 'immigrants' and their imputed 'allies' on the political left are differentiated from a unitary understanding of 'the people', while Teo's (2000) study of Australian news reporting traces the associations made between Asian immigrants and criminality.

## ANALYSIS OF RIGHT-WING DISCOURSES ON IMMIGRATION

Van der Valk (2003) examines how a notion of 'the people' was mobilised within political debates in France so as to exclude certain groups. She argues that not only did these discourses represent immigrant 'others' in a negative light (especially in terms of criminality), but these negative associations were transferred to those seen as 'allies' of immigrants – specifically, the political left. The invocation of 'the people' works not only to legitimise the anti-immigration discourses of sections of the right, but also to question the legitimacy and the loyalties of the left. References to such abstract notions as 'the people', 'the community' or 'family life' in political discourses are hard to rebut, because they seem to embody values which no one would want to dispute but at the same time are often imprecise. For these reasons, they can become powerful carriers of meaning.

Differences within an account also point us to the work that is being done to reconcile conflicting ideas, to cope with contradiction or uncertainty, or to counter alternatives. By paying attention to such variations the analyst disrupts the appearance of a coherent or 'watertight' piece of discourse, allowing insights into the text's internal hesitations or inconsistencies, and the way that the discourse excludes alternative accounts. Huckin's (2002) study of homelessness illustrates this (Box 23.5).

## ANALYSIS OF MEDIA DISCOURSE ON HOMELESSNESS

Huckin's (2002) study of media discourse on homelessness uses an example from a newspaper editorial. He argues that the text emphasises substance abuse and mental illness as two of the chief causes of homelessness, but does not include strategies for addressing these problems in its discussion of appropriate public responses. Rather, the text concentrates on charity and voluntary action, on jobs, and on policing and criminalisation. There is a mismatch, then, between the account of the causes of homelessness, and the account of possible solutions. Huckin reads this mismatch in terms of a conservative political agenda that stresses the role of charity, opportunity and private enterprise over public welfare programmes. Indeed, the solutions highlighted in the text are strongly associated with law and order, which the researcher suggests may be inappropriate as a response to problems of mental illness and substance abuse.

In reading for variation in the text, Huckin develops an argument about the way dominant policy solutions for homelessness are advanced even if these are at odds with how the problem is understood. Looking for associations and reading for variations or contrast represent two tactics for analysing what Foucault called 'the play of internal relationships' within a text. The two studies demonstrate each in turn: in her account of right-wing political discourse (Box 23.4), Van der Valk analysed patterns of association, showing how these were created between 'the people' and the parties of the right, and between immigrants and the left. In the study of homelessness (Box 23.5), Huckin's patterns of variation included inconsistency between the diagnosis of a problem (mental illness and substance abuse) and the endorsement of practical solutions (charity and policing).

### Characterisation and agency

Patterns of association within a text are frequently used to characterise particular individuals or groups. This leads us to a third tool for opening up a discourse for analysis: exploring how social actors are spoken about and positioned within a text. This involves asking the following questions:

- What characteristics, problems or concerns are associated with different social actors or groups?
- From what standpoint does the speaker or author develop their account?
- How is agency attributed or obscured within the text?

Effects of characterisation are partly about how certain values, problems or qualities – illegality, threat, order or patriotism, for example – come to be associated with certain groups. Other strategies of characterisation work through more specific effects of 'personalisation' – giving people names and individual histories – or depersonalisation (see Box 23.6). KhosraviNik's (2009: 486) study contrasts press accounts where refugees or immigrants are represented in depersonalised and mass terms – 'Albania flooded by the rising tide of refugees' – with others where they are 'personalised' – '[Bajric's] mother had carried him in her arms through snowdrifts up to three feet deep, with her other children and their grandmother trailing behind, to become unwilling refugees of war'.

The author or speaker's own standpoint may also be of analytic interest. Press accounts frequently depersonalise the author's voice: one of the ways in which authority is established in media discourses is through presenting these accounts as impersonal, distanced or objective. This implies that the journalist's standpoint is neutral, detached and disinterested – they merely *report* on events rather than providing an interpretation of them. KhosraviNik (2009: 488–489), for example, examines a piece in the *Daily Mail* in 2005 with the provocative headline 'White flights grows from cities divided by race' that describes a 'serious and urgent' situation involving white residents leaving areas whose racial make-up is being changed by 'chain migration'. While the headline and the content uses controversial language, however, the account it offers is largely attributed to 'a report' and 'evidence' provided by a 'think-tank', distancing the story's authorship.

In contrast to this impersonal or objective standpoint, political discourse often draws on strategies of association and personalisation to position the author in a positive way. The *authority* of a political discourse is less likely to rely on distancing strategies than on associating the speaker with such values as statesmanship, the nation or the people, or by personalising their account in terms of their biography, their family or their hardships (see the workshop and discussion exercise associated with this chapter).

---

**|  BOX 23.6  |**

## CHARACTERISATION OF REFUGEES AND ASYLUM SEEKERS IN MEDIA DISCOURSE

KhosraviNik's (2009) study offers good examples of 'personalisation' and association. In his analysis of how British press covered the Kosovo conflict of 1999, KhosraviNik notes how the newspapers in his sample give Kosovar refugees individual or family stories in which people's names are used, and their ages or aspects of their personal histories given. In examining the coverage of the 2005 British General Election campaign, he identifies a similar strategy in an account of one local group's support for a single Malawian asylum seeker threatened by deportation. Here, the liberal *Guardian* newspaper intervenes in the broader political debate by highlighting the personalised story of an African woman who has settled in Dorset (a rural English county with a very small black and minority ethnic population). The local group is associated with a church, and the woman is a mother of four children who does voluntary work in a charity shop – drawing on a series of positive associations with community, church, family and charity.

The third analytic strategy in respect of characterisation and agency is to examine how agency is depicted within the text. Who is seen as active or passive in producing the problems, processes or solutions described? This dynamic can work in different ways: agency often has positive associations within a text, but passivity may also have positive connotations. KhosraviNik notes how the newspapers he analyses from 1999 commonly represent Khosovar refugees as innocent, passive or powerless: 'He was doing his homework when the tanks stormed the village, a five-year-old boy sitting quietly at the table with his mother'; 'The Serbian special police burst through the door and handcuffed a man, a simple Albanian farmer whose family had lived there for generations' (2009: 484).

Critical discourse analysts also point to more technical linguistic strategies of nominalisation and passivisation in establishing or obscuring agency and causality (see Billig, 2008). Nominalisation refers to the use of nouns instead of verbs to describe events: in the example Billig suggests, a headline such as 'Attack on protesters' (where attack is a noun) has a different force from one reading 'Police attack protesters' (where attack is a verb). In a similar way, a speaker's use of the *passive* rather than the active voice can obscure agency: 'Protesters were attacked' as opposed to 'Police attacked protesters' – in the latter case, using an active verb requires a subject or agent. The discourse analyst can look for instances where the text substitutes abstract nouns or concepts for social actors: think of how often finance reporters tell us that 'the markets responded positively' to news of job cuts at a certain company, or of references to how 'globalisation' is threatening jobs. In each case the abstract category (markets, globalisation) replaces the social actors (stockbrokers, investors, corporate executives) who make decisions about the benefits of layoffs to share value or whether to move their firm's production to cheaper labour markets.

Specific forms of agency by real social actors are attributed to abstract or impersonal processes.

## Attending to emphasis and silences

The final tool for opening up a text for analysis is to look for patterns of emphasis and for silences. KhosraviNik highlights the references to large numbers, uncontrollable quantities or irresistible forces in media representations of refugees and immigrants, especially through metaphors of 'flooding' – with references to 'influx', 'pouring in', 'ever-swelling numbers' and a 'rising tide' (2009: 486). It is worth noting here that, while discourse analysis is a qualitative method of social research, researchers at times use a quantitative logic of argument in noting the frequency or consistency with which various terms, metaphors or associations are used. With a relatively large sample of textual data such as KhosraviNik's, it becomes possible to trace these patterns across different texts.

Huckin's (2002) example points us to the telling silences in the media account of homelessness. He argues that the text's neglect of the systematic lack of affordable housing support a reading of homelessness as involving individual pathologies (mental illness) and illicit behaviour (substance abuse). Similarly, Van Dijk (2000, 2002) refers to the frequent 'silence' of ethnic minorities in media coverage of race. Minority voices are seldom heard in mainstream media, he argues, and when they do appear they are often marginal or treated with scepticism. KhosraviNik (2009: 492) offers an interesting inversion of this kind of silence in his account of a report in *The Times* of a televised public debate with the opposition Conservative (Tory) Party Leader during the 2005 British election campaign. Three of the contributors from the audience are named (while a fourth is described as a 'disillusioned Tory voter'); of these, one individual is referred to as 'an Afro-Caribbean' and another as 'a young Asian man'. The silence in this case is around the ethnic identities of the other two audience members mentioned in the article, with the implication that they are white. The journalist considers it relevant to identify the minority ethnicity of two individuals, whereas the ethnicity of the others is taken for granted or not deemed relevant to the public debate on immigration.

These kinds of analysis require the researcher to adopt a rather 'split' approach to the text. That is, it is necessary to read *along* with the meanings that are being created, to look to the way the text is organised and to pay attention to how things are being said. At the same time, discourse analysis can require the researcher to read *against* the grain of the text, to look to silences or gaps, to make conjectures about alternative accounts which are excluded by omission, as well as those which are countered by rhetoric. While I have argued that we cannot force our data to say things that are not there, we can as critical researchers point out those places where the text is silent, to think about what remains 'unsaid' in the organisation of a discourse. Such a move can help to place the discourse in a wider interpretive context.

## Presenting the analysis

The final stage of the research process involves developing and presenting an argument on the basis of your discourse analysis. It is at this point that the researcher is concerned with using language to construct and **warrant** their own account of the data (that is to say, to back it up with persuasive evidence and authority). This aspect of the process provides a useful context in which to consider the relation of discourse analysis to issues of validity, writing and reflexivity (see Chapter 30).

Social researchers can think about research validity in terms of both **internal** and **external validity** (see Chapter 30), referring to the coherence and consistency and the evidence base of a piece of research on the one hand, and the generalisability of the research on the other.

Discourse analysts have a particular concern with issues of internal validity. Their reliance on close textual work means that they develop arguments on the basis of detailed interpretation of data. One can therefore ask:

- How coherent is the interpretive argument?
- Is it soundly based in a reading of the textual evidence?
- Does it pay attention to textual detail?
- How plausible is the movement from data to analysis?
- Does the researcher bring in arguments from outside the text, and if so how well supported are these claims?

Discourse analysis is concerned with the examination of meaning, and the often complex processes through which social meanings are produced. In evaluating discourse analytic research we should therefore be looking for interpretive rigour and internal consistency in argument. Analytic claims need always to be supported by a sound reading of data. In this sense, good discourse analyses stand up well to the demands of internal validity. However, this is not to say that discourse analysis aims to offer a 'true' or objective account of a given text. The discourse analyst aims to provide a persuasive and well-supported account, offering an insightful, useful and critical interpretation of a research problem. The discourse analyst seeks to open up statements to challenge, interrogate taken-for-granted meanings, and disturb easy claims to objectivity or common sense in the texts they are reading. It would therefore be inconsistent to contend that the analyst's own discourse was itself wholly objective, factual or generally true.

Discourse analysts often deal with relatively small data sets emerging from specific social settings. Like much qualitative case study research, they are therefore unlikely to support claims of being more widely representative, so raising problems regarding generalisation and external validity as conventionally conceived, though their capacity for theoretical generalisation (see Chapter 9) is likely to be strong.

Discourse analysis involves a commitment to examining processes of meaning in social life, a certain modesty in analytic claims, and an approach to knowledge which sees this as open and contestable rather than closed. By adopting such an approach to knowledge, the analyst and the reader may be confident of the internal validity and wider relevance of a particular account while remaining open to other critical insights and arguments. Discourse analysis fits into a broader field of social research methods (e.g. conversation analysis) which seek to analyse general social patterns through a close investigation of detail.

A critical and open stance towards data and analysis may also be understood as part of a reflexive approach to social research (see Chapter 5). In aiming to be reflexive in their research practice, social researchers question their own assumptions, critically examine their processes of inquiry, and consider their effect on the research setting and research findings – whether in terms of their presence in a fieldwork situation, the way they select their data, or how their theoretical framework shapes the process of data collection and analysis. Reflexivity also involves attention to the writing strategies that researchers employ to construct a research account, and here the insights of discourse analysis are very useful.

## Conclusion

In writing this chapter, I have drawn on various discursive strategies in an effort to make my account fit into a methods textbook. I have suggested that discourse analysis does not sit easily with hard-and-fast rules of method. At the same time, however, I have drawn on a particular language (data, evidence, analysis, validity) and on particular forms of textual organisation (moving from theory to empirical examples, using subheadings, boxes, numbered and bulleted lists) so as to explain discourse analysis in the form of a fairly orderly research process. An attention to the way that language is put to work is a useful tool for any reader or researcher who wants to think critically about social research processes and to evaluate research findings.

## FURTHER READING

Wetherell et al. (2001a) collects together pieces by key writers on different approaches to discourse theory, while (2001b) offers a practical guide to discourse analysis; Fairclough (2003) is another extremely useful textbook; Van Dijk (2007, 2008), Wodak and Meyer (2001) and Wodak and Krzyżanowski (2008) are further useful references from a critical discourse analysis and discourse-historical standpoint. For shorter introductions, Gill (1996) and Potter and Wetherell (1994) remain clear and very helpful. Both provide detailed examples of the use of discourse analysis in media research.

### Student Reader (Seale, 2004b): relevant readings

1   Michael Billig: 'Methodology and scholarship in understanding ideological explanation'

51  Stuart Hall: 'Foucault and discourse'

52  Jonathan Potter and Margaret Wetherell: 'Unfolding discourse analysis'

53  Norman Fairclough and Ruth Wodak: 'Critical discourse analysis'

54  H.G. Widdowson: 'The theory and practice of critical discourse analysis'

See also Chapter 13, 'Discourse analytic practice' by Alexa Hepburn and Jonathan Potter and Chapter 14, 'Critical discourse analysis' by Ruth Wodak in Seale et al. (2004).

## Journal articles illustrating or discussing the methods described in this chapter

Johansson, K., Lilja, M., Park, M. and Josephsson, S. (2010) 'Balancing the good – a critical discourse analysis of home modification services', Sociology of Health & Illness, 32 (4): 563–582.

Maier, C.D. (2011) 'Communicating business greening and greenwashing in global media: a multimodal discourse analysis of CNN's greenwashing video', International Communication Gazette, 73: 165–177.

Rogers, R., Malancharuvil-Berkes, E., Mosley, M., Hui, D. and Joseph, G.O. (2005) 'Critical discourse analysis in education: a review of the literature', Review of Educational Research, 75: 365–416.

## Web links

Discourse Analysis Online: www.shu.ac.uk/daol

Discourseanalysis.net: www.discourseanalysis.net

Language on the Move: www.languageonthemove.com

## KEY CONCEPTS FOR REVIEW

**Advice:** Use these, along with the review questions in the next section, to test your knowledge of the contents of this chapter. Try to define each of the key concepts listed here; if you have understood this chapter you should be able to do this. Check your definitions against the definition in the glossary at the end of the book.

| | |
|---|---|
| Agency | Nominalisation |
| Critical discourse analysis | Passivisation |
| Discourse | Patterns of association |
| External validity | Patterns of variation |
| Internal validity | Reflexivity |
| Interpretive repertoires | Silences (attending to) |
| Keyword | Warrant |

### Review questions

1 What kinds of data might discourse analysts collect?
2 What are the main considerations in selecting these data for analysis?
3 What questions does a discourse analyst ask of a text?

## Workshop and discussion exercise

1 The extract in Box 23.7 is from a speech given in Philadelphia by the Democratic Senator Barack Obama in March 2008. Obama responds in this speech – often referred to as his 'race speech' – to the controversy surrounding comments made by his local pastor Reverend Jeremiah Wright, including remarks suggesting that the United States had provoked the terrorist attacks of September 2001. Obama was elected as the USA's first African-American president in November 2008. Read the extract and consider the following questions:

(a) Consider the different *discourses* or *interpretive repertoires* that are being drawn upon to construct the speaker's arguments: for example, which moral, historical and political ideas are being mobilised in order to support the speaker's position?

(b) How does the speaker construct a particular 'identity' or 'voice' for himself? What is the potential effect of such a voice – how might it *be heard* – within discourses of race?

(c) Which other individuals are invoked in this extract? How are their stories positioned in relation to this account? You should look here not only for references to specific individuals, but also 'types' – such as 'fathers' or 'lobbyists'. How do the references to these types of actors draw on other discourses from outside the text?

(d) How does the speech use variation and patterns of emphasis to create its rhetorical effect?

(e) Can you identify strategies of *nominalisation* or *passivisation* in this speech – that is, where agency is imputed not to social actors but to impersonal nouns or abstract processes? Alternatively, can you identify moments where agency is imputed to individuals or groups? What is the effect of these contrasting versions of agency in the speech?

(f) In what ways does the speaker characterise America and Americans?

---

**▌ BOX 23.7 ▌**

### EXTRACT FROM A SPEECH MADE BY SENATOR BARACK OBAMA, 18 MARCH 2008 IN PHILADELPHIA

And this helps explain, perhaps, my relationship with Reverend Wright. As imperfect as he may be, he has been like family to me. He strengthened my faith, officiated my wedding, and baptized my children. Not once in my conversations with him have I heard him talk about any ethnic group in derogatory terms, or treat whites with whom he interacted with anything but courtesy and respect. He contains within him the contradictions—the good and the bad—of the community that he has served diligently for so many years.

I can no more disown him than I can disown the black community. I can no more disown him than I can disown my white grandmother—a woman who helped raise me, a woman who sacrificed again and again for me, a woman who loves me as much as she loves anything in this world, but a woman who once confessed her fear of black men who passed her by on the street, and who on more than one occasion has uttered racial or ethnic stereotypes that made me cringe.

These people are a part of me. And they are part of America, this country that I love.

[…]

The fact is that the comments that have been made and the issues that have surfaced over the last few weeks reflect the complexities of race in this country that we've never really worked through—a part of our union that we have not yet made perfect. And if we walk away now, if we simply retreat into our respective corners, we will never be able to come together and solve challenges like health care or education or the need to find good jobs for every American.

.... We do not need to recite here the history of racial injustice in this country. But we do need to remind ourselves that so many of the disparities that exist between the African-American community and the larger American community today can be traced directly to inequalities passed on from an earlier generation that suffered under the brutal legacy of slavery and Jim Crow.

Segregated schools were and are inferior schools; we still haven't fixed them, 50 years after Brown v. Board of Education. And the inferior education they provided, then and now, helps explain the pervasive achievement gap between today's black and white students.

Legalized discrimination—where blacks were prevented, often through violence, from owning property, or loans were not granted to African-American business owners, or black homeowners could not access FHA mortgages, or blacks were excluded from unions or the police force or the fire department—meant that black families could not amass any meaningful wealth to bequeath to future generations. That history helps explain the wealth and income gap between blacks and whites, and the concentrated pockets of poverty that persist in so many of today's urban and rural communities.

A lack of economic opportunity among black men, and the shame and frustration that came from not being able to provide for one's family contributed to the erosion of black families—a problem that welfare policies for many years may have worsened. And the lack of basic services in so many urban black neighborhoods—parks for kids to play in, police walking the beat, regular garbage pickup, building code enforcement—all helped create a cycle of violence, blight and neglect that continues to haunt us.

This is the reality in which Reverend Wright and other African-Americans of his generation grew up. They came of age in the late '50s and early '60s, a time when segregation was still the law of the land and opportunity was systematically constricted. What's remarkable is not how many failed in the face of discrimination, but how many men and women overcame the odds; how many were able to make a way out of no way, for those like me who would come after them.

For all those who scratched and clawed their way to get a piece of the American Dream, there were many who didn't make it—those who were ultimately defeated, in one way or another, by discrimination. That legacy of defeat was passed on to future generations—those young men and, increasingly, young women who we see standing on street corners or languishing in our prisons, without hope or prospects for the future. Even for those blacks who did make it, questions of race and racism continue to define their worldview in fundamental ways. For the men and women of Reverend Wright's generation, the memories of humiliation and doubt and fear have not gone away; nor has the anger and the bitterness of those years. That anger may not get expressed in public, in front of white co-workers or white friends. But it does find voice in the barbershop or the beauty shop or around the kitchen table. At times, that anger is exploited by politicians, to gin up votes along racial lines, or to make up for a politician's own failings.

[…]

In fact, a similar anger exists within segments of the white community. Most working- and middle-class white Americans don't feel that they have been particularly privileged by their race. Their experience is the immigrant experience—as far as they're concerned, no one handed them anything. They built it from scratch. They've worked hard all their lives, many times only to see their jobs shipped overseas or their pensions dumped after a lifetime of labor. They are anxious about their futures, and they feel their dreams slipping away. And in an era of stagnant wages and global competition, opportunity comes to be seen as a zero sum game, in which your dreams come at my expense. So when they are told to bus their children to a school across town; when they hear an African-American is getting an advantage in landing a good job or a spot in a good college because of an injustice that they themselves never committed; when they're told that their fears about crime in urban neighborhoods are somehow prejudiced, resentment builds over time.

*(Continued)*

*(Continued)*

Like the anger within the black community, these resentments aren't always expressed in polite company. But they have helped shape the political landscape for at least a generation. Anger over welfare and affirmative action helped forge the Reagan Coalition. Politicians routinely exploited fears of crime for their own electoral ends. Talk show hosts and conservative commentators built entire careers unmasking bogus claims of racism while dismissing legitimate discussions of racial injustice and inequality as mere political correctness or reverse racism.

Just as black anger often proved counterproductive, so have these white resentments distracted attention from the real culprits of the middle class squeeze—a corporate culture rife with inside dealing, questionable accounting practices and short-term greed; a Washington dominated by lobbyists and special interests; economic policies that favor the few over the many. And yet, to wish away the resentments of white Americans, to label them as misguided or even racist, without recognizing they are grounded in legitimate concerns—this too widens the racial divide and blocks the path to understanding.

This is where we are right now. It's a racial stalemate we've been stuck in for years. Contrary to the claims of some of my critics, black and white, I have never been so naïve as to believe that we can get beyond our racial divisions in a single election cycle, or with a single candidacy—particularly a candidacy as imperfect as my own.

But I have asserted a firm conviction—a conviction rooted in my faith in God and my faith in the American people—that, working together, we can move beyond some of our old racial wounds, and that in fact we have no choice if we are to continue on the path of a more perfect union.

For the African-American community, that path means embracing the burdens of our past without becoming victims of our past. It means continuing to insist on a full measure of justice in every aspect of American life. But it also means binding our particular grievances—for better health care and better schools and better jobs—to the larger aspirations of all Americans: the white woman struggling to break the glass ceiling, the white man who has been laid off, the immigrant trying to feed his family. And it means taking full responsibility for our own lives—by demanding more from our fathers, and spending more time with our children, and reading to them, and teaching them that while they may face challenges and discrimination in their own lives, they must never succumb to despair or cynicism; they must always believe that they can write their own destiny.

[...]

The profound mistake of Reverend Wright's sermons is not that he spoke about racism in our society. It's that he spoke as if our society was static; as if no progress had been made; as if this country—a country that has made it possible for one of his own members to run for the highest office in the land and build a coalition of white and black, Latino and Asian, rich and poor, young and old—is still irrevocably bound to a tragic past. But what we know—what we have seen—is that America can change. That is the true genius of this nation. What we have already achieved gives us hope—the audacity to hope—for what we can and must achieve tomorrow.

In the white community, the path to a more perfect union means acknowledging that what ails the African-American community does not just exist in the minds of black people; that the legacy of discrimination—and current incidents of discrimination, while less overt than in the past—are real and must be addressed, not just with words, but with deeds, by investing in our schools and our communities; by enforcing our civil rights laws and ensuring fairness in our criminal justice system; by providing this generation with ladders of opportunity that were unavailable for previous generations. It requires all Americans to realize that your dreams do not have to come at the expense of my dreams; that investing in the health, welfare and education of black and brown and white children will ultimately help all of America prosper.

In the end, then, what is called for is nothing more and nothing less than what all the world's great religions demand—that we do unto others as we would have them do unto us. Let us be our brother's keeper, scripture tells us. Let us be our sister's keeper. Let us find that common stake we all have in one another, and let our politics reflect that spirit as well.

For we have a choice in this country. We can accept a politics that breeds division and conflict and cynicism. We can tackle race only as spectacle—as we did in the O.J. trial—or in the wake of tragedy—as we did in the aftermath of Katrina—or as fodder for the nightly news. We can play Reverend Wright's sermons on every channel, every day and talk about them from now until the election, and make the only question in this campaign whether or not the American people think that I somehow believe or sympathize with his most offensive words ...

That is one option. Or, at this moment, in this election, we can come together and say, 'Not this time.' This time, we want to talk about the crumbling schools that are stealing the future of black children and white children and Asian children and Hispanic children and Native American children. This time, we want to reject the cynicism that tells us that these kids can't learn; that those kids who don't look like us are somebody else's problem. The children of America are not those kids, they are our kids, and we will not let them fall behind in a 21st century economy. Not this time.

This time we want to talk about how the lines in the emergency room are filled with whites and blacks and Hispanics who do not have health care, who don't have the power on their own to overcome the special interests in Washington, but who can take them on if we do it together.

This time, we want to talk about the shuttered mills that once provided a decent life for men and women of every race, and the homes for sale that once belonged to Americans from every religion, every region, every walk of life. This time, we want to talk about the fact that the real problem is not that someone who doesn't look like you might take your job; it's that the corporation you work for will ship it overseas for nothing more than a profit.

This time, we want to talk about the men and women of every color and creed who serve together and fight together and bleed together under the same proud flag. We want to talk about how to bring them home from a war that should have never been authorized and should have never been waged. And we want to talk about how we'll show our patriotism by caring for them and their families, and giving them the benefits that they have earned.

I would not be running for President if I didn't believe with all my heart that this is what the vast majority of Americans want for this country. This union may never be perfect, but generation after generation has shown that it can always be perfected. And today, whenever I find myself feeling doubtful or cynical about this possibility, what gives me the most hope is the next generation—the young people whose attitudes and beliefs and openness to change have already made history in this election.

# 24

# ANALYSING CONVERSATION

## Tim Rapley

---

### Chapter Contents

---

At first sight, the idea that an analysis of conversation may be a useful way to make sense of society and culture may seem strange. As part of our everyday life we are bombarded with the obvious truth that talk is 'just talk'. As a child you may have heard the rhyme 'Sticks and stones may break my bones but words can never hurt me.' When we ask someone to account for something they have said they may reply, 'Oh well, it is just something I say.' From this perspective, any focus on conversation may appear to be one of the most trivial of things. However, if you stop and think for a moment, it is not hard to see that conversation – or interaction, for

want of a more general description – is potentially *the* central way through which we make friends, have relationships, learn things, do our jobs – as Moerman explains it: '[T]alk is a central part of social interaction, and social interaction is the core and enforcer, the arena and teacher, the experienced context of social life' (1992: 24).

The analysis of conversation has been undertaken by people working within various theoretical and methodological traditions, including interactional socio-linguistics, the ethnography of communication, discursive psychology and critical discourse analysis. (Chapter 23 in this book outlines discourse analysis; Wetherell,

Taylor and Yates (2001a) also provide an overview.) However, for the purposes of this chapter I am going to outline how the research tradition called *conversation analysis* studies talk and interaction. And in this chapter, you will be shown how people have analysed audiotapes and videotapes of action and interaction taken from everyday settings, including friends talking on the phone, doctors talking to parents of a sick child, news interviewers questioning politicians and lawyers working in courtrooms. By reading this chapter, you will learn:

- some basic features of how conversation analysts conduct line-by-line analysis of action and interaction
- what conversation analysts mean when they talk about focusing on 'naturally occurring' action and interaction
- how to read and create a conversation analysis style transcript of talk, following the transcription system developed by Gail Jefferson
- about the role and value of single-case analysis and comparative analysis in conversation analysis.

## Some background to conversation analysis

I want to begin by exploring some of the central issues for conversation analysis. To do that we need to focus on its parent, ethnomethodology, and explore a few of the key concerns for this approach to social life. As Melvin Pollner notes:

One of ethnomethodology's contributions to the understanding of social life is its capacity to produce a deep wonder about what is often regarded as obvious, given or natural. Whether it be the interpretation of documents, the utterance 'uh-huh' or the flow of everyday interaction, ethnomethodology has provided a way of questioning which begins to reveal the richly layered skills, assumptions and practices through which the most commonplace (and not so commonplace) activities and experiences are constructed. (1987: ix)

There are three things of particular relevance to us in that quote:

- The notion of an attitude of 'deep wonder'.
- A focus on 'what is often regarded as obvious, given or natural'.
- An appreciation of the practices of social life being immensely 'richly layered'.

Conversation analysis and ethnomethodology involve fascination with the local production of social reality (i.e. its ongoing production in particular moments, situations, times, places and contexts) and explore how it is finely crafted and intimately ordered; they seek to 'step back' in order to gain purchase on just *how* everyday realities are produced.

Conversation analysis requires researchers to consider how elements of our social life – our talk, tasks and identities – are locally accomplished in and through talk and interaction. This approach routinely involves detailed analysis of audio- and video-recorded social interactions. Sometimes it also uses ethnographic fieldwork (see Chapter 14). Harvey Sacks, one of the founders of conversation analysis, outlines the central research strategy for conversation analysis. He 'simply' says: 'Just try to come to terms with how it is that the thing comes off. ... Look to see how it is that persons go about producing what they do produce' (1992: Fall 64: 11).

To begin to explore Sacks's advice, take the talk in Example 1 below (see also the transcription conventions in Box 24.1). So Sue, in Example 1, wonders out loud about how the person known as 'he' found out about something. I take that most people would hear Fiona as saying 'My *hunch* is that that they found out through work or Kay'. Whether Fiona does in fact know but is unwilling to admit this is open to question.

However, we can see that she is *displaying* or *doing uncertainty*. In and through the action of displaying or doing uncertainty, Fiona works to say 'Don't hold me accountable for the accuracy of this information'. Let's view another instance of this, Example 2, taken from a trial for rape. We join the sequence as the defence attorney is cross-examining the alleged rape victim.

---

### Example 1

*Sue*:  Wonder how he found out an all that (0.4)

*Fiona*:  I:::: I don't know through work or Kay probably

*Source*: Beach and Metzinger 1997: 569 – simplified transcript

### Example 2

*Attorney*:  Well didn't he ask you if uh on that night that uh::: he wanted you to be his girl (0.5)

*Attorney*:  Didn't he ask you that? (2.5)

*Witness*:  I don't remember what he said to me that night (1.2)

*Attorney*:  Well you had some uh uh fairly lengthy conversations with the defendant uh did'n you? (0.7)

*Attorney*:  On the evening of February fourteenth? (1.0)

*Witness*:  We were all talking.

*Source*: Drew, 1992: 478–479

---

Again, we can begin to see how the words 'I don't remember' are not necessarily tied to the working of the individual speaker's memory, but rather can be understood as a *social action*. Through the answer 'I don't remember' she avoids confirming the question and so avoids both confirming and disconfirming information that could be potentially damaging or discrediting to her case. The attorney then follows up this line of argument and she answers that 'We were all talking'. In and through displaying her lack of memory or certainty, she displays the lack of importance she gave to the defendant's actions towards her. The defendant's actions, his asking her 'to be his girl' and their 'lengthy conversations', are only unmemorable to her because, at the time, they went unnoticed. The implication is that, at that time, she had no special interest in him or particular reason to notice him; above all, she should not be accused of 'leading him on'.

As with discourse analysis (Chapter 23), conversation analysis does not treat language as a neutral, transparent, medium of communication. Conversation analysis focuses on how social actions and practices are accomplished *in and through* talk and interaction. As the above examples begin to show, apparently mundane, trivial or innocent words or phrases like 'I don't know', 'probably' and 'I don't remember' do work for participants – they can work to say (among many other things) 'Don't hold me that accountable for what I'm saying'. And this work is *not* tied to individual character, personality or psychology. To be sure, some people might use these words more often than others, but the social action that happens in and through the use of these words, in these specific contexts, is independent of individual characteristics.

So conversation analysis looks with wonder at some of the taken-for-granted – seen but unnoticed – ways that we 'do' social life. It seeks to describe the richly layered practices of social life through the close and detailed observation of people's action and interaction. The central source of these observations are recordings of *naturally occurring* talk and interaction.

## Recording social life

Schegloff offers the following story about an aphasiologist (someone who deals with speech disorders caused by dysfunction of the language areas of the brain):

> [W]hile engaged in testing aphasic patients, he would ordinarily use rest periods during which patients had a coffee break to go and check his mail, etc. One day he happened to join the patients in the coffee room during the break and was astonished to hear the patients doing things while talking amongst themselves or with relatives which they had just shown themselves to be 'unable' to do in the preceding test session. (1999: 431)

This story nicely demonstrates the potential benefits of a focus on what people do in the context of their everyday lives. By using observations of naturally occurring action and interactions over, say, experiments, interviews or imagining you already know, you can gain a different perspective on people's actions and interactions.

It is important to note what conversation analysts mean when they say that they prefer to focus on naturally occurring action and interaction. Some people take it to mean that you should only use data that is *not* researcher-led or researcher-prompted. However, what they mean is that you should try to discover how some action or interaction – be it a police interrogation or a qualitative interview – occurs as 'natural', normal or routine. So, rather than asking a focus group moderator about how they run focus groups, you can gain a better understanding of 'how they run focus groups' through recordings of them actually running focus groups. Equally, rather than asking counsellors about how they counsel, you would want to base your observations on recordings of them actually doing counselling. From this perspective, researcher-led information (from interviews or other sources) is still potentially of use in trying to describe how counsellors do counselling, or how focus group moderators run focus groups, but the primary source of data would be audio- or video-recordings of what they actually do.

Sacks outlines the rationale behind using recording equipment:

> I started to work with tape-recorded conversations. Such materials had a single virtue, that I could replay them. I could transcribe them somewhat and study them extendedly – however long that might take. The tape-recorded materials offered a 'good enough' record of what happened. Other things, to be sure, happened, but at least what happened on tape had happened. I started with tape-recorded conversations ... simply because I could get my hands on it and I could study it again and again, and also, consequentially, because others could look at what I had studied and make use of it what they could, for example if they wanted to be able to disagree with me. (1984: 26)

Audio, and increasingly video, recordings of talk and interactions, although never a comprehensive record of what's going on, allow us access to many of the practices of social life.

As Sacks notes, people can only transcribe recordings 'somewhat'; transcripts are by their very nature *translations*, are always partial and selective textual re-presentations. The actual process of making detailed transcripts enables you to become familiar with what you are observing. You have to listen/watch the recording again and again (and again). Through this process you begin to notice the interesting and often subtle ways that people interact. These are the taken-for-granted features of people's talk that without recordings you would routinely fail to notice, fail to remember or be unable to record in sufficient detail by taking hand-written notes as it happened. What is key to remember is that you base your analysis on the actual inter-actions and the recordings of those interactions. Transcripts are only, to borrow Spiegelberg's phrase, 'aids for the sluggish imagination' (cited in Garfinkel, 1967: 39); they can help you remember 'what was going on' on the recording. The subsequent benefit of making transcripts is that you can use them in the presentations of your findings.

---

**BOX 24.1**

## SIMPLIFIED TRANSCRIPTION SYMBOLS

| Symbol | Example | Explanation |
|---|---|---|
| (0.5) | that (0.5) is odd? | Length of silence measured in tenths of a second |
| (.) | right (.) okay | Micro-pause, less than two-tenths of a second |
| ::: | I:::: I don't know | Colons indicate sound-stretching of the immediately prior sound. The number of rows indicates the length of prolonged sound |
| _____ | I know that | Underlining indicates speaker's emphasis or stress |
| [ | T: [Well 'at's R: [I mean really | Left brackets indicate the point at which one speaker overlaps another's talk |
| = | you know=that's fine | Equal signs indicates that there is no hearable gap between the words |
| WORD | about a MILLION | Capitals, except at beginnings indicate a marked rise in volume compared to the surrounding talk |
| ? | Oh really? | Question mark indicates rising intonation |
| . | Yeah. | Full stop indicates falling intonation |
| hhh | I know how .hhh you | A row of 'h's prefixed by a dot indicates an inbreath, without dot, an outbreath. The number of 'h's indicates the length of the in- or out-breath |
| ( ) | What a ( ) thing | Empty brackets indicate inability to hear what was said |
| (word) | What are you (doing) | Word in brackets indicates the best possible hearing |
| (( )) | I don't know ((shrugs)) | Words in double brackets contain author's descriptions |

---

Conversation analysts are often faced with certain dilemmas, including what to record, how to record it, which parts to transcribe and the level of detail of the transcript. There are no definitive answers to any of these questions and most depend on what your analytic interest is. For example, people working with readily available talk (e.g. live radio broadcasts) can only use audio recordings and can only transcribe the verbal interaction. For those who focus on interactions that occur in different places at different times (such as nursing work in a hospital ward), a period of ethnography may be essential in order to establish what might be relevant to record and what type of recording – audio or video – is feasible and acceptable to the participants.

When it comes to the transcription, most analysts use parts of the transcription system developed by Gail Jefferson for recording verbal interaction (see Box 24.1 for transcription symbols). This level of technical detail is used to try to re-present the highly dynamic and complex lived interactional work we all engage in when talking to others. Non-verbal interaction, including direction of gaze, gestures, bodily movement and use of artefacts, requires a further layer of description (see Heath et al., 2010).

## Exploring a mundane moment in talk

In order to explore some of the ways talk can be analysed, let's focus on a rather 'trivial', ordinary moment of talk, shown in Example 3.

---

### Example 3

1  *John*:    So what do you think about bicycles on campus?

2  *Judy*:    I think they're terrible.

3  *John*:    Sure is about a MILLION of 'em

4  *Judy*:    eh heh

*Source*: Maynard, 1991: 461

---

At first glance this might not be that interesting. However, note *how* John works to display his thoughts about bicycles on campus. Rather than just tell Judy what he thinks about them, he asks Judy a question (1). So John *invites* Judy to offer her thoughts or opinions about bicycles. Judy then *replies*, that she thinks 'they're terrible' (2). Then, and only then, does John report his *perspective*.

So, why should that interest us at all? What we've got here is some rather lovely work – these people are actively doing something we all routinely do. We can re-produce the opening lines of their talk as follows:

> John invites Judy to talk about a topic (1) Judy talks about the topic (2) John then gives his perspective on the same topic and his perspective closely fit's with Judy's (3).

Now, it does not take a great leap of imagination to think about a moment when we all do similar work. Think about the times when you leave the cinema or a lecture. Often what happens is, rather than say outright 'I hated that film/lecture', you ask the person you are with a question like 'What did you think', they then tell you that they 'thought is was excellent' and then you may 'fit' your response around what they have just said: 'I liked the start but some of it was quite boring'.

This way of talking, that Maynard (1991) calls the perspective-display sequence, can be a wonderful way that we *do caution*. Rather than just giving your opinion 'outright' without knowing whether the other person agrees or not, *once you have heard their opinion* you can then deliver yours in a 'hospitable environment' (1991: 460) as you can tie what they have said into your own report.

This is one example of how people analyse conversations – they focus on *how* speakers interact. A lot of conversation analysis has focused on what Heritage (1997: 162) calls 'the social institution *of* interaction' (author's emphasis) *how* everyday interaction is locally and collaboratively produced. A lot of work also focuses on 'the management of social institutions *in* interactions' (1997: 162), *how* specific institutions – be they law, medicine, education – and institutional activities – be they testimony, consultations, teaching – are locally and collaboratively produced.

Box 24.2 shows how interactional management of diagnosis works in an institutional setting.

---

**BOX 24.2**

## THE INTERACTIONAL MANAGEMENT OF DIAGNOSIS IN AN INSTITUTIONAL SETTING

Maynard (1992) notes how the perspective-display sequence (see Example 3) can occur when doctors deliver 'bad' diagnostic news. He recorded some consultations where parents are given a diagnosis about their child's health:

### Example 4

| 1 | *Dr*: | How's Bobby doing. |
|---|---|---|
| 2 | *Mo*: | Well he's doing pretty good you know |
| 3 | | especially in the school. |
| | | … |
| 4 | | Now [the teacher] thinks he's not |
| 5 | | gonna need to be sent to another school. |
| 6 | *Dr*: | He doesn't think he's gonna need to be |
| 7 | | sent |
| 8 | *Mo*: | Yeah that he was catching on a little bit uh |
| 9 | | more you know like I said I– I– I know that |
| 10 | | he needs a– you know I was 'splaining to her |
| 11 | | that I'm you know that I know for sure that |
| 12 | | he needs some special class or something. |
| 13 | *Dr*: | Wu' whatta you think his problem is. |
| 14 | *Mo*: | Speech. |
| 15 | *Dr*: | Yeah. Yeah his main problem is a – you know a |
| 16 | | <u>lan</u>guage problem |
| 17 | *Mo*: | Yeah language. |

*Source*: Maynard, 1992: 339 – modified transcript

The doctor asks an open question about how this mother's child, Bobby, is 'doing' (1). She then replies that he is 'doing pretty good' (2) and goes on to give evidence for this by referring to what Bobby's teacher has been saying (4–5). The doctor asks a question about this (6–7). In the course of replying to his question, she offers her own opinion – that she knows 'for sure he needs some special class or something' (11–12).

---

The doctor then asks another question, inviting her to talk about what she thinks is Bobby's 'problem' (13). She replies that it is 'Speech.' (14). Then, and only then, does the doctor report his perspective. He agrees with the mother's understanding 'Yeah.' (15) and then reformulates the problem as 'a language problem' (15–16). She then agrees with this and reformulates her description of the problem in alignment with the doctor's terminology (17).

Rather than just offer his perspective at the start of their talk, the doctor delays giving his perspective. Initially the mother just produces 'good' news about her son. She then offers some 'bad' news, which the doctor invites her to elaborate on, which she does. Note how he only delivers the 'bad' news diagnosis once the 'hospitable environment' of 'bad' news talk has been developed. Also, he delivers the 'bad' news diagnosis as a confirmation of what the mother already knows. As Maynard notes, a doctor can use a perspective-display sequence to co-implicate or confirm a parent's view in the delivery of a 'bad' news diagnosis. In this way, the parent is produced as 'already having some knowledge of their child's condition' and 'good' parents should be experts on their children. Interestingly, the perspective-display sequence can be used by doctors to confirm the parent's own thoughts when they then go on to deliver a diagnosis that is alternative to the parent's own thoughts.

## Building a case

Maynard's work also shows us something about one of the methods that conversation analysts use. You focus on a single episode of talk to explore in detail how that specific moment of interaction happens. You notice something interesting, something that you think might be an 'organised' way of talking. You then go and look for other examples, in other settings, between different speakers to see if you can find other examples of this type of work. In this way, you attempt to build a case that this organised way of talking is something that people do as part of their everyday lives – that this thing is part of the social institution of interaction. Refusals and disagreements have been investigated in this way.

## The social institution of refusal and disagreement

A considerable body of work has been undertaken that collects together many instances of talk where people are either accepting or refusing something, be it an invitation, offers, requests, proposals (Davidson, 1984; Drew, 1984) or agreeing or disagreeing with assessments (Pomerantz, 1984; see also Sacks, 1987). They have documented the routine ways that people do acceptance and refusal and agreement and disagreement in Anglo-American talk.

As you can see, acceptance (Example 5) and agreement (Example 6) are routinely done immediately, with no gap in the talk (and sometimes overlapping the other speaker's talk) and are relatively 'forthright', in that they are simple and straightforward. Compare this to how refusals and disagreements are often produced (Examples 7, 8 and 9).

---

Example 5

A:    Well, will you help me [out

B:    [I certainly will

*Source*: Davidson, 1984: 116 – simplified transcript

*(Continued)*

---

*(Continued)*

Example 6

J:   It's really a clear lake, isn't it?

R:   It's wonderful

*Source*: Pomerantz, 1984: 60

Example 7

B:   Wanna come down 'n have a bite a' lunch with me?
     I got some beer en stuff.

A:   Wul yer real <u>sweet</u> hon, uhm, let-=

B:   [D'you have sumpn else?

A:   [I have-

A:   No, I have to uh call Bill's mother

*Source*: Pomerantz, 1984: 101

Example 8

*(S's wife has just slipped a disc)*

H:   And we were wondering if there's anything we can do to help

S:   [Well 'at's

H:   [I mean can we do any shopping for her or
     something like tha:t?
     (0.7)

S:   Well that's most kind Heatherton .hhh
     At the moment <u>no</u>:. because we've still got the bo:ys at home.

*Source*: Heritage, 1984: 271

Example 9

B:   I think I'll call her and ask her if she's
     interested because she's a good nurse, and I
     think they would like her don't you?

A:   Well, I'll tell you, I haven't seen Mary for
     years. I should – As I remember, yes.

B:   Well do you think she would fit in?

A:   Uhm, uh, I don't know, What I'm uh
     hesitating about is uh – – uhm maybe she would.
     (1.0)

A:   Uh but I would hesitate to uhm –

*Source*: Pomerantz, 1984: 73

The difference is clear. With a refusal or disagreement you routinely get some combination of the following actions:

- *Delays:* a gap before a response or a gap within a response, a delay before an answer is given.
- *Hesitations:* like 'mm' 'erm' 'uhm' and in-breath or out-breaths.
- *Prefaces:* like 'Well' and 'Uh', agreement tokens like 'Yeah'.
- *Mitigations:* apologies and appreciations.
- *Accounts:* excuses, explanations, justifications and reasons.

Interestingly, a lot of the time we say 'no' without ever explicitly saying it and other speakers understand us to be saying 'no' without ever having to hear us say it out loud.

Researchers have documented how we can 'notice' a potential or upcoming refusal or disagreement prior to someone actually producing one. For instance, in Example 10 below, note how speaker Z works to make their invitation more 'inviting'. Even after the micro-pause (around two-tenths of a second), Z works to *upgrade* their invitation with the 'sweetener' of providing 'beer and stuff'.

---

**Example 10**

Z:      C'mon down here,=it's okay (0.2)

Z:      I got lotta stuff,=I got beer and stuff 'n

*Source*: Davidson, 1984. 105 – simplified transcript

---

In this case, Z has heard this pause as a potential refusal and shows the other speaker (and us) what she has taken it to mean. We have seen related work in Example 7. Just after A's appreciative comment 'Wul yer real <u>sweet</u> hon, uhm, let-=', B asks the question 'D'you have sumpn else?'. B's question marks indicate that they have heard A's talk as a preface to an upcoming rejection of the invitation. So we are able to monitor other people's talk for the finest of distinctions.

Through the detailed comparative analysis of instances of talk, conversation analysts have outlined how the work of agreeing/accepting and disagreeing/refusing is routinely done. This is not to say they we all behave like robots and that this is *the only* way that people do this work – but rather, when doing social life we routinely work with and against this specific normative interaction order, or set of obligations and expectations of each other. We only have to think of the multiple ways that a quick and plain 'no' can be interpreted as the speaker being blunt or rude, as

someone who holds a heartfelt opinion on that specific topic or as someone who is being mischievous. Note, though, that in some cases, a quick and plain 'no' may be the preferred (rather than dispreferred) response, say for example when someone makes the self-assessment 'My new hair cut makes me look terrible'.

These two alternative, but non-equivalent, courses of actions – preferred actions that are direct and plain responses and dispreferred actions that are delayed and embellished responses – document what conversation analysts call preference organisation. This concept of 'preference' does not refer to inner psychological or subjective experiences of individual speakers. Rather, it describes one of the systematic ways that speakers in general, across a range of actions, contexts and situations, work to organise an aspect of the social institution of talk and interaction.

Before going on to see how conversation analysts have looked at talk in some institutional settings, we will examine some work (in Box 24.3) which shows the potential insights that can be gained from a detailed focus on *what people actually do*, rather than what we imagine they might or should do.

---

**BOX 24.3**

## 'JUST SAY NO': CONVERSATION ANALYSIS AND DATE RAPE

Kitzinger and Firth have taken the observation that in Anglo-American interaction there 'is an organised and normative way of doing indirect refusal' (1999: 310) and begun to question the 'refusal skills' training advocated by many date rape prevention programmes. As you have seen, as part of our everyday lives we routinely understand and orientate to people saying 'no' without them ever having to necessarily say 'no' out loud. Kitzinger and Firth suggest that

> the insistence of date rape prevention (and other refusals skills) educators on the importance of saying 'no' is counter-productive in that it demands that women engage in conversationally abnormal actions which breach conventional social etiquette, and in allowing rapists to persist with the claim that if a woman has not actually said 'NO' (in the right tone of voice, with the right body language, at the right time) then she hasn't refused to have sex with him. (1999: 310)

As they outline, for a man to claim that because the woman didn't actually say 'no' he 'just didn't understand' or 'wasn't clear whether' she was refusing sex produces him as socially ignorant and interactionally incompetent. It is not that these men are cultural dopes (i.e. don't understand normative interaction order) or that these men just don't understand 'women's ways' of communicating; rather, these men do not like being refused sex. As the authors note, '[t]he problem of sexual coercion cannot be fixed by changing the way women talk' (1999: 311).

---

## The organisation of social institutions in interaction

From the perspective of conversation analysts, institutions are organised and *produced* through action and interaction. At their most extreme, some institutions pre-allocate specific talk, tasks and identities to people. Take, for example, courtrooms or the British House of Commons, where, once in session, only specific individuals can speak at specific times. In courtrooms, the judge determines who is 'out of order', who is in 'contempt of court' and directs others to 'answer the question'. Those not allocated the right to talk should, at all times when in session, be silent witnesses to the proceedings. If they do not perform this action, they can, potentially, be removed or incarcerated. However, the social organisation of most institutions – be it medicine, education, counselling, news interviews, market research, academic research, sexuality, gender, race, friendship, family, relationships – is not as rigidly fixed and policed in terms of the rights and responsibilities of those involved.

What is of interest to conversation analysts is how specific institutions are locally produced in and through the collaborative actions of people. Let us focus briefly on news media interviews. As Clayman notes, news interviewers are meant to be

> interactionally 'adversarial' while remaining officially 'neutral', that is, to introduce viewpoints that contradict those of the interviewees, not as a matter of personal expression, but as a way of further soliciting interviewees' own views. (1988: 490)

One of the ways that interviewers achieve this is to distance themselves from being heard as 'the author' of any controversial statement. This can be seen in Example 11.

---

**Example 11**

IR: Reverend Boesak lemme a pick up a p<u>oi</u>nt the ambassador made.　　　←1

　　Wh<u>a</u>t assurances can y<u>ou</u> give <u>u</u>s that t<u>a</u>lks between m<u>o</u>derates in that country

　　will take pl<u>a</u>ce when it s<u>ee</u>ms that <u>a</u>ny black leader who is w<u>i</u>lling to talk to

　　the government <u>i</u>s br<u>a</u>nded

　　as the ambassador said a coll<u>a</u>borator　　　←2

　　and is then p<u>u</u>nished.

IE: The amb<u>a</u>ssador has it wr<u>o</u>ng. It's n<u>o</u>t the people ...　　　←3

(*Source*: Clayman, 1988: 483)

---

Note how the interviewer (IR) prefaces the question (arrow 1). IR is just following 'up a point the ambassador made', he is *not* to be heard as the 'author' of the question. Again, at arrow 2, he repeats this action; the interviewer is not personally calling someone 'a collaborator', rather he is just following up on something 'the ambassador said'. The interviewee (IE) collaborates in this (arrow 3); the 'target' of his answer, and therefore the person responsible for the content and opinions embedded in the question, is 'The ambassador' and not IR.

Put simply, rather than say something like 'you're an idiot', news interviewers routinely say something like 'Mr Smith says you're an idiot' or 'Some people say you're an idiot'. This is just one of the practices that *locally produces* the impartiality of news interviewing and so sustains the impartial status of the institution of news interviews. As Heritage and Greatbatch (1991) note, a question remains: clearly these news interviewers are *doing* impartiality/neutrality, but does that mean they are *being* impartial/neutral in any conventional sense?

Such a practice – a speaker distancing themselves from being heard as responsible for the content of a question – does not only occur in news interviewing. Example 12 shows some talk from a pre-test HIV counselling session.

---

**Example 12**

1　C:　er: I have to ask you this have you ever injected

2　　　drugs.

3　P:　No.

4　C:　Because they're the sort of highest ris:k (.)

*Source*: Silverman, 1996: 155

---

The counsellor (C) prefaces their question with 'er: I have to ask you this' (1). This preface works to say 'I would not normally ask such a question and I am only asking it now as this is part of my job.' Note the talk that follows the patient's (P) answer, where the counsellor works to further account for 'why I asked this question'.

In both cases the questioners try to say 'I'm not wholly responsible for this action'. However, the practical reasoning of doing such work is tied to the specific institutional tasks and identities they are engaged with: news interviewers when doing interviewing should be seen and heard as impartial; counsellors when doing counselling should try to build rapport. And this is a key point, when studying talk and interaction the idea is not to say 'here's an example of a perspective-display sequence' and 'there's an example of preference organisation' but rather to document the work that specific organisation of talk does

in *locally producing* specific tasks, identities and contexts. To outline what such analysis can look like, I want to look at a study of interaction in a courtroom.

## Making sense of evidence in courtrooms

Goodwin (1994) undertook an analysis of the trial of Rodney King. Four white American police officers had stopped King, an African American, and then physically assaulted the man. Unknown to the officers, a man across the street had made a videotape of the incident. How to 'make sense' of the video-record of the police officers' and Rodney King's actions became a central feature of the trial. Example 13 is a transcript from part of the defence's case. We join the talk as the videotape of the incident is being played, stopped and commented on.

---

**Example 13**

| 1 | *Defence*: | Four oh five, oh one. |
| 2 | | We see a blow being delivered= |
| 3 | | =Is that correct. |
| 4 | *Expert*: | That's correct. |
| 5 | | The – force has again been escalated (0.3) |
| 6 | | To the level it had been previously, (0.4) |
| 7 | | And the de-escalation has ceased. … |
| 8 | *Defence*: | And at– |
| 9 | | At this point which is, |
| 10 | | for the record four thirteen twenty nine, (0.4) |
| 11 | | We see a blow being struck |
| 12 | | and thus the end of a period of, de-escalation? |
| 13 | | Is that correct Captain. |
| 14 | *Expert*: | That's correct. |
| 15 | | Force has now been elevated to the previous level, (0.6) |
| 16 | | After this period of de-escalation. |

*Source*: Goodwin, 1994: 617

---

This small fragment contains two sequences (1–7 and 8–16) which share very similar features – the defence lawyer does some description then asks a question about that description, and the expert witness answers that question and in so doing produces some re-description. What is important to note is how, through their actions, they collaborate to build a way of how to 'make sense' of the images on the video.

With the first sequence, the defence lawyer calls out the time of the image, 'Four oh five, oh one.' (1) and then describes the image, 'We see a blow being delivered=' (2). Note how he describes the action in the image – this is to be seen and understood as a single blow – this is not a beating or an attack. He then asks for confirmation of his description, '=Is that correct.' (3). The expert witness confirms this (4) and then re-describes the action in the image. This is not to be seen only as a 'blow', but as a moment when 'The – force has again been escalated … the de-escalation has ceased.' (5–7). With this re-description, the single image of the blow is now to be seen as a precise moment of 'escalation' to a precise 'level' (6) of force. With the second sequence (8–14), similar work goes on, except in this sequence the defence lawyer also uses the description 'the end of a period of, de-escalation' (12) to account for the police officers' actions.

In this example, the defence's case works around coding and highlighting each specific blow on the video ('Four oh five, oh one' and 'four thirteen twenty-nine') as separate, distinct, actions. The multiple strikes to Rodney King's body, that happen seconds apart, are transformed by the interaction between the defence lawyer, the police expert and the video technology, as separate, distinct uses of force.

This 'individual' strike is *only* to be understood as a moment of elevation or escalation of force, a moment when the period of de-escalation has ceased. The seconds between blows are to be understood as 'an assessment period' (Goodwin, 1994: 617), where the officers are analysing Rodney King's actions for signs of cooperation. As the defence went on to argue, 'Rodney King

and Rodney King alone was in control of the situation' (Goodwin, 1994: 618).

One of the things that Goodwin's analysis highlights is how things do not 'speak for themselves' but rather that they are always spoken for. In the case of the Rodney King trial, the defence lawyer and the expert police witness collaborated in producing a specific way to 'make sense' of the images on the tape. Throughout the trial, the case for the defence argued that the video tape was an objective record of the incident and used the testimony produced with a range of expert witnesses to instruct the jury to understand the video of the beating of King as an example of 'good' police work. The defence argued, successfully in the first court case, that the video displayed that the officers where *only* engaged in 'careful, systematic police work' (1994: 617).

## Conclusion

As these examples begin to show, from a conversation analytic perspective, the focus is on *how* institutions are produced in and through the collaborative actions and interactions of people. So what the analysis of conversation allows us to do is to try to document the ways that people organise specific institutions and institutional tasks and identities. Importantly, the analysis is based on what the participants do, to what they themselves are attending within their talk, what outcomes they achieve, and is not based on *a priori* assumptions of what the analyst thinks 'should be' going on.

Conversation analysts are constantly preoccupied with describing the *lived work* of talking and interacting. They begin to show us that the work of being an ordinary member of society is made up of masses of tacit, taken-for-granted, knowledges and practices. Such an approach is not going to be for everyone, as it often produces rather modest, descriptive, claims about things we all already just know 'at a glance'. What those researching society and culture can take away from their investigations is that talk is not just a 'trivial' medium for social life, but rather it is *in and through* our talk and interactions that we experience, produce and maintain social life. As Sacks notes:

[I]n every moment of talk, people are experiencing and producing their cultures, their roles, their personalities. … [Y]ou and I live lives of talk, experience the social world as motivated talkers and listeners, as tongued creatures of the social order; each with our own bursts of pleasure and pain, each with our proud differences of personal style. (cited in Moerman, 1988: xi)

Here are some key points to remember about conversation analysis:

- People doing conversation analysis focus on how social actions and practices are locally accomplished in and through talk and interaction. They closely analyse audio and videoing recordings of interaction, often making very detailed transcripts.

- They often focus on features of interaction like: how speakers take turns at talk; how talk is shaped by prior actions and shapes what follows it; how talk is designed to perform certain actions; how institutional tasks and identities shape the organisation of talk.

- They sometimes do detailed analysis of single cases of talk. They also collect and compare similar instances of talk to identify some of the systematic ways that speakers in general, across a range of actions, contexts and situations, work to organise the social institution of talk and interaction.

## FURTHER READING

Excellent book-length introductions to conversation analysis have been provided by Hutchby and Wooffitt (2008), and ten Have (2007) and Rapley (2007). Silverman's (1998) account of the writings of Harvey Sacks is a good way into the theoretical background of conversation analysis, as well as giving an account of important methodological procedures. For examples of empirical research related to some of the themes of this chapter, see: Speer & Hutchby's (2003) discussion of peoples' awareness and orientation to audio and video recording equipment.

Kitzinger (2000) and Stokoe and Smithson (2001) for examples of gender, feminism and conversation analysis.

Clayman (2002) for an analysis of a specific form of news interview questions.

Edwards (2006) and Antaki (2004) for conversation analysis applied to psychological ideas.

Heath (2002) and Hindmarsh and Pilnick (2007) for video-based work in healthcare settings.

### Student Reader (Seale, 2004b): relevant readings

47 David Silverman: 'Harvey Sacks: social science and conversation analysis'

48 Anssi Peräkylä: 'Reliability and validity in research based on tapes and transcripts'

58 Paul Atkinson: 'Transcriptions'

See also Chapter 11, 'Ethnomethodology', by Paul ten Have and Chapter 12, 'Conversation analysis' by Anssi Peräkylä in Seale et al. (2004).

### Journal articles illustrating use of the the methods described in this chapter

Weathersbee, T.E. and Maynard, D.W. (2009) 'Dialling for donations: practices and actions in the telephone solicitation of human tissues', Sociology of Health & Illness, 31 (6): 803–816.

Burns, A. and Radford, J. (2008) 'Parent–child interaction in Nigerian families: conversation analysis, context and culture', Child Language Teaching and Therapy, 24: 193–209.

Stokoe, E. (2010) '"I'm not gonna hit a lady": conversation analysis, membership categorisation and men's denials of violence towards women', Discourse & Society, 21: 59–82.

## Web links

Ethno/CA news – information on ethnomethodology and conversation analysis: www2.fmg.uva.nl/emca

An introduction to Conversation Analysis (Charles Antaki): www-staff.lboro.ac.uk/~ssca1/sitemenu.htm

Nick Llewllyn's Tutorial – Analysing Observational 'Real Time' Data: http://sites.google.com/site/llewellyn-nick/tutorial

Emanuel Schegloff's Transcription Module: www.sscnet.ucla.edu/soc/faculty/schegloff/TranscriptionProject/index.html

Alexa Hepburn and Jonathan Potter's Transcription Guide: www.staff.lboro.ac.uk/~ssah2/transcription/transcription.htm

TalkBank – CA Bank – Database of audio or video clips with transcripts: http://talkbank.org/CABank/

Australian Institute for Ethnomethodology and Conversation Analysis: http://aiemca.net

The International Institute for Ethnomethodology and Conversation Analysis: www.iiemca.org

Methods@manchester – ethnomethodology: www.methods.manchester.ac.uk/methods/ethnomethodology/index.shtml

e-Source – Chapter 9 on 'Conversation analysis' by John Heritage: www.esourceresearch.org

---

## KEY CONCEPTS FOR REVIEW

**Advice:** Use these, along with the review questions in the next section, to test your knowledge of the contents of this chapter. Try to define each of the key concepts listed here; if you have understood this chapter you should be able to do this. Check your definitions against the definition in the glossary at the end of the book.

Collaborative production of talk

Doing aspects of social life

Ethnomethodology

Local production/accomplishment

Naturally occurring action, interaction or data

Normative interaction order

Perspective-display sequence

Pre-allocation of roles, identities etc.

Preference organisation; preferred/dispreferred utterances and actions

Transcription symbols

---

## ■ Review questions

1 What do conversation analysts mean when they say they focus on 'naturally-occurring action and interaction'?
2 Why is the perspective-display sequence a good way to 'do' caution?
3 What are the common ways by which we produce refusals?

1 This is a task designed to help you familiarise yourself with the transcription conventions used in conversation analysis. As a consequence, you should start to understand the logic of transcribing this way and be able to ask questions about how the speakers are organising their talk.

Tape-record no more than five minutes of talk in the public domain. One possibility is a radio call-in programme. Avoid using scripted drama productions as these may not contain recurrent features of natural interaction (such as overlap or repair). Do not try to record a television extract as the visual material will complicate both transcription and analysis.

Now go through the following steps:

(a) Attempt to transcribe your tape using the conventions in Box 24.1. Try to allocate turns to identified speakers where possible but don't worry if you cannot identify a particular speaker (put ? at the start of a line in such cases).

(b) Encourage a colleague or fellow student to attempt the same task independently of you. Now compare transcripts and listen again to the tape recording to improve your transcript.

(c) Using the chapter as a guide, attempt to identify in the talk and your transcript any features in the organisation of the talk (e.g. preference organisation, perspective-display sequences, features of institutional talk, strategies used to appear neutral and so on).

2 Examine Examples 14 and 15 below (drawn from Atkinson and Drew, 1979: 52, and discussed in Heritage, 1984: 248–249):

(a) Why does Heritage argue that these extracts demonstrate that 'questioners attend to the fact that their questions are framed within normative expectations which have sequential implications' (1984: 249)?

(b) In Example 2, what are the consequences of *Child* naming the person to whom his utterance is addressed? Why might children often engage in such naming?

---

Example 14

| 1 | A: | Is there something bothering you or not? |
|---|----|------|
| 2 | | (1.0) |
| 3 | A: | Yes or no. |
| 4 | | (1.5) |
| 5 | A: | Eh? |
| 6 | B: | No. |

Example 15

| 1 | Child: | Have to cut the:se Mummy. |
|---|--------|------|
| 2 | | (1.3) |
| 3 | Child: | Won't we Mummy? |
| 4 | | (1.5) |
| 5 | Child: | Won't we? |
| 6 | M: | Yes. |

---

# 25

# NARRATIVE ANALYSIS AND INTERPRETATIVE PHENOMENOLOGICAL ANALYSIS

## Ann Griffin and Vanessa May

This chapter focuses on two approaches, narrative analysis and interpretative phenomenological analysis (IPA), which are typically used for analysing texts, though narrative analysis can also be used to analyse visual materials. Both methods are relatively new arrivals within the social sciences and can be seen as part of the resurgence of humanist approaches that are person-centred, using case studies. They also draw on postmodern or poststructuralist schools of thought which have involved a renewed interest in the role that language plays in social interaction and its place in structures of power.

Narrative analysis originates from the disciplines of linguistics and literary criticism, where this has involved looking at the narrative structure of literary works such as novels. The approach has become increasingly popular within the social sciences since the 1990s and there are a number of textbooks on narrative analysis (listed under 'Further reading' at the end of this chapter) and even a dedicated journal called *Narrative Inquiry*. IPA, which originates from the philosophical field called phenomenology (which seeks to understand what it is like for an individual to experience at first hand the phenomena of the world). This perspective, has been developed particularly within psychology and is a more recent addition to the social science methods toolkit. Both methods are used within a range of disciplines including sociology, psychology, health and education.

These approaches have some important similarities in that both are interpretative, and often concentrate on first-person accounts, though narrative is also used to analyse public, official and collective accounts. Furthermore, people who use both narrative analysis and IPA are interested in meaning and understanding, that is, in how individuals interpret and make sense of their experiences, as well as in understanding how the context in which accounts are produced influences the telling of stories. These methods also require you to see meaning as something which is co-constructed, that is, an active process in which both the teller and audience participate, often in situations of unequal power.

There are, however, also some key differences between the two methods. Narrative analysis draws on a range of theories and in fact contains within it several different varieties of analysis, so that it is hard to specify overall rules about what kind of data ought to be analysed, or even how any one narrative analysis should proceed. IPA, on the other hand, is a more precisely specified approach which draws on phenomenology. Furthermore, whereas the stated aim of IPA is to come as close as possible to an individual's experience, among narrative analysts there is a debate over the extent to which this can be done, and many social scientists using the method are instead particularly interested in the social aspects of narrative, that is, the social origins of the narratives that individuals tell and the social impacts that narratives have.

First we are going to describe narrative analysis and then move on to IPA. Towards the end of the chapter we will show you how each of these approaches might be applied to an extract from a research interview – the personal story told by Wendy to Jocelyn Cornwell, shown in Box 21.8.

## Narrative analysis

One very broad way of defining narrative analysis is to say that it is 'any study that uses or analyses narrative materials' (Lieblich et al., 1998: 2). The term narrative materials, though, needs to be defined: these can include 'naturally occurring' narratives such as everyday conversations between people, life stories collected for research purposes in interviews, or written narratives found the private, public or political realms (e.g. diaries, letters and policy documents). Although narrative analysis mainly involves written or oral texts, photographs, films or even dance performances can also be used as data. This section will cover: what constitutes a narrative; why we use narrative analysis in the social sciences; and examples of the different approaches to analysing narratives.

## What is narrative and why study it?

Although the definition of the term narrative is under some dispute, key characteristics that are included in many definitions are that a narrative is an account of a non-random sequence of events that conveys some kind of action and movement through time. Thus, narratives are generally understood to have some form of chronology. The sequence of events is made non-random with the help of a 'plot' that creates a logical or meaningful connection between them so that prior events seem to inevitably lead to later ones, thus providing a sense of causality. This plot is often constructed around a particular point or meaning that the narrator wishes to convey to their audience.

All narratives have a narrator. Narratives also have an audience, who may be actual or imagined. In many ways, narrators shape their narratives with the intended or actual audience in mind, and therefore tend to tell different stories to different audiences such as a partner, a friend, a colleague or a stranger. Furthermore, narratives may be interpreted differently by different audiences. Narratives are thus collaboratively performed events between narrator and audience (earlier, we referred to this as the 'co-constructed' nature of this kind of data). As a consequence, narratives are not 'fixed texts', but change with each telling.

As will be evident, narrative analysis is a very 'broad church' within the social sciences, including a variety of approaches and techniques. However, narrative analysis is based on some key principles that do contribute to a sense of coherence in the method, as outlined below.

Jerome Bruner (1987, 1991) has argued that one of the main reasons to be interested in studying narratives is because narrative is a basic human way of making sense of the world. It can be argued that rather than understanding our lives as an unconnected series of events, we make sense of our experiences and organise our memories on a fundamental level in story form; that is, we lead 'storied lives'. Consequently, many narrative analysts maintain that narratives do not give us access to what 'really' happened or to underlying psychological motives, but rather they can be used to show us *how* experiences are reconstructed and interpreted once they have occurred.

Because narrative is so crucial to how we understand and communicate our experiences, narratives are everywhere, and much of the qualitative data that social scientists collect is actually in narrative form. Social scientists who have used narrative analysis often say that they were drawn to this method because it respects this fundamental feature of much of their data. Narrative analysis keeps stories intact, and in this respect this way of analysing qualitative data is different from qualitative thematic analysis (see Chapter 21), which breaks up stories into bits in order to fit them into coding categories.

Narratives are also inherently social in that they are one of our main means of communicating with each other. It is this social aspect of narratives, as a collective way of constructing reality, which interests many social scientists. When communicating our experiences to other people, we use narrative frameworks to structure the many events that happen to us in a manner that renders them easily understandable to others. Examples of narrative frameworks are the romantic story of falling in love that many people use to make sense of their couple relationships or the narrative frameworks that are used to make sense of illness, such as the primary narrative for breast cancer described in Box 25.2. These narrative frameworks do not originate from the individual but are shared cultural tools that offer us a repertoire of possible stories and set limits on what can be told. There is a sense in which, as we use these culturally shared narratives to make sense of our lives, culture 'speaks itself' through our story (Riessman, 1993: 5).

An example of this can be found in the study that Ken Plummer (1995) conducted on the changing shape of the 'coming out' stories that gay men of different ages tell. He proposes that the stories people tell about a particular issue reflect how that issue is viewed in society. Plummer found that the older men told accounts of long-term denial and secrecy about their homosexuality, followed by a late acceptance and a gradual shift towards leading openly gay lives. In contrast, the young men's life stories were quite different, telling of positive acceptance of their own sexuality and 'coming out' at a relatively young age. Plummer argues that this difference can be seen as a result of the successes of the gay rights movement, which has meant that more and more gay men, especially public figures, have been open about their sexuality, which in turn has allowed these younger men to draw upon sociocultural narratives of homosexuality in their own lives.

This overlap between individual and sociocultural narratives means that one fruitful avenue of analysis for social scientists is to study the social context within which a narrative is told. The sociocultural frameworks that individuals employ to make sense of their own lives are the result of social processes where different social groups try to make their interpretation of reality 'stick'. Thus the social world is also 'storied'. There are, for example, collective narratives about who 'we' are and where 'we' come from: as a nation, an ethnic group, a class or a gender.

These are often incorporated into media or political narratives, but can also be found in everyday talk.

Some groups have more narrative authority than others. For example, some professions have persuasive power when it comes to offering explanations: medical doctors are generally understood to provide authoritative narratives of how illnesses come about and how they can best be prevented and cured; social scientists are regarded by some people (though not all) as providing authoritative explanations of social problems, like drug use or social inequality. Certain narratives are, in other words, attached to certain professional groups and social institutions, and their use requires a degree of narrative competence and authority. At the same time, some social groups develop counter narratives that act as forms of resistance to the narratives told by the powerful. Thus many narrative analysts are interested not only in how sociocultural narratives are constructed, but also in inequalities in the power of different people to use narrative to achieve their objectives.

Because of this link between social relations of power and narratives, a further reason for analysing narratives is to examine what a narrative accomplishes. An example of this is given in Box 25.1. It should be clear by now that narratives are strategic, functional and purposeful, and narrating is often done in order to achieve certain ends. Personal narratives may aim to tell others who the narrator is; collective narratives may aim to mobilise people into action, or to foster a sense of community and belonging.

---

**BOX 25.1**

## PRESENTING A MORAL SELF: AN EXAMPLE OF NARRATIVE ANALYSIS

### The research problem

Vanessa May aimed to understand how mothers who have breached or have considered breaching social norms that constitute 'good' motherhood present a self.

### The data

May studied written life stories by Finnish women born between 1910 and 1960: 18 life stories were written by married women with children who had considered divorce, and 17 life stories by lone mothers.

### The analysis

This focused on the dialogue the narrators held with dominant social norms. The focus was on accounts of times when the narrator had breached or risked breaching social norms surrounding 'good' motherhood.

### Presenting a moral self in relation to one's wish to divorce

The 18 narrators writing about possible divorce placed their children's well-being as a central consideration in their eventual decision to either divorce or remain married, thus adhering to the central definition of 'good' motherhood. It would thus appear that the ethic of care for dependent children presents a non-negotiable moral norm.

### Presenting a moral self in relation to lone motherhood

None of the 17 lone mothers negated the widespread assumption that two parents are better than one, indicating that this is another non-negotiable moral norm. Therefore these narrators needed to salvage a moral self despite going against one of the cornerstones of 'good' motherhood. They did so by showing that they had done their utmost to secure their children's well-being.

### Conclusions

May concluded that personal narratives offer a forum for presenting oneself as a moral actor and offering justifications for (potential) breaches of norms. Personal narratives allow narrators to preserve a positive social identity, something the narrators accomplished by aligning their behaviour with alternative definitions of 'good' motherhood.

*Source*: adapted from May, 2008

## Two approaches to narrative analysis in the social sciences

Within this disparate methodological field, one key distinction can be made, namely between studies that focus mainly on the 'textual' elements of the narrative itself (be this oral, written or visual) and those studies that also focus on the interactional context within which the narrative is told.

The first group, that is, studies mainly focusing on the narrative itself, can further be divided along two axes: first, from *thematic* to *holistic* analyses, and second, from analysing the *content* of what is said to analysing *how* it is said. Narrative analysts are interested in sequences of text as a whole because they wish to pay attention to the sequencing of themes within narratives, thus foregrounding the 'specifically narrative aspects of texts' meaning' (Squire, 2008: 50). Even when narrative analysts take a more thematic approach and focus on themes across different narratives, they tend to analyse these in relation to the whole narrative within which they appear. Such an approach differs somewhat from the type of categorical or thematic analysis that many social scientists have traditionally been engaged in where texts are broken up into thematic chunks which are then analysed out of context. Such analyses have been criticised for eliminating 'the sequential and structural features that are hallmarks of narrative' (Riessman, 2008: 12).

Regarding the second axis, many social scientists end up doing a bit of both: focusing on both the told (the content of what is said) and on the telling (how it is told). An analyst may focus on the narrative structure of a story, using for example Labov's (1972) definition of the six elements that comprise a fully-formed narrative (see the analysis of Wendy's story later in this chapter for more details of Labov's six elements). Or another approach might be to focus on the genres that a narrator is making use of, or on the regressions, progressions and turning points of a narrative as indicators of the main argument that the narrator is trying to convey. Box 25.2 provides an example of a study that uses a holistic approach to narrative, focusing on both the narrative structure and the content, and also examining to what end the narratives are told.

---

## BOX 25.2

### NARRATIVE STRUCTURE: CONSTRUCTING THE IDEAL BREAST CANCER PATIENT

#### The research problem

Elizabeth Davis (2008) analysed 11 documents produced by the National Cancer Institute (US) on the topic of breast cancer. Davis argued that it was important to analyse narratives because they are a product of, and therefore reflect, social values, and medical narratives in particular because of the legitimacy and power that the medical institution holds.

#### The analysis

Davis identified a primary narrative based on six structural dimensions of narrative: characters, setting, events, audience, causal relations and themes. For example, in terms of characterisation, she found that the documents presented breast cancer as the villain of the story, which the (competent and knowledgeable) doctor as hero and the patient as (fearful yet strong) heroine were trying to defeat with the help of medical technology. The patient was also depicted as being surrounded by a team of helpful and supportive family members, friends and various health-care and volunteer workers. The events constructed a plot with six stages from pre-symptomatic to post-recovery through which the patient would journey, and identified how the patient should behave and what she should feel at each stage. For example, during the treatment stage the patient is meant to educate herself about cancer and treatment, communicate with her doctor and address her fears. The overarching themes that Davis identified were those of risk (all women are at risk of breast cancer and should behave accordingly) and control (the doctor is presented as the one ultimately in control, while the patient can exercise some control by educating herself about her illness).

#### Conclusions

Davis argues that in constructing the ideal breast cancer patient, the primary narrative medicalises the lives of women beyond the cancer. First, the patient is encouraged to address all her concerns (also non-medical) to her doctor, although in reality doctors are often ill-trained to deal with the psychological or social issues that their patients might face. Second, the breast cancer patient's life post-cancer is also medicalised: she is urged to keep monitoring herself for signs of a reoccurrence of the cancer.

*Source*: adapted from Davis, 2008

---

When analysing 'narratives in action', that is, how the interaction context in which a narrative is performed shapes the narratives, the main focus is on oral narratives, and on how narratives are produced and performed in dialogue (see Box 25.3). Analysts who focus on this dimension of narrative try to understand how the context of talk shapes what is said, and therefore take account of the setting and the social circumstances of the speakers as well as the actual dialogue or interaction that occurs between them. For example, when analysing a research interview situation, the role of the researcher in producing the narrative is taken into account. Who the researcher is (in terms of, for example, gender, class or ethnicity) and their role in the interaction will shape what the interview participant says.

---

**BOX 25.3**

## NARRATIVE AS CO-CONSTRUCTION

### The research problem

Lois Presser (2005) conducted longitudinal qualitative interviews with men who had committed serious violent crimes, including murder, assault and rape. She argues that the relations of power between interviewer and participant should be seen as part of interview data and systematically analysed.

### Analysing the 'what' and the 'how'

Presser's analysis was a mixture of analysing the 'what' and the 'how' of talk. In terms of the 'what', she, for example, coded the data according to sociologically interesting themes (e.g. what the men said about their peers). From these, Presser distilled eight key aspects that the men focused on, including 'social distinctions that the men drew, the men's talk about their true selves, talk about the self over time' (2005: 2074). She then developed a second generation of themes that focused on the men's constructions of a moral self. In terms of the 'how', Presser analysed the coherence of the narratives and also the interaction between herself and the men she interviewed In order to capture the flow of the interview. She constructed a running summary of how the men's accounts unfolded and what appeared to be going on between herself and the research participant. Presser examined her own role as a collaborator in producing the men's narratives and came to see the accounts they provided as a 'situated, collaborative negotiation of narrated identities' (2005: 2070).

### 'Doing' gender in interaction

Presser felt that both she and the men she interviewed were using 'their gender relations with each other to affirm an appropriately gendered self' (2005: 2073). In enacting their 'decent selves' to her, the men she interviewed were also positioning her 'in terms of hegemonic femininity, encompassing vulnerability and heterosexuality' (2005: 2079) as well as asserting their male authority over her, for example, through their performances of 'chivalrous masculinity' such as offering Presser advice on men. But Presser also positioned herself in gendered ways by, for example, alleviating tension in situations and not challenging the men's accounts. Why is it important to study the interactional nature of narratives? Such an approach rests on the assumption that social reality is constructed through everyday interaction. Narratives can be used to sanction certain forms of knowledge, to exclude or include particular social groups, or to construct social roles. Narrative analysis can therefore be used to examine how narrative not only reflects, but also shapes social contexts.

---

## Interpretative phenomenological analysis

Interpretative phenomenological analysis (IPA) is a method for interpreting people's accounts of their own experiences. As its name implies, IPA has been inspired by the philosophy of phenomenology and the theory of interpretation (sometimes known as hermeneutics). Phenomenology concerns the attempt to understand lived experience, that is, what it is like for an individual to experience phenomena. The approach therefore places experience as central to the development of analytic understanding and involves the investigation of subjectivity in the form of a first-person account. The hermeneutic viewpoint involves the belief that there is no such thing as a pure description; every communicative act involves interpretation, and therefore when a social researcher writes about an experience, this is always an act of reconstruction.

After a brief discussion of phenomenology and how it has shaped IPA research, the remainder of this section will focus on how these principles are applied in IPA work, as well as the ways in which relevant data are gathered, and how the results of analysis can be presented.

## What is phenomenology?

A phenomenological enquiry places peoples' lived experience as the starting point for investigation and meaning-making. The researcher using this approach attempts to enter the individual's lifeworld, which is the place where people are directly involved with the world and from which position their experience originates, in order to understand what 'being-in-the-world' is like ('being-in-the-world' is a term used by the German philosopher Martin Heidegger). 'Being-in-the-world' is an active process; human beings need to formulate meaning based on their experience of daily events and these understandings are unique, being both personal and situated at the particular location of each person, either geographically or in society. Phenomenological studies are often referred to as idiographic, which means that their mission is to explore the specific and the subjective nature of an experience rather than produce generalisable explanations of objective phenomena. Phenomenological philosophers and social scientists have purposely sought to redress the limitations they perceive in the scientific method, or positivistic approach, which conceives the world as concrete, out there,

with an objectivity that renders the world measureable. Phenomenology instead positions the world as experienced, as subjective and in our minds. For the phenomenologist, experience is therefore everything, and the basic stepping stone in the construction of our reality is our interpretation of the objects or things in the world. This interpretation depends on our subjective encounter, mediated through our consciousness, with these objects.

## What is IPA?

IPA work draws on these broad principles and is therefore a research method in which the analyst seeks to explore particular, personal stories, accepting that they are the product of individual acts of interpretation and that their retelling is itself an act of reconstruction. It is therefore inductive, rather than deductive: theory arises from the exploration of the lived experience and a study ought not to be driven by pre-determined theoretical perspectives. IPA seeks to know how the world appears to the individual and to convey this unique meaning by placing the informant as the expert or the 'knower'. This means, too, that IPA research has a sensitive and contemplative focus; the researcher, by attentively tuning in to the teller's account, attempts to highlight those areas regarded by the narrator as everyday events, but which to the analyst may reveal important insights that require further interrogation. For example, in Wendy's story (Box 21.8) there is much 'matter of fact' talk about her hysterectomy. Wendy's reportage presents the idea of surgery and any subsequent impact on her female identity as unproblematic. This appears at odds with the more widely accepted discourses about feminine subjectivity and the loss of childbearing potential that accompanies hysterectomy. IPA is often used in researching marginalised groups because it involves attending carefully to the experiences of such people, whose voice may otherwise be suppressed by the prevailing assumptions that others may make about them.

Context too, the 'situated' nature of experience, is central to the work of a researcher using IPA. An individual's subjective awareness of a particular phenomenon is at least in part the product of contextual factors, such as the individual's social or institutional position, network of formal and informal relationships, or physical location. The experience occurs in relation to others and will differ according to social relationships, such as those that involve power differentials. For example, in Box 25.4, Eatough and Smith (2006) demonstrate the changing expression of anger that is brought about by the birth of Marilyn's son, who is of course powerless in relation to his mother, which sees her actively protecting him from her own outbursts of rage and thus changing her experience of anger. Similarly, a focus on the biological, social and psychological contexts all importantly contribute to our understanding of what an experience is like for that person.

The IPA researcher takes an exploratory, open-minded approach but is aware that she or he is not a neutral agent in the research process.

It is acknowledged that the researcher will have their own preconceptions but that as a result of thoughtful practice these beliefs should not unduly overwhelm their work. Within the mainstream phenomenological tradition there is the practice of writing an 'epoché statement', a written confessional which declares the researcher's assumptions and forethoughts about the study and is meant to guard against these assumptions overly determining the analysis.

IPA researchers recognise that we cannot directly enter into another person's lifeworld and have first-hand knowledge of their experiences, but they believe that we can come closer to their experience by attending carefully to what we are told. The researcher and informant thus work together, intersubjectively, each reconstructing and co-constructing meaning through the ongoing dialogue. The process of empathetically engaging with the story of another person's lifeworld experience is seen as permission to the researcher to interpret and reconstruct their informant's narrative in order to present a sensitive third-person account.

---

**BOX 25.4**

## UNDERSTANDING EMOTIONS USING IPA

### The research problem

To demonstrate how the emotion of anger and its sequelae, that is, the feelings and behaviours it generates, are experienced by an individual and how these are changed by motherhood.

### Background

Emotions are externally focused, that is, they are directed towards somebody or something and therefore are shaped by the environment that provokes them. Because they are so specific, to the individual's psychological makeup and to the context in which they arise, they can be studied by the investigation of an individual experience.

### Data

One woman's experience of anger was explored. Marilyn was interviewed on two occasions, using a semi-structured topic guide.

*(Continued)*

**Data analysis**

A close reading was followed by a more literal analysis which looked for 'psychological concepts and abstractions'. Marilyn talked about a variety of issues around feeling angry. 'Trembling', 'feeling hot' and 'blood-pressure boiling' were the initial descriptions that lead to higher order conceptualisations, or themes, about the bodily experience of emotions. 'Trash the bedsit', 'swipe the ornaments', 'break down and cry' were the behaviours Marilyn demonstrated when angry, the later one being an adaptation since the birth of her son, and these early themes helped provide the super-ordinate themes of expression and suppression of emotion.

**Findings**

The authors use Marilyn's subjective experience of anger to position anger as a deeply physical, felt emotion. Anger is experienced through the body and the body holds a central place in our personal understanding and communication of this emotion.

*Source:* adapted from Eatough and Smith, 2006

## Gathering data

The one-to-one qualitative interview is the technique most widely used by IPA researchers, as it is seen as the best way by which the lived experience may be communicated, affording a relatively rapid admission to rich individual stories, as well as having the capacity to re-examine intriguing responses. Other methods have been used too, such as focus groups, observational data, postal questionnaires and e-mail correspondence, but the potential thinness by which these media may portray an experience needs to be considered carefully. IPA researchers usually limit the number of people in their studies because this allows them to look in detail at small numbers of cases rather than dissipating their effort superficially across more cases. Smith and Osborne (2008: 56) suggest a range from one to six cases, but advise the novice IPA researcher to limit their sample to three in order to achieve full justice to the complexity of the material. Purposive sampling (see Chapter 9) is the active means by which IPA researchers select individuals who have been exposed to a particular phenomenon; those who are uniquely placed

to give their own insights into the experience under interrogation.

## Analysing data

In general terms the IPA approach, like other qualitative methods, employs the constant revisiting and re-questioning of the data, until you can 'do justice to the fullness and the ambiguity of the lifeworld' (van Manen, 1990: 131). An understanding of the meanings that the data hold is reached through a thoughtful, reflective process which begins with immersion in and close scrutiny of the material. The IPA approach recommended by Jonathan Smith (2008) is a four-staged procedure. After the close-reading phase the researcher is advised to proceed incrementally to first describe, then interpret and then, if more than one participant is involved, begin to work across cases. By taking these sequenced steps there is an enhanced transparency and, hopefully, increased coherence by which meanings are revealed from their original text. Structuring the textual material, as illustrated in Figure 25.1, shows the way in which transcript,

| Description | | | Interpretation |
|---|---|---|---|
| | 96 | J: Did you have any idea, have you ever had any idea | |
| Usually Wendy demonstrates a deep understanding of her body and the effects of interventions, but not here – she doesn't know why it started. | 97 | about why you have always bled so much, why, why your | |
| | 98 | periods haven't ever been regulated? | |
| | 99 | W: No, I'd never, from the time mine started when I was at | |
| Unpredictable periods, heavy loss. | 100 | school, I never knew when I would start, I never knew | *'MEDICAL KNOWLEDGE'* |
| | 101 | how heavy I would lose. I used to be at home maybe for | |
| Making her ill. | 102 | three or four days in bed. I was that ill. And the only time I | |
| The pill stopped this. | 103 | wasn't was when I was on the pill. The doctor at the family | Pill as a mechanism to control her experience of lived body. |
| Being told by a doctor they would regulate. | 104 | planning said like they will regulate. I said I'm thirty! If they | |
| Disbelief. | 105 | haven't regulated in fifteen years I said I don't think they're | Wendy's long experience of heavy periods shapes her belief that they will not regulate. |
| Given a choice – pills or smoking. | 106 | going to now. But she just didn't want me to have it no | *'I KNOW MY OWN BODY'.* |
| 'That was that.' | 107 | more cos I smoked. That was it. She wanted me to stop | Power relations and autonomous reaction, expressed her own agency, changed doctor |
| | 108 | smoking and I wouldn't. So I got my pills from my doctor | to achieve her own agenda. |
| Went to her own doctor. | 109 | instead! Just changed. | *'MY CHOICE'.* |

FIGURE 25.1 IPA coding of Wendy's story

description and interpretation can remain united and persistently visible to the researcher, thus requiring them to constantly re-evaluate the credibility of their interpretative moves.

To set up this way of displaying the data, the first step is to insert line numbers to the transcript and then put two wide margins on both sides of the document. The margin on the left is used to record the researcher's initial thoughts; these first ideas should be literal and closely related to the text, picking out the key ideas that invite curiosity about the person's experience. When this stage is completed the interpretive phase begins. This phase builds on what has been identified and described previously to generate more abstracted or conceptualised notions about the lived experience. These ideas are documented in the far right margin of the transcript. It is, however, quite likely that some interpretative thoughts will have seeped into the researcher's mind before this point, but this process allows an opportunity to question and double-check the merit of these higher order interpretations. The display of the data in this manner also permits others to inspect the data and the analysis (sometimes called 'auditing'), so permitting credibility and dependability of the analysis to be evaluated. The themes that have been identified can be further ordered into clusters and grouped under super ordinate themes. Qualitative data analysis software, such as NVivo, can be used to aid IPA analysis in arranging units of meaning into clusters or themes. Other helpful features are its ability to visually model either individual cases or entire data sets, showing how the units of meaning relate to each other (see Chapter 21).

Box 25.5 looks at how research into the experience of illness can be implemented.

---

**BOX 25.5**

## THE EXPERIENCE OF ILLNESS

### Research problem

To explore the lived experience of a common chronic neurological disorder – Parkinson's disease

### Data

A single case study, comprising three semi-structured interviews with 'Beth'.

### Data analysis

This identified themes relating to the various manifestations of Parkinson's disease: movement problems, the mental effects of the disease and the impact of medication. These generated the super ordinate theme of 'mind and body'. In addition, Beth talked about herself pre-Parkinson's, made comparisons with how she appeared now and expressed her internal self as unchanged. These generated the second super ordinate theme of 'self and agency'.

### Results

Beth's experience of Parkinson's disease involves the expression of organic problems, her individual cognition and the social surroundings in which she lives. IPA in this study identified how Beth's sense of herself was important in determining how she coped with the challenges of Parkinson's disease. Furthermore, the study of Beth's experience identified some rarely reported symptoms of the disease (hot sweats). This sort of detailed work, which situates the patient as central, can provide important insights into the experience of illness and potential interventions that contribute to patient care.

*Source*: adapted from Bramley and Eatough, 2005

Fundamental to IPA is that the presentation of analysed data should contain substantial verbatim quotations which illustrate the importance of the participant's voice. Quotations permit transparency, allowing the reader insight into the basis of an author's interpretation. Appropriately chosen quotes can describe and symbolise the essence of the experience, often in a more direct, nuanced way than if presented through academic writing. On the other hand, it should be recognised that quotations are not a neutral route into the informant's world: they can also be chosen by the analyst for rhetorical effect if they are selected in a way that will create a certain impression.

Participant validation (called 'member validation' in Chapter 21), as a method for demonstrating the credibility of data analysis, is congruent with the IPA approach. Giving back the analysis to the informant in order to hear their responses to the picture painted by the researcher recognises the central place occupied by the informant in the research process. Also the data analysis should be a transparent demonstration which links the participant's talk and the researcher's thoughts, making it more straightforward for the informant to concur or refute the researcher's interpretation.

In addition, IPA researchers are not averse to applying other theoretical perspectives on the lived experience (Hughes, 2007). Bramley and Eatough (2005) and Eatough and Smith (2006) use theories of the self and agency, whilst Robinson et al. (2005) have used theories of loss (see Box 25.6).

---

**BOX 25.6**

## MAKING SENSE OF DEMENTIA – APPLYING THEORIES OF LOSS TO AN IPA ANALYSIS

### Research problem

To explore couples' shared experiences of dementia with a particular focus on their psychological reaction of loss.

### Data

Nine couples, where one partner had been given the diagnosis of early stage dementia, were jointly interviewed.

### Results

The couples' talk generated two main themes. One key theme referred to the couples' detection of a change in mental capacity, how they made sense of it and their subsequent adaption. The second major theme identified the fluctuant nature of the pair's readjustment. The alternating nature of the process swung between highlighting the positive aspects, for example, their new coping strategies and successful adjustments, and the negative effects of the illness, that of depression, frustration and challenges in ordinary daily living.

### Discussion

The authors argue that the experience of loss in their study of dementia can be understood with reference to existing theories of loss. They refer to Stroebe and Schut's (1999) work 'The dual process model of coping with bereavement'. This model says that the adaptation to loss relies on two processes: *loss orientation*, which is the work people do to cope with whatever has gone, and *restoration orientation*, which is the work of rebuilding and moving on.

*Source*: adapted from Robinson et al., 2005

## Comparing narrative analysis and IPA

In order to illustrate how, despite their similar focus on the stories that people tell, narrative analysis and IPA can be used to draw out different aspects of a story, we discuss how the two methods might go about analysing an excerpt from the same qualitative research interview. Before you read further, please turn to Wendy's story (shown in Box 21.8 on page 389 onwords) and make some notes on how you would use narrative analysis and IPA to analyse the text. Below, we briefly explore the elements of the interview that the two methods of analysis might focus on.

### Narrative analysis and Wendy's story

This is a qualitative interview between Jocelyn, the interviewer, and Wendy, the research participant. Both were white women in their 30s; Jocelyn was upper-class, Wendy working-class. The interview was conducted for Jocelyn's PhD study of 'hard earned lives' (Cornwell, 1984) and was captured on video-camera. Jocelyn and Wendy met several times – we can conclude from Jocelyn's opening statement that this is at least the third time she and Wendy have met. In the following brief sketch of an analysis we examine the narrative structure, the co-construction of the narrative between Jocelyn and Wendy, and the use of sociocultural narrative frameworks.

#### Narrative structure

At the beginning, Jocelyn sets the agenda for the interview (Wendy's hysterectomy). Narratives have a beginning, middle and end, and Jocelyn indicates that she wants Wendy to produce a chronological illness narrative that begins in the time before the operation (lines 5–6).

The narrative follows Labov's six elements of a fully formed narrative (Labov, 1972). Labov outlined these as an abstract, an orientation, a complicating action, a resolution, a coda and an evaluation. Jocelyn and Wendy together provide the *abstract* by establishing that the narrative is about Wendy's hysterectomy. Wendy provides an *orientation* in lines 8–16 that introduces the main actors: Wendy, her doctor, her periods and her smoking. The *complicating action* and turning point comes when the pill becomes less effective in controlling her bleeding. The *resolution* of the narrative is that Wendy's hysterectomy has not had a negative impact on her feminine subjectivity. The *coda* returns the narrative to the present (prompted by Jocelyn's question on lines 121–122): Wendy feels healthier now than before the operation.

The sixth element contained in Wendy's account is that of *evaluation*, or the main argument of the story, which positions her as an autonomous subject who decides for herself and acts on her own without consulting even friends or family. Wendy indicates that this trait is hard-wired into her personality (lines 42–43). Most importantly in this narrative, Wendy does not listen to doctors' advice (lines 107–109 and lines 64–66). Her autonomy is also apparent in the manner with which she rejects cultural frameworks on the benefits of talking and the negative impact that a hysterectomy has on a woman's subjectivity.

### Use of sociocultural frameworks and co-construction of narrative

This narrative is a co-construction, where Jocelyn brings in well-known cultural frameworks such as the therapeutic narrative on the importance of talking about one's worries (lines 31–32, 34, 37–38, 40) and the narrative on hysterectomies as robbing a woman of her essential female subjectivity and therefore as something that a woman would not voluntarily choose (lines 69–71, 89–90, 126). These interjections by Jocelyn to some degree take Wendy away from the narrative she wishes to tell, yet Wendy does not merely brush these aside. This is perhaps partly due to Jocelyn's insistence, but possibly also because of the cultural dominance of the narrative frameworks that Jocelyn introduces. Wendy instead stops to consider and counter Jocelyn's interpretations: she is the type of person who does not talk about her problems but rather sorts them out for herself (lines 41–42, 46–50), and her hysterectomy did not damage her womanhood because she had already had children, which is why she had no more need for her womb (lines 91–95, 127–131). On the contrary, Wendy feels healthier now that her womb has been removed (lines 130–131). One might also want to consider the effect that the class difference between Jocelyn and Wendy might have had on this interaction that comes across as somewhat of a power struggle.

This interaction can be interpreted as Wendy offering an account of her seemingly unusual behaviour when questioned by Jocelyn. It is in instances where people are made aware that they have breached a social norm that they tend to offer accounts to justify their behaviour and offer counter-narratives (Scott and Lyman, 1968).

It would seem that there was some tension between Jocelyn and Wendy when discussing the significance that a womb has for feminine subjectivity, as indicated by Jocelyn's abrupt change of subject to the more neutral topic of the reason for why Wendy had bled so much (lines 96–98). Jocelyn then goes on to further build rapport with Wendy by echoing Wendy's words (line 117), thus indicating that she agrees with Wendy's interpretation of causality.

## IPA and Wendy's story

Wendy's lived experience of menstruation will be used to illustrate how her story might be coded using IPA and how this analysis can be understood with reference to the psychological attributes associated with coping. Figure 25.1 shows a limited section of Wendy's story. It has the descriptive coding in the left-hand column. These are phenomenological; that is, they are more descriptive, or literal, in that they relate directly to what Wendy reports as her lived experience, its characteristics, her understanding and concerns. The right-hand column begins to identify themes.

One coding theme that comes across clearly in the data is Wendy's 'medical knowledge' of menstruation; most of her talk demonstrates a comprehensive understanding of her irregular bleeding and its treatment (lines 8–12, 14–16, 69–73, 75–76, 113–116, 124–125). The only caveat to this is her lack of knowledge about its aetiology (lines 99–101). This technical comprehension is balanced by a more contextual theme, 'I know my own body' (lines 13–16, 20–22, 25–30, 103–106, 117), where Wendy is able to predict the effects of treatments, or their withdrawal, and the precise onset of her periods; indeed, it was the failure of this regular pattern that made her think something was wrong (lines 24, 28–30). Her approach to dealing with the problem is interesting; under the theme 'speaking with others' (lines 33–41, 43–44, 46), Wendy clearly articulates that she does not consult with either family or friends. In the theme 'my choice' she describes how she sorts things out for herself and uses her own health beliefs and values to decide on her best course of action (lines 42–44, 47–50, 53–65, 80–84, 91, 108–109, 118–120). This agentic behaviour is illustrated particularly well by her decision to go to her general practitioner (GP) to get a repeat prescription of her oral contraceptive pill despite having been denied this treatment, on health grounds, by the family planning doctor (lines 108–109). The final coding category, for the purpose of this illustration, is 'no loss to me' (lines 91–95, 123–124, 127–131), where Wendy defends her choice to have surgery and articulates, in a particularly matter-of-fact way, that having a hysterectomy had not impacted on her sense of self, indeed quite the opposite as her womb had done its job and her physical health was improved.

Wendy's experience, one could argue, is of someone who has coped successfully with her menstrual disorder and its management; the analysis of her transcript reveals a range of actions and thought processes that Wendy used to achieve this end. Billings and Moos (1981) suggest three main coping constructs: active-cognitive strategies and active-behaviour strategies (ways of thinking and acting that promote the ability to cope with stressful life events), whilst the third one, avoidance strategies (e.g. persistent anger or comfort eating) is associated with maladaptive coping strategies. If we reflect on Wendy's active-cognitive strategies, we can see she draws on her past experience, *'I know my own body'*, and uses her extensive *'medical knowledge'* to problem-solve, resulting in *'my choices'*, which sometimes challenge medical advice. *'No loss to me'* expresses an objective, pragmatic stance to having undergone a hysterectomy, one that is unusual, being unencumbered by the more popular discourse of loss of womanhood. Active behaviours involve *'speaking to others'*: Wendy consults with doctors, but not with friends and family, denying herself access to her own social networks. Included in *'my choices'* is another active behaviour, that of getting the pill from her GP when it has been refused by the family planning clinic. Avoidance strategies are rare, taking to her bed and being ill (lines 101–102) possibly being the only example.

So Wendy does indeed demonstrate many features which are attributed to coping successfully with life events; her thoughts and behaviours demonstrate a strong self-belief and internal locus of control. Her matter-of-fact approach is without emotional baggage that is often associated with avoidance strategies. What makes her account unique, idiographic? Three things stand out: her success appears not to rely on her accessing her social networks – these are an extremely important factor widely associated with successful coping. Her highly adaptive behaviour and problem-solving skills are more typically associated with higher socioeconomic groups, and her atypical reaction to loss counters the norm.

## Conclusion

This chapter has reviewed two approaches to the analysis of (mainly) first-person accounts, narrative analysis and IPA. Whereas narrative analysis contains different approaches, IPA is more linked to a singular philosophical thread and has developed a more unified methodological approach. What connects narrative analysis and IPA is not so much the particular way in which the analysis is conducted, but their approach to studying people: interpretative analysis of first-person accounts focusing on meaning (though narrative analysis can also be used to analyse other types of narrative, but this is done less frequently) and setting them within the social, political and cultural contexts in which the teller's story emerges. Despite their procedural differences, they both seek to shed light on meaning, and to study the interface between individual and social context (i.e. how individuals use socio-cultural narratives to make sense of their experiences) and how these individual narratives in turn help shape social contexts and collective ways of constructing social reality. They both acknowledge that the researcher, as audience and as orator, impacts on the research process in a variety of ways, yet this is not wholly viewed as problematic but rather something to be systematically and reflexively analysed by the researcher.

## *FURTHER READING*

Concerning IPA, Smith et al. (2009), Smith and Osborn (2008) and van Manen (1990) provide helpful overviews and guidance. For narrative analysis, consult Andrews et al. (2008), Lieblich et al. (1998) and Riessman (2008).

## Student Reader (Seale, 2004b): relevant readings

55 Catherine Kohler Riessman: 'Strategic uses of narrative in the presentation of self and illness: a research note'

See also Chapter 8, 'Narrative research' by Molly Andrews, Shelley Day Sclater, Corinne Squire and Maria Tamboukou in Seale et al. (2004).

## Journal articles using or discussing the methods described in this chapter

Boserman, C. (2009) 'Diaries from cannabis users: an Interpretative Phenomenological Analysis', Health, 13: 429–448.

Boudens, C.J. (2005) 'The story of work: a narrative analysis of workplace emotion', Organization Studies, 26: 1285–1306.

Frost, N. (2009) '"Do you know what I mean?": the use of a pluralistic narrative analysis approach in the interpretation of an interview', Qualitative Research, 9: 9–29.

Hydén, L-C. (1997) 'Illness and narrative', Sociology of Health & Illness, 19 (1): 48–69.

Lomsky-Feder, E. (1995) 'The meaning of war through veterans' eyes: a phenomenological analysis of life stories', International Sociology, 10: 463–482.

## Web links

Centre for Narrative Research, University of East London: www.uel.ac.uk/cnr/index.htm

Narrative Research @ Anglia Ruskin University containing support materials for narrative analysis. http://web.anglia.ac.uk/narratives/index.phtml

A web resource for narrative psychology: http://web.lemoyne.edu/~hevern/narpsych/narpsych.html

Katherine Cohler Riessman's webpage containing pdf files of her publications on narrative analysis: www2.bc.edu/~riessman/papers.html

Halla Beloff at Edinburgh University who does visual narrative analysis: http://homepages.ed.ac.uk/halla/

Narrative Analysis: http://staff.bath.ac.uk/psscg/QM-Nar-lec.htm

The Interpretative Phenomenology Analysis webpage at Birkbeck: www.ipa.bbk.ac.uk

IPA discussion groups: http://groups.yahoo.com/group/ipanalysis/

Brief overview of IPA; also contains descriptions and links to other qualitative methodologies: http://onlineqda.hud.ac.uk/methodologies.php#Interpretative_Phenomenological_Analysis

Van Manen's webpage (phenomenology): www.phenomenologyonline.com

## KEY CONCEPTS FOR REVIEW

**Advice:** Use these, along with the review questions in the next section, to test your knowledge of the contents of this chapter. Try to define each of the key concepts listed here; if you have understood this chapter you should be able to do this. Check your definitions against the definition in the glossary at the end of the book.

*(Continued)*

| | |
|---|---|
| Co-construction of meaning | Narrative |
| Hermeneutic viewpoint | Narrative frameworks |
| Idiographic | Narrative materials |
| Lifeworld | Phenomenology |

## Review questions

1 What are the major points of difference in narrative and IPA work?
2 What kinds of question can narrative analysis answer?
3 What is the difference between a holistic and a thematic narrative analysis?
4 Why is it important to include the social and interactional context in an analysis of narratives produced in dialogue?
5 What are the main principles of phenomenology?
6 How does phenomenology inform the practice of IPA research?
7 What understanding of the role played by the researcher in influencing the account provided by the informant is evident in narrative and IPA approaches?
8 Describe the stages of data analysis in IPA research.
9 Write a research question that would suit either a narrative analysis or an IPA approach and give three reasons why this would be your preferred methodology, compared with the alternative.

## Workshop and discussion exercises

1 Conduct your own narrative analysis of the interview with Joanna in Box 12.12 (pp. 224–6). You can focus, for example, on narrative structure, the dialogue that the narrators hold with dominant norms around motherhood, and on the interaction between the interviewer and the research participant.
2 Conduct your own IPA of the interview with Joanna in Box 12.12. Discuss with others your descriptive coding and how you came to generate your interpretative themes. What does your analysis tell you about her lived experience?

# 26

# CONTENT AND COMPARATIVE KEYWORD ANALYSIS

## Clive Seale and Fran Tonkiss

---

### Chapter Contents

---

This chapter focuses on two related methods of textual analysis: content analysis and keyword analysis. These techniques share a common interest in the use of language in social contexts, providing insights into the way speech and texts help to shape and reproduce social meanings and forms of knowledge. Methods of textual analysis are relevant to a range of research subjects, in such fields as sociology, psychology, media and communications, history, politics and social policy, cultural studies, socio-linguistics, law, education, management and organisation studies.

The discussion begins by outlining content analysis in the study of textual data. We look at different ways of approaching textual content, how this method can be used in conjunction with other forms of analysis, and consider key problems of validity. We then outline keyword analysis, a method made possible by the widespread availability of personal computers, initially developed within the discipline of linguistics but now increasingly used by social scientists in a variety of disciplines.

## Content analysis

Content analysis is a quantitative method for studying textual data. It seeks to analyse texts in terms of the presence and frequency of specific terms, narratives or concepts. This can involve counting items (specific words or categories) or measuring the number of lines or amount of space given to different themes. Content analysis has a long pedigree in psychology and in communications research (see Berelson, 1952). It is still frequently used in the analysis of media texts – such as newspaper articles, radio and television reports – and is closely associated with the study of visual content in photographic, film and television images (see Chapter 16). In this discussion, however, we are concerned with the use of content analysis in relation to speech and written texts.

The principal strength of this approach lies in the clear and systematic study of textual content as a basis for analysis and interpretation. Content analysis is the primary method used for large-scale and comparative study of textual data. It potentially has a high degree of validity and reliability in terms of precise sampling, providing clear empirical evidence for research findings, and in allowing for replication and generalisation (see Chapter 30). In grounding analysis on empirical content rather than on interpretive argument, furthermore, this can be seen as one of the most objective methods for the study of texts.

Content analysis, however, while it shares many of the advantages of quantitative social research (including, it might be said, certain claims on academic legitimacy), has been subject to a number of criticisms. Chief amongst these is the objection that such analysis is concerned simply with 'crass' content: with *what* is said rather than with *how* it is said; with the description of texts rather than their interpretation, meanings or effects. In this respect, debates over content analysis bear on a central methodological issue in social and cultural research. Content analysis can be placed within a broadly empiricist and positivist tradition of inquiry, concerned with the analysis of observable features or facts, rather than with less observable and often highly subjective questions of meaning. At the same time, in their focus on texts and speech, content analysts are clearly interested in the production and reproduction of meaning. The method therefore raises quite sharply the question of whether a 'scientific' model of social research can be appropriate to the study of social and cultural objects that are in large part defined by the meanings they hold for social actors. In what follows we examine how content analysis can help to address these questions of qualitative meaning and potential readings.

Content analysis adopts a fairly standard model of research design. Having formulated a research topic, the researcher defines the relevant population of interest and then draws an appropriate *sample* from it (see also Chapter 9). In this case, though, the research will be based on a sample of texts rather than a sample of people. This might come from a number of sources, for example:

- political debates and speeches
- media texts
- policy and legal documents
- archival sources and other historical documents
- tourist guides
- publicity literature
- press statements.

In many instances the potential sample will be vast, given the scale on which texts are produced and circulated. Random sampling is a challenging task even for researchers working on a large scale, and often is not feasible for researchers involved in smaller studies. It is important, therefore, for researchers to delimit their sample very clearly by:

- setting time limits, choosing, for example:
  - television coverage over a one-week period
  - three issues of a magazine each year for 20 years defining the type of text as precisely as possible, choosing, for example:
  - a particular piece of legislation
  - presidential speeches or party political broadcasts
  - newspaper editorials or front pages.

When working with samples of these kinds, the researcher needs to make very clear the rationale for the selection of texts. Moreover, this selection should aim to produce a sample that is *relevant* to the research problem, *representative* of the field of interest, and *manageable* for the researcher to analyse in detail.

## Coding content

Counting and analysing textual data can proceed in various ways. A common starting-point is to define categories of analysis and to code the data using these categories. The categories may be preset by the researcher in advance of reading the data, or they may be based on an initial reading of the texts (see Chapter 21 for an account of how a coding scheme like this can be developed).

In many cases, coding categories emerge from a combination of these two processes: some will be pre-set to reflect the aims and the theoretical framing of the research; further categories will arise from detailed reading and coding of textual content. This stage of the research requires intensive work to ensure that coding categories will capture the content of the texts in ways that are clear (reducing ambiguity and overlap) and exhaustive (including all relevant content). A key aim in constructing and applying codes is to limit the margin for interpretation on the part of individual researchers.

## Inter-rater reliability

The reliability of the coding process is an important consideration in content analysis: will different researchers code the data in the same way? Content analysts frequently use tests of inter-rater reliability to ensure that codes are matched to content in a consistent manner. At the pilot stage of the research, and as a further check in the course of data analysis, a number of researchers will code sample texts using the same set of coding categories and guidelines for their use. The degree of agreement between researchers acts as a test of the reliability of the content analysis as a whole (see Neuendorf, 2002 for a more detailed discussion of validity and reliability in content analysis).

A widely accepted measure of inter-rater reliability when applying a coding scheme is the kappa statistic. This delivers a single number, ranging between 0 and 1, which indicates the degree to which two coders have made the same coding decisions. Kappa is usually interpreted as follows:

| | | |
|---|---|---|
| 0 | = | poor agreement |
| 0.01–0.20 | = | slight agreement |
| 0.21–0.40 | = | fair agreement |
| 0.41–0.60 | = | moderate agreement |
| 0.61–0.80 | = | substantial agreement |
| 0.81–1 | = | almost perfect agreement |

An example (Parke et al., 2011) which involved applying a coding scheme containing codes to a sample of newspaper articles illustrates the calculation of *kappa*. This was study in which 37 different arguments for and against a health policy had been identified. Each argument was therefore a code. Hannah Parke and Clive Seale, working together on this project, independently read 10 articles and marked every time they thought text relating a particular argument was present in the article. There were therefore 370 coding decisions to be made by each rater, in deciding whether an argument was 'yes' (present) or 'no' (not present) in each article. The results of the coding decisions are shown in Table 26.1. You can see that there were 55 'yes + yes' decisions, indicating that both raters applied a given code to an article, and 295 'no + no' decisions, indicating both raters did *not* apply a given code to an article. The 'yes + no' decisions indicates a disagreement between the two raters, where one applied a code that the other did not. You can see that there were 12 + 8 = 20 such decisions.

Around the edges of the table are the row and column marginals (see Chapter 19), which add together the totals for the rows and the columns. For example, Rater 2 made 63 'Yes' decisions.

The equation for *kappa* (κ) is:

$$\kappa = \frac{\Pr(a) - \Pr(e)}{1 - \Pr(e)},$$

where $\Pr(a)$ is the relative observed agreement among raters, and $\Pr(e)$ is the hypothetical probability of chance agreement, using the observed data to calculate the probabilities of each observer randomly saying each category.

To calculate $\Pr(a)$ note that there were 55 + 295 = 350 occasions on which both raters agreed. This is 350/370 = 0.94 or 94 per cent of the time.

To calculate $\Pr(e)$ (the probability of random agreement), note that:

Rater 1 said 'Yes' to 67 decisions and 'No' to 303. This rater thus said 'Yes' 67/370 = 18 per cent of the time.

Rater 2 said 'Yes' to 63 decisions and 'No' to 307. This rater thus said 'Yes' 63/370 = 17 per cent of the time.

Therefore the probability that both raters would say 'Yes' randomly is $0.18 \times 0.17 = 0.03$. The probability that both of them would say 'No' is $0.82 \times 0.83 = 0.68$. The overall probability of random agreement is therefore $\Pr(e) = 0.03 + 0.68 = 0.71$ or 71 per cent.

$\Pr(a)$ – $\Pr(e)$ is therefore 0.94 – 0.71 = 0.23 and 1 – $\Pr(e)$ is 1 – 0.71 = 0.29

Kappa is therefore 0.23/0.29 = 0.79

This level of agreement is at the top end of 'substantial agreement', so we decided that the arguments identified by the coding scheme was sufficiently well defined for us to trust that they were objective and did not require further development before being applied to the whole collection of articles.

## Using word counts

The development of a coding scheme and its refinement until an acceptable kappa statistic is produced is one way in which a content analysis can proceed. An alternative starting-point for content analysis is for the researcher to compile a simple word count. This involves beginning analysis with a frequency count of the main items in the text. This often is done using

TABLE 26.1   Results of an inter-rater reliability exercise

|          |       | Rater 1 |     |   |       |
|----------|-------|---------|-----|---|-------|
|          |       | Yes     | No  |   | Total |
| Rater 2  | Yes   | 55      | 8   | = | 63    |
|          | No    | 12      | 295 | = | 307   |
|          |       | =       | =   |   | =     |
|          | Total | 67      | 303 | = | 370   |

computer searching. There is a variety of software available to assist in content analysis, which will analyse texts in a number of ways, including producing keyword lists and word frequencies, identifying main ideas, analysing patterns of word use, comparing vocabulary between texts, and producing full concordances that list and count *all* words that appear in a text and then enable the context of particular words to be explored. Figure 26.1 shows a keyword-in-context (KWIC) display for the word 'heart' as it is used in a poem by Philip Larkin. On the left hand side you can see a word list, indicating the number of times particular words occur in the poem. 'Heart' appears 25 times. The larger box indicates that the first use of 'heart' is in the context of 'That my own heart drifts and cries'. Note, too, that 'hearts' occurs 7 times. It is often important to consider variations to words that

arise from prefixes and suffixes, or (as in this case) plural forms, if the full range of meanings attached to a word in a particular text are to be understood. As you can see from this display, concordance software offers the capacity to assess this in a quick visual scan.

Such computer-assisted approaches are extremely useful when researchers are dealing with a large amount of material – the initial 'reading' of the texts is done by computer, measuring the frequency of specific words and providing a broad picture of the texts as a basis for analysis. In this way they organise a large body of data for the researcher in a manageable form. Moreover, this approach can be seen to minimise researcher bias by grounding the initial analysis in the manifest content of the texts – that is, in the content as it has been written or spoken by the producer, rather than as it has been read by

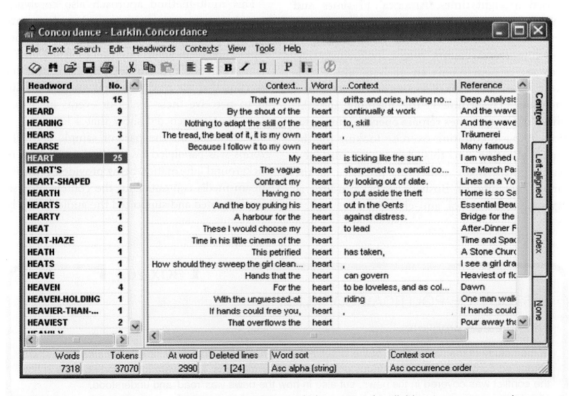

**FIGURE 26.1** Concordance software showing keywords in context (available at www.concordance software.co.uk)

the researcher (sometimes called the latent content). Taken further, word counts and concordances can be developed into full-scale keyword analysis, described later in this chapter.

These techniques are not limited to researchers working on large-scale studies or with extensive resources. More and more textual material is available in electronic form over the Internet and in electronic archives. Newspaper articles, policy documents and political speeches are three key resources that researchers can retrieve at little or no cost, and internet material in general is a growing field for analysis. Concordance software such as that shown in Figure 26.1 is commonly used to give a broad-brush account of politicians' speeches. Thus, Beard and Payack (2000) counted the words used in the US presidential debate between candidates George W. Bush and Al Gore in the run-up to the 2000 election. They found that George Bush used the words 'abortion' eight times, 'America' 17 times, and 'taxes' 33 times. Al Gore said 'abortion' once, 'America' twice, and 'taxes' 25 times.

While these counts might look suggestive, they are of course only an 'analysis' in the simplest sense – in terms of sorting and enumerating the data. The context, the meaning and the effect of the speeches remain open to interpretation. A basic counting exercise looking for the term 'abortion' in this debate, for instance, would not capture either the presence or the larger meaning of Bush's use of 'pro-life' as against Gore's use of 'anti-choice'.

## Content analysis and interpretation

Content analysis therefore should not just be about producing simple counts of things, but should also involve an attempt to take in issues of meaning and context. This can sometimes work by combining content analysis with other methods, or by using it as a framework for the more interpretive analysis of texts. Two examples illustrate this.

Philo's research (Box 26.1), the first example, is particularly interesting in taking the analysis beyond the counting of manifest content. The content analysis formed part of a larger study that involved audience focus groups with 85 people, and survey questionnaires conducted with 300 17–22-year-olds in Scotland. The aim of these other parts of the study was to examine where people got their information about the Israeli/Palestinian conflict, and to explore their understanding and perceptions of what was going on.

This multi-method approach also combined quantitative (content and survey) analysis with qualitative (focus group) analysis for further exploration of audience interpretation and understanding. While this did not provide a basis for asserting that the media content *causes* individuals to perceive these issues or events in certain ways, the research did show that a low level of understanding on the part of sample audience groups was paralleled by the limited amount of background information being provided by mainstream media content. Thus the content analysis supplemented and supported the audience study.

---

**BOX 26.1**

## A STUDY OF POLITICAL CONFLICT

### The research problem

In their study of media coverage of the Israeli/Palestinian conflict, Philo et al. (2003; see also Philo, 2001) combined content analysis with focus group and survey methods. They were interested not only in how the conflict was covered in the news, but also in how the news was 'read' and understood.

### Sampling

The content analysis centred on television news reports of the Intifada that began in September 2000, based on a clearly defined sample. This was drawn from major news programmes (lunchtime, early evening and late night bulletins) on two British television channels with the largest news audiences (BBC1 and ITN) over an 18-day period from the start of the Intifada. The sample yielded 89 reports, which were recorded and transcribed in full.

### Coding

Philo et al. then set up a number of themes to code the content of the news stories, including fighting/violence, origins of the crisis and peace negotiations. News content was then analysed in terms of how much coverage was given to these different themes. Here the researchers used the measurement of space as the basis for their content analysis.

### Finding from content analysis

They found that, of 3,536 lines of text in the reports, only 17 lines included any account of the history or causes of the conflict. This is in itself a striking finding, based on a fairly straightforward coding and counting exercise: less than 0.5 per cent of the mainstream news coverage in this sample contained information on the background to the conflict.

### Finding from audience survey

A survey of 300 young people, involving respondents who said their main source of information was television news, found that many of those questioned knew very little about the origins or character of the conflict. For example, 71 per cent of those surveyed did not know who were 'settlers' and who was occupying the 'occupied territories'; 11 per cent thought that the settlers were Palestinian and the occupation a Palestinian occupation, while only 9 per cent knew that it was an Israeli occupation.

In the second example, a different approach to content analysis is illustrated by Seale's (2002) work on news reports of people with cancer (see Box 26.2). It is important to note the degree of interpretive work being done in Seale's study in assigning content to different codes. How is one to assess, for example, the difference between showing a fighting spirit (a 'good' emotion) and anger (a 'bad' emotion)? These categories are not necessarily clear-cut, and their different meanings will in part come from the *context* in which they are used (see Chapter 3 for a discussion of contextual sensitivity). A quantitative content analysis in this way can be used together with a more qualitative analysis of textual meaning to formulate an interpretive content analysis (similar to the qualitative thematic analysis described in Chapter 21). By looking not only at the number of times different emotional states are mentioned, but also the ways in which they are talked about, Seale developed an interpretive analysis of how gender inflected the representation of cancer in the press. He argues that the texts tended to reproduce ideas of gender difference in stressing 'women's skills in the emotional labour of self-transformation', developing personal resources to deal with their situation, while for men 'cancer is more commonly portrayed as a test of pre-existing character' (2002: 107). The analysis of media content was therefore informed by theoretical perspectives on gender and selfhood, and by the interpretation of textual meanings.

BOX 26.2

# NEWS REPORTS OF PEOPLE WITH CANCER

## The research problem

To discover how news coverage differs in its treatment of men and women with cancer (Seale, 2002).

## Sampling

358 articles published in the English-language press during a one-week period.

## Counting and coding

In contrast to Philo – who pre-selected categories or themes to code his data – Seale began his content analysis by running a word concordance on the media texts (see Figure 26.1). The text is reorganised so that it reads not as a narrative but as a count of individual words. Such computer searching sorts the text in terms of its quantitative content without the researcher imposing any categories on the initial analysis.

Seale used this basic analysis to identify the different themes and uses of language that were evident in the texts. For example, Seale noted the frequency with which the language of emotions occurred in the news content. He went on to code the texts in terms of the presence of a range of items indicating different states of emotion. Such items as joking or being humorous, feeling supported by others, accepting one's illness or showing a fighting spirit were coded as positive or 'good' emotions. References to fear or anxiety, anger, isolation, misery or depression were coded as negative or 'bad' emotions.

## Finding

The content analysis suggested that the emotions of women with cancer were discussed in the news texts more frequently than those of men; this was particularly the case for 'bad' emotions and especially for feelings of fear and anxiety.

*Source*: Seale, 2002: 110

---

This raises critical questions about the objectivity of content analysis. As discussed earlier, the validity of this method tends to rest on claims about the neutrality of the researcher's role and the objectivity of the results. There are a number of points to be made here:

1 The 'objectivity' of content analysis can be questioned in that qualitative judgements often underlie the definition of coding categories.

2 Even where researchers use more 'neutral' keyword counts, content analysis will tend to reproduce a repertoire of dominant themes or narratives (e.g. in political and media discourse), and therefore can help to reinforce the power of these categories.

3 Content analysis can be seen to assume a shared world of meaning that is accessible in the content of texts. It is not at all clear, however, that statements about content tell us very much about either producers' intentions or consumers' interpretations.

It needs to be asked how far the categories used in content analysis reflect the intentions of the author, the understanding of the reader, or merely the perceptions of the analyst. One cannot simply read from intentions via content to audience readings: simply, we do not necessarily all read the news in the same way. In these respects, content analysis encounters the problems of meaning that run through all analyses of social texts.

## Keyword analysis

We have already illustrated the usefulness of word counts, concordances and (briefly) KWIC displays for content analysis. Building on these and other techniques, keyword analysis is an increasingly popular computer-assisted method for analysing texts. It exploits both the widespread availability of large volumes of electronic text as material for analysis, and the power of personal computers. Both of these things have become increasingly available in the past 10 or 20 years, and the method therefore offers opportunities to social and cultural researchers that are unprecedented. The method goes beyond content analysis and in some applications has supported discourse analysis (Baker, 2005, 2006; Adolphs, 2006), described more fully in Chapter 23 in this book. Before going into the detail of how to do keyword analysis, we will outline some general characteristics of the method.

## General characteristics

We are all used to the idea that special instruments are required by scientists. The astronomer needs a telescope, the microbiologist needs a microscope, the biomedical scientist needs a stethoscope. Instrumentation allows the scientist to see or hear things that the eye and ear cannot apprehend without such technological assistance. Sometimes, of course, imagination and theoretical knowledge are needed to visualise things that existing scientific instruments cannot make more directly available for human perception. Scientific theories lead us to believe that certain objects will have a particular appearance if we were able to make instruments powerful enough to visualise them. Other objects can be 'seen' more directly through telescopic or microscopic instruments. Still others can be seen by the naked eye.

If natural science operates like this, can the same be said for social research? Clearly, the status of social research as science is a popular topic for debate, with passionate positions often being held. Whatever the final conclusion of such debate (and we suspect it may never be resolved once and for all), it isn't hard to find at least some examples where special techniques, and sometimes instrumentation, allows the social researcher to perceive phenomena that are otherwise invisible. Conversation analysis (see Chapter 24) does this through the technology of the audio or video recording, supported by detailed transcription techniques. This allows things to be perceived which otherwise happen too fast to notice. Keyword analysis provides something more akin to an 'aerial view.'

The free availability of large volumes of text, which keyword analysis exploits, brings with it problems associated with the sheer volume of material a researcher may assemble. Keyword analysis can provide a quick way into key features of text collections, allowing a more fine-grained analysis to focus on those parts of texts most likely to yield rich insights. This can be illustrated with an example taken from our research into cancer narratives on the Internet.

## Providing an aerial view

In May 2005, Clive Seale (2006; Seale et al., 2006) downloaded the entire contents of two internet archives concerning cancer, containing messages written by people communicating with each other about their experiences of breast and prostate cancer. Cutting a long story short, the postings of 900 women with experience of breast cancer and 153 men with experience of prostate cancer were available for analysis. Together, these comprised 1,361,911 words about breast cancer and 267,459 words about prostate cancer, a total of over 1.6 million words spread over nearly 13,000 separate messages or postings.

Let us imagine what it would take to read and code this amount of material in a conventional qualitative thematic analysis of the sort described in Chapter 21. To help put this into proportion, at the time we did this study there was just one other study in the research literature that compared the online postings of people with breast and prostate cancer (Klemm et al., 1999). This study used eight codes to categorise postings including, for example, whether these involved giving or receiving information, providing encouragement and support, or described personal experience. Thus the codes were a priori ones, designed near the start of the analysis to reflect the concerns and expectations of the authors about what might be important. This study by Klemm et al., then, analysed 1,541 postings in total, with coding involving reading all of the material and deciding whether each code could be applied to each posting. The authors do not report how long this took them, but no doubt it took a considerable amount of time, especially as Klemm's project involved an interrater reliability exercise.

Keyword analysis, though, dispenses with much of this labour-intensive and somewhat uncertain work, using computing power to deliver an objective, replicable and inference-free account of the contents of texts within seconds. *Wordsmith Tools*, software developed to support this kind of work (see www.lexically.net/wordsmith), is most commonly used for keyword analysis. It takes some work to make sense of the computer output and turn it into something recognisable as 'analysis', but the rapidity with which meaningful results are generated by keyword procedures is one of the major attractions of the method.

Returning to our archive of about 1.6 million words, Tables 26.2 and 26.3 show output from *Wordsmith Tools* software that give the top keywords in breast and prostate cancer texts, when compared with each other, respectively. By **keywords** we mean the words that occur more commonly in one set of texts than in the other. The first row of numbers in Table 26.2 relates to the word 'PSA', which is a shorthand form for 'prostate

specific antigen' as is usually found in the two-word phrase 'PSA test'. This word occurs 1,164 times in the prostate cancer text, which is 0.42 per cent of all of the words in the prostate text. The 'RC.Freq' column indicates that the word 'PSA' occurred just once in the breast cancer text ('RC' stands for 'reference corpus'). This was a woman with breast cancer who wrote the following message:

> I have been really upset lately because a friend of mine was told he had a high PSA (which can indicate prostate cancer) way back in September and yet there have been so many delays in his care that he won't find out until Monday whether his cancer has spread or not. He is not yet in treatment!!!

But apart from this single mention, Table 26.2 shows that the PSA test is not a topic for women with breast cancer. As there are 1,361,911 words in the breast cancer text, the software does not calculate the percentage with a single case represents as there would be too many decimal places in a number very close to zero, so the 'RC. %' column is left blank. Finally, at the right-hand side there is a 'Keyness' statistic. This is a statistic based on a log-likelihood calculation which is a handy indicator of how 'key', statistically speaking, is a difference between the two texts. Table 26.3 shows that the top breast cancer keyword, then, is the word 'chemo', which occurs 3,578 times in the breast cancer text but just 16 times in the PSA text.

Comparative keyword lists like this are one of the most common forms of output in keyword analysis. Although only the top few on each side of the comparison are shown here, it is normal to consider the top 100, 200 or even 300 in most keyword analyses. In this analysis, which compared the text produced by people with cancer on the two types of web forum, the top 200 keywords from each side of the comparison were examined and grouped into categories, shown in Table 26.4.

**TABLE 26.2**  Top prostate cancer keywords: comparison of people with prostate and breast cancer in web forums

| Key word | Freq. | % | RC.Freq.** | RC. % | Keyness |
|---|---|---|---|---|---|
| *Positive* | | | | | |
| PSA* | 1,164 | 0.42 | 1 | | 4,141.74 |
| PROSTATE | 1,080 | 0.39 | 28 | | 3,606.20 |
| RP* | 339 | 0.12 | 2 | | 1,186.17 |
| PC* | 377 | 0.14 | 30 | | 1,142.48 |
| GLEASON* | 285 | 0.10 | 0 | | 1,017.19 |
| PCA* | 299 | 0.11 | 6 | | 1,010.35 |
| REGARDS | 393 | 0.14 | 111 | | 912.12 |
| RT* | 290 | 0.10 | 44 | | 790.90 |
| BRACHYTHERAPY | 151 | 0.05 | 0 | | 538.87 |
| MEN | 286 | 0.10 | 180 | 0.01 | 465.20 |
| SCORE | 154 | 0.06 | 31 | | 393.73 |
| CATHETER | 128 | 0.05 | 14 | | 370.49 |
| UROLOGIST | 89 | 0.03 | 0 | | 317.60 |
| BLADDER | 110 | 0.04 | 15 | | 306.32 |
| PROSTATECTOMY | 83 | 0.03 | 0 | | 296.18 |
| HORMONE | 214 | 0.08 | 193 | 0.01 | 271.52 |
| DAD | 177 | 0.06 | 125 | | 267.95 |

*Notes*:

* PSA = Prostate specific antigen, RP = Radical prostatectomy, PC and PCA = Prostate cancer, RT = Radiotherapy, Gleason = the Gleason test.

** RC.Freq = Reference corpus frequency (i.e. frequency in the breast cancer text, in this case).

**TABLE 26.3**  Top breast cancer keywords: comparison of people with prostate and breast cancer in web forums

| Key word | Freq. | % | RC.Freq.** | RC. % | Keyness |
|---|---|---|---|---|---|
| CHEMO* | 3578 | 0.26 | 16 | | 1169.09 |
| BREAST | 3653 | 0.27 | 40 | 0.01 | 1045.87 |
| I | 53671 | 3.91 | 8174 | 2.95 | 624.75 |
| BC* | 1702 | 0.12 | 2 | | 602.35 |
| MASTECTOMY | 1594 | 0.12 | 0 | | 586.45 |
| SHE | 3330 | 0.24 | 167 | 0.060 | 479.34 |
| HER | 2797 | 0.20 | 113 | 0.041 | 476.60 |
| TAMOXIFEN | 1270 | 0.09 | 0 | | 467.20 |
| LOVE | 1681 | 0.12 | 55 | 0.020 | 326.67 |
| IT | 20472 | 1.49 | 2988 | 1.08 | 300.87 |
| LUMP | 1008 | 0.07 | 9 | | 299.87 |
| DCIS* | 792 | 0.06 | 0 | | 291.31 |
| HAIR | 834 | 0.06 | 6 | | 256.91 |
| I'M | 3508 | 0.26 | 303 | 0.11 | 256.03 |
| WOMEN | 1060 | 0.08 | 22 | | 253.44 |
| MOLE | 662 | 0.048 | 0 | | 243.48 |
| RECONSTRUCTION | 648 | 0.05 | 0 | | 238.33 |
| ME | 8757 | 0.64 | 1127 | 0.41 | 228.16 |
| X* | 1085 | 0.08 | 34 | 0.01 | 215.86 |
| MUM | 706 | 0.05 | 7 | | 205.98 |
| THINK | 3800 | 0.28 | 386 | 0.14 | 199.65 |

*Notes*:

* Chemo = Chemotherapy, BC = Breast Cancer, DCIS = Ductal carcinoma in situ, X = mostly kiss.

** RC.Freq = Reference corpus frequency (i.e. frequency in the prostate cancer text, in this case).

**TABLE 26.4**  Coding scheme identifying meaningful categories of keywords

| Keyword category | Examples of keywords |
|---|---|
| Greetings | Regards, thanks, hello, welcome, [all the] best, regs (= regards) |
| Support | Support, love, care, XXX, hugs |
| Feelings | Feel, scared, coping, hate, bloody, cry, hoping, trying, worrying, nightmare, grateful, fun, upset, tough |
| Health care staff | Nurse, doctor, oncologist, urologist, consultant, specialist, Dr, Mr |
| Clothing and appearance | Nightie, bra, wear, clothes, wearing |
| Internet and web forum | www, website, forums, [message] board, scroll |
| Knowledge and communication | Question, information, chat, talk, finding, choice, decision, guessing, wondering |
| Research | Study, data, trial, funding, research |
| Lifestyle | Organic, chocolate, wine, golf, exercise, fitness, cranberry [juice] |
| Superlatives | Lovely, amazing, definitely, brilliant, huge, wonderful |

*Notes:*

[ ] square brackets are used to give commonly associated word showing a word's predominant meaning.

(=) rounded brackets with = sign used to explain a term's (predominant) meaning.

Category labels indicate words which appear to share a common characteristic, usually a semantic one (e.g. all words referring to people) but also sometimes a grammatical category (e.g. all personal pronouns, all superlative adjectives). This is the point at which keyword analysis is reminiscent of conventional qualitative thematic coding, in which the researcher allocates labels to segments of text according to whether that text has a particular characteristic relevant to the research question (as did Klemm et al., (1999) when they marked up text that involved the exchange of information, or the giving of support). But in comparative keyword analysis (CKA) like this, the 'codes' are used to label groups of words rather than segments of text.

The assignation of words to categories requires investigation of the predominant way in which they are being used in the text concerned. For example, perhaps the word 'support' refers to a device used to 'support' a part of the body, such as a 'support stocking' rather than a supportive relationship between people. Perhaps 'xxx' has nothing to do with kisses, but has been used to delete references to the names of individuals whose anonymity must be preserved. 'Best' could refer to a positive evaluation of a medical treatment rather

than forming part of a formulaic closing sequence. At this point a critic might feel that this is a method that fails to take account of the context in which a word occurs, something normally acquired through a close reading of the text being analysed.

Fortunately, it is not difficult in keyword analysis to discover the context in which words are being used in order to assess predominant meanings. To appreciate this, it is necessary to understand keyword-in-context (KWIC) displays, and the idea of collocation.

## Keywords-in-context (KWIC) and collocation

The English linguist John Firth is famous for his saying 'You shall know a word by the company it keeps' (1957: 11). Collocation is the term that has developed to refer to the company a word keeps, that is, the other words with which it is typically found. In statistical terms, collocates are therefore words that occur together with a higher frequency that would be expected by chance alone.

Concordance software allows us to explore the 'company that words keep'. KWIC displays are a standard type of output in most concordance software. They allow a specified number of words, or concordances, occurring on either side of a particular word to be displayed. Below are KWIC displays of the first 5 of 24 instances 'xxxxx' in the breast cancer web postings:

for kind replies, was sad to read of Jean's passing, she wrote so well lurve Anne xxxxx Where do you live? I'm going to Skye tomorrow for AGES, hurrah!

breast cancer, I hope we can as much as possible, enjoy Christmas. Annette. XXXXX I have been diagnosed with invasive ductal carcinoma, grade 3,

can. As the saying goes: Life is for living! Good health to you all Love Sarah xxxxx Hi It was the vodka that kept me going! I was on the tango trial

up, not that I think that is going to happen. Good health to you all. Love Sarah xxxxx

thanks to both of you. Seen the liver specialist on the 21st sep

fed in the Breast Unit. My operations have been cancelled. much love to you all xxxxx Hi Yes the boxes and ingredients do differ on the tamoxifen.

It is clear from this (and from the other 19 instances not shown) that 'xxxxx' is being exclusively used to indicate kisses at the end of messages, with new messages generally beginning straight after the xxxxx. The KWIC display thus allows for no other interpretation.

But in the case of 'x' where there are 1,085 instances in the breast cancer web postings things are more complicated. First, reading through this many KWIC displays would take quite a bit of time. To estimate the predominant meanings of 'x' we can therefore take a look at its most common collocates – words frequently located near 'x'. This is displayed in Table 26.5

**TABLE 26.5** Top 10 words adjacent to 'x'; left hand side (L1), right hand side (R1)

| Word | L1 | Centre | R1 |
|------|-----|--------|-----|
| Descending order of L1 | | | |
| BELINDA | 48 | 0 | 0 |
| JOY | 45 | 0 | 0 |
| JEAN | 40 | 0 | 0 |
| PEARLY | 38 | 0 | 3 |
| 4 | 32 | 0 | 1 |
| 6 | 32 | 0 | 10 |
| JANE | 28 | 0 | 2 |
| CLAIRE | 26 | 0 | 0 |
| MELANIE | 26 | 0 | 0 |
| WENDY | 23 | 0 | 2 |
| Descending order of R1 | | | |
| HI | 0 | 0 | 192 |
| I | 0 | 0 | 122 |
| RAY | 1 | 0 | 56 |
| RAYS | 0 | 0 | 47 |
| FEC | 5 | 0 | 26 |
| THANKS | 4 | 0 | 26 |
| X | 23 | 1,085 | 22 |
| HELLO | 0 | 0 | 20 |
| I'M | 0 | 0 | 19 |
| JUST | 1 | 0 | 14 |

The 'Descending order of L1' display shows that women's names were very commonly placed just before 'x', consistent with the interpretation of 'x' as a farewell kiss. But the occurrence of the numerals '4' and '6' on further inspection turned out to be instances where 'x' was being used as a multiplication sign. The 'Descending order of R1' display shows with the words 'Hi', 'I', 'thanks', 'hello', 'I'm' and 'just' that 'x' occurred at the end of a message, these being words with which next messages typically begin. The occurrence of 'x' as a collocate of itself is also consistent with the 'kiss' interpretation, as this occurs where 'x x x' is written rather than 'xxx'. But the occurrence of 'ray and 'rays' indicates the term 'X-ray' and the occurrence of 'FEC' indicates the use of 'x' as a multiplication sign, as in the phrase '4 x FEC' used by women to describe the frequency of their chemotherapy treatments.

Thus the sign 'x' is predominantly a kiss, but not exclusively so. As linguists would say, we have disambiguated the meaning of this term and discovered that it has various subsidiary meanings, as well as its predominant one as a kiss. Even when employed as a kiss, there may be variation and significance in the number of times it occurs in sequence: more kisses convey the meaning of more affection. A similar analysis of 'x' in the postings of men with prostate cancer reveals that only four of the 34 instances of 'x' in the men's text were used to denote a kiss, finally confirming the view that women are much more likely to end their messages with a kiss.

KWIC and collocation are, therefore, important ways in which words can be investigated in their contexts so that valid inferences are drawn about how they are being used. The raw collocation display shown in Table 26.5 is usually sufficient to provide disambiguation evidence, but more sophisticated ways of displaying collocation statistics are also sometimes used.

For example, extremely common words like 'the' or 'and' often appear as collocates of words, simply because they are common. A mutual information (MI) score is designed to adjust for this phenomenon, indicating which collocates co-occur more often than might be expected by chance alone. This is helpful where fairly uncommon words are involved, such as those used in medical jargon.

An MI score can also take account of words occurring within a specified distance of the keyword being analysed (not just the immediately adjacent ones). This can be very useful in establishing common connotations, or semantic prosodies for words. The semantic prosody of a given word is determined by the frequency it occurs in the context of other words that have positive or negative evaluations (Louw, 1993). A type of 'leakage' occurs whereby the positive or, more usually, negative senses of these other words 'overflows' onto the given word with which they co-occur. This is a way of communicating covert evaluations that are often not merely idiosyncratic, but highly constitutive of cultural stereotypes with ideological implications (Stubbs, 2001; Charteris-Black, 2004, 2005). Thus Baker (2006), in an investigation of a collection of representative usage of the English language, used a procedure similar to the MI score to show that the word 'bachelor' is disproportionately found within three words of 'eligible', 'confirmed', 'flat', 'days' and 'party', indicating fairly positive connotations of youth or freedom. But the word 'spinster' is collocated with 'elderly', 'widows', 'sisters' and 'three', this last being reminiscent of the three witches in Macbeth. This example demonstrates the use of collocation to expose and reveal aspects the persuasive and ideological character of texts and provides a link between keyword and discourse analysis.

## Comparative Keyword Analysis (CKA)

Equipped with a coding scheme to categorise keywords that characterise a text, known as comparative keyword analysis (CKA), it

**TABLE 26.6** Keywords by gender in web forums: selected categories*

**Research**

| Prostate | Breast |
| --- | --- |
| study, data, funding, median | NO KEYWORDS |

**The Internet**

| Prostate | Breast |
| --- | --- |
| www, justgiving, http, prostatecancerwatch-fulwaiting, .com, cancerwww, [message] board, htm, co, topic, .org, .asp | Forums, Bacup |

**Feelings**

| Prostate | Breast |
| --- | --- |
| Beat | feel, feeling, scared, hard, cope, coping, feels, brave, hate, felt, wanted, glad, nice, upset, tough, scary, bad, loved, lost, fear, losing, [better] safe [than sorry], luckily, cry, bloody, liked, fun, nightmare, living [with], try, deal [with], grateful, nasty, crying, bear, funny, blame, hoping, trying, worrying |

**People**

| Prostate | Breast |
| --- | --- |
| men, dad, wife, his, dads, he, man, patients, dad's | I, she, her, I'm, women, me, mum, they, my children, I've, them, people, ladies, women, family, mother, you, sister, friends, baby, husband, kids, daughter, I'm, myself, girls, friend, partner, someone, you've, person, yourself, married, I'd, hubby, you've, son, lady, boys, he's, mine, she's, everyone |

**Clothing and appearance**

| Prostate | Breast |
| --- | --- |
| NO KEYWORDS | wear, clothes, wearing |

| | Superlatives |
| --- | --- |

| Prostate | Breast |
| --- | --- |
| NO KEYWORDS | Lovely, amazing, definitely, brilliant, huge, wonderful |

Note:

* Keywords are words appearing proportionately more frequently in one text than the other. Each section lists keywords in descending order of 'keyness'; words with two or more predominant meanings are excluded.

becomes possible to compare texts to identify key areas of difference. In our study of breast and prostate cancer texts we showed that men with prostate cancer were more likely to use words that referred to research and the Internet, whereas women were more likely to use words referring to feelings, people, clothing and appearance, as well as use 'superlatives' (shown in Table 26.6).

Now these findings fit in with a very large literature on 'gender differences' in both linguistics (e.g. Coates, 2004) and health behaviour (e.g. Gray et al, 1996; Kiss and Meryn, 2001). In this sense, they are not surprising. Nor is it uncontroversial to focus on gender 'difference'. Gender is one of the easiest dimensions on which human beings can be divided and many social researchers have succumbed to the temptation to compare males and females. Some now feel that this tends to reinforce ideas about difference rather than recognise similarity and overlap (Cameron, 2007). It also tends to essentialise the idea of gender difference as a universal and context-free phenomenon, missing the fact that in many social contexts gender is 'performed' differently. As well as being influenced by upbringing and social expectations, individuals can often resist these influences and increasingly do so in relation to gendered identities in (e.g.) urban, secular and more wealthy environments. The desire to recognise this has become particularly acute for some gender researchers (Butler 1990; Speer, 2005; Kiesling, 2005).

This leads us to recognise two main methodological issues relevant for comparative keyword analysis (CKA) of the type we have described here: the need to discover more than what is already known or obvious, and the tendency of the method to emphasise difference at the expense of similarities.

## Choosing interesting comparison groups

We have said that the initial analysis of crude gender differences between men and women with these two types of cancer told us, broadly speaking, what we might have expected. This is not entirely fair, as this study provided what was probably the first empirical confirmation about women's higher usage of superlative adjectives, something long ago predicted by Lakoff (1975) (she called them 'empty adjectives' and gave 'divine' and 'charming' as examples from her own experience). But our experience with the method has shown that much of the art of producing unusual and unexpected findings with CKA lies in choosing interesting comparison groups. The success of this strategy can be illustrated by further work done on the web forum

postings (Seale, 2006) in which the postings of men on the breast cancer forum and women on the prostate cancer forum were examined.

Regarding women on the prostate cancer forum, it was striking that they constituted almost half the people posting to this forum and that they posted more words, overall, than did men. These were, on the whole, people who identified themselves as the wives, daughters, other relatives and friends of men with prostate cancer. There were some men on the breast cancer forum too, and for the most part these were also relatives and friends of people with the disease, although men constituted only a small proportion of the participants on the breast cancer forum. We decided to use CKA to investigate these people and, first of all, compared them with their 'own' gender on the other forum. Thus men male relatives and friends on the breast cancer forum were compared with men with prostate cancer on the prostate cancer forum; female relatives and friends on the prostate cancer forum were compared with women with breast cancer on the breast cancer forum.

The women relatives and friends on the prostate cancer forum showed very little difference from women elsewhere (apart from referring to prostate cancer a lot more, of course). But we noticed one interesting feature of their keywords, in that these contained the words 'welcome', 'thank you' and 'hello'. A KWIC display and associated collocational analysis revealed that these words were being used as part of the following phrases:

> 'welcome to this [board/forum/message board]'
>
> 'thank you for your [words/kind words/ message/replies]'
>
> 'hello [all/everyone/again/(name of person)]'

Thus these women were more frequently fulfilling a 'hostess' function, oiling the wheels of sociability so that interaction could proceed smoothly. In Fishman's (1997) terms, women turned out to be doing a lot of the 'interactional shitwork' on this forum, pacifying quarrels and making newcomers feel welcome. Particular women, usually people who had been participating in the groups over a long period of time, tended to contribute more of these phrases.

Examining the men on the breast cancer forum provided more of a surprise, as they demonstrated many points of difference with men elsewhere. These men, according to the CKA results, were more likely to refer to feelings, a wide range of other people including children, friends and family, to use words indicating an interest in interpersonal communication and to talk about 'love', 'care', 'support' and 'help'. Thus they appeared to be less like conventional 'men' and more like conventional 'women' in their choice of words and topics. Yet CKA showed that these men were also different in key respects from women relatives and friends on the prostate forum, using the following keywords more often:

> want, wanted, feel, feels, wants, scared, lost, strong, angry, upset, feelings, cope, emotional, hard, feeling

Faced with this keyword evidence it became relevant to investigate the stories of these men further through a conventional reading of their stories. They turned out to be people who were often facing or responding to loss of a partner, or in some case loss of a mother. They responded by becoming particularly communicative about their feelings (which often involved anger) and concerned about other people, these frequently being the children that they had to look after now that their partner was unable to do so. Interestingly, many of these men reflected on their 'new man' identity, and the final research report contained several quotes illustrating this, of which the following are two examples:

> I suppose it is a fact that some men find it hard to get it across as well as they should!

After all we went through it has left me with some sort of feeling of opening up more and just saying whatever I feel. This thing has some strange side effects on emotions that I don't think you can read or learn about other than experience them personally.

> I gave up work to look after [our children] and am now a full time carer. I found it very difficult to come to terms with my wife's original diagnosis (about 2 and a half years ago). I concentrated purely on being practical (very male!) and denied not only my wife's emotional needs but mine too. Matters came to a bit of head and I had to seek counselling which I think was the bravest thing I've ever done!!! ... I'm in touch with my feminine side which I think is important too!

Thus CKA enabled a very large quantity of text to be scanned for promising features that could be investigated further, identifying interesting and somewhat unusual phenomena located in small parts of the larger corpus that could then be read and analysed conventionally. Contrary to expectations that an emphasis on 'difference' would result in a stereotyped and 'essentialised' picture of gender, it in fact led to a discovery of people 'doing gender' in non-conventional ways in response to biographical circumstances and social context. Additionally, because the method is backed up by counts of keywords, the classic problem of anecdotalism that affects much qualitative research (only showing quotations that support the writer's argument at the expense of negative or deviant cases) is avoided. In this respect, CKA fulfils the promised benefits of counting in qualitative research perceived by Silverman (1993) and the advantages of mixed method research (see Chapter 27).

Figure 26.2 shows in diagrammatic form the different comparisons made in the course of this project.

| Men with PC on PC forum | ←→ | Women with BC on BC forum |
|---|---|---|
| Men relatives/friends on BC forum | ←→ | Men with PC on PC forum |
| Women relatives/friends on PC forum | ←→ | Women with BC on BC forum |
| Men relatives/friends on BC forum | ←→ | Women relatives/friends on PC forum |

FIGURE 26.2 Multiple comparisons made in CKA study of breast and prostate cancer (BC and PC) web forums

## Conclusion

This chapter introduced, first, content analysis. This is an approach to textual analysis that values objectivity and replicability, usually delivered by generating a demonstrably reliable coding scheme, although word counting can also contribute to this. Examples of studies building on the strengths of content analysis but also providing the opportunity for interpretive work on the part of the analyst, were shown. Keyword analysis was then described. This approach enables much larger amounts of material to be analysed than in conventional content or qualitative thematic analysis, while retaining a commitment to in-depth, interpretive analysis of key aspects of these larger collections of text. It exploits the ready availability of electronic text in archives or on the Internet, something which may be particularly attractive as an alternative to collecting texts by recording speech and transcribing it, which is very time consuming. It is a method that helps respond to criticisms that reports of qualitative analysis select anecdotes that are not representative of the texts analysed. The method also often show things that are hard to see in a conventional reading of text, and the analyst's pre-existing ideas are sometime disturbed or extended in surprising ways. Like any method, there are things to guard against, chief amongst which is the need to investigate the variable meanings of words in their original contexts before drawing conclusions.

## FURTHER READING

Neuendorf (2002) provides a comprehensive guide to content analysis, while Berger (2011) offers a concise introduction to the method in communication research. The book most likely to help social researchers using keyword analysis – particularly if they want to use it to pursue discourse analytic projects – is by Paul Baker (2006). Other books (e.g. Adolphs, 2006; McEnery et al., 2006) are more geared towards linguists, but nevertheless make useful reading for social researchers interested in health issues. Seale and Charteris-Black (2010) also provide an overview.

### Student Reader (Seale, 2004b): relevant readings

14  Robert Philip Weber: 'Content analysis'
45  Graham R. Gibbs: 'Searching for text'

## Journal articles using the methods described in this chapter

Baker, P., Gabrielatos, C., KhosraviNik, M., Krzyżanowski, M., McEnery, T. and Wodak, R. (2008) 'A useful methodological synergy? Combining critical discourse analysis and corpus linguistics to examine discourses of refugees and asylum seekers in the UK press', Discourse & Society, 19: 273–306.

Bridges, A.J., Wosnitzer, R., Scharrer, E., Sun, C. and Liberman, R. (2010) 'Aggression and sexual behavior in best-selling pornography videos: a content analysis update', Violence Against Women, 16: 1065–1085.

Seale, C. (2008) 'Mapping the field of medical sociology: a comparative analysis of journals', Sociology of Health & Illness, 30 (5): 677–695.

Seale, C. and Charteris-Black, J. (2008) 'The interaction of class and gender in illness narratives', Sociology, 42: 453–469.

## Web links

The Content Analysis Guidebook Online, by Kimberley A. Neuendorf: http://academic.csuohio.edu/kneuendorf/content

Resources related to content analysis and text analysis: www.content-analysis.de

Inter-coder reliability: http://astro.temple.edu/~lombard/reliability

Analysing website contents: www.boxesandarrows.com/view/content-analysis

*Wordsmith Tools*: www.lexically.net/wordsmith

The software for keyword analysis – Wmatrix: http://ucrel.lancs.ac.uk/wmatrix/ – web-based software that automatically categorises ('tags') words into semantic and grammatical categories before enabling wordlists and comparative keyword lists to be produced. Warning: can be useful to think with, but always check out the meanings of individual words thus categorised.

Concordance: www.concordancesoftware.co.uk – produces wordlists and KWIC displays.

## KEY CONCEPTS FOR REVIEW

**Advice:** Use these, along with the review questions in the next section, to test your knowledge of the contents of this chapter. Try to define each of the key concepts listed here; if you have understood this chapter you should be able to do this. Check your definitions against the definition in the glossary at the end of the book.

| | |
|---|---|
| Anecdotalism | Kappa statistic |
| Collocation | Keyword |
| Comparative keyword analysis (CKA) | Keyword-in-context (KWIC) display |
| Concordance | Latent content |
| Content analysis | Manifest content |
| Disambiguation of meaning | Marginals (of a table) |
| interpretive content analysis | Mutual information (MI) score |
| Inter-rater reliability | Semantic prosody |

## ■ Review questions

1 What are the strengths and weaknesses of (a) content analysis and (b) keyword analysis?
2 What is the kappa statistic used for?
3 How can word counts assist in doing a content analysis?
4 What are keywords and how are they identified?
5 What techniques allow the content and keyword analyst to investigate the meaning of words in their context?

## ■ Workshop and discussion exercises ■

1 This exercise involves doing a content analysis of dating advertisements. Your raw materials will be a page or two of such advertisements taken from a newspaper or other publication containing such advertisements. The focus of the analysis will be on documenting the way in which gender and sexual preference are constructed in the advertisements.

(a) *Defining categories:* Look through the advertisements and discuss them with others with whom you are doing this analysis. Develop a list of categories and keywords which describe the main attributes that people seek for in partners (e.g. words that relate to physical appearance, to character, to social status, to expectations of the desired relationship).

(b) *Assigning categories:* Once your list is complete, go through each advertisement indicating whether each category applies to each one. Where there are disagreements over the assignment of categories, discuss these. Keep a tally of how many advertisements are assigned to each category.

(c) *Analysis:* Look at the overall distribution of advertisements across the various categories and try to draw some conclusions about the attributes sought for in partners. Which attributes predominate? How do the attributes vary according to whether men, women, heterosexual or homosexual partners are sought for? Why do you think this is? Have your categories worked well? What different story would other categories have told? Do you think your findings can be generalised to other magazines or media that contain such personal advertisements?

(d) You can apply this process to a variety of other media and to topics other than personal ads. It is often illuminating to make statistical comparisons of different media, or to compare a medium in the past with the same genre today.

2 This is an exercise that requires you to use *Wordsmith Tools* software, available at www.lexically.net/wordsmith:

(a) Download some electronic text that you are interested in, and divide it into two groups (A and B) sharing common characteristics (e.g. text produced by men and women; articles appearing in 'serious' and 'popular' newspapers). Try to ensure that you have at least 50,000 words in each group.

(b) Use *Wordsmith Tools* to produce a word list of each of the two groups of text, and save them.

(c) Use the software to produce keyword lists, first of A compared with B, then of B compared with A. Inspect the top 100 keywords in these lists to see if you can group words into categories sharing similar characteristics. This will require investigation of some of the words whose predominant meaning in the relevant texts may be unclear, or ambiguous. KWIC displays will be useful here.

(d) For each significant group of words, divide the words into those that are 'key' in group A texts, and those that are 'key' in group B texts.

(e) What has this told you about the characteristics of these texts? Has it revealed anything you would not have known already, or by a brief reading of a few of the texts? What further investigations might you conduct to examine the context in which particular words are being used?

# 27

# COMBINING QUALITATIVE AND QUANTITATIVE METHODS

## Neil Spicer

---

### Chapter Contents

---

Social and cultural researchers often emphasise differences between qualitative and quantitative methods. Qualitative methods tend to be linked with interpretivism and postmodernism, while quantitative methods tend to be linked to positivism. However, focusing on the *differences* between these approaches reinforces their apparent incompatibility. In this chapter I want to uggest a number of ways in which the qualitative–quantitative divide might be destabilised so

as to open up the possibilities for combining qualitative and quantitative methods within a single research project. I will use the term combined methods research to mean research that combines *both* qualitative and quantitative methods.

I will start by looking at the differences between qualitative and quantitative research and suggest that these can be over-emphasised and that considerable overlap between the two approaches can be found in the practice of social research. In addition to concerns of methodology, pragmatic and political considerations legitimately influence whether qualitative or quantitative methods or both are used in a research project. Methodological assumptions therefore should not be seen as dictating your decision whether to use qualitative or quantitative social research methods, or to combine them.

In the second half of the chapter I will look more closely at four possible approaches to combined methods research in practice, although the list is by no means definitive. The four approaches that I will be looking at are:

- *The triangulation of methods:* Triangulation implies combining more than one method in looking at a particular research question to cross-check results for consistency and enhance confidence in the research findings.

- *The use of multiple methods:* In contrast to triangulation, multiple methods entails exploring different facets of a broad research question or addressing a research question from a number of different perspectives.

- *Combining methods to generalise:* Quantitative methods can usefully be used to establish generalizations from predominantly qualitative studies (see also Chapter 7).

- *The facilitative combination of methods:* Qualitative and quantitative methods can be used sequentially. By this I mean the use of qualitative methods to facilitate or inform primarily quantitative research and/or using qualitative methods to extend a quantitative component of a study.

## Arguments for combining qualitative and quantitative methods

### Revisiting the qualitative–quantitative divide

Researchers have traditionally adopted either quantitative or qualitative research methods in a single research project. Box 27.1 summarises a number of commonly used methods. There is, however, a growing trend in social research to use a combination of both quantitative and qualitative approaches; this chapter explores the reasons for doing this and offers a number of practical examples of how it might be done.

---

**BOX 27.1**

### KEY QUANTITATIVE AND QUALITATIVE METHODS

| Quantitative | Qualitative |
|---|---|
| Structured interview survey | Semi- or unstructured interviews |
| Statistical analysis of secondary quantitative data | Focus group discussions |
| Quantitative content analysis | Discourse analysis and semiotic analysis |
| Structured observation | Ethnographic methods including participant observation |

---

Writers have put forward arguments both for and against combined quantitative and qualitative methods research. A key question relates to the differences between the approaches to qualitative and quantitative research and whether these differences matter. Critics of combined methods research argue that the assumptions behind qualitative and quantitative methods are fundamentally different both in terms of what we are able to know and how we can know it (issues of epistemology) together with assumptions about the nature of the social world (issues of ontology). Box 27.2 summarises the main distinctions between the two approaches, and issues of epistemology and ontology are discussed in Chapter 2. It could be argued that the distinction makes the approaches incompatible:

> [this view holds that] … research methods are ineluctably rooted in epistemological and ontological commitments … the epistemological positions in which the two [qualitative and quantitative] methods are grounded constitute *irreconcilable views* about how social reality should be studied. (Bryman, 2001: 445; emphasis added)

But are the assumptions underlying qualitative and quantitative methods really mutually exclusive? Bryman (2001) suggests that the linkages between ontological and epistemological assumptions and research methods are rarely as deterministic, fixed and dualistic in practice as they are sometimes imagined to be. Hammersley notes in relation to the conventional qualitative–quantitative divide that: 'the distinction is … misleading in my view because it obscures the breadth of issues and arguments involved in the methodology of social research' (1992a: 39). He argues that qualitative and quantitative methods often share more common ground in practice than the conventionally held dichotomy would suggest. Recognising this destabilises the distinction between the two approaches and therefore their apparent incompatibility (Philip, 1998).

---

**BOX 27.2**

## SOME COMMONLY PROPOSED DIFFERENCES BETWEEN APPROACHES

| Quantitative | Qualitative |
| --- | --- |
| Positivist | Interpretivist/postmodernist |
| Artificial | Naturalistic |
| Deductive | Inductive |
| Objectivist | Constructionist/subjective |
| Structured | Exploratory |
| Theory testing | Theory generating |
| Controlling | Subjective |

---

One example is the assumption that qualitative research involves the study of people in naturally occurring social settings or situations (naturalism). This is often seen as contrasting with the approach taken in quantitative research (Box 27.2), which is associated with studying artificial settings established especially for the purpose of research in which extraneous variables are controlled for as they would be in a natural science experiment (see Chapter 8). This distinction, however, overly caricatures research in practice. Whilst ethnographic research, for example, may be closer to capturing 'naturally occurring' settings or situations than other methods, it is inevitable that there will be reactivity among research participants; in other words, they will alter their behaviour as a result of their awareness that they are participating in research. A researcher will therefore not be participating in and observing a naturally occurring setting.

Likewise, whilst unstructured interviews or focus groups tend to be more informal in style, giving them the feel of 'naturally occurring' conversations, they are not normal situations. As with ethnographic methods, reactivity will inevitably occur in that interview participants are conscious that they are taking part in interviews and adjust the way they talk accordingly. Furthermore, it is important to remember that *all* research, whether qualitative or quantitative, is part of the social world that it is studying (that definitely does not conform to laboratory standards), which, it could be argued, makes the distinction between 'artificial' and 'naturally occurring' irrelevant (Hammersley, 1992a).

A further example of the way in which the differences between the two approaches tend to be characterised is that quantitative research entails constructing hypotheses and subsequently testing them through empirical research (in other words, a deductive process). Qualitative research, on the other hand, is assumed to involve an inductive process in which theory is derived from (or 'grounded' in) empirical data. In practice, however, quantitative research, rather than a linear process of hypothesis constructing and testing, is often very much more exploratory than is generally appreciated; unexpected patterns, interconnections between concepts and ideas may emerge from the data during the analysis stage that were not conceived during the design stage of a research project. Conversely, qualitative methods such as unstructured interviews and ethnographic methods are inevitably based on pre-formulated theories, propositions or 'hunches' (whether they are made explicit or not). Hence, all research, whether qualitative or quantitative, tends to be an *iterative* process in practice whether this is acknowledged or not. As Hammersley puts it: 'all research involves both deduction and induction in the broad sense of those terms; in all research we move from ideas to data as well as from data to ideas' (1992a: 48).

In addition to epistemological and ontological concerns, more pragmatic factors such as the institutional context in which research is practiced, researchers' skills and the views of research funders influence which methods are chosen (Brannen, 1992). For example, the current preference of qualitative methods in many social science departments in academic institutions may not encourage the creative use of quantitative methods. Conversely, policy makers and programme implementers such as project managers often do not recognise the value of qualitative research since it is believed to be more subjective and less generalisable than quantitative research. Box 27.3 shows how some feminist researchers have sought to use combined methods to give their research a greater chance of influencing policies.

---

| BOX 27.3

## FEMINIST RESEARCHERS AND THE QUALITATIVE–QUANTITATIVE DIVIDE

The feminist approach to social research in particular emphasises the political motivations for conducting research using qualitative methods (see Chapter 3). A number of feminist scholars have been influential in re-establishing the profile of quantitative as well as combined methods research.

In a debate edited by Hodge (1995), 'Should women count?', which appeared in *Professional Geographer*, it was argued that quantitative methods can make gender inequalities more visible. They can therefore be used to inform and influence policy makers with a view to affecting social change and to challenge discrimination. A feminist geographer who took part in this debate summarised the advantages of using quantitative methods in combined methods research:

> [Q]uantitative methods can contribute by describing and analysing the broad contours of difference, by providing a basis for informed policy making and progressive political change, by identifying people and places for in-depth study, and by situating [qualitative] research in a broader context. (McLafferty, 1995: 436)

Whilst I have suggested that there are more similarities between qualitative and quantitative approaches than the divide usually implies, I do not want to lose sight of the differences. Indeed, these differences can be put to good use in combined methods research. Postmodernism in social research implies diversity, both in terms of embracing multiple truths and that there are, and should be, multiple standards by which the human and social world can be understood (this is known as epistemological relativism). Postmodernism offers the opportunity to adopt a *diversity* of methods in generating knowledge of the human and social world within a single research project. Philip (1998), for example, who argues in favour of combined methods research, says that:

> employing a range of methodological strategies means that the researcher does not necessarily privilege a particular way of looking at the social world … I would suggest that such [postmodernist] diversity encompasses methodological plurality as well as postmodernism encouraging different voices to be heard and facilitating the exploration of different truths. (1998: 261)

In a similar vein, Bryman suggests that the differences between qualitative and quantitative methods should be the rationale behind their combination within a single research project:

> [Q]uantitative and qualitative research are different, otherwise there would be no point in even discussing the possibility of combining them. They each have distinctive characteristics that make the possibility of combining them especially attractive. (1992: 75)

## Interpretivism and quantitative methods?

The claim that the use of quantitative methods in a positivistic framework has a monopoly in gaining knowledge of the human and social world contradicts the idea of epistemological relativism that I suggest should guide the adoption of combined qualitative and quantitative research. If quantitative methods are to be combined with qualitative methods in a single research project it is important to revisit a number of key critiques and assumptions about quantitative research, and to ask whether quantitative methods might be used with a more interpretive framework thereby making the approach more compatible with qualitative methods.

Key to doing this it is important to recognise the rhetorical devices that often reinforce the authority of quantitative research writing and conceal the influence of researchers' subjectivity. A good example of this is where quantitative research papers and reports rarely use the first person ('I' or 'we') in describing how a study was designed or conducted, thereby downplaying the inherent subjectivity of the researcher(s) and the fact that interpretation of data plays a big part in arriving at conclusions. This concealment therefore reproduces the myth that (quantitative) social research can be done objectively. Indeed, it is worth remembering that the use of rhetoric is not unique to quantitative research; its use in qualitative research writing, in particular ethnographic writing, is now widely recognised (Back, 2004).

In adopting quantitative methods within combined methods research, I strongly encourage you to adopt a critical sensitivity to the problems and limitations of quantitative analysis. Think carefully about what is actually being measured through the use of numbers and be aware of the problems of numerical data quality and the limitations of what can be concluded from these. In line with this interpretivist, non-positivist approach to using quantitative methods, research writing should incorporate the recognition that analytical categories (such as options in a structured interview questionnaire) are constructs. That is to say, they shape how we see the human and social world as well as reflect it. While some generalisations are often possible and different groups have different experiences that can be represented, although imperfectly, through the use of numbers by using numbers, you do not necessarily have to make the ontological assumption that universalistic laws govern the human and social world as would be the case in a positivistic framework. Revisiting claims about the status of quantitative research therefore means taking a more reflexive approach, conventionally associated with qualitative research. This involves the researcher making their subjective values and assumptions explicit when writing up research, and acknowledging the role that their values and assumptions had in the design of a study (including the categories within a structured questionnaire), and in the interpretation of data. Once again, feminist scholars have outlined an approach to this:

[T]o be objective in feminist terms means to make one's position *vis à vis* research *known* rather than invisible, and to limit one's conclusions rather than making grand claims about their universal applicability. The call to *limit* and locate one's truth claims is as relevant to researchers who use qualitative methods as to those who [use quantitative methods]. (Mattingly and Falconer-Al-Hindi, 1995: 428–429)

## Combined methods research in practice: the best of both worlds?

### The triangulation of methods

Triangulation of methods is an approach to combining two or more quantitative and/or qualitative methods in addressing a research question in order to cross-check results for consistency and to offset any bias of a single research method (see also Chapter 30). The aim is to increase confidence in the conclusions drawn from a study thereby enhancing its overall validity. This is relatively straightforward in cases where the findings of two methods agree; in cases where findings from two or more methods appear contradictory, a researcher would typically either re-examine existing data more carefully or carry out follow-up data collection to understand these contradictions. The concept of triangulating methods is not new. Campbell and Fiske (1959), for example, used more than one quantitative method in a psychological study. Triangulation is commonly applied to qualitative research methods, such as ethnographies consisting of participant observation and unstructured interviews, as well as to combined qualitative and quantitative methods such as structured interview surveys combined with in-depth interviews and focus-group discussions. Box 27.4 gives an example.

The triangulation of methods has, however, come under considerable criticism. The most fundamental criticism is that the approach is based on the 'naive realist' assumption that a single, fixed and coherent reality can be converged on through the use of more than one method (Blaikie, 1991). This approach assumes, for example, that the language used by respondents in research interviews directly reflects (if not perfectly) a reality outside that interview. It fails to recognise that different findings are likely to emerge from each method and that any individual is likely to interpret data and write research accounts in very different ways. Seale (1999) calls this the ethnomethodological critique of triangulation. A further criticism of triangulation is that even if research employing different methods generates consistent findings, it is by no means certain that a further method would not reveal different, contradictory findings. Seale (1999) refers to this as the 'philosophical critique' of triangulation.

## AN EXAMPLE OF TRIANGULATION OF METHODS

The triangulation of methods was used in a study that examined social scientists' attitudes to media coverage of their research (Deacon et al., 1998). A cross-section of quantitative and qualitative research methods were combined, including a structured mail questionnaire survey and semi-structured interviews. A number of inconsistencies between the quantitative and qualitative components of the study were, however, revealed in the analysis of the data. The quantitative method (the mail questionnaire) suggested that the social scientists were generally positive about how the media covered their work, whilst the more qualitative (semi-structured) interviews revealed their views to be far more negative. Instead of privileging the accuracy of one set of findings over another, the data were re-examined in order to understand the inconclusive results. The study concluded that whilst the social scientists were generally satisfied with the media reporting of their research, they were much more critical of specific instances in which they felt the media had represented their research in a negative light.

It is important, then, to recognise that qualitative and quantitative methods can rarely be used to address exactly the same research question: '[I]t is highly questionable whether quantitative and qualitative research are tapping the same things even when they are examining apparently similar issues' (Bryman, 1992: 64). It is wise, therefore, to use triangulation exercises either to closely re-examine the data or to open up new lines of inquiry, without imagining that triangulation will produce a definitive account of the 'truth'.

## Multiple methods

Triangulation can be distinguished from multiple methods research, which is informed by the postmodernist idea that there should be multiple standards for understanding the social world (epistemological relativism) and therefore diversity and contradictions should be incorporated within research accounts. This involves *not* (necessarily) aiming to converge on a single, definitive account: if different methods *do* produce what appear to be consistent results, these results should not be seen as unassailably coherent, fixed and definitive. Denzin (1989) rejects

the goal for the triangulation of methods, outlining instead what he calls strategies of multiple triangulation:

> [T]he researcher using different methods should not expect findings generated by different methods to fall into a coherent picture … [t]hey will not and they cannot, for *each method yields a different slice of reality*. What is critical is that different pictures be allowed to emerge … The goal of multiple triangulation is a fully grounded interpretive research approach. Objective reality will never be captured. In-depth understanding, not validity, is sought in any interpretive study. (1989: 246; emphasis added)

In practice, this approach recognises that each qualitative or quantitative method has its own strengths and weaknesses and hence can appropriately address different kinds of research question that constitute different facets of an overall research problem. This allows for a broader range of issues to be addressed than might otherwise be possible in using a single method.

One way of applying multiple methods is to use qualitative approaches to examine small-scale or micro-level phenomena that underlie the large-scale or macro-level regularities that quantitative methods may reveal. Qualitative methods (such as ethnographic methods or unstructured interviews) can be helpful in capturing complexity and processes as well as diversity and contradiction in the human and social world within local settings. Quantitative analysis of official statistics, for example, as often used for secondary analysis (see Chapter 17), can be used to highlight aspects of people's lives that are measurable (such as spatial, temporal and socio-economic inequalities in income or health, perhaps at neighbourhood, regional, national or international levels). McLafferty highlights the advantages of combining methods in this way by suggesting: 'By coupling the power of the general with the insight of the particular, such research illuminates people's lives and the larger contexts in which they are embedded' (1995: 440). Qualitative methods are often then effective in interpreting patterns emerging from quantitative analysis.

Box 27.5 shows an example of multiple methods research conducted in Jordan in which both quantitative and qualitative interviews were carried out to look at different but related research questions. In this example, qualitative interviews helped to explain the broader patterns revealed in the quantitative interview survey. Box 27.6 presents a further example of a study that assessed the effects of global health initiatives for HIV/AIDS in the Central Asian country of Kyrgyzstan to explore different aspects of a number of inter-related themes.

---

**BOX 27.5**

## AN EXAMPLE OF MULTIPLE METHODS RESEARCH 1

A multiple methods approach involving both quantitative and qualitative methods was used in my own research to examine the ways in which pastoral mobility excluded families from health service provision in rural Jordan (Spicer, 1998, 1999). I carried out a structured questionnaire-interview survey to compare patterns of health service and 'traditional' Arabic medicine use between semi-nomadic and settled groups. This approach usefully allowed the broad differences in health service use and experiences between groups of families to be explored. However, the method provided limited explanation of the patterns it revealed. A number of semi-structured and unstructured interviews were used on a complementary basis in order to draw out far more experiential accounts of health, illness and health care-seeking activities and related family biographies to changing 'lay' discourses of health and illness. The qualitative methods therefore provided a deeper, more nuanced understanding of the broader differences and similarities that the quantitative aspect of the study revealed.

---

**BOX 27.6**

## AN EXAMPLE OF MULTIPLE METHODS RESEARCH 2

A study exploring the effects of global health initiatives for HIV/AIDS including the Global Fund to Fight AIDS, Tuberculosis and Malaria in the Central Asian country of Kyrgyzstan employed a range of quantitative methods (structured interview surveys with clients using HIV/AIDS services, service providers and service managers, and an analysis of quantitative secondary data) and qualitative methods (in-depth semi-structured interviews with policy makers, development agencies and HIV/AIDS service clients) to explore a number of inter-related themes (Murzalieva et al. 2008, 2009). One of these themes was human resources. Drawing on data derived from a structured survey of service providers and service managers, the study examined the effects of the scale up in funding for HIV/AIDS programmes on the numbers of health and social workers staffing HIV/AIDS services, showing that increases had been most significant in the capital, Bishkek. Qualitative interviews with service managers and national level actors explored the multiple connected health systems drivers of service providers' performance including poor salary incentives, unfair bonus scales in governmental organisations and weak legal protection among medical staff.

The study was influential in informing the Kyrgyzstan proposal for a Global Fund HIV/AIDS programme; policy makers and development partners indicated that they valued the broad patterns revealed in the quantitative elements of the work which provided a clear overview of the scale of the effects of the HIV/AIDS control programme. The qualitative interviews with service managers and national level actors offered explanatory insight on different aspects of the programme, and the in-depth semi-structured interviews with clients were seen as valuable in providing a rich narrative understanding of individuals' lived worlds and their experiences of accessing HIV/AIDS services and associated experiences of stigma and discrimination – which were hitherto poorly understood by policy makers and development agencies.

Multiple method research also involves bringing different perspectives to bear on an overall research problem. Bryman (2001), for example, shows that quantitative and qualitative methods can be used to provide a balance between exploring researchers' and participants' perspectives respectively. Thus quantitative methods (such as structured questionnaires/interviews) can be usefully drawn on in exploring the specific concerns of the researcher. Qualitative methods, such as unstructured interviews and participant observation that tend to be open-ended, are more effective in grounding research in participants' perspectives without filtering these views through researchers' pre-established constructs and categories.

## Combining research methods to generalise

For research to influence policy makers or public service providers who often need to make judgments on the spending of resources, the level of generality or relative significance of findings usually needs to be presented as part of a research study. Hence, quantitative research is commonly favoured over qualitative studies, the latter of which generally draw on data from far smaller study populations than the former. In practice, the *quasi-quantification* of qualitative research reports is quite common: that is, an indication of the relative significance of phenomena being discussed by using phrases such as 'the majority' and 'very few' is common, but lacks precision. One way to tackle this problem is to introduce what some researchers call the limited quantification of qualitative studies by making the frequencies of phenomena identified explicit in research accounts, even if these frequencies are relatively low. This adds a degree of precision to a reader's appreciation of the generality of phenomena being discussed in a research account (Box 27.7). However, care should be taken in assuming that the precision that comes with using numbers *necessarily* equates to greater accuracy – something that critics of quantitative methods have always maintained. In particular, you should take care in using numbers selectively in research accounts to support a particular line of argument without accounting for contradictions and inconsistencies. Seale calls this selective presentation of numbers 'counting to mislead', and suggests that 'counting on its own is not enough; it must be supported by a genuinely self-critical, fallibilistic mindset, involving a commitment to examine negative instances' (1999: 131). As I said earlier in this chapter, it is particularly important that you make explicit in combined research methods writing the limitations of what numbers appear to show.

---

**BOX 27.7**

## LIMITED QUANTIFICATION IN A QUALITATIVE REPORT

Presenting simple counts of events can help readers gain a sense of how representative and widespread particular instances are. This was shown in a study of 163 elderly people living alone in their last year of life, where relatives and others were interviewed after the deaths of the people concerned. Here is an extract from the report of this study:

> It was very common for the people living on their own to be described either as not seeking help for problems that they had (65 instances covering 48 people), or refusing help when offered (144 instances in 83 people). Accounts of this often stressed that this reflected on the character of the person involved, although other associations were also made. In particular, 33 speakers gave 44 instances where they stressed the independence which this indicated: '[She] never really talked about her problems, was very independent …'; '[She] was just one of those independent people who would struggle on. She wouldn't ask on her own'; 'She used to shout at me because I was doing things for her. She didn't like to be helped. She was very independent.' Being 'self sufficient', 'would not be beaten', and being said to 'hate to give in' were associated with resisting help. (Seale, 1996: 84)

---

Quantitative methods can also be used in combination with qualitative methods to assess whether a specific case or small number of cases studied in-depth using qualitative methods are more generally typical at a wider 'population' level (in other words to assess the external validity of a qualitative study; see Chapter 30). An in-depth discourse or semiotic analysis of selected documents or visual images, for example, could be combined with a quantitative content analysis of a wider cross-section of documents or images in order to judge the extent to which the cases examined in depth are representative (e.g. Bell, 2002). Similarly, in-depth interviews could be combined with a large-scale questionnaire survey, with the aim of the latter being to assess the scale of the phenomena revealed in the former. An example of this approach is shown in Box 27.8, where quantitative methods are used to generalise from a qualitative component of a study.

---

**BOX 27.8**

## AN EXAMPLE OF USE OF QUANTITATIVE METHODS TO GENERALISE

A study of a community-based initiative in London that piloted a number of innovative models of community participation was conducted by Hewitt et al. (2003). Unstructured focus group interviews and observational work with young people provided insights into their experiences of a number of selected projects, each of which represented one of the models of community participation from a larger number

---

of projects supported by the community-based initiative. This was complemented with a structured telephone questionnaire survey with project workers from all sampled projects in order to gain an appreciation of their perspectives on the effectiveness of the different models of participation as well as to highlight the relative frequency of each of the models. This provided an appreciation of the scale of generality of the issues examined qualitatively. Importantly, care was taken to ensure that the qualitative cases were representative of the categories used in the quantitative part of the study. This provided a convincing basis for the generalisations made within a well-defined population.

## The facilitative combination of research methods

Qualitative and quantitative methods can also be combined *sequentially*, and is known as facilitative combination of research methods. Qualitative methods can be used as the first stage of a wider researcher project in order to facilitate, inform or prepare the ground for primarily quantitative research. For example:

- Qualitative methods can provide contextual awareness of research settings and research participants and inform the development of analytical categories for quantitative surveys. In this way, analytical categories can be more closely grounded in the perspectives of research participants.

- Qualitative methods can be drawn on to help generate research questions and hypotheses used in quantitative work. The first example in Box 27.9 shows qualitative methods being used to inform quantitative research in this way.

- Qualitative methods can inform the design of structured questionnaire or interview surveys by giving a researcher greater sensitivity in framing specific interview questions using appropriate language to minimise the possibility of misunderstanding and to avoid sensitive or offensive questions.

Quantitative methods can be used to facilitate qualitative research. For example:

- Quantitative methods can be used in revealing broader patterns that are subsequently investigated through the use of in-depth qualitative methods in order to understand and explain these patterns.

- Quantitative methods can be used to establish or refine research questions that could be subsequently addressed through the use of in-depth qualitative methods.

- Quantitative surveys and the analysis of official statistics can be used to identify groups or geographical settings for qualitative research or to provide profiles of groups or settings for selecting comparative cases for in-depth study using qualitative methods. The second example in Box 27.9 shows this.

---

**BOX 27.9**

## TWO EXAMPLES OF THE FACILITATIVE COMBINATION OF METHODS

### Qualitative methods facilitate a quantitative study

Qualitative methods were used by Dressler (1991) to inform a quantitative study that looked at the complex relationships between factors such as economic conditions and social support resources that affected depression among African Americans in a community in the southern United States. Exploratory

*(Continued)*

unstructured interviews were used in the first instance to provide insights into the perceptions of community members. These were explored further in a structured interview survey that formed the second stage of the research. The fact that the initial interviews were open-ended meant that many of the categories measured in the quantitative study were derived from the accounts of interview respondents of the qualitative interviews.

## Quantitative methods facilitate a qualitative study

McLafferty (1995) carried out research into patterns and causes of low birth weights in a number of neighbourhoods of New York City in which the analysis of quantitative data informed the use of qualitative methods. As a first stage of the research she looked at the spatial unevenness in low birth weights and changes in these patterns over time that were apparent through analysis of secondary statistical data sources. She was therefore able to pinpoint a number of neighbourhoods in which low birth weights had risen, which were therefore appropriate locations for detailed empirical analysis involving qualitative methods in order to identify factors that had caused these localised changes.

## Conclusion

Ontological and epistemological differences lie at the heart of the argument not to combine quantitative and qualitative research methods in a single study. However, as this chapter has argued, this need not be the case: these methodological differences are fluid and frequently remain unspoken or explicit in conducting and writing quantitative and qualitative research. Thinking through and making explicit your methodological assumptions is an essential part of writing combined methods research, since failing to do so leaves you open to criticism from those who point to what they see as irreconcilable differences between quantitative and qualitative approaches to conducting research.

In addition to ontological and epistemological issues, your *research questions* should pragmatically guide your choice of qualitative and quantitative research methods. Philip summarises this approach:

Researchers should think beyond the myopic quantitative–qualitative divide when it comes to designing a suitable methodology ... I am not trying to say that all research should combine methods, but urge that the *research topic itself* should play a prominent role in leading the researcher to design a methodology ... as opposed to a researcher automatically using certain methodologies because their epistemological positioning stresses a particular approach to collecting information and data analysis. (1998: 273–274; emphasis added)

You should not assume that combined methods are inherently better than research based on a single method in all circumstances, but combine qualitative and quantitative methods where this is appropriate to your research questions. Finally, I strongly encourage you to develop ways of combining methods that have not been discussed in this chapter or elsewhere: the ability to innovate lies at the heart of creative research practice, and is a central part of combined methods research.

Seale (1999) is very useful further reading on a number of issues that I have touched on in this chapter. He provides a detailed critique of triangulation, explores a number of approaches to generalising from qualitative research as well as using numbers to improve the quality of qualitative research. He also discusses reflexivity in research writing. Hammersley (1992a) details a number of ways in which conventionally held assumptions about the differences between qualitative and quantitative methods can be destabilised. Bryman (2001) provides a comprehensive classification of approaches to combining qualitative and quantitative methods. See also a special issue of *Professional Geographer* (47 (4): 1995) devoted to this subject. Other contributions to these debates which include a wealth of examples are Creswell and Clark (2011), Teddlie and Tashakkori (2008) and Bergman (2008).

## Student Reader (Seale, 2004b): relevant readings

76  John K. Smith and Lous Heshusius: 'Closing down the conversation: the end of the qualitative–quantitative debate among educational inquirers'

77  Alan Bryman: 'Quantitative and qualitative research: further reflections on their integration'

78  Ann Oakley: 'Who's afraid of the randomised controlled trial? Some dilemmas of the scientific method and "good" research practice'

79  Maureen Cain and Janet Finch: 'Towards a rehabilitation of data'

See also Chapter 21, 'Working qualitatively and quantitatively' by Julia Brannen in Seale et al. (2004).

## Journal articles using or discussing the methods described in this chapter

Bryman, A. (2007) 'Barriers to integrating quantitative and qualitative research', Journal of Mixed Methods Research, 1: 8–22.

Hall, J.N. and Ryan, K.E. (2011) 'Educational accountability: a qualitatively driven mixed-methods approach', Qualitative Inquiry, 17: 105–115.

Johnson, R.B., Onwuegbuzie, A.J. and Turner, L.A. (2007) 'Toward a definition of mixed methods research', Journal of Mixed Methods Research, 1: 112–133.

## Web links

Methods@manchester – mixed methods: www.methods.manchester.ac.uk/methods/mixed-methods.shtml

Research design and mixed-method approach – a hands-on experience: www.socialresearchmethods.net/tutorial/Sydenstricker/bolsa.html

*Forum: Qualitative Social Research* – a special issue on 'Qualitative and quantitative research: conjunctions and divergences': www.qualitative-research.net/fqs/fqs-e/inhalt1–01-e.htm

*Journal of Mixed Methods Research*: http://mmr.sagepub.com

British Educational Research Association – mixed methods research: www.bera.ac.uk/mixed-methods-research

**Review questions**

1 Summarise the arguments for and against combining methods.
2 What differences are there between quantitative and qualitative methods?
3 What have feminist researchers contributed to the debate about mixed methods?
4 What is the difference between the triangulation of methods and the use of multiple methods?
5 How can methods be combined in order to generalise?
6 What is meant by the facilitative combination of methods?

## Workshop and discussion exercises

1 Identify and discuss both the methodological *differences* and *similarities* between qualitative and quantitative approaches to social research. Is quantitative research *always* positivistic? In what ways might qualitative research adopt the assumptions of positivism?

2 How would you justify conducting a piece of research using combined methods to an audience of policy making or practitioners?

3 Design a research project in which qualitative and quantitative methods are combined in an advantageous way. Discuss whether you would use *triangulation* or the *multiple methods* approach in combining the methods and the implications this has for the knowledge you generate from the research.

4 Which of the research topics listed in Box 27.10 would be appropriately investigated using:

(a) Quantitative methods only?
(b) Qualitative methods only?
(c) Combined methods?

BOX 27.10

### SOME RESEARCH TOPICS

- The causes and consequences of homelessness for single people.

- The effectiveness of community service orders as a means of rehabilitating offenders.

- The way of life of travellers.

- Assessment of the way the police deal with sexual crime.
- How policy is made in a political party.
- How EEG (electro-encephalogram) readings correlate with emotional states.
- Children's reading preferences.
- Students and how they manage their academic work.
- Quality of terminal care of cancer patients.
- Sexual activity in public settings (e.g. public toilets)
- The experience of trainee nurses.
- School bullying.
- Racism in football.
- Victims of domestic violence.
- Sex discrimination at work.
- Right-wing political groups.
- New-age religion.
- The experience of boys in a ballet school.
- Analysis of archived qualitative interviews with elderly people recollecting wartime experiences.
- Analysis of media representations of ideal female body shape.
- Conversation analysis of calls to a computer help line.
- Ethnographic study of an on-line support group for parents of children with disfiguring conditions.
- Comparative analysis of discourse on immigration in US presidential and British prime ministerial speeches.

# PART THREE

## WRITING, PRESENTING, REFLECTING

# 28

# WRITING A RESEARCH REPORT

## Carol Rivas

<table>
<tr><td colspan="2" align="center">**Chapter Contents**</td></tr>
</table>

This chapter is designed to guide you in writing up your research. The recommendations apply to writing at undergraduate and postgraduate degree level, but are also relevant to those seeking to publish their work more formally. The main aim of the chapter is to aid you in writing up research effectively. The same principles apply to formal and informal writing, and to reports of qualitative or quantitative social research studies using primary or secondary sources of data as well as purely library-based or 'theoretical' write-ups (see also Chapter 10).

Writing is important to research for many reasons. It is the product of your study and as such may be required by your examiners if you are a student submitting work for assessment, or by your funders or employers if you are a research worker. It is a way of informing others about your findings (although not the only way – you should also consider alternatives such as workshops and oral presentations). It is a demonstration of your research abilities to examiners, employers, or the scientific community at large.

Writing is also part of the research process. By working and reworking a report, you may realise that your argument has holes in it and that you need to go back and re-analyse some of your data, or gather more. Trying a variety of arrangements of your data or your arguments may help you to see things in a different light and give you that 'eureka' moment. In the words of the sociologist Laurel Richardson:

Although we usually think about writing as a mode of 'telling' about the social world, writing is not just a mapping-up activity at the end of the research project. Writing is also a way of 'knowing' – a method of discovery and analysis. By writing in different ways, we discover new aspects of our topic, and our relationship to it. Form and content are inseparable. (2000: 923)

This chapter begins by examining writing as a tool used to impart a message or to aid analysis. This is followed by: tips on writing up the different sections of a research report; citing other people's work; and how to avoid plagiarising. Although Richardson refers specifically to sociological writings based on empirical fieldwork in the excerpt above, what she says – and what is said throughout this chapter unless I flag it up as otherwise – applies equally to qualitative and quantitative, empirical and theoretical works.

## Writing as a tool

Writing has been described by the sociologist Carol Smart as 'a creative act which is frankly terrifying' (2010: 4). Part of this terror, Smart explains, often comes from having to reduce masses of data to something manageable, interesting and informative. But part, she says, comes from the onus on the writer to reliably and authentically represent their subjects (for which also read 'topic' or 'field' or 'experiments', although Smart is writing about qualitative studies).

In any kind of research reporting, the researcher must appropriately select one from among a number of possible stories, accurately re-present the evidence (which may consist of, for example, numbers, texts or images if an empirical report or the work of others if library-based), and include sufficient contextual information to enable an in-depth understanding of what is being described and the limitations and implications of the descriptions. Although this is true across disciplines, it is within the social sciences that writers seem most troubled about the perceived and real authenticity of their representations. For example, the sociologist Clifford Geertz was concerned about authors who claimed to have 'actually penetrated other worlds' (1988: 4–5) and about the way words have the power to distort, stating that it is appropriate to possess

> a worry about the legitimacy of speaking for others, a worry about the distorting effects of Western assumptions on the perception of others, and a worry about the ambiguous involvements of language and authority in the depiction of others. (1995: 128–129)

Over the last three decades, these worries have resulted in considerable discussion about the social, linguistic and rhetorical structures of social scientific writing and how these affect the reliability and validity of what we write. Do we tell the truth or manipulate it, consciously or not? Is there a truth or truths? Are we qualified to represent our research participants? Can we control the way people interpret what we write? Where each individual stands in these debates depends on their ontological and epistemological perspectives (see Chapter 2). Here I consider how you can attempt to address some of the issues in your writing.

## Reflexivity

One way of dealing with worries about authenticity is to reflect on them and then voice your concerns so that others can read about them and also reflect on them. This is known as reflexive writing. Commonly within the social sciences it is used to explore the biases you bring to your research, such as relevant professional and personal experiences, preferences and knowledge. Such biases may affect the way you interpret your data, and also the content of the data you gather. For example, it is often claimed that researchers should be matched according to such variables as race, gender, age and socioeconomic status with the people from whom they are directly gathering observational or interview or survey data. However, there are also arguments against this. Reflexive reporting of such matches and mismatches helps the researcher to consider the (co-)constructed nature of their findings. In this way, reflections on bias and the authentic voice (i.e. how much you can speak on behalf of others) helps you to enrich your analysis and your readers to judge the credibility and validity of your interpretations and conclusions.

Reflections on bias are common to and good practice in all science reporting. However, within sociology, reflexivity has also been taken up as a new form of writing. Sometimes whole papers have been devoted to reflection on how a study has been done, without any actual reporting of the results. Or large sections of reports have been devoted to reflexivity on the basis that, if we accept that knowledge is socially and culturally produced and historically contingent, reflection on the current and past social and cultural influences on the knowledge that we are reproducing in our report should take centre stage.

This form of reflexive writing may be helpful in developing more robust methods or informing others how to do novel research, but it may become narcissistic and self-indulgent waffle, or as the sociologist and philosopher Pierre Bourdieu called it, 'pretext for text' (2003: 282). I recommend limiting reflexive writing unless it is the purpose of your report as in the following example, in which even then, the writer notes, it should be undertaken with care:

> This is an article about the fact that I wrote two versions of the sentence that came just before this one, and about the fact that, as I type this sentence, I don't really know where my argument will lead. Not yet. Like me, you may be worried. How will this article move from false start to completed product? Even more anxiety producing: How will I write an article about writing an article—an article that simultaneously serves up a finished product and the process that leads to it—*without collapsing under the weight of self-reference?* Shouldn't the finished article, if it is done right, hide that process from view? And most urgently, *why* am I writing this article? (Colyar, 2009: 2; emphasis added)

## Writing and the art of rhetoric

Rhetoric in the way I refer to it in this chapter means the art of persuasion or effective communication. It has been argued variously that we cannot control what effect our writing has on the reader (Barthes, 1977b: 148) or that we can tightly manipulate the reader through particular devices (Gowers, 1973), but reality probably lies somewhere between. Researchers use writing conventions – structures and rhetorical devices that are associated with research authority and trustworthiness – to convince readers about the factual correctness or facticity of their written argument. You can see an example of this in Box 28.1, which is from a *British Medical Journal* article written in the terse style commonly used in reports of quantitative analyses, with economy of word use and no reflexive passages.

---

**BOX 28.1**

### INTRODUCTION TO A SCIENTIFIC JOURNAL ARTICLE

While little demonstrable difference exists between antidepressants in terms of efficacy,[1] toxicity in overdose varies widely.[2] We compared the fatal toxicities of antidepressants currently available in Britain individually and by group during 1987–92, during which time the selective serotonin reuptake inhibitors were introduced. (Henry et al., 1995)

---

The type of writing shown in Box 28.1 can be quickly skimmed and key points extracted by people who do not have the time or inclination to read more literary styles. Tutors, examiners, editors and funders might require it. But there is sometimes an argument for writing in a more evocative and descriptive style. Roald Hoffmann, a Nobel prize-winning chemist, was also a published poet. He said that no research article need be written in such an 'ossified stylistic mode', and that we should aim to create 'an emotional or aesthetic response' in our readers, as well imparting scientific facts. He argued that since no-one can fully reproduce real events in their writings, it was appropriate to create the sensations of reality (1988: 1–2). Carol Smart (2010) agrees, saying that when we evoke in our reader the sentiments and feelings that help them imagine, we aid understanding. More literary forms of writing may make research more accessible.

## Metaphor and imagery as literary styles

Writers commonly deploy metaphor and imagery in less 'ossified' scientific writing. Richard Dawkins is a successful exponent, beginning with his book *The Selfish Gene* (1976) and continuing with *River out of Eden* where he makes extensive use of the metaphor of a river of life:

> The river of my title is a river of DNA, and it flows through time, not space. It is a river of information, not a river of bones and tissues; a river of abstract instructions for building bodies, not a river of solid bodies themselves. (1996: x)

Significantly, as well as being an evolutionary biologist and popular science author, Dawkins was formerly Professor for Public Understanding of Science at Oxford University. Dawkins uses metaphor as a way of explaining something technical to lay people, drawing on common understandings of usual everyday things to make accessible the less known. But metaphors are subjective and so easy to criticise. They often provide limited insights and have the potential to block both analyst and reader from a complete understanding. These are good reasons for avoiding them in formal essays and reports. Tutors are more likely to criticise than be impressed by them.

## Simply accessible

Something in between the 'ossified' and the literary can be effective in getting your message across. Pick up patient leaflets next time you visit your doctor, or political party leaflets, or information booklets for gym members, anything designed for lay consumption, and examine the writing style. Good examples will be easy to read, but also informative. They will probably use devices to draw the reader in, such as a question-and-answer format in which the person asking the question is 'me' (e.g. 'How many times a day should I take the medicine?').

Looking at these may help you to write your report better even if you do not follow their style too closely. Use them also as direct models of the style you should adopt for information sheets and consent forms for a research study (see Chapter 5), and to produce newsletter publications and articles for local groups – for example, those where you did your research. You might also submit an article to a practitioner publication such as the *Nursing Times* or the *Times Education Supplement*, aimed at professionals unlikely to subscribe to academic or specialist journals (see Box 28.2). You could even use a similar style to put up information about your study on your college website.

---

**BOX 28.2**

### AN EXCERPT FROM A *NURSING TIMES* ARTICLE

A hard-hitting video on YouTube last month appeared to show a young girl giving birth on a school playing field. For many, it made very uncomfortable viewing. But, although the video looked like it had been filmed on a pupil's mobile phone, it had been created by a Leicester PCT to raise awareness of the issue of teenage pregnancy in the area. (Lomas, 2009)

If this article had been written for an academic publication or for policy makers and funders within the NHS, it would have probably begun with an 'ossified' paragraph on the prevalence of teenage pregnancy and the economic cost to society. But in this practitioner journal the aims are to grab the reader's interest with a shockingly evocative statement, to appeal to their everyday practice, and to use simple language that they can take in and enjoy after a busy day at work.

## Choosing which style to adopt

You should find examples of writing in this chapter that resonate with your own natural style, or that you aspire to. However, the dictates and fashions of your discipline, your audience and its requirements (e.g. whether you need to write a short report or a dissertation) may mean you have to use a different style from the one you might prefer. Establish the relevant requirements before you begin writing.

To adopt particular styles you must emulate their structure, vocabulary, narrative approach and other rhetorical devices. Box 28.3 shows how the same story may be handled very differently for different audiences. The extracts come from a newspaper report of a scientific study and the scientific journal article on which the newspaper story is based.

The newspaper piece comes from the British *Daily Telegraph* and is written by a reporter, David Moore. Note the use of headlines that act as a summary of the story, which is then fleshed out, using rhetoric to engage a lay audience, including eyewitness reportage (i.e. an apparent interview). Contrast this with the scientific report on which it is based. The newspaper report focuses on the human interest – its first statement is 'socialising with others' and the first phrase in the main article is about 'cancer patients'. The scientific article comes from a 2010 scientific report by the neurologist Lei Cao and colleagues in molecular biology in the scientific journal *Cell*. It talks almost entirely about laboratory experiments with mice; the entire paper contains only two sentences referring to the implications of the research for humans, one of which is reproduced in the extract shown (the phrase 'potential therapeutic relevance'). Note also the use of single-sentence paragraphs in the newspaper which contrasts with bigger blocks of text in the scientific article, and the difference in the language used to report the same findings.

---

**BOX 28.3**

## COMPARISON OF NEWSPAPER REPORTING OF A SCIENTIFIC ARTICLE AND THE ORIGINAL ARTICLE

Newspaper report (Moore, 2010)

Socialising with others 'can help fight cancer'

Socialising with others may help fight cancer, according to research showing that the stress of interaction causes tumours to shrink and even go into remission.

Cancer patients who change their lifestyle to keep company with more people could see substantial improvements in their condition, the study suggests.

The findings challenge accepted wisdom that stress is damaging to health, indicating that a manageable level of stress can help the body fight disease. [...]

Matthew During of The Ohio State University, who led the experiments on mice, said that the results had substantial implications for how people with cancer should live after diagnosis.

Researchers found that moving mice with cancer from their standard laboratory lodgings – where they live in groups of five – to more spacious accommodation shared with up to 20 other rodents had a significant positive effect on the progress of their condition.

Their tumours shrunk in weight by an average of 77 per cent (43 per cent by volume), while five per cent of the mice showed no evidence of cancer after three weeks.

The mice's 'enriched' environment also included more space for them to exercise and toys with which to play, but the researchers identified the stress of socialising as the key factor in suppressing the cancers.

Science journal report (Cao et al., 2010)

Results

[...] In the mice housed in EE for 3 weeks prior to tumor implantation, the mean volume of the tumor was 43 per cent smaller than those in the control housing ($p < 0.05$; Figure 1E C). For the 6 week groups, the tumor mass in EE mice was reduced by 77.2 per cent (Figure 1E D, $p < 0.001$). Notably, all mice in the control groups developed solid tumors, whereas 5 per cent of mice with 3 weeks of EE had no visible tumors, and this tumor-resistant group reached 17 per cent with 6 weeks EE (Figure 1E). [...]

Discussion

[...] Our results demonstrate that EE significantly reduces cancer burden in both a syngeneic melanoma as well as a colon cancer model. Moreover, the intervention was further generalisable to a spontaneous cancer model, the Apcmin/+ mouse, whose mutation is a common and early event of human colon cancer progression. Moreover, a significant subset of EE mice remained tumor free while all the controls had tumors. In addition, EE was effective even though it was initiated after the establishment of the peripheral tumor, suggesting potential therapeutic relevance.

## Getting it down

If you like structure or your report needs to be structured in a very specific way, write down broad headings before you do anything else. Then begin to write! Some people mull over their ideas in their head and are relatively quick and efficient at actually writing. Others do not have much idea of what they will write until they start and the process then seems more laboured. If you get writer's block, depending on how you prefer to work, either write headline sentences and key thoughts and then try to fill them out, or jot down anything until you get into writing mode and the real work can begin. Don't stop the flow. Can't think of a word? Put in a 'placeholder', as Julia Colyar describes below. Flag up problems, but keep going. You can discard the rubbish later. Expect to draft, revise, resequence, redraft 5–15 times.

Most of my writing starts with that first sentence, followed by several placeholder notes to myself, including: 'I need a quote' and 'problem statement here.' [...] Sometimes my notes are less specific, more whimsical, as I insert nonsense words (finkle and whateverness), blank spaces (_____), or symbols (@@@) intended to help me figure out the length of a particular sentence if it is to be placed next to the problem statement or the intriguing quote. I'll highlight them in bold so that I won't forget to fix them later. (2009: 1–2)

If you find yourself stuck after the first draft, brainstorm different ways of saying the same thing or use a thesaurus; this may stimulate your creative processes.

It is often said that the opening sentence of a book is the most important. The same cannot be claimed for research reports, where the introduction is often not the first part to be read. Instead, the first sentences of each section assume most importance, then the first sentences of each paragraph within the section. They should introduce a main point which the remainder of the section or paragraph then substantiates. This is a bit like the newspaper report in Box 28.3 – the same broad principles may be said to apply to all writing.

## Structuring the different sections

Mostly, reports will contain all the elements described for dissertations in Chapter 10 – and considered here – even if the way these fit together varies. But do check whether you need to include additional sections. Remember that structure is used as a tool in writing. Examine the hidden as well as explicit structure of particular articles that you wish to emulate for a more individual approach. But make sure the style you use fits any formal requirements you need to adhere to. Read the related part of Chapter 10 which is complementary to this chapter.

Many people begin by writing the methods or analysis and then 'top and tail' these with the introduction and discussion sections. Always write any abstract only once you have finalised your text, otherwise it may more closely reflect your early ideas than their refinement.

## Abstract

An abstract should briefly summarise your report, with the emphasis on *key* findings and conclusions. Don't include references, tables or figures; abstracts are stand-alone. Write it in the past tense. Keep mention of the method to one sentence if possible. Cut out all unnecessary words. But don't lose the sense and readability – people often read the abstract first to decide whether or not to look at the rest of the text, or refer back to it when reading the main report to remind themselves of the big picture.

Sometimes abstracts are single paragraphs of continuous text, but you may be required to structure it with subheadings. Usually these would be *Introduction*, *Methods*, *Results*, *Conclusions*, but you may need to include others such as *Setting*, *Implications*. Check the style guide you are required to follow.

## Executive summary

Consider writing an executive summary if the report is big. It should only include key points – usually as bulleted or numbered brief paragraphs – not their substantiation, and should be no more than two pages long. Remember to represent all the sections of your report. If you get writer's block here, one technique you might use is to try writing down the first sentence of each key paragraph of your report. Word-processing software that has an executive summary function does this. Whether or not this works well depends on how you have written the report. Alternatively, write down the key points of your study without referring to your report, then check it to add in points and facts you have forgotten.

## Introductory and background sections

These explain why the research was done; that is, they establish your rationale for and choice of research problem, research question and approach. They are usually structured to form a logical argument. The sociologist Jennifer Mason (2002) broke this down into parts; her list is modified in Box 28.4. Most, if not all, items occur in both qualitative and quantitative reports:

## TYPICAL ELEMENTS OF INTRODUCTORY AND BACKGROUND SECTIONS

1 General claims or appeal to common-sense knowledge ('It is well known that', 'Thirty years of research have shown', 'For many people .'). This is usually the opening line.

2 Outlining gaps in knowledge, problematising the literature.

3 Invoking personal experience or authenticity: 'In an earlier study I ...', 'My own interest in this is .'

4 Linking the personal back to general points and to the beginnings of a theoretical proposition or argument: 'As this suggests ...'

5 Drawing on other studies to substantiate the proposition or argument: 'This is supported by studies X and Y', 'Other studies have shown ...'

6 Developing specific questions, concepts or, in quantitative research, hypotheses, and also aims and objectives – the rationale for the bulk of the report.

7 Explication of what the report will do or contain (may include definitions and a theoretical framework).

*Source*: adapted from Mason, 2002

## Methods

Methods sections explain how the research was done and generally differentiate method (what you did) from methodology (the theory and analysis of your method). Assume that your reader has only a very general understanding of the process and no knowledge of the details. You may need to, or find it better to, write according to subtopic rather than chronologically, for example with separate subsections for research governance (outlining conformity to regulations that researchers are obliged to follow, such as data protection or the management of risks of harm), setting, the source and type of materials, forms and questionnaires used, recruitment and follow-up, statistics, analysis. Do not include any results, even if they look like methods. For example, don't say 'By only counting honeybees between 10am and 11am we missed 2 per cent of the total population'. Say 'We restricted counting honeybees to the period between 10am and 11am as this was when most visited flowers' and then in the results say this missed 2 per cent of the total and explain how you know this and what the implications are for your findings. Similarly, the demographic details of your participants are results even if they are used to consider the representativeness of your sample population or to compare control and intervention groups in sampling.

## Results

If your results or 'findings' section is long and complex, begin with a quick overview or with a signposting of what it will consider. This is an example from a paper I wrote:

It was clear from the interviews that the [...] intervention was not necessarily at the forefront of interviewees' minds when they discussed collaboration [within the UK National Health Service]. Here we report what interviewees said about collaboration in general under the three headings: inter-organisational collaboration, intra-organisational and inter-professional collaboration, and inter-individual collaborations. Under each of these headings we also consider the influence of the [intervention] on collaboration. (Rivas et al., 2010)

People new to research writing are often unclear about how to incorporate data in a qualitative report. The golden rule is to be selective. Restrict extracts to a few lines and use them to illustrate what you say, not as the dominant text. Don't over-quote from one or a few cases. Saying how many respondents provided data supporting your key points demonstrates that your arguments are grounded in the data. But don't overuse counts. The aim in qualitative research is to give voice to a wide range of perspectives and experiences, rather than the dominant or most frequent ones. Providing counts throughout may lead your reader to consider the report as if it were quantitative, and therefore to discount examples provided by only one or two of your respondents. With interview data, include your question in extracts if it affected your participant's answers. If you follow these principles, your reader will be confident that you have systematically and rigorously filtered and reduced your data and will be better able to judge the reliability and validity of your work.

You do not usually need to adhere to linear narratives as rigidly in qualitative reports as in quantitative reports. You could weave data from several respondents into a composite narrative, that is, a constructed 'case' (making sure you are explicit about this), use cross-sectional data (the most common approach), or present your argument with reference to your entire data set and then demonstrate its validity by testing it in more detail with a case study. You may choose to use data to support your arguments, but you may also use them to enliven your writing. Charts and tables may be helpful, although they

are more common in quantitative research reports. It is a good idea to see how your tutors or examiners write if you are submitting a student report or dissertation. For example, some people hate to see tables and charts in qualitative reports, others welcome them, and still others are ambivalent.

You may think it straightforward to present more numerical data, but as the experienced social survey worker Cathy Marsh (1988) made clear, authors often get it wrong. Again, the golden rules are to choose the most informative statistical analyses and ways of presenting the data and to match them with the text so they support and illustrate it. If data can be simply summarised in one or two sentences, do so – tables that provide very little information may actually confuse rather than aid understanding. But complex data often benefit from being displayed in figures and tables. Always number the figures consecutively and tables also consecutively, and include a mention of them in the main text so the reader knows when it is optimal to consider them. Remember to make it clear why they should be looking (e.g. 'Table 1 shows that there were more married women in sample 1 than in sample 2'). Figures and tables should be self-explanatory, that is, they should be comprehensible without reference to the main text. They should have titles that accurately explain what they are showing in one or two sentences (e.g. 'Table 1: Annual UK alcohol deaths 2006–2010 per thousand population, age-standardised and raw data'). Don't include complicated narrative analyses within the figure or table; these should be in the main text. It is best to put titles above figures and tables since footnotes and comments are conventionally placed below them.

Use a maximum of five lines or sets of data in charts and graphs. If you want to show more, use a series of graphs all formatted in exactly the same way and to the same size, so they can be compared. It can be hard to tell small and large dotted lines apart. Use contrasting rather than similar intensity colours to distinguish different sets of data or they won't photocopy well (you should assume this may be necessary); it may be better to use different symbols and types of shading, and greytone. Do a test photocopy if unsure.

Make sure you label figures and tables fully, including all axes and their units of measurement. Don't squash them up or let titles get confused with the main text. Avoid having text from the main body of the report to the left or right of the graph or figure and let them take up around one-third of a page. If you are using a word processing programme and this results in a lot of white space, with text sent to the next page, slightly reduce their size to see if that helps.

## Drawing on theory and interpretation

Research writing is, generally speaking, strengthened when it appeals to particular theories (Chapter 3 provides more details). The theories may be obviously related to your work or contradictory (which opens up further discussion that you can use to support your argument), or they may come from a different substantive area but have application to your own research. Be careful not to squeeze your data to fit a theory but rather use mismatches to develop and refine the theory or produce your own. Always substantiate any criticisms you have of the work of others (so that they become critiques) with counter-arguments and suggestions for improvement.

In quantitative research reports, the data are often presented in the findings or results section, and then interpreted, perhaps with reference to theory, in a further section called the *Discussion*. In qualitative and mixed method reports, interpretation and data reporting are often more intermingled. You can see an example in Box 28.5, where Smart's analysis of family life produces multiple layers of meaning. I have highlighted Smart's interpretations using bold text, with straight reporting of the data in normal font. The data extract is indented. You might realise that it is important to distinguish between interpreted and literal data; Smart gives clues as to what is interpretation here, using terms and phrases such as 'concept', 'it was clear', 'one might say'.

---

> ■ BOX 28.5 ┌
>
> ## AN ANALYSIS OF FAMILY LIFE
>
> [T]hese grandparents were faced with some quite troublesome conflicts of values. As members of an older generation they disapproved of the way in which the younger generation 'easily' left their marriages, re-partnered, separated again and so on. **Yet as parents they occupied a rather different moral universe** and they were unwilling to place their own children in the ranks of the feckless and selfish 'others' who apparently carelessly abandoned their vows and families. With the possible exception of one case, all the grandparents thought that their adult daughters had been right to leave or give up on their marriages. [...] In addition, some started to wonder whether women of their own generation or their parents' generation might not have been forced to stay in very unhappy, even oppressive, marriages.
>
> > *Amelia:* I think with Jill's marital disasters, as you might say, I've learnt a lot about marriages ending and accepting that sometimes it has to be and that you haven't got to be judgmental about it
>
> *(Continued)*

*(Continued)*

and you've just got to accept that people just sometimes don't love each other anymore and there's no point. You see, these days it's the way women are; they have incomes, they can be independent, they're not tied to a chap because they've nowhere to go and no money where they couldn't leave. And a lot of, an awful lot of, women must have been stuck in horrendous marriages going back generations, mustn't they really? (aged 65)

Although redefining the 'golden age' was important as a strategy for managing the present, it was clear that these grandparents also had to find a philosophy to guide them. The concept that kept recurring throughout their narratives was the idea that families are, or should be, 'close' and should stay close. Closeness meant a range of things, not necessarily physical proximity of course, although that could be part of it as divorced daughters often gravitated back to be near their parents' home. Being close meant that grandparents felt they had to support their children, even though their lives had taken a wrong turn in some way. […] One might say that their commitment to their children outweighed their identification with a generation which in general deplored divorce.

*Source*: adapted from Smart, 2005

In Box 28.6 you can see how the educationalist Drew Ross (2007) has done the same thing with theory and data. This excerpt is from Ross's report of an institutionally independent organic online learning community (OOLC) founded and populated by London cabbies-in-training, also known as 'Knowledge Boys and Girls' (KB/KG). Theory is shown by bold text (not in the original).

If you use this style, make sure your report remains clear and accessible to someone who is not as well acquainted with the subject matter as you are. Theory should generally be used in the findings section only to mark out the relevance of your data as Ross has done. Save your critique and in-depth exploration of theory to the discussion.

---

**BOX 28.6**

## INTEGRATING THEORY AND DATA IN THE FINDINGS SECTION OF A REPORT

**According to Goffman, high-stakes, often formal performances take place in what he calls front-regions (FRs) or frontstages. […] Opposed, and often proximal to a FR is the back-region (BR), or backstage [...] The back-region is hidden from the front-region audience to a greater or lesser extent and is the locale where three primary practices occur: rehearsals for FR performances, training and prop gathering for competent FR performances, and catharsis/relaxation [...]** in Knowledge Schools (when these are employed), KB/KGs place themselves in positions where they are scrutinized by an audience of authorities who possess the capacity to alter the trajectory of their training. **These settings are, as Goffman (1959) and Meyrowitz (1985) describe: formal, marked**

by decorum and politeness, and dedicated to displaying competence. In the same vein, riding around on their motor scooters, visibly engaged in the authentic learning tasks that comprise the bulk of their training places Knowledge Boys and Girls in the public eye, [...] much of what takes place in the backstage acknowledges [these] frontstage perform- ances. What follows here are four excerpts from CabbieCall that help illustrate how members are able to utilize their shared online space as textual backstage.

*Source*: Ross, 2007: 317

Compare the styles in Boxes 28.5 and 28.6 with the more scientific style of Box 28.7, which keeps results separate from interpretation or theory. This example comes from a paper I co-authored about the marked rise in alcohol-related deaths in the 1990s compared with previous years. Note that the key numerical finding is restated and then cautiously unpicked in the discussion, whereas the reporting of results is confined to pure descriptions of the data.

---

**BOX 28.7**

## AN EXAMPLE OF SCIENTIFIC STYLE

### Results

Fifty two per cent of the increase in deaths in men aged 40 to 59 years resulted from increases in the ICD9 category 571.3; other categories of alcohol related mortality showed smaller increases and none showed a decrease (Table 1).

### Discussion

The rise in alcohol related deaths between 1993 and 1999 was largely the result of increases in the ICD9 category 571.3 (alcoholic liver damage unspecified), whereas other causes of alcohol related mortality showed relatively small increases. The descriptor for ICD9 571.3 suggests that the precise nature of the pathology included in this category may not have been verified. We can only presume that there were reasonable grounds for suspecting a large alcohol intake by the deceased, and that any pathology found was consistent with alcoholic liver disease. The progressive rise in deaths each year since 1993 strongly suggests that it is not an artefact. It may be that doctors and pathologists cite alcohol more freely as a cause of death because of changes in social factors. However, even if this were the case, it would be unlikely to cause such a dramatic rise in the numbers of deaths. Several studies have indicated the unre- liability of death certification with respect to liver disease.[3] However, the rises in both overall alcohol related deaths and deaths confined to category ICD 571.3 suggest that the increase is real.

*Source*: adapted from Henry et al., 2002

---

Theoretical analyses (Box 28.8) do not focus on the reporting of original data, although some may occasionally be included to illustrate particular points. The literature review shown in Box 28.9 is similar in this respect. This review was a 'systematic review' (see Chapter 6) that aimed to be exhaustive in its search for relevant materials and included aggregation of the results from studies it reviewed, using mathematical meta-analysis.

---

**BOX 28.8**

## THEORETICAL WRITING

What I am concerned with for purposes of deliberative education theory is not public deliberation as the sole (or the best) tool of democratic decision-making,[86] but rather deliberation as a process of public communication, analysis, and decision making in a democratic society [...] In classical deliberative democracy models, deliberation usually entails justification through argument and reasoning.[87] For purposes of the deliberative education theory, however, I adopt Iris Marion Young's modification to this definition. Young argues that reliance solely on pure reason as the language of deliberation inevitably excludes those whose language of deliberation and social perspectives are different. Young posits that gender, class and ethnicity produce different speech cultures.

*Source*: Fisher, 2004

---

**BOX 28.9**

## LITERATURE REVIEWING

Theoretical frameworks are not explicit in all the primary studies we considered, nor can they always be deduced. In general the frameworks for the woman-centred interventions [...] were pragmatic, promoting adjustment of the intervention to the wants or needs of individual women. There was wide variation in the detail provided for each model. For example, all professionals using the psychological intervention designed by Kubany[96;97] had to adhere to an identical procedure as detailed in a proscriptive manual. By contrast Tutty[72] used a more open-ended approach, which gave advocates the choice of whether or not to involve the woman's family and friends. The individual level advocacy offered by Sullivan in her pilot and main study[65–71] goes beyond individual support or empowerment of women to focus on making the community more responsive to the woman's needs, brokering structural changes. This dual focus, Sullivan and colleagues believe, helps explain the success of their intervention.

*Source*: Ramsay et al., 2005

---

## Discussion and conclusion

These explain what your research has achieved (see also Chapter 10). Begin with a summary statement about your findings, followed by your interpretation, including consideration of whether your original hypothesis is supported or not (as in the example in Box 28.7) if relevant. If you followed the styles shown in Boxes 28.5 or 28.6, interweaving data and interpretation or theory, now is the time to expand on your ideas and draw more heavily on the literature. Remember your data will support or problematise your initial ideas or other research, but never prove or disprove them.

Here, it is also appropriate to critique your study with a consideration of both its strengths and its limitations. Some people prefer this to come at the start of the discussion (in which case commence with the strengths), some at the end (in which case you could begin with the limitations so you end on a positive note). If there are problems with your study, always suggest solutions that might be implemented in future research. Few studies are perfect, and it is valuable to show where improvements might be made and pointless to gloss over the problems in the hope that your reader won't notice. End with your key finding and its implications.

If you are expected to write a separate discussion and conclusion, briefly summarise the discussion in a short paragraph at the start of the conclusions, ending with one or two sentences on the implications of your research (even if this is just that you have been able to explore and add to data relating to your research question or hypothesis).

## Acknowledgements

Acknowledgements should be used to show recognition for people who have made valuable contributions to your research or report. This does not of course include the cat for being warm and cuddly when you most needed comfort, or your mother for making it all possible by giving birth to you. It should include people who advised you, helped with the analysis, provided materials, data or transcriptions, or proof-read or critiqued your drafts. Avoid over-flowery language.

## Appendices

Appendices are for information that is helpful but not essential to your report. They are not a catch-all for those bits of information you want to include but that make you go over your word count. Each separate appendix should be lettered (e.g. Appendix A, Appendix B, etc.), according to the order they are referred to in the main body of the report, which may be with text such as 'For the full interview, see Appendix A', or 'For more details on the equipment used, see Appendix B'.

## Using headings and subheadings

Using headings and subheadings makes your report easier to read and navigate through, and helps the reader to see that you have included everything of importance. It can also make it easier for you to check that you have organised your text properly and have given the appropriate weight (length of text) to different parts. For example you may realise, using subheadings, that you have written about something very minor over two pages and only allowed one paragraph to discuss the main finding.

## Citing other people's work

Library-based reports need to cite many more references than do empirical reports; as a rule of thumb, a short review should contain at least 30 relevant references if it is to have a reasonable chance of covering the topic sufficiently comprehensively. Longer reviews and theoretical critiques will usually have over 100 references (see Boxes 28.8 and 28.9 for examples of a theoretical dissertation and a literature review respectively, and Chapter 10 for further details on their design). Chapter 10 also contains advice on how to present correctly formatted references and citations, and Chapter 6 has information on the use of bibliographic software that can help with this.

On the whole it is best to avoid referring to magazines and newspapers unless they add something that more formal references cannot. Reference only a few textbooks; most references should be from journals or books in the relevant field, and it will often be wise to give priority to more recently published ones. Don't just read abstracts – your reader may be well be acquainted with the original publication and able to tell this. If you cannot obtain the full reference, look for similar publications that you can get (unless it is a must-read piece, in which case you may have to pay for it through your library or online via the publisher's website). Try not to include lecturers' handouts as references. Instead, find out where they got their information and seek it out yourself.

## Avoiding plagiarism

Plagiarism – writing as if someone else's work is your own – is a form of theft and also prevents you from thinking for yourself and from writing well. Note that you need not be afraid of being accused of plagiarism if you have not committed it, or if you have inadequately referenced material because of poor referencing skills but are clearly not passing it off as your own. The following tips will help you avoid plagiarising:

1   Fully reference all the information you use, from the first draft onwards, including unusual or clever or particularly illustrative words or phrases you wish to adopt from someone else – these should additionally be in quotes.

2   Instead of copying other people's text into your notes, read a small bit, then rewrite it in your own words without looking at the original; you can check after to make sure you did not misrepresent it or forget important detail. Alternatively, summarise the text by writing down key words (but only single words or phrases!) as you read, then make these into sentences later without looking at the original.

3   From the start, use a method for indicating exactly which text or ideas you have copied verbatim from others or paraphrased closely in your notes, just in case you forget to change or delete it in your final draft or in case you separate it from its reference. For example, use highlighters or asterisks. Beware of using something like italics in a word-processed document – even if you are careful not to reformat

the paragraph, software programmes sometimes try to be 'clever' and may 'autoformat' it without you realising. Don't forget to mark out clever ideas which are your own (e.g. by putting (ME) after them); otherwise in your final draft you may waste time trying to work out the source – this sounds silly, but even the cleverest or most experienced of writers may re-read their own text a couple of weeks after writing it and find it hard to recognise their own insights!

4   Start your paraphrased text with a crediting comment such as 'According to Jemima Puddleduck …'.

5   Short quotes should be enclosed in 'quotation marks'. Longer quotes should be separated from your own text as a new paragraph, and perhaps indented from the left-hand margin or written using a different font type, size or spacing. In this case it is not necessary to use quotation marks.

6   Be selective with quotes. It is better to demonstrate your understanding in your own words.

7   When paraphrasing it is plagiarism to include too many words from the original text, even if you provide a reference. Consider using a quote instead.

8   It is not necessary to provide a reference when you write about something that is common knowledge in your field of study or the wider world, but if in doubt, always provide a reference. Being in a Wiki does not constitute common knowledge.

9   To add an explanation or word to a quote that was not in the original, place it in [square brackets]. Only do this where it is necessary for the quote to make sense.

10  Don't let anyone else copy your work – make sure others do not have access to digital versions on your computer or disks or memory sticks, and do not let anyone else doing the same work keep a hard copy.

11  Do not save different drafts of your work using the same name, but name them Project X draft 1, Project X draft 2 etc, with consecutive numbering. Even better, include the date in the title. This may be useful should you ever be accused of plagiarism or if you lose information on a source between one draft and the next.

12  Password-protect your computer, and use encrypted memory sticks; if you have to leave your computer unattended briefly and others can access it, hold

down the Windows key and L to lock it without logging out. This may be a data governance requirement when you have confidential information on your computer.

13  Leave enough time to write your assignment – often people cut and paste (and hence plagiarise) simply because they have run out of time.

## The final draft

When you think you have a final draft, read it from the perspective of your audience. Will they understand it. Does anything raise questions that are not answered? Leave your draft for two weeks and read it again. When revisions involve only small changes to words and sentences, you have reached the law of diminishing returns and should stop. Follow the required style rules, double-checking referencing, footnotes, chapter headings and numbering, and font size. If in doubt:

- type/word-process reports double spaced on one side of paper, left-justified in a 10–12pt readable font such as Arial, Verdana or Times New Roman

- use three or fewer heading levels (e.g. Section 1.1.1)

- leave margins of at least 25mm on the left (or you risk losing text inside any binding), 20mm elsewhere. Keep the top margin smaller than the bottom or the page will look unbalanced

- number pages

- provide a contents list if your report is long, or to give it a more polished look

- don't over-format the text

- avoid colours (they don't photocopy), although they are useful while you write

- if transferring files electronically, ensure you send them in formats that can be opened using other or older software

- make sure all acronyms have been explained and don't use them in headings

- make sure you have been consistent with your use of particular formats and abbreviations

- keep within any specified word count or you may be penalised.

If you are too close to your work to cull words effectively, write down your top three arguments or conclusions, then go through each paragraph asking yourself whether its deletion would destroy these arguments. Be ruthless – but keep old drafts in case you change your mind. Also use the 'does anyone care?' rule – delete the interesting but obscure. I write twice as much as I need, then cut down, but some people prefer to keep within the specified limits at all times. Choose the approach that works for you.

Once you have a final draft, systematically delete superfluous words. This enhances readability, even if you are within your word count. For example 'and then' can usually be reduced to 'then' or (even) omitted entirely. See Table 28.1 for more suggestions. If in doubt, and you are over your word count, ask yourself if literary flourishes take priority over content, rhetoric or data!

Automated proof-reading is possible with software such as Microsoft Word. But remember that software programmes miss some things, and sometimes make errors, for example if you set one to correct all instances of the error 'em' for 'me', you may find that unwittingly the word 'remember' has been changed to 'rmemeber' throughout!

If you quote more than 5 per cent of the content of another article or directly reproduce a figure or a table that someone else has created, it is not enough to simply acknowledge the source. Before you submit your work, you must obtain written permission from the copyright holder. Usually this will be the publisher rather than author of the piece. This permission will not be necessary if you are simply writing the report for examination, but does become vital if you distribute the report more widely in professional circles. Alternatively, shorten the quote. Remove unnecessary information using three points in ellipsis (…) to indicate text

**TABLE 28.1** Ways to reduce your word count and write clearer text

| Avoid | Example | Replacement |
|---|---|---|
| Words that don't add meaning | Basically | [nothing] |
| Circumlocutions – using many words when a few will do | Prior to, in anticipation of, following on from | Before, after, as |
| Tautologies – combinations of two or more words with the same meaning | Safe haven, future prospects | Haven, prospects |
| Long-winded or clumsy clauses | The service with the most attendances | The most attended service |
| 'It was', and 'There is' | It was Freud who said … | Freud said … |
| | There is a tendency among clinicians to … | Clinicians tend to … |
| Multiple noun strings | Women-directed non-directive evaluation techniques | Non-directive evaluation techniques aimed at women |
| Passive forms of verbs | An improvement in performance was recorded | Performance has been improved |

omitted within a sentence, or four points (....) to show the gap is between sentences.

Get feedback. Give 15 people your draft and you will get back 15 different suggestions for revision, many in direct conflict! So ask only one or two. You could ask a family member or best friend if lay people should be able to understand it, but bear in mind that they may be worried about hurting you and so may not be critical enough, or they may be overcritical because they do not understand your task properly. Ask fellow students – you can reciprocate – but not if they have done a similar project as you may then influence each other's final report and your examiners may accuse you of plagiarism or mark you down for copying each other. Take advantage of formative assessments, where tutors critique your work without giving it a mark. Present your paper at a conference or seminar to test the strength of your argument or the way you present the data.

Do take full notice of the feedback. If your tutor fails to understand something, perhaps you have not crafted your paragraph as well as you thought. Amend it and you will produce a better draft. Even if you do not agree with all the points raised, consider how you might address them.

Remember that if you don't, your final examiner may have the same criticisms (and if the person who gave the feedback is also marking your work, they will not be impressed by your inaction).

If you do not get much feedback from your tutor or lecturer from a formative assessment, ask them why not. Is it really because your report is so good that it requires no changes? Some tutors prefer to set you thinking critically about your work, with a few broad statements and no detail.

If you receive a low mark and you feel this is not justified, take a deep breath before you take any action. After you have recovered from the initial shock, read the feedback that you have been given, in detail, then consider whether, maybe, your mark might be fair after all. If you are still unhappy with it, see your tutor and ask for their advice – or if your tutor was the one doing the marking and you do not want more detailed feedback, but rather a second opinion, contact the student office and ask what to do next.

You need to think of your exam or coursework as a means to an end and be strategic in following your tutor's advice (and also the advice in this book). Now is not the time to stand your ground on principle – save this till after you have passed your exams and have the status, authority, and also the wisdom that comes with experience, and most importantly your qualification! Journal editors allow you to opt out of some of the changes a peer reviewer suggests, if you can fully justify why. But with exams there is no second chance.

## Conclusion

Reading and writing are subjective experiences, but the primary purpose of research reports is to be read and understood by your target audience. This chapter has shown how to use literary and rhetorical devices to accomplish this. But while suggesting ways that you may experiment with style so that you can reach different audiences, it stresses that you must stick to any specific style and structuring requirements that you are asked to follow. Tips are provided for following convention in structuring a research report and in avoiding some pitfalls of presentation, such as putting too much theory and interpretation in your findings section as well as inappropriate referencing. Ideas are given for avoiding plagiarism and for using feedback on your work constructively, or at least strategically.

## FURTHER READING

Wolcott (2009) has written a popular book providing advice to people writing up qualitative research. Those wanting help with a scientific writing style will benefit from Day and Gastel's (2006) book on writing a scientific paper, now in its sixth edition. For advice that covers different styles of writing, consult Thody (2006).

### Student Reader (Seale, 2004b): relevant readings

28  John M. Swales: 'Episodes in the history of the research article'

34  Clifford Geertz: 'Being there'

57  James Clifford: 'Partial truths'

60  Laurel Richardson: 'The consequences of poetic representation'

75  William Foote Whyte, Laurel Richardson and Norman K. Denzin: 'Qualitative sociology and deconstructionism: an exchange'

See also Chapter 37, 'Writing a social science monograph' by Barbara Czarniawska and Chapter 38, 'Publishing qualitative manuscripts' by Loseke and Cahill in Seale et al. (2004),

### Journal articles discussing the issues raised in this chapter

Caulley, D.N. (2008) 'Making qualitative research reports less boring: the techniques of writing creative nonfiction', Qualitative Inquiry, 14: 424–449.

Fuchs, L.S. and Fuchs, D. (1993) 'Writing research reports for publication: recommendations for new authors', Remedial and Special Education, 14: 39–46.

*(Continued)*

*(Continued)*

Kashy, D.A., Donnellan, M.B., Ackerman, R.A. and Russell, D.W. (2009) 'Reporting and interpreting research in PSPB: practices, principles, and pragmatics', *Personality and Social Psychology Bulletin*, 35: 1131–1142.

## Web links

The Research Paper: www.trinity.edu/mkearl/research.html

Writing up research: www.rdinfo.org.uk/flowchart/Section10.htm

A Guide for Writing Research Papers Based on Modern Language Association (MLA) Documentation: www.ccc.commnet.edu/mla

Social Research Update Issue 5 on Ethnographic Writing, by Martyn Hammersley: http://sru.soc.surrey.ac.uk/SRU5.html

Writing in the Social Sciences: www.abacon.com/compsite/subjects/ssciences.html

AuthorAid – some social science writing resources: www.authoraid.info/news/some-social-science-writing-resources

## KEY CONCEPTS FOR REVIEW

**Advice:** Use these, along with the review questions in the next section, to test your knowledge of the contents of this chapter. Try to define each of the key concepts listed here; if you have understood this chapter you should be able to do this. Check your definitions against the definition in the glossary at the end of the book.

| | |
|---|---|
| Abstract | Plagiarism |
| Authenticity | Reflexivity |
| Executive summary | Research governance |
| Facticity | Rhetoric |
| Interpreting vs. reporting data | Subheadings |

 **Review questions**

1 How can reflexivity by writers help readers of research reports?

2 How does scientific or quantitative research reporting differ from qualitative research reporting? In what ways are they similar?

3 Why might it be important to separate the reporting of data from its interpretation? Why might it be important not to separate them?

4 **What are the key components and characteristics of the following things: an abstract, an executive summary, an introductory section, a methods section, a results section, a concluding section?**

5 **What are appendices and acknowledgements for?**

6 **How can plagiarism be avoided?**

---

## Workshop and discussion exercises

1 **The following extracts in Box 28.10 show writing in different styles by the sociologist Kathy Charmaz. The first comes from an article in which she demonstrates that placement in a moral hierarchy of suffering affects whether and how an ill person's stories will be heard. The second is for an academic journal article about the experience of chronic illness.**

**Compare and contrast the narrative voice, textual quality and 'empirical facts' in these two extracts. In each case consider:**

(a) **How does the writer achieve authority and persuasiveness?**

(b) **What are the rhetorical aspects of each extract?**

(c) **How does the writer appeal to the reader and how much emotion does she evoke in each piece?**

(d) **Why might she have done this?**

---

**⌐ BOX 28.10 ⌐**

## TWO CONTRASTING STYLES OF REPORTING

Style 1

Imagine Christine walking slowly and determinedly up the short sidewalk to my house. See her bent knees and lowered head as she takes deliberate steps. Christine looks weary and sad, her face as burdened with care as her body is encumbered by pain and pounds. Always large, she is heavier than I have ever seen her, startlingly so.

Christine has a limited education; she can hardly read. Think of her trying to make her case for immediate treatment – without an advocate. Christine can voice righteous indignation, despite the fatigue and pain that saps her spirit and drains her energy. She can barely get through her stressful workday, yet she must work as many hours as possible because she earns so little. (Charmaz, 1999: 363)

Style 2

A rhetoric of self claims certain attributes, values, and beliefs about past and/or present self as defining it. This rhetoric makes truth claims, posits a specific logic, and aims to sway views. Serious illness raises questions about self and identity. People who once could take their personal and social identities as givens now may need to reclaim or revise them. The identity claims embedded in illness stories form the basis for a rhetoric of self. (Charmaz, 2002: 302)

1 Choose articles reporting two research studies, one largely quantitative, the other largely qualitative. If possible, they should be on similar subjects. How do they compare in terms of structure (look at the subheadings) and rhetorical devices to persuade the reader of the author's point of view? How are data and theory used in each one?

# 29

# GIVING ORAL PRESENTATIONS

## David Silverman

---

### Chapter Contents

As the previous chapter showed, writing a research report is never a solitary activity – although this is certainly how it can seem as we labour in front of our computer screen in the small hours. In practice, writing involves entering a series of social relationships, between students and professors, between students and other students, and with members of the wider academic community – other researchers, editors, readers of research reports and, if you are doing research, with research participants in the field.

Such relationships need not just be viewed as potential or real sources of 'trouble'. Instead, they can and should be treated as important sources of insight into how well we are practising our research skills. Effective feedback is an essential resource for effective research. As two psychologists have put it:

> Adults learn best in situations where they can practise and receive feedback, in a controlled, non-threatening environment. So

a good principle to aim for is: no procedure, technique, skill, etc., which is relevant for your thesis project should be exercised by you there for the first time. (Phillips and Pugh, 1994: 52)

Non-threatening feedback can also work if your writing seems to have dried up. 'Writer's block' is something we all experience from time to time. So don't despair. If you can't face feedback, I have found that a complete break for a week or two usually works (for more discussion of writer's block, including solutions, see Ward, 2002: 96–100).

Feedback can come in a variety of forms: written comments from others on drafts that you have produced, conversations in which you express your ideas and gain reactions to these, and the responses of referees to grant proposals or journal articles you submit for funding or for publication. Another important source of feedback is the response of audiences to an oral presentation. Giving a talk is one way of networking, allowing you to make links with people both inside and outside your own department or university (see Churchill and Sanders, 2007: 95–104). So take every opportunity to present your research at any setting that arises, from an informal meeting of fellow students, to interested laypersons, to a scientific conference in your field. Watch out for 'calls for papers' and regularly inspect the sites where they are posted.

This chapter aims to help you understand the nature and importance of shaping your work with an audience in mind, and learn practical skills to help you make an effective oral presentation.

## The 'awful academic talk' and how to avoid it

Paul Edwards has described something that we have all experienced. He calls it: 'The Awful Academic Talk'. The features of this talk are familiar to anyone who has attended an academic conference or university seminar:

> The speaker approaches the head of the room and sits down at the table. (You can't see him/her through the heads in front of you.) S/he begins to read from a paper, speaking in a soft monotone. (You can hardly hear. Soon you're nodding off.) Sentences are long, complex, and filled with jargon. The speaker emphasizes complicated details. (You rapidly lose the thread of the talk.) With five minutes left in the session, the speaker suddenly looks at his/her watch. S/he announces – in apparent surprise – that s/he'll have to omit the most important points because time is running out. S/he shuffles papers, becoming flustered and confused. (You do too, if you're still awake.) S/he drones on. Fifteen minutes after the scheduled end of the talk, the host reminds the speaker to finish for the third time. The speaker trails off inconclusively and asks for questions. (Thin, polite applause finally rouses you from dreamland.) (Edwards, 2004: 1)

This chapter aims to help you to avoid presenting this kind of awful, soporific talk. But first we need to know what lies behind such poor presentations. Stupidity is rarely the reason; poor presenters are unlikely to be stupid. Instead, as Edwards suggests, we need to find an answer to the puzzle of 'why … otherwise brilliant people give such soporific talks? (2004:1). He comes up with two good answers to this question:

- *Fear:* reading a paper seems like offering you a suit of armour which can conceal your stage fright.

- *Academic culture,* which erroneously equates oral presentations with 'giving a paper'.

In this challenging environment, a number of simple strategies can help you avoid giving yet another 'awful academic talk':

- Remembering the needs of this particular audience.

- Good time management.

- Never read out a talk.

- Use effective visual aids.

- Grabbing your audience's attention at the outset.

And as Gary Marx has written:

> Take your oral presentations as seriously as you do your writing. Speak to your audience with clarity, logic, vigour, and examples that will grab them. (Marx, 1997: 107)

## Audience needs

When you speak, tailor what you say for your audience. Early on in my academic career, I was invited to talk about my research at a seminar at another university. I had already grasped the need to tailor my remarks to a particular audience and so had prepared two different talks on my research. One was highly specialist, the other was non-technical. Unfortunately, on that day, I had misjudged my audience and brought with me what turned out to be the 'wrong' talk. Faced with a heavyweight group of specialists, I was insufficiently experienced to improvise and was forced to present the 'Mickey Mouse' version of my research.

I still cringe when I think of this experience. However, although I failed embarrassingly on this occasion, I had at least been partially correct in my method: I had attempted to prepare a talk with an audience in mind (see Cryer, 2006: 133). Just as we design our ordinary conversation for particular recipients (children, colleagues etc.), so recipient design should always go into your oral presentations. As Gary Marx comments: 'Try to remember who you are talking to, and the differential stake you and your audience have in your topic. Gear your talk to your audience' (1997: 107).

Following Marx, you will clearly want to give different kinds of talks to experts in your field,

participants in your research or to general but non-specialist academic audiences. For each audience, you should choose a particular focus (e.g. theory, method, substance) and an appropriate vocabulary (see Strauss and Corbin, 1990: 226–229).

## Good time management

Many have had the experience of speakers who only have time to get through a small part of their material or who overrun and then use up the time for questions. Good time management is a quality possessed by effective speakers. If you think you will not have the confidence to improvise to beat the clock, then it is wise to try out your talk beforehand with a watch nearby.

The usual experience is that it takes far longer to get through your material than you expect. So take the minimum of material in one file and, if necessary, bring a 'comfort blanket' of additional material in another file to use in the unlikely event that you need it. Bear in mind the following wise advice if time runs out: 'If you find that you are running out of time, do not speed up. The best approach is normally to abort the presentation of your findings … and move straight to your conclusion' (Watts and White, 2000: 445).

## Never read out a talk

I know having your full script is a source of comfort. As Gary Marx puts it: 'The fact that you get only one chance with a live audience may engender anxiety and the written word is a safety net. But it has a pre-determined, even stultifying quality, which denies the fluid and interactive nature of live presentations' (1997: 107).

But think back to all those boring talks you have attended in which the speaker had his head buried in his script. Do you really want to inflict that on your audience? More positively: 'You will never know what verbal riffs lie buried in your consciousness if you always cling to the security of the page' (Ibid.).

## Use effective visual aids

Try to present your points through uncluttered visual aids. Where you need to provide extensive material (e.g. long transcripts or tables), then distribute handouts. Take on board the following wise suggestions (adapted from Edwards, 2004: 2) about PowerPoint slides:

- Keep each slide concise (six lines of text as a maximum).
- If you need more space, use more slides.
- Pictures or other images help keep your audience interested.
- Don't talk to the screen.
- Have a paper version of your talk in front of you.
- Don't just read out slides but illustrate with interesting examples.

Box 29.1 summarises much of what I have been saying so far. Note that Edwards' advice here is marked as provisional with the word 'usually'. He indicates that it is 'usually worse' to read rather than talk, yet some of the most powerful speeches are made by politicians essentially reading from autocues. However, such speakers have often been trained in how to deliver such material so that they speak slowly, with appropriate pauses for dramatic effect and audience understanding; most academic talks that involve reading do not do this. Similarly, the use of visual aids and summaries at the start and finish of a talk, advocated as 'usually better' by Edwards in Box 29.1, can in some circumstances be overdone, resulting in a talk that members of the audience may feel patronises them with an over-simple approach. Like most lists of advice, Box 29.1 should be interpreted as providing guidance rather than rigid rules.

---

**BOX 29.1**

### GOOD AND BAD PRESENTATION TECHNIQUES

*Usually better*

- Talk
- Stand
- Move
- Vary the pitch of your voice
- Speak loudly and clearly, toward the audience
- Make eye contact with the audience
- Focus on main arguments
- Use visual aids: outlines, pictures, graphs
- Finish your talk within your time limit. Corollary: rehearse your talk
- Summarise your main arguments at the beginning and end
- Notice your audience and respond to its needs

*Usually worse*

- Read
- Sit
- Stand still
- Speak in a monotone
- Mumble facing downward
- Stare at the podium
- Get lost in details
- Have no visual aids
- Run over time. Don't practice.
- Fail to provide a conclusion
- Ignore audience behaviour

*Source*: Edwards, 2004: 2

## Grab your audience's attention at the outset

Responding to your audience's needs means paying attention to what parts of your talk seem to be grabbing their attention or boring them and spending more time on the attention-grabbing material. But you can also build in features to your talk which will make them sit up and listen from the start.

There are many tactics you can use at the start of your talk to grab your audience's attention:

- begin with a puzzle, as in a detective novel

- start with an interesting data extract

- start with a personal anecdote about how you became interested in your topic

- if you are not the first speaker, try to relate what you have to say to what has gone before

- tell an apposite witty story (but only if this comes naturally).

Finally, remember that both you and your audience need to get something out of your talk. Avoid the temptation just to give talks based on a paper already approved by your teachers. If the paper is really finished, what will you gain from audience feedback? A much better strategy is to send such a chapter to a journal. Instead, try to use early work or working papers. Here the responses of your audience may well help you to see a way ahead. As Watts and White suggest:

> in giving … conference papers from your project … present incomplete work. In this way, you can seek guidance from your audience and receive stimulus for thinking about the next stage of your work … In your paper you can direct the discussion towards particular issues on which you would like other people's opinions by drawing attention to them. (2000: 443)

Let me now illustrate these suggestions by some examples.

## The art of presenting research

You will have gathered already that, in my view, even the most astounding research can sound dull if not properly presented. Unfortunately, this does not mean that poor research can be retrieved if you are a witty and effective speaker, because you will eventually be found out. But effective presentation of good research should be your aim.

To flesh out the bare bones of my argument, I have taken extracts from my reports on presentations by research students completing their first year in my own department. Naturally, to protect the innocent, I have given these students false names. Each student was allowed up to 15 minutes to make a presentation to their fellow students on their progress during their first year and their plans for further work; 10–15 minutes were allowed for questions.

Just as we tend to preface 'bad' news by 'good' news when giving information in everyday life, let me begin by some reports of 'good' practice. In Box 29.2 are some extracts from my reports on this kind of presentation.

---

**BOX 29.2**

### REPORTS ON GOOD PRESENTATIONS

1   Pat's talk was lively and clear, making good use of overhead transparencies. She responded well to questions. This was a well-focused presentation, lively and interesting. The handouts were helpful and the video data was fascinating.

---

2   Derek gave a lively and relatively clear talk, making good use of his overheads. He spoke with some humour, gave an 'agenda' to his audience and explained the difficulties of his project.

3   This was highly professional, with good use of overheads and handouts. Anna used her limited time well, managing to accommodate her talk to the 15 minutes available. Her answers to questions were most effective, giving me the impression that she is already in control of her topic.

4   This was a well-focused presentation, lively and interesting. Sasha's answers to questions were good. Overall, I felt this was an excellent presentation based upon a piece of highly professional research. My views seem to be shared by the students present, one of whom remarked that she hoped her own work would be up to this standard in a year or two's time. Congratulations are due to Sasha and her supervisor.

5   This was a well-focused presentation, lively and interesting and improvised rather than read. The audience's attention was held throughout. Ray's answers to questions were thoughtful and helpful. In particular, he was able to establish a dialogue with students from a range of backgrounds and was at home responding to theoretical and practical issues. I especially liked Ray's attempt to derive methodological issues from the data analysis. There were time problems, from which Ray will have learned something. Overall, I felt this was an excellent presentation based upon a piece of highly professional research.

These are the qualities that impressed me in these 'good practice' presentations:

- liveliness
- not reading out a prepared text
- recipient design for the audience
- clarity
- effective visual aids
- humour
- explaining your agenda
- not minimising your difficulties
- good time management
- good response to questions.

Now for the 'bad' news (Box 29.3)!

## BOX 29.3

### REPORTS ON BAD PRESENTATIONS

1   John was hampered by lack of preparation. His extempore presentation may have confused the audience by introducing too many topics and using too many examples which were not fully explained. His habit of turning his back on the audience to address the (empty) blackboard was unfortunate and, I am afraid, added to the impression of a non user-friendly talk. This is disappointing given John's breadth of reading and excellent understanding. I think the only solution is to work harder on trying to relate his concerns to the interests and knowledge of particular audiences.

2   This was an interesting presentation. However, Bruce made things a little difficult for his audience by offering no initial agenda, not using overheads and by having only one copy of some data extracts. He

*(Continued)*

*(Continued)*

also ran into time problems, which better planning could have obviated. This presentation will have given him the opportunity in future talks to think through his objectives and to offer more user-friendly methods.

3   This was probably too specialised for a mixed audience, although Larry responded clearly to questions. The talk came to life when Larry departed from his script and gave an example (about record production) which brought to life the abstract concepts he was using. I strongly suggest that, in future, for such an audience, he uses more overheads and then talks around them, using such helpful examples.

The following qualities concerned me in this group of 'bad practice' presentations:

- lack of preparation
- too much material
- not looking at the audience
- lack of recipient design
- no agenda
- no visual aids
- poor time planning.

Most presentations fell between these extremes. I will conclude with some 'mixed' examples (Box 29.4).

---

**BOX 29.4**

## REPORTS ON 'MIXED' PRESENTATIONS

1   Maurice gave a clear presentation using handouts and overheads. His delivery was good and appropriately recipient designed. My only suggestion is that he should try to type overheads and put less material on each sheet.

2   Stan had taken the trouble to prepare handouts. However, it was disappointing that, perhaps because of time limitations, he did not have time to analyse the data provided. I would also have preferred him not to read out a paper. It is important to practice the art of talking using only a few props, like overheads, if you want to keep the audience's attention. Nonetheless, Stan's talk was well-organised and timed, and he offered interesting responses to questions, showing a pleasing ability to admit when he was unsure about a point.

3   As in an earlier talk, this was very professional, combining good overheads with helpful illustrations from video and audiotape. My only suggestion is that it might be helpful to give more guidance to the audience about the issues to look for before offering data.

4   Mary gave a confident, well-prepared talk based on a handout. She responded well to questions. My only suggestion is that, in future, she works more on integrating any handout with her talk so that her audience is not confused about what they should be attending to at any one time.

5   Yoko had thoughtfully prepared overheads, but these were not as clearly related to her talk as they might have been. Although it is always very difficult to speak in one's second language, it is difficult to

keep the audience's attention when a paper is read. In my view, it is worth Yoko practising at giving presentations simply by talking around her overheads. One way to do this would be to focus on the nice examples of texts and images that she presented and to pull out her analytic and methodological points from them rather than to attempt to read a somewhat abstract paper.

6   Julia gave an engaging, lively presentation which held her audience throughout. I liked her explanation of the personal reasons behind her research and admired her ability to speak without notes. Her overheads were useful. Some minor suggestions for future talks: remember to avoid turning away from the audience to look at the screen; think about using other information sources as well as overheads (handouts of definitions would have been useful); try out a talk beforehand so as to avoid time problems.

7   This was an interesting talk which carefully explained the issues involved for a non-specialist audience. Jane's account of how her interest in the topic 'coalesced' was very useful, as were her overhead transparencies (although, in future, she should note that these can be most effectively used by covering up parts of each slide until she gets on to them). She ran into some time difficulties and this is also something to watch in future. Overall, a good account of a fascinating topic.

8   Luigi made a good attempt to explain a difficult topic to a non-specialist audience. I particularly liked his account of his intellectual and personal background. In future, he will need to pay more attention to explaining his concepts and to time constraints.

The following were the good and bad news about these 'mixed' presentations:

- Using visual aids *but* these are poorly prepared.
- Well organised *but* reading out a prepared text.
- Giving examples of data *but* not explaining what to look for.
- Using handouts *but* not integrating them in the talk.
- Explaining the background *but* not explaining your concepts.
- Using overheads *but* turning away to look at them or having too much material on the screen.

## Conclusion

For each problem about presentations that I have identified, there is a solution. A key problem is that of losing your audience; the solution is to pay attention to recipient design using some of the techniques this chapter has outlined. Another key problem is that of overrunning; solution: don't prepare too much material. And to avoid boring your audience, use well-designed visual aids and don't read out a talk. All of this is in the context of giving presentations in order to gather feedback, so it is appropriate to remind ourselves about why feedback matters.

There are two reasons why students write papers and give talks: to pass some internal assessment or to get feedback on their work. Unfortunately, in our assessment-obsessed university culture, students tend to forget that feedback from peers and advanced scholars serves both normative and instrumental ends. In a normative sense, offering material for feedback recognises the community of scholars to which scientific work aspires. Instrumentally, such feedback will undoubtedly help improve your work. If you have long-term academic ambitions, it will also help you to improve your teaching skills and, perhaps, to plant the seeds of future journal articles.

So never think of this as 'mere' presentation or the 'boring' bit that has to be got through in order to get your degree. If we cannot use what we have learned to engage others in dialogue, maybe we are in the wrong business!

## FURTHER READING

Wolcott (2009) covers feedback as well as many other practical matters. Cryer (2006: Ch.13) and Chapter 29 by Watts and White in Burton (2000) discuss giving presentations on your work. Phelps et al. (2007) provide very useful advice on using software in your presentations. Gary Marx's paper (Marx, 1997) is a lively and extremely helpful guide for the apprentice researcher.

### Journal articles discussing the issues raised in this chapter

Knoblauch, H. (2008) 'The performance of knowledge: pointing and knowledge in PowerPoint presentations', Cultural Sociology, 2: 75–97.

Othman, Z. (2010) 'The use of okay, right and yeah in academic lectures by native speaker lecturers: Their "anticipated" and "real" meanings', Discourse Studies, 12: 665–681.

Stark, D. and Paravel, V. (2008) 'PowerPoint in public: digital technologies and the new morphology of demonstration', Theory, Culture & Society, 25: 30–55.

### Web links

Conference Presentation – Judo: http://perl.plover.com/yak/presentation/

Making Good Powerpoint Slides: www.microsoft.com/atwork/skills/presentations.aspx

How to Make Good Presentations: www.cmos.ca/presentationse.html

## KEY CONCEPTS FOR REVIEW

Advice: Use these, along with the review questions in the next section, to test your knowledge of the contents of this chapter. Try to define each of the key concepts listed here; if you have understood this chapter you should be able to do this. Check your definitions against the definition in the glossary at the end of the book.

| | |
|---|---|
| Feedback | Time management |
| Recipient design | Visual aids |

 **Review questions**

1 What is recipient design and how can you achieve it?
2 What principles are likely to produce good visual aids?

3   How can you ensure good time management when giving an oral presentation?

4   What are the purposes of giving oral presentations?

<hr>

## Workshop and discussion exercises

1   This exercise will help you answer the question 'Who is my audience?' You are trying to persuade someone or some group of the value of your argument and conclusions. Ask yourself:

(a) Would you present the same thing in the same way to all audiences?

(b) What changes might you make and why?

(c) Can you identify your audience (in advance of making your argument)?

(d) If not, what could you do?

(e) Are audiences uniform or mixed?

(f)  How should you pitch your argument for a mixed audience?

*Source*: adapted from an unpublished paper by Duncan Branley

2   This will help you think about recipient design. Select two articles in your area of academic interest from two different journals or books. Work out the audience(s) at which the journal or book is aimed by reading the journal's 'Instructions to contributors' or a book's introductory editorial chapter. Then go through the steps below:

(a) In what way does each article attempt to reach its appropriate audience(s)?

(b) How successful is it in doing so?

(c) How could it be improved to appeal more to its target audience(s)?

3   Get invited to give a talk on your work and make sure that somebody attends who is prepared to give you good feedback. Plan the talk to reach the audience (e.g. students, staff, laypeople or a mixture). Having given your talk, ask the attending person for feedback on the success of your talk. Then consider how you could have improved the talk to appeal more to its target audience.

# 30

# VALIDITY, RELIABILITY AND THE QUALITY OF RESEARCH

## Clive Seale

Discussions of the quality of social and cultural research often begin with the ideas of validity and reliability. These derive from the scientific (sometimes thought of as 'positivist') tradition. Thus validity refers to the truth-value of a research project; can we say whether the reported results are true? Reliability, on the other hand, concerns the consistency with which research procedures deliver their results (whether or not these are true). Thus we can ask whether a particular questionnaire, if applied on two different occasions to the same person, would generate the same answers. When the concept of reliability is applied to whole research projects, we are asking questions about their replicability. That is to say, if we repeated the research project exactly, would we get the same result again? In the scientific tradition, replicable studies using reliable research instruments have been considered essential preconditions for studies that produce valid or true knowledge. Many procedures and techniques have been devised in order to test validity and reliability and this chapter will demonstrate some of these.

However, the scientific discussion of validity and reliability makes assumptions that sit uncomfortably with many conceptions of qualitative social and cultural research. As was shown in Chapter 2, some researchers in the interpretivist tradition reject realism as an adequate basis for judging the value of research studies, substituting a variety of idealist philosophical conceptions, or indeed political conceptions, of the value of research. Scientific discussions of validity and reliability are firmly rooted in the realist tradition. Here, the task of the researcher is to find something out about the world and report findings in an objective, value-free manner. If, however, research knowledge itself is treated as a social construction, it is hard to sustain a commitment to realism and objectivity. Other criteria must then be used to judge the quality or value of a research study. Perhaps, for example, the quality of a study can be judged according to whether it promotes insight, understanding or dialogue, or in terms of whether it gives voice to particular social groups whose perspective has been hidden from public view. This chapter will first introduce you to scientific conceptions of validity, reliability and replicability and will then show you how a variety of qualitative researchers in the interpretive tradition have approached the issue of

judging the quality of their work. The chapter will conclude with some comments about how you may be able to use these discussions to inform your own research practice.

## The scientific tradition

In the scientific tradition, validity is understood to have various components. These are indicated in Box 30.1.

### Measurement validity

The measurement validity of questions in interviews and questionnaires can be improved by various methods (see Chapter 11 for an account of how to design questions for social surveys). The first and perhaps most common method is known as face validity, whereby the researcher thinks hard about whether the questions indicate the intended concept. The assessment of face validity may be helped by asking people with practical or professional knowledge of the area to assess how well questions indicate the concept, including their judgements of how comprehensively the various aspects of the concept have been covered. Thus a sequence of questions designed to indicate a person's health status might be assessed by a group of nurses or doctors (the term content validity is also sometimes used to describe such assessment by experts).

---

BOX 30.1

## THE COMPONENTS OF VALIDITY

- *Measurement validity*: the degree to which measures (e.g. questions on a questionnaire) successfully indicate concepts.

- *Internal validity*: the extent to which causal statements are supported by the study.

- *External validity*: the extent to which findings can be generalised to populations or to other settings.

Criterion validity involves comparing the results of questions with established indicators of the same concept. Criterion validity can be concurrent or predictive. Concurrent criterion validity might, for example, involve comparing the results of an interview survey of people's health status with the results of a doctor's examination of the same people done at around the same time. If the interview results differ from the doctor's assessment, the interview would be judged to have poor validity. Predictive criterion validity involves comparisons with what happens in the future. For example, the validity of examinations at school in measuring academic ability might be judged by seeing whether these are good at predicting eventual degree results.

Construct validity evaluates a measure according to how well it conforms to expectations derived from theory. Thus, if we have reason to believe that health status is related to social class, we would expect our measure of health status to give different results for people from different social classes. The construct validity of certain questions may only be established after a series of studies and analyses in which researchers build up a greater understanding of how the questions relate to other constructs.

None of these methods of improving measurement validity is perfect. Argument about the face validity of indicators often reveals disagreement about the meaning of concepts. For example, what do we mean by 'health'? Although our indicator may agree with some external criterion, who is to say that the external criterion is valid? Thus a doctor's judgement about health status is not infallible; sometimes people get poor degrees for reasons other than their academic ability. Construct validity depends both on a theory being correct and on other measures of other concepts in the theory being valid. If social class is not related to health, or if our measure of social class is itself not valid, then associations between health and social class cannot show the validity of our measure of health.

## Internal validity

It is important to have valid measures if internal validity is to be sustained, but this is not the only necessary component. In order to prove that one thing (A) has caused another (B) three basic conditions must be met. First, A must precede B in time (the problem of time order). Second, A must be associated with B. That is to say, when the measure of A changes, the measure of B must also change. Third, the association must not be caused by some third factor C (the problem of spurious causation).

Thus, in examining the hypothesis that people with a higher educational level (A) therefore subsequently achieve higher income levels (B), it is no good if a person's income is assessed before their education is complete (a time order problem). Additionally, there is unlikely to be a causal relationship if people with a high educational achievement do not differ from those with a low educational achievement in their incomes (in which case we would say that there is no association between the variables). Most difficult to establish in social research, however, is the issue of whether some third variable – such as parental social class (C) – is associated with both educational achievement (e.g. rich parents send their children to private schools) and income (e.g. a private income from family wealth). In this case, an apparent relationship between education and income may be spurious since both educational achievement and income have been affected by the third variable. Ensuring that causal statements are valid is a matter of research design (see Chapter 8) and the adequacy of statistical analysis (see Chapters 18–20). The example in Box 30.2 will also help you understand the ideas involved.

## External validity

In social survey work external validity is ensured by representative sampling, techniques for which are described in Chapter 9. Since a researcher cannot study everyone in a population (unless they do a complete census of all members of that population), there is inevitably a degree of selection involved in choosing people (or settings) to study. Representative sampling seeks to ensure that the people (or settings) studied are not unusual or atypical in any way, so that what is discovered about them may also hold true for others in the population. Usually, statistical inference is used to make a probabilistic estimate of the likelihood that a result in a randomly selected sample is a freak occurrence (see Chapter 19).

---

BOX 30.2

### CONNECTICUT TRAFFIC FATALITIES

#### The causal proposition

In 1960 the Governor of Connecticut announced that a police crackdown on speeding and drunk drivers had resulted in a dramatic reduction from the alarmingly high rate of traffic fatalities that had been evident in 1955.

#### Threats to internal validity

Campbell (1969) listed a number of 'threats' to this as a causal claim, including:

- *History*: For example, the weather might have been better in later years resulting in fewer accidents.
- *Maturation*: Drivers may have been getting more careful anyway.
- *Instability and regression*: Traffic fatality rates go up and down from year to year anyway; 1956 just happened to have a high number of fatalities. In subsequent years a 'regression towards the mean' was therefore pretty likely.
- *Testing*: Perhaps publishing the high 1955 death rate made people more careful when driving.
- *Instrumentation*: Perhaps the method for estimating number of deaths changed. For example, in 1955 death could have been recorded according to whether people resided in Connecticut, whereas in 1956 death might have been recorded according to place of death (or vice versa).
- *Selection*: This would occur, for example, if the population of Connecticut had undergone a change. Perhaps an economic boom produced an influx of young male drivers with cheap cars during the high fatality year.
- *Experimental mortality*: Perhaps fewer counties in the state returned death statistics in one year compared to the other.

---

However, it is quite common for there to be shortcomings in the degree to which social and psychological research done from within the scientific tradition deals with external validity. This can be particularly evident in experiments where people are recruited as volunteers. An experimenter may discover that a group of volunteers behave in a certain way under experimental conditions, but if the volunteers are different from the people to whom the result is to be generalised, external validity may be poor. Additionally, an experimental situation may not be very good at mimicking the conditions of real life.

Consider the traffic fatalities example (Box 30.1). Imagine that the problems of internal validity were overcome. As a complete census of Connecticut drivers, there would be no problem then in drawing conclusions about police influence on drivers' behaviour in Connecticut. But if drivers' attitudes to the police, or indeed police behaviour during crackdowns were different in other places, a different impact on driver behaviour might be experienced.

## Reliability and replicability

A study can be reliable without being valid. Consider an archery target: arrows can strike it consistently (reliably) in the wrong place. Thus a measurement can be consistently wrong. At the same time, as the second target shows, a valid measure is not necessarily reliable if the object being measured is changing: perhaps the target is moving? Figure 30.1 shows these ideas in visual form. See if you can interpret the third and fourth targets.

In the realist, scientific tradition it is important to get consistent results when observations are being made, or questions are being asked. If different researchers use the same interview schedule it is no good if they get different results with the same person (assuming that the person has not changed their views between interviews). Similarly, if researchers applying a coding scheme (see Chapter 21) for analysing data disagree amongst each other about how to assign codes, it is hard to place much faith in their objectivity. For this reason, questionnaires, interview schedules, measuring devices of various sorts and coding schemes are often subjected to tests of their reliability, sometimes involving inter-rater reliability tests (described in detail in Chapter 26). Thus a questionnaire designed to measure political preferences might be tested by being applied to the same group of respondents twice by different researchers. If the results are the same each time, even though different researchers have used it, the questionnaire is said to be reliable. If different researchers categorise the same qualitative answers from a survey in the same way, inter-coder reliability is said to be high.

More broadly, replicability is at stake when comparing different studies of the same problem that have used the same or similar methods. In the early days of scientific studies it was considered important to develop a style of research reporting so that other investigators could repeat studies and, hopefully, get the same results. This would then increase faith in the truth-value of the findings because they would be seen to have been replicated by other investigators. For this reason, accounts of method in research reports may be quite detailed.

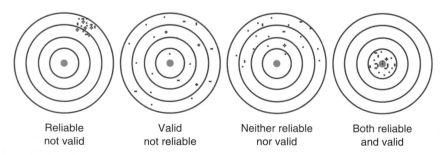

**FIGURE 30.1** The relationship between reliability and validity (Trochim, 2003)

## The interpretivist tradition

It would be wrong to say that all qualitative, interpretivist approaches to research make a radical break with the conceptions of validity and reliability thus far outlined. Quite a lot of qualitative researchers pursue a broadly *realist* and scientific agenda, and so can often apply the ideas of internal and external validity and reliability to their work, though some modifications may be necessary. In other cases, though, particularly if associated with idealist and social constructionist perspectives, this is a greater problem and quite different notions of quality come into play. These reflect profoundly different conceptions about the purposes and status of the knowledge that researchers produce and ultimately relate to differing philosophical and political considerations. I will therefore first describe modifications and then radical breaks from the scientific tradition.

## Modifications

Realist qualitative or interpretivist research often involves intensive study of single settings (case studies) or a small number of people. In ethnography, for example, a researcher may spend a considerable amount of time participating in the everyday life of a particular social group so that it can be studied in considerable depth (see Chapter 14). The advantage of doing this is often claimed to be that of naturalism: the capacity to reveal how people behave as they ordinarily ('naturally') go about their lives. This is felt to contrast with less naturalistic methods (such as interviews) which temporarily extract people from their daily lives so that they can answer questions about events that they may not actually have to face in real life, or about which they may give misleading answers. Qualitative, exploratory interviews, though, are sometimes said to be superior to the structured ones favoured by survey researchers in the scientific tradition in that they allow the perspectives and priorities of individuals to be revealed, without imposition of the pre-conceptions of the researcher (see Chapter 12).

Both ethnographic method and qualitative interviewing are very time-consuming, though, and can normally only be applied to very few cases, settings or people. In other words, the *breadth* of a social survey may be sacrificed for *depth*, meaning that representativeness and therefore external validity may be seen as questionable. At the same time, an exploratory approach can reveal phenomena that have not been predicted in advance. Thus it can be said that quantitative research often establishes the prevalence of things already known about, whereas in-depth case study research can find things that no one has ever noticed before. Originality and discovery, then, might be seen as indicators of the quality of qualitative research, with external validity being of lesser importance. Some people (e.g. Mitchell, 1983) have expressed this as theoretical generalisation, contrasting this with the 'empirical generalisation' of statistical studies. This is because, when a new phenomenon is discovered, its importance can only be judged by reference to its contribution to some existing body of knowledge, or 'theory'. Thus, discovering a black stone on a pebble beach may seem to be of no great importance in its own right, but if such a discovery is made in an area where geological conditions were thought to make black stones impossible, the finding acquires greater significance. This is why some qualitative researchers nowadays like to speak about 'theorising' an area of inquiry: only when a finding is placed in a relevant theoretical context can it acquire significance, so a knowledge of social theory may be particularly important for qualitative inquirers. Chapter 3 discusses a variety of ways in which social theory can be incorporated into research practice.

Additionally, internal validity may take on a different meaning in interpretivist research. Causal inquiry has got itself a bad name in some qualitative research circles, being associated with a deterministic model of human agency that denies the capacity of people to exercise free will and fails to explore meaning-making activities in social life. Yet causal statements are pretty much inevitable in any discussion of human social and cultural life. If you look closely at research reports they will always contain implied causal mechanisms. Box 30.3 contains an illustration of this. Additionally, not all statistical work is devoted to proving causality, but instead is descriptive. It is true to say, though, that proving the existence of causality is only very rarely an interest of qualitative researchers, so scientific notions of internal validity are not much use in assessing the quality of such studies.

---

### BOX 30.3

## IMPLICIT CAUSAL REASONING IN A QUALITATIVE STUDIES

The general region from which the immigrant came was also important in the organization of Cornerville life. The North Italians, who had greater economic and educational opportunities, always looked down upon the southerners, and the Sicilians occupied the lowest position of all. (Whyte, 1943/1981: xvii)

Whyte, in this passage of 'description', is proposing a causal relationship between region of origin and Cornerville pecking order. Further, he is suggesting that economic and educational differences between Italian regions influence this.

---

Measurement validity, which has been shown to be an essential precondition for the internal validity of statistical studies, might be seen quite straightforwardly as an important aspect of quality in qualitative research. Of course, measurement may not be something attempted by qualitative researchers (although they may sometimes count things), but the underlying issue in measurement validity is the adequacy of links between concepts and their indicators (concept–indicator links). These links are important in qualitative research too, and grounded theory is an approach that prioritises the creation of good concept–indicator links. Chapter 22 describes grounded theory in depth, but for the moment you should note that it is based on creating new concepts and ideas and the relations between them (in other words, theory) from observations of social settings. This contrasts with an approach that starts with theory and then seeks empirical examples. As a result, research reports based on grounded theorising generally exhibit excellent links between concepts and the examples drawn from data. In this sense, qualitative researchers can be thought of as being concerned with a form of 'measurement validity'. A good qualitative report exemplifies concepts with good examples.

Yet there are recognisable difficulties in applying the scientific paradigm to qualitative research work. Various authors have therefore proposed modified schemes. Lincoln and Guba's (1985) account of quality issues in what they call 'naturalistic inquiry' (drawing on the meaning of naturalism that refers to the study of people in their normal or 'natural' settings) is one such effort and is shown in Box 30.4.

These authors are critical of the notion of 'truth-value,' saying that it assumes a 'single tangible reality that an investigation is intended to unearth and display' (1985: 294), whereas the naturalistic researcher makes 'the assumption of multiple constructed realities' (1985: 295). In this respect they reveal a dissatisfaction with crude realism and appear to be moving towards a social constructionist epistemological position (see Chapter 2). They argue, then, that credibility should replace 'truth-value'. Through prolonged engagement in the field, persistent observation and triangulation exercises, as well as exposure of the research report to criticism by other researchers and a search for negative instances that challenge emerging hypotheses and demand their reformulation, credibility is built up.

---

**BOX 30.4**

## LINCOLN AND GUBA'S TRANSLATION OF TERMS

| Conventional inquiry | Naturalistic inquiry |
| --- | --- |
| Truth-value (Internal validity) | Credibility |
| Applicability (External validity) | Transferability |
| Consistency (Reliability) | Dependability |
| Neutrality (Objectivity) | Confirmability |

---

Triangulation is a technique advocated by Denzin (1978) for validating observational data. Denzin outlines four types of triangulation:

1  *Data triangulation* involves using diverse sources of data, so that one seeks out instances of a phenomenon in several different settings, at different points in time or space. Richer descriptions of phenomena then result.

2  *Investigator triangulation* involves team research; with multiple observers in the field, engaging in continuing discussion of their points of difference and similarity, personal biases can be reduced.

3  *Theory triangulation* suggests that researchers approach data with several hypotheses in mind, to see how each fares in relation to the data.

4  *Methodological triangulation* is the most widely understood and applied approach. This, for Denzin, ideally involves a 'between-method' approach, which can take several forms but, classically, might be illustrated by a combination of ethnographic observation with interviews. Additionally, methodological triangulation is frequently cited as a rationale for mixing qualitative and quantitative methods in a study (see Chapter 27).

Box 30.5 gives an example of methodological triangulation.

---

**BOX 30.5**

## AN EXAMPLE OF METHODOLOGICAL TRIANGULATION

Rossman and Wilson (1994) describe a project to investigate the impact on school organisation of state authorities' introduction of minimum competency tests in schools. This combined qualitative interviews with school teachers and other educationists in 12 school districts with a postal questionnaire of a larger sample. Analysis of the questionnaire results suggested that curricular adjustments were more common in school districts where teachers reported that their relationship with state educational authorities was 'positive'. The qualitative interviews sought and found corroboration of this. Thus, for example, in a district where no changes occurred in the curriculum, a local administrator said, 'The state has become someone we have to beat rather than a partner to work with' (1994: 320–321). The authors go on to say:

> On the other extreme was a district that accepted the state's increased role in monitoring educational outcomes and worked hard to find creative instructional techniques to improve student performance. The qualitative descriptions of how these two districts responded to the state mandate corroborated and offered convergence to the quantitative findings. (1994: 321)

---

Negative instances are instances of data (sometimes also called 'deviant cases') that contradict emerging analyses, generalisations and theories. Discovery of these can have a variety of effects, sometimes leading to the abandonment of ideas, but more often to a deeper analysis that accounts for a wider variety of circumstances. An example of a negative instance found in a research study that extended an initial analysis produced by another investigator is shown in Box 30.6.

---

**BOX 30.6**

## TYPIFICATIONS AND PERSONAL RESPONSIBILITY IN HOSPITAL CASUALTY DEPARTMENTS

### The initial generalisation (Jeffery, 1979)

In hospital casualty departments, staff categorise patients as 'bad' if they have problems deemed to be trivial, or are drunks, tramps or victims of self-harm. On the other hand, if patients have problems which allow doctors to practise and learn new clinical skills, or test the professional knowledge of staff, they are categorised as 'good'.

### The negative instance (Dingwall and Murray, 1983)

Children in casualty departments often exhibit the qualities identified by Jeffery as being those of the 'bad' adult patients, being uncooperative for example, or suffering from mild or self-inflicted injuries. Yet staff do not treat them harshly.

---

Labels applied by staff depend on a prior assessment of whether patients are perceived as being able to make choices (children are not, adults are, on the whole). Children are therefore generally 'forgiven' behaviour that in adults would be deemed reprehensible on the grounds that children are understandably irresponsible. Additionally, staff assess whether the situation is such that patients are able to make choices. Thus, some adults might be categorised as being present in casualty inappropriately, rather than being 'bad' patients if the events that led them there are not their 'fault' (e.g. they had been given poor advice to go to casualty from a person in authority).

Returning to Lincoln and Guba (Box 30.4), these authors also advise researchers to 'earmark' a portion of data to be excluded from the main analysis, returned to later once analysis has been done in order to check the applicability of concepts. But 'the most crucial technique for establishing credibility', they say, is through 'member checks' (1985: 314), showing materials such as interview transcripts and research reports to the people on whom the research has been done, so that they can indicate their agreement or disagreement with the way in which the researcher has represented them (this can also be called member validation).

'Applicability', in Lincoln and Guba's view, depends on generalising from a sample to a population on the untested assumption that the 'receiving' population is similar to that of the 'sending' sample. The naturalistic inquirer, on the other hand, would claim the potential uniqueness of *every* local context. This means study of both sending and receiving contexts so that transferability is established. This is clearly quite demanding and, apart from theoretical generalisation (see above), other conceptions of transferability in qualitative research are possible. For example, it can be argued that a very detailed or thick description of a setting can give a reader of a research report the vicarious experience of 'being there', in the same way as a good travel writer can facilitate armchair 'travelling' (Geertz, 1973, 1988). The reader is then well equipped to assess the similarity of the setting described in the research report to settings in which she or he has personal experience (see Chapter 14 for a discussion of thick description).

To replace consistency, or reliability as conventionally conceived, Lincoln and Guba propose dependability, which can be achieved by a procedure they call auditing. This involves 'auditors' scrutinising the adequacy of an 'audit trail', consisting of the researchers' documentation of data, methods and decisions made during a project, as well as its end product. Auditing is also useful in establishing confirmability, Lincoln and Guba's fourth criterion, designed to replace the conventional criterion of neutrality or objectivity. Auditing is also an exercise in reflexivity which involves the provision of a methodologically self-critical account of how the research was done. The authors conclude by pointing out that the trustworthiness of a qualitative, naturalistic study is always negotiable and open-ended, not being a matter of final proof whereby readers are compelled to accept an account.

Lincoln and Guba's philosophical position is (at this stage in their writing) half-way between realism and idealism. As we saw, they are dissatisfied with the crude realism that they feel characterises the conventional, scientific view of validity and reliability and, at some points, speak of 'multiple realities,' something which is normally associated with a social constructionist, idealist view (see Chapter 2). Another way of describing such half-way positions is Hammersley's (1992b) term: subtle realism. Here, there is recognition of the existence of a social world that exists independently of the researcher's mind, but also recognition of the impossibility of knowing this world in any final, certain sense. Research reports can only approach reality in various ways.

This subtle realist position, for Hammersley, leads to an emphasis on the plausibility and the credibility of research reports. In assessing the claims made in a research report, Hammersley argues that we should first assess how plausible these are in the light of what is already known about the subject. If a research study contradicts existing knowledge, we need quite compelling evidence in support of its claims. Credibility refers to the adequacy of the links between claims and evidence within the report. It is important to provide the strongest of evidence for the most important claims; lesser claims may need less stringent proof. Additionally, we may wish to assess the relevance of a research study for political, policy-related or practical concerns (see Chapter 4).

Hammersley has been described as a post-positivist, signalling his position as one who modifies 'positivist' or 'scientific' conceptions of validity and reliability in order to apply somewhat similar thinking to qualitative, interpretivist research work. Also within this post-positivist tradition can be placed the work of Becker (1970) and Glaser and Strauss (1967). A later writer who adopts a somewhat scientific conception of the quality of qualitative research is Silverman (2001). These authors represent a tradition that has advocated a number of practical ways in which the quality of qualitative research may be enhanced, listed in Box 30.7 along with references to fuller discussions. Some of these have been mentioned in this chapter or are explained more fully elsewhere in this book. Not all of these authors would agree on all of these things, and their discussions of them contain many subtleties and reservations that cannot be discussed fully here, but you can use the items as a guide to further exploration of these issues and techniques.

---

> **BOX 30.7**
>
> ## WAYS OF ENHANCING THE QUALITY OF QUALITATIVE RESEARCH
>
> - *Triangulation* (Seale, 1999a: Ch. 5; see also Box 30.5)
>
> - *Member validation* (Seale, 1999a: Ch. 5)
>
> - Search and account for *negative instances* or deviant cases that contradict emerging ideas (Seale, 1999a: Ch. 6; see also Box 30.6)
>
> - Produce *well-grounded theory* with good examples of concepts (Seale, 1999a: Ch. 7; Chapter 22 in this book)
>
> - Demonstrate the *originality* of findings by relating these to current social issues or social theories (Seale, 1999a: Ch. 8; Mitchell, 1983; Chapters 3 and 4 in this book)
>
> - *Combine* qualitative and quantitative methods (Seale, 1999a: chs 8 and 9; Chapter 27 in this book)
>
> - Use *low inference descriptors* that show the reader a very full account of observations made, reducing the extent to which the researcher's interpretations are involved in recording raw data, as in conversation analytic transcriptions (Seale, 1999a: Ch. 10; Chapter 24 in this book)
>
> - Present a *reflexive* account of the research process so that the reader can see where the ideas and claims come from (Seale, 1999a: Ch. 11; Chapter 5 in this book)

## Radical conceptions

Lincoln and Guba occupy an interesting position in these debates because, even in their 1985 book, they sat rather uneasily in the post-positivist or subtle realist camp. In later work (Guba and Lincoln, 1994) they reveal a more radical position and it is worth examining the shift in their thinking that occurs here since it gets to the heart of the difference between the modified and the radical views.

As we saw, at one point they referred to 'multiple constructed realities' lying at the heart of their position, thus revealing themselves to be, at the philosophical level, occupying a relativist or social constructionist position (see Chapter 2). In this respect they differ from post-positivists like Hammersley, though by 1985 it seems they had not fully worked through the implications of this for research practice. Relativism, if applied to the truth status of research reports themselves, suggests that these are humanly constructed 'versions' of the world, perhaps written out of a commitment to certain value positions or political interests. This contrasts with a view of research as an objective report on the world. Instead, research reports are really no more than 'representations' of the social and cultural world and should be assessed as 'partial truths' (Clifford and Marcus, 1986). Chapter 14 assesses the application of this view to ethnography, demonstrating that – particularly in the discipline of anthropology – a view of research as representation has led to a deeper understanding of the political uses of research knowledge. In the case of anthropology, for example, a view has emerged that is highly critical of the involvement of this (supposedly 'objective') discipline in supporting oppressive colonialist views.

Bauman (1987) is another writer who has thought deeply about the politics of research knowledge. He distinguishes between two positions on this, which can be broadly equated with those of post-positivism and postmodernism:

- One view of research knowledge, Bauman argues, is that it is an attempt to *legislate* on the truth, so that debates can be resolved once and for all. The researcher occupies a superior position, employing methods that provide a better, more authoritative view than those employed in everyday life.

- A second view, though, is that researchers are more like *interpreters*, who generate conversations between groups of people who may not yet have communicated. Thus a researcher or an intellectual, Bauman says, occupies a facilitative role in society, encouraging debate rather than ruling on the truth.

Research understood from this second perspective starts to lose its distinction from social commentary. The distinction between 'data' and 'theory' begins to break down, being revealed as a hangover from a past scientific age. Data, after all, is pre-constituted by the theories and values of the researcher so that it cannot be regarded as an objective account of reality (see Chapter 2). Rather than looking to the inner qualities of a research account in order to judge its quality, some say that it would therefore be better to examine the effects of a research study in society in order to see whether it is good or bad. In their 1994 book, Guba and Lincoln begin to outline this view by presenting a fifth criterion for judging the quality of naturalistic inquiry: authenticity.

In describing this, Guba and Lincoln reveal a sympathy for political conceptions of the role of research that goes several steps beyond Hammersley's concern with political and practical relevance (see earlier). Authenticity, they say, is demonstrated if researchers can show that they have represented a range of different realities ('fairness'). Research should also help people develop 'more sophisticated' understandings of the phenomenon being studied ('ontological authenticity'), be shown to have helped people appreciate the viewpoints of people other than themselves ('educative authenticity'), to have stimulated some form of action ('catalytic authenticity') and to have empowered people to act ('tactical authenticity').

Of course, the view that fairness, sophistication, mutual understanding and empowerment are generally desirable is itself a value-laden position. It represents an attempt to pull back from the relativist abyss by founding research practice on a bedrock of political values. Attempts to implement 'democratic' values like this are not always appreciated by people who prefer to organise their lives and political systems according to alternative values. But it can be seen that Guba and Lincoln have travelled on a path beginning with a rejection of positivist criteria and the substitution of interpretivist alternatives. Dissatisfied with the limitations of these, constructionism has been embraced, introducing an element of relativism. Political versions of the value of research have then been imported to save facing the logical implications of relativism, which might end in a nihilistic vision and abandonment of the research enterprise.

This is a path that other qualitative researchers have trodden. Working together with Yvonna Lincoln, Norman Denzin has been influential in promoting political conceptions of the research enterprise, arguing that qualitative research has reached a moment in its development where postmodernist and constructionist influences have resulted in a 'crisis of legitimation'. They argue that

> [t]he qualitative researcher is not an objective, authoritative, politically neutral observer standing outside and above the text ... Qualitative inquiry is properly conceptualized as a civic, participatory, collaborative project. This joins the researcher and the researched in an ongoing moral dialogue. (Denzin and Lincoln, 2000: 1049)

This follows on from an earlier statement in which they say that a central commitment of qualitative researchers remains

> in the humanistic commitment of the qualitative researcher to study the world always from the perspective of the interacting

individual. From this simple commitment flow the liberal and radical politics of qualitative research. Action, feminist, clinical, constructivist, ethnic, critical and cultural studies researchers are all united on this point. They all share the belief that a politics of liberation must always begin with the perspectives, desires, and dreams of those individuals and groups who have been oppressed by the larger ideological, economic, and political forces of a society, or a historical moment. (Denzin and Lincoln, 1994: 575)

As a criterion for judging the quality of research it is immediately obvious that this is open to dispute. It is not difficult to imagine a well-conducted study that enabled people in positions of power to achieve their aims. The vision of society as no more than a system inhabited by oppressors and oppressed also seems naive (see also Hammersley, 1995a). Research can at times be more relevant to direct political projects, at others less relevant, but its quality is an issue somewhat independent of this.

## Conclusion

As a practising researcher you may be wondering which of these conceptions suits you best. Are you going to commit yourself to a scientific vision in which you prioritise objectivity and replicability, or to a post-positivist position in which you retain some of this commitment in a modified form, or will you reject these in favour of a political conception of the research process? Clearly, the views of the various authors are often incompatible. It seems wrong to develop a measuring instrument that can be judged reliable and valid if the measuring instrument is really no more than an imposition of a particular, value-laden vision of the world on oppressed people. It seems foolish to assess a research report solely according to its political consequences if its findings and claims are poorly supported with evidence, or if the analysis of evidence is clearly influenced by the researcher's values.

In these disputatious circumstances many researchers seem to feel that they must belong to one camp or another, to identify themselves as 'scientists', 'subtle realists' or 'radical constructionists' before they begin their research activities. In my view this is a mistake. Many of the disputes that exist at the level of methodological debate are simply not resolvable by further discussion, but are a matter of preference. Depending on the actual topic of the research and the problems that are seen to be central, certain considerations will always be more important than others. The personal biographical situation and local circumstances of researchers and their likely audiences are the main influences on how projects proceed and quality is judged. Exposure to methodological discussions such as the ones outlined in this chapter can help in producing generalised methodological awareness that can be helpful when actually carrying out a research project or intellectual inquiry. Thus a researcher who is aware of these debates is more likely than one who is not to produce a research study that is sophisticated. That is to say, it will be a study that is sensitive to a variety of ways in which it is possible to proceed, show awareness of the consequences of particular decisions made during the course of the study, and the eventual report will demonstrate to a variety of potential audiences that something of value has been created.

## FURTHER READING

This chapter is a condensed and simplified version of a book on the quality of qualitative research which I wrote (Seale, 1999a) and which is the best place to start in expanding your knowledge of this area. The book contains an account of validity and reliability in the quantitative tradition as well. There are relevant chapters by Gobo, Flybjerg and Seale in *Qualitative Research Practice* (Seale et al., 2004).

### Student Reader (Seale, 2004b): relevant readings

6   Thomas D. Cook and Donald T. Campbell: 'Validity'

25  R.C. Lewontin: 'Sex lies and social science'

35  Martyn Hammersley: 'Some reflections on ethnography and validity'

48  Anssi Peräkylä: 'Reliability and validity in research based on tapes and transcripts'

62  Zygmunt Bauman: 'Intellectuals: from modern legislators to post-modern interpreters'

65  Patti Lather: 'Fertile obsession: validity after poststructuralism'

66  Thomas A. Schwandt: 'Farewell to criteriology'

79  Maureen Cain and Janet Finch: 'Towards a rehabilitation of data'

See also Chapter 27, 'Quality in qualitative research' by Clive Seale in Seale et al. (2004).

### Journal articles discussing the issues raised in this chapter

Seale, C. (1999b) 'Quality in qualitative research', Qualitative Inquiry, 5: 465–478.

Meyrick, J. (2006) 'What is good qualitative research?: a first step towards a comprehensive approach to judging rigour/quality', Journal of Health Psychology, 11: 799–808.

*(Continued)*

*(Continued)*

Decker, S.H. and Pyrooz, D.C. (2010) 'On the validity and reliability of gang homicide: a comparison of disparate sources', Homicide Studies, 14: 359–376.

Walwyn, R. and Roberts, C. (2010) 'Therapist variation within randomised trials of psychotherapy: implications for precision, internal and external validity', Statistical Methods in Medical Research, 19: 291–315.

## Web links

Research methods knowledge base: www.socialresearchmethods.net

Validity and reliability in quantitative research: http://allpsych.com/researchmethods/variablesvalidity reliability.html

A Framework for Assessing the Quality of Qualitative Research: www.nationalschool.gov.uk/policyhub/news_item/qual_framework.asp

Methods@manchester – What is quality in qualitative research?: www.methods.manchester.ac.uk/methods/qualityinquali/index.shtml

e-Source – Chapter 7 on 'Observational studies' by Richard Berk: www.esourceresearch.org

## KEY CONCEPTS FOR REVIEW

**Advice:** Use these, along with the review questions in the next section, to test your knowledge of the contents of this chapter. Try to define each of the key concepts listed here; if you have understood this chapter you should be able to do this. Check your definitions against the definition in the glossary at the end of the book.

| | |
|---|---|
| Auditing | Naturalism |
| Authenticity | Negative instances |
| Concept–indicator links | Plausibility |
| Confirmability | Post-positivism |
| Construct validity | Reflexivity |
| Credibility | Reliability |
| Criterion validity (concurrent and predictive) | Replicability |
| Dependability | Spurious causation |
| External validity | Subtle realism |
| Face validity | Theoretical generalisation |
| Inter-coder/inter-rater reliability | Time order |
| Internal validity | Transferability |
| Measurement validity | Triangulation |
| Member validation | Validity |

## Review questions

1. What is the difference between validity, reliability and replicability?
2. Outline different ways of improving (a) measurement validity, (b) internal validity, and (c) external validity.
3. Describe what is meant by each of the following terms: credibility, transferability, dependability and confirmability. How do they differ from more scientific conceptions of reliability and validity?
4. How can triangulation and searching for negative instance help improve the quality of qualitative research?
5. What is authenticity and how might it be achieved in a research study?

## Workshop and discussion exercises

1. How would you design a study of the causal influence of police crackdowns on driving behaviour that overcame the threats to internal validity listed in Box 30.2 and the threat to external validity mentioned later in the chapter?
2. Seek out and read two studies that represent different 'moments' in the history of qualitative research. For example, choose a study that involves grounded theorising and another where the author situates him- or herself within postmodernism. How do the studies differ in their conception of what makes a good research study? How might each author apply these criteria to the other's work?
3. Choose a research study in an area of work where you have some knowledge of existing literature and assess it in the light of the following questions:

   (a) How consistent are the findings with what is already known?
   (b) What evidence is supplied to support the credibility of the conclusions and how persuasive is this?
   (c) What relevance might the study have for political or practical affairs?

4. In relation to a specific study, consider whether its quality would be improved by attention to the issues raised under the 'positivist' headings of measurement validity, internal and external validity and reliability. To what extent could the modified interpretivist criteria outlined in the chapter be applied to the study? Do these lead you to consider different issues from those raised under the 'positivist' headings?
5. This exercise requires you to work with others on some qualitative data, such as some interview transcripts.

   - Without discussing your ideas with others in your group, read one part of the data transcript (e.g. a single interview) and draw up a list of key themes you perceive in the data.
   - Compare the themes you have identified with those of others in your group. What are the similarities and differences?
   - Take four or five themes from those identified by members of the group and, working individually again, apply them to some new data (e.g. a second interview) by marking parts of the transcript which you believe exemplify each theme.
   - Compare what you have done with others in the group. What difficulties are there in consistently applying the themes? Does inconsistency matter?

# 31

# WHEN THINGS GO WRONG

## Mike Michael

This chapter is an attempt to present some pointers in coping with what happens when things go wrong in a research project. While there are many methodology books that usefully describe the choice and proper use of particular research methods to answer particular research questions, rather less attention is paid to the variety of routine problems that can arise in any research project. One of the results of this relative neglect is that novice researchers can feel rather inadequate. Everything that goes wrong thus becomes a matter of one's own inexperience, lack of skill, or downright incompetence.

This negative attribution to self is unsurprising when what is very often presented is a more or less idealised picture of methodological procedure. A little reflection on the fact that things go wrong even for seasoned researchers would go some way to dispelling the sense of overbearing methodological mystique. To appreciate that even one's supposed intellectual elders and betters have also made mistakes in the process of data collection and analysis can be of considerable reassurance. That is to say, some consideration of the ways that seasoned researchers can 'repair' research that has gone wrong so that eventually interesting and useful things might be said (interesting and useful to the relevant research community or to users such as policy makers), might serve to make the whole research process a little less fraught.

Of course, the phrase 'when things go wrong' covers a multitude of disasters:

- At the grandest level, there might be such huge disparities between the research question posed and the research method chosen that one generates no relevant data.

- At a very practical level there are issues of thwarted access: people simply refuse to speak to you, or do not allow you to speak to those for whom they effectively act as gatekeepers.

- At the interpersonal data-gathering level, there might be respondents who simply do not answer the questions, or who disorient you in some way.

One of the points of this chapter is to suggest that there might still be 'interesting and useful things to be said' about the social world despite this apparent lack of data. As we shall see, this means having a feel for how to judge just what counts as 'interesting' and 'useful', and a reflexive sensibility that can help draw out the more general value of one's methodological problems.

So, this chapter is about exploring some of these variants of 'when things go wrong'. It will, of course, not be possible to be exhaustive – things go wrong in many, many surprising and disparate ways. The aim, rather, is to provide a sense of how one can turn a bad situation into a 'do-able' project that can be intellectually interesting. In what follows, I start with some thoughts on what it means to do 'interesting' and 'useful' research in a cultural community of social scientific scholars. After this, I present a catalogue of disasters – well, three anecdotes actually – that draw on my own painful research experience (which has largely been interview-based). In the process, I consider the ways that I managed to get out of what were, in one or two

cases, very sticky empirical situations. For example, I suggest that even when it seems self-evident that one has no data, if the research question is properly reformulated, it is possible to discover that one is actually in possession of some fascinating data.

## Saying 'interesting' and 'useful' things

Let me start with a brief foray into the doings of science. This is because science is still in many ways the benchmark by which social scientific research is judged, not least in terms of its rigour (if not its forms of explanation). As sociologists of scientific knowledge have shown, the rigour of science is considerably looser than would appear from the outside. For example, Harry Collins (1985) has documented how methods are *always* contestable in science and how, indeed, in a scientific controversy closure or resolution is attained not by simply following methodological rules but by the social processes of argumentation by which other 'opponent' scientists are discredited. To be sure, this might draw on accounts of their methodological strengths or weaknesses, but it will also involve arguments about the quality of opponents' institutional affiliation, assessments of their reputation, and even aspersions about their sanity.

In all this, the resolution of the controversy is, ironically, not decided by the facts of nature as revealed by implementing proper methodological procedure; rather, once the controversy is resolved – that is, once all but one faction in a controversy have been discredited, marginalised or silenced – *then* the facts of nature are known.

There are a number of lessons to draw from this digression into the sociology of scientific knowledge:

- *Methods are always disputable* and claims about the research 'going wrong' are just part and parcel of the character of science.

- As such, *methodology is just one form of argumentation* out of several.

- What makes a fact a fact is crucially *dependent on social and cultural processes.*

Now, one important aspect of these social and cultural processes is the perception that one's work is 'useful' or 'interesting'. That is, if one's findings, ideas, conceptions, frameworks, data and so on contribute to, or in some way enable, colleagues' work, then these are deemed valuable. As Mulkay (1979) noted, whether scientists conform to norms of scientific good conduct is subordinate to whether their work can be judged 'useful' or 'interesting'. The upshot of this is that even when 'things go (disastrously) wrong', if one can find a way of showing how one's work is 'useful' or 'interesting', then it will be seen to be valuable. Inevitably, however, what counts as 'useful' or 'interesting' is difficult to pin down.

Box 31.1 shows the contrary ways, over and above methodological rectitude, in which work can be judged 'useful' or 'interesting' in social science.

---

**| BOX 31.1 |**

## SOME DIMENSIONS ON WHICH SOCIAL SCIENCE MAY BE JUDGED 'USEFUL' AND 'INTERESTING'

- *Theoretical sophistication:* for example, does your research demonstrate a thoroughgoing engagement with cutting edge theoretical debates? Versus

- *Empirical usefulness:* for example, does your research contribute to quality of life, illuminate people's actual social conditions?

- *Radicalism:* for example, does your work 'push the envelope' politically or epistemologically (in other words, does it exhibit political radicalism or epistemological radicalism)? Versus

- *Relevance:* for example, does your research contribute to the making of policy or the production of advice?

---

These contrasting assessments are rhetorical commonplaces that are constantly drawn upon as a means of congratulating or denigrating peers and colleagues. They are also, as is shown in Chapters 3 and 4, relevant considerations from the outset in planning research. And, of course, the *valency* of each commonplace can be reversed. Thus:

- *theoretical sophistication* can be called *ivory tower thinking*

- *empirical usefulness* can be called *over-simplification*

- *radicalism* can be called *utopianism*

- *relevance* can be called *selling out.*

The point is that saying 'interesting' things or staking claims to doing 'useful' work is always a fraught business. Indeed, to complicate matters still further, the capacity to reflect on these different commonplace practices of academic judgment is likewise subject to judgment. As ethnomethodologists have long argued, there is no time out: none of us moves outside of the criteria of judgment in order to judge them – this very act is subject to judgment. This chapter will be no less subject to such scrutiny than your research reports.

The commonplaces listed above, for all their slipperiness, do nevertheless suggest ways in which it might be possible to recover a research project even when it has gone horribly wrong. When respondents do not respond, when they do not respond in the expected way, when you realise you have been asking the wrong questions, indeed using the wrong methods, then it might still be possible to say something interesting or useful. In what follows, I will present three anecdotes of research gone wrong with a view to showing how it was, or could have been, turned into something other than mere failure:

- In the first, I relate an interview where everything that could go wrong did go wrong and, to all intents and purposes, no data was collected at all. This episode was in large part due to the 'recalcitrance' of the respondent who simply did not want to talk about the things the interview was supposed to address.

- In the second anecdote, I consider a case where the method was inappropriate and led, once more, to what seemed like a distinct lack of data.

- In the third anecdote, we found that in focus groups with school students, we were getting data that were not at all what we were expecting, but which, as it turned out, could be used to raise some interesting and useful questions within the research field as a whole.

## Anecdote 1: 'recalcitrant' respondents

In 1989, I was working as a researcher at Lancaster University with Rosemary McKechnie and Brian Wynne looking into the public understanding of science, specifically, ionising radiation. Most of this research entailed conducting interviews with members of the public to derive the 'mental models' that underpinned their understanding of ionising radiation. One sample of respondents was drawn from the electoral register. This particular example of a disastrous piece of fieldwork involved an interview with a respondent at her home and is described in Box 31.2.

Now, this was undoubtedly a rather eccentric fieldwork episode. There seemed to be no relevant data that could be salvaged from the interview, even if the recorder had managed to pick up our voices above the cat's activities. For a long time this interview was consigned to a bin in the back of my mind labelled 'put down to experience'. However, more recently I have been reflecting on the role of non-humans in the production of social ordering. In other words, I have been interested in how entities such as technologies, objects, animals, 'natural' environments of various sorts contribute to what we understand to be more or less routine social events. Suddenly, in the context of this new set of concerns, this 'disastrous interview episode' has become rather interesting.

---

**BOX 31.2**

### A DISASTROUS INTERVIEW?

This was our second interview. Between this and the first interview, the circumstances of the respondent had changed insofar as she had got a job at Burger King. I was seated on the sofa, the respondent was in an armchair to my right, and the tape recorder was placed on the floor between us. During the preliminary conversation, her pit bull terrier entered the room and made its way slowly over to where I was sitting. It turned itself around and proceeded to sit on my feet. According to the respondent, 'she liked to know where people were'. My main aim in this interview was to get the respondent to talk about how she saw ionising radiation in a broader context, not least that of the local nuclear power installations at Heysham and Sellafield. However, it very quickly became clear that she would much rather talk about her new job at Burger King. She felt that there were excellent opportunities for rapid promotion. While this conversation was going on, we were joined by her cat, who ambled over to the tape recorder. After a few moments of clawing at the tape recorder, it began to pull it along the ground by its strap, taking it further and further

*(Continued)*

away from the interview. Needless to say, the combination of the pit bull terrier on my feet, the respondent's evident intentness to speak only about the excellent career structure at Burger King, and the disappearing tape recorder all conspired to make this a non-interview. Certainly, I did not feel I could intervene further in this scene of domestic harmony by insisting that we talk about the ionising radiation. After an hour or so, the 'interview' came to an end and I paid the interviewee and, with considerable relief, left.

## Re-interpretation of the interview

What this anecdote demonstrates is that a whole array of entities need to behave themselves in a particular way, and a peculiar range of relations need to be instituted, in order for there to be any 'relevant social data' (in this case, interview material of a specific sort) at all. That is to say, companion animals such as cats and dogs, technologies such as tape recorders and TVs, persons such as interviewees, neighbours, relatives, friends and, of course, interviewers need to be disciplined in such a way that out of their various inter-relations are yielded 'relevant social data'. The 'disastrous interview episode' illustrates what happens when this discipline breaks down. 'Normally' an interview is so organised by both interviewer and, crucially, interviewee that all manner of possible interruptions are kept at bay.

The obvious upshot is that, if an interview (or, indeed, any form of fieldwork) has gone wrong, one could ask the question: What has *enabled* this to go wrong? In other words, rather than see this as a failure of methodological procedure, one could inquire into the ways in which persons, objects, natures and technologies have started to behave in an 'undisciplined' way such that it becomes impossible to collect 'relevant social data'. As a corollary, one can also begin to examine what has had to be disciplined in order to allow one to collect such data in more successful fieldwork episodes.

Additionally, to say that the 'disastrous interview episode' is an instance of things going wrong is obviously to take the perspective of the interviewer. For the interviewee, this episode might well be characterised as anything from an enjoyable social encounter to a triumphant opportunity to make a particular point. This raises the further issue of how the interviewee interprets the interviewer. For example, the interviewee in the previous example could be said to be ignoring the topic of ionising radiation and focusing upon the career prospects of Burger King because she wants to display that she no longer needs the fee that comes with the interview. In other words, she might be interpreting me as a representative of the university and hence elitist or privileged and the source of something like a humiliating largesse (payment for an interview on a topic she is not interested in). Moreover, this interpretation on the part of the interviewee, and the self that is implicated in the 'doing' of such an interpretation, might be partly enabled by the way she is relating to her animals. The point is that one can attempt to re-interpret this disaster as a successful interaction. The question to ask is: How, from the perspective of the 'recalcitrant' respondent, can the 'disastrous' interview be seen to be a 'success'?

Of course, this sort of question generalises to other situations where respondents, participants, gatekeepers and so on have been 'obstructive' in some way or other. Rather than see such 'obstructions' primarily as a matter of personal failure or incompetence, consider how the 'obstruction' might be reframed as a social encounter that has worked more or less successfully for the 'subject of study'. After all, the scrutiny of everyday social life by a whole host of social and human scientists (some academic, some commercial, some government or charity-sponsored) seems to be becoming comparatively common (Rose, 1999). In such a context, the seeming failure of respondents' engagement can be regarded as an indication of *skilfulness* on their part, as opposed to *skillessness* on the part of the researcher. Another question, then, that one can address is: What sort of social skill has been deployed by the respondent in 'doing' such recalcitrance or accomplishing such obstruction? Relatedly, one could also pose the question: What sorts of 'interests' – personal, social, institutional – are being enacted through such obstructiveness?

The analysis suggested above entails, as it were, 'going meta': it involves interrogating the social arrangements that make the method (e.g. interview) 'work'. In terms of our various criteria for saying interesting or useful things (Box 31.2), one could make the following points:

- The interrogation is epistemologically radical because it has placed on to the sociological agenda (along with various authors such as Latour, 1999 and Haraway, 1997) the role of non-humans in the making of society and social knowledge.

- The interrogation is potentially politically radical (and certainly controversial) because it raises, albeit in simplified form, the issue of where agency (the freedom to act and to interpret the meaning of action) and rights lie.

The general lesson, then, is that failures in fieldwork that are precipitated by the 'misbehaviour' of respondents can be recovered when these failures are re-interpreted as an insight into, indeed, an interrogation of when 'things go right'. See Box 31.3, however, for a reversal of this logic, in which interviews that appeared unproblematic at the time were later seen as quite ambiguous.

---

**BOX 31.3**

## CODA: PROBLEMATISING 'SUCCESSFUL' INTERVIEWS

In a series of interviews conducted with scientists about the rights and wrongs of animal experimentation (Michael and Birke, 1994a, 1994b), when we came to interpret our data, we were faced with a problem. While the interviews were, on the whole, very 'successful', the data were interpretable in a number of ways depending on how we interpreted the interviewees' interpretations of us as interviewers. This depended on whether we regarded them as addressing themselves to us as:

- social scientists (both of us were attached to social science departments)

- scientists (my colleague was also a biologist)

- representatives of a science magazine (the research was commissioned by the *New Scientist*)

- pro- or anti-animal experimentation (the funding of the research was provided by both pro- or anti-organisations).

The broader question is, to what extent were the responses addressed to, as it were, the 'wrong' or 'mistaken' versions of the interviewers? Or, to put it in another more positive way, what has the interviewer been 'constructed as' by the interviewee and to what ends?

---

## Anecdote 2: 'reckless' researchers

In 1987, I took my first research job proper. After finishing my PhD in social psychology, I was hired to do research on the public understanding of science. My main qualification for this was, I suppose, having some (rather limited) experience of interviewing, and an interest in discourse analysis. The project was the same as that mentioned in Anecdote 1; Box 31.4 describes the source of a new problem with this project.

BOX 31.4

## FAILURE TO GET RELEVANT DATA

The project's aim was to unpick people's mental models of particular 'scientific' phenomena. At stake was how people understood a phenomenon such as 'ionising radiation' through particular cognitive representations – images, metaphors, analogies and so on. The procedure was to pose a series of quite difficult, almost technical, questions in order to see what sort of models were applied and how. The further aim was to see whether and how these mental models were shaped by social factors such as people's understanding of, or trust in, the sources of information about those phenomena (e.g. the nuclear industry).

In outline, at least, this seemed like a splendid project. I certainly thought so. However, there was one thing that we neglected to register. Many of the existing studies of mental models either applied to social phenomena, or to medical, physical or technological phenomena (such as the common cold, electricity or central heating systems), with which people were generally very familiar. Recklessly, we had general-ised this approach to address understandings of ionising radiation – a phenomenon with which people were, in general, very unfamiliar.

In response to our questions about even the most apparently elementary aspects about radiation (whether it was made up of particles or rays), we were met with a chorus of 'don't knows'. In other words, instead of even the most tenuous effort at answering our questions, our respondents preferred to insist upon their ignorance. It looked as if we had no data from which to derive our mental models. It looked as if the entire research project would prove to be a disaster.

## Rescuing the project

However, in the context of the main studies in public understanding of science, these 'don't know' responses actually proved very interesting. At the time, the majority of studies in public understanding of science tended to be questionnaire-based quizzes which treated any answer of 'don't know' as a simple absence of, or deficit in, scientific knowledge and understanding. In contrast, what we found was that on answering with a 'don't know', respondents would then go on to provide a series of *reasons* for not knowing (for more detail see Michael, 1992, 1996). These included the three 'discourses of ignorance' shown in Box 31.5, each of which reflected a different relationship with scientific authority.

BOX 31.5

## THREE DISCOURSES OF IGNORANCE

1   *I can't understand:* 'Ignorance' was said to be a reflection of mental constitution – they did not possess a 'scientific mind' and thus they could not understand such knowledge. But in 'admitting' this, they were simultaneously demonstrating that they were aware of the fact, that they were 'rational' about their ignorance. This reflects subordination to science.

2   *I don't need to understand:* 'Ignorance' was said to reflect a division of labour: scientists did one thing, other people did other things. Each could not be expected to know the details of the other's job – lay people simply did not need to know the science. Indeed, some respondents claimed that such patterns of knowledge and ignorance allowed institutions to work to everyone's benefit. This reflects functional co-habitation with science.

3 *I don't want to understand:* 'Ignorance' was represented as a deliberate choice – they did not want to come to grips with the scientific knowledge. In these interviews scientific knowledge was consciously bracketed, ignored, jettisoned or avoided because it was perceived as essentially peripheral to, or a distraction from, what the respondent considered to be the real issue at stake. This reflects a challenge to science.

This analysis (albeit rather condensed here), in taking the 'don't know' responses seriously, served as a critical commentary on those questionnaire studies which treated 'don't knows' merely as signs of the absence of knowledge. Indeed, it further suggested that the questionnaires could be used as 'prompts', to get people not so much to answer the questions as remark on the meanings of such questions and their perceived relations to those who would ask or be interested in such questions.

In terms of saying something 'interesting' or 'useful', this shift of analytic emphasis meant that we could now observe apparent lack of knowledge as something that was itself performed in order to accomplish certain ends. Indeed, the ostensible absence of knowledge, contrary to the then orthodox view in the public understanding of science field, does not stop people from being effective citizens. Instead of assuming that lack of scientific knowledge meant that lay people were disabled from contributing to science policy debates, one could say that such a lack of knowledge might be an *expression* of citizenship insofar as it reflected a challenge to, or disaffection with, the very terms of such policy debates. At the time, at least, this seemed like an important and useful contribution.

So, from a study that seemed to have generated very little data indeed, a slight shift in perspective meant that a somewhat different set of questions could be formulated which revealed that we were actually in possession of some very good data. This shift of perspective was partly enabled by our knowledge of how others were studying the public understanding of science. Reports about people's ignorance of science were

(and still are) a regular feature in the media. Treating ignorance as something that could be rationalised, explained and deployed by lay people allowed us to see how ignorance could also be represented as positive and even productive.

There are a number of broader principles (for want of a better term) that we might draw from the above example:

- First, it is important to go back and examine why a seemingly standard methodology and conceptual framework (in the above case, mental models) failed to generate the expected data. It might be the case that there are limits to the uses of such approaches, and that is itself an important observation.

- Second, cultivating an awareness of broader debates within the substantive field or sub-discipline can trigger off a sense of the possible value of one's (lack of) data. One can ask, how would others treat this (lack of) data? Can I say something interesting about this apparent absence which others have missed?

- Third, do not be discouraged by people's inability or unwillingness to answer your questions (even when you are asking the wrong questions). Being incapable, self-denigration, hostility and so on – all these are social *accomplishments*. One can pose the following questions: *how* have these presentations of self been accomplished and to *what* ends? Is it possible to read these performances as reflecting particular sorts of relations (such as relations of power with scientific institutions)?

## Anecdote 3: 'deviant' data

One could say that the 'don't know' responses were 'deviant data' insofar as they were certainly not anticipated. Finding data that one does not expect is, of course, what makes research so exciting. However, sometimes data are gathered which are often difficult to interpret, especially when one begins the research with expectations that are otherwise pretty standard for the research area within which one is working. Chapter 30 in this book discusses a variety of uses to which *deviant cases* or *negative instances* can be put. Box 31.6 shows how this affected another project with which I was involved.

---

**BOX 31.6**

## DISCOVERY OF DEVIANT DATA

In a research project conducted with Simon Carter, we were aiming, amongst other things, to explore what sources of information (about genetics and illness) were trusted by older school students. In a series of focus groups, we attempted to ascertain the extent to which, for instance, the Web, family members, GPs or medical journals were trusted. Our expectation was that there would be some consensus around the, albeit ambivalent, trustworthiness of certain sources. Instead what we found was that as soon as one possible source was mentioned by one participant, another would raise problems with it and suggest another possible source, the trustworthiness of which would, in its turn, be questioned by another student, and so on.

---

### Re-thinking the research problem

This made us re-think what was going on and reconsider our initial expectations, which were grounded in the assumption that such sources of information would be used to inform certain understandings about genetics and illness. In other words, we (and the subdiscipline of public understanding of science) would be expecting to see such sources being treated as if they contributed to the emergence of a certain *product* – namely, knowledge (after all, the students were motivated to derive such knowledge, not least for the purposes of passing biology exams). Instead, what we seemed to be witnessing was a *collective performance of contingency and movement*. Against seeing any of these sources as leading to a *product-like* knowledge, the students were engaged in a *process* of picking up, comparing, stringing together and criticising without necessarily reaching any conclusion or resolution about the trustworthiness of these sources (Michael and Carter, 2001). What looked like 'problematic' data (which perhaps cast aspersions on our ability to conduct focus groups – we could even be accused of letting the focus groups get out of control) could be usefully re-interpreted as raising issues about the very way in which the subdiscipline thought about knowledge and trust. By treating these focus groups as social events, and by shifting our 'take' on the data from 'product' to 'process', we could begin to explore how sometimes it is important for people to evoke a sense of shared scepticism. The social uses of this shared, collectively performed scepticism remain to be studied in detail.

The broader principle that is raised by this final anecdote is that one should not be afraid to innovate. If one's data makes no sense, then it is not necessarily because one has improperly generated or collected that data. It might be the case that the data that have been collected point to the limits of, or poverty of theory within, one's subdiscipline. Even if the punchline to such a study is that there is 'something' further to be investigated, this might still be an 'interesting and useful thing to say'.

## Conclusion

In the course of this chapter, I have attempted to deal with three things that can go wrong when doing research:

- When respondents do not 'behave' themselves.
- When the researcher has mis-designed the project.
- When expectations about the sort of data that should be collected are not met.

Obviously, the examples I have offered are but a small selection of what could go wrong. If there is a key lesson to draw, it is 'don't panic'. There are ways and means by which an apparent disaster can be turned around so that 'interesting and useful things' can be said. I have tried to indicate what some of these might be by drawing out some more general principles from the ways my colleagues and I have managed to get out of some tricky situations.

Of course, if such problems do arise, do not feel shy of seeking advice from peers, colleagues and supervisors. At the very least, they might be able to alert you to other concerns and debates within your field to which your data (or 'lack' of it) might be able to contribute. In the end, however, there is a calculation that will need to be made: is the extra work you must do to put yourself in a position to reinterpret your (lack of) data justified, or should you start your project afresh? This is perhaps the thorniest question of all, but it is one that has to be faced: sometimes it is just better to start again from scratch.

There is one final point to make. What counts as 'interesting and useful' is also a matter of *how* one writes. John Law (1994), reflecting on his ethnography of a large physics laboratory, admitted to feeling that wherever he was must be where the action *was not*. In other words, whatever data one is gathering, there is a pervasive sense that the *real* data, the *really good* data, are elsewhere. Conveying a sense of the limits of, and absences in, one's data is not an admission of failure but a sign of reflexivity and self-criticism. Another, more formal, way of putting this is in terms of auto-ethnography (e.g. Chang, 2008) in which the self is situated within an array of sociocultural dynamics, and interpreted and analysed in relation to a range of others (e.g. in terms of relations of similarity, difference, or opposition). In some ways, the present chapter is just such an exercise in auto-ethnography. The self that is implicated in the various research 'failures' I have described can be re-worked in terms of its relationships not only to the empirical cases (e.g. Why did that participant refuse to answer my questions?), but also to the process of research itself (e.g. What are the taken-for-granted parameters of a 'successful' piece of fieldwork?). Properly done, such reflexive, self-critical and modest analyses are an invitation to a complex and variegated dialogue about one's (lack of) findings, one's research and social scientific research in general: and after all, in the end, all research is work 'in progress'.

---

### *FURTHER READING*

Becker (1998) provides advice and a series of helpful anecdotes from his own research experience, many of which involve the kind of 'lateral thinking' described in this chapter. Janesick (2003) outlines a series of 'stretching exercises' for researchers, designed to feed creativity and loosen trapped thoughts.

*(Continued)*

*(Continued)*

## Student Reader (Seale, 2004b): relevant readings

2 C. Wright Mills: 'On intellectual craftsmanship'

26 Paul Feyerabend: 'Against method'

## Web links

Lateral Thinking Problems: www.folj.com/lateral

Lateral thinking the de Bono way: www.debonoconsulting.com/lateral_thinking.asp

## KEY CONCEPTS FOR REVIEW

**Advice:** Use these, along with the review questions in the next section, to test your knowledge of the contents of this chapter. Try to define each of the key concepts listed here; if you have understood this chapter you should be able to do this. Check your definitions against the definition in the glossary at the end of the book.

Epistemological radicalism

Political radicalism

Reflexivity

 **Review questions**

1 What kinds of thing can 'go wrong' in a research project?
2 What makes research useful and interesting?
3 What can you do to rescue a project if you find that you can't collect data directly relevant to the original research questions?

## Workshop and discussion exercises

1 This is an exercise designed for people who are at least half way through a project. However, if you are at the start of a project, you might find it useful to use your imagination to think of ways you can 'rescue' your project if what you are planning doesn't work out. Although you can do this exercise alone by writing things down, it is best done in a group with friends or others involved in the same kind of work:

(a) Identify the things that have 'gone wrong' so far in your research project.

(b) Do the same for the things that have 'gone right' so far (this is just to cheer you up if the previous part of the exercise has made you feel depressed!).

(c) Use the examples and advice in the chapter to identify (i) what you have already done to put things right, and (ii) what you can do in the future to put things right.

# GLOSSARY

Compiled by Milind Arolker and Clive Seale

**Abstract:** A summary of a journal article, appearing at the start of the article and reproduced in bibliographic indexes. Abstracts can also sometimes be found in other publication formats, such as chapters or theses. (See *Boxes* 6.3 and 7.4).

**Action research:** A multi-stage type of research, in which a problem is researched, changes are made, the problem and the effects of the changes are studied, more changes are made and so on, through a number of cycles, until the problem is solved or alleviated.

**Action theory:** Social theory in which action, its purposive nature and its meaning to people, is taken to be of central importance. Action theory is often associated with the name of Max Weber, who developed the interpretive tradition in social science. (See *Chapter 4* from the second edition of this book, by Filmer *et al*, available on the website for this current edition: www.rscbook.co.uk)

**Agency:** The capacity of individual 'agents' to construct and reconstruct their worlds, and to act independently from, or in opposition to, social forces and social structures (such as family, religious or institutional norms). Discourse analysis can involve looking for the way in which texts portray agency.

**Alert service:** A service offered by some bibliographic databases and journals which will send you a message about new publications that relate to your literature review, your recorded interests, or that have appeared recently in the journal.

**Allocation concealment:** Used in randomised controlled trials (RCTs) to prevent selection bias. This involves concealing information from trial organisers/researchers about which intervention/treatment or control group potential RCT participants will be assigned to until the last minute.

**Allocation sequence:** See *Randomisation sequence*

**Analysis of variance** or ANOVA: a method for analysing the relationship between two or more variables where the dependent variable is interval-level and the independent variable(s) is or are nominal. It proceeds by testing the significance of any differences between the mean values of the dependent variable within the different groups described by the independent variable. ANOVA is useful where the independent variable has three or more categories, and can then be understood as an extension of the logic of the *t*-test.

**Analytic memos:** Notes made by a researcher to record emergent ideas during a research project.

**Anecdotalism:** Only showing quotations that support the writer's argument at the expense of negative or deviant cases that might go against the case being made, or require its further elaboration.

**Anthropological strangeness:** The art or mental trick of making a social setting and behaviour within it appear as if the observer is encountered as a stranger. If applied to mundane 'taken-for-granted' events, this can lead to unusual and original insights.

**Anti-essentialism:** See *Essentialism*

**Archives:** Repositories of a variety of materials, such as documents, photographs and films, often of an historical nature, catalogued and filed for the use of researchers, scholars and other investigators.

**Association:** A quantifiable relationship between two variables. This can be linear, in which case it is a correlation, or another shape (e.g. curvilinear).

**Auditing:** The systematic scrutiny of material gathered within a qualitative or 'naturalistic' study that allows others, such as peer reviewers, to follow the methodological decisions and evaluate the quality of a research study. (This should be distinguished from another use of the term 'audit' common in health services, which refers to an exercise collecting and assessing data which measures the performance of a particular aspect of a health service against a defined standard.)

**Authenticity:** In general, this refers to the truthfulness of information, or of a research report (as opposed to falsity), but the term has also been used by Guba and Lincoln (1994) to refer to a political conception of the research process, whereby a study is judged good if it succeeds in enhancing participants' understanding and empowering them to act to change their circumstances.

**Autonomy:** See *Ethical principles*

**Axial coding:** A term used by grounded theorists to refer to exploration of the interconnections of coding categories that have been identified through open coding.

**Bar chart:** A graph displaying a frequency distribution. (See *Figure 19.5*)

**Beneficence:** See *Ethical principles*

**Beta coefficient:** See *Standardised coefficient*

**Bias:** Any systematic error that obscures correct conclusions about the subject being studied. Typically, such bias may be caused by the researcher's own pre-judgments, or by procedures adopted for data gathering. For example, a qualitative researcher might select anecdotes that support his or her preferred argument, ignoring others. A researcher carrying out an experimental design may allocate respondents to the different intervention groups in the study non-randomly, or a social survey researcher may study a non-representative sample. In qualitative research provision of a reflexive account of the research process can help in addressing the issue of whether one can trust the researcher to have been rigorous and fair.

**Bibliographic indexes:** A searchable database of published sources, such as journal articles. Examples include PubMed, Social Science Citation Index, Google Scholar.

**Bivariate statistics:** Analysis and statistical tests involving two variables, as in the cross-tabulation of two variables, a simple correlation, a chi-square statistic or a correlation coefficient.

Blinding (or masking): A method used primarily in trials to prevent bias, by ensuring that some of those involved in the research process are not aware of the treatment or intervention that a participant is receiving. The three types of blinding that are common are: participant blinding, treatment deliverer blinding, and blinding of outcome assessors.

Boolean searches: Searches for material (such as references or segments of coded text) using combinations of keywords linked by operators such as 'and', 'or' or 'not'. Databases (e.g. library catalogues) and qualitative analysis software (such as *NVivo*) commonly support such searches.

Bracketing: Used in semiotics to indicate the suspension of interest (for analytic purposes) in the relationship between signs and their referents. The term is also helpful in understanding the mental attitude required when doing discourse analysis or any analytic approach that treats text as a topic rather than a resource. Instead of considering the claims made in texts about reality outside the text, bracketing forces the analyst to consider the 'reality' the text constructs.

Break characteristics: Categories that distinguish groups from each other. When allocating participants to focus groups, a researcher can ensure that the groups are differentiated by some characteristic, such as gender. For example, a researcher may try to ensure that the groups contain an equal mix of male and female participants. (See *Box 13.7*, and also *Control categories*)

Career: Used, primarily, by symbolic interactionists and ethnographers to describe a person's progress through a social setting, as stages in learning how to experience the drug, or mental patients pass through a series of institutional settings.

Case study: The study of a single 'case' – for example, a person, an institution, an event. How 'case-ness' is defined depends on the logic of the particular research inquiry. For example, a nation might be thought of as a 'case' for certain purposes, even though a nation contains many people, each of which might be understood as a 'case' in some other inquiry. It is not a method of research as such because the data being offered can have been gathered using a variety of different methods (questionnaire, qualitative data, quantitative data).

Case-control: A research design in which the researcher selects a group of people who have the event or characteristic of interest (cases) and a comparable group of people who do not (controls). A comparison of the past exposures between the cases and controls will indicate whether there is an association between exposure and the event or characteristic that you want to explain. Usually, the cases are persons. But they can also be groups, departments, organisations and so on. (See *Box 8.8*)

Categorical variable: A variable which naturally falls into categories which do not have a sense of order or magnitude (e.g. a person's gender or a person's marital status). Also called a *Nominal variable*.

Categories: A term which, when used within grounded theory, refers to phenomena with shared characteristics, which are therefore placed together (see *Box 22.3*). Examples are friendship, awareness context, social loss story. (See also *Properties*)

Causality: A generative rather than accidental link between successive states of affairs (as where A is seen to have brought about B). Randomised controlled trials (RCTs), which are a type of experimental design, are generally seen as the best design for establishing causality.

**Cell:** The point within a contingency table showing the value of an intersection between variables.

**Census:** A count of the characteristics of every member of a given population (as opposed to a survey of a selected sample from that population). (See also *Sample survey*)

**Central tendency:** See *Measures of central tendency*

**Charts:** Visual displays of statistical information including bar charts, pie charts and histograms.

**Chi-square test:** A test of statistical significance commonly used for contingency tables, but also adaptable to see if a frequency distribution deviates significantly from what one would expect by chance alone. A chi-square enables a *p*-value to be calculated.

**Cleaning data:** Checking statistical data entry for errors and remedying these.

**Clinical trial:** An experiment designed to test the efficacy or effectiveness of a clinical treatment. (See also *Randomised controlled trial*)

**Clinically important difference:** A difference in a quantitative variable which will be clinically important to those in whom the variable is measured. For example, a new medication may cause a 1% reduction in blood pressure, but this may be so small that it is insignificant for preventing diseases like stroke or heart attack, so is not clinically important.

**Closed questions:** Question which can normally be answered by a single word or phrase, such as 'yes' or 'no'. (See *Box 11.6*, and also *Fixed-choice questions* and *Open questions*)

**Cluster randomised trial:** A randomised trial in which the units that are randomised are clusters (or groups) of individuals rather than the individuals themselves, for example hospitals or schools might be randomised rather than patients or pupils.

**Cluster sampling:** A probability sampling strategy involving successive sampling of units (or clusters); the units sampled progress from larger ones to smaller ones. For example, a researcher might first select schools from a list of all schools in the country, and then select pupils from those schools to interview, taken from a list of all of the pupils in the previously selected schools. (See also *Multistage cluster sampling*)

**Co-construction of meaning:** Refers to the way in which people interact to produce the meaning of things. (*See Box 25.3*)

**Coding:** The procedures whereby observations, segments of text, visual images or responses to a questionnaire or interview are collected into groups which are like one another, and a symbol is assigned as a name for the group. Data may be 'coded' as they are collected, as where respondents are forced to reply to fixed-choice questions. Alternatively, the coding of qualitative data can form a part of an interpretive, theory building approach.

**Coding stripes:** A term used in *NVIVO* software for qualitative analysis referring to coloured lines, with code labels, indicating an area of text to which coding has been applied.

**Coherence theory of truth:** Maintains that truth is primarily a property of whole systems of propositions, and can be ascribed to individual propositions only according to their coherence with the whole.

**Cohort study:** A research design in which a group of individuals (the cohort) are followed up over a period of time and measurements taken at several time points, to try to identify associations between attributes of the individuals and/or test hypotheses. (See also *Longitudinal study*)

**Collaborative production of talk:** Similar to *Co-construction of meaning*, but referring in particular to the way in which this is done through talk.

**Collocation:** Collocated words are ones which are commonly found next to, or near, a particular word.

**Column marginal:** The sum of a column in a contingency table. (See *Figure 19.10* and associated discussion)

**Column percentage:** The percentage of the total number of cases contained in a cell located in a column of a contingency table. (See *Figure 19.10* and associated discussion)

**Column variable:** A variable whose values are laid out across the top of a contingency table, thus forming the columns of a table as opposed to the rows. (See *Figure 19.10* and associated discussion)

**Combination to generalise:** Combining methods (e.g. qualitative and quantitative methods) in order to enhance the capacity to make generalisations.

**Combined or multiple methods research:** Research that uses more than one method (e.g. a survey using fixed choice questionnaires, followed up by qualitative interviews with a small number of the survey participants).

**Combining concepts:** A useful mental trick to develop the originality of research questions. Instead of just exploring one concept (e.g. sexism), think of another concept that could be combined with it (e.g. poverty) to come up with an unusual idea (e.g. to investigate the effect of poverty on the rate at which sexism occurs).

**Comparative keyword analysis (CKA):** Keyword analysis in which two texts of interest are compared with each other, rather than with a reference corpus.

**Comparative method:** The comparison of people's experiences of different types of social structure or social setting in terms of historical points in time, or across cultures at a single point in time. This is an approach which can shed light on the particular arrangements of both sides of the comparison. (See also *Constant comparison*)

**Computer assisted telephone interviewing (CATI):** Interviewing people over the telephone, using computer prompts for questions and entering data as answers are produced.

**Concept:** An idea located within a model. For example, the concept 'stimulus-response' is derived from behaviourism.

Concept map: A visual display of the ideas being developed in a research project. (*See Figures 21.4 and 21.5 for an example*)

Concept–indicator links: Refers to how well the form in which data are collected (e.g. items on a questionnaire) indicate the concepts they are intended to measure. Good links of this sort are important in achieving validity in measurement. For example, if you are trying to discover how fast someone reads (the concept 'reading speed'), a good indicator of this would be to time them reading something aloud. There would be a less direct link if you just asked them how many books they had read in the past year, as this may be unrelated to reading speed.

Concordance: A list of all of the words appearing in a text, often shown in their immediate context.

Conditional or first-order tables: Where an initial tabulation (a *Zero-order table*) is broken down by the values of a third variable to investigate the conditions under which relationships appearing in the zero-order table may apply, or be modified.

Confidence interval: Shows the range of values which include the true population value of a particular variable at a specified probability (usually 95%). For example, if we say 25% (95% CI: 20%–30%) of people live in poverty, this indicates we are 95% certain that the true value in the population from which our sample was drawn lies between 20% and 30%.

Confidentiality: Promises made to research participants about who will be told about what participants reveal to the researcher about themselves or their experiences. This will sometimes involve a guarantee of anonymity in any report of the research.

Confirmability: Used by Lincoln and Guba (1985) to refer to whether the results of a qualitative research project could be confirmed by others. This may be helped by providing an audit trail. (See also *Auditing*)

Confounder/confounding variable: A variable, other than the variable(s) under investigation, which is not controlled for and which may distort the results of experimental research because it is independently associated with both the outcome (dependent) and the predictor (independent) variables.

Connotation: Used in semiotics to indicate the interpretive meanings of signs, which may be ideological. Thus a picture of a soldier saluting a flag connotes nationhood and patriotism as well as the more straightforward things such as 'soldier' and 'flag' that it denotes. (See also *Denotation*, and *Figures 16.2* and *Box 16.5*)

Constant comparison: Used in grounded theory studies to describe how an item of data that is coded as a particular category is examined and its similarities with and differences from other items in the category are noted. In this way categories can be differentiated into new and more clearly defined ones and subcategories established. (See *Box 22.3*)

Construct validity: Evaluates a measure according to how well it conforms to expectations derived from theory. Thus, if we have reason to believe that health status is related to social class, we would expect our measure of health status to give different results for people from different social classes.

Constructionism: See *Social constructionism*

Consumption, production and representation: Terms from media studies to describe study of (1) the way 'audiences' of mass media respond to media messages (consumption), (2) the actions and influences on those who create media messages, such as journalists, script writers, website designers (production) and (3) the content of media messages themselves (representation).

Content analysis: Normally used in methods texts to refer to the quantitative analysis of texts or images, content analysis is in practice often combined with *Qualitative thematic analysis* to produce a broadly interpretive approach in which quotations as well as numerical counts are used to summarise important facets of the raw materials analysed.

Content validity: See *Measurement validity*

Contextual sensitivity: An important perspective of social science which helps a researcher appreciate that apparently uniform institutions like 'a tribe', 'a market', 'family' or 'identity' take on a variety of meanings depending on context. (See also *Historical sensitivity* and *Political sensitivity*)

Contingency table: A table of numbers in which the relationship between two variables is shown. Contingency tables can usefully be broken down into rows and columns. Percentages placed in the cells of the table, giving the proportion which each cell contributes to the sum of particular rows or columns, are often helpful in detecting the strength and direction of relationships.

Continuous variable: A characteristic, such as height or weight, that can have an infinite number of values arranged as a continuum.

Control categories: Used when allocating participants to focus groups according to some characteristic which the researcher wishes to remain constant or unchanged across the groups, such as a common gender or a common voting preference. (See *Box 13.7* for an example, and also *Break characteristics*)

Control group: In assessing the effects of an intervention (e.g. a new drug) using an experimental design a researcher will need to allocate participants to a control group to be confident that any change measured in the intervention group would not have happened anyway. The control group will match the intervention group as closely as possible.

Control lists: A list of literature search terms, or keywords, that are linked together for a particular concept, within a catalogue or indexing system. They can function like a thesaurus.

Controls: The group of participants in a case-control study who do not have the attribute (usually a medical condition) that the cases have, and against whom characteristics or previous exposures of the cases are compared to ascertain if there is any difference in these characteristics and exposures between the two groups.

Convenience sampling: (Also referred to as 'accidental sampling'.) A non-probability sampling strategy that uses the most easily accessible people (or objects) to participate in a study.

**Copyleft:** The opposite of 'copyright', being a term used to indicate initiatives that allow people to share materials in different ways without infringing copyright.

**Correlation:** In social statistics this term refers to a situation where two variables vary together, displaying a linear association. A correlation may be positive (in which case the two variables rise together) or negative (where one goes down the other goes up). Correlation coefficients (or tests of association) exist to indicate the strength and direction of linear relationships like this. Association includes linear relationships like this, but also includes curvilinear relationships.

**Correlation coefficient:** An indicator, ranging between $-1.0$ and $+1.0$, of the linear association between two variables. Karl Pearson's formula (for Pearson's $r$) can indicate a perfect positive relationship (a coefficient of $+1$), a perfect negative relationship (a coefficient of $-1$), or no relationship at all (a coefficient of zero).

**Correspondence theory of truth:** One of a number of different conceptions of 'truth', in relation to scientific explanations, which proposes an interchangeable connection between objectivity and truth. (See *Box 2.7*)

**Count:** When SPSS provides a cross-tabulation table for a contingency table, the count for each column and variable indicates the frequency pertinent to those two categories. (See *Figure 19.11*)

**Covert research:** Research that involves the deliberate intention not to inform those under study of their participation in research, either prior or during the research.

**Credibility:** A term coined by Lincoln and Guba (1985) applicable to the work of researchers carrying out studies of people in normal, or 'natural' settings. The credibility, or trustworthiness, of a researcher's report can be built up through several techniques: peer review; prolonged field experience; data triangulation; rejection of hypotheses during data analysis; ensuring claims are linked to strong evidence and so on. (See also *Member validation*, *Plausibility* and *Validity*)

**Criterion validity:** This is enhanced when a researcher identifies an independent, relevant, reliable and valid proxy measure or, 'gold standard', which can be used to compare a researcher's chosen method of measurement. The proxy measurement can be taken at the same time (to enhance concurrent criterion validity) or deferred to the future (predictive criterion validity). (See also *Validity*)

**Critical case:** Having set parameters for what should count as a case to study to answer a research question, just one specific critical, or single, case might be selected, particularly if the researcher wishes to confirm or challenge a theory. (See also *Unique case*, *Representative case*, *Revelatory case* and *Longitudinal case*)

**Critical discourse analysis:** Taking the perspective that people's use of written or spoken language reflects and influences their version of the world, society, events, or inner feelings, critical discourse analysis involves an engaged and committed examination of the relationship between language and its use within social, historical, political or ideological contexts. (See also *Discourse* and *Semantic prosody*)

**Cross-sectional study:** A study designed to capture data on measures of interest at one particular point in time from a selected sample. Correlations between measures can be made; for example, the relationship between employment status and health. Note that this type of study does not always reveal the direction of the relationship. (See *Box 8.3* for an example)

Cross-tabulation: An output produced by SPSS which is similar to a contingency table enabling comparisons between two categorical variables to be made. (See also *Contingency table*)

Cultural relativism: A position popular within the discipline of anthropology holding that values and norms of any given society cannot be compared with those of another society, perhaps to gauge superiority or inferiority, because such individual cultures have internal logic of their own.

Cultural scripts or texts: Terms used by those concerned to analyse cultural objects, such as pictures, films, sports events, fashions, food styles, to indicate that these can be viewed as containing messages in a manner comparable to a piece of written text.

Curvilinear relationship: A measure of association between two variables which demonstrates a line of best fit which curves rather than being exclusively positive or negative. (See *Figure 19.14*)

Data: The plural of datum, which refers to a record of an observation. Data can be numerical (and thence analysed within a quantitative paradigm) or consist of words, images or objects (perhaps for qualitative analysis).

Data analysis: A broad term referring to the processing and handling of data with the aim of drawing conclusions.

Data archives: can be distinguished from the more general term 'archive' in that they contain quantitatively coded material from surveys, or qualitative material collected as part of social research studies, made available through the archive for secondary analysis.

Data collection vs. data generation: Two possible views of the status of data. 'Collection' implies that the data are 'out there' waiting to be collected by the researcher. 'Generation' implies that data are co-produced by researcher and researched, or shaped in some other way by the ideas or methods that lead to their eventual presentation as 'data'. (See also *Topic versus resource*)

Data entry: The transfer of responses observed as part of a research process (e.g. a telephone survey) directly onto a computer.

Data matrix: The tabulation of observed responses, or research data (often from a questionnaire), in a particular way to permit comparison of variables against respondents or cases and to facilitate statistical testing. (See *Box 18.1* and *Figure 18.1*)

Database: A structure way of holding related information, where the structure is explicit enough to allow for quick searching to locate specific items of information. (See also *Fields*)

Deconstruction: An approach to social analysis that undermines claims to authority by exposing rhetorical strategies used by social actors, including the authors of research reports themselves. It has been promoted in particular by the post-modernist Derrida.

Deduction (and deductive reasoning): A form of logic or reasoning, amongst other metaphysical premises of science, which allows for the inference of a particular instance when a pre-existing law, or premise, holds true (i.e. if A, then B, where A is the premise/law and B represents the inferred instance). (See also *Hypothetico-deduction*)

Deductive coding: An approach to analysis of qualitative data, demanding that the researcher is pre-appraised and informed, usually from existing literature, of potential ideas, themes or concepts, or even gaps in knowledge, against which data can be appraised, analysed and thus coded. (See *Box 21.1*, and also *Inductive coding*)

Deductive-nomological (D-N) model: A model purporting to describe all scientific explanations of particular phenomena, and which specifically refers to the capacity of a law (or theory) to infer particular instances. (See *Box 2.6*, and also *Explanandum* and *Explanans*)

Denotation: In the analysis of an image, denotation refers to what the picture shows at a factual, descriptive level. This contrasts with connotation, where the analysis involves a use of a framework to guide a search for meaning, perhaps ideological, that can be 'coded' from the image. (See *Connotation*, *Figure 16.2* and *Box 16.5*)

Dependability: Proposed by Lincoln and Guba (1985) as a term closely related to reliability, and pertinent to data gathered within a qualitative or 'naturalistic' study. A researcher can enhance the dependability of their work by producing documentation of data, findings and decisions made during the research regarding methods chosen and any other issues. This documentation can be audited to assess the clarity of the account of the research process, including the researcher's thinking and conclusions.

Dependent variable: See *Variable*

Depth interview: A type of research interview aiming to understand an interviewee's personal framework of beliefs and values, why he or she acts as they do and the significance or meaning they associate with their activities and experiences.

Derived variables: The creation of new variables that measure new concepts by combining existing variables in a dataset, often when engaged in secondary analysis (See *Box 17.7*)

Descriptive accounts: See *Normative and descriptive accounts of science*

Descriptive statistics: These include the mean, mode, median, range and standard deviation for a particular sample of raw, parametric data, which help to summarise their distribution or pattern. (See *Figures 9.1, 19.2* and *19.6*, and also *Standard error* and *Standard deviation*)

Determinism: is the view that everything that happens is caused. When applied to human action, it suggests that our perception of having a free will is an illusion, and that the task of social research is to expose the true causes of action.

Dewey decimal system: A leading index system, used by libraries, which allocates specific number codes to various disciplines. (See also *Library of Congress system*)

**Diachronic vs. synchronic analysis:** Two distinct concepts identified by Saussure (1974) in his study of structural linguistics which forms the basis for semiotic analysis. Diachronic analysis looks at the arrangements of elements of a system, whereas synchronic analysis focuses on how the meaning of words evolves over time within a language. (See *Box 16.4*)

**Dichotomous variable:** A variable that has two values (e.g.. Yes/No; male/female).

**Differential bias:** Any type of bias, for example recall, or selection bias, that leads to one sample in a research study being handled differently to another group.

**Direct effect:** Where variables are regarded as having a direct influence on each other without any other variable intervening in the chain of causation. (See *Figure 20.4* and *Table 20.2*, and also *Indirect effect*)

**Directional hypothesis (or one-tailed hypothesis):** A hypothesis that makes a specific prediction, for example a positive or negative correlation, about the relationship between two variables. (See also *Non-directional hypothesis*)

**Disambiguation of meaning:** A word is said to be disambiguated when the various meanings which it is used to convey have been adequately identified. For example, the word 'bank' may mean the side of a river, or a financial institution. (See *Figure 26.4*, and also *Collocation* and *Keyword-in-context display*)

**Discourse:** This has come to refer, under the influence of Foucault, to systems of knowledge and their associated practices. More narrowly, it is used by discourse analysts to refer to particular systems of language, with a characteristic terminology and underlying knowledge base, such as medical talk, psychological language, or the language of democratic politics.

**Discursive repertoires:** Collections of phrases and linguistic choices that are derived from, or associated with, a set of ideas, such as ideas about 'race'. (See *Box 12.6*)

**Disproportionate stratification:** A method of selecting a sample from a population which deliberately contains a disproportionate number of a particular group of interest to the researcher, but which is numerically rather rare. Members of such groups may otherwise not be included in sufficient numbers in a simple random sample that gives every person in the population an equal chance of being selected.

**Dissemination:** The various ways in which research findings are broadcast to audiences, or helped to influence people to whom they apply. Plans for dissemination are often required by funding bodies considering research proposals, so that they can anticipate that research findings being shared as widely as possible. (See also *Research proposal* and *Signposts*)

**Divine orthodoxy:** See *Explanatory and divine orthodoxies*

**Documents for internal/external consumption:** A distinction which categorises documents drawn up for the internal use of organisations, and not necessarily for external publication. Such documents may be found in an archive.

**Doing aspects of social life:** (For example, caution, uncertainty, disagreement, neutrality as opposed to being cautious, uncertain, neutral and so on.) A choice of words designed to convey the orientation of conversation analysts in focusing on how social actions and practices are accomplished (done) in and through close observation and attention to the detail of talk and interaction.

**Double blind:** In experimental studies, blinding refers to restricting knowledge about who has been allocated to each trial arm once allocation has been carried out. If neither the participants nor the person supplying the intervention knows which treatment the participants have been allocated to, the trial is said to be double blinded.

**Effectiveness:** The extent to which an intervention, when used under defined circumstances, does what it is intended to do. Experimental studies are designed to assess this.

**Efficacy:** In general terms, this refers to the capacity of an intervention to bring about a beneficial or therapeutic change.

**Elaboration paradigm:** A structured approach to the exploration of causal relationships between variables through the examination of contingency tables. By introducing third variables to bivariate tabulations, arguments about causal direction and spuriousness are tested. The logic of this approach underlies most multivariate statistical analysis.

**Email surveys:** An internet-based method of administering a survey, involving attachment of a set of questions to an email to respondents who fill in the answers and return their responses. (See *Box 11.3*)

**Emic perspective:** Terminology used by anthropologists which refers to a research participant's own conceptions of social reality or culture. (See also *Etic perspective*)

**Empirical dissertation:** A study written in an educational context involving data collection and analysis, as opposed to a theoretical study which does not. (See *Box 10.1*, and also *Theoretical dissertation*)

**Empiricism:** The view that knowledge is derived from sensory experience, for example visual observation, and asserts that *objective* knowledge is 'true' knowledge. More loosely, it has been used to describe research that contains little in the way of reflection or theory, preferring to report 'facts' as they appear to be (as in the term 'abstracted empiricism') and assuming they exist first before any theories do. (See also *Objectivity*)

**Encoding and decoding:** When creating images or other kinds of message (e.g. a news article), the producers of these intend them to convey certain meanings and so 'encode' them into the image or the message. Consumers or audiences then 'decode' or interpret these images or messages, but may do so in a variety of ways not anticipated by the encoder.

**Epistemic responsibility:** An argument elaborated by Doucet and Mauthner (2002) that researchers take note of ethical issues related to the knowledge gained from data analysis, and engage with social, institutional and political contexts, as well as intellectual frameworks to do so.

**Epistemological radicalism:** Research which stretches the boundaries of philosophical questions concerning how we understand knowledge. (See *Box 31.1*, and also *Political radicalism*)

**Epistemology:** This refers to philosophical ideas about knowledge, consisting of attempts to answer questions about how we can know what we know, and whether this knowledge is reliable or not. Debates about the adequacy of empiricism, for example, are epistemological debates.

**Essentialism:** This is now increasingly used in order to explain why anti-essentialism is preferable, though in more purely philosophical discussion the term has greater usefulness. Amongst social and cultural researchers, anti-essentialism involves the rejection of a scientific quest for universal essences, such as the discovery of a universal psychological makeup, or generally applicable sex differences, in preference for a view that human 'nature' is a social construction.

**Ethics committee:** A committee tasked with assessing the rigour with which a researcher has considered ethical issues inherent in their research proposal. Major concerns of the ethics committee include preventing participants from suffering harm, and ensuring that informed consent has been gained from participants.

**Ethical principles (beneficence, non-maleficence, autonomy and justice):** Four fundamental principles of medical ethics, set out by Beauchamp (1994: 3). They also underlie the development of social research ethics. *Beneficence* refers to the obligation to provide benefits and balance benefits against risks; *non-maleficence* refers to the obligation to avoid the causation of harm; respect *for autonomy* refers to the obligation to respect the decision-making capacities of autonomous persons; *justice* refers to obligations of fairness in the distribution of benefits and risks.

**Ethnocentrism:** This refers to the practice of judging a different society by the standards and values of one's own. This is seen, particularly by ethnographers, as inhibiting understanding of other ways of life.

**Ethnography:** Taken literally, this means highly descriptive writing about people. Ethnographers collect data systematically through observation of people, and interaction with them, as these people carry on their tasks in their usual (or natural) setting. An ethnographic account may contain theories which explain the behaviour of those thus observed. (See also *Participant observation*)

**Ethnomethodology:** Involves the examination of the ways in which people produce orderly social interaction on a routine, everyday basis. It provides the theoretical underpinning for conversation analysis. Despite its name, it is not a 'methodology', but rather a particular theoretical framework or model guiding how to explore data.

**Etic perspective:** Terminology used by anthropologists which refers to the researcher's own conceptions of social reality or culture. (See also *Emic perspective*)

**Evaluation:** A form of research used to assess the value or effectiveness of social interventions or programmes. This research can be quantitative, in which case it most usually takes the form of a trial, or qualitative, involving investigators who, while remaining largely outside the development and implementation of an intervention, investigate its effectiveness using qualitative or mixed methods.

**Evidence-based:** Clinical or policy decisions are said to be evidence-based when they are based on empirical evidence that supports the decision.

**Executive summary:** The key points of a research report produced in summary form. This is usually longer than an abstract.

**Expected and observed values:** Referring to the numbers within cells of a contingency table, the expected values are those that would occur by the action of chance alone, given the values contained in the marginals of the table. The observed values are the numbers that actually appear, as the results of the observations made by the researcher during data collection. Where there is a large discrepancy between what is expected and observed, the relationship between the variables in the table is likely to be statistically significant, although this also depends on the overall sample size.

**Experimental study design:** One of two main categories of study design in which the researcher usually imposes an intervention on some of the study participants and measures the effects. (See *Figure 8.1*, and also *Randomised controlled trial*)

**Explanans:** The sentence containing the explanation for the explanandum (see *Box 2.6*), including a general law and conditions relevant to the specific explanandum. For example: for the explanandum that 'smoke has appeared from within a building', the general law part of the explanans would be 'fire generates smoke', and the relevant conditions part of the explanans would be 'the building is on fire thus causing the smoke' (explaining why smoke has appeared). (See also *General and specific explanations*)

**Explanandum:** The sentence describing the phenomenon to be explained (see *Box 2.6*). For example: 'smoke appears from within a building' (explained by the explanans).

**Explanations (scope, form, structure, testability and validity of):** These are five general ways of categorising scientific explanations. (See *Box 2.5*)

**Explanatory and divine orthodoxies:** These 'modes of thinking' about social research result in the failure to access the issue of how social institutions work. The explanatory orthodoxy asserts that how people act is defined by 'society' and can be reduced to variables such as class, ethnicity or gender. The divine orthodoxy stresses that research participants' knowledge is inherently unreliable or imperfect and that a researcher can always spot and see through these issues and take them into account when designing research.

**Explanatory trial:** A trial conducted under ideal conditions in which a treatment (very often a drug, surgery or other therapy) is administered to a select group of patients in whom compliance with treatment is strictly monitored, to ascertain whether or not the treatment is efficacious (works in ideal conditions).

**External validity:** See *Validity*

**Face validity:** See *Measurement validity*

**Facilitative combination of methods:** The sequential use of qualitative and quantitative research methods in particular order. Whichever method is carried out first will provide results that inform subsequent methodological choices when using the next method in line.

Facticity: The process whereby certain perceptions or phenomena achieve the status of uncontroversial fact. Phenomenological analysis attempts to reduce facticity, as does the method of deconstruction, by exposing the social practices that generate it. Achieving facticity may involve both the objectification and the naturalisation of something as a fact. The use of passive voice in official documents ('it is noted that', rather than 'we note') confers facticity associated with bureaucracy.

Falsificationism: Coined by the philosopher and empiricist, Karl Popper (1902–1994), it regards explanations or theories as scientific if they are testable and refutable. Popper regarded this as an important component of scientific progress, adopting norms associated with the hypothetico-deductive method to get closer to the 'truth' through rejection of existing theories so that new and better theories might then be formulated. (See also *Hypothetico-deduction* and *Verificationism*)

Feedback: Comments or criticisms invited by the researcher on any aspect of their work, whether written or oral.

Field notes: Descriptions (which are as precise as possible) of social processes and their contexts (e.g. things people do or say in social settings) which set out to capture their various properties and features. Researchers typically record this type of data when carrying out observation as part of an ethnographic study.

Fields: The subsections that create the structure of a database and against which records are stored.

Fixed choice questions: Questions that require respondents to pick an answer from a given set of options. (See *Box 11.6*, and also *Closed questions* and *Open questions*)

Flanders Interaction Analysis Categories (FIAC): A structured observation tool that characterises teaching styles in terms of how teacher-centred they are. The observer records the predominant activity observed in the preceding three seconds. (See *Box 11.12*, and also *Roter interaction analysis system* and *Structured observation*)

Focus group: An interview or discussion with a group of participants. These allow researchers to examine people's different perspectives as they operate within a social network and they permit exploration of how the articulation of accounts is influenced by group norms.

Foreshadowed problems: Issues or problems, related to the research question, which are identified upfront before carrying out ethnographic fieldwork. (See also *Funnel structure*)

Fragmentation: A term coined by Ranajit Guha (1997) to refer to the accidental or deliberate destruction of documents as they undergo filing in an archive.

Framework approach to analysis: A method for managing qualitative data developed by the National Centre for Social Research. It involves summarising data in charts developed from a thematic framework. See: www.natcen.ac.uk/about-us/our-approach/framework.

Frequency distribution (or frequency count): A count of the number of times each value of a single variable occurs. Thus, the proportion of the population fitting into each of six categories of social class may be given as a frequency distribution. The distribution can be presented in a variety of ways, including, for example, a raw count, percentages or a pie chart.

**Functionalism:** An approach to explaining social phenomena in terms of their contribution to a social totality. Thus, for example, crime is explained as necessary for marking the boundary of acceptable behaviour, reinforcing social order. Prominent functionalists include Durkheim and Parsons.

**Funnel structure:** Referring to the way ethnographic research progresses, the researcher may begin with a rudimentary idea about the sort of problem to be investigated, which is liable to change (i.e. the 'funnel' narrows) over the course of fieldwork, particularly as problems are transformed or emerge in the field.

**Gatekeepers:** The people or institutions that oversee and may obstruct or enable access to the setting in which the researcher wishes to carry out observation or other research methods.

**Genealogy of ideas:** Historical research can help trace the roots and development of ideas, systems of knowledge or discourses that are considered relevant today. For example, Foucault has carried out 'genealogical' studies of ideas about sexuality and madness in European societies over time. Foucault suggested in a further metaphor that an *archaeological* approach towards the elucidation of these be adopted.

**General and specific explanations:** A general explanation relates to a general explanandum. A specific explanation relates to specific parts of an explanandum. (See also *Explanans*)

**Generalisability:** Also referred to as 'external validity'. The extent to which the results of a study are useful in settings other than the setting in which the research was conducted; the extent to which the results derived from a sample may hold true in the population from which that sample was selected.

**Genre conventions:** The particular conventions associated with certain types of document. For example, research methods textbooks may typically make liberal use of bullet points, figures and boxes. This would not be a common convention in a novel or a poetry collection.

**Grey literature:** Useful materials, often reporting research, other than books and journal articles. They include newspapers, conference proceedings and abstracts, theses and documents produced by governments, private organisations and charities.

**Grounded theory:** a term coined by Glaser and Strauss to describe the type of theory produced by their methods of ethnographic data collection and analysis. The approach emphasises the systematic discovery of theory from data by using methods of constant comparison and theoretical sampling, so that theories remain grounded in observations of the social world rather than being generated in the abstract. This they propose as an inductive alternative to hypothetico-deductive approaches.

**Group administered self-completion surveys:** The administration of a survey instrument to a group of respondents who then complete the survey individually. Typically, this may involve a researcher distributing a questionnaire to pupils in a school at the start of a lesson and then collecting the completed questionnaires at the end of the lesson.

**Harvard referencing system:** A standard system for citing references and ordering reference information in a bibliography.

**Hawthorne effect:** The modification of participants' behaviour due to the presence of the researcher studying them. Named after a study carried out at the Western Electrical Company's Hawthorne Works in Chicago in the 1930s. (See also *Placebo effect*)

**Helsinki (Declaration of):** Produced in 1964 and repeatedly revised by the World Medical Association since, it sets out international standards for carrying out medical research involving people. The current sixth version (2008) is the only official one and replaces all previous versions.

**Hermeneutic viewpoint:** This view stresses that all description is based on interpretation, and this includes an individual's description of phenomena they experience. Any social researcher collecting data about an individual's experience will, by definition of the viewpoint, be reconstructing the experience.

**Histogram:** A graph made up of bars which help visualise a frequency distribution.

**Historical sensitivity:** An important perspective of social science which demands that the researcher appreciates any historical evidence relevant to the current issue or research problem of interest. (See also *Contextual sensitivity* and *Political sensitivity*)

**Holism:** The philosophical view that individual parts of an entity are interconnected and cannot exist, nor can they be understood independently of their whole entity. Aristotle, in Metaphysics, elaborated on the concept of 'wholeness' when asking what makes up living things. (See *Reductionism*)

**Household drop-off survey:** A method for administering a survey which involves going to the respondent's home or business address and handing them the survey instrument to complete and return. This allows the respondent to consider their responses in private and permits the researcher personal contact with their potential respondents. This method may improve the survey response rate. (See also *Group administered questionnaire*)

**Hypothesis:** A statement that specifies a relationship between two or more variables. When assessed through relevant data collection and analysis under a quantitative paradigm, hypotheses can be accepted or rejected according to whether a statistical relationship is found or not. (See *Directional hypothesis*, *Hypothetico-deduction*, *Non-directional hypothesis* and *Null hypothesis*)

**Hypothetico-deduction (and Hypothetico-deductive method):** The view that (or process by which) science progresses by starting with hypotheses based on theories, which are then tested for truth or falsity by observation and experimentation, eventually leading to hypotheses that survive rejection and then add up to an aggregate of positive knowledge. (See also *Falsificationism*, *Induction*, *Deduction* and *Scientific revolution*)

**Idealism:** Often opposed to realism, this term describes the view that the world exists only in people's minds. (See also *Realism*)

**Idiographic:** Referring to the aim of phenomenological studies to explore the subjective nature of experience, rather than to produce generalisable explanations of objective phenomena. (See *Lifeworld* and *Phenomenology*)

**Immersion:** Researchers are said to have 'immersed' themselves in either the field (the setting studied) or their data if they spend a long time in the field, or studying their data, and thus get to know it extremely well. The repeated reading of qualitative data is designed to encourage such immersion so as to become sensitive to its meaning.

**Import filters:** Used by bibliographic software to facilitate reference importing, so that relevant items of the reference (such as title, abstract or author) map to the appropriate part of the software's database.

**Importing references:** An alternative to manually entering references into bibliographic software.

**Impression management:** A researcher carrying out participant observation needs to give due consideration to this. It refers to developing insight into how they are perceived by the research participants being observed. A balance may need to be struck between establishing normal social intercourse and rapport, meeting any relevant norms or customs, and not appearing threatening when seeking research data or information.

**In loco parentis:** Literally 'in place of parents'. Researchers carrying out research with children as participants need to be aware that under certain circumstances they may be held responsible if the child is harmed in any way.

**In-depth interview:** See *Depth interview*

**Incidence:** A quantitative measure which indicates the rate at which new cases of a disease or event occur. (See also *Prevalence*)

**Inclusion criteria:** Criteria, defined by a research question, for including people in a study (or including studies in a systematic review).

**Independent variable:** See *Variable*

**Indexes to archives:** Indexes allow researchers to search archives using keywords or dates.

**Indirect effect:** A variable is said to have an indirect effect on another variable when it exerts this influence through another ('intervening') variable.

**Induction:** A metaphysical premise of science, and means of 'scientific' explanation, that permits the inference of laws, or theories or generalisations from multiple observations. It is the opposite of deduction, but appeals to empiricism, and verificationism in particular. (See *Deduction*, *Empiricism*, *Rationalist epistemology* and *Verificationism*)

**Inductive coding:** An approach to qualitative data analysis which tends to be followed when studies begin with a broad research question and precise themes emerge empirically from the data rather than presenting themselves at the outset. (See *Box 21.1*, and also *Deductive coding*)

Inductive reasoning: A form of reasoning in which a generalised conclusion is formulated from particular instances.

Informed consent: The process of obtaining voluntary participation of individuals in research based on a full understanding of the aims of the research study, its possible benefits and risks, and the handling of information which the participant helps create.

Instrumentalism: A philosophy maintaining that scientific theories are useful conceptual constructs that have no truth value. Instead their evaluation rests on how well they explain and predict phenomena.

Intention to treat analysis: Analysis in which data from randomised individuals are analysed with the individuals remaining in the groups to which they are randomised, regardless of whether they actually receive the intervention. Participants may have a variety of different reasons for not participating in the intervention after originally agreeing to do so. In health care interventions this makes the study closer to reality, since people often do not turn up for appointments, or cease following treatment recommendations.

Interaction: At its broadest, interaction is the basis of all social life. Much more narrowly, and in relation to focus group research, interaction can be considered a key feature of this form of data collection. Rather than being a means to interviewing several people at once, focus groups are concerned with exploring the formation and negotiation of accounts within a group context, and how social interaction acts as a medium through which people define, discuss and contest issues.

Interactionism: An approach to studying social life which emphasises the exploration of the ways in which it is organised around events and symbols to which people orient themselves.

Inter-coder/inter-rater reliability: See *Reliability*

Internal validity: See *Validity*

Interpreting vs. reporting data: Interpretation of data in the quantitative research paradigm is often perceived to be separate from the reporting of data. Here, interpretation can consist of comments on what the researcher believes to be significant about the patterns in data (the 'findings') that have been reported. For researchers who, by contrast, believe that data is generated at least in part by the instrumentation employed to create it, all 'reporting' of data involves interpretation. One therefore sometimes sees, in qualitative research writing, less distinction between the two. (See *Boxes 28.5* and *28.6*)

Interpretive content analysis: See *Content analysis*

Interpretive repertoires: The ways of speaking about and understanding a topic that organise the meanings of a text. (See also *Discursive repertoires*)

Interpretivism/interpretive methods: Refers to approaches emphasising the meaningful nature of people's participation in social and cultural life. The methods of natural science are seen as inappropriate for such investigation. Researchers working within this tradition analyse the meanings people confer upon their own and others' actions.

**Inter-quartile range:** A descriptive statistic, defined as two figures which indicate the range within which the middle 50% of measurements for individuals within the study lie.

**Intersubjectivity:** The common-sense, shared meanings constructed by people in their interactions with each other and used as an everyday resource to interpret the meaning of elements of social and cultural life.

**Intertextuality:** A term referring to the ways in which documents or other texts are related to one another, and whether the connections are explicit (e.g. 'matters arising' as part of a set of a meeting's minutes) or implicit (e.g. the shared conventions or style between documents). (See *Box 15.8*)

**Interval variables:** These variables have the properties of identity, magnitude and equal intervals between points. The Celsius scale of temperature is an example. (See also *Nominal variables* and *Ratio scales*)

**Intervening variable:** A variable that is affected by one variable and then transmits this effect to another variable in a chain of causation. Within the elaboration paradigm, this type of variable must be caused to vary by an independent variable in the zero-order relationship, and in turn must cause variation in the dependent variable. (See *Box 20.3*)

**Intervention group:** A group within a trial which receives a specified intervention. Very often in a clinical trial there are only two groups to which individuals are randomised; the control group and the intervention group.

**Interview:** A form of communication with the aim of producing different forms of information with individuals or with groups. An interview can take a flexible approach or a highly structured approach to asking questions.

**Interview guide:** See *Topic guide*

**In vivo codes:** Codes, or terms, taken directly from data, when that data takes the form of words. They help the analyst, when carrying out an inductive approach to analysis, avoid imposing their own interpretations of the meaning of data.

**Justice:** See *Ethical principles*

**Kappa statistic:** A measure of inter-rater reliability when applying a coding scheme for content analysis of text. The value range is from zero to one, and a value of 0.81 or greater indicates almost perfect agreement. (See *Table 26.1*, and also *Content analysis*)

**Keyword analysis:** Referring to computer-assisted methods for analysing texts, keywords are words that occur more commonly in one set of texts when compared to a reference text. (See *Box 26.2*, and also *Comparative keyword analysis* and *Keyword-in-context display*)

**Keyword-in-context (KWIC) display:** Using computers to facilitate content analysis, a researcher can produce an output displaying and counting all contexts (surrounding words) in which a particular word appears within a text or set of texts. A large body of textual data can be thus made more manageable for the researcher to carry out further analysis. (See *Figure 26.1*, and also *Collocation* and *Manifest content*)

**Knowledge of context:** Knowledge about the surrounding structures in which an event which is being studied takes place. For example, a contextual factor that might inform a study of doctor–patient interaction and help understand the talk that takes place may be whether the setting is public or private health care. A first-hand researcher can often use the knowledge of context, which they pick up without at the time realising it, to interpret the data they have collected. Any subsequent researcher approaching the data second-hand may not be able to access such background knowledge.

**Langue and parole:** Two concepts identified by Saussure (1974) in his study of structural linguistics which forms the basis for semiotic analysis. Langue, or language, is the system of signs, whereas parole, or speech, is the individual instances of use of language to make particular speech acts or utterances. (See *Box 16.4*, and also *Sign*, *Signified* and *Signifier*)

**Latent content:** An analysis of text informed by the interpretation of the researcher (e.g. whether a text conveys a particular idea), rather than being a report of manifest content (e.g. the number of times a particular word occurs). (See also *Manifest content*)

**Law, theorem and theory:** Within the hierarchy of scientific explanations, a law lies below a principle (or *explanans*). A theorem comes below law and can be deduced from laws. A theory, however, is a set of laws pertaining to a composite explanandum. (See also *Deduction*, *Explanandum* and *Explanans*)

**Library classification systems:** A means of organising a library's references.

**Library of Congress system:** A leading index system developed in the United States, used by libraries, which allocates specific Roman letter codes to various disciplines. (See also *Dewey Decimal system*)

**Lifeworld:** The place where a research participant (an individual) is directly involved with the world and from which position their experience originates. It is important, in a phenomenological enquiry, for the researcher to enter this.

**Limited quantification:** Making the frequencies of phenomena encountered in qualitative research accounts explicit, irrespective of how low the frequencies are. This may provide an appreciation of generality for the reader. One should guard against the notion that quantifying qualitative findings improves accuracy, however, and such analysis should be supported by a self-critical approach, involving perhaps, a search for negative instances. (See *Box 27.7*)

**Linguistic repertoire:** A term used in discourse analysis to refer to the resources (discourses, intersubjective meanings etc.) on which people draw in order to construct accounts.

**List format:** A way of presenting themes identified within qualitative data by listing them and giving quotes illustrating those themes. (See also *Careers* and *Typologies*)

**Literature review:** A narrative describing an appraisal of previous research or literature on a subject.

**Local production/accomplishment:** Conversation analysts (and ethnomethodologists) are interested in how social reality is created in particular moments, situations, places and contexts (i.e. its local production) as well as how talk and interaction that occur in particular locations constitute the identities of participants, in other words, their local accomplishment.

**Logical positivism:** A pro-science epistemology which asserts that all theories and scientific explanations should be testable by contact with an external reality. Logical positivists support the view that theory can be created through verificationism. 'Facts' are assumed to have a higher status in comparison to 'values' or 'beliefs', irrespective of how the latter might underpin the former. (See also *Realism* and *Verificationism*)

**Logistic regression:** see *Regression*

**Longitudinal case:** A single case studied at two or more points in time for answering a research question which involves examining changes over time. (See also *Critical case*, *Representative case*, *Revelatory case* and *Unique case*)

**Longitudinal study:** See *Cohort study*

**Loss to follow-up:** A term referring to decreasing participation in longitudinal studies, such as cohort studies which require repeated questioning of participants, sometimes for many years.

**Manifest content:** The surface characteristics of content, described with the minimum of interpretive judgement (e.g. how long a text is, how many times a particular word occurs, which words are often to be found together). (See also *Latent content*)

**Margin of error:** See *Confidence interval*

**Marginality:** Used to describe the typical position of the ethnographer, who exists on the margins of the social world being studied, in that he or she is neither a full participant nor a full observer. Also used to describe groups of people living outside mainstream culture.

**Marginals (of a table):** The edges of a table which sum the values for their respective rows and columns.

**Matching:** A process by which units (usually individuals) within a quantitative research study are formed into pairs (or sometimes in case-control studies groups of three or four) within which some attributes of the units are identical. The aim of matching is to reduce bias.

**Materialism:** The philosophical view that the only thing that exists is matter, so that all things (including our ideas) are the result of material interactions (in the case of ideas, these might be chemical interactions in the brain).

**Maximum variation sampling:** A type of non-probability sampling suited to small samples where no sampling frame exists. Selection is based on the researcher's existing knowledge of the subject being studied with the aim of finding people with widely varying experiences. (See *Box 9.6*, and also *Non-probability sampling*)

**Mean:** A descriptive statistic used as a measure of central tendency. All measurements in a set of measurements are added together and divided by the number of people or things that have been studied.

**Measurement scale:** Measurement of a phenomenon or property means assigning a number or category to represent it. The methods used to display and/or analyse numerical (quantitative) data will depend on the type of scale used to measure the variable(s). There are four scales of measurement: nominal, ordinal, interval or ratio. The data associated with each measurement scale are referred to as nominal data, ordinal data, interval data and ratio data respectively.

**Measurement validity:** The extent to which a measuring instrument appears to measure what it claims to measure. For example, to assess the measurement validity of a set of questions contributing to a measurement device, a researcher may deliberately target individuals acknowledged to be experts in the topic area to give their opinions on how well various aspects of the concepts have been covered. This is sometimes called an assessment of its face, or content validity. (See also *Operationalisation*)

**Measures of association:** Statistics used to indicate the strength and direction of an association between variables.

**Measures of central tendency:** Statistics such as the mean, median or mode which in various ways indicate the central point in a frequency distribution.

**Media genres:** Categories of media output. Examples include soap operas, television documentaries, news and current affairs. In media analysis it is important to understand the genre conventions of different media genres.

**Median:** A descriptive statistic used as a measure of central tendency. It is the middle value in a list of quantitative measurements when these measurements are ordered from smallest to largest.

**Member validation:** The act of giving your research participants a chance to examine and comment on themes you have derived from the data they helped contribute, before findings are written up. Although it can be argued that there are many ways of 'seeing' the data, this form of validation may prove useful if the goal of the research is to identify and apply themes that are recognised or used by participants.

**Memos:** Informal notes drafted and retained by the researcher as data is coded. They help capture impressions, ideas, working theories, personal comments and any problem codes. (See also *Analytic memos*)

**Meta-analysis:** An agglomeration of existing empirical research evidence which is synthesised with the aim of providing a robust and reliable summary of disparate research evidence. Quantitative systematic reviews often involve meta-analysis so as to pool the results of different studies, thus increasing the likelihood of finding significant patterns in data.

**Metadata:** Literally, 'data about data'. Metadata associated with documents in an archive might include the date of their production and the author. Metadata attached to research interview data files uploaded into qualitative analysis software might include relevant demographic details about the participants or the location of the interviews. Such metadata can be used to 'filter' searches of uploaded research data.

**Metaphysics:** The branch of philosophy concerned with fundamental questions of existence, of being in the world, and of the nature of objects. A metaphysician, for example, might ask 'What is time?' or 'How is it that we are beings?' Unlike science, which deals with explanations and empirical data, philosophy often deals with untestable justifications, and this implies that it deals with metaphysical phenomena.

**Method:** A specific research technique (e.g. a social survey, interviews, experimental design).

**Methodology:** Concerns the theoretical, political and philosophical roots and implications of particular research methods or academic disciplines. Researchers may adopt particular methodological positions (e.g. concerning epistemology or political values) which establish how they go about studying a phenomenon. This can be contrasted with *method*, which generally refers to matters of practical research technique.

**Micro vs. macro levels of analysis:** The micro level of social life generally involves small-scale interactions, such as occur when people meet face-to-face. The macro level, on the other hand, involves the study of social structures, social organisations, or historical changes in society. It is sometimes said that qualitative studies are good for investigating the small-scale (micro) phenomena that potentially underlie large-scale (macro) observations and conclusions revealed in quantitative studies.

**Mis-en-scène:** The spatial organisation of a visual image, including camera angle, point of view, focus and so on. These elements can be analysed to understand how they work to create the 'gaze' of protagonists and spectators. (See *Box 16.1*)

**Mode:** A descriptive statistic that is a measure of central tendency; it is the value that occurs most frequently in a distribution of measurements.

**Model:** In social theory, this refers to an overall framework for looking at reality, indicating what reality is like and the basic elements it contains. Examples are functionalism, behaviourism, symbolic interactionism or ethnomethodology. This is distinct from its meaning in statistics (as in 'statistical modelling') where it refers to the attempt to discover rules that govern the patterns found in some numerical data.

**Multidimensional concept:** A concept made up of several different sub-concepts or ideas. For example, to find indicators for assessing 'alienation', a researcher would have to assess its different components (e.g. powerlessness, loss of moral conviction, isolation).

**Multiple regression:** See *Regression*

**Multiple response item:** A fixed-choice question format which allows the respondent to select one or more items to answer the question. At the analysis stage, each response can be considered a dichotomous variable, and given a code for 'selected' or 'not selected'. (See *Box 18.2*)

**Multistage cluster sampling:** Cluster sampling involving more than one stage. For example, a researcher may choose five local government districts from a list of all of those in a country, then choose five schools from the many within those districts, then choose five classrooms from each of the many classrooms in each school, and then choose five pupils to interview in each of those classrooms.

**Multivariate analysis/statistics:** Analysis of the relationships between three or more variables (as opposed to bivariate analysis, which involves two variables, or univariate analysis, which involves one). This might involve the cross-tabulation of two variables by different values of a third variable, multiple or logistic regression with two or more independent variables.

**Mutual information (MI) score:** An adjustment made for the phenomenon whereby common words, such as 'the' or 'and', routinely appear as collocates of keywords, indicating which collocates co-occur more often than might be expected by chance alone. (See also *Collocation* and *Keyword-in-context display*)

**Narrative:** A narrative is an account of a non-random sequence of events that conveys some kind of action and movement through time. (See *Narrative frameworks* and *Narrative materials*)

**Narrative frameworks:** Used by individuals to structure the experiences they wish to convey to others in order to make the events easily understandable to others. The romantic story of 'falling in love' is an example of a narrative framework a person might draw upon in order to tell the story of their own experience. (See *Box 25.2*)

**Narrative materials:** The materials, or 'data', that narrative analysts analyse. These can include 'naturally occurring' narratives such as everyday conversations between people, life stories collected for research purposes in interviews, or written narratives found in the private, public or political realms (e.g. diaries, letters and policy documents).

**Naturalism:** Naturalists take the view that the methods of the natural sciences are appropriate to the study of the social and cultural world. This should be distinguished from another meaning of the term *naturalism* or *naturalistic* which is sometimes used to refer to the claim of ethnographers to collect naturally occurring data. It should be further distinguished from the term 'naturalising'. (See also *Naturalising*)

**Naturalising:** This is the process whereby matters that are in fact socially constructed and were once fluid and changeable come to be perceived as a part of the natural order and therefore fixed, inevitable and right (or 'natural'). It can be observed in official documents, where items noted are worded in a way that confers objectivity and an unquestionable status. By contrast, social researchers often wish to 'denaturalise' phenomena (such as sexual identity, for example) by exposing the human processes whereby they are constructed. (See also *Facticity*)

**Naturally occurring action, interaction or data:** Action, interaction or the recording of data which is not researcher-led or researcher-prompted but rather takes place in a usual, 'normal' or routine setting. An example of naturally occurring data might be an audio recording of a consultation between a doctor and patient as it proceeds in a consulting room.

**Negative association or relationship:** A quantifiable linear relationship between two variables, which indicates that as one variable rises, the other falls. This is sometimes called an 'inverse relationship'.

**Negative instances:** instances of data (sometimes also called 'deviant cases') that contradict emerging analyses, generalisations and theories.

**Nesting:** A technique involving enclosure of one pair of parentheses within another pair, in order to refine a search of an index or database.

**Nominal variables:** Also called categorical variables, these are variables that simply categorise or name things, such as colour, or gender, or ethnicity, or marital status. There is no sense of ordering, size or magnitude between the different values of such variables. (See also *Ordinal variables*)

**Nominalisation:** A technical linguistic strategy noted by critical discourse analysts, which involves use of nouns in place of verbs to describe events. For example, instead of 'Fascists riot against Muslims in Bradford' (where 'riot' is a verb) a headline might read 'Riot against Bradford Muslims' (where 'riot' is a noun), which lends a different force to the meaning. (See also *Passivisation*)

**Non-directional hypothesis (or two-tailed hypothesis):** A hypothesis that does not make a specific prediction, for example a positive or negative correlation, about the relationship between two variables. (See also *Directional hypothesis* and *Null hypothesis*)

**Non-experimental study design:** One of two main categories of study design in which the researcher does not directly influence the behaviour of the study participants, but observes and measures the study participants. (See *Figure 8.1*)

**Nonfoundationalism:** The philosophical viewpoint that is impossible to uncover or define a criterion for the satisfactory assessment of truth. From a science perspective, this becomes relevant if it can be argued that it is impossible to test a scientific hypothesis in isolation, as tests are based on assumptions which themselves require testing ad infinitum. Nonfoundationalists may thus end up by arguing that science can never be superior to other forms of knowledge.

**Non-maleficence:** See *Ethical principles*

**Non-parametric tests:** Statistical tests that can be used to analyse descriptive statistics concerning data samples for which no assumption can be made concerning the distribution of the measure within its parent population.

**Non-probability sampling:** A type of sampling method in which some people have an unknown, or no chance of being selected. Examples include snowball sampling or sampling by case study. (See *Box 9.1*)

**Non-response:** The problem that arises from participants not taking part in research. This problem can lead to biased interpretation of results. It can be minimised by re-considering the research design, and mitigated by investigating the characteristics of non-responders, reporting how they compare with responders and thinking through how this might have affected the results gathered from responders. (See also *Response rate*)

**Non-significant result:** The outcome of a statistical test, which results in a $p$-value greater than a specified level (e.g. $p>0.05$), indicating that the observed difference or association between two or more variables could have occurred by chance, and may not be true of the population from which the sample was drawn.

Normal curve: A theoretical probability distribution of a variable with specific properties: perfect symmetry and no skew towards a particular direction.

Normative and descriptive accounts of science: Normative accounts of science explain what science ought to do, whereas descriptive accounts explain what it actually does.

Normative interaction order: Revealed by conversation analysts, this is a set of obligations and expectations that people tend to work with and against, particularly evident in conversations involving agreement/acceptance and disagreement/refusal, where it is usually found that there is an overriding preference for agreement.

Null hypothesis: A hypothesis that states there to be no predicted relationship between two variables. (See also *Directional hypothesis* and *Non-directional hypothesis*)

Numeric variables: See *String and numeric variables*

Objectives: Having drawn up a research proposal and identified aims of the research, objectives can be defined to describe what the researcher needs to do to achieve the aims and thus address the research question or problem.

Objectivity: Knowledge, for example theories or scientific explanations, which approximate closely to 'truth' when it conforms to reality, perhaps through empirical observation. Note that from a transcendentalist perspective, 'truth' is seen as distinct from 'objectivity'. (See also *Empiricism, Epistemology, Rationalist epistemology* and *Transcendentalism*)

Observational study: Within a quantitative paradigm or methodology, observational studies include any non-experimental study that involves the researcher observing and sometimes measuring what occurs without directly influencing the behaviour of the study participants. An example would be a cross-sectional survey. Within the qualitative paradigm, observational research involves seeing or recording events directly, perhaps by audio or video recording them, or by taking part in them and writing up field notes describing what happened.

Observed value: See *Expected and observed values*

Observer expectation bias: Bias that arises when an observer who is collecting data in a quantitative study has information about the individuals on whom the data are being collected which will make him/her record data in a different way for different participants.

Odds ratio: 'Odds' means the probability of an event occurring divided by the probability of this event not occurring. If the odds for an event are calculated for two different samples and then divided, the result represents a ratio of the odds. A result of one indicates that the odds in both groups are equal. Odds ratios are used to express the results of logistic regression.

One-tailed test: Used by a researcher when testing a specific prediction related to two variables. The statistical test used to assess the probability of the prediction occurring will use only one tail of a frequency distribution of values. (See also *Directional hypothesis* and *Two-tailed test*)

**Ontology:** A branch of philosophy concerned with what can be said to exist. This can be distinguished from *epistemology*, which concerns how we may know what exists. For example, is social class, or race or gender a thing that exists independently of us, or is it something that we create/construct, or perhaps just use to think with?

**Open coding:** Coined by Glaser and Strauss (1967), this is the first stage of thematic coding of qualitative data when using a grounded theory approach. (See *Box 21.2*)

**Open questions:** A question providing space or time for the respondent to answer in their own terms. (See *Box 11.6*, and also *Closed questions* and *Fixed-choice questions*)

**Operationalisation:** The process of developing indicators for concepts. Thus a concept such as 'alienation' might be indicated by questions on a questionnaire about powerlessness, isolation or moral deviance. The adequacy of operationalisation is an aspect of measurement validity, but can also be applied usefully to assess the adequacy of links made in qualitative research between ideas and examples.

**Oral vs. documentary sources:** Oral sources involve recording narratives, memories and stories directly from respondents so as to build a picture of history or the past as retold by people. Documentary sources are text-based and exist in a wide range of formats: diaries, letters, reports, memoranda, legislation and so on. (See *Box 15.2*)

**Ordinal variable/scale:** These are variables that function as categories in a particular rank order. The interval between the categories is neither fixed nor equal. Example scales: strongly agree, agree, neither agree nor disagree, disagree, strongly disagree; social class I professional, II semi-professional, IIIa non-manual, IIIb manual, IV semi-skilled, V unskilled. (See *Box 11.8*, and also *Interval variables* and *Nominal variables*)

**Outcome:** The endpoint of a study an investigator is most interested in. Used most often in relation to quantitative studies, particularly trials which assess treatments or other interventions, in which there may be several outcomes, for example mortality, a clinical measurement such as blood pressure, or quality of life.

**Overt vs. covert role:** These are different roles which an observer can take when doing fieldwork in a social setting. Adopting a covert role entails denying research participants the information that they are being watched, and is rare in ethnographic studies carried out nowadays. By contrast, adopting a fully overt role may influence the behaviour of the people under study and invalidate findings.

*p*-value: *p* stands for probability, and refers most commonly to the probability of obtaining a statistical test's value by chance. Having defined a hypothesis that asserts a particular relationship which one is interested in testing, and its corresponding null hypothesis, the researcher collects relevant data from selected samples and a statistical model is chosen that best fits the data. Depending on the type of data, a particular statistical test is chosen to assess the model. SPSS outputs for statistical tests provide a significance value, which equates to the *p*-value. Values of *p* less than 0.05 indicate a less than 5% probability of obtaining statistical test's value by chance, implying that the model fitted to the sample data is likely to fit the parent population, and that observed difference in data is likely to be real.

**Panel study:** A type of longitudinal, non-experimental, observational study, similar to a cohort study in that changes over time are measured and described. Panel studies differ from cohort studies due to the method of selection of a sample: representative samples are taken across the whole population of interest to maximise generalisability of findings to the population of interest. (See *Box 8.5*, and also *Cohort study*)

**Paradigms (Kuhnian):** The overall conception and way of working shared by workers within a particular discipline or research area. In this regard, paradigm shifts occur from time to time as scientific communities experience revolutions of thought. (See *Scientific revolution*)

**Parallel group design:** The commonest design choice for a randomised controlled trial in which participants are randomly allocated to groups which are followed up in parallel over the course of the trial. (See *Figure 8.4*, and also *Randomised controlled trial* and *Trial arms*)

**Parametric tests:** Statistical tests, such as the *t*-test, which are used to assess descriptive statistics concerning data samples whose measurements are believed to fit a normal distribution for the measure within the parent population.

**Participant expectation bias:** Bias that occurs when participants in a quantitative research study are aware of some characteristics of the research study (e.g. which intervention group they are in as part of an intervention study, or the purpose of an observational study) which makes them provide data that is different from the data they would have provided without this information.

**Participant observation:** Used to describe the method most commonly adopted by ethnographers, whereby the researcher participates in the life of a community or group, while making observations of members' behaviour.

**Partisan vs. scholar:** These are two extreme (or elitist) positions which can affect the perspective of a social scientist or influence social science research work. The scholar position asserts that the researcher should appeal to his or her own conscience alone when judging the value of his or her academic work, rather than being tied or influenced by any public debate or social policy. The partisan perspective seeks to ensure that research outputs promote a particular policy view or side of a debate.

**Passivisation:** A technical linguistic strategy noted by critical discourse analysts, which involves use of passive voice instead of active voice to obscure agency. For example 'The couple were hijacked', instead of 'Somalians hijacked the couple'. (See also *Nominalisation*)

**Path analysis:** A procedure associated with multiple regression involving a diagram indicating the strength and direction of influences between several variables, enabling calculation of direct and indirect causal pathways.

**Patterns of association:** Connections between concepts, groups, individuals, institutions and so on, which a researcher can reveal through a process of discourse analysis of a written or spoken text. (See *Box 23.4*, and also *Patterns of variation*, *Discourse* and *Critical discourse analysis*)

**Patterns of variation:** Inconsistencies, hesitations or contradictions that a researcher can reveal through a process of discourse analysis of an ostensibly coherent written or spoken text. (See *Box 23.5*, and also *Critical discourse analysis*, *Discourse* and *Patterns of association*)

**Pearson's *r*:** A measure of correlation. (See also *Correlation coefficient*)

**Percentage of variance explained:** This is calculated by squaring the value of Pearson's *r*, when carrying out statistical tests of association between two variables. The variance in the data represented on the y-axis of a scattergram, expressed as the percentage $r^2$, can be explained by the variable represented on the x-axis. (See *Figure 19.14*, and also *Correlation coefficient*)

**Perspective-display sequence:** Coined by Maynard (1991), this particular sequence refers to the way in which an individual can offer their opinion (or perspective), having listened to another's, and thus be informed as to how to 'couch' the opinion, rather than admitting it 'outright' in the first place. This is a way of 'doing caution' in social contexts.

**Phenomenology:** A philosophical orientation frequently informing qualitative studies concerned to understand what it is like for an individual to experience, first-hand, phenomena in the world. Phenomenology positions the world as experienced, as subjective and in our minds. As a philosophical viewpoint, it sets out to redress the positivistic outlook of the world and knowledge. (See also *Facticity*, *Idiographic* and *Positivism*)

**Photo elicitation:** The use of images in conjunction with other research methods, such as research interviews or focus groups, as stimulus material to encourage comments on a subject. (See also *Photo-voice*)

**Photo-voice:** A research method requiring participants to create their own photographs or images in order to encourage comments on a subject. (See *Box 16.6*, and also *Photo elicitation*)

**Pie chart:** A way of presenting a frequency distribution visually by showing the proportion of a circle occupied by each value of a variable.

**Placebo effect:** From Latin, meaning 'I will please', this is a putative explanation for an observed and usually desirable change in a measured variable within a group when in fact the group received no 'intervention' to account for the change. For example, sick people given a 'dummy' pill with no active ingredients may start to feel better, just because they feel they are being treated with something. The effect can be mitigated, or controlled for, by comparing an experimental group receiving a 'real' treatment with a suitably designed control group who receive a 'placebo' (e.g. a pill with no active ingredient) and where participants are kept guessing ('blinded') as to whether they are receiving the dummy or the real treatment. (See also *Hawthorne effect*)

**Plagiarism:** Presentation of someone else's work as if it were your own. This can be done by direct copying without citation of the original work, or by summarising another person's ideas and presenting them as if they were your own. *Self-plagiarism* occurs when a person presents or publishes the same piece of work more than once without indicating the first source. Plagiarism is generally used to indicate the idea of copying, although failing to acknowledge another person's contribution to a work that is being presented or published for the first time may be considered plagiarism; it is certainly a dishonest practice. Other forms of cheating include fabrication of quotations, data and other results.

Plausibility: An important term relating to the quality of research which appeals to a subtle realist epistemological position. A paper can be judged as plausible by assessing its claims against what is already known on the subject. (See also *Credibility*)

Political radicalism: Social science research might be judged useful using this criterion, implying that the research results significantly alter the political landscape in which the research has been carried out. (See *Box 31.1*, and also *Epistemic radicalism*)

Political sensitivity: An important perspective of social science which demands that the researcher maintains awareness of vested, political interests behind problematised issues in order to question how 'official' definitions of problems arise. (See also *Contextual sensitivity* and *Historical sensitivity*)

Polysemy: A linguistic term referring, literally, to 'many meanings or signs'. One person's interpretive analysis of data may be different to another's interpretation, reflecting such multiplicity of perspectives.

Population: A group of things, not necessarily people, which a researcher can define and from which a sample can be drawn in order to make research concerning the population practicable.

Positive association or relationship: A quantifiable linear relationship between two variables, which indicates that as one variable rises, the other rises too. (See *Figure 19.14*)

Positivism: In its looser sense this has come to mean an approach to social inquiry that emphasises the discovery of laws of society or external stimuli that determine human behaviour, often involving an empiricist commitment involving a combination of quantitative methods with traditional methods employed by the natural scientist.

Postmodernism: A social movement or fashion amongst intellectuals centring around a rejection of modernist values of rationality, progress and a conception of social science as a search for overarching explanations of human nature or the social and cultural world. Postmodernists celebrate the fall of such oppressive grand narratives, emphasising the fragmented and dispersed nature of contemporary experience and the difficulty of obtaining certain knowledge.

Post-photography: Manipulation of photographic images, for example digitally enhancing a picture after it has been taken.

Post-positivism: This can be considered as a development of or amendment to positivism, in tune with the working assumptions about the status of knowledge made by many natural scientists and most social scientists these days. For example, whereas positivists are generally realists, post-positivists adopt a position of critical realism: that all observation is theory-laden and fallible. Post-positivists also still stress the importance of objectivity, recommending the breaking-down of relativistic mindsets that separate different disciplines and using data to test theoretical approaches to understanding phenomena.

Post-structuralism: See *Structuralism*

**Power calculations:** An important calculation carried out for planning randomised controlled trials, which helps trialists work out how many participants they must recruit in order to show a significant difference in outcome measures between trial arms. (See *Box 8.10*)

**Pre-allocation of roles, identities etc.:** From the perspective of conversation analysts, institutions are organised and produced through action and interaction. Some institutions assign (pre-allocate) specific talk, tasks and identities to people in a normative manner. For example, in a courtroom, the judge can determine who is 'out of order' and can direct others to 'answer the question'.

**Pre-coding and post-coding:** These terms relate to the meaningful preparation (coding) of datasets, for statistical analysis, from responses to questionnaires. Questions that require the respondent to pick answers from a list of options (as in fixed-choice questions) to be pre-coded. Questions that allow for free-text responses require post-coding by the researcher in order to categorise answers after the respondent has completed the questionnaire.

**Predictor:** A variable that is assumed a priori to predict the outcome (or outcomes) in a research study, and that the researcher is particularly interested in investigating.

**Preference organisation; preferred/dispreferred utterances and actions:** Preference organisation refers to one of the systematic ways that speakers generally organise social talk and interaction. Preferred utterances/actions might be direct and plain, for example 'No', and dispreferred actions might include hesitations, delays, or mitigations.

**Preferred readings:** The interpretation of images that producers (or creators of those images) want their consumers (or audience) to appreciate. (See also *Encoding and decoding*)

**Prevalence:** A quantitative measure which indicates how widespread a certain attribute (e.g. a medical condition) is in a population. For example, the prevalence of Alzheimer's disease would be calculated as the number of people with Alzheimer's disease divided by the total population. (See also *Incidence*)

**Primary outcome:** The most important outcome that investigators want to investigate, usually as part of a quantitative experimental trial.

**Primary sources:** See *Secondary sources*

**Principle:** See *Law, theorem and theory*

**Privacy:** The capacity to keep personal matters or information out of view from others. Social researchers carrying out ethical research on humans must consider to what extent their methods invade participants' privacy (e.g. the extent to which disclosure of personal matters may be embarrassing for participants).

**Probability sampling:** A sampling method which demands that each member of a population has a known chance of being selected into a sample. This method is generally regarded as being likely to produce a sample that is representative of the population from which the sample is drawn. A simple random sample means that the chance of being selected for the sample is equal for each member of the population. Other methods of probability sampling include stratified and cluster sampling. (See also *Cluster sampling, Simple random sample* and *Stratified sample*)

Production: See *Consumption, production and representation*

Properties (of categories): A term used in grounded theory to describe the characteristics of phenomena identified as important. For example, pain may have the property of intensity, as may friendship. Friendship may have also the property of duration or depth.

Proximity operators: Words such as 'near' or 'adjacent' or 'after' which can be used to facilitate and narrow down a search of literature using an index and its keywords. (See *Box 6.2*)

Purposive/purposeful sampling: A non-probability sampling strategy in which the researcher selects participants who are considered to be typical of the wider population or have a significant relation to the research topic. (It is sometimes referred to as 'judgmental sampling'). (See also *Quota sampling*)

QDA software: Computer programs that support the handling of most, if not all types of qualitative data, enabling thematic coding, database organising, concept mapping and other components of qualitative data analysis.

Qualitative interview: This term generally refers to an in-depth, loosely or semi-structured interview, encouraging the interviewee to talk at length, largely in their own terms, about a topic, such as one derived from their own experience.

Qualitative research: Research primarily dealing with non-numerical data, such as images, fieldnote observations, texts, video and audio. It encompasses a large range of methods of data collection and analysis.

Qualitative thematic analysis: Analysis based on the identification of themes in qualitative material, often identified by means of a coding scheme. A widely used approach to qualitative analysis, often (though not by necessity) treating accounts as a *resource* for finding out about the reality or experiences to which they refer; this is similar to *interpretive content analysis*. (See also *Topic versus resource*)

Quantitative research: Research which primarily involves the collection and analysis of numerical data. It often, though not always, is set within a positivist framework, using deductive reasoning. (See also *Positivism* and *Deduction*)

Quasi-experimental design: Involves control of spurious variables by means of statistical operations at the analysis stage, rather than the design stage (as occurs in randomised controlled trials). The approach is often used to analyse survey data, or in situations where strict experimental designs may be impractical or unethical.

Query: An output created by a catalogue, or index, which is being searched. The query lists the search terms entered, plus any proximity operators usually as a summary before the results of the search.

Questionnaire: A research tool or method given to research participants to complete by answering questions related to the research topic. Consideration must be given to the method for administering a questionnaire, for example whether face-to-face, over the telephone or through self-completion.

**Quota sampling:** A purposive, non-probability sampling strategy where the researcher identifies the proportions in various strata of a population (e.g. people placed into age groupings by gender) and ensures that all these strata are proportionately represented within the sample to increase its representativeness. (See also *Purposive sampling*)

**$R^2$:** This is similar to $r^2$, in that it represents the percentage of variance explained. Unlike $r^2$, which is applied to bivariate relationships, it refers to multiple regression analysis, involving three or more variables. (See *Figure 20.2*, and also *Percentage of variance explained*)

**$r^2$:** See *Percentage of variance explained*

**Random sampling:** See *Probability sampling*

**Randomisation:** The process whereby, in a randomised controlled trial, participants are allocated at random to the trial arms (e.g. the treatment and the control group) to ensure that the only difference between people in each arm is the treatment they receive. Random allocation ought to ensure that all other variables are similar across both groups. Randomisation protects trial conclusions from bias and confounding.

**Randomisation sequence/list:** A sequence or a list trial arms, usually randomly ordered, which are used to assign participants to different arms as they are recruited to a randomised controlled trial. For example, in an RCT of a psychological counselling intervention, this may be used to assign participants either (a) to a group receiving the counselling that is being evaluated, or (b) to another group not receiving this counselling, or (c) to a group receiving some other psychological treatment.

**Randomised controlled trial (RCT):** An experimental method whereby participants are randomly allocated to either a group receiving an experimental treatment or another which acts as a 'control', or to some other treatment with which the experimental treatment is being compared, so that the effects of the experimental treatment can be compared with the other groups, or trial arms. The method is effective in ruling out spurious causation.

**Range:** This describes the minimum and maximum value of 100% of a numerical data sample. (See also *Inter-quartile range*).

**Ratio scales:** These have all the properties of interval scales as well as a true zero point. Examples include height, weight, heart rate, age and so on. (See also *Interval scales*, *Nominal variables* and *Ordinal variables*)

**Rationalism:** Unlike empiricism, rationalism gives preference to reason over any sensory experience as a source of knowledge. Concrete objects or phenomena must be deduced from any general concepts that describe them, and unlike the transcendentalist viewpoint, such phenomena are thought to be fixed.

**Rationalist epistemology:** A philosophical approach to the nature of knowledge arguing that concepts or objects are produced from reason, and specifically by deduction from any general concepts or theories/laws. (See also *Deduction*)

Reactivity: The reactions of people being studied to the presence of an observer, often perceived to be a source of bias, in that behaviour may become artificial as a result. (See also *Naturally occurring action, interaction or data*)

Realism: The view that a reality exists independently of our thoughts or beliefs. The language of research is seen to refer to this reality, rather than purely constructing it, though more subtle realists recognise constructive properties in language as well. (See also *Logical positivism*, *Positivism* and *Post-positivism*)

Recall bias: A phenomenon particularly relevant to case control studies (though more general problems with recall are also of concern in any study involving retrospection by participants). In case control studies recall bias may occur if either cases or controls have an unequal ability to recall their histories.

Recipient design: Designing messages, such as research reports or presentations, so that the needs of audiences (e.g. people who read a research report, people who listen to a presentation) are taken into account. Preparing and displaying a visual aid, such as a PowerPoint slide, so that audience members have enough time to study it and take in its message before the next one is shown, is an example of good recipient design.

Recoding variables: Re-numbering or re-grouping the categories of an existing variable. Recoding often reduces the number of categories, as where respondents answers about their age in years are re-grouped into age bands. Recoding, for example, may make it possible to convert a variable with number of values into a more dichotomous variable. (See *Box 18.5*)

Record: The content of the fields which belong together for a particular row in a database. For example, a record might contain a person's name, address and phone details. Compiling a database involves putting together lots of records. (See *Figure 6.1*)

Reductionism: The identification of a basic explanation for a complex phenomenon. Thus sexual identity may be explained by reference to genetic determinants alone, or social life explained in terms of economic relations alone. (See also *Holism*)

Reference management software: Software that helps create databases for bibliographic references. Records can be kept for different types of source, such as journal articles or books, because of the program's flexibility in the organisation of its database fields. This means the software can produce output in a variety of different reference styles.

Reference styles: The way in which references are laid out within the main body of a scholarly text, as citations, and at the end of the text, as a bibliography or reference list. Reference management software can automate reference styles for authors, depending on the conventions they have chosen, or might be obliged to follow (by a publisher, for example). (See *Box 10.8*)

References: An overall term for bibliographic sources which a researcher wishes to drawn upon when presenting an argument. The sources need not be restricted to printed materials; they can be in electronic or web-based formats.

**Referents:** Defined by Saussure (1974) as the things that words or signs refer to.

**Reflexivity:** In its broad meaning, this is used to refer to the capacity of researchers to reflect upon their actions and values during research, whether in producing data or writing accounts. More narrowly, ethnomethodologists use the term to describe a property of language, which reflects upon actions to make them appear orderly.

**Regression line or line of best fit:** A line that runs through a scattergram plot of two or more variables that involves the least distance between it and all the points. It is useful for making predictions.

**Regression:** A statistical technique for using the values of one variable to predict the values of another, based on information about their relationship, often given in a scattergram. Multiple regression involves the prediction of an interval-level variable from the values of two or more other variables. Logistic regression does this too, but predicts the values of nominal or ordinal variables.

**Relationships of sequence vs. relationships of hierarchy:** Two ways in which documents (found, for example, in an archive) relate to one another. A relationship of sequence can arise from the order in which the text was produced or filed. A relationship of hierarchy may concern information about who writes a document, to whom it is sent, who reads it and who has to act on it. (See *Box 15.8*)

**Relative risk:** This is one way in which categorical variables can be summarised, particularly when a researcher wants to compare proportions. The relative risk of an event occurring is calculated by the risk of the event occurring in one group divided by the risk of the event occurring in another group, each risk representing a proportion.

**Relativism:** This can be epistemological (or 'conceptual'), cultural or moral. The first of these involves the rejection of absolute standards for judging truth. The second suggests that different cultures define phenomena in different ways, so that the perspective of one culture cannot be used to understand that of another. The third implies that perceptions of good and evil are matters of social agreement rather than having universal validity.

**Reliability:** The capacity of a measuring device, or indeed of a whole research study, to produce the same results if used on different occasions with the same object of study. Reliability enhances confidence in validity, but is insufficient on its own to show validity, since some measurement strategies can produce consistently wrong results. Establishing *intercoder* or *inter-rater reliability* may be important in some studies where unambiguous meanings for codes in a coding scheme are at stake, so that exercises in which the same material is coded by more than one person and the results compared for consistency may be carried out. (See also *Kappa statistic*)

**Replicability/replication:** Replicability is closely linked to reliability, concerned with the consistency with which research procedures deliver results. A replicable study is one which produces similar results if the study were repeated, most likely as a consequence of using reliable methods of analysis or measurement. A less common meaning, and largely confined to the term 'replication', occurs in the context of the elaboration paradigm, referring to when a relationship identified in a zero-order table has also been identified in a first-order table.

**Representative case:** Having set parameters for what should count as a case to study for answering a research question, just one specific representative, or single, case might be selected, particularly when it has many features common to other cases and offers some potential to generalise findings. (See also *Critical case*, *Longitudinal case*, *Revelatory case* and *Unique case*)

**Representative sample:** A limited number of cases from a population, selected by a researcher, which accurately reflects the whole population and from which generalisations can be made. (See also *Probability sampling*)

**Representation:** See *Consumption, production and representation*

**Research design:** The collection of decisions about method and methodology that a researcher must make when setting out to do a research study. The design of the research will depend on the most appropriate methodological approach pertinent to the topic or question, and the particular methods required in order to collect, analyse and report the data and its conclusions.

**Research governance:** Standards intended to promote good and transparent research practice, imposed by regulations and formal requirements made that govern the conduct of a research study. Such procedures are aimed at enhancing public confidence in research and minimising misconduct, poor performance and adverse effects. Examples of areas subject to research governance are studies that involve children (where the researcher may have to prove that he or she has no criminal record), or studies with the potential for invasion of privacy (where data protection laws may require certain procedures to be followed).

**Research problem:** A disciplined researcher will narrow the focus of their particular area of interest to a definable problem from which a research question can be formulated. Defining and narrowing a research problem may be aided by brainstorming ideas and literature concepts until a definable and researchable problem becomes clear. (See *Box 10.3*, and also *Research process* and *Research question*)

**Research process:** A set of steps starting from a particular problem (social or otherwise), or puzzle, leading to a generation of a research problem which usually includes elaborating or creating concepts or theory based on a review of the literature. A research method can then be chosen to address a specific research problem. Finally, the process, including data collection, analysis and interpretation, is written up as a report. (See also *Research problem* and *Research question*)

**Research proposals:** These are developed around a particular research question (or questions) and allow the researcher to present their research design strategy or design for both informal (for advice) and formal (for research funding) appraisal. Most research appraisals follow a defined format using specific subtitles or signposts. (See also *Signposts*)

**Research questions:** The questions that a researcher wants to answer by doing a study. These may be regarded as foundational to a research project, although the point at which they are identified can be quite variable. In many quantitative studies, they are fixed before data collection begins. In many qualitative or exploratory studies, research questions change and develop as the study proceeds. (See *Box 7.1*, and also *Research process* and *Research problem*)

Response rate: The number of people taking part in a research study, such as a survey, divided by the total number asked to take part. The higher the rate, the more representative the sample is likely to be of the population being studied. To maximise response rates, due consideration should be given to elements of research design that are likely to influence it (e.g. guarantees of confidentiality, financial incentives to take part). (See also *Non-response*)

Retrospective study: A study that looks back at events in the past, either by examining data collected in the past, or requiring participants to recall past events. (See also *Recall bias*)

Revelatory case: Having set parameters for what should count as a case to study for answering a research question, a revelatory case (or cases) might be selected because the researcher believes it has unique potential as a source of data, perhaps because it contains members of otherwise hard-to-reach groups. (See also *Critical case*, *Longitudinal case*, *Representative case* and *Unique case*)

Rhetoric: The linguistic strategies used by speakers or authors of text to convey particular impressions or reinforce specific interpretations, most commonly in support of the authority of the text to speak the truth.

Roter Interaction Analysis System (RISA): A structured observation tool for coding talk in health care encounters. (See *Box 11.10*, and also *Structured observation*)

Row marginal: The sum of a row in a contingency table. (See *Figure 19.10* and associated discussion)

Row percentage: The percentage of the total number of cases contained in a cell located in a row of a contingency table. (See *Figure 19.10* and associated discussion)

Row variable: A variable whose values are laid out along the vertical axis of a contingency table, thus forming the rows going across a table as opposed to the columns. (See *Figure 19.10*)

Sample: A defined number of members of a population of interest which will be smaller, and more manageable, to study than a whole population. Samples may or may not be representative of the population, depending on the purpose of the research study.

Sample size calculation: A calculation appropriate to quantitative research which aims to determine the sample size needed in advance of the research in order that the investigators can achieve their primary aim, for example to detect a statistically significant difference of a certain size between two groups. Getting this right can save studying an unnecessarily large number of cases and, conversely, failing to study enough.

Sample survey: A survey of a sample taken from a population (usually, though not always, by means of a probability sampling method). (See *Sampling theory*)

Sampling: The selection of units of analysis (e.g. people or institutions) for study. Sampling can involve attempts to statistically represent a population, in which case a variety of random or probability methods are available. Alternatively, sampling can be opportunistic, or formed by emerging theoretical concerns of a researcher.

Sampling fraction: A number which helps a researcher to systematically select a random sample from a sampling frame. For example, if a sample of 100 students were required from a year group of 400 students, the sampling fraction is 4. Taking a random number below 4, the researcher selects the first person to be included in the sample (say, person number 2). Then the sampling fraction is added (2 + 4 = 6) and the next student (in this case, the 6th on the list) is selected. Then the sampling fraction is added again, and the procedure is repeated until a sample of 100 has been chosen.

Sampling frame: A list of items or individuals constituting the population that the researcher is interested in studying, from which a sample can be derived. (See *Box 9.3*)

Sampling theory: The underlying principles of probability, applied by means of mathematical calculations, to provide rationales for different sampling methods, and for making inferences from samples to populations.

Saturation of themes: During thematic coding and analysis of qualitative data, the process of data collection and analysis can be said to end when no new themes emerge from the data. At this point, saturation of themes occurs.

Scattergram or scatterplot: A graphical representation of numerical data, showing how two variables relate to each other. The position of each point is determined by the value of a case on both vertical and horizontal axes, showing where these values intersect. (See *Figure 19.14*)

Scheduling: When administering a face-to-face structured interview, a schedule refers to asking the questions in the same order for each participant. (See *Standardising*)

Scholar: See *Partisan vs. scholar*

Scientific paradigm: Defined by Thomas Kuhn (1922–1996) as a set of theoretical premises, methods and practices pertaining to a particular theoretical discipline or generation of scientists within which cumulative scientific work takes places largely under unquestioned or routine conventions.

Scientific revolution: Thomas Kuhn (1922–1996) proposed a transcendentalist perspective that science progresses through a number of these critical situations when scientific research produces knowledge that results in a shift, or change, in paradigm. (See also *Falisificationism, Hypothetico-deductive method* and *Transcendentalism*)

Search terms: Words, keywords or phrases a researcher uses to retrieve entries from a database or index when searching for references, publications or other kids of document. Some indexes/databases provide pre-defined search terms organised in hierarchies.

Search tools: These are included in qualitative data analysis software to facilitate retrieval of particular sections of text or image and their surrounding contexts, contained in a collection of materials being analysed.

Secondary analysis: Analysis of data by researchers unconnected with the original purposes of the data collection, as where non-government researchers use datasets gathered as a part of government social surveys.

**Secondary sources:** Analyses or restatements of primary sources (records of events as they are first described or original data) by other authors or researchers. Secondary sources might take the form of research reports, news articles, biographies, documentaries or history books) used to gain an understanding of a topic. Primary sources might be poems, raw tabulations of census data, video recordings or other records of observation. The use of secondary sources should be distinguished from secondary analysis of other researchers' original data (a primary source). (See *Box 15.1*)

**Selection bias:** This refers to systematic differences between participants entered into different groups that form trial arms of an experimental trial. If eligible participants are entered into an experimental trial randomly, this should minimise selection bias. (See also *Randomised Controlled Trial* and *Randomisation*)

**Selective coding:** A coding activity used by grounded theorists, associated most closely with the emergence of themes or categories, under which subsidiary codes or categories can be grouped. Constant comparison is an important associated activity. (See *Box 22.5*, and also *Axial coding* and *Open coding*)

**Semantic prosody:** A positive or negative connotation for a particular word, determined by its common collocates. Identification of this can expose ideological uses of language, as in keyword and discourse analysis. (See also *Collocation*, *Critical discourse analysis*, *Keyword-in-context display* and *Mutual information score*)

**Semi-structured interview:** An interview in which the researcher asks open questions relating to a pre-determined range of themes, listed in a topic guide. There is flexibility as to the order in which questions are asked.

**Serialisation:** The particular way and order in which documents are filed in an archive. Of itself, it can reveal something about the political structures or context that shape the actual production of the documents. (See *Box 15.13*, and also *Fragmentation*)

**Significance level:** Statistical tests provide a probability of obtaining a particular test result, which enables researchers to accept or reject hypotheses that concern the data being investigated. It is common to see a probably level of 0.05 as a cut-off for defining a significance level, meaning that if the probability works out as less than 0.05 (written as '$p<0.05$'), then the probability of obtaining such a statistical test result by chance must be very low (less than 5%), and that either a null hypothesis can be rejected or an experimental hypothesis can be accepted.

**Signified and signifier:** Defined by Saussure (1974) as two components of a sign. The signifier is the sound or the image of a particular word, and the signified is the concept people attach to the signifier. Members of the same linguistic group will tend to 'agree' to use a particular relationship between signifier and signified. (See also *Signs*)

**Signposts:** Features of a written text designed to help readers find their way around it easily. In relation to research proposals, signposts may take the form of subheadings such as: Title, Abstract, Background, Literature review etc. More loosely, 'signposting' can refer to paragraphs or sentences at the start or end of sections which tell the reader what he/she is about to read about, or summarising what he/she has just read, or stating how a particular section fits into a larger structure of ideas in a document.

**Signs:** A concept identified by Saussure (1974) in his study of structural linguistics which forms the basis for semiotic analysis. These generate the meaning of linguistic units and the mode of thought in which people in a particular linguistic culture operate. (See also *Signified* and *Signifier*)

**Silences (attending to):** Discourse analysts may search for 'silences' when analysing texts. The silences may concern people, institutions or issues that are not raised by authors when discussing a particular topic, for example minority ethnic groups whose views are not reported in media coverage of race.

**Simple random sample:** A sample drawn up in such a way that every member of the relevant population has an equal chance of being selected. Methods for drawing up a sample may involve use of a lottery system, a systematic sampling approach using a sampling fraction, or a table of random numbers. (See also *Cluster sampling*, *Stratified sampling* and *Systematic sample*)

**Single blind:** In experimental studies, blinding refers to restricting knowledge about who has been allocated to each trial arm once allocation has been carried out. If only one group of people is thus 'blinded' (e.g. the participants) but others are not (e.g. the people supplying the intervention, or measuring the outcome), they are single blinded. (See also *Double blind*)

**Situated knowledge:** An epistemological position that rejects the positivist approach that knowledge or facts can be understood from a neutral and objective position. Instead, producers of knowledge about the social world are themselves seen as part of the social world being studied, so that the knowledge produced by research will reflect values 'situated' by the context within which is has been carried out.

**Skewed distribution:** An asymmetrical spread of numerical data represented, for example, on a histogram. (See *Figure 19.8*)

**Skip instructions:** Instructions to respondents to 'skip' over certain questions on a questionnaire that earlier answers have shown are not relevant for them. For example, a respondent may be instructed not to answer questions about smoking habits if they have said they do not smoke. When built into a web survey, these automatically jump over parts of the questionnaire that are no longer relevant so that the respondent does not see the irrelevant items.

**Snowball sampling:** A non-probability sampling strategy which relies on referrals from earlier participants to others whom they know. To mitigate the effects of finding participants in just one network or missing isolated members of a network, the researcher can try finding multiple starting points for snowballing to access different networks.

**Social constructionism:** The view that the phenomena of the social and cultural world and their meanings are created in human social interaction. Taken further, social constructionism can be applied to social research itself, prompting debates about whether social research and fiction differ. The approach often, though not exclusively, draws on idealist philosophical orientations.

**Social facts:** Regularities of social life that appear to have an independent existence, acting to determine or constrain human behaviour. Norms of conduct or religious rules are examples. The concept is of particular importance in relation to functionalism and positivism.

**Social problems:** Social arrangements or processes that people regard as problematic, unwanted or causing harm. Social problems are often defined by the media or by politicians, as well as by administrators or managers. Examples include: homelessness, poor communication by an institution, and uncontrolled immigration. The relationship between social problems and research problems is not always direct.

**Social structure:** Ordered interrelationships that are characteristic of particular societies, such as its class structure or system of economic or political relations.

**Specific:** See *General and specific explanations*

**Specification or interaction:** Within the elaboration paradigm, the inclusion of a test variable can specify the conditions under which a relationship holds true. For example, a relationship between poverty and racism may only hold true for men. There is therefore said to be an interaction between gender and poverty in explaining racism. (See also *Table 20.1*)

**Specificity of scientific explanations:** For a scientific explanation to be informative or useful, it needs to be specific, rather than general. For an explanandum, the explanans will include specific conditions under which the explanans can be applied. (See *Explanans*)

**Spider diagrams:** A visual method for linking concepts or codes created from an initial process of open coding of a text, during qualitative data analysis. (See *Figure 21.2*)

**Sponsorship:** In the context of observational or ethnographic research, access to the field may rely on help from a member of the group being observed, particularly if they otherwise act in the role of 'gatekeeper'. When such help is received, perhaps in the form of introductions to other members of the group, the person can be considered an informal 'sponsor'. (See *Gatekeeper*)

**Spurious causation:** Finding this can threaten the extent to which causal statements between variables are supported by a study. To suggest that A causes B, when in fact some third factor, C, causes both A and B to vary, would mean that one is spuriously asserting a causal relationship between A and B. (See *Internal validity*)

**Spurious variable:** Within the elaboration paradigm, having identified a relationship between two variables in a zero-order table, this can be shown to be spurious if conditional tables involving a third variable fail to demonstrate replication of the original relationship. (See also *Intervening variable* and *Replication*)

**Standard deviation:** A statistic showing how close the data points in a distribution are to the mean. A high standard deviation indicates that data are spread out over a wide range of values; a low one indicates that they tend to be quite close to the mean.

**Standard error:** The amount of variability for a given descriptive statistic, for example the mean, measured across several samples from a population. Large values may indicate that a sample is not representative of its population.

**Standardised coefficient (Beta coefficient):** A statistic produced as part of multiple regression output allowing the relative impact of the independent variable on the dependent variable to be assessed.

This coefficient refers to the expected change in the dependent variable for each standard deviation increase in the independent or predictor variable.

**Standardising:** When administering a structured interview, standardising refers to wording the questions the same way for each participant. (See *Scheduling*)

**Standpoint models:** These involve the assumption that different social positions produce different experiences and therefore lead to different types of knowledge. Because of this, researchers often engage with the experiences of socially oppressed and marginalised groups. The knowledge derived from this is felt to provide a more valid account of the social world than adopting an apparently 'neutral' or 'objective' stance. (See also *Situated knowledge*)

**Statistical inference:** The generalisation of findings from a sample to the broader population from which the sample has been randomly drawn. A variety of statistical tests, such as the chi-square, help in estimating the level of probability that such inferences about the population are true, given the sample size. This is expressed as the statistical significance of the finding. (See also *p-value* and *Confidence interval*)

**Statistical significance:** See *Significance level*

**Statistical test:** A mathematical calculation that provides information about a characteristic of a numerical relationship found in data. Statistical tests can, for example, summarise patterns such as the strength or direction of associations or support statistical inference. Examples include a chi-squared test or a regression coefficient. The choice of statistical test will depend, amongst other things, on the level at which variables have been measured (e.g. whether they are ordinal or interval variables).

**Steering group:** A group with the remit of advising and monitoring the progress of a (usually large) collaborative and possibly multi-disciplinary research project.

**Stratified sample:** Individuals in the population are first divided into groups or *strata* (e.g. men and women, old and young) and a random sample is selected from within each *stratum*. The sample thus selected will be a more accurate reflection of the population being studied, as it will be representative on the stratifying variables. (See *Box 9.4*)

**Stratifying factor:** A factor, such as gender or age, used to divide a sampling frame into *strata*. Possible factors may be defined from the information available about the sampling frame being used. (See *Disproportionate stratification* and *Sampling frame*)

**String and numeric variables:** In data entry, variables may be in entered into a spreadsheet, database or SPSS as numbers (numeric) or as letters (string) to indicate the different values. Gender may thus be recorded as 'male' or 'female' (string) or '1' and '2' (numeric).

**Structuralism:** The view that behind the social and cultural realities we perceive, such as clothes or food fashions, kinship organisation and even language itself, deep structures exist which, through combinations of their elements, produce the surface complexity of the relevant phenomena. Post-structuralism retains elements of structuralism (its interest in surface signs, for example) but abandons the quest for deep structures. (See *Chapter 4* from the second edition of this book, by Filmer et al., available on the website for this current edition: www.rscbook.co.uk.)

Structured observation: To do this the researcher determines at the outset precisely what behaviours are to be observed and typically uses a standardised checklist to record the frequency with which those behaviours occur during the time spent observing. This results in quantitative data. (See also *Flanders Interaction Analysis Categories* and *Roter Interaction Analysis System*)

Subheadings: In the context of writing a research report, subheadings, such as 'introduction', 'methods', 'results',and 'conclusions', may be required to support the structure of an abstract or the body of the report itself. (See also *Signposts*)

Subjectivity: The thoughts, feelings, preferences and perceptions held by a person. (See *Hermeneutic viewpoint* and *Phenomenology*)

Subjects: A broad term referring to those people or institutions taking part in a research study. 'Research participants' is a term generally used in this book because it has connotations of agency which the editor prefers.

Substantive and formal theories: Described by Glaser and Strauss (1967), and broadly interpreted as a move towards generality within qualitative research, substantive theory relates to and explains the phenomena of immediate interest to the researcher. Formal theory refers to an extrapolation of the theory to other contexts or settings, perhaps elaborating the original substantive theory to broaden its scope.

Subtle realism: The recognition of the existence of a social world that exists independently of the researcher's mind, but also combined with the recognition of the impossibility of knowing this world in any final, certain sense, not least without some element of interpretation or construction.

Suppression: When examining a zero-order relationship between two variables against separate values of a third, test variable, suppression is said to have been removed if a relationship appears that was previously unseen in the original zero-order relationship.

Survey research: This type of research method tends to fit into a quantitative paradigm, involving collection of data that is as highly replicable as possible. Surveys can be conducted face-to-face, by post, by telephone or online, and each respondent is approached with the same questions in the same order (in general). Although studies involving qualitative interviews are also often 'surveys', they are not generally referred to as such, and they are less frequently done on samples chosen by probability methods than is usual in the social survey.

Symbolic interactionism: A body of theory that emphasises the organisation of everyday social life around events and actions, that act as symbols to which actors orient themselves. Interactionists frequently study this through observation of face-to-face interaction, and a preferred method for doing this is ethnography. (See *Chapter 4* from the second edition of this book, by Filmer et al., available on the website for this current edition: www.rscbook.co.uk.)

**Systematic review:** A type of literature review which aims to retrieve all available evidence published on a subject, evaluate the quality of the studies that have produced that evidence, and summarise the accumulated findings of the higher quality studies to support clinical or policy decisions, rendering them evidence based.

**Systematic sample:** A specific method of random sampling which requires the calculation of a sampling fraction to help determine which elements of those listed of a sampling frame to select. It is important to ensure that the list of elements in the sampling frame is not already structured in a particular way which could systematically bias the sample. For example, taking every other person in a list that contains men and women alternately would fail to represent one gender in the sample. (See also *Sampling fraction*, *Simple random sampling* and *Stratified sampling*)

**Teleological:** Outcome or ends-based reasoning, revealing a purpose rather than an explanation. For example, the statement 'Humans evolved intelligence in order to cope with complexity' is teleological, as it suggests a fundamental cause or design lying behind such evolution.

**Test variable:** A third variable whose values can be used to examine a known relationship drawn up between two other variables (e.g. in a zero-order contingency table).

**Testable explanation:** An explanation that makes rigorous and specific predictions which could be verified or falsified by observation.

**Text:** Although this term includes the kind of thing we usually mean by 'text' (e.g. a written document), in recent times the term has been applied to almost any object in the world. Semioticians, for example, have considered items as diverse as wrestling matches and Coca-Cola cans as 'texts', worthy of analysis for their cultural connotations.

**Thematic content analysis:** An approach to qualitative data analysis which identifies and categorises themes in texts such as interview or focus group transcripts, or documents.

**Theorem:** See *Law, theorem and theory*

**Theoretical dissertation:** A study written in an educational context involving critical appraisal of the theoretical literature pertaining to a particular area or discipline, but no empirical element. These are sometimes also called 'library-based' studies. (See *Box 10.1*, and also *Empirical dissertation*)

**Theoretical framework:** A set of ideas and concepts that offers researchers a way of thinking about research problems. For example, functionalist theory points the researcher in the direction of social structure and its causative role in forming human experience, whereas interactionist theory leads the researcher to study how meanings are created through interactions between people.

**Theoretical generalisation:** An important concept concerning the contribution made by qualitative research studies. Whereas statistical research can often assert external validity in a transparent empirical sense ('empirical generalisation'), the capacity of qualitative studies to discover and understand new phenomena means that their relevance for existing theories ('theoretical generalisation') can be claimed.

**Theoretical sampling:** Choosing a sampling element (e.g. a person, a social setting) on the basis of its likely contribution to a (grounded) theory emerging during the course of a study.

**Theoretical saturation:** A criterion pertinent to data that has been coded into categories, allowing the researcher to judge that they have sampled sufficient things (or groups, or individuals) and that further sampling will not reveal additional data regarding properties of the category. Like 'theoretical sampling', this criterion was coined and built into the processes of grounded theory by Glaser and Strauss (1967). (See also *Theoretical sampling*)

**Theoretical sensitivity:** The capacity to perceive how social and other theories may relate to the research problem at hand. Such sensitivity can alert the researcher to new ways of seeing old problems, and enhance capacity to make theoretical generalisations. (See *Contextual sensitivity*, *Historical sensitivity* and *Political sensitivity*)

**Theory:** Assumptions, sets of concepts or explanations that guide our understanding of knowledge or phenomena. Although empiricists may value objective facts more than theory, it is generally agreed nowadays that theory can help inform a particular approach to researching a problem.

**Thick description:** A term adapted by the anthropologist Clifford Geertz to convey the essence of his semiotic approach to ethnography, based on intensive observation of social life from which interpretations of cultural signs can be generated, as for example in the many layered meanings of a Balinese cock fight.

**Time management:** The capacity to pace a research project or other episode of work so that all elements are completed to a satisfactory level within a given time period. For example, when giving oral presentations time management is important, and contributes to good recipient design. This will invariably involve thinking about the quantity of content that can be covered in the time available.

**Time order:** When proving that an association exists between two variables, A and B, A must precede B in time. Cross-sectional studies, which capture data as a snap-shot in time, are not always useful for establishing causality as it can be hard to establish a temporal relationship between variables measured; longitudinal studies are better for this. However, some variables (such as family income at birth) inevitably occur earlier in time than others (such as family income now), so if gathered in a cross-sectional survey they do not present time-order problems.

**Time series:** A study design in which, at two or more points in time, the same method for sampling a population and same questions are used, but the people studied are (or may be) different. This enables trends over time to be established. Many government surveys are time-series studies.

**Topic guide:** An aide-memoire for an interviewer when carrying out semi-structured research interviews or focus groups. Rather than a list of questions that the researcher reads out, they are a list of topics which act as prompts or reminders to ask about these things. They ensure that each interviewee is asked to talk about similar issues.

**Topic vs. resource:** These are two ways in which accounts, such as those that are contained in interview transcripts, can be viewed and used. If a researcher regards the social world as having an existence independent of language, to which the language of accounts refers, interviewees' descriptions can be treated as a resource and assessed for accuracy in reporting on events. However, a researcher might approach the accounts as particular representations of events and therefore take a close interest in the ways in which such 'discourse' is generated. In this case, the account is treated as a topic. (See also *Data collection vs. data generation* and *Discourse*)

**Total effect:** The sum of direct and indirect effects of one variable on another. In path analysis this can be calculated by multiplying the standardised Betas in the relevant indirect paths and adding the product of this to the standardised Beta value of the direct effect. (See *Figure 20.4* and *Table 20.2*)

**Transcendentalism:** An epistemological position (concerning the nature of knowledge) which combines elements of empiricism and rationalism, arguing that objects or concepts must be formed in our consciousness not just as a result of using our senses, but also as a process of construction involving pre-existing reasoning. Knowledge is thus never fixed, but constantly evolves. (See also *Empiricism*, *Epistemology*, *Scientific revolution* and *Rationalist epistemology*)

**Transcription symbols:** Punctuation symbols and other text conventions used by most conversation analysts to represent and help detail the highly dynamic and complex nature of interactional work involved in naturally occurring talk. Overlaps of talk, in-breaths and out-breaths, quiet and loud speech are examples of things indicated by such symbols.

**Transferability:** Lincoln and Guba (1985) use this term to refer to what other researchers may call 'generalisability'. In qualitative research, they say, a study is transferable if the findings apply also to settings other than the one studied. It is enhanced by providing a dense or 'thick' description of the setting being studied.

**Trial arms:** Another term for groupings that participants can be assigned to as part of a randomised controlled trial. One arm, for example, might contain people receiving an experimental treatment; another arm might be people receiving the treatment that is normal for the condition the study participants suffer from; or they might be a control group receiving no treatment.

**Triangulation:** A metaphor derived from surveying and navigation to indicate the convergence of two or more viewpoints on a single position or, in social research, truth. A triangulation exercise might, for example, involve seeing whether the results of a questionnaire are repeated in observational data. Associated with a realist approach and, largely, with early qualitative discussions of validity, triangulation is treated with scepticism by non-realists who reject the view that revelation of a single truth is the object of a research account.

**Truncation:** Deliberately limiting the number of characters of a particular search term when searching an index or database, for example Psychol*, to retrieve terms like 'Psychology', 'Psychological', 'Psychologist' etc. This technique broadens the scope of a search, but may provide results that are not relevant specifically to the desired research area. (See *Wildcards*)

**Trustworthiness:** See *Credibility*

**t-test:** A test used for numerical and normally-distributed data to establish whether two means differ significantly. The means being compared may come from the same sample (or individuals), for which a paired *t*-test is required, or may come from separate samples, in which case an unpaired *t*-test is used.

**Two-tailed test:** Used by a researcher when testing a non-directional hypothesis. This statistical test will assess both tails of a frequency distribution of values to capture both positive and negative statistical relationships. (See also *Non-directional hypothesis* and *One-tailed test*)

**Type I error:** The erroneous rejection of a null hypothesis which leads a researcher to falsely conclude that a genuine directional and statistically significant relationship exists between variables of interest in the population being studied. (See also *Null hypothesis*)

**Type II error:** The erroneous acceptance of a null hypothesis which leads a researcher to falsely conclude that no statistically significant relationship exists between variables of interest in the population being studied. (See also *Null hypothesis*)

**Typologies:** Classifications of people, events or processes according to their characteristics. Such classifications may emerge during qualitative data analysis. Examples are the division of university students into 'deep' and 'surface' processors according to characteristics of typical learning styles, classification of diseases according to whether they are chronic or acute, or a typology of arguments according to whether they are ad hominem, evidence-based, from reasoning alone and so on.

**Unexplained variance (or the) error term:** When carrying out multivariate statistical analysis, this figure represents the variance of the dependent variable that is not explained by independent variables in the model.

**Unique case:** Having set parameters for what should count as a case to study for answering a research question, just one specific unique, or single, case might be selected for investigation, particularly when instances of the case are rare. (See also *Critical case*, *Representative case*, *Revelatory case* and *Longitudinal case*)

**Universal law:** A law that applies to all cases relevant to an explanation.

**Unstandardised coefficient (B):** A number representing the impact of a one-unit change in an independent variable on a dependent variable, in multiple regression output. (See also *Standardised coefficient (Beta coefficient)*)

**Utilitarian ethics:** John Stuart Mill published 'Utilitarianism' in 1861, and provided the principle of utility which offers a criterion for moral judgments about 'right' and 'wrong': 'Actions are right in proportion as they tend to promote happiness; wrong as they tend to produce the reverse of happiness. By happiness is intended pleasure and the absence of pain; by unhappiness, pain and the privation of pleasure.'

**Univariate statistics:** Analysis and statistical tests involving a single variable, such as a frequency distribution or a mean.

**Validity:** At its most simple, this refers to the truth status of research reports. However, a great variety of techniques for establishing the validity of measuring devices and research designs have been established, both for quantitative and qualitative research. More broadly, the status of research as truth is the subject of considerable philosophical controversy, lying at the heart of the debate about postmodernism.

A convenient way of categorising concerns about validity is to divide these into *internal* and *external*. The former refers to the internal design of a study (e.g. can it prove causality?); the latter refers to the generalisability of a study (e.g. does the sample represent a population adequately?).

Value labels: The name, or label, given to the values of a variable. For example, value labels for the variable 'Gender' might be 'Male' and 'Female'. (See *Figures 18.1* and *18.3*)

Variables: Qualities on which units of analysis vary. Thus, if a person is the unit of analysis in, say, a social survey, examples of variables might be their social class, gender, attitudes to politics and so on. Variables can be measured at a variety of levels, according to which they can be subjected to specific mathematical operations. In considering relationships between variables, it is important to define which is a causal (or independent) variable, and which is an effect (dependent) variable.

Variance: An estimate of the average variability or spread of data from the mean, calculated by the sum of the squared differences between observed data and their mean, divided by the number of observations/values minus 1. Given that measure is in 'units squared', the square root of the variance is used instead – this gives a standard deviation for the data. (See also *Standard error*)

Verificationism: An empiricist's approach to justifying the scientific value of an explanation, stating that generalisations, or theories, are basic units of genuine (or 'true') knowledge since they can be predicted from one or more confirmatory observations. (See also *Empiricism, Falsificationism* and *Induction*)

Verstehen: Max Weber used this word to describe the study of intersubjectivity, involving an attempt to understand the meaning of social action from the actor's viewpoint. (See also *Intersubjectivity*)

Visual aids: These include not only slides and PowerPoint shows, but also other materials, such as data transcripts and handouts, usually used to support the delivery of a verbal presentation.

Visual ethics: This concerns questions about confidentiality, anonymity and consent when considering carrying out research using visual materials, particularly if people or places are identifiable from images that you wish to publish or exhibit.

Visuality: Argued by Gillian Rose (2007) as the socially constructed nature of what and how we see things.

Volunteer sample: A non-probability method of sampling which allows for recruitment of interested participants into a study, perhaps after seeing an advertisement about the proposed research. While participants are likely to be well-motivated to take part, the disadvantage with this approach is the failure to capture views of those who don't volunteer.

Vulnerable groups: A term broadly defined as groups who are at particular risk in society. The concept of vulnerability refers to issues of relative disempowerment within the social setting, and studies of vulnerable groups may raise particular ethical concerns. (See *Box 5.5*)

Warrant: A verb meaning to back up and provide persuasive evidence for a claim. In formulating an argument, or providing a justification, warrants are often important. Discourse analysts often look out for them.

**Web surveys:** These are surveys carried out on the Internet. The respondent is sent a link to a webpage which contains the questionnaire to which they can respond. (See also *Email surveys* and *Skip patterns*)

**Weight, weight factor:** A number used to restore sample population data to reflect the parent population more accurately. It is important to include weights to statistical analyses of research data, particularly if conclusions are being generalised to a whole population from samples that do not reflect the proportions of members of that population, either because of non-response or because disproportionate stratification was used to select the sample. (See *Box 18.6*)

**Weighting:** A way of handling data to allow for disproportionality inherent in the sampling method, or caused by non-response. The weighting of sample survey responses or variables, for example, allows for certain variables to contribute more or less to the statistical tests being used to make inferences about the population being studied. (See also *Disproportionate stratification* and *Non-response*).

**Wildcards:** These are punctuation symbols, such as a question mark or an asterisk, which can be included in place of actual letters of search terms entered when querying a database or index. They are useful if there are alternative spellings of a particular search term and a researcher seeks to maximise the chances of a retrieving all relevant items indexed by the words concerned. (See *Truncation*)

**x-axis:** The horizontal axis of a graph. For a histogram, the x-axis is used to list categories, usually in ascending order if appropriate to the data.

**y-axis:** The vertical axis of a graph. For a histogram, the y-axis is used to show the frequencies of categories listed on the x-axis.

**Zero-order table:** A contingency table showing data for values of two variables which may demonstrate an association. The term is used in the context of the elaboration paradigm, which involves creating a zero-order table and then seeing if the relationship it demonstrates holds true under different conditions. (See *Table 20.1*)

**Zigzag approach:** A method relevant to qualitative methodology whereby a researcher switches between data collection and data analysis in alternate steps. This approach encapsulates an important principle of grounded theorising which recommends that data collection ought not to occur at one point in time, but rather should be interspersed with periods of data analysis in order to inform further (theoretical) sampling. (See *Figure 21.1*)

# REFERENCES

Adolphs, S. (2006) Introducing Electronic Text Analysis: A Practical Guide for Language and Literary Studies. London: Routledge.

Akobeng, A.K. (2005) 'Understanding systematic reviews and meta-analysis', Archives of Disease in Childhood, 90: 845–848.

Alderson, P. and Morrow, V. (2004) Ethics, Social Research and Consulting with Children and Young People. Ilford: Barnado's.

Ali, S. (2003) 'Mixed-Race' Postrace: Gender, New Ethnicities and Cultural Practices. New York and Oxford: Berg.

Allen, L. (2005) 'Managing masculinity: young men's identity work in focus groups', Qualitative Research, 5: 35–57.

Allison, G.T. (1971) Essence of Decision: Explaining the Cuban Missile Crisis. Boston, MA: Little Brown.

Anderson, M. and Fienberg, S.E. (1999) The History of the First American Census and the Constitutional Language on Census-taking: Report of a Workshop. http://lib.stat.cmu.edu/~fienberg/DonnerReports/FirstCensus.pdf.

Andrews, H. (2005) 'Feeling at home: embodying Britishness in a Spanish charter tourist resort', Tourist Studies, 5: 247–266.

Andrews, M., Squire, C. and Tamboukou, M. (eds) (2008) Doing Narrative Research. London: Sage.

Antaki, C. (2004) 'Reading minds or dealing with interactional implications', Theory & Psychology, 14: 667–683.

Arber, S. and Ginn, J. (1991) Gender and Later Life: A Sociological Analysis of Resources and Constraints. London: Sage.

Arber, S., Gilbert, N.G. and Dale, A. (1985) 'Paid employment and women's health: a benefit or a source of role strain?', Sociology of Health and Illness, 7 (3): 375–400.

Atkinson, P. and Coffey, A. (1997) 'Analysing documentary realities', in D. Silverman (ed.), Qualitative Research: Theory, Method and Practice. London: Sage.

Atkinson, J.M. and Drew, P. (1979) Order in Court: The Organisation of Verbal Interaction in Judicial Settings. London: Macmillan.

Atkinson, P., Coffey, A., Delamont, S., Lofland, J. and Lofland, L. (eds) (2001) Handbook of Ethnography. London: Sage.

Back, L. (1996) New Ethnicities and Urban Culture: Racisms and Multiculture in Young Lives. London: UCL Press.

Back, L. (2004) 'Reading and writing research' in C. Seale (ed.), Researching Society and Culture (2nd edition). London: Sage.

Back, L. (2007) The Art of Listening. Oxford, New York: Berg.

Baez, B. (2002) 'Confidentiality in qualitative research: reflections on secrets, power and agency', Qualitative Research, 2 (1): 35–58.

Baker, P. (2005) Public Discourses of Gay Men. London: Routledge.

Baker, P. (2006) Using Corpora in Discourse Analysis. London: Continuum.

Baker, P., Gabrielatos, C., KhosraviNik, M., Krzyżanowski, M., McEnery, T. and Wodak, R. (2008) 'A useful methodological synergy? Combining critical discourse analysis and corpus linguistics to examine discourses of refugees and asylum seekers in the UK press', Discourse & Society, 19: 273–306.

Barbour, R.S. and Kitzinger, J. (eds) (1999) Developing Focus Group Research: Politics, Theory and Practice. London: Sage.

Barnett, V. (2002) Sample Survey: Principles and Methods. London: Arnold.

Barthes, R. (1977a) Elements of Semiology. New York: Hill and Wang.

Barthes, R. (1977b) The Death of the Author: Image-Music-Text. Trans. Stephen Heath. New York: Hill and Wang, 142–148.

Barthes, R. (1986) Mythologies. London: Paladin.

Baruch, G. (1981) 'Moral tales: parents' stories of encounters with the health professions', Sociology of Health & Illness, 3 (3): 275–296.

Bauman, Z. (1987) Legislators and Interpreters. Cambridge: Polity.

Beach, W.A. and Metzinger, T.R. (1997) 'Claiming insufficient knowledge', Human Communication Research, 23: 562–588.

Bear, L. (2007) Lines of the Nation: Indian Railway Workers, Bureaucracy, and the Intimate Historical Self. New York: Columbia University Press.

Beard, R. and Payack, P.J.J. (2000) Presidential Debates Mirror Long-term School Decline. www.yourdictionary.com/library/presart1/html.

Beauchamp, T.L. (1994) 'The "four-principles" approach', in R. Gillon (ed.), Principles of Health Care Ethics. Chichester: Wiley.

Beauchamp, T.L., Faden, R.R., Wallace, R.J. and Walters, L. (eds) (1982) Ethical Issues in Social Science Research. Baltimore, MD: Johns Hopkins University Press.

Becker, H.S. (1963) Outsiders: Studies in the Sociology of Deviance. New York: Free Press.

Becker, H.S. (1970) Sociological Work: Method and Substance. Chicago, IL: Aldine.

Becker, H.S. (1998) Tricks of the Trade: How to Think about Your Research While You're Doing It. Chicago, IL: University of Chicago Press.

Becker, H.S. and Richards, P. (1986) Writing for Social Scientists: How to Start and Finish your Thesis, Book or Article. Chicago, IL: University of Chicago Press.

Beecher, H.K. (1955) 'The powerful placebo', Journal of the American Medical Association, 159 (17): 1602–1606.

Bell, J. (2005) Doing your Research Project: A Guide for First-time Researchers in Education and Social Science. Buckingham: Open University Press.

Bell, P. (2002) 'Content analysis of visual images', in T. van Leeuwen and C. Jewitt (eds), Handbook of Visual Analysis. London: Sage.

Bell, V. (1993) Interrogating Incest: Foucault, Feminism and the Law. London: Routledge, 126–149.

Benatar, S. and Singer, P.A. (2000) 'A new look at international research ethics', British Medical Journal, 321: 824–846.

Berelson, B. (1952) Content Analysis in Communication Research. Glencoe, IL: Free Press.

Berg, B.L. (2004) Qualitative Research Methods for the Social Sciences. Boston, MA: Allyn and Bacon.

Berger, A.A. (2000) 'Content analysis', in Media and Communication Research Methods: An Introduction to Qualitative and Quantitative Approaches. London: Sage.

Berger, A.A. (2011) Media and Communication Research Methods: An Introduction to Qualitative and Quantitative Approaches (2nd edition). London: Sage, 205–220.

Bergman, M. (2008) Advances in Mixed Methods Research: Theories and Applications. London: Sage.

Berlin, J.M. and Carlström, E.D. (2008) 'The 20-minute team – a critical case study from the emergency room', Journal of Evaluation in Clinical Practice, 14 (4): 569–576.

Bernard, H. Russell (2000) Social Research Methods: Quantitative and Qualitative Approaches. Thousand Oaks, CA: Sage.

Billig, M. (1987) Arguing and Thinking: A Rhetorical Approach to Social Psychology. Cambridge: Cambridge University Press.

Billig, M. (2008) 'The language of Critical Discourse Analysis: the case of nominalization', Discourse & Society, 19 (6): 783–800.

Billings, A.G. and Moos, R.H. (1981) 'The role of coping responses and social resources in attenuating the stress of life events', Journal of Behavioral Medicine, 4,(2): 139–157.

Blaikie, N.W.H. (1991) 'A critique of the use of triangulation in social research', Quality & Quantity, 25: 115–136.

Blaxter, M. (1990) Health and Lifestyles. London: Routledge.

Bloch, A. (1992) The Turnover of Local Councillors. York: Joseph Rowntree Foundation.

Bloch, A. (2004) 'Doing social surveys', in C. Seale (ed.) Researching Society and Culture (2nd edition). London: Sage.

Bloch, A. and John, P. (1991) Attitudes to Local Government. York: Joseph Rowntree Foundation.

Bloor, M. (1983) 'Notes on member validation', in R. Emerson (ed.), Contemporary Field Research: A Collection of Readings. Boston, MA: Little, Brown.

Bond, G.C. (1990) 'Fieldnotes: research in past occurrences', in R. Sanjek (ed.), Fieldnotes. New York: Cornell University Press.

Bonell, B. (2002) 'The politics of the research-policy interface: randomised trials and the commissioning of HIV prevention services', Sociology of Health & Illness, 24 (4): 385–408.

Booth, C. (1894) Correspondence with Alfred Marshall. (Senate House Library MS797/I/1352). http://booth.lse.ac.uk/static/a/2.html.

Booth, C. (1902) Life and Labour of the People in London, Volume 10. London: Macmillan.

Booth, C. (1902–1903) Life and Labour of the People in London (17 volumes). London: Macmillan.

Boserman, C. (2009) 'Diaries from cannabis users: an Interpretative Phenomenological Analysis', Health, 13: 429–448.

Boudens, C.J. (2005) 'The story of work: a narrative analysis of workplace emotion', Organization Studies, 26: 1285–1306.

Bourdieu, P. (2003) 'Participant objectivation', Journal of the Royal Anthropological Institute, 9: 282–294.

Bourgois, P. (1998) 'Just another night in a shooting gallery', Theory, Culture & Society, 15: 37–66.

Bowley, A.L. and Burnett-Hurst, A.R. (1915) Livelihood and Poverty: A Study in the Economic Conditions of Working-class Households in Northampton, Warrington, Stanley and Reading. London: Bell.

Bradshaw, J., Ditch, J., Holmes, H. and Vilhiteford, P. (1993) 'A comparative study of child support in fifteen countries', Journal of European Social Policy, 3: 255–271.

Bramley, N. and Eatough, V. (2005) 'The experience of living with Parkinson's disease: an interpretative phenomenological analysis case study', Psychology & Health, 20 (2): 223–235.

Brannen, J. (ed.) (1992) Mixing Methods: Qualitative and Quantitative Research. Aldershot: Avebury.

Bridges, A.J., Wosnitzer, R., Scharrer, E., Sun, C. and Liberman, R. (2010) 'Aggression and sexual behavior in best-selling pornography videos: a content analysis update', Violence Against Women, 16: 1065–1085.

Bringer, J.D., Johnston, L.H. and Brackenridge, C.H. (2006) 'Using computer-assisted qualitative data analysis software to develop a grounded theory project', Field Methods, 18: 245–266.

British Sociological Association (2002) Statement of Ethical Practice. www.britsoc.org.uk/about/ ethic.htm.

Brown, G. (1973) 'Some thoughts on grounded theory', Sociology, 7: 1–16.

Brown, G. and Harris, T. (1978) Social Origins of Depression. London: Macmillan.

Brown, R.H. and Davis-Brown, B. (1998) 'The making of memory: the politics of archives, libraries and museums in the construction of national consciousness', History of the Human Sciences: Special Issue 'The Archive', 11 (4): 17–32.

Bruner, J. (1987) 'Life as narrative', Social Research, 54: 11–32.

Bruner, J. (1991) 'The narrative construction of reality', Critical Inquiry, 18: 1–21.

Bryman, A. (1992) 'Qualitative and quantitative research: further reflections on their integration', in J. Brannen (ed.), Mixing Methods: Qualitative and Quantitative Research. Aldershot: Avebury.

Bryman, A. (2001) Social Research Methods. Oxford: Oxford University Press.

Bryman, A. (2007) 'Barriers to integrating quantitative and qualitative research', Journal of Mixed Methods Research, 1: 8–22.

Bryman, A. and Cramer, D. (2001) Quantitative Data Analysis for Social Scientists. London: Routledge.

Bryman, A. and Cramer, D., (2008) Quantitative Data Analysis with SPSS 14, 15 and 16: A Guide for Social Scientists. London: Routledge.

Buckingham, R.W., Lack, S.A., Mount, B.M., Maclean, L.D. and Collins, J.T. (1976) 'Living with the dying: use of the technique of participant observation', Canadian Medical Association Journal, 115: 1211–1215.

Burns, A. and Radford, J. (2008) 'Parent–child interaction in Nigerian families: conversation analysis, context and culture', Child Language Teaching and Therapy, 24: 193–209.

Burton, D. (2000) Research Training for Social Scientists. London: Sage.

Burton, M.L., Croce, M.D., Masri, S.A., Bartholomew, M. and Yefremian, A. (2005) 'Sampling from the United States Census Archives', Field Methods, 17: 102–118.

Busfield, S. (2000) 'Irving loses Holocaust libel case', Guardian, 11 April 2000.

Butler, J.P. (1990) Gender Trouble: Feminism and the Subversion of Identity. New York and London: Routledge.

Cameron, D. (2007) The Myth of Mars and Venus. Oxford: Oxford University Press.

Campbell, D.T. (1969) 'Reforms as experiments', American Psychologist, 24: 409–429.

Campbell, D.T. and Fiske, D.W. (1959) 'Convergent and discriminant validation by the multitraitmultimethod matrix', Psychological Bulletin, 56 (2): 81–105.

Cantor, M.G. and Pingree, S. (1983) The Soap Opera. London: Sage.

Cao, L., Liu, X., Lin, E.J., Wang, C., Choi, E.Y., Riban, V., Lin, B. and During, M.J. (2010) 'Environmental and genetic activation of a brain-adipocyte BDNF/leptin axis causes cancer remission and inhibition', Cell, 142: 52–64.

Cartwright-Hatton, S., Roberts, C., Chitsabesan, P., Fothergill, C. and Harrington, R. (2004) 'Systematic review of the efficacy of cognitive behaviour therapies for childhood and adolescent anxiety disorders', British Journal of Clinical Psychology, 43 (4): 421–436.

Caulley, D.N. (2008) 'Making qualitative research reports less boring: the techniques of writing creative nonfiction', Qualitative Inquiry, 14: 424–449.

Chakrabarty, D. (1989) Rethinking Working-class History. Princeton, NJ: Princeton University Press.

Chambliss, W. (1975) 'On the paucity of original research on organized crime', American Sociologist, 10: 36–39.

Chandler, D. (2007) Semiotics: The Basics. London: Routledge.

Chang, H. (2008) Autoethnography as Method. Walnut Creek, CA: Left Coast Press.

Chapple, A. and Ziebald, S. (2010) 'Viewing the body after bereavement due to a traumatic death: qualitative study in the UK', British Medical Journal, 340:c2032.

Charmaz, K. (1983) 'Loss of self: a fundamental form of suffering in the chronically ill', Sociology of Health & Illness, 5 (2): 168–195.

Charmaz, K. (1999) 'Stories of suffering: subjective tales and research narratives', Qualitative Health Research, 9: 362–382.

Charmaz, K. (2002) 'Stories and silences: disclosures and self in chronic illness', Qualitative Inquiry, 8: 302.

Charmaz K. (2006) Constructing Grounded Theory: A Practical Guide through Qualitative Analysis. London: Sage.

Charteris-Black, J. (2004) Corpus Approaches to Critical Metaphor Analysis. Basingstoke and New York: Palgrave-MacMillan.

Charteris-Black, J. (2005) Politicians and Rhetoric: The Persuasive Power of Metaphor. Basingstoke and New York: Palgrave-MacMillan.

Christie, B (2000) 'Doctors revise Declaration of Helsinki', British Medical Journal, 321: 913.

Churchill, H. and Sanders, T. (2007) Getting Your PhD: A Practical Insider's Guide. London: Sage.

Cicourel, A.V. and Kitsuse, J.I. (1963) The Educational Decision Makers. New York: Bobbs Merrill.

Clayman, S.E. (1988) 'Displaying neutrality in television news interviews', Social Problems, 35: 474–492.

Clayman, S. (2002) 'Tribune of the people: maintaining the legitimacy of aggressive journalism,' Media, Culture, & Society, 24: 191–210.

Clifford, J. and Marcus, G.E. (eds) (1986) Writing Culture: The Poetics and Politics of Ethnography. Berkeley, CA: University of California Press.

Coates, J. (2004) Women, Men and Language: A Sociolinguistic Account of Gender Differences in Language. London: Pearson Education.

Code, L. (1991) What Can She Know? Feminist Theory and the Construction of Knowledge. Ithaca, NY: Cornell University Press.

Coffey, A. (1999) The Ethnographic Self: Fieldwork and the Representation of Identity. London: Sage.

Coffey, A. and Atkinson, P. (1996) Making Sense of Qualitative Data: Complementary Research Strategies. London: Sage.

Coffey, A., Holbrook, B. and Atkinson, P. (1996) 'Qualitative data analysis: technologies and representations', Sociological Research Online, 1 (1) www.soc.surrey.ac.uk/socresonline.

Cohen, S. and Taylor, L. (1972) Psychological Survival: The Effects of Long-term Imprisonment. London: Allen Lane.

Collins, H.M. (1985) Changing Order: Replication and Induction in Scientific Practice. London: Sage.

Colyar, J. (2009) 'Becoming writing, becoming writers', Qualitative Inquiry, 15: 421–436.

Coolican, H. (2004) Research Methods and Statistics in Psychology. London: Hodder & Stoughton.

Corbin, J. (1987) 'Women's perceptions and management of a pregnancy complicated by chronic illness', Health Care for Women International, 84: 317–337.

Cornwell, J. (1984) Hard Earned Lives: Accounts of Health and Illness from East London. London: Tavistock.

Corrigan, O. (2003) 'Empty ethics: the problem with informed consent', Sociology of Health & Illness, 25 (7): 768–792.

Corsaro, W. (1981) 'Entering the child's world: research strategies for field entry and data collection in a pre-school setting', in J.L. Green and C. Wallats (eds), Ethnography and Language in Education Settings. Norwood, NJ: Ablex.

Corti, L. and Thompson, P. (2004) 'Secondary analysis of archived data', in C. Seale, G. Gobo, J.F. Gubrium and D. Silverman (eds), Qualitative Research Practice. London: Sage.

Courtney, C. and Thompson, P. (1996) City Lives. London: Methuen.

Creswell, J. (2007) Qualitative Inquiry and Research Design: Choosing among Five Approaches. Thousand Oaks, CA: Sage.

Creswell, J. and Clark, V.P. (2011) Designing and Conducting Mixed Methods Research. Thousand Oaks, CA: Sage.

Croll, P. (1986) Systematic Classroom Observation. Brighton: Falmer.

Cryer, P. (2006) The Research Student's Guide to Success (3rd edition). Buckingham: Open University Press.

Dahl, E. and Malmberg-Heimonen, I. (2010) 'Social inequality and health: the role of social capital', Sociology of Health & Illness, 32 (7): 1102–1119.

Dale, A., Arber, S. and Proctor, M. (1988) Doing Secondary Analysis. London: Unwin Hyman.

Daley, B., Griggs, P. and Marsh, H. (2008) 'Reconstructing reefs: qualitative research and the environmental history of the Great Barrier Reef, Australia', Qualitative Research, 8: 584–615.

Davidson, J.A. (1984) 'Subsequent versions of invitations, offers, requests, and proposals dealing with potential or actual rejection', in J.M. Atkinson and J. Heritage (eds), Structures of Social Action: Studies in Conversation Analysis. Cambridge: Cambridge University Press.

Davis, E.M. (2008) 'Risky business: medical discourse, breast cancer, and narrative', Qualitative Health Research, 18 (1): 65–76.

Dawkins, R. (1976) The Selfish Gene. Oxford: Oxford University Press.

Dawkins, R. (1996) River Out of Eden: A Darwinian View of Life. London: Harper Collins.

Day, R.A and Gastel, B. (2006) How to Write and Publish a Scientific Paper. Cambridge: Cambridge University Press.

De Vaus, D.A. (2002a) Surveys in Social Research. London: Routledge.

De Vaus, D.A. (2002b) Analysing Social Science Data: 50 Key Problems in Data Analysis. London: Sage.

Deacon, D., Bryman, A. and Fenton, N. (1998) 'Collision or collusion? A discussion of the unplanned triangulation of quantitative and qualitative research methods', International Journal of Social Research Methodology, 1: 47–63.

Decker, S.H. and Pyrooz, D.C. (2010) 'On the validity and reliability of gang homicide: a comparison of disparate sources', Homicide Studies, 14: 359–376.

DeCuir-Gunby, J.T., Marshall, P.L. and McCulloch, A.W. (2010) 'Developing and using a codebook for the analysis of interview data: an example from a professional development research project', Field Methods. Published online before print 27 December, doi: 10.1177/1525822X10388468.

Dennett, D.C. (1996) Darwin's Dangerous Idea: Evolution and the Meaning of Life. London: Penguin.

Denzin, N.K. (1978) The Research Act: A Theoretical Introduction to Sociological Methods (2nd edition). New York: McGraw-Hill.

Denzin, N.K. (1988) 'Qualitative analysis for social scientists', Contemporary Sociology, 17 (3): 430–432.

Denzin, N.K. (1989) The Research Act: A Theoretical Introduction to Sociological Methods (3rd edition). Englewood Cliffs, NJ: Prentice-Hall.

Denzin, N.K and Lincoln, Y.S. (eds) (1994) Handbook of Qualitative Research. Thousand Oaks, CA: Sage.

Denzin, N.K and Lincoln, Y.S. (eds) (2000) Handbook of Qualitative Research (2nd edition). Thousand Oaks, CA: Sage.

Derrida, J. (1996) Archive Fever: A Freudian Impression. Chicago: University of Chicago Press.

Dey, I. (1993) Qualitative Data Analysis: A User-friendly Guide for Social Scientists. London: Routledge Kegan Paul.

Dickson-Swift, V., James, E.L., Kippen, S. and Liamputtong, P. (2007) 'Doing sensitive research: what challenges do qualitative researchers face?', Qualitative Research, 7: 327–353.

Dingwall, R. (1977) The Social Organisation of Health Visitor Training. London: Croom Helm.

Dingwall, R. and Murray, T. (1983) 'Categorisation in accident departments: "good" patients, "bad" patients and children', Sociology of Health & Illness, 5 (12): 121–148.

Doucet, A. and Mauthner, M. (2002) 'Knowing responsibly: linking ethics, research practice and epistemology', in M. Mauthner, M. Birch, J. Jessop and T. Miller (eds), Ethics in Qualitative Research. London: Sage.

Douglas, M. (1975) 'Self-evidence', in M. Douglas (ed.), Implicit Meanings. London: Routledge.

Downward, P. and Riordan, J. (2007) 'Social interactions and the demand for sport: an economic analysis', Contemporary Economic Policy, 25 (4): 518–537.

Dressler, W.W. (1991) Stress and Adaptation in the Context of Culture: Depression in a Southern Black Community. Albany, NY: State University of New York Press.

Drew, P. (1984) 'Speakers' reporting in invitation sequences', in J.M. Atkinson and J. Heritage (eds), Structures of Social Action: Studies in Conversation Analysis. Cambridge: Cambridge University Press.

Drew, P. (1992) 'Contested evidence in courtroom cross-examination: the case of a trial for rape', in P. Drew and J. Heritage (eds), Talk at Work: Interaction in Institutional Settings. Cambridge: Cambridge University Press.

Durkheim, E. (1970) Suicide: A Study in Sociology. London: Routledge and Kegan Paul (originally published 1897).

Durkheim, E. (1982) The Rules of Sociological Method. London: Macmillan.

Eatough, V. and Smith, J. (2006) '"I was like a wild, wild person": Understanding feelings of anger using interpretative phenomenological analysis', British Journal of Psychology, 97: 483–498.

Edwards, P. (2004) How to Give an Academic Talk: Changing the Culture of Public Speaking in the Humanities. http://pne.people.si.umich.edu/PDF/howtotalk.pdf.

Edwards, D. (2006) 'Discourse, cognition and social practices: the rich surface of language and social interaction', Discourse Studies, 8 (1): 41–49.

ESRC (Economic and Social Research Council) (2003) ESRC Mission Statement. www.esrc.ac.uk/esrccontent/postgradfunding/ mission.asp.

ESRC (Economic and Social Research Council) (2009) Research Ethics Framework. www.esrc.ac.uk/ESRCInfoCentre/Images/ESRC_Re_Ethics_Frame_tcm6–11291.pdf.

Fabian, J. (2002) Time and the Other: How Anthropology Makes Its Object. New York: Columbia University Press.

Fairclough, N. (1995) Critical Discourse Analysis. New York: Longman.

Fairclough, N. (2003) Analysing Discourse: Text Analysis for Social Research. London: Routledge.

Fairclough, N. and Wodak, R. (1997) 'Critical Discourse Analysis: an overview', in T.A. van Dijk (ed.), Discourse and Interaction. London: Sage.

Field, A. (2009) Discovering Statistics using SPSS for Windows (3rd edition). London: Sage.

Fielding, N. (1981) The National Front. London: Routledge and Kegan Paul.

Fielding, N. and Fielding, J. (2000) 'Resistance and adaptation to criminal identity: using secondary analysis to evaluate classic studies of crime and deviance', Sociology, 34 (4): 671–689.

Fielding, N. and Gilbert, N. (2000) Understanding Social Statistics. London: Sage.

Filmer, P., Jenks, C., Seale, C., Thoburn, N. and Walsh, D. (2004) 'Developments in social theory', in C. Seale (ed.), Researching Society and Culture, (2nd edition). London: Sage.

Finnis, J. (1983) Fundamentals of Ethics, Washington, DC: Georgetown University Press.

Firth, J.R. (1957) Papers in Linguistics 1934–1951. Oxford: Oxford University Press.

Fisher, A. (2004) 'The content of the right to education – theoretical foundations'. Center for human rights and global justice working paper: Economic, Social and Cultural Rights Series, Number 4. www.chrgj.org/publications/docs/wp/Fisher%20The%20Content%20of%20the%20Right%20to%20Education.pdf.

Fishman, P.M. (1977) 'Interactional shitwork', Heresies, 2: 99–101.

Flanders, N. (1970) Analyzing Teaching Behavior. Reading, MA: Addison-Wesley.

Flick, U. (2003) Designing Qualitative Research. London: Sage.

Flick, U. (2006) An Introduction to Qualitative Research. London: Sage.

Forsey, M.G. (2010) 'Ethnography as participant listening', Ethnography, 11: 558–572.

Foster, J. and Sheppard, J. (1994) British Archives: A Guide to Archive Resources in the UK. Basingstoke: Macmillan.

Foster, L.H. (2010) 'A best kept secret: single-subject research design in counseling', Counseling Outcome Research and Evaluation, 1: 30–39.

Foucault, M. (1972) The Archaeology of Knowledge. London: Tavistock.

Foucault, M. (1977) Discipline and Punish. Harmondsworth: Penguin.

Foucault, M. (1980) Power/Knowledge: Selected Interviews and Other Writings 1972–1977. New York: Pantheon.

Foucault, M. (1984) 'What is an author?' in P. Rabinow (ed.), The Foucault Reader. Harmondsworth: Penguin.

Foucault, M. (2000) 'Lives of infamous men', in P. Rabinow (ed.), Essential Works of Foucault, 1958–1984, Volume III: Power. London: Penguin.

Fox, N., Ward, K. and O'Rourke, A. (2005) 'Pro-anorexia, weight-loss drugs and the Internet: an "anti-recover" explanatory model of anorexia', Sociology of Health & Illness, 27 (7): 944–971.

Frankenberg, R. (1993) White Women, Race Matters: The Social Construction of Whiteness. London: Routledge.

Franz, C., McClelland, D. and Weinberger, J. (1991) 'Childhood antecedents of conventional social accomplishment in midlife adults: a 36-year prospective study', Journal of Personality and Social Psychology, 60 (4): 586–595.

Frost, N. (2009) '"Do you know what I mean?": the use of a pluralistic narrative analysis approach in the interpretation of an interview', Qualitative Research, 9: 9–29.

Frost, N.A, Nolas, S-M., Brooks-Gordon, B., Esin, C., Holt, A., Mehdizadeh, L. and Shinebourne, P. (2010) 'Pluralism in qualitative research: the impact of different researchers and qualitative approaches on the analysis of qualitative data', Qualitative Research, 10 (4): 441–460.

Fuchs, L.S. and Fuchs, D. (1993) 'Writing research reports for publication: recommendations for new authors', Remedial and Special Education, 14: 39–46.

Garfinkel, H. (1967) Studies in Ethnomethodology. Englewood Cliffs, NJ: Prentice-Hall.

Garnett, M. (2000) Out of This World: An Exploration Into the Use of Complementary Therapies by Those Who Nurse the Dying. PhD thesis, University of London.

Garnett, M. (2003) 'Sustaining the cocoon: the emotional inoculation produced by complementary therapies in palliative care', European Journal of Cancer Care, 12: 129–136.

Geer, B. (1964) 'First days in the field', in P. Hammond (ed.), Sociologists at Work. New York: Basic Books.

Geertz, C. (1973) The Interpretation of Cultures. London: Fontana.

Geertz, C. (1988) Works and Lives: The Anthropologist as Author. Stanford, CA: Stanford University Press.

Geertz, C. (1995) After the Fact: Two Countries, Four Decades, One Anthropologist. Cambridge: Harvard University Press.

Gerth, H.H. and Wright Mills, C. (eds) (1948) From Max Weber: Essays in Sociology. London: Routledge & Kegan Paul.

Gibbs, G.R. (2002) Qualitative Data Analysis: Explorations with NVivo. Buckingham: Open University Press.

Giddens, A. (1991a) Modernity and Self-Identity: Self and Society in the Late Modern Age. Cambridge: Polity Press.

Giddens, A. (1991b) The Consequences of Modernity. Cambridge: Polity Press.

Giddens, A. (1993) Sociology. Cambridge: Polity Press.

Gill, R. (1996) 'Discourse analysis: methodological aspects', in J.E. Richardson (ed.), Handbook of Qualitative Research Methods for Psychology and the Social Sciences. Leicester: British Psychological Society.

Glaser, B.G. (1978) Theoretical Sensitivity: Advances in the Methodology of Grounded Theory. Mill Valley, CA: Sociology Press.

Glaser, B.G. (1992) Emergence versus Forcing: Basics of Grounded Theory Analysis. Mill Valley, CA: Sociology Press.

Glaser, B.G. and Strauss, A.L. (1964) 'The social loss of dying patients', American Journal of Nursing, 64 (6): 119–121.

Glaser, B.G. and Strauss, A.L. (1965) Awareness of Dying. Chicago, IL: Aldine.

Glaser, B.G. and Strauss, A.L. (1967) The Discovery of Grounded Theory: Strategies for Qualitative Research. Chicago, IL: Aldine.

Glaser, B.G. and Strauss, A.L. (1968) Time for Dying. Chicago, IL: Aldine.

Gobo, G. (2008) Doing Ethnography. London: Sage.

Goffman, E. (1959) The Presentation of Self in Everyday Life. New York: Doubleday Anchor.

Goodwin, C. (1994) 'Professional vision', American Anthropologist, 96 (3): 606–633.

Gowers, E. (1973) The Complete Plain Words (2nd edition revised by Bruce Fraser). London: HMSO.

Grady, J. (2008) 'Visual research at the crossroads', Forum: Qualitative Social Research, 9 (3). www.qualitative-research.net/index.php/fqs/article/viewArticle/1173/2618.

Gray, R., Fitch, M., Davis, C. and Phillips, C. (1996) 'Breast cancer and prostate cancer self-help groups: reflections on differences', Psycho-Oncology, 5: 137–142.

Greenhalgh, S. (1994) 'Controlling births and bodies', American Ethnologist, 21: 3–30.

Greenhalgh, T. (1997) 'How to read a paper: papers that summarise other papers (systematic reviews and meta-analyses)', British Medical Journal, 315: 672–675.

Griffin, C., Bengry-Howell, A., Hackly, C., Mistral, W. and Szmigin, I. (2009) '"Every time I do it I absolutely annihilate myself": loss of (self-)consciousness and loss of memory in young people's drinking narratives', Sociology, 43 (3): 457–476.

Guba, E.G. and Lincoln, Y.S. (1994) 'Competing paradigms in qualitative research', in N.K. Denzin and Y.S. Lincoln (eds), Handbook of Qualitative Research. Thousand Oaks, CA: Sage, 105–117.

Gubrium, J. and Holstein, J. (1987) 'The private image: experiential location and method in family studies', Journal of Marriage and Family, 49: 773–786.

Gubrium, J. and Holstein, J. (1997) The New Language of Qualitative Method. New York: Oxford University Press.

Gubrium, J. and Holstein, J. (eds) (2002) Handbook of Interview Research: Context and Method. Thousand Oaks, CA: Sage.

Guha, R. (1997) 'Chandra's death', in R. Guha (ed.), Subaltern Studies Reader, 1986–1995. Minneapolis, MN: University of Minnesota Press.

Guise, J., McVittie, C. and McKinlay, A. (2010) 'A discourse-analytic study of ME/CFS (Chronic Fatigue Syndrome) sufferers' experiences of interactions with doctors', Journal of Health Psychology, 15 (3): 426–435.

Hakim, C. (2000) Research Design: Successful Designs for Social and Economic Research. London: Routledge.

Hall, J.N. and Ryan, K.E. (2011) 'Educational accountability: a qualitatively driven mixed-methods approach', Qualitative Inquiry, 17: 105–115.

Hall, S. (1980) 'Encoding/decoding', in S. Hall (ed.), Culture, Media, Language. London: Hutchinson, 128–38.

Hall, S. (1992) 'The West and the rest', in S. Hall and B. Gieben (eds), Formations of Modernity. Cambridge: Polity Press.

Hallam, E. and Street, B. (eds) (2000) Representing Otherness. London and New York: Routledge.

Halse, A. and Honey, A. (2005) 'Unraveling ethics: illuminating the moral dilemmas of research ethics', Signs: Journal of Women in Culture and Society, 30 (4): 2141–2162.

Hammersley, M. (1992a) 'Deconstructing the qualitative–quantitative divide', in J. Brannen (ed.), Mixing Methods: Qualitative and Quantitative Research. Aldershot: Avebury.

Hammersley, M. (1992b) What's Wrong with Ethnography: Methodological Explorations. London: Routledge.

Hammersley, M. (1995a) The Politics of Social Research. London: Sage.

Hammersley, M. (1995b) 'Theory and evidence in qualitative research', Quality & Quantity, 29: 55–66.

Hammersley, M. (1997) 'Qualitative data archiving: some reflections on its prospects and problems', Sociology, 31 (1): 131–142.

Hammersley, M. (2002) Discourse Analysis: A Bibliographical Guide. www.cf.ac.uk/socsi/capacity/Activities/Themes/In-depth/guide.pdf.

Hammersley, M. and Atkinson, P. (1995) Ethnography: Principles in Practice (2nd edition). London: Routledge.

Hammersley, M. and Atkinson, P. (2007) Ethnography: Principles in Practice (3rd edition). London: Routledge.

Hansen, E.C. (1977) Rural Catalonia Under the Franco Regime. Cambridge: Cambridge University Press.

Haraway, D. (1991) Simians, Cyborgs and Women: The Reinvention of Nature. London: Free Association Books, 149–182.

Haraway, D. (1997) Modest Witness, Second Millennium: FemaleMan Meets OncoMouse: Feminism and Technoscience. London: Routledge.

Harding, S. (1991) Whose Science? Whose Knowledge?: Thinking From Women's Lives. Milton Keynes: Open University Press.

Harkness, S., Machin, S. and Waldfogel, J. (1997) 'Evaluating the pin money hypothesis: the relationship between women's labour market activity, family income and poverty in Britain', Journal of Population Economics, 10 (2): 137–158.

Harper, D. (1998) 'An argument for visual sociology', in J. Prosser (ed.), Image-based Research: A Sourcebook for Qualitative Researchers. London: Falmer, 24–41.

Harris, C. (1991) 'Configurations of racism: the Civil Service, 1945–60', Race & Class, 33 (1): 1–29.

Harrison, B. (2002) 'Seeing health and illness worlds – using visual methodologies in a sociology of health and illness: a methodological review', Sociology of Health & Illness, 24 (6): 856–872.

Hart, C. (1998) Doing a Literature Review: Releasing the Social Science Research Imagination. London: Sage.

Hart, C. (2001) Doing a Literature Search: A Comprehensive Guide for the Social Sciences. London: Sage.

Heath, C. (2002) 'Demonstrative suffering: the gestural (re)embodiment of symptoms', Journal of Communication, 52: 597–617.

Heath, C., Hindmarsh, J. and Luff, P. (2010) Video in Qualitative Research. London: Sage.

Heaton, J. (1998) 'Secondary analysis of qualitative data', Social Research Update Issue 22. http://sru.soc.surrey.ac.uk/SRU22.html.

Heaton, J. (2004) Reworking Qualitative Data. London: Sage.

Hegel, G.W.F. (2010) The Science of Logic. Cambridge: Cambridge University Press.

Henry, G.T. (1990) Practical Sampling. Newbury Park, CA: Sage.

Henry, J.A., Alexander, C.A. and Sener, E.K. (1995) 'Relative mortality from overdose of antidepressants', British Medical Journal, 310: 221–224.

Henry, J.A., Moloney, C., Rivas, C. and Goldin, R.D. (2002) 'Increase in alcohol related deaths: is hepatitis C a factor?', Journal of Clinical Pathology, 55: 704–707.

Henz, U. (2009) 'Couples' provision of informal care for parents and parents-in-law: far from sharing equally?' Ageing & Society, 29 (3): 369–395.

Heritage, J. (1984) Garfinkel and Ethnomethodology. Cambridge: Polity Press.

Heritage, J. (1997) 'Conversation analysis and institutional talk: analysing data', in D. Silverman (ed.), Qualitative Research: Theory, Method and Practice. London: Sage, 161–182.

Heritage, J. and Greatbatch, D. (1991) 'On the institutional character of institutional talk: the case of news interviews', in D. Boden and D.H. Zimmerman (eds), Talk and Social Structure: Studies in Ethnomethodology and Conversation Analysis. Berkeley, CA: University of California Press.

Hesmondhalgh, D. and Baker, S. (2008) 'Creative work and emotional labour in the television industry', Theory, Culture & Society, 25: 97–118.

Hewitt, R. (1996) Routes of Racism: The Social Basis of Racist Action. Stoke-on-Trent: Trentham Books.

Hewitt, R., Spicer, N. and Tooke, J. (2003) Projects, Participation and Partnerships: An Analysis of LSL HAZ Activities. London: Goldsmiths, University of London.

Hey, V. (1994) 'Telling tales: methodological issues arising from doing research on decision making and the frail elderly', in P. Alderson (ed.), Sharing Health and Welfare Choices with Old People. London: SSRU Consent Series no 7: 46–56.

Hill, M.R. (1993) Archival Research Strategies and Techniques. London: Sage.

Hindmarsh, J. and Pilnick, A. (2007) 'Knowing bodies at work: embodiment and ephemeral teamwork in anaesthesia', Organization Studies, 28: 1395–1416.

Hine, C. (1998) Virtual Ethnography. Paper presented at the Research and Information for Social Scientists Conference, 25–27 March 1998, Bristol. www.intute.ac.uk/socialsciences/archive/iriss/papers/paper16.htm.

Hodge, D.C. (1995) 'Should women count? The role of quantitative methodology in feminist geographic research', Professional Geographer, 47 (4): 426.

Hoffmann, R. (1988) 'Under the surface of the chemical article', Angewandte Chemie International Edition, 27 (12): 1593–1602.

Hoffmaster, B. (1994) 'The forms and limits of medical ethics', Social Science & Medicine, 39 (9): 1155–1164.

Holdaway, S. (1982) 'An inside job: a case study of covert research on the police', in M. Bulmer (ed.), Social Research Ethics: An Examination of the Merits of Covert Participant Observation. London: Macmillan.

Holland, J. (1991) 'Introduction: history, memory and the family album', in P. Holland and J. Spence (eds), Family Snaps: The Meanings of Domestic Photography. London: Virago, 1–14.

Holland, J. and Ramazanoglu, C. (1994) 'Coming to conclusions: power and interpretations in researching young women's sexuality', in M. Maynard and J. Purvis (eds), Researching Women's Lives from a Feminist Perspective. London: Taylor and Francis.

Hollander, J.A. (2004) 'The social contexts of focus groups', Journal of Contemporary Ethnography, 33 (5): 602–637.

Hollis, M. (1994) The Philosophy of Social Science: An Introduction. Cambridge: Cambridge University Press.

Holmes, T.H. and Rahe, R.H. (1967) 'The social readjustment rating scale', Journal of Psychosomatic Research, 11: 213–218.

Holosko, M.J. (2010) 'What types of designs are we using in social work research and evaluation?', Research on Social Work Practice, 20: 665–673.

Holstein, J. and Gubrium, J. (eds) (2008) Handbook of Constructionist Research. New York: Guilford Press.

Homan, R. (1991) The Ethics of Social Research. London: Longman.

Horrocks, S., Anderson, E. and Salisbury, C. (2002) 'Systematic review of whether nurse practitioners working in primary care can provide equivalent care to doctors', British Medical Journal, 324: 819–823.

Hsieh, H-F. and Shannon, S.E. (2005) 'Three approaches to qualitative content analysis', Qualitative Health Research, 15: 1277–1288.

Huckin, T. (2002) 'Textual silence and the discourse of homelessness', Discourse & Society, 13 (3): 347–372.

Hughes, C. (2007) 'The pleasures of learning at work: Foucault and phenomenology compared', British Journal of Sociology of Education, 28 (3): 363–376.

Humphrey, L. (1970) Tearoom Trade: A Study of Homosexual Encounters in Public Places. London: Duckworth.

Hutchby, I. and Wooffitt, R. (2008) Conversation Analysis. Cambridge: Polity Press.

Hydén, L-C. (1997) 'Illness and narrative', Sociology of Health & Illness, 19 (1): 48–69.

Im, E-O. and Chee, W. (2005) 'A descriptive internet survey on menopausal symptoms: five ethnic groups of Asian American University faculty and staff', Journal of Transcultural Nursing, 16: 126–135.

Israel, M. and Hay, I. (2006) Research Ethics for Social Scientists. London: Sage.

James, N. and Busher, H. (2009) Online Interviewing. London: Sage.

Janesick, V. (2003) 'Stretching' Exercises for Qualitative Researchers (2nd edition). Thousand Oaks, CA: Sage.

Jeffery, R. (1979) 'Normal rubbish: deviant patients in casualty departments', Sociology of Health & Illness, 1 (1): 90–107.

Johansson, K., Lilja, M., Park, M. and Josephsson, S. (2010) 'Balancing the good – a critical discourse analysis of home modification services', Sociology of Health & Illness, 32 (4): 563–582.

Johnson, R.R. (2011) 'Suspect mental disorder and police use of force', Criminal Justice and Behavior, 38: 127–145.

Johnson, R.B., Onwuegbuzie, A.J. and Turner, L.A. (2007) 'Toward a definition of mixed methods research', Journal of Mixed Methods Research, 1: 112–133.

Jones, J.H. (1993) Bad Blood: The Tuskegee Syphilis Experiment. New York: Free Press.

Junker, B. (1960) Fieldwork. Chicago, IL: University of Chicago Press.

Kaczorowski, J. (2009) 'Standing on the shoulders of giants: introduction to systematic reviews and meta-analyses', Canadian Family Physician, 55: 1155–1156.

Kaplan, A. (1991) 'Gone fishing, be back later', in W.B. Shaffir and R. Stebbins (eds), Experiencing Fieldwork. Newbury Park, CA: Sage.

Kashy, D.A., Donnellan, M.B., Ackerman, R.A. and Russell, D.W. (2009) 'Reporting and interpreting research in PSPB: practices, principles, and pragmatics', Personality and Social Psychology Bulletin, 35: 1131–1142.

Keddie, N. (1971) 'Classroom knowledge', in M. Young (ed.), Knowledge and Control. London: Collier-Macmillan.

Kelle, U. (1997) 'Theory building in qualitative research and computer programs for the management of textual data', Sociological Research Online, 2: 2. www.soc.surrey.ac.uk/socresonline.

Keller, C., Fleury, J. and Rivera, A. (2007) 'Visual methods in the assessment of diet intake in Mexican American women', Western Journal of Nursing Research, 29: 758–773.

Kelly, M. (2010) 'The role of theory in qualitative health research', Family Practice, 27 (3): 285–290.

Kelman, H.C. (1982) 'Ethical issues in different social science methods', in T.L. Beauchamp, R.R. Faden, R.J. Wallace and L. Walters (eds), Ethical Issues in Social Science Research. Baltimore, MD: Johns Hopkins University Press.

Kendall, G. and Wickham, G. (1999) Using Foucault's Methods. London: Sage.

Kennedy, B.L. (2011) 'The importance of student and teacher interactions for disaffected middle school students: a grounded theory study of community day schools', Urban Education, 46: 4–33.

KhosraviNik, M. (2009) 'The representation of refugees, asylum seekers and immigrants in British newspapers during the Balkan conflict (1999) and the British General Election (2005)', Discourse & Society, 20 (4): 477–498.

Kiesling, S.F. (2005) 'Homosocial desire in men's talk: balancing and re-creating cultural discourses of masculinity', Language in Society, 34: 695–726.

Kingery, W.D. (1998) Learning From Things: Method and Theory of Material Culture Studies. Washington, DC: Smithsonian Institute.

Kirkwood, J. (1993) 'Investing ourselves: use of researcher personal response in feminist methodology', in J. deGroot and M. Maynard (eds), Women's Studies in the 1990s: Doing Things Differently? Basingstoke: Macmillan.

Kiss, A. and Meryn, S. (2001) 'Effect of sex and gender on psychosocial aspects of prostate and breast cancer', British Medical Journal, 323: 1055–1058.

Kitzinger, J. (1994a) 'Focus groups: method or madness?', in M. Boulton (ed.), Challenge and Innovation: Methodological Advances in Social Research on HIV/AIDS. London: Taylor and Francis, 159–175.

Kitzinger, J. (1994b) 'The methodology of focus groups: the importance of interaction between research participants', Sociology of Health & Illness, 16 (1): 103–121.

Kitzinger, C. (2000) 'Doing feminist conversation analysis', Feminism & Psychology, 10: 163–193.

Kitzinger, C. and Firth, H. (1999) '"Just say no?" The use of conversation analysis in developing a feminist perspective on sexual refusal', Discourse & Society, 10 (3): 293–316.

Klemm, P., Hurst, M., Dearholt, S.L and Trone, S.R. (1999) 'Gender differences on Internet cancer support groups', Computers in Nursing, 17 (2): 65–72.

Knepper, P. and Scicluna, S. (2010) 'Historical criminology and the imprisonment of women in 19th-century Malta', Theoretical Criminology, 14: 407–424.

Knoblauch, H. (2008) 'The performance of knowledge: pointing and knowledge in PowerPoint presentations', Cultural Sociology, 2: 75–97.

Knowles, C. and Sweetman, P. (eds) (2004) Picturing the Social Landscape: Visual Methods and the Sociological Imagination. London: Routledge.

Koppel, R., Localio, A., Cohen, A. and Strom, B. (2005a) 'Neither panacea nor black box: responding to three papers on computerized physician order entry systems', Journal of Biomedical Informatics, 38 (4): 267–269.

Koppel, R. Metlay, J.P., Cohen, A., Abaluck, B., Localio, A.R., Kimmel, S.E. and Strom, B.L. (2005b) 'Role of computerized physician order entry systems in facilitating medical errors', Journal of American Medical Association, 293 (10): 1197–1202.

Krathwohl, D.R. (1988) How to Prepare a Research Proposal: Guidelines for Funding and Dissertations in the Social and Behavioral Sciences. Syracuse, NY: Syracuse University Press.

Krauss, R. (1991) 'A note on photography and the simulacral', in C. Squiers (ed.), The Critical Image: Essays in Contemporary Photography. London: Lawrence and Wishart, 15–27.

Krueger, R.A. and Casey, M.A. (2008) Focus Groups: A Practical Guide for Applied Research. London: Sage.

Kuhn, A. (1995) Family Secrets: Acts of Memory and Imagination. London and New York: Verso.

Kuhn, T. (1970) The Structure of Scientific Revolutions (2nd edition, enlarged). Chicago, IL: University of Chicago Press.

Kvale, S. and Brinkmann, S. (2009) Interviews: Learning the Craft of Qualitative Research. London: Sage.

Kynaston, D. (2001) The City of London, IV: A Club No More, 1945–2000. London: Pimlico.

Labov, W. (1972) Language in the City: Studies in the Black English Vernacular. Philadelphia, PA: University of Pennsylvania Press.

Lakoff, R. (1975) Language and Women's Place. New York: Harper and Row.

Landsberger, H.A. (1958) Hawthorne Revisited: Management and the Worker: Its Critics, and Developments in Human Relations in Industry. Ithaca, NY: New York State School of Industrial and Labor Relations, Cornell University.

Larkin, M. (2009) 'Life after caring: the post-caring experiences of former carers', British Journal of Social Work, 39 (6): 1026–1042.

Latour, B. (1999) Pandora's Hope: Essays on the Reality of Science Studies. Cambridge, MA: Harvard University Press.

Latour, B. and Woolgar, S. (1979) Laboratory Life: The Production of Scientific Facts. Princeton, NJ: Princeton University Press.

Laslett, P. (1965) The World We Have Lost. London: Methuen.

Law, J. (1994) Organizing Modernity. Oxford: Blackwell.

Lee, V.E. and Smith, J.B. (1997) 'High school size: which works best and for whom?', Educational Evaluation and Policy Analysis, 19: 205–227.

Leiss, W., Kline, S. and Jhally, S. (1990) Social Communication in Advertising: Persons, Products and Images of Well-Being (2nd edition). London: Routledge.

Li, S. and Seale, C. (2007) 'Learning to do qualitative data analysis: an observational study of doctoral work', Qualitative Health Research, 17: 1442–1452.

Li, S. and Seale, C. (2008) 'Acquiring a sociological identity: an observational study of a PhD project', Sociology, 42: 987–1002.

Lieblich, A., Tuval-Maschiach, R. and Zilber, T. (1998) Narrative Research: Reading, Analysis, and Interpretation. Thousand Oaks, CA: Sage.

Liebow, E. (1967) Tally's Corner Washington DC: A Study of Negro Streetcorner Men. London: Routledge & Kegan Paul.

Lincoln, Y.S. and Guba, E. (1985) Naturalistic Enquiry. Beverly Hills, CA: Sage.

Lipstadt, D. (1993) Denying the Holocaust: The Growing Assault on Truth and Memory. New York: Free Press/Macmillan.

List, D. (2004) Maximum Variation Sampling for Surveys and Consensus Groups. Audience Dialogue: Adelaide. www.audiencedialogue.net/maxvar.html.

Lister, M. (ed.) (1995) The Photographic Image in Digital Culture. London: Routledge.

Livingston, E. (1987) Making Sense of Ethnomethodology. London: Routledge.

Llobera, J. (1998) 'Historical and comparative research', in C. Seale (ed.), Researching Society and Culture. London: Sage, 72–81.

Lofland, J. (1971) Analysing Social Settings: A Guide to Qualitative Observation. Belmont, CA: Wadsworth.

Lomas, C. (2009) Beyond Getting the Message – Why the NHS is Adopting Social Marketing. www.nursingtimes.net/whats-new-in-nursing/primary-care/beyond-getting-the-message-why-the-nhs-is-adopting-social-marketing/5002452.article.

Lomsky-Feder, E. (1995) 'The meaning of war through veterans' eyes: a phenomenological analysis of life stories', International Sociology, 10: 463–482.

Louw, B. (1993) 'Irony in the text or insincerity in the writer? The diagnostic potential of semantic prosodies', in Baker, M., Francis, G. and Tognini-Bonelli, E. (eds), Text and Technology: In Honour of John Sinclair. Philadelphia, PA and Amsterdam: John Benjamins.

Lunt, P. and Livingstone, S. (1996) 'Rethinking the focus group in media and communications research', Journal of Communication, 46 (2): 79–98.

Lynd, R.S. and Lynd, H.M. (1929) Middletown: A Study in Contemporary American Culture. New York: Harcourt Brace.

Lynd, R.S. and Lynd, H.M. (1937) Middletown in Transition: A Study in Cultural Conflicts. New York: Harcourt Brace.

Machamer, P. and Silberstein, M. (2002) Blackwell's Guide to Philosophy of Science. Oxford: Blackwell.

Maier, C.D. (2011) 'Communicating business greening and greenwashing in global media: a multimodal discourse analysis of CNN's greenwashing video', International Communication Gazette, 73: 165–177.

Mansergh, G., Naorat, S., Jommaroeng, R., Jenkins, R.A., Jeeyapant, S., Kanggarnrua, K., Phanuphak, P., Tappero, J.W. and van Griensven, F. (2006) 'Adaptation of venue-day-time sampling in Southeast Asia to access men who have sex with men for HIV assessment in Bangkok', Field Methods, 18: 135–152.

Margolis, E. (2000) 'Class pictures: representations of race, gender and ability in a century of school photography', Education Policy Analysis Archives, 8 (31). http://epaa.asu.edu/epaa/v8n31/.

Marsh, C. (1982) The Survey Method: The Contribution of Surveys to Sociological Explanation. London: Allen and Unwin.

Marsh, C. (1988) Exploring Data. Cambridge: Polity.

Martin, M. and McIntyre, L.C. (eds) (1994) Readings in the Philosophy of Social Science. Cambridge, MA: MIT Press.

Marx, G. (1997) 'Of methods and manners for aspiring sociologists: 37 moral imperatives', The American Sociologist, 28 (1): 102–125.

Marx, K. (1967) Capital. London: International.

Marx, K. and Engels, F. (2004) The German Ideology. London: Lawrence & Wishart.

Mason, J. (1996) Qualitative Researching. London: Sage.

Mason, J. (2002) Qualitative Researching, (2nd edition). London: Sage.

Mattingly, D.J. and Falconer-Al-Hindi, K. (1995) 'Should women count? A context for the debate', Professional Geographer, 47 (4): 427–435.

Mauthner, M. (1998) 'Bringing silent voices into a public discourse: researching accounts of sister relationships', in J. Ribbens and R. Edwards (eds), Feminist Dilemmas in Qualitative Research: Public Knowledge and Private Lives. London: Sage.

Mauthner, M., Birch, M., Jessop, J. and Miller, T. (eds) (2002) Ethics in Qualitative Research. London: Sage.

May, V. (2008) 'On being a "good" mother: The moral presentation of self', Sociology, 42: 470–486.

Maynard, D.W. (1991) 'On the interactional and institutional bases of asymmetry in clinical discourse', American Journal of Sociology, 97: 448–495.

Maynard, D.W. (1992) 'On clinicians co-implicating recipients' perspective in the delivery of diagnostic news', in P. Drew and J. Heritage (eds), Talk at Work. Cambridge: Cambridge University Press.

Maynard, M. and Purvis, J. (eds) (1994) Researching Women's Lives from a Feminist Perspective. London: Taylor and Francis.

McCall, G.J. and Simmons, J.L. (eds) (1969) Issues in Participant Observation: A Text and Reader. Reading, MA: Addison-Wesley.

McEnery, T., Xiao, R. and Tono, Y. (2006) Corpus-based Language Studies: An Advanced Resource Book. London: Routledge.

McLafferty, S. (1995) 'Counting for women', Professional Geographer, 47 (4): 436–442.

McWhinney, I.R., Bass, M.J. and Donner, A. (1994) 'Evaluation of palliative care service: problems and pitfalls', British Medical Journal, 309: 1340–1342.

Medical Research Council (Streptomycin in Tuberculosis Trials Committee of the Medical Research Council) (1948) 'Streptomycin treatment of pulmonary tuberculosis', British Medical Journal, 2 (4582): 769–782.

Mellick, M. and Fleming, S. (2010) 'Personal narrative and the ethics of disclosure: a case study from elite sport', Qualitative Research, 10: 299–314.

Mercer, K. (1994) Welcome to the Jungle: New Positions in Black Cultural Studies. London and New York: Routledge, 171–220.

Merton, R.K. (1987) 'The focused interview and focus groups: continuities and discontinuities', Public Opinion Quarterly, 51: 550–566.

Meyrick, J. (2006) 'What is good qualitative research?: a first step towards a comprehensive approach to judging rigour/quality', Journal of Health Psychology, 11: 799–808.

Michael, M. (1992) 'Lay discourses of science: science-in-general, science-in-particular and self', Science, Technology & Human Values, 17: 313–333.

Michael, M. (1996) 'Ignoring science: discourses of ignorance in the public understanding of science', in A. Irwin and B. Wynne (eds), Misunderstanding Science? The Public Reconstruction of Science and Technology. Cambridge: Cambridge University Press, 105–125.

Michael, M. and Birke, L. (1994a) 'Animal experimentation: enrolling the core set', Social Studies of Science, 24 (1): 81–95.

Michael, M. and Birke, L. (1994b) 'Accounting for animal experiments: credibility and disreputable "others"', Science, Technology & Human Values, 19 (2): 189–204.

Michael, M. and Carter, S. (2001) 'The facts about fictions and vice versa: public understanding of human genetics', Science as Culture, 10 (1): 5–32.

Milgram, S. (1974) Obedience to Authority. New York: Harper and Row.

Miller, D. (1994) Modernity, an Ethnographic Approach: Dualism and Mass Consumption in Trinidad. Oxford: Berg.

Miller, D. (1995) 'The young and the restless and mass consumption in Trinidad', in R.C. Allen (ed.), To be Continued … Soap Operas Around the World. London: Routledge.

Miller, D. (1998) Material Cultures: Why Some Things Matter. London: UCL Press.

Mills, M., Davies, H.T.O., Macrae, W.A. (1994) 'Care of dying patients in hospital', British Medical Journal, 309: 583–586.

Millsted, R. and Frith, H. (2003) 'Being large-breasted: women negotiating embodiment', Women's Studies International Forum, 26 (5): 455–465.

Mitchell, J.C. (1983) 'Case and situational analysis', Sociological Review, 31 (2): 187–211.

Moerman, M. (1974) 'Accomplishing ethnicity', in R. Turner (ed.), Ethnomethodology. Harmondsworth: Penguin.

Moerman, M. (1988) Talking Culture: Ethnography and Conversational Analysis. Philadelphia, PA: University of Pennsylvania Press.

Moerman, M. (1992) 'Life after CA: an ethnographer's autobiography', in G. Watson and R.M. Seiler (eds), Text in Context: Contributions to Ethnomethodology. London: Sage.

Moisander, J. and Valtonen, A. (2006) Qualitative Marketing Research. London: Sage.

Moore, D. (2010) 'Socialising with others "can help fight cancer"', Daily Telegraph, 9 July. www.telegraph.co.uk/health/healthnews/7879031/Socialising-with-others-can-help-fight-cancer.html.

Moreira, T. (2007) 'Entangled evidence: knowledge making in systematic reviews in healthcare', Sociology of Health & Illness, 29 (2): 180–197.

Morgan, D. (1993) Successful Focus Groups. London: Sage.

Morgan, D. (1997) Focus Groups as Qualitative Research (2nd edition). London: Sage.

Morley, D. (1980) The 'Nationwide' Audience. London: British Film Institute.

Morton, R.L., Tong, A., Howard, K., Snelling, P. and Webster, A.C. (2010) 'The views of patients and carers in treatment decision making for chronic kidney disease: systematic review and thematic synthesis of qualitative studies', British Medical Journal, 340: c112.

Moss, S. (2000) 'History's verdict on Holocaust upheld: historians claim victory after rigorous courtroom test', Guardian, 12 April.

Mulkay, M. (1979) Science and the Sociology of Knowledge. London: Allen and Unwin.

Mulkay, M. and Gilbert, G.N. (1981) 'Putting philosophy to work: Karl Popper's influence on scientific practice', Philosophy of the Social Sciences, 11: 389–407.

Mulvey, L. (1975) 'Visual pleasure and narrative cinema', Screen, 16 (3): 6–8.

Munday, J. (2006) 'Identity in focus: the use of focus groups to study the construction of collective identity', Sociology, 40 (1): 89–105.

Murray, P.J. (1997) 'Using virtual focus groups in qualitative research', Qualitative Health Research, 7 (4): 542–549.

Murzalieva, G., Aleshkina, J., Temirov, A,. Samiev, A., Kartanbaeva, N., Jakab, M. and Spicer, N. (2009) Tracking Global HIV/AIDS Initiatives and their Impact on the Health System: The Experience of the Kyrgyz Republic Final Report. Centre for Health System Development, Kyrgyzstan and London School of Hygiene and Tropical Medicine.

Murzalieva, G., Kojokeev, K., Samiev, A., Aleshkina, J., Kartanbaeva, N., Botoeva, G., Ablezova, M. and Jakob, M. (2008) Tracking Global HIV/AIDS Initiatives and their Impact on the Health System: the Experience of the Kyrgyz Republic Interim Report. Centre for Health System Development, Kyrgyzstan and London School of Hygiene and Tropical Medicine.

Narcisse, M-R., Dedobbeleer, N., Contandriopoulos, A-P. and Ciampi, A. (2009) 'Understanding the social patterning of smoking practices: a dynamic typology', Sociology of Health & Illness, 31 (4): 583–601.

Neal, R.D., Ali, N., Atkin, K., Allgar, V.I., Ali, S. and Coleman, T. (2006) 'Communication between South Asian patients and GPs: comparative study using the Roter Interaction Analysis System', British Journal of General Practice, 56 (532): 869–875.

Neill, S.J. (2010) 'Containing acute childhood illness within family life: a substantive grounded theory', Journal of Child Health Care, 14: 327–344.

Nelson, B. (1984) Making an Issue of Child Abuse: Political Agenda Setting for Social Problems. Chicago, IL: University of Chicago Press.

Neuendorf, K.A. (2002) The Content Analysis Guidebook. London: Sage.

Nichols, E. and Childs, J.H. (2009) 'Respondent debriefings conducted by experts: a technique for questionnaire evaluation', Field Methods, 21: 115–132.

O'Leary, Z. (2010) The Essential Guide to Doing your Research Project. London: Sage.

Oakley, A. (1981) 'Interviewing women: a contradiction in terms?', in H. Roberts (ed.), Doing Feminist Research. London: Routledge.

Olwig, K.F. (1987) Cultural Adaptation and Resistance on St. John: Three Centuries of Afro-Caribbean Life. Gainesville, FL: University of Florida Press.

Othman, Z. (2010) 'The use of okay, right and yeah in academic lectures by native speaker lecturers: Their "anticipated" and "real" meanings', Discourse Studies, 12: 665–681.

Parke, H., Ashcroft, R., Brown, R., Marteau, T.M. and Seale, C. (2011) 'Financial incentives to encourage healthy behaviour: an analysis of UK media coverage', Health Expectations. Early view online before print 20 July, doi: 10.111/j.1369-7625.2011.00719.x.

Passerini, L. (1991) 'Memory', History Workshop Journal, 15 (Spring): 1983.

Payne, J. (1987) 'Does unemployment run in families? Some findings from the General Household Survey', Sociology, 21: 199–214.

Pearson, G. (1983) Hooligan: A History of Respectable Fears. Basingstoke: Macmillan.

Peek, L. and Fothergill, A. (2009) 'Using focus groups: lessons from studying daycare centers, 9/11, and Hurricane Katrina', Qualitative Research, 9 (1): 31–59.

Phelps, R., Fisher, K. and Ellis, A. (2007) Organizing and Managing Your Research: A Practical Guide for Postgraduates. London: Sage.

Philip, L. (1998) 'Combining quantitative and qualitative approaches to social research in human geography – an impossible mixture?', Environment and Planning, 30: 261–276.

Phillips, E. and Pugh, D. (1994) How to Get a PhD. Buckingham: Open University Press.

Philo, G. (2001) 'Bad news from Israel: media coverage of the Israeli/Palestinian conflict', Glasgow University Media Group. www.gla.ac.uk/ departments/sociology/Israel.pdf.

Philo, G. and Beattie, L. (1999) 'Race, migration and media', in G. Philo (ed.), Message Received. London: Longman.

Philo, G., Gilmour, A., Rust, S., Gaskell, E. and West, L. (2003) 'The Israeli/Palestinian Conflict: TV news and public understanding', in D.K. Thussu and D. Freedman (eds), War and the Media: Reporting Conflict 24/7. London: Sage.

Phoenix, A. (1994) 'Practising feminist research: the intersection of gender and "race" in the research process', in M. Maynard and J. Purvis (eds), Researching Women's Lives from a Feminist Perspective. London: Taylor and Francis, 49–70.

Pink, S. (2007) Doing Visual Ethnography: Images, Media and Representation in Research. London: Sage.

Plummer, K. (1995) Telling Sexual Stories: Power, Change and Social Worlds. London: Routledge.

Pocock, S.J. (1983) Clinical Trials: A Practical Approach. Chichester: Wiley.

Pollner, M. (1987) Mundane Reason: Reality in Everyday Life and Sociological Discourse. Cambridge: Cambridge University Press.

Pomerantz, A. (1984) 'Agreeing and disagreeing with assessments: some features of preferred/dispreferred turn shapes', in J.M. Atkinson and J. Heritage (eds), Structures of Social Action: Studies in Conversation Analysis. Cambridge: Cambridge University Press.

Potter, J. (1984) 'Testability, flexibility: Kuhnian values in scientists' discourse concerning theory choice', Philosophy of the Social Sciences, 14: 303–330.

Potter, J. (2003) 'Studying the standardized survey as interaction', Qualitative Research, 3: 269–278.

Potter, J. and Wetherell, M. (1987) Discourse and Social Psychology: Beyond Attitudes and Behaviour. London: Sage.

Potter, J. and Wetherell, M. (1994) 'Analyzing discourse, in A. Bryman and B. Burgess (eds), Analyzing Qualitative Data. London: Routledge.

Pratt, J., Bloomfield, J. and Seale, C. (1984) Option Choice: A Question of Equal Opportunity. Windsor: NFER/Nelson.

Presser, L. (2005) 'Negotiating power and narrative in research: implications for feminist methodology', Signs, 30: 2067–2090.

Price, R. and Price, S. (1991) Two Evenings in Saramaka. Chicago: University of Chicago Press.

Prior, L. (2003) Using Documents in Social Research. London: Sage.

Prior, L. (2008) 'Repositioning documents in social research', Sociology, 42: 821–836.

Prosser, J. (ed.) (1998) Image-based Research: A Sourcebook for Qualitative Researchers. London: Falmer.

Prosser, J. and Loxley, A. (2007) 'Enhancing the contribution of visual methods to inclusive education', Journal of Research in Special Educational Needs, 7 (1): 55–68.

Prosser, J., Loxley, A. (2008) Introducing Visual Methods. ESRC National Centre for Research Methods Review Paper. http://eprints.ncrm.ac.uk/420/1/MethodsReviewPaperNCRM-010.pdf.

Puchta, C. and Potter, J. (2004) Focus Group Practice. London: Sage.

Punch, K.F. (2006) Developing Effective Research Proposals. London: Sage.

Punch, M. (1986) The Politics and Ethics of Fieldwork: Muddy Boots and Grubby Hands. Newbury Park, CA: Sage.

Puwar, N. (2007) 'Social cinema scenes', Space and Culture, 10 (2): 253–270.

Quinn, N. (1996) 'Culture and contradiction: the case of Americans reasoning about marriage', Ethos, 24 (3): 391–425.

Rabiee, F. (2004) 'Focus-group interview and data analysis', Proceedings of the Nutrition Society, 63: 655–660.

Ramsay, J., Rivas, C. and Feder, G. (2005) 'Interventions to reduce violence and promote the physical and psychosocial well-being of women who experience partner violence: A systematic review of controlled evaluations'. Final Report. www.dh.gov.uk/assetRoot/04/12/74/26/04127426.pdf.

Rapley, T. (2007) How to Study Conversations, Discourse and Documents. London: Sage.

Rhodes, T. (1997) 'Risk theory in epidemic times: sex, drugs and the social organisation of "risk behaviour"', Sociology of Health & Illness, 19 (2): 208–227.

Reay, D. (2004) '"Mostly roughs and toughs": social class, race and representation in inner city schooling', Sociology, 38 (5): 1005–1023.

Renzetti, C. and Lee, R.M. (1993) Researching Sensitive Topics. London and New York: Sage.

Ribbens, J. (1989) Interviewing – an "unnatural situation"?', Women's Studies International Forum, 12 (6): 579–592.

Richardson, L. (2000) 'Writing: a method of inquiry', in N. Denzin and Y. Lincoln (eds), Handbook of Qualitative Research. Thousand Oaks, CA: Sage.

Riessman, C.K. (1987) 'When gender is not enough: women interviewing women', Gender & Society, 1 (2): 172–207.

Riessman, C.K. (1993) Narrative Analysis. Newbury Park, CA: Sage.

Riessman, C.K. (2008) Narrative Methods for the Human Sciences. Los Angeles, CA: Sage.

Rivas, C., Abbott, S., Taylor, S.J.C., Clarke, A., Roberts, C.M., Stone, R. and Griffiths, C. (2010) 'Collaborative working within UK NHS secondary care and across sectors for Chronic Obstructive Pulmonary Disease and the impact of peer review: qualitative findings from the UK National COPD Resources and Outcomes Project (NCROP)', International Journal of Integrated Care, 10. www.ijic.org/index.php/ijic/article/view/573/1073.

Robinson, L., Clare, L. and Evans, K. (2005) 'Making sense of dementia and adjusting to loss: psychological reactions to a diagnosis of dementia in couples', Aging & Mental Health, 9 (4): 337–347.

Robson, C. (2002) Real World Research. Oxford: Blackwell.

Rogers, R., Malancharuvil-Berkes, E., Mosley, M., Hui, D. and Joseph, G.O. (2005) 'Critical discourse analysis in education: a review of the literature', Review of Educational Research, 75: 365–416.

Rollnick, S., Seale, C., Rees, M., Butler, C., Kinnersley, P. and Anderson, L. (2001) 'Inside the routine general practice consultation: an observational study of consultations for sore throats', Family Practice, 18 (5): 506–510.

Rose, G. (1982) Deciphering Social Research. London: Macmillan.

Rose, G. (2007) Visual Methodologies: An Introduction to the Interpretation of Visual Materials. London: Sage.

Rose, N. (1999) Powers of Freedom: Reframing Political Thought. Cambridge: Cambridge University Press.

Rosenberg, M. (1968) The Logic of Survey Analysis. New York: Basic Books.

Ross, D.A.R. (2007) 'Backstage with the knowledge boys and girls: Goffman and distributed agency in an organic online community', Organization Studies, 28 (3): 307–325.

Rossman, G.B. and Wilson, B.L. (1994) 'Numbers and words revisited: being "shamelessly eclectic"', Quality & Quantity, 28: 315–327.

Roter, D.L. (2000) The Roter Interaction Analysis System (RIAS) Handbook 2000. Baltimore, MD: Johns Hopkins School of Public Health, Department of Health Policy and Management.

Rubin, H.J. and Rubin, I.S. (2005) Qualitative Interviewing: The Art of Hearing Data. Thousand Oaks, CA: Sage.

Ryan, R.M. and Niemiec, C.P. (2009) 'Self-determination theory in schools of education: can an empirically supported framework also be critical and liberating?', Theory and Research in Education, 7: 263–272.

Ryen, A. (2004) 'Ethical issues', in C. Seale (ed.) Social Research Methods: A Reader. London: Routledge.

Sacks, H. (1984) 'Notes on methodology', in J.M. Atkinson and J. Heritage (eds), Structures of Social Action: Studies in Conversation Analysis. Cambridge: Cambridge University Press.

Sacks, H. (1987) 'On the preferences for agreement and contiguity in sequences in conversation', in G. Button and J.R.E. Lee (eds), Talk and Social Organisation. Clevedon: Multilingual Matters.

Sacks, H. (1992) Lectures on Conversation, Volume 1. Oxford: Blackwell.

Salmons, J. (2010) Online Interviews in Real Time. London: Sage.

Sandelowski, M. and Barroso, J. (2003) 'Writing the proposal for a qualitative research methodology project', Qualitative Health Research, 13: 781–820.

Saussure, F. de (1974) Course in General Linguistics. London: Fontana.

Savage, M. (2007) 'Changing social class identities in post-war Britain: perspectives from Mass Observation', Sociological Research Online, 12 (3). www.socresonline.org.uk/12/3/6.html.

Sayers, S.M., Mackerras, D., Singh, G., Bucens, I., Flynn K. and Reid, A. (2003) 'An Australian Aboriginal birth cohort: a unique resource for a life course study of an indigenous population. A study protocol', BMC International Health and Human Rights, 3: 1.

Scambler, G. (2009) 'Health-related stigma', Sociology of Health & Illness, 31 (3): 441–455.

Schegloff, E.A. (1999) 'Discourse, pragmatics, conversation, analysis', Discourse Studies, 1: 405–436.

Schlesselman, J.J. and Stolley P.D. (1982) Case Control Studies: Design, Conduct, Analysis. Oxford: Oxford University Press.

Schu, A. (1964) Collected Papers, Volume 2. The Hague: Martinus Nijhoff.

Scott, J. (1990) A Matter of Record: Documentary Sources in Social Research. Cambridge: Polity Press.

Scott, J. (2006) Documentary Research. London: Sage.

Scott, S. (1984) 'The personable and the powerful', in C. Bell and H. Roberts (eds), Social Researching: Politics, Problems, Practice. London: Routledge.

Scott, M.B. and Lyman, S.M. (1968) 'Accounts', American Sociological Review, 33: 46–62.

Seale, C. (1996) 'Living alone towards the end of life', Ageing & Society, 16: 75–91.

Seale, C. (1999a) The Quality of Qualitative Research. London: Sage.

Seale, C. (1999b) 'Quality in qualitative research', Qualitative Inquiry, 5: 465–478.

Seale, C. (2001) 'Sporting cancer: struggle language in news reports of people with cancer', Sociology of Health & Illness, 23 (3): 308–329.

Seale, C. (2002) 'Cancer heroics: a study of news reports with particular reference to gender', Sociology, 36 (1): 107–126.

Seale, C. (ed.) (2004a) Researching Society and Culture (2nd edition). Sage.

Seale, C. (ed.) (2004b) Social Research Methods: A Reader. London: Routledge.

Seale, C. (2006) 'Gender accommodation in online cancer support groups', Health 10 (3): 345–360.

Seale, C. (2008) 'Mapping the field of medical sociology: a comparative analysis of journals', Sociology of Health & Illness, 30 (5): 677–695.

Seale, C. (2009a) 'End-of-life decisions in the UK involving medical practitioners', Palliative Medicine, 23 (3): 198–204.

Seale, C. (2009b) 'Legalisation of euthanasia or physician-assisted suicide: survey of doctors' attitudes', Palliative Medicine, 23 (3): 205–212.

Seale, C. (2010) 'Secondary analysis of qualitative data', in D. Silverman (ed.), Qualitative Research (3rd edition). London: Sage, 347–364.

Seale, C. and Addington-Hall, J. (1994) 'Euthanasia: why people want to die earlier', Social Science & Medicine, 39 (5): 647–654.

Seale, C. and Addington-Hall, J. (1995a) 'Euthanasia: the role of good care', Social Science & Medicine, 40 (5): 581–587.

Seale, C. and Addington-Hall, J. (1995b) 'Dying at the best time', Social Science & Medicine, 40 (5): 589–595

Seale, C. and Charteris-Black, J. (2008) 'The interaction of class and gender in illness narratives', Sociology, 42: 453–469.

Seale, C. and Charteris-Black, J. (2010) 'Keyword analysis: a new tool for qualitative research', in I.L. Bourgeault, R. DeVries and R. Dingwall (eds), The Sage Handbook of Qualitative Methods in Health Research. London: Sage.

Seale, C., Charteris-Black, J. and Ziebland, S. (2006) 'Gender, cancer experience and internet use: a comparative keyword analysis of interviews and online cancer support groups', Social Science & Medicine, 62 (10): 2577–2590.

Seale, C., Gobo, G., Gubrium J.F. and Silverman D. (eds) (2004) Qualitative Research Practice. London: Sage. (Paperback 'student' version published in 2007)

Shaffir, W.B. (1985) 'Some reflections on approaches to fieldwork in Hassidic communities', Jewish Journal of Sociology, 27 (2): 115–134.

Shippee, T.P. (2009) '"But I am not moving": transitions in a continuing care retirement community', The Gerontologist, 49: 418–427.

Sieber, S. (1979) 'The integration of fieldwork and survey methods', American Journal of Sociology, 78 (6): 1135–1159.

Silverman, D. (1975) 'Accounts of organisations – organisational structures and the accounting process', in J.B. McKinley (ed.), Processing People: Cases in Organisational Behaviour. London: Holt, Reinhart & Winston, 269–302.

Silverman, D. (1984) 'Going private: ceremonial forms in a private oncology clinic', Sociology, 18: 191–202.

Silverman, D. (1987) Communication and Medical Practice: Social Relations in the Clinic. London: Sage.

Silverman, D. (1993) Interpreting Qualitative Data: Methods for Analysing Talk, Text and Interaction. London: Sage.

Silverman, D. (1996) Discourses of Counselling: HIV Counselling as Social Interaction. London: Sage.

Silverman, D. (1998) Harvey Sacks. Cambridge: Polity Press.

Silverman, D. (1999) Doing Qualitative Research: A Practical Handbook. London: Sage.

Silverman, D. (2001) Interpreting Qualitative Data (2nd edition). London: Sage.

Silverman, D. (2006) Interpreting Qualitative Data (3rd edition). London: Sage.

Silverman, D. (2007) A Very Short, Fairly Interesting, Reasonably Cheap Book about Qualitative Research. London: Sage.

Silverman, D. (2010) Doing Qualitative Research (3rd edition). London: Sage.

Silverman, D. (ed.) (2011) Qualitative Research. London: Sage.

Silverman, D. and Jones, J. (1976) Organisational Work: The Language of Grading and the Grading of Language. London: Collier/Macmillan.

Singer, P.A. and Benatar, S.R. (2001) 'Beyond Helsinki: a vision for global health ethics', British Medical Journal, 322: 747–748.

Skeggs, B. (1994) 'Situating the production of feminist ethnography', in M. Maynard and J. Purvis (eds), Researching Women's Lives from a Feminist Perspective. London: Taylor and Francis.

Slater, D.R. (1998) 'Analysing cultural objects: content analysis and semiotics', in C. Seale (ed.), Researching Society and Culture. London: Sage, 233–244. (1st edition).

Smart, C. (2005) 'Textures of family life: further thoughts on change and commitment', Journal of Social Policy, 34 (4): 541–556.

Smart, C. (2010) Disciplined Writing: On the Problem of Writing Sociologically. ESRC National Centre for Research Methods NCRM Working Paper Series #13, 02/10, Morgan Centre, University of Manchester.

Smith, H.P. and Kaminski, R.J. (2011) 'Self-injurious behaviors in state prisons: findings from a national survey', Criminal Justice and Behavior, 38: 26–41.

Smith, J. (ed.) (2008) Qualitative Psychology: A Practical Guide to Research Methods. London: Sage.

Smith, J. and Osborn, M. (2008) 'Interpretative phenomenological analysis', in J. Smith (ed.), Qualitative Psychology: A Practical Guide to Research Methods. London: Sage.

Smith, J., Flowers, P. and Larkin, M. (2009) Interpretative Phenomenological Analysis: Theory, Method, Research. London: Sage.

Smith, M.J. (1998) Social Science in Question. London: Sage.

Smith, M.V. (2008) 'Pain experience and the imagined researcher', Sociology of Health & Illness, 30 (7): 992–1006.

Smith, S.W., Brownell, M.T., Simpson, R.L. and Deshler, D.D. (1993) 'Successfully completing the dissertation: two reflections on the process', Remedial and Special Education, 14: 53–59.

Sokal, A. (1996) 'Transgressing the boundaries: towards a transformative hermeneutics of quantum gravity', Social Text, 46/47: 217–252.

Song, M. (1998) 'Researching Chinese siblings', in J. Ribbens and R. Edwards (eds), Feminist Dilemmas in Qualitative Research: Public Knowledge and Private Lives. London: Sage.

Speer, S. (2005) Gender Talk: Feminism, Discourse and Conversation Analysis. London: Routledge.

Speer, S.A. and Hutchby, I. (2003) 'From ethics to analytics: aspects of participants' orientations to the presence and relevance of recording devices', Sociology, 37 (2): 315–337.

Spicer, N.J. (1998) 'Sedentarization and accessibility to health services', in R.W. Dutton, J.I. Clark and A.M. Battikhi (eds), Arid Land Resources and Their Management: Jordan's Desert Margin. London: Kegan Paul International.

Spicer, N.J. (1999) 'Pastoral mobility, sedentarization and accessibility of health services in the northeast Badia of Jordan', Applied Geography, 19 (4): 299–312.

Spicker, P. (2011) 'Ethical covert research', Sociology, 45 (1): 118–133.

Squire, C. (2008) 'Experience-centred and culturally-oriented approaches to narrative', in M. Andrews, C. Squire and M. Tamboukou (eds), Doing Narrative Research. London: Sage.

St Louis, B. (2007) Rethinking Race, Politics and Poetics: C.L.R. James' Critique of Modernity. New York and Abingdon: Routledge.

Stacey, J. (1988) 'Can there be a feminist ethnography?', Women's Studies International Forum, 11 (1): 21–27.

Standerwick, K., Davies, C., Tucker, L. and Sheron, N. (2007) 'Binge drinking, sexual behaviour and sexually transmitted infection in the UK', International Journal of STD and AIDS, 18: 810–813.

Stark, D. and Paravel, V. (2008) 'PowerPoint in public: digital technologies and the new morphology of demonstration', Theory, Culture & Society, 25: 30–55.

Stewart, K. and Williams, M. (2005) 'Researching online populations: the use of online focus groups for social research', Qualitative Research, 5 (4): 395–416.

Stokoe, E.H. and Smithson, J. (2001) 'Making gender relevant: conversation analysis and gender categories in interaction', Discourse & Society, 12 (2): 243–269.

Stokoe, E. (2010) '"I'm not gonna hit a lady": conversation analysis, membership categorization and men's denials of violence towards women', Discourse & Society, 21: 59–82.

Strauss, A.L. (1987) Qualitative Analysis for Social Scientists. Cambridge: Cambridge University Press.

Strauss, A.L. and Corbin, J. (1990) Basics of Qualitative Research: Grounded Theory Procedures and Techniques. Newbury Park, CA: Sage.

Strauss, A.L. and Corbin, J. (eds) (1997) Grounded Theory in Practice. Thousand Oaks, CA: Sage.

Stretesky, P.B. (2009) 'National case-control study of homicide offending and methamphetamine use', Journal of Interpersonal Violence, 24 (6): 911–924.

Stroebe, M.S. and Schut, H. (1999) 'The dual process model of coping with bereavement: Rationale and description', Death Studies, 23: 197–224.

Strunk, W. and White, E.B. (2000) The Elements of Style (4th edition). Harlow: Longman. (First published with Strunk as sole author, 1918)

Stubbs, M. (2001) Words and Phrases: Corpus Studies of Lexical Semantics. Oxford and Malden, MA: Blackwell.

Sudnow, D. (1965) 'Normal crimes: sociological features of the penal code in a public defender's office', Social Problems, 12: 255–276.

Swales, J.M. (1990) Genre Analysis: English in Academic and Research Settings. Cambridge: Cambridge University Press.

Symons, C. (2009) The Gay Games: A History. London: Routledge.

Tagg, J. (1988) The Burden of Representation: Essays on Photographies and Histories. Basingstoke: Macmillan Education.

Taussig, M. (1987) Shamanism, Colonialism and the Wild Man. Chicago, IL: University of Chicago Press.

Teddlie, C. and Tashakkori, A. (2008) Foundations of Mixed Methods Research: Integrating Quantitative and Qualitative Approaches in the Social and Behavioral Sciences. Thousand Oaks, CA: Sage.

ten Have, P. (2007) Doing Conversation Analysis: A Practical Guide. London: Sage.

Teo, P. (2000) 'Racism in the news: a Critical Discourse Analysis of news reporting in two Australian newspapers', Discourse & Society, 11 (1): 7–49.

Teplin, L.A., McClelland, G.M., Abram, K.M. and Weiner, D.A. (2005) 'Crime victimization in adults with severe mental illness: comparison with the National Crime Victimization Survey', Archives of General Psychiatry, 62 (8): 911–921.

Thody, A. (2006) Writing and Presenting Research. London: Sage.

Thomas, G. (2009) How to do your Research Project: A Guide for Students in Education and Applied Social Sciences. London: Sage.

Thomas, M., Bloor, M. and Frankland, J. (2007) 'The process of sample recruitment: an ethnostatistical perspective', Qualitative Research, 7: 429–446.

Thomas, W. and Znaniecki, F. (2007) The Polish Peasant in Europe and America: Organization and Disorganization in America. Whitefish, MT: Kessinger.

Thompson, E.P. (1966) The Making of the English Working Class. London: Vintage.

Thompson, P. (1988) The Voice of the Past: Oral History (2nd edition). Oxford: Oxford University Press.

Travers, M. (2009) 'New methods, old problems: a sceptical view of innovation in qualitative research', Qualitative Research, 9: 161–179.

Tonkiss, F. (2004) 'History of social statistics and the social survey', in C. Seale (ed.), Researching Society and Culture (2nd edition). London: Sage.

Toulmin, S.E., Rieke, R. and Janik, A. (1979) An Introduction to Reasoning. London: Macmillan.

Trochim, W.M. (2003) Reliability and Validity. www.socialresearchmethods.net.

Trochim, W.M. (2010) The Research Methods Knowledge Base. www.socialresearchmethods.net/kb/.

Ungar, M. (2006) '"Too ambitious": what happens when funders misunderstand the strengths of qualitative research design', Qualitative Social Work, 5: 261–277.

Van der Valk, I. (2003) 'Right-wing parliamentary discourse on immigration in France', Discourse & Society, 14 (3): 309–348.

Van Dijk, T.A. (1993) 'Principles in Critical Discourse Analysis', Discourse & Society, 4 (2): 249–283.

Van Dijk, T. (ed.) (1997) Discourse Studies: A Multidisciplinary Introduction. London: Sage.

Van Dijk, T. (2000) 'New(s) racism: a discourse analytical approach', in S. Cottle (ed.), Ethnic Minorities and the Media. Buckingham: Open University Press, 33–49.

Van Dijk, T.A. (2001) 'Critical Discourse Analysis', in D. Schiffrin, D. Tannen and H.E. Hamilton (eds), Handbook of Discourse Analysis. Oxford: Blackwell.

Van Dijk, T. (2002) 'Discourse and racism', in D. Goldberg and J. Solomos (eds), The Blackwell Companion to Racial and Ethnic Studies. Oxford: Blackwell, 145–159.

Van Dijk, T.A. (ed.) (2007) Discourse Studies. London: Sage.

Van Dijk, T.A. (2008) Discourse Reader. London: Sage.

van Manen, M. (1990) Researching Lived Experience: Human Science for an Action Pedagogy. Albany, NY: State University of New York Press.

Van Zoonen, L. (1994) Feminist Media Studies. London: Sage.

Walliman, N. (2001) Your Research Project: A Step-By-Step Guide for the First-time Researcher. London: Sage.

Walwyn, R. and Roberts, C. (2010) 'Therapist variation within randomised trials of psychotherapy: implications for precision, internal and external validity', Statistical Methods in Medical Research, 19: 291–315.

Warburton, N. (1996) Thinking From A to Z. London: Routledge.

Ward, A. (2002) 'The writing process', in S. Potter (ed.), Doing Postgraduate Research. London: Sage.

Ware, V. and Back, L. (2001) Out of Whiteness: Color, Politics, and Culture. Chicago, IL: Chicago University Press.

Watts, H.D. and White, P. (2000) 'Presentation skills', in D. Burton (ed.), Research Training for Social Scientists. London: Sage.

Weathersbee, T.E. and Maynard, D.W. (2009) 'Dialling for donations: practices and actions in the telephone solicitation of human tissues', Sociology of Health & Illness, 31 (6): 803–816.

Weber, M. (1949) 'Objectivity in social science', in E.A. Shils and H.A. Finch (eds), The Methodology of the Social Sciences. London: The Free Press.

Weber, M. (2002) The Protestant Ethic and The Spirit of Capitalism. Trans. Peter Baehr and Gordon C. Wells. Harmondsworth: Penguin. (First published 1905 in German)

Weinberg, M.S. (1994) 'The nudist management of respectability', in P. Kollock and J. O'Brien (eds), The Production of Reality: Essays and Readings in Social Psychology. Thousand Oaks, CA: Pine Forge Press.

Wengraf, T. (2001) Qualitative Research Interviewing: Biographic Narratives and Semi-Structured Methods. London: Sage.

West, P. (1990) 'The status and validity of accounts obtained at interview: a contrast between two studies of families with a disabled child', Social Science & Medicine, 30 (11): 1229–1239.

Wetherell, M. and Potter, J. (1992) Mapping the Language of Racism: Discourse and the Legitimation of Exploitation. London: Harvester Wheatsheaf.

Wetherell, M., Taylor, S. and Yates, S.J. (eds) (2001a) Discourse Theory and Practice: A Reader. London: Sage.

Wetherell, M., Taylor, S. and Yates, S.J. (eds) (2001b) Discourse as Data: A Guide for Analysis. London: Sage.

White, J. (1980) Rothschild Buildings. London: Routledge.

White, J. (1986) The Worst Street in North London: Campbell Bunk, Islington, Between the Wars. London: Routledge.

Whyte, W.F. (1943) Street Corner Society: The Social Structure of an Italian Slum. Chicago, IL: University of Chicago Press (3rd edition 1981).

Wiener, C.L. (1975) 'The burden of rheumatoid arthritis: tolerating the uncertainty', Social Science & Medicine, 9: 97–104.

Wiles, R., Prosser, J., Bagnoli, A., Clark, A., Davies, K., Holland, S. and Renold , E. (2008) Visual Ethics: Ethical Issues in Visual Research. ESRC National Centre for Research Methods Review Paper. http://eprints.ncrm.ac.uk/421/1/MethodsReviewPaperNCRM-011.pdf.

Wodak, R. (2001) 'The discourse-historical approach', in R. Wodak and M. Meyer (eds), Methods of Critical Discourse Analysis. London: Sage.

Wodak, R. (2004) 'Critical discourse analysis', in C. Seale, G. Gobo, J.F. Gubrium and D. Silverman (eds), Qualitative Research Practice. London: Sage.

Wodak, R. and Krzyżanowski, M. (eds) (2008) Qualitative Discourse Analysis in the Social Sciences. Basingstoke: Palgrave Macmillan.

Wodak, R. and Meyer, M. (eds) (2001) Methods of Critical Discourse Analysis. London: Sage.

Wolcott, H. (2009) Writing Up Qualitative Research. Newbury Park, CA: Sage.

Wolf, E. (1982) Europe and the People Without History. Berkeley, CA: University of California Press.

Woodward, S. (2008) 'Digital photography and research relationships: capturing the fashion moment', Sociology, 42: 857–872.

Wutich, A., Lant, Y., White, D.D., Larson, K.L. and Gartin, M. (2010) 'Comparing focus group and individual responses on sensitive topics: a study of water decision makers in a desert city', Field Methods, 22: 88–110.

Yin, R.K. (2003) Case Study Research: Design and Methods. Thousand Oaks, CA: Sage.

Young, L. (1996) Fear of the Dark: 'Race', Gender and Sexuality in the Cinema. London: Routledge.

Ziebland, S. and McPherson, A. (2006) 'Making sense of qualitative data analysis: an introduction with illustrations from DIPEx (personal experiences of health and illness)', Medical Education, 40: 405–414.

# NAME INDEX

# SUBJECT INDEX

The page numbers of terms in blue in the text (normally where a definition of that term is given), are in bold type.

Deduction, deduce 10, 11, 15, 16, 21, 100, 248, 448, 481, 482, **564**, *see also* Induction
   Deductive coding, *see* Coding
   Deductive-nomological (D-N) model **15–16**, **546**
   Hypothetico-deductive method **22**, **571**
Definitive concept, *see* Concepts
De-naturalising, *see* Naturalise
Denotation, *see* Semiotics
Dependability, *see* Validity
Dependent variable, *see* Variable, types of
Depth interviews, *see* Interviews, types of
Derived variables, *see* Variable, types of
Descriptive accounts of science, *see Normative and descriptive accounts of science*
Descriptive statistics 330, **331**, 333, 334, **564**
Design of research, *see* Research design
Determinism, deterministic 16, 23, 481, 534, **564**
Deviant cases, *see* Negative instances
Dewey Decimal library classification system 81, **564**
Diachronic *versus* synchronic analysis **291**, **565**
Dichotomous variable, *see* Variable, types of
Differential bias **565**
Direct effect, *see* Path analysis
Directional hypothesis (or one-tailed hypothesis) **580**
Disambiguation of meaning **472**, **565**
Discourse **406**, 550–1, **565**
   Discursive repertoires **211–12**, 218, **565**
Discourse analysis 30, 34, 108, 164, 222, 293, **406–23**, 424, 467, 480
Dispreferred actions, *see* Conversation analysis
Disproportionate stratification, *see* Sampling
Dissemination 72, **110**, **565**
Dissertations 154–77
   *passim* based on Secondary analysis 154, 161–3 *passim*
   based on Secondary sources 154, **173**
   Empirical **154–6**, 157, **160**, 170, **566**
   Structure of 170–2
   Theoretical **154–5**, 161, **174**, **599**
Divine orthodoxy, see *Explanatory and divine orthodoxies*
Documents 265–80, 287
   Documentary sources **265**
   in ethnography 255
   Internal versus external **265**, **565**
   Public versus private 251
Documentary films 285
'Doing' aspects of social life 447, 548, **433**, 434, **435**, **549**, **566**
Double barrelled question, *see* Questions
Double blind, *see* Randomised controlled trial

Effectiveness 129, **566**
Efficacy **566**
Elaboration paradigm **351**, 352–7, 395, **566**
   Conditional relationships **353**, 356, **560**
   First order relationships **353**, 357, **560**
   Interaction **356**
   Intervening variable 38, **355**, 356, **360**, **574**
   Replication **353**, 354, 357, **590**
   Specification 354, **356**, 357, **596**

Elaboration paradigm *cont.*
   Spurious causation, spurious relationships **353–5**, 356, 357, 361, 362, **530**, **596**
   Suppression 355, **356**, 357, **598**
   Test variable **353**, **355–7**, **599**
   Zero order table 353–57, **604**
Electronic and email interviews, *see* Interviews, types of
Emic perspective **566**
Empiricism **10–12**, 15, **18–20**, **22–24**, 30, 33, 460, **566**
Encoding and decoding 293, **566**
Epistemic responsibility 71, **566**
Epistemological
   Anarchism 23
   Radicalism **546**, **567**
   Relativism *see* Relativism
Epistemology 9, **481–2**, 490, 535, **567**
   and Interviews 208, 210–11
   Constructionist **108**
   Empiricist *see* Empiricism
   Rationalist **11**
   Transcendental **11**
Error term
   *see* Unexplained variance
Essentialism 49, 474, 475, **567**
   Anti-essentialism **49**, 55
Ethical principles 61, 66, 109
   Autonomy **62**, 66, 67, 69, **556**, **567**
   Beneficence **62**, **567**
   Non-maleficence **62**, **567**
   Justice **62**, **567**
Ethics committees, *see* Research ethics committees
Ethnic identification devices **32–3**, 36, 49, 350
Ethnocentrism 246, **249–50**, **567**
Ethnography 33, 34, 64, 163–4, 246–262 *passim*, 401, 533, 553, **567**
   and Focus groups 233–5
   Autoethnography, *see* Ethnography 553
   *see also* Participant Observation
Ethnomethodology 31, **35–6**, **247**, **425**, 484, 546, **567**
Etic perspective **567**
Evaluation research 229, 237
Executive summary **504**, **568**
Expected value, *see* Chi Square test
Experimental method 101, 350–1, *see also* Randomised controlled trial (RCT)
   Quasi experiments 119, 350–1, **587**
Explanations, 9, 10, 12, 13–14
   General and specific **15**, **570**, **596**
   Testable 8, 9, 12, 15, 18–19, **599**
Explanatory and divine orthodoxies **53–4**, **568**
Explanatory trial, *see* Randomised controlled trial
Explanans / explanandum 13, 14, **15–16**, 17, 18, **568**
External validity, *see* Validity

Face validity, *see* Validity
Facebook, 66, 160, 166, 167
Facilitative combination, *see* Combined methods
Facticity **274–5**, **500**, **569**
Falsificationism **18–19**, **22**, 23, 36, **569**
   *see also* Verificationism

Interviews *cont.*
    Interview schedule 192–8, 208, 395, 532
    Qualitative 105, 108, 111–12, 163, 206–26, 323–4,
        389–92, 547–9, **587**
    Scheduling **183**, **593**
    Semi–structured **183**, 208, 452, **594**
    Standardising **183**, **597**
    Structured 165, 182–97, 320, 322
    Telephone interviews 108, 168, 183–4, 191, 218
    Topic guide 109, 163, 219, **600**

Justice, *see* Ethical principles

Kappa statistic **461–2**, **574**
Keyword analysis 386, 467–72
    Comparative keyword analysis (CKA) 470,
        **472–4**, **559**
    Keyword-in-context (KWIC) display 470–2, **574–5**
Knowledge of context 256, **308**, 313, **575**, *see also*
    Contextual sensitivity

Langue *versus* parole **291**, **575**
Latent content **464–5**, **575**
Law, theorem and theory **15**, **575**
Leading question, *see* Questions
Library catalogues 80–3, 318
Limited quantification **487–8**, **575**
Lifeworld **448–50**, **575**
Line of best fit, *see* Regression line
Linguistic repertoire **508**
Linguistic repertoire **575**
List format **379**, **575**
Literature review 78–93, 170, 368, **575–6**
    Searching for literature 80–7, 102, 106
    Systematic review **92–3**, **599**
    Writing 91, 106–7, 510
Local production *or* local accomplishment **425**, **576**
Logical positivism, *see* Positivism
Logistic regression, *see* Regression
Longitudinal case, *see* Case study
Longitudinal study 119, 122, **123**–5, 351–2, 576
Loss to follow-up 123, **124**, 125, 127, **576**
Low inference descriptors 538
Macro *versus* micro levels of analysis **485–6**, **578**
Manifest content **463**, 464, **576**
Margin of error **137**–8, 576, see also *Confidence interval*
Marginality **254**, **576**, *see also* Field relations
Marginals (of a table), *see* Contingency table
Market research 54, 144, 207, 228, 237, 242
Marxism, 22, 12, 23, 24, 280
Matching **126**, **576**
Material culture 163, 164–5
Materialism 14, **576**
Maximum variation sampling, *see Sampling, types of*
Mean, *see* Measures of central tendency
Means, comparing 342–4 *see also* Statistical tests
Measurement 353
    Levels of 196–7, 338
    Measurement scale **577**
Measurement validity, *see* Validity

Measures of association, *see* Statistical tests
Measures of central tendency **331**–2, **577**
    Mean **331**, **577**
    Median **331–2**, **577**
    Mode **332**, **578**
Media genres **285**, **577**
Median, *see* Measures of central tendency
Member validation, *see* Validity
Memos, see *Analytic memos*
Meta-analysis **93**, 510, **577**
Metadata 279, **384–5**, **577**
Metaphysics **9–10**, 13, 14, 15, 18, 20, 21, **578**
Method, *see* Methodology
Methodology 22–3, 36, **37**, 38, **160–1**, 170, 174, 271,
    480, 505, **578**
Micro *versus* macro levels of analysis **486**, **578**
Mis-en-scène **288**, **578**
Missing values 321, 330
Mixed methods research, *see* Combined methods
Mode, *see* Measures of central tendency
Model 12, 13, 34, **36–8**, 460, **578**, *see also* Theory
    in Statistical analysis **259**, 360, **578**
Modeller, modelling tools 379, 385–6
Multidimensional concepts, *see* Concepts
Multiple methods research 480, **485–7**, **559** *see also*
    Combined methods
Multiple regression, *see* Regression
Multiple response item, *see* Questions
Multivariate statistical analysis **333**, 352–363, **579**
    *see also* Variables, relationships between; Multiple and
        Logistic regression
Murray Research Center, see Archives 305–6, 307
Mutual information (MI) score **472**, **579**

Narrative frameworks **443–4**, 454, 455, **579**
Narrative materials **442**, **579**
Natural science, *see* Science
Naturalism (in philosophy) **23–4**, 25, **248**, 274, **579**
Naturally occurring action, interaction or data **34–5**, 36,
    **234**, 240, **248**, 254, 274, **427**, 481, **533**, 535,
    537, 539
Naturalising 39, **274**, 275–6, 292, 407, **579**
Negative instances, *see* Validity
Negative association or relationship, *see* Variables,
    relationships between
Nesting, *see* Search terms
Network sampling, *see* Sampling
Nominal variable, *see* Variables, types of
Nominalisation **419**, **580**, *see also* Passivisation
Non-directional hypothesis (or two-tailed hypothesis)
    **341**, **580**, *see also* Directional hypothesis
Non-experimental study design 119–127, 129, 580
Nonfoundationalism **21**, **580**
Non–maleficence, *see* Ethical principles
Non-parametric tests **580**
Non-probability sampling, *see* Sampling
Non response, *see* Response rate
Non-significant result *see* Statistical significance
Normal curve **332**, **581**
Normal science, *see* Science

Normative interaction order **433**, 434, **581**
Normative and descriptive accounts of science
    8, **22**, **581**
Null hypothesis, *see* Hypothesis
Numeric variable, *see* Variables, types of
NVivo *see* QDA software

Objectives, *see* Research objectives
Objectives of science 8, 9, 13, 15
Objectivity, objective knowledge **19–20**, 24, 59–60,
    71, 246, 247, 290, 400, 415, 417, 466, 481, 535,
    539, **581**
    *see also* Bias; Value-freedom
Observational study
    In Qualitative research 32, 163–4, 250, 385, 400, **581**
    In Quantitative study design **581**
    *see also* Structured observation 197–202
Observed value, *see* Chi square test
Observer categories, *see* Folk categories
Odds ratio 93, **360**, 362, **581**
Observer expectation bias **581**
Official statistics 30, 31, 38, 255, 303–5, 486
One-tailed test or hypothesis, *see* Directional hypothesis
Ontology 10, 480–1, 484, 482
Open coding, *see* Coding
Open question, *see* Questions
Operationalisation 185, 230, **582**
Ordinal variable, *see* Variables, types of
Originality 91–2, 160, 533, 538
Outcome, outcome variable, see Variables, types of
Overt research **249**, 250, **582**

*p*-value, *see* Statistical tests
Panel study 119, **123–4**, 303, **583**, *see also* Cohort study
Paradigms (Kuhnian), paradigm shift **22**, 23, 41, **583**
Parallel group design **128**, **583**
Parametric tests **583**
Parole, *see* Langue
Participant expectation bias **583**
Participant observation 34, 67–9, 119, 163–4, 198,
    233–4, **246**, 393, 480, 484, **583**
    Roles in 250
Partisan *versus* scholar **51–2**, **583**
Passivisation **419**, **583**, *see also* Nominalisation
Path analysis **359–60**, **583**
    Direct effects **360**, **565**
    Indirect effects **360**, **572**
    Total effects **360**, **601**
Patterns of association **413–4**, **583**
Patterns of variation **413–4**, **584**
Pearson's correlation coefficient (*r*), *see* Statistical tests
Percentage of variance explained **342**, 358, **584**
Perspective–display sequence **429–31**, **584**
Phenomenology **246**, **442**, 447–8, **584**, *see also*
    Interpretative Phenomenological Analysis (IPA)
Photo elicitation **293–5**, **584**
Photography 31, 68, 164, 269, 284, 286–9, 292–9, *see*
    *also* Post-photography
Photo-voice **295**, **584**
Photo-elicitation **276**

Pie chart, *see* Charts
Piloting, *see* Questionnaire
Placebo effect **128**, 130, **584**
Plagiarism **176**, **512–13**, 514, **584–5**
Plausibility, *see* Validity
Policy and research 45–55, 110
Politics and research 59–60
    *see also* Sensitivity, political
Political radicalism 546, **585**
Polysemy **293**, **585**
Polyvocality 289, 402
Population, *see* Sampling
Positive association or relationship, *see* Variables,
    relationships between
Positivism 23–4, 30, 248, 395, 448, 460, 479, 481, 483,
    528, 538, **585**
    Logical positivism **9**, 11, 20, 23, **576**
    Post-positivism **538**, 539, 540, **585**
Post coded question, *see* Questions
Postmodernism 23, **24**, 30, 53, 174, 248, 400, 401, 442,
    479, 481, 483, 485, 539, 540, **585**
Post–photography **286**, **585**
Post-positivism, *see* Positivism
Post-structuralism **442**
Power calculations **130**, **586**
Pre-allocation of roles, identities etc. **434**, **586**
Pre-coded question, *see* Questions
Predictive validity, *see* Validity
Predictor variable, *see* Variable, types of
Preference organisation **433–4**, **586**
    Preferred and dispreferred actions **433–4**, **586**
Preferred reading **293**, **586**
Prevalence 121, 122, 128, 289, 358, 533, **586**
Primary outcome **586**
Primary sources *versus* secondary sources **264–5**, 269,
    287, **594**
Privacy **64**, 70–1, 109, 163, **586**
Probability sampling, *see* Sampling
Probe question, *see* Questions
Project management 114–15
Properties, *see* Grounded Theory
Proximity operators, *see* Boolean searches

QDA software 375, **384**, **587**
    NVivo 384–6
    Coding stripes **384**, **558**
    Modelling tool 385, 386
    Search tool **385**, **593**
Qualidata, *see* Archives
Qualitative data archives, *see* Archives
Qualitative thematic analysis 163, 221–2, 366–92
    *passim*, 443, 465, 467, 476, **587**
Qualitative research 34–9, 53,4, 101, 480–4,
    533–40, **587**
Quantitative research 100–1, 480–4, 529–32, **587**
Quasi-experimental design, *see* Experimental
    method
Query, *see* Search terms
Question Bank 304, 307
Question order 193–4

Questionnaires 182–91
  Design 192–8
  Email and web based 188–91
  Postal 187–8
  Self completed 184–5
Questions, question design
  Closed **195–6**, 208–9, **558**
  Fixed choice 136, 193, **195–6**, 318, **569**
  Open **195–6**, 322–3, **582**
  Pre-coded **318**, 321, **322**, **586**
  Post-coded 193–4, 322, **586**
Quota sample, *see* Sampling, types of

$r^2$ , *see* Statistical tests
$R^2$ , *see* Statistical tests
Randomisation/random allocation, *see* Randomised
  controlled trial
Random sampling, see *Sampling*
Randomisation sequence/list, *see* Randomised
  controlled trial
Randomised controlled trial 92, 119, 123, 127–30, **588**,
  *see also* Experimental method
  Blinding **129–30**, **557**
  Control group 128, 129–30, **561**
  Explanatory **568**
  Single and double blinding **129**, **566**, **595**
  Intervention or treatment group 101, **127**,
    128–30, **574**
  Randomisation/random allocation **129**, **588**
  Randomisation sequence/list **129**, **588**
  Selection bias **129**, **594**
  Trial arms **128**, 129, **601**
Range, **331–2**, **588**
  Inter-quartile range **574**
Rationalist epistemology **10–12**, 20, **588**
Reactivity 68, 201, **249**, 250, 255, 351,
  481–2, **589**
Realism 10, **19**, 271, 529, 535, 537, **589**
  Subtle realism **537–8**, **598**
Recall bias *see* Bias
Recipient design 55, **520**, 523, **589**
Recoded variable, *see* Variable, types of
Reductionism 14, **17–18**, **589**
Reference management software, *see* Bibliographic
  software
Reference styles **89**, **589**
References **80**, 82, 83, 87, 88–9, 110, 174–5,
  511–12, **589**
Referents **291**, **590**
Reflexivity, reflexive **36**, **59**, 60, 71, 162, **213**, 214, 218,
  **418**, **499–500**, **537**, 553, **590**
Regression
  Logistic regression **360–2**, **590**
  Multiple regression **357–9**, **590**
  Regression line, line of best fit **339–341**, 342, **590**
Relativism **11–12**, **15**, **16**, 16–17, 19, 80, 81, 296, **509**
Relative risk **590**
Relativism **24**, 539, 540, **590**
  Cultural **246**, **563**
  Epistemological 20, 483, 485

Reliability 108–9, 162, 170, 271–2, 460, **528**, **532**,
  534–9, **590**
  Inter-coder or rater reliability 199, 200, 202, **381**,
    **461–2**, **532**
Replicability 308, **528–9**, 532, **590**
Representation, studies of 155, 156, 164, 172, 284, 285,
  286, 290, 410, 413, 416, **561**
Representative case, *see* Case study
Representative sample, *see* Sampling
Research design 73, **98**, 103, 119–131, 160–1, 250, **591**
  in Qualitative research 101, 250, 307
  in Quantitative research 38, 100–1, 350–2
Research ethics committees 73, 103, 109, 112–13, 166, **567**
Research governance **505**, 513, **591**
Research objectives **106–7**, 108, 122, 124, **581**
Research problem 35–8, 46, 99, 107, **158–60**, 161, 170,
  173, 251, 409–10, 552, **591**
Research process **157–8**, 171, 409, **591**
Research proposal 103–13, **591**
Research questions 31, 35, 78–80, **99–102**, 160–1,
  185–6, **591**
Respondent validation, *see* Member validation
Response rate **141–3**, 185, 187–8, 191, 192, 325, 351, **592**
  Non-response **122–3**, 142, **580**
Retrospective study **126**, **592**
Revelatory case, *see* Case study
Reviewing literature, *see* Literature reviews
Rhetoric 211, 248, 412, 453, **500**, 502, **592**
Roter Interaction Analysis System (RIAS) **198–200**, **592**
Row marginal, variable or percentage, *see*
  Contingency table

Sample survey **136**, 142, **592**
Sampling, sampling theory 134–152
  Population *versus* sample 123–7 *passim*, 135–7,
    **138**, 139–150 *passim* 161, 165, 185, 216, 325,
    336, 342, 531, **585**
  Sampling fraction **139**, 140, **593**
  Sampling frame **138–9**, 140–1, 144, **593**
  Sample size calculation 130, **592**
  Types of
    Cluster 139, **141**, 147, **558**
    Convenience **561**
    Maximum variation sampling 135, 145–6, **576**
    Multi-stage cluster **141**, **578**
    Network 145, 239–40, 252, *see also* Snowball
      sampling
    Non-probability sampling **135**, 136, 138,
      144–6, **580**
    Probability **135–141**, 215–16, **586**
    Purposive 161, **237**, 450, **587**
    Quota **144–5**, 237, **588**
    Random 129, 135–141, 161, 165, **236–7**, 325, 337,
      342, 461
    Representative 123–4, **135**, 141, 144, 147, 531, **591**
    Simple random **139**, 140
    Snowball 135, **145**, 218, **595**
    Stratification, stratified **140–1**, **597**
    Stratifying factor **140**, **597**
    Systematic **139**, 140, **599**